Evaluating Fetal Alcohol Spectrum Disorders in the Forensic Context

Natalie Novick Brown
Editor

Evaluating Fetal Alcohol Spectrum Disorders in the Forensic Context

A Manual for Mental Health Practice

Springer

Editor
Natalie Novick Brown
Federal Way, Washington, USA

ISBN 978-3-030-73627-9 ISBN 978-3-030-73628-6 (eBook)
https://doi.org/10.1007/978-3-030-73628-6

This Springer imprint is published by the registered company Springer Nature Switzerland AG
The registered company address is: Gewerbestrasse 11, 6330 Cham, Switzerland

For my beloved children, Lisa and Peter,
and for all children, everywhere.

Foreword

This book commemorates nearly 50 years of research on fetal alcohol spectrum disorders (FASD), brain-based neurodevelopmental disorders caused by prenatal alcohol exposure. Fetal alcohol syndrome (FAS), one of the disorders under the FASD umbrella, was first discovered in the United States in the early 1970s when colleague David W. Smith and I—both dysmorphologists at the University of Washington in Seattle—identified 11 unrelated children from three racial backgrounds with a similar pattern of symptoms (craniofacial anomalies, growth deficiency, and central nervous system dysfunction). The birth mothers of all these children were alcoholics. By the late 1970s, animal studies had established that alcohol was a teratogen (i.e., a substance that produces physical and functional deficits in the human embryo or fetus upon exposure), and necropsy studies on children with FAS revealed the vulnerability of the fetal brain to alcohol exposure in utero. By 1978, it had been determined that prenatal alcohol exposure was the most frequent known cause of mental deficiency. However, it was not until the 1990s when Dr. Ann Streissguth at the University of Washington's Fetal Alcohol and Drug Center recognized the connection between FASD and the law did researchers start to examine those links empirically.

Although the first major hurdle children with FASD must face in their young lives is the educational system, not far behind are problems with the law. In fact, Streissguth, Barr, Kogan, and Bookstein (1996) documented the rate of "trouble with the law" in persons with FASD between 12 and 51 years of age to be 68% for males and 52% for females. With respect to prevalence in the general population, a recent study estimated FASD in up to 5.0% of students in regular first- and second-grade classes in four US communities, three rural and one urban, making it a burgeoning public health problem (May et al., 2018). Studies (mostly Canadian) of FASD prevalence in the legal system show youths with FASD are 19 times more likely to be incarcerated than youths without FASD (Popova, Lange, Bekmuradov, Milhic, & Rehm, 2011). Adult studies in correctional institutions find similar rates. Unfortunately, our justice system is ill-equipped to deal appropriately with this disorder, which occurs in individuals through no fault of their own, causing lifelong brain damage totally beyond their control.

There are a variety of reasons for this situation. To begin with, there is an appalling lack of awareness regarding this disorder by attorneys, which results in cases where well-meaning lawyers might fail to consider the possibility that prenatal alcohol exposure may have contributed to their clients' offense conduct. There also is a lack of knowledge regarding FASD by the judiciary, which can lead to situations where judges have never heard of FASD and therefore fail to distinguish it from disorders such as attention-deficit/hyperactivity disorder (ADHD). FASD is a highly stigmatized disorder, leading to the possibility that juries might hold prejudicial stereotypes about affected individuals. Finally, there is a lack of understanding that the full spectrum of defects associated with FASD involves FAS at one end of the spectrum and alcohol-related neurodevelopmental disorder (ARND) at the other end. Whereas FAS is associated with a pattern of growth deficiency and structural birth defects plus neurobehavioral and neurodevelopmental impairments, ARND—the far more common disorder—is associated with neurobehavioral and neurodevelopmental impairments but lacks the structural birth defects and growth deficiency. Although both conditions involve the same degree of brain damage and functioning seen in intellectual disability, because there are no outward physical signs of FAS in ARND, judges, lawyers, and jurors may not be open to considering prenatal alcohol exposure as a contributing factor in criminal conduct.

This practical *hands-on* manual comes at an important time for the justice system as well as for the field of FASD. In 2010, the Canadian Bar Association passed a resolution urging the legal system to avoid ongoing criminalization of people with FASD and recommending the allocation of additional resources to develop policies and solutions regarding FASD and access to justice. Two years later, the American Bar Association passed a similar resolution, urging attorneys and judges to help identify and respond effectively to FASD in children and adults through training to expand awareness of FASD's devastating impact and emphasize the value of collaboration among medical, mental health, and disability experts. Approximately ten years now since those resolutions were approved, we are, in my opinion, at a tipping point relative to this disorder. Awareness by the general population that prenatal alcohol exposure is not a rare occurrence is increasing exponentially. Within the medical profession, it generally is accepted that there is no safe amount of alcohol to consume during pregnancy and that FASD has been used effectively as a mitigating factor in a number of criminal cases. Much of what the two Bar Association resolutions proposed ten years ago is explored in the chapters that follow.

Kenneth Lyons Jones
Department of Pediatrics, Division of Dysmorphology/Teratology
University of California, San Diego School of Medicine
La Jolla, CA, USA

References

May, P. A., Chambers, C. D., Kalberg, W. O., Zellner, J., Feldman, H., Buckley, … Hoyme, H. E. (2018). Prevalence of fetal alcohol spectrum disorders in 4 US Communities. *Journal of the American Medical Association, 319*(5), 474–482. https://doi.org/10.1001/jama.2017.21896

Popova, S., Lange, S., Bekmuradov, D., Mihic, A., & Rehm, J. (2011). Fetal alcohol spectrum disorder prevalence estimates in correctional systems: A systematic literature review. *Canadian Journal of Public Health, 102*(5), 336–340. https://doi.org/10.1007/bf03404172

Streissguth, A. P., Barr, H. M., Kogan J., & Bookstein, F. L. (1996). *Understanding the occurrence of secondary disabilities in clients with fetal alcohol syndrome (FAS) and fetal alcohol effects (FAE): Final report*. Seattle: University of Washington. http://lib.adai.uw.edu/pubs/bk2698.pdf

Preface

Welcome, reader! Natalie Novick Brown, PhD, a dedicated and talented psychologist and forensic mental health professional, was inspired to create this book to assist clinicians faced with the challenge of evaluating youths and adults in forensic settings with possible fetal alcohol spectrum disorder (FASD)—most of whom are undiagnosed at the point of entry into the legal system. This book also is intended for legal professionals who want to improve their understanding of why FASD can make a difference in case outcome. Luminaries in their respective fields, contributors to this book represent a variety of perspectives (medical, psychological, psychiatric, criminal defense, prosecution, judicial) who together provide a compendium of practical procedures and evidence-based strategies for competent multidisciplinary assessment in legal matters. Like Dr. Novick Brown, all of the contributors to this collection have considerable expertise in FASD, gained experientially and/or through formal training, and share the same deep concerns about the large numbers of undiagnosed people with serious brain injury acquired before birth: how can we find others to competently expand and carry on this extraordinarily important work and provide the specialized tools and information they need? In short, how can we, working together, achieve justice for those whose often-invisible disability sometimes leads to calamitous outcomes?

The groundbreaking secondary disabilities study by Psychologist Ann Streissguth et al. (1996) established that well over half of persons with FASD had been in trouble with the law (Streissguth, Barr, Kogan, & Bookstein, 1996). Prior to this study, efforts to raise FASD in criminal cases had met with little success. The failure of such efforts contrasted significantly with the long-standing willingness of courts to recognize the special needs of children with FASD in family law (Golden, 2005). Since 1996, defense attorneys have invoked FASD in criminal cases with increasing effectiveness, particularly in litigation about appropriate sentencing in capital cases. Understanding the reasons for this evolution in effectiveness is essential for forensic work in FASD today.

A 1988 habeas hearing in the Bobby Francis case (*Francis v. Barton*, 1991) was one of the earliest cases where defense counsel tried to raise FASD. James Merikangas, MD, mental health expert for the defense in the case, reported in a recent phone conversation with one of the authors that at the time he testified in 1988, the only thing he knew about FASD was a summary about fetal alcohol syndrome (FAS) he had read in *Recognizable Patterns of Human Malformation*, which was written by dysmorphologists David Weyhe Smith and Kenneth Lyons Jones. In the summary, Smith and Jones (1982) described FAS as a medical condition with characteristic facial features and brain damage. Their knowledge about FAS had begun in 1973 when medical resident Christine Ulleland asked them to examine a group of unrelated infants with similar facial features whose mothers were alcoholics. Shortly thereafter, the three medical colleagues and psychologist Ann Streissguth published a paper in *Lancet*, describing the condition they were seeing as FAS (Jones, Smith, Ulleland, & Streissguth, 1973).

Most of the early research work in FASD during the 1970s and 1980s focused on infants and young children with FAS or fetal alcohol effects (FAE), another condition caused by prenatal alcohol exposure that involved the same brain damage but not all of the outward physical characteristics seen in FAS (i.e., facial features and growth deficit) (Smith & Jones, 1982). Because little was known in 1988 about how prenatal alcohol exposure could affect adult behavior, Merikangas had no clear way to connect FAS with the defendant's offense conduct. According to court records, the judge found the defendant "did not suffer from fetal alcohol syndrome" (*Francis v. Barton*, 1991, p. 24) and accepted the State expert's testimony rather than that of Merikangas.

Although other early efforts to raise FASD at trial generally were similarly unsuccessful, they drew the attention of capital punishment litigators, and in 1990, Streissguth was invited to speak at a major national conference of capital defense lawyers. Later, in conversation with one of the authors in 2010, Streissguth recalled that while her description of FASD interested the audience, lawyers in attendance advised her it would be difficult to raise FASD in criminal cases without data connecting the disability to criminal conduct. According to Streissguth, discussions with many dedicated attorneys who were seeking better outcomes for clients facing the death penalty motivated her to rethink her research priorities, and a couple years later, she and her colleagues obtained funding from the Centers for Disease Control (CDC) for a large study of children, adolescents, and adults with FASD. Generally called the "secondary disabilities study," the research investigated the developmental consequences of FASD and was published to worldwide acclaim in 1996 (Streissguth et al., 1996).

Discovery in the secondary disabilities study that a high percentage of youths and adults with FASD had been arrested or convicted at least once in their lives was only the first step. Since then, researchers have sought to identify the specific cognitive and adaptive difficulties in FASD that interact with environmental factors to cause criminal conduct. Ability to make this connection in a given case (i.e., identifying the nexus between the disability and a defendant's unlawful actions) has been the key factor in determining whether proof of FASD through multidisciplinary diagnosis and testimony affects case outcome. Identifying the nexus is an interdisciplinary as well as multidisciplinary endeavor, involving legal professionals and mental health experts. Mental health professionals inform counsel about the cognitive and behavioral manifestations of FASD that lead to misconduct, and lawyers understand how to best present such information to the court. This collection describes the investigative steps found to be important in attaining successful outcomes based on FASD as well as legal and judicial perspectives regarding how FASD applies to the forensic context.

The way FASD affects behavior in affected individuals varies widely and is influenced by context as well as brain functioning. People with FASD can be eager to please, vulnerable to suggestion, and easily led by others to join in criminal activity. Such characteristics also make this population susceptible to manipulation during police interrogation, causing them to confess to crimes they did not commit or exaggerate their criminal responsibility with no awareness of consequences. Most people with FASD also are impulsive. While typically this impulsivity results in relatively minor offenses such as shoplifting or theft, under certain conditions impulsivity can lead to catastrophic offenses. In such cases, FASD can explain behavior that otherwise is inexplicable.

In 2001, the Fetal Alcohol Syndrome/Fetal Alcohol Effects (FAS/FAE) Legal Issues Resource Center (now FASD Legal Issues Resource Center) was established at the University of Washington in the Fetal Alcohol and Drug Unit (FADU), then headed by Streissguth. Founded by Streissguth, law professor Eric Schnapper, and the Center's director Kathryn Kelly, the Center's goal was to consult with defense lawyers and prosecutors, explaining the nature and general consequences of FASD and helping legal professionals determine the manner in which FASD might be related to their cases. Additionally, the Center also has provided FASD training for thousands of judges, lawyers, and other legal professionals, such as mitigation specialists, investigators, probation officers, and corrections staff. Around the time the Center began operating, William (Billy) Edwards, a Los Angeles County Public Defender, initiated pro bono FASD trainings for attorneys and others. Edwards gathered a group of experts in FASD to join him, and these dedicated professionals—many of whom contributed chapters for this collection—regularly paid their own expenses to travel throughout the United States in order to improve understanding of FASD in the judicial, mental health, medical, law enforcement, probation, and disability communities.

In 2007, encouraged by Streissguth and assisted by Kelly, Novick Brown assembled an informal team of professionals in Seattle to provide attorneys with expert advice, testing, and diagnostic assessment as well as testimony in criminal cases involving individuals with FASD. In addition to Novick Brown, this team included Neuropsychologist Paul Connor, Psychiatrist Richard Adler, and retired Superior Court Judge Anthony Wartnik. In 2010, this group published a proposed "gold standard" protocol for multidisciplinary FASD assessment in the forensic context, which was based upon a similar protocol in the clinical setting (Novick Brown, Wartnik, Connor, & Adler, 2010). Since then, these professionals have worked together and with other professionals around the United States, some of whom contributed to this book, to improve and expand upon the original protocol to provide the highest caliber of services in civil and disability as well as criminal contexts—making diagnoses and treatment recommendations where warranted, providing trial testimony about the direct links between FASD and offense conduct, and training mental health professionals to do similar work. The multidisciplinary approach to FASD assessment has proven very effective in such things as achieving disability eligibility for affected persons and persuading juries to reject the death penalty in favor of a sentence of life without the possibility of parole.

A striking illustration of the potential effectiveness of this "best practices" multidisciplinary approach came in the case of Timothy Flowers. Flowers originally was convicted of murder and sentenced to death in 2002. Because Flowers' original attorneys failed to offer evidence of his FASD at trial, the judge who originally sentenced him decided in 2015 that he should be resentenced. At the resentencing hearing, Merikangas—the same expert who testified in the 1988 *Francis v. Barton* case but was unable then to persuade the judge that Francis was severely impaired as a result of FAS—testified about the nature of FASD and provided a specific account of the connection between the disability and Flowers' offense. After hearing testimony about "fetal alcohol exposure and brain damage" from Merikangas as well as two neuropsychologists, the judge in *Flowers* determined it had been "prejudicial error not to present such evidence at trial" (*Flowers v. State*, 2015, p. 88), noting:

> If the Court and the jury had the benefit of knowing the multitude of mitigating factors which trial counsel failed to adequately investigate and identify – in particular expert testimony explaining how Mr. Flowers' brain damage impairs his ability to exercise judgment, make independent decisions, or process information in stressful circumstances, such as Mr. Flowers' experts were able to provide based on the relevant background evidence – there is a reasonable probability that Mr. Flowers would have received a lesser sentence. (*Flowers v. State*, 2015, pp. 88-89).

The judge then changed Flowers' sentence from death to life imprisonment without the possibility of parole. Beyond *Flowers*, the body of legal case history from 1988 to today demonstrates the extraordinary importance of forensic testimony for defendants with FASD. In certain US states, such testimony truly has meant the difference between life and death.

While FASD awareness was gradually increasing in the US legal field over the past three decades, similar awareness in Canada also was growing, assisted by frequent interchange among researchers in both countries. For example, at the University of Washington conference in 1996 to introduce the results of Streissguth's secondary disabilities research for the Centers for Disease Control (CDC), many attendees were from Canada. At an impromptu lunch meeting on the first conference day for those interested in FAS/FAE and legal issues, British Columbia researchers Julianne Conry, Diane Fast, and Christine Loock joined 40 other conference attendees and Michael Dorris (1990), adoptive father of three children with FASD and author of best-selling FASD book, *The Broken Cord*. The group held a riveting hour-long discussion about links between FASD, criminal behavior, and the law. A few years later, Fast, Conry, and Loock (1999) published results of their groundbreaking prevalence study, which found over 23% of youths in an inpatient forensic facility met diagnostic criteria for an FASD. In 2011, Ab Chudley et al. (2011) from the University of Manitoba in Canada reported similar research on the prevalence of FASD in an adult Canadian correctional facility (MacPherson, Chudley, & Grant, 2011). More recently, Kaitlyn McLachlan et al. (2019) examined the prevalence of FASD in another adult correctional population in Canada, finding FASD in approximately 18% to possibly 31% of the sample. Unfortunately, there has been no similar prevalence research in comparable US correctional settings.

In 2008, a national government-sponsored conference on FASD was held in Whitehorse, Yukon, Canada, to explore FASD in the context of the criminal justice system. Titled "The Path to Justice – Access to Justice for Individuals With FASD," the conference identified a need to address gaps in the criminal justice system for this population. The conference report concluded there were significant barriers to justice for those with FASD and recommended an action plan involving the justice system, First Nations Communities, rural communities, and FASD researchers (Canada, Department of Justice, 2008). Judge Heino Lilles of Whitehorse was a catalyst for this conference and instrumental in the decision of Whitehorse attorney Rod Snow to select FASD and Justice as his signature issue when he was elected President of the Canadian Bar Association (CBA). Judge Lilles was one of the judges who developed the first therapeutic court in Whitehorse called the Community Wellness Court, which was designed for defendants with FASD, addictions, and mental health problems. In operation since 2007 and presided over by Judge Karen Ruddy, the Community Wellness Court has been so successful that in 2018, the Court was given robust and permanent annual operational funds. During Snow's CBA Presidency in 2010, the organization developed and passed a resolution on FAS that called for awareness of FAS and changes in how courts dealt with this disability. This Canadian resolution led to Howard Davidson, then Director of the American Bar Association's (ABA) Center on Children and the Law, drafting a similar FASD resolution in 2012, which was adopted that year by the ABA. The ABA resolution calls for US courts and court professionals to identify FASD and respond effectively to the disability by initiating training programs to enhance awareness of FASD and its impact on individuals in child welfare, juvenile justice, and adult criminal justice systems (ABA, 2012).

In 2012, the Institute of Health Economics (IHE) in Edmonton, Alberta, Canada, held a Consensus Development Conference on Legal Issues of FASD. Honorable Ian Binnie, former justice of the Supreme Court of Canada, led the development of a Consensus Statement with recommendations for policy and law (Canada, Institute of Health Economics, 2013). One question discussed at the conference concerned how courts could better address the specific needs of persons with FASD. In 2019, a problem-solving "FASD Court" for juveniles and adults was established in Winnipeg, Manitoba, Canada. According to Judge Mary Kate Harvie, chair of the committee that developed the specialized court and current presiding judge, there is an ever-increasing demand for the court's FASD-informed approach and services (CBC, 2020, January 13). In late 2020, a three-year pilot program was launched in Manitoba to provide FASD diagnostic assessments for justice-involved adult defendants ages 18 to 25 years. In this program, if defendants are found to have FASD, they then are eligible for FASD Court, which qualifies them for special services and supports (CBC, 2020, September 13).

Canada also has developed an FASD website (www.fasdjustice.ca) in both French and English "for justice system professionals and others who want to understand more about FASD." The website provides information about FASD, including background data, case law, legal resources, and strategies for effective intervention (Canada, 2020). In the United States, the Department of Health and Human Services, Health Resources and Services Administration (HRSA), funded the development of a directory of FASD-related resources in the States and U.S. Trust Territories and Associated States. Edited by Barbara Morse and Corinne Barnwell under the auspices of Boston University's School of Medicine, the original directory was published in 2000 and currently is in the process of being updated by Morse. Ultimately, the updated directory will include state-by-state listings of psychologists and medical doctors who are experienced in diagnosing juveniles and adults with FASD as well as FASD-informed legal professionals. It will include lists of national and state resources, treatment programs, and prevention programs and also will feature a listing of FASD-knowledgeable residential programs for children, adolescents, and young adults with FASD. The updated directory will be available in 2021 on FADU's website (fadu.psychiatry.uw.edu) and on the website of the National Organization on Fetal Alcohol Syndrome (NOFAS; www.nofas.org).

In conclusion, this impressive compilation, the culmination of decades of research and forensic experience, is intended to give you, the reader, the information and tools you need to effectively evaluate and understand persons in the legal context who have a brain-based disability acquired before birth through no fault of their own. We hope this collection will inspire you, whatever your profession, to specialize in FASD and spread the word. Your efforts will be deeply appreciated by those whose lives you touch as well as by those who love and care for this population. The professionals whose chapters comprise this collection warmly welcome you as a colleague and commit to providing whatever assistance you need as you begin to incorporate into your professional lives the information acquired from reading this remarkable, singularly important, and literally life-saving collection.

Seattle, WA, USA

Kathryn Kelly
Eric Schnapper

References

American Bar Association. (2012). Resolutions with Reports of the House of Delegates, ABA 2012 Annual Meeting, Chicago, Il., # 112B.

Canada. (2020). Fetal alcohol spectrum disorder & justice. https://www.fasdjustice.ca

Canada. Department of Justice. (2008). Executive summary of conference, The path to justice – Access to justice for individuals with FASD. *SCICS*. https://scics.ca/en/product-produit/final-report-to-federalprovincialterritorial-ministers-responsible-for-justice-and-public-safety/

Canada. Institute of Health Economics. (2013). Consensus statement on legal issues of fetal alcohol spectrum disorder (FASD). Edmonton, AB. https://www.ihe.ca/publications/consensus-statement-on-legal-issues-of-fetal-alcohol-spectrum-disorder-fasd-

CBC News. (2020, January 13). As demand explodes, Manitoba's new FASD court expands to meet need. https://www.cbc.ca/news/canada/manitoba/manitoba-fasd-court-expansion-1.5386229

CBC News. (2020, September 30). Manitoba launches FASD pilot program to help young adults get diagnosed. https://www.cbc.ca/news/canada/manitoba-justice-fasd-diagnosis-1.5744521

Dorris, M. (1990). *The broken cord*. New York: Harper Perennial.

Fast, D. K., Conry, J., & Loock, C. A. (1999). Identifying fetal alcohol syndrome among youth in the criminal justice system. *Journal of Developmental & Behavioral Pediatrics*, 20(5), 370–372. https://doi.org/10.1097/00004703-199910000-00012

Francis v. Barton, 581 So. 2nd 583 (F.L. App. Div. 1991). Retrieved from http://murderpedia.org/male.F/images/f/francis_bobby_marion/78068amicus.pdf

Flowers v. State of Alabama, Case No. CC-01-169.60 (Circuit Ct., Baldwin County, Ala. 2015). Order, May 22, 2015.

Golden, J. (2005). *Message in a bottle: The making of fetal alcohol syndrome*. Cambridge, MA: Harvard University Press.

Jones, K. L., Smith, D. W., Ulleland, C. N., & Streissguth, A. P. (1973). Pattern of malformation in offspring of chronic alcoholic mothers. *Lancet*, *301*(7815), 1267–1271. https://doi.org/10.1016/s0140-6736(73)91291-9

McLachlan, K., McNeill, A., Pei, J., Brain, U., Andrew, G. & Oberlander, T. F. (2019). Prevalence and characteristics of adults with fetal alcohol spectrum disorder in corrections: A Canadian case ascertainment study. *BMC Public Health*, *19*, 43. https://doi.org/10.1186/s12889-018-6292-x

MacPherson, P. H., Chudley, A. E., & Grant. B. A. (2011). Fetal alcohol spectrum disorder (FASD) in a correctional population: Prevalence, screening and characteristics. Research Report R-247. Ottawa, ON: Correctional Service Canada. https://www.csc-scc.gc.ca/005/008/092/005008-0247-eng.pdf

Novick Brown, N., Wartnik, A. P., Connor, P. D., & Adler, R. S. (2010). A proposed model standard for forensic assessment of FASD. *Journal of Psychiatry and Law*, *38*(4), 383–418. https://doi.org/10.1177/009318531003800403

Smith, D. W., & Jones, K. L. (1982). *Recognizable patterns of human malformation: Genetic, embryologic, and clinical aspects.* (3rd ed.). Philadelphia: Saunders.

Streissguth, A. P., Barr, H. M., Kogan J., & Bookstein, F. L. (1996). *Understanding the occurrence of secondary disabilities in clients with fetal alcohol syndrome (FAS) and fetal alcohol effects (FAE): Final report*. Seattle, WA: University of Washington Publication Services. http://lib.adai.uw.edu/pubs/bk2698.pdf

Acknowledgments

This book would not have been possible without the giant in the FASD field upon whose shoulders I stand, Dr. Ann Streissguth. Ann, from the moment I started my postdoctoral fellowship with you at the University of Washington and you learned I was interested in forensic psychology, you would not let me consider any career pathway but *FASD* and forensic psychology. You shared with me your groundbreaking secondary disabilities research and vision that FASD, like intellectual disability, should matter in the legal world. I "saw the light" and am forever grateful to you for the loving push you gave me back then and the extraordinarily fulfilling work I have done over the past 25 years since that push.

This book also would not have been possible without another loving "push" from two wonderful friends and colleagues, Kay Kelly and Eric Schnapper. Kay and Eric also are giants in the FASD field—Kay for her tireless FASD advocacy and capacity to help legal professionals understand FASD as a crisis situation in the criminal and disability fields and Eric for his extraordinary ability to convert the science of FASD into legal language the higher courts can appreciate.

I am grateful to Claudia Van Wyk, the brilliant federal habeas attorney who in 2005 recognized FASD in her death row client and pulled me into the capital defense world to educate the court on how the disability had influenced his offense conduct. Claudia, my solo testimony in your case made me realize the importance of a multidisciplinary team in the capital context. Immediately after your case, I began building an informal team of professionals with Kay's eager assistance and connections.

This book would not exist but for my dear friend and colleague, Paul Connor, who was the first in our informal team of forensic experts to jump on board with me in 2006. Thank you, Paul, for the years you have spent teaching me about the neuropsychology of FASD from your unique vantage point as the *only* neuropsychologist in the United States with formal postdoctoral training in FASD as well as neuropsychology.

My heartfelt thanks also go to the other members of our informal multidisciplinary "team," who came on board with Paul and me in 2007: Richard Adler, Tony Wartnik, and Julian Davies. Beloved colleagues, we have been on an amazing adventure since we started working together many years ago. (Thank you from the bottom of my heart, Kay, for bringing us together.) Rich, you truly have inspired as well as educated me about the critical role neuroimaging can play in FASD. Working with you since 2007 has been an exciting adventure into the inner workings of the human brain. Thank you for allowing me to ride along on your coattails. Julian, words cannot describe what a joy it has been to work with you. Your compassion, unsurpassed knowledge of FASD, and consummate ability to explain the disability to legal professionals and juries is humbling. Tony, I believe you were the very first judge to "see the light" back in the 1990s. Thank you for your guidance, your wisdom, and always being there for us whenever we had questions about FASD in the legal context.

I am ever so grateful to the many esteemed authors whose chapters in this collection are filled with relevant data and creative applications that move the science and forensic applicability forward. I so appreciate your putting up with my nit-picky edits (due to journalism training during my undergrad days). You should know that each time I read your chapters during the editing process, I always came away thrilled by the fresh ideas you brought to this volume.

I thank my pre-Springer editor Sam Brawand. I really could not have done this book without you, Sam. Your editing was stellar, and your humor along the way was pure delight.

I thank Judith Newlin, Springer editor, for reaching out to me with this "book idea." Thank you, Judith, for seeing and supporting the critical need for a book like this to educate professionals to carry on our work.

Finally, I want to thank my family—my children Lisa and Peter, their partners (and also my children) Niko and Maria, and my husband Stu. You all put up with me working on this book for a solid year when I should have been spending more time with you. I am sorry and I am grateful. I so love you.

Natalie Novick Brown
December 30, 2020

Contents

List of Figures

List of Tables

About the Contributors

Brian R. Abbott, PhD holds a doctorate in psychology and a master's degree in social work. Abbott is licensed by the states of California and Washington as a clinical psychologist and as a clinical social worker in California and is a licensed sexual offender evaluator in Illinois. He is in independent practice, based in San Jose, California, and has worked forensically in nine states. Over his 42-year career, Abbott has performed more than 2,200 forensic evaluations for criminal, civil, dependency, delinquency, and family courts in a wide variety of areas. For the past 18 years, he has conducted sexually violent predator (SVP) evaluations and provided consultation and training to forensic practitioners and attorneys. He has been sought out to testify as an expert in Daubert and Frye admissibility hearings in multiple states related to diagnosis and risk assessment issues with sexually violent predators. He has conducted research and published peer-reviewed journal articles related to SVP risk assessment.

Richard S. Adler, MD is an adult, child, and adolescent forensic psychiatrist and clinical instructor at the University of Washington, School of Medicine, Seattle, Washington. In 2007, Adler was approached to join a nascent forensic diagnostic group. The need for a physician to assist in establishing legally relevant medical diagnoses had been identified. His background in physiological psychology, toxicology/pathology, and attention-deficit/hyperactivity disorder came in handy. Forensic psychiatry training director, Bruce C. Gage, MD, provided key guidance at an early phase in this group, urging the importance of developing and disseminating a proposed forensic model standard developed along the lines of the clinical standard. Ultimately, Adler became the psychiatrist for FASDExperts, an ensemble diagnostic team composed of psychologist Natalie Novick Brown, neuropsychologist Paul D. Connor, and Judge (retired) Anthony P. Wartnik. Since 2007, FASDExperts has conducted FASD assessments in well over 200 capital defense cases around the United States, pre- and post-conviction, as well as in felony cases involving vulnerable victims.

Larry G. Anderson of the Provincial Court of Alberta, Edmonton Criminal Division, Alberta, Canada, was a criminal defense lawyer for 25 years before being appointed to the bench in 2006. While practicing law and building a criminal law firm with a core group of lawyers, he was active in many community, professional, and educational organizations and initiatives, including a term as president of the Law Society of Alberta, the body governing the legal profession in the province. As a judge, he recently completed a term as Assistant Chief and has been involved in numerous educational roles at the provincial, national, and international level. He helped establish the Edmonton Mental Health Court where, as a judge of the Provincial Court of Alberta, he continues to sit.

Larry Burd, PhD received his doctoral degree in Community Health Sciences from the University of Manitoba Health Science Center in Winnipeg, Manitoba. Burd currently is professor, Department of Pediatrics, University of North Dakota School of Medicine, and director of the North Dakota Fetal Alcohol Syndrome Center and FAS Clinic. He has been with the Pediatric Therapy Program for 40 years, where he has evaluated more than 18,000 children with birth defects, developmental disorders, and mental illness. He has conducted research in 41 countries around the world, including current ongoing longitudinal studies (now in their 28th consecutive year of data collection) in subjects with Tourette syndrome, autism, fetal alcohol syndrome, and infant mortality risk. He has published over 220 professional papers on topics dealing with development and behavior in children and adolescents, and for over 30 years, he has sponsored clinics on Tribal nations for children with developmental disabilities and mental health disorders.

Radhika Chimata, MD completed her bachelors degree in Religion and Psychology at Northwestern University in 1996. She then worked in the not-for-profit arena before joining a doctoral program in Clinical-Community Psychology at DePaul University in 1999. She left with a masters degree and was busy with her two boys until 2011, when she started medical school. She completed her psychiatry residency at Rush University Medical Center in 2019. She is a board-certified adult psychiatrist who specializes in trauma and addictions. She currently works as an inpatient psychiatrist at Streamwood Behavioral Health Services, Streamwood, Illinois, and is an instructor at the Psychiatry residency program at Loretto Hospital, Chicago, Illinois.

Paul D. Connor, PhD is a licensed psychologist/neuropsychologist in private practice and courtesy clinical assistant professor at the University of Washington, Seattle. He received a PhD in clinical psychology with specialization in neuropsychology from Brigham Young University and completed an internship at Henry Ford Health System, specializing in neuropsychology. He also received postdoctoral training in neuropsychology and fetal alcohol spectrum disorders (FASD) at the University of Washington, where for over 13 years, he conducted research involving the effects of prenatal alcohol exposure (PAE) on brain structure and associated neuropsychological and mental health functioning. After entering private practice in 2007, he joined psychologist Natalie Novick Brown, psychiatrist Richard Adler, and retired judge Anthony Wartnik in forming FASDExperts, an informal multidisciplinary team that has conducted FASD assessments in various venues across the United States. He presents and consults internationally about FASD assessment and diagnosis and has authored or coauthored nearly 20 peer-reviewed articles and three book chapters on FASD. In his private practice, he conducts neuropsychological evaluations in clinical and forensic settings, using an empirically based test battery shown to be sensitive to the effects of PAE.

Julian K. Davies, MD is a clinical professor of pediatrics at the University of Washington, Seattle, where for the past 17 years, he has evaluated children and adults at the longest-running FASD diagnostic clinic in the United States. Davies has helped train FASD diagnostic teams from around the world, published articles in the peer-reviewed literature on prenatal alcohol/drug exposures, and presented on FASD at regional and national conferences. In the forensic arena, he has been retained by defense counsel across the country as well as by the U.S. Attorney's Office in Seattle. He co-directs the Center for Adoption Medicine and has a faculty pediatric practice where most of his patients are fostered or adopted. His interest in adoption, foster care, and FASD began in Russia, where he started a summer arts and clown camp for Russian orphans. He was trained at Yale, University of California at San Francisco, and the University of Washington.

Tom Donaldson is the CEO and president of the Washington, DC-based National Organization on Fetal Alcohol Syndrome (NOFAS), a public health advocacy, nonprofit organization striving to prevent prenatal alcohol exposure and support individuals and families living with fetal alcohol spectrum disorders (FASD). Since 1994, he has helped formulate and carry out NOFAS strategic and business plans and all FASD programmatic and policy initiatives. He has extensive experience in nonprofit governance, public policy, government affairs, media relations, social marketing, coalition building, and public health. Under his leadership, NOFAS has established a network of over 30 affiliated organizations, served families in all 50 states, and strengthened federal and state investment in FASD-related research, public health, and services. Donaldson has lectured extensively, hosted or moderated countless forums, appeared in numerous media interviews, and written feature articles, position statements, testimony, and narratives on all facets of FASD. He has served as a member or liaison representative to nearly all federal and national FASD committees and on several disability and maternal and child health charitable boards of directors. In 2014, he was honored with the Senator Harold Hughes Memorial Award by the National Institute on Alcohol Abuse and Alcoholism (NIAAA).

William J. Edwards Billy deputy public defender in the Los Angeles County Office of the Public Defender and Mental Health Court, is a member of the Board of Directors for the National Organization on Fetal Alcohol Syndrome (NOFAS) and Chair of the NOFAS Justice Task Force. He is considered one of the early pioneers in the training of attorneys around issues involving fetal alcohol spectrum disorders (FASD). As Deputy Public Defender, he works in Los Angeles County's Mental Health Court, representing clients with mental illness and developmental disorders. Previously, his professional work involved capital habeas appeals in Florida. A paper he coauthored on death row inmates with intellectual disabilities was cited by the United States Supreme Court in *Atkins v. Virginia*, the case that exempted defendants with intellectual disabilities from the death penalty. In 2006, he was appointed to serve on the Committee for People with Intellectual Disabilities, a federal advisory committee established by Executive Order to advise the U.S. President and Secretary of Health and Human Services on issues concerning citizens with intellectual disabilities. While serving on this committee, he initiated a series of national and international workshops (still ongoing) for attorneys on FASD. In 2011, he served as editor of a landmark two-volume issue of the *Journal of Psychiatry and Law*, which focused on the legal aspects of FASD. In 2012, he helped draft and secure passage of the American Bar Association's resolution on FASD. In 2014, he was presented in Seattle with the Dr. Ann Streissguth Annual Award for Outstanding Contribution to the Field of FASD and the Law. That same year, NOFAS inducted him into the Tom and Linda Daschle FASD Hall of Fame. In 2019, he was invited to assist the U.S. Department of Health and Human Services Office of the Assistant Secretary for Planning and Evaluation (ASPE) in developing policies aimed at reducing the lifelong burden on children with FASD and their families.

John Matthew Fabian, PSY.D., J.D., ABPP is double board-certified by the American Board of Professional Psychology and practices as a forensic neuropsychologist. Dr. Fabian was formerly director of a state court psychiatric clinic and has worked and testified in adult and juvenile court psychiatric clinics, a maximum-security state forensic hospital, and a Federal Bureau of Prison forensic studies center. He has testified in state and federal courts throughout the United States and conducted evaluations in approximately 700 adult and juvenile murder cases. He has faculty appointments in the Forensic Psychiatry Fellowship Training Program at the University of Texas Health Sciences Center at Houston, McGovern Medical School, Department of Psychiatry and Behavioral Sciences, and in the Forensic Psychology Postdoctoral Fellowship program at Walter Reed National Military Medical Center, Center for Forensic Behavioral Science.

Anthony J. FitzGerald of the District and Youth Court, Auckland District Court, New Zealand, was appointed a District Court Judge in 1999. He currently spends his time divided equally between working in the Youth Court and in adult criminal courts. He has a strong interest in solution-focused approaches to judicial rulings in both jurisdictions and has been involved in establishing and presiding in such courts since 2007, which included a mental health court within Youth Court and "crossover lists" for young people in the Youth Court who have care and protection status in the Family Court. In the adult jurisdiction, he helped establish a court for homeless offenders in 2010 and has presided in that court ever since then. He is the patron of the FASD Care Action Network in New Zealand.

Frances Gordon retired Crown Counsel, practiced criminal and human rights law for over 35 years as defense counsel, prosecutor, senior manager in the British Columbia (Canada) Prosecution Service, and independent British Columbia Police Complaints Commissioner. In the latter, she was responsible for civilian oversight of municipal police conduct. Internationally, she served as the executive director of the United Nations (U.N.)-affiliated International Centre for Criminal Law Reform and Criminal Justice Policy (UBC) and Vietnam's Director of the Canadian International Development Agency-funded JUDGE Project. Recently retired from the practice of law, she has continued to act as consultant to the U.N. Office of Drugs and Crime (UNODC) programme on effective prosecutions of sexual and gender-based crimes in Egypt, Palestine, and Myanmar.

Stephen Greenspan, PhD received his doctorate in developmental psychology from the University of Rochester and post-doctoral certificate in developmental disabilities from the Neuropsychiatric Institute at the University of California, Los Angeles (UCLA). He is emeritus professor of Educational Psychology at the University of Connecticut and currently resides in Northern California. A leading authority on intellectual disability (ID) and most-cited researcher in the ID section of *DSM-5*, much of his work has focused on social incompetence, gullibility, and risk-unawareness in people with ID and related disorders like fetal alcohol spectrum disorder (FASD). These themes are emphasized in two recent books: *Annals of Gullibility* (Praeger, 2009) and *Anatomy of Foolishness* (Hamilton, 2019). His coauthored chapter "FASD and the Concept of ID Equivalence" in *Fetal Alcohol Spectrum Disorders in Adults* (Springer, 2016) was cited as a basis for his induction into the NOFAS Tom and Linda Daschle Hall of Fame. He has provided expert testimony on behalf of several death penalty defendants with FASD and ID, which is the focus of an in-process book, *Naïve Criminal Offenders* (Springer, expected 2021). Because of his dedication to understanding those with neurodevelopmental disorders, he was awarded the John Jacobson Award for Creative Thinking from the ID Division of the American Psychological Association and Gunnar and Rosemary Dybwad Award for Humanitarianism from the American Association on Intellectual and Developmental Disability.

Dilys Haner, PhD, C Psych is a registered psychologist in Ontario, Canada, who specializes in clinical and forensic psychology. She conducts clinical and forensic assessments for London Family Court Clinic (LFCC), London, Ontario, Canada, a unique clinic that works with children and families involved with legal/clinical systems, and also does psychological assessments for Moosonee Area District School Board, James Bay Lowlands Secondary School Board, and Child and Youth Milopemahtesewin Services through Boniferro and Associates Psychological Services. Her professional work includes comprehensive assessments of parenting capacity under Section 98 of the *Child, Youth, and Family Services Act*; parenting plan evaluations under Section 30 of the *Children's Law Reform Act*; and youths mental health evaluations under Section 34 of the *Youth Criminal Justice Act*, as well as assessments for mental health problems, trauma, neurodevelopmental disorders (e.g., fetal alcohol spectrum disorder [FASD], attention-deficit hyperactivity disorder, autism spectrum disorder), learning, and risk of violence. She provides psychotherapy to children, adolescents, adults, and families with a variety of mental health and behavioral disorders and problems of daily living in trauma, separation, and divorce contexts. She also conducts program evaluation research, provides clinical training to students and residents, consults with youths residential facilities, facilitates a support group for caregivers of children and adolescents with FASD, lectures to professional groups on FASD and related topics, and does trainings for front-line workers and families on mental health and behavioral problems in children and adolescents.

Kimberly Harris, PhD, C Psych is the assistant executive director at the London Family Court Clinic, Ontario, Canada. Director of a multi-year grant to support children and families in living with FASD, she has provided leadership for a number of community collaborations related to FASD and culturally responsible/collaborative assessment. As a licensed forensic psychologist, she maintains an active caseload, including assessments for court where she has been declared an expert witness in FASD. She conducts training and program development on FASD in the child welfare and justice sectors. An adjunct professor in the Faculties of Education and Social Science at Western University, she mentors graduate students and has published research articles, clinical guides, and a book chapter in *Juvenile Justice: Advancing Research, Policy, and Practice* (Wiley, 2011).

Kaylee Husark is an undergraduate in her senior year at the University of North Dakota, majoring in electrical engineering, with a biomedical engineering and premedicine focus. She hopes to attend the University of North Dakota School of Medicine after graduation. Her career interests are biomedical engineering, emergency medicine, and geriatrics. Husark was awarded the Lillian Elsinga Outstanding Student Leader Award in spring of 2020. Since 2019, she has worked with Dr. Larry Burd in his research involving fetal alcohol spectrum disorders (FASD). Their first publication, coauthored by several others, was a fact sheet on FASD in North Dakota.

Kenneth Lyons Jones, MD is a Distinguished Professor of Pediatrics and chief of the Division of Dysmorphology and Teratology in the School of Medicine at the University of California, San Diego, and co-director of the Center for Better Beginnings. Jones is one of two physicians who first described the fetal alcohol syndrome (FAS) in 1973, and he has clinically evaluated hundreds of children who were prenatally exposed to alcohol in the United States, Russia, Ukraine, Italy, South Africa, South Korea, and Poland. He has also led numerous research studies involving pregnant women, environmental exposures, and birth and child health outcomes. He serves as the principal investigator on a National Institute on Alcohol Abuse and Alcoholism U24 that is part of the Collaborative Initiative on Fetal Alcohol Spectrum Disorder (CIFASD). CIFASD's overall aim is to form and develop effective interventions and treatment approaches for FASD, through multidisciplinary research involving basic, behavioral, and clinical investigators and projects.

Kathryn (Kay) Kelly is project director of the FASD Legal Issues Resource Center in the Fetal Alcohol and Drug Unit, University of Washington, Seattle, and also is a Research Coordinator for a National Institute on Alcohol Abuse and Alcoholism (NIAAA)-funded 5-year study titled *Health and Neurobehavior in Adults With Prenatal Alcohol Exposure*. She first learned about FASD at a 1996 training provided by Ann Streissguth for capital defense attorneys and other court professionals, including the staff of the Capital Habeas Unit in the Office of the Federal Public Defender in Los Angeles, where Kelly was a mitigation specialist/investigator. Prior to that, she served for 29 years as a probation officer, state and then federal.

Marilyn G. Klug, PhD received her doctoral degree from the University of North Dakota, Grand Forks, North Dakota, in research methodologies. An associate professor, Department of Population Health, University of North Dakota School of Medicine, she has assisted the Departments of Pediatrics, Rural Health, Occupational Therapy, Gerontology, Biomedicine, and Family Medicine in designing research for publication for the past 25 years. She teaches research methods and biostatistics to students and residents in the Geriatrics, Physicians' Assistant, and Occupational Therapy programs and has published over 70 papers in peer-reviewed health care journals.

Erica Madore, Esq. is an Assistant County Attorney in Milaca, Minnesota. She has practiced as a prosecutor in Minnesota since 2016, with a caseload including adult criminal defendants, youths involved in juvenile delinquency, civil commitment, and treatment court. She is affiliated with the American Institute for the Advancement of Forensic Studies, based in St. Paul, Minnesota. She received a bachelor's degree in History and Sociology from the University of Minnesota and is a graduate of the University of Minnesota Law School.

Valerie McGinn, PhD received her doctoral degree from the University of Auckland and is a Clinical Neuropsychologist and Clinical Director of the FASD Centre, Aotearoa, New Zealand, where she is part of a multidisciplinary FASD diagnostic and treatment team. She is an Honorary Senior Research Fellow at the Department of Population Health, Centre for Addiction Studies at the University of Auckland, and FASD Advisor to the Health Coalition, Aotearoa. McGinn has diagnosed and advised in the management of hundreds of at-risk children and adolescents with FASD, many in state care or before the courts. Her evidence in the New Zealand courts has resulted in FASD now being widely recognized and accommodated within the legal system. She has a special interest in false confessions, youths who have killed, and imprisoned women with FASD. Her FASD evidence to the Privy Council resulted in the quashing of a murder conviction. She also is an expert advisor for the FASD-Care Action Network (FASD-CAN), an organization in New

Zealand that was created to support and advocate for people with FASD and their families and caregivers.

Kaitlyn McLachlan, PhD, C Psych trained as a clinical psychologist with a forensic specialization at Simon Fraser University, after which she completed a postdoctoral fellowship with concurrent appointments at the University of Alberta and University of British Columbia. Currently an assistant professor in the Department of Psychology at the University of Guelph, Ontario, Canada, she is a member of both the College of Psychologists of Ontario and College of Psychologists of British Columbia (out-of-province status). The core of her research has focused on improving outcomes for vulnerable populations (including those with fetal alcohol spectrum disorder) in both community and criminal justice settings. Currently, she is a Research Lead in Justice with the Canada Fetal Alcohol Spectrum Disorder Research Network.

Mansfield Mela, MBBS, FRCPC, FWACP, MRCPsych is the director of the Center for Forensic Behavior Science and Justice Studies and professor in the Department of Psychiatry, College of Medicine, University of Saskatchewan, Saskatoon, Canada. He also is diagnostic research lead of the Canada FASD Research Network and a forensic psychiatrist at the Regional Psychiatric Centre in Saskatoon, Canada. His research focuses on psycholegal aspects of forensic mental health, with specific interests and expertise in the area of fetal alcohol spectrum disorder (FASD). He brings a clinical perspective to his research questions and seeks to generate research and implement knowledge to achieve evidence-based practice among forensic mental health and FASD populations. He is the author of *Prenatal Alcohol Exposure: A Clinician's Guide* (American Psychiatric Association, March 2021).

Natalie Novick Brown, PhD is a licensed clinical and forensic psychologist in Washington State, Florida, and Alaska and clinical assistant professor (courtesy staff) in the Department of Psychiatry and Behavioral Sciences, School of Medicine, University of Washington, Seattle. Her doctoral training in clinical psychology at the University of Washington included an internship in forensic psychology, which was followed by formal post-doctoral training and ultimately, certification, in forensic evaluation and treatment of sex offenders. She was awarded a postdoctoral fellowship in fetal alcohol spectrum disorder (FASD) with pioneer researcher Dr. Ann Streissguth at the University of Washington's Fetal Alcohol and Drug Unit (FADU), which involved participation in research that led to publication by Streissguth and coauthors of *Understanding the Occurrence of Secondary Disabilities in Clients with Fetal Alcohol Syndrome (FAS) and Fetal Alcohol Effects (FAE)*. A licensed psychologist in private practice since 1996 and certified evaluator and treatment provider for the State of Washington's Division of Developmental Disabilities (now, Developmental Disabilities Association), Novick Brown has specialized in FASD, neurodevelopmental disorders, and sex offender treatment/evaluation while consulting with and conducting research at FADU's Parent-Child Assistance Program, an intervention for high-risk alcohol and drug abusing mothers. In 2007, with colleagues Paul Connor, Richard Adler, and Anthony Wartnik, she co-founded *FASDExperts*, an informal multidisciplinary group that conducts forensic evaluations in capital cases around the United States. In 2012, she helped author the American Bar Association's resolution on FASD. Over the course of her career, she has published nearly 40 peer-reviewed journal articles and book chapters on FASD, mentored and supervised graduate students regarding FASD, evaluated nearly 500 adolescents and adults with FASD, testified in scores of pre- and post-conviction capital cases involving FASD, and conducted trainings on FASD at national and international conferences.

Ann Marie O'Connell, BS, MS-2 received a bachelor of arts degree in biology from Concordia College, Moorhead, Minnesota. O'Connell currently attends the University of North Dakota School of Medicine and Health Sciences as a second-year medical student. She works on research with Dr. Larry Burd at the FAS Clinic and is interested in child development and preventive health care in pediatrics.

Amanda Palme, BS, M2-2 is a second-year medical student at the University of North Dakota School of Medicine and Health Sciences in Grand Forks, North Dakota. She received her bachelor of science degree in cell and molecular biology, with a minor in psychology, from the University of Minnesota, Duluth, Minnesota. During the summer between her first and second years of medical school, she participated in research on fetal alcohol spectrum disorder with Dr. Larry Burd at the North Dakota FAS Center at the University of North Dakota. She is interested in the pursuing the fields of internal medicine or psychiatry.

Cecil R. Reynolds, PhD ABN, ABPdN earned a doctoral degree from the University of Georgia in 1978, with a major in school psychology and minors in statistics and in clinical neuropsychology. He interned at the Medical College of Georgia (Pediatric Neurology section and Neurological Surgery section) and the Rutland Center for Severely Emotional Disturbed Children. Prior to joining Texas A & M University in 1981, he served as associate director and acting director of the Buros Institute of Mental Measurement, after writing the grants and proposals to move the Institute to Nebraska following the death of its founder, Oscar Buros. His primary research interests are in all aspects of psychological assessment. He has authored more than 300 scholarly publications and over 50 books in psychology, including *The Energetic Brain, The Clinician's Guide to the BASC, Clinical Applications of Continuous Performance Tests*, *Handbook of School Psychology*, *Encyclopedia of Special Education*, and *Handbook of Clinical Child Neuropsychology*. He is also the author of several widely used tests of personality and behavior including the Behavior Assessment System for Children (the most widely used measure of its kind in the English-speaking world) and Revised Children's Manifest Anxiety Scale. He also is senior author of the Test of Memory and Learning, the Clinical Assessment Scales for the Elderly, the Reynolds Intellectual Assessment Scales (RIAS), and more than 40 other tests. He maintained a clinical practice treating trauma victims and individuals with traumatic brain injury (TBI) for 25 years before retiring from clinical work at the end of 2003 to extend his forensic practice. Reynolds is a diplomate in clinical neuropsychology of the American Board of Professional Neuropsychology and of the American Board of Pediatric Neuropsychology (and is a past President of both Boards). He was elected a Distinguished Practitioner and Fellow of the National Academies of Practice in 2012 and is a past president of the National Academy of Neuropsychology, and APA Divisions 5, 40, and 16. He served as editor in chief of *Archives of Clinical Neuropsychology* (1990–2002), *Applied Neuropsychology* (2004–2008), and the prestigious APA journal *Psychological Assessment* (2009–2015). In 2015, he became editor of APA's open-access journal, *Archives of Scientific Psychology*, and in 2019, editor of the *Journal of Pediatric Neuropsychology.* Reynolds has received multiple national awards recognizing him for excellence in research including the Society for the Psychological Study of Social Issues Robert Chin Award and a MENSA best research article award, the Senior Scientist Award from APA Division 16 (School Psychology), the National Academy of Neuropsychology's Distinguished Clinical Neuropsychologist Award, the Academy's highest award for research accomplishments, and the Buros Institute Distinguished Reviewer Award among others. His service to the profession and to society has been recognized through the President's Gold Medal for Service to the National Academy of Neuropsychology, the Academy's Distinguished Service Award, and the University of North Carolina at Wilmington Razor Walker Award for Service to Youth. He received the Jack I. Bardon Award for Lifetime Distinguished Service Contributions to school psychology, the APA Div. 5 Samuel Messick Award for Distinguished Contributions to Measurement Science, and the Div. 12 Award for Distinguished Contributions to Clinical Assessment. In 2017, Reynolds received the APA D16 Nadine Murphy Lambert Award, which is given only every two to three years for a lifetime of distinguished contributions of "unusual depth and breadth" to the field. He is currently an Emeritus Professor of Educational Psychology, Professor of Neuroscience, and Distinguished Research Scholar at Texas A & M University and practices forensic neuroscience in Austin, Texas.

Anne L. Sandstrom, BS is a third-year medical student at the University of North Dakota School of Medicine and Health Sciences, pursuing a career in surgery. She received a bachelor of science in biology and psychology from Baylor University in 2018. Her research interests include fetal alcohol spectrum disorders, substance use in pregnancy, and maternal and social determinants of infant outcomes.

Eric Schnapper, PhD is professor of law at the University of Washington in Seattle. He serves as the legal consultant to the University of Washington's Fetal Alcohol and Drug Unit. In addition to his teaching responsibilities, he represents plaintiffs in civil rights and employment discrimination litigation. Prior to joining the University of Washington School of Law, he served for 25 years as assistant counsel at the NAACP Legal Defense and Educational Fund, Inc., in New York.

Karen A. Steele, Esq. is a lawyer in Salem, Oregon. Her legal practice focuses on capital and other complex cases that include neurodevelopmental issues such as fetal alcohol spectrum disorder (FASD), late adolescent brain development and consequent behavioral attributes, and the forensic implications of these and similar conditions/developmental states—integrating and presenting neuroscientific information in forensic contexts. She is a graduate of Washington University School of Law in St. Louis, Missouri, and received her bachelor of arts degree in political science and journalism from the University of Wisconsin-Madison. In 2015, she was presented in Seattle with the Dr. Ann Streissguth Annual Award for Outstanding Contribution to the Field of FASD and the Law.

Douglas Waite, MD, FAAP is chief of developmental pediatrics at Bronxcare Health System and assistant clinical professor of pediatrics at Mount Sinai Hospital, New York. He serves on several FASD task forces for the American Academy of Pediatrics (AAP) and is a member of the executive committee for the AAP Council on Foster Care, Adoption and Kinship Care; Vice Chair of the Board of Directors for the National Organization for Fetal Alcohol Syndrome; and past member of the Board of Directors of the Child Welfare League of America. He has special interests in neurodevelopmental disorders associated with prenatal alcohol and substance exposure, posttraumatic stress disorder, and effects of child abuse and neglect on child development.

Anthony P. Wartnik served as a trial court judge for 34 years prior to retiring in 2005 as senior judge of King County Superior Court in Seattle, Washington. As a Superior Court judge for close to 25 years, in the early 1990s he was assigned the first case to be filed involving an FASD diagnosis in a juvenile, after which he developed and chaired a multidisciplinary task force to establish protocols for determining competency to stand trial in youths with organic brain damage. In the late 1990s, he was asked to serve on and then chaired the Washington State Governor's Advisory Panel on FAS/FAE. As chair of the state's annual judicial conference education planning committee, he implemented and presented FASD training sessions for the Washington judiciary in the early 2000s. Following retirement, he consulted with the Fetal Alcohol and Drug Unit in the School of Medicine at the University of Washington. As a certified trainer for the Substance Abuse and Mental Health Services Administration (SAMHSA), he has conducted national and international workshops on FASD and the law and has authored and coauthored articles and book chapters on the same subject. He currently serves as an adjunct professor in the Human Services Department at Concordia University, St. Paul, Minnesota, where he teaches the legal aspects of Forensic Report Writing and Special Needs Populations, both of which include units on FASD.

Abbreviations

AAIDD	American Association on Intellectual and Developmental Disabilities
AAMR	American Association of Mental Retardation
AB	Adaptive behavior
ABA	American Bar Association
ABAS	Adaptive Behavior Assessment System
ABAS-3	Adaptive Behavior Assessment System, 3rd edition
ABC	Alcohol Related Neurodevelopmental Behavioral Checklist
ACC	Anterior cingulate cortex
ACE	Adverse Childhood Experience
ACS:SC	Advanced Clinical Solutions' Social Cognition Test
ACT	Auditory Consonant Trigrams Test
ADA	*American Disabilities Act of 1990*
ADHD	Attention Deficit Hyperactivity Disorder
APA	American Psychiatric Association
ARBD	Alcohol-related birth defects
ARND	Alcohol-related neurodevelopmental disorder(s)
ASD	Autism spectrum disorder
BAC	Blood alcohol concentration
BRIEF	Behavior Rating Inventory of Executive Function
BRIEF-2	Behavior Rating Inventory of Executive Function, 2nd edition
BRIEF-A	Behavior Rating Inventory of Executive Function, Adult version
BVMT-R	Brief Visuospatial Memory Test-Revised
CAST-MR	Competence Assessment for Standing Trial with Mental Retardation
CATA	Conners Auditory Test of Attention
CBA	Canadian Bar Association
CD	Conduct disorder
CDC	U.S. Centers for Disease Control and Prevention
CFA	Confirmatory factor analysis
CIFASD	Collaborative Initiative on Fetal Alcohol Spectrum Disorders

CMA	Chromosomal microarray
CNS	Central nervous system
CNS-VS	Computer-Based Neuropsychological Screening Test
Code	Canadian *Criminal Code*
COVID-19	Coronavirus disease 2019
COVR	Classification of Violence Risk
COWAT	Controlled Oral Word Association Test
CPS	Child Protective Service
CPT-3	Conners Continuous Performance Test, 3rd edition
CST	Competency to Stand Trial
CT	Computerized tomography
CVLT-3	California Verbal Learning Test, 3rd edition
CYPM	Crossover Youth Practice Model
DD	Developmental disability
DD/ID	Developmental delays and intellectual disabilities
DEAR	Direct Language/Engage Support System/Accommodate Needs/Remain Patient
DGR	Diagnostic-related group
D-KEFS	Delis-Kaplan Executive Function System
DOC	Department of Corrections
DSM-5	*Diagnostic and Statistical Manual of Mental Disorders*, 5th edition
DSM-IV	*Diagnostic and Statistical Manual of Mental Disorders*, 4th edition
DSM-IV-TR	*Diagnostic and Statistical Manual of Mental Disorders*, 4th edition, text revision
DTI	Diffusion tensor imaging
ECST-R	Evaluation of Competency to Stand Trial-Revised
EEG	Electroencephalogram
EF	Executive functioning
ERP	Event-related potential
FA	Fractional anisotropy
FABS	Fetal Alcohol Behavior Scale
FADU	Fetal Alcohol and Drug Unit, University of Washington
FAE	Fetal alcohol effects
FAI	Forensic assessment instrument
FAS DPN	Fetal Alcohol Syndrome Diagnostic and Prevention Network
FAS	Fetal alcohol syndrome
FASD	Fetal alcohol spectrum disorder(s)
FBA	Functional Behavior Evaluation
FDA	U.S. Food and Drug Administration
F-FDG	Radio-labelled glucose
FIT-R	Fitness Interview Test-Revised
fMRI	Functional magnetic resonance imaging
FM-UE	Fugl-Meyer Upper Extremity Scale of Motor Impairment
FSIQ	Full-Scale Intelligence Quotient
FT	Finger Tapping Test

GABA	Gamma aminobutyric acid
GP	Grooved Pegboard Test
GSS	Gudjonsson Suggestibility Scale
HCR-20	Historical, Clinical, and Risk Management-20
HCR-20V3	Historical, Clinical, and Risk Management-20, Version 3
HHS	U.S. Department of Health and Human Services
HPA	Hypothalamic–pituitary–adrenal
IAC	Ineffective Assistance of Counsel
ICD	International Classification of Diseases
ICD-10	World Health Organization's International Classification of Diseases
ICV	Intracranial volume
ID	Intellectual disability
IDEA	*Individuals with Disabilities Education Act of 1990*
IEP	Individual Educational Plan
IHE	Institute of Health Economics, Edmonton, Alberta, Canada
ILS	Independent Living Scales
IMG	Intensive Monitoring Group (Auckland Youth Court)
IOM	Institute of Medicine
IQ	Intelligence quotient
ISB	Inappropriate sexual behavior
IUGR	Intrauterine growth restriction
LORETA	Low-Resolution Electromagnetic Tomographic Analysis
LTO	Long-term offender order
Mac-CAT-CA	MacArthur Competence Assessment Tool for Criminal Adjudication
MDA	Multidisciplinary assessment
MDMA	3,4-Methylenedioxymethamphetamine
MICR	*Miranda Rights Comprehension Instruments*
MR	Mental retardation
MRI	Magnetic resonance imaging
NAB:AC	Neuropsychological Assessment Battery: Auditory Comprehension Test
NAS	Neonatal abstinence syndrome
NCR	Not Criminally Responsible
ND/AE	Neurobehavioral disorder/alcohol-exposed
ND-PAE	Neurobehavioral disorder associated with prenatal alcohol exposure
NEPSY	Developmental Neuropsychological Assessment
NFB	Neurofeedback
NIAAA	National Institute on Alcohol Abuse and Alcoholism
NICU	Neonatal intensive care unit
NOFAS	National Organization on Fetal Alcohol Syndrome
NOS	Not otherwise specified (cognitive disorder)
NSCAW	National Survey of Child and Adolescent Well-Being

ODD	Oppositional defiant disorder
OFC	Occipital frontal circumference
PAE	Prenatal alcohol exposure
PASAT	Paced Auditory Serial Addition Test
PCE	Prenatal cocaine exposure
PET	Positron emission tomography scan
pFAS	Partial fetal alcohol syndrome
PFC	Prefrontal cortex
PFL	Palpebral fissure length
PKU	Maternal phenylketonuria
PME	Prenatal marijuana exposure
PPV	Positive predictive value
PTSD	Posttraumatic stress disorder
PVT	Performance Validity Test
qEEG/QEEG	Quantitative electroencephalogram
RBANS	Repeatable Battery for Neuropsychological Status
RCFT	Rey Complex Figure Test
RFF	Ruff's Figural Fluency Test
RMA	Recovering Mothers Anonymous
RNR	Risk-need-responsivity
ROC	Receiver operating curve
ROI	Regions of interest
RYFS	Regional Youth Forensic Service (Auckland)
SAMA	Standardized Assessment of Miranda Abilities
SAMHSA	[U.S.] Substance Abuse and Mental Health Services Administration
SARA	Spousal Assault Risk Assessment
SAS	Statistical Analysis Software
SAVRY	Structured Assessment of Violence Risk in Youth
SD	Standard deviation
SDIC-SVB	Serious Difficulty In Controlling Sexually Violent Behavior
SDP	Smoking during pregnancy
SE/AE	Static encephalopathy/alcohol-exposed
SEM	Standard error of measurement
SOI	Severity of illness
SOCCPN	Sex Offender Civil Commitment Programs Network
SPJ	Structured Professional Judgement
SS	Standard score
SSI	Supplemental Security Income
SSRI	Selective serotonin reuptake inhibitor
START	Short-Term Assessment of Risk and Treatability
STROOP	Stroop Color Word Test
SVP	Sexually violent predator
TBI	Traumatic brain injury
TFLS	Texas Functional Living Scale
TMT	Trail Making Test

TOGRA	Test of General Reasoning Abilities
TOVA	Test of Variables of Attention
VAS	Vocabulary Assessment Scales
Vineland-3	Vineland Adaptive Behavior Scales, 3rd edition
VMI	Visual-Motor Integration Test
VRAG	Violence Risk Appraisal Guide
VRAG-R	Violence Risk Appraisal Guide-Revised
VSD	Ventricular septal defect
WAIS-IV	Wechsler Adult Intelligence Scale, 4th edition
WASI	Wechsler Abbreviated Scale of Intelligence
WCST	Wisconsin Card Sorting Test
WES/WGS	Whole exome or whole genome sequencing
WIAT-III	Wechsler Individual Achievement Test, 3rd edition
WJ-III	Woodcock Johnson Test, 3rd edition
WRAT	Wide Range Achievement Test
WRAT-4	Wide Range Achievement Test, 4th edition

Chapter 1
Diagnostic History: Prenatal Exposure to Alcohol and Other Teratogens

Tom Donaldson

Abstract From the time the constellation of impairments associated with prenatal alcohol exposure was first described in the medical literature as fetal alcohol syndrome (FAS) in 1973, science has refined our understanding of the physical and behavioral signs and symptoms of this brain-based disorder and the consequences for affected individuals through the lifespan. Although phenotype variability remains in medical and behavioral health diagnostic guidelines, it generally is understood that the disability, now generally called fetal alcohol spectrum disorder (FASD), is a multisystem condition that involves the entire body, with the most common and significant impairments related to structural and functional brain damage. Despite its significance as the leading preventable nonhereditary cause of developmental disabilities, affecting as many as one in 20 school-age children in the United States, complex clinical and societal factors contribute to inadequate diagnostic capacity and limited awareness of FASD from the classroom to the courtroom. Systemic ignorance of FASD compounds the untreated progression of disabilities inherent in the disorder and underlies discriminatory treatment of individuals vulnerable to mental and substance use disorders and victimization, who lack accountability beyond their cognitive capacity. This chapter describes an evolution in our understanding of FASD and the models developed to clinically identify the disability. An increase in diagnostic accuracy is noted as well as a need for expanded research and scientific translation. Corresponding advances are essential in recognizing FASD across systems of care and non-medical settings to increase attention to and investment in the disorders, so affected children and adults achieve the outcomes and equitable treatment they deserve.

Keywords Fetal alcohol spectrum disorder · FASD · Prenatal alcohol exposure · Secondary disabilities

T. Donaldson (✉)
National Organization on Fetal Alcohol Syndrome (NOFAS), Washington, DC, USA
e-mail: donaldson@nofas.org

N. Novick Brown (ed.), *Evaluating Fetal Alcohol Spectrum Disorders in the Forensic Context*, https://doi.org/10.1007/978-3-030-73628-6_1

1.1 Introduction

Decades of research have established a robust body of knowledge about maternal alcohol consumption, alcohol's teratogenic effects on embryonic and fetal development, criteria to reliably identify fetal alcohol spectrum disorders (FASD) and their debilitating effects on development and functioning, and prevalence of postnatal comorbid disorders. However, the proposition that alcohol could interfere with prenatal development was met initially with doubt among researchers and practitioners who were skeptical science and medicine could have previously overlooked the risks associated with prenatal alcohol exposure (PAE). Although this premise has been confirmed overwhelmingly during the past 50 years, there remains widespread confusion about the scope of the problem and lifelong implications for affected individuals.

In the United States, one in nine *pregnant* women report drinking alcohol in the previous month, and approximately one-third of these women engage in frequent binge drinking (Denny, Acero, Naimi, & Kim, 2019). Based upon these data, at least 400,000 pregnancies in the United States are alcohol-exposed each year, with as many as 125,000 births jeopardized by high-risk binge drinking. Alcohol is a confirmed teratogen, an agent that can cause embryonic or fetal malformations. In particular, PAE can produce permanent brain damage that manifests as cognitive and behavioral impairments, including diminished IQ in many individuals as well as deficits in learning, memory, attention, perception, processing speed, motor skills, and executive functioning (e.g., problem-solving and self-regulation). A 1996 Institute of Medicine (IOM) report found, "of all the substances of abuse, including heroin, cocaine, and marijuana, alcohol produces by far the most serious neurobehavioral effects in the fetus" (Stratton, Howe, & Battaglia, 1996, p. 35).

Although at least as pervasive as autism spectrum disorders (Wozniak, Riley, & Charness, 2019), FASD often is portrayed as rare. As a result, FASD has not attracted attention and investment commensurate with its public health impact. As predicted by the number of pregnancies exposed to alcohol, FASD is widespread, and related costs to society are vast. A recent wide-ranging active case ascertainment cross-sectional study of over 13,000 first-grade students in mixed race populations in four regions of the United States found the most conservative FASD prevalence estimate was 1 in 20 children (May et al., 2018). Comparable rates have been found in surveillance studies in Italy, Russia, South Africa, and other countries. The total annual expense for health care and special services for children and adults in the United States with FASD is estimated to be $6 billion (Greenmyer, Klug, Kambeitz, Popova, & Burd, 2018). Individualizing this estimate, the average yearly cost to treat a person with FASD is nearly 30% higher than treating someone with autism and 13% higher than treating someone with diabetes.

From a public health standpoint, it is critical to understand the amount and pattern of alcohol consumption that presents a risk of FASD. Early research found less than an ounce of alcohol per day was associated with growth deficiency and physical anomalies (Davis, Partridge, & Storrs, 1982). Later research found the amount of alcohol in *one alcoholic beverage* interfered with the binding of cells critical to fetal development, including brain development (Charness, Riley, & Sowell, 2016). Rather than a threshold above which alcohol consumption becomes harmful, risk now is viewed as a dose–response relationship incorporating a range of effects corresponding to a range of exposures. Research has not identified a level of prenatal alcohol exposure known to be without risk (Charness et al., 2016). This empirical situation was the basis for the U.S. Surgeon General's health advisory on alcohol and pregnancy in 1981 (Food and Drug Administration (FDA), 1981), the first public health message recommending abstinence from alcohol during pregnancy due to the risk of birth defects, and subsequent health advisory in 2005 (U.S. Department of Health and Human Services (HHS), 2005). Whenever alcohol is present during gestation, it has the potential to interfere with whatever embryonic and fetal development is occurring at that time, as described in Fig. 1.1.

Diagnostic accuracy and caregiver knowledge are two factors that determine clinical management, recognition across systems, and ultimate awareness and acceptance of a condition in society. Diagnosis is critical because it enables decisions about treatment and prognosis, helps professionals and society to empathize with affected patients, and increases the likelihood other patients will seek treatment. This chapter highlights the evolution, current standing, and obstacles to diagnosing FASD as well as the implications for individuals with this disability in the criminal justice system and other domains.

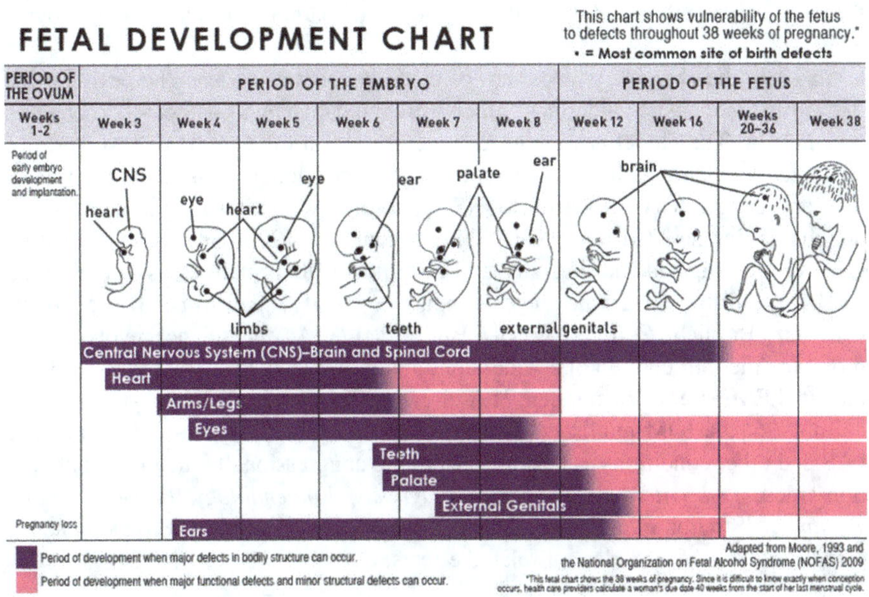

Fig. 1.1 Unlike other sites, the brain and spinal cord develop throughout the entire pregnancy

1.2 Diagnosing Fetal Alcohol Spectrum Disorders

Although research has yet to provide the decisive knowledge necessary to establish universal diagnostic criteria, there are sound evidenced-based methods in place for diagnosing conditions arising from PAE. Countless individuals, mostly children, have received a proper diagnosis that has enabled them to obtain beneficial medical and behavioral health treatments. Unfortunately, when adults are first diagnosed with FASD, the diagnosis often occurs in the forensic context. Whether child or adult, it is acknowledged generally that multidisciplinary assessment constitutes best practice because of the medical and mental health components in FASD.

Fetal alcohol syndrome (FAS) was first documented in the medical literature in France in 1968 (Lemoine, Harousseau, Borteyru, & Menuet, 1968). The publication did not include diagnostic criteria, nor did the article lead to recognition of FAS in France or anywhere else in Europe (Calhoun & Warren, 2007). In 1973 and 1974, three articles published in *The Lancet* (Jones & Smith, 1973; Jones, Smith, Streissguth, & Myrianthopoulos, 1974; Jones, Smith, Ulleland, & Streissguth, 1973) described a characteristic pattern of structural characteristics and functional deficits stemming from PAE, which they described as FAS. Because this diagnostic label did not adequately describe partial effects when a diagnosis of FAS could not be made, the term fetal alcohol effects (FAE) was introduced in 1978 (Clarren & Smith, 1978) to describe children suspected of being exposed prenatally to alcohol but without the full sentinel features and growth deficiencies known to be associated with FAS. Although not intended as a diagnostic term, in time FAE came to be used to diagnose unspecified birth defects and developmental delays when alcohol was the suspected etiology, often at the insistence of parents and caregivers (Hoyme et al., 2005).

In 1980, the characteristic pattern of birth defects in FAS was the basis for the first formal diagnostic guidelines, which were published by the Research Society on Alcoholism. The guidelines involved three criteria in the context of PAE: pre- or postnatal deficiency in height or weight, distinct constellation of facial abnormalities, and central nervous system (CNS) abnormality manifesting as neurological deficits in infancy (Rosett, 1980). Throughout the 1980s and 1990s, ongoing research investigated the diversity and severity of abnormalities associated with PAE, from stillbirth to a wide range of cognitive deficits and neurobehavioral effects (Jarmasz, Basalah, Chudley, & Del Bigio, 2017). As the science evolved, this prompted the introduction of a wider continuum of effects to supplant misused and outdated FAE (Benz, Rasmussen, & Andrew, 2009).

In 1996, the IOM published the first comprehensive diagnostic guidelines for FAS and other conditions caused by PAE in the congressionally mandated publication titled, *Fetal Alcohol Syndrome: Diagnosis, Epidemiology, Prevention, and Treatment* (Stratton et al., 1996). The IOM study group developed five diagnostic categories for FAS and alcohol-related effects:

1. FAS with confirmed maternal alcohol exposure;
2. FAS without confirmed maternal alcohol exposure;

3. Partial FAS (pFAS) with confirmed maternal alcohol exposure, consisting of some of the cardinal facial features and either growth deficiency, CNS neurodevelopmental abnormalities, and/or behavioral or cognitive impairments;
4. Alcohol-related birth defects (ARBD), referring to congenital anomalies including malformations and dysplasias; and
5. Alcohol-related neurodevelopmental disorders (ARND), a complex pattern of cognitive and behavior abnormalities and/or CNS dysfunction.

All diagnoses except FAS required a confirmed history of PAE (Benz et al., 2009). While the IOM classifications provided a diagnostic framework, they did not include specific guidance for clinicians (e.g., detailing how "impairment" was defined). Eventually, the term "fetal alcohol spectrum disorders" or FASD was introduced in the late 1990s to capture the range of deficits and dysfunction associated with PAE.

In 1997, the first edition of the FASD 4-Digit Diagnostic Code was developed by the Washington State FAS Diagnostic and Prevention Network (FAS DPN). Like the IOM guidelines, the 4-Digit Code identified and validated the complete range of alcohol-induced impairments in children and adults with FASD. The 4-Digit Code uses a four-point Likert scale to assess the four fundamental domains: PAE, facial features, growth, and CNS structural/functional abnormalities (Astley, 2004). One of the strengths of the 4-Digit Code is it objectively quantifies assessment, so any clinician can be trained to implement the system—a critical consideration for increasing diagnostic capacity. Today, the 4-Digit Code is in its third edition (Astley, 2004) and widely used in the clinical setting in the United States.

Responding to a lack of diagnostic clarity in the IOM guidelines, in 2004 the National Task Force on FAS and FAE published *Fetal Alcohol Syndrome: Guidelines for Referral and Diagnosis* in an effort to standardize criteria for FAS. This landmark publication, which was sponsored by the Centers for Disease Control, achieved widespread consensus and operationalized the diagnostic process with clinical specificity for FAS (Bertrand et al., 2004). In 2005, guidelines were published which operationalized diagnosis of disorders under the IOM framework (Hoyme et al., 2005). In 2016, these guidelines were updated (Hoyme et al., 2016). The new guidelines, which clarified and expanded upon the 2005 guidelines, were used in a surveillance project that found 1 in 20 school-age children had FASD (May et al., 2018). These guidelines adopted a new definition of PAE, a new scale for evaluating physical anomalies including facial dysmorphia, and a requirement for neurobehavioral impairment (Wozniak et al., 2019).

Meanwhile, federally mandated guidelines based upon appraisal of the leading diagnostic approaches at the time (i.e., 4-Digit Code and IOM framework) were published in Canada in 2005 (McLennan, 2015). Through a process of implementation and review, the Canada Fetal Alcohol Spectrum Disorder Research Network published an update to the Canadian diagnostic guidelines in 2016, condensing all diagnostic categories under one category: fetal alcohol spectrum disorder, either with or without sentinel facial features (Cook et al., 2016). One of the divergent features of the Canadian guidelines is use of the singular diagnosis "FASD" to incorporate all diagnoses under the FASD umbrella.

Increasingly, scientists and practitioners were finding the neurocognitive, self-regulation, and adaptive functioning impairments associated with PAE presented the most difficulty for affected individuals through the lifespan (Doyle & Mattson, 2015). Since observable facial abnormalities usually were not present in those with FASD, thereby ruling out diagnoses of FAS and pFAS, it was apparent further study was needed to either define ARND for use in clinical settings or develop a novel classification to identify the neurobehavioral characteristics associated with PAE. This issue was examined by the task force that developed the *Diagnostic and Statistical Manual of Mental Disorders* (*DSM-5*; American Psychiatric Association (APA, 2013), which resulted in the mental health diagnosis *neurodevelopmental disorder associated with prenatal alcohol exposure* (ND-PAE). Although diagnostic criteria for ND-PAE were included in *DSM-5* on a provisional basis as a condition requiring further study, the criteria have become widely accepted in the mental health field and now are the standard of practice for diagnosing the CNS impairment in FASD (Doyle & Mattson, 2015; Hagan Jr et al., 2016; Kable et al., 2016; Olson, 2015). Generally, the objective of ND-PAE is to clarify the neurodevelopmental and behavioral health symptoms associated with FASD, specifically evidence of broad deficits in executive functioning, neurologically based skills involving mental control and self-regulation, and adaptive behavior (e.g., ability to manage appropriate social and personal behavior), which currently is beyond the reach of diagnostic schemes emphasizing physical anomalies (Kable et al., 2016).

A diagnosis of ND-PAE would be suitable for a child or adult with impairments in neurocognitive functioning, self-regulation, and adaptive behavior who was exposed to more than minimal amounts of alcohol at any time during gestation. Further, the impairments must be associated with clinically significant problems that are not better explained by other known medical, pharmacological, or environmental conditions or exposures. Diagnostic criteria include neurocognitive dysfunction (e.g., evidence of impairment in one or more of the following: global intellect, executive functioning, learning, memory, or visual–spatial reasoning), self-regulation problems (e.g., at least one impairment in mood, behavior, attention, or impulse control), and at least two impairments in adaptive functioning (e.g., language, socialization, daily living skills, or motor skills). Clinicians may diagnose patients with ND-PAE by recording "Other specified neurodevelopmental disorder," followed by a specific reason such as ND-PAE and using code 315.8 (F88). A summary of the categories and criteria associated with the IOM and *DSM-5* diagnostic systems is shown in Table 1.1.

The emergence of ND-PAE has raised questions about the necessity of further elucidating both ND-PAE and ARND as there is considerable overlap in their constructs (Johnson, Moyer, Klug, & Burd, 2018). While the diagnostic criteria in both systems are quite similar, there are two principle differences: theoretically, ARND could be diagnosed in an individual without any psychiatric issues (i.e., medical diagnosis only), while ND-PAE is strictly a mental health diagnosis that does not require a multidisciplinary team. In other words, ND-PAE involves a format and

Table 1.1 Fetal Alcohol Spectrum Disorders (FASD)—Diagnostic Categories and Criteria, adapted from Stratton et al., 1996; Hoyme et al., 2016; American Psychiatric Association (APA, 2013)

Fetal Alcohol Spectrum Disorders (FASD)—Diagnostic Categories and Criteria
Fetal alcohol syndrome (FAS)·with or without documented alcohol exposure
I. Facial anomalies A. Short palpebral fissures B. Thin vermilion border C. Smooth philtrum II. Growth deficiency (prenatal or postnatal) A. Height and/or weight ≤ tenth percentile for chronological age III. Abnormal brain growth (including one or more of the following) A. Head circumference ≤ tenth percentile B. Brain structure anomalies C. Recurrent nonfebrile seizures IV. Evidence of neurobehavioral impairment (either cognitive or behavioral impairment required) A. Cognitive impairment 1. Presence of global impairment (general conceptual ability, or performance, verbal, or spatial IQ ≥ 1.5 standard deviations [SD] below the mean) or cognitive impairment in at least one neurobehavioral domain (executive function, learning, memory, or visual-spatial) 1.5 SD below the mean B. Behavioral impairment 1. Evidence of behavioral deficit in at least one domain of self-regulation (mood or behavioral regulation, attention, or impulse control) ≥ 1.5 SD below the mean
Partial Fetal alcohol syndrome (pFAS)—With documented alcohol exposure
I. Facial anomalies (including two or more of the following) A. Short palpebral fissures B. Thin vermilion border C. Smooth philtrum II. Evidence of neurobehavioral impairment (either cognitive or behavioral impairment required) A. Cognitive impairment 1. Presence of global impairment (general conceptual ability, or performance, verbal or spatial IQ ≥ 1.5 SD below the mean) or cognitive impairment in at least one neurobehavioral domain (executive function, learning, memory, or visual-spatial) ≥ 1.5 SD below the mean B. Behavioral impairment 1. Evidence of behavioral deficit in at least one domain of self-regulation (mood or behavioral regulation, attention, or impulse control) ≥ 1.5 SD below the mean

(continued)

Table 1.1 (continued)

Fetal Alcohol Spectrum Disorders (FASD)—Diagnostic Categories and Criteria
Partial Fetal alcohol syndrome (pFAS)—Without documented alcohol exposure
I. Facial anomalies (including two or more of the following) A. Short palpebral fissures B. Thin vermilion border C. Smooth philtrum II. Growth deficiency or abnormal brain growth A. Height and/or weight ≤ tenth percentile for chronological age, or B. Head circumference ≤ tenth percentile, brain structure anomalies, or recurrent nonfebrile seizures III. Evidence of neurobehavioral impairment (either cognitive or behavioral impairment required) A. Cognitive impairment 1. Presence of global impairment (general conceptual ability, or performance, verbal or spatial IQ ≥ 1.5 SD below the mean) or cognitive impairment in at least one neurobehavioral domain (executive function, learning, memory, or visual-spatial) ≥ 1.5 SD below the mean B. Behavioral impairment 1. Evidence of behavioral deficit in at least one domain of self-regulation (mood or behavioral regulation, attention, or impulse control) ≥ 1.5 SD below the mean
Alcohol-related neurobehavioral disorder (ARND)
I. Documented alcohol exposure II. Evidence of neurobehavioral impairment (either cognitive or behavioral impairment required) A. Cognitive impairment 1. Presence of global impairment (general conceptual ability, or performance, verbal, or spatial IQ ≥ 1.5 SD below the mean) or cognitive impairment in at least two neurobehavioral domains (executive function, learning, memory, or visual-spatial) ≥ 1.5 SD below the mean B. Behavioral impairment 1. Evidence of behavioral deficit in at least two domains of self-regulation (mood or behavioral regulation, attention, or impulse control) ≥ 1.5 SD below the mean
Alcohol-related birth defects (ARBD)
I. Documented alcohol exposure II. One or more physical abnormalities that have been demonstrated to be a result of prenatal alcohol exposure through either animal models or human studies.
Neurobehavioral disorder associated with prenatal alcohol exposure (ND-PAE)
I. Documented alcohol exposure during gestation II. Evidence of neurocognitive impairment (including one or more of the following) A. Global intellectual impairment B. Executive functioning deficit C. Learning impairment D. Visual-spatial reasoning deficit E. Memory deficit III. Evidence of self-regulation deficit (including one or more of the following) A. Mood or behavioral regulation impairment B. Attention deficit C. Impulse control deficit IV. Evidence of adaptive functioning deficit (two or more required; ND-PAE diagnosis requires presence of a or b) A. Communication impairment B. Social communication and interaction deficit C. Daily living skills deficit D. Motor skills deficit

structure familiar to mental health clinicians, which makes diagnosis more accessible (Hoyme et al., 2016). To date, research has not determined if both methods have utility as diagnostic tools and are sufficiently distinct or if they will be merged.

As this chapter has noted, there are a number of broadly recognized and similar approaches to diagnosing FASD. Each system has significant advantages and minor limitations. No authoritative body has recommended one approach over another, but it generally is agreed that a multidisciplinary team is necessary to conduct the most comprehensive assessment (American Academy of Pediatrics, 2013), particularly in the forensic context, where there must be an expert who can explain to the court why the diagnosis matters with respect to offense conduct. While these diagnostic systems have been implemented successfully in forensic as well as clinical settings, there is general agreement among researchers, clinicians, and public health professionals that to advance the field it is necessary to validate a single set of diagnostic guidelines that are recognized internationally (Astley, 2013; Mattson, Bernes, & Doyle, 2019). Without commitment to a universal standard, diagnostic capacity is impeded, and affected individuals continue to be undiagnosed or misdiagnosed. Essential interventions and benefits that could yield better outcomes are missed (Manning & Hoyme, 2007; Streissguth et al., 2004; Wozniak et al., 2019), and affected individuals often are misunderstood by mental health, educational, and criminal justice professionals (Kable et al., 2016). Lack of consensus also hinders assessment of research data, creates uncertainty among care providers, and provides policymakers with a rationale for inaction. Most importantly, the absence of accord has stranded more than 90% of individuals with FASD without proper diagnosis and treatment (Chasnoff, Wells, & King, 2015).

1.3 Diagnostic Challenges

Because the effects of PAE are determined in large part by quantity, timing, and pattern of alcohol exposure, which often is difficult to determine, and the relative influence of other factors such as genetics, nutrition, environment, ethnic variability, and societal disparities are not fully understood, diagnostic precision has not been achieved. Many signs and symptoms are nonspecific, and the disorders often present with broad variability and go unnoticed clinically (Mattson et al., 2019). Common signs of FASD are suggestive of many disorders, requiring careful differential diagnosis to rule out competing diagnostic possibilities. As a result, FASD has been called a diagnosis of exclusion.

A high rate of polysubstance use among women with substance use disorders also may complicate identification of FASD. Studies show polysubstance use as high as 50% among women who consume substances known to be harmful during pregnancy. Nicotine is used most often in conjunction with other substances, followed by alcohol, marijuana, and cocaine (Forray & Foster, 2015). Among users of multiple illicit drugs, high rates of binge drinking are common (Elliott, Haddock, Campos, & Benoit, 2019). Memory, learning, and behavior changes in children are linked to prenatal exposure to nicotine as well as tetrahydrocannabinol, the psychoactive compound of marijuana. Prenatal exposure to marijuana also is related to broad cognitive deficits (Scott-Goodwin, Puerto, & Moreno, 2016), while cocaine, amphetamine, Ecstasy, and opiates can affect both structural and functional brain development associated with learning and behavioral health disorders (Ross, Graham, Money, & Stanwood, 2015). As many as half of pregnant women who use marijuana also consume alcohol (Breit, Zamudio, & Thomas, 2019), and animal studies show dual exposure to alcohol and marijuana produces a greater incidence of birth defects than either substance alone (Fish et al., 2019). This synergetic effect on brain development beyond the harm resulting from each substance in isolation, including persistent effects on behavior, has been widely recognized (Breit et al., 2019; Fish et al., 2019; Gautam, Warner, Kan, & Sowell, 2015). Amid the opioid crisis, when a woman is using both alcohol and opiates, the effects of alcohol on the mother and her offspring often are obscured by treatment for opiate withdrawal.

Stigma, financial incentives, and absence of an accurate alcohol usage history from birth mothers are among other factors inhibiting accurate identification of FASD. Research strongly suggests women who use alcohol during pregnancy face condemnation from the general public (Corrigan et al., 2017). Overt and discreet discrimination shames women, discourages treatment for alcohol use disorder, and divides biological and adoptive families, all of which has restricted formation of an effective family-led FASD advocacy movement. Including the etiology or cause of the disorder in the name (e.g., fetal alcohol spectrum disorders, neurobehavioral disorder associated with prenatal alcohol exposure) was anticipated to promote awareness and prevention. However, in some instances such terminology also has increased the stigma faced by birth mothers of offspring with FASD. Several jurisdictions have sought to criminalize maternal alcohol use rather than prioritize access to therapeutic rehabilitation for women who need help to stop drinking, claiming decades of public health advisories to abstain from alcohol during pregnancy have established a societal norm that should be punished if violated. Birth mother stigma and the role of alcohol in society as a lifestyle choice can trigger resistance to abstinence messages and create significant barriers to reducing exposure and public recognition of FASD.

Another consequence of diagnostic variability is that FASD-related health-care utilization is unknown due to lack of specific medical billing and coding (Burd, Klug, Coumbe, & Kerbeshian, 2003). Other than ND-PAE criteria, FASD diagnostic schemes generally are not tailored to fit classification systems used by medical and behavioral health practitioners and public and private insurance providers. "Fetal alcohol syndrome, dysmorphic" (Q86.0) is noted in the tenth revision of the World Health Organization's International Classification of Diseases (ICD-10), a medical classification coding system used globally. However, ICD-10 does not mention the other conditions that make up the spectrum of disorders associated with PAE. Accordingly, providers must provide and bill for services using existing diagnostic categories and codes that might compromise the needs of individuals with FASD (Olson, 2015).

Obtaining an accurate maternal usage history can be problematic. Due to the instability and progressive nature of alcohol use disorder, affected individuals often are not with their birth mothers at the time of assessment. Moreover, environmental influences are known to affect outcomes but are difficult to quantify. There also is a growing concern that in the clinical setting, it is not realistic to train multidisciplinary teams on the scale necessary to meet the needs of children born each year with PAE, let alone the current population of undiagnosed children, adolescents, and adults (Burd, 2016; Cook et al., 2016).

Unfamiliarity with FASD among practitioners, diagnostic inconsistency, and a high proportion of affected individuals who present with unique constellations of symptoms result in a high rate of misdiagnosis. A systematic review of 127 FASD studies identified 428 comorbid diseases and conditions co-occurring in individuals with FASD, including congenital malformations, deformities, chromosomal abnormalities, and mental and behavioral disorders (Popova et al., 2016). Missed or inaccurate diagnosis condemns affected individuals to debilitating secondary disabilities such as mental health disorders, learning and behavioral problems that result in disrupted school experiences, trouble with the law, incarceration, inappropriate sexual behavior, alcohol and substance use disorders, dependent living, and problems with employment and parenting in adulthood (Streissguth, Barr, Kogan, & Bookstein, 1996).

1.4 FASD and the Justice System

People with FASD often end up in the criminal justice system as either victims or offenders (Burd, Selfridge, Klug, & Bakko, 2004). In fact, most individuals with FASD are not identified with the disability until entry into the child welfare, education, or judicial system. Due to diminished cognitive capacity, they often are susceptible to exploitation and manipulation, unable to read social cues or recognize social or physical risk, and have trouble making "cause and effect" connections. Executive dysfunction may impair understanding of appropriate behavior or reduce ability to conform to social customs and laws (Edwards & Greenspan, 2010). Defendants with FASD can be victimized by the justice system when they naively admit crimes they did not commit, are unable to effectively participate in their own defense because of cognitive limitations, or are victimized by other offenders during incarceration (Brown, Haun, Zapf, & Novick Brown, 2017).

Changes in social behavior in individuals prenatally exposed to alcohol, recognized as early as infancy, signal potential for aberrant behavior later in life (Kelly, Day, & Streissguth, 2000). Effects of social maladjustment in childhood tend to increase through adolescence into adulthood, causing multiple problems at home, in school, and in the community. Attention problems, hyperactivity, poor impulse control, and defiance are among behaviors that can foreshadow substance use and criminality. Estimates suggest well over half of individuals with FASD will be arrested for at least one crime (Streissguth et al., 1996; Streissguth et al., 2004).

Significant adaptive dysfunction renders those with FASD functionally equivalent to persons with intellectual disability (Greenspan, Novick Brown, & Edwards, 2016), which explains much of the offense conduct in FASD. Adaptive functioning refers to skills necessary to function independently, assimilate into society, and appropriately interact with others (Fagerlund et al., 2012). Individuals with FASD tend to display significant deficits in communication, socialization, and daily living skills, with somewhat less severe deficiency in the latter (Streissguth et al., 1996). Socialization deficits worsen with age to the point of stagnation (Crocker, Vaurio, Riley, & Mattson, 2009). Because of their cognitive deficits, children with FASD tend to have deficient response inhibition and often are unable to control inappropriate reactions (Connor, Sampson, Bookstein, Barr, & Streissguth, 2000). When solving problems, they tend to violate rules and employ inefficient strategies (Green et al., 2009). Adaptively, these impairments manifest in ways that significantly increase likelihood of social misconduct (Moore & Riley, 2015) such that by adulthood, this population has high rates of psychopathology as well as impaired coping behavior (e.g., alcohol and drug use disorders) and trouble with the law (Streissguth, 1997) stemming from adaptive dysfunction (Chudley, Kilgour, Cranston, & Edwards, 2007).

In some US states, an FASD diagnosis may be considered a mitigating factor during the sentencing phase of criminal prosecution. While the presence of an FASD does not justify or excuse criminal acts, criminal responsibility is grounded in a defendant's capacity to form intent. If judgment is impaired due to compromised cognitive functioning, as it typically is in FASD, experts have concluded the disorder should be considered in criminal proceedings (Mansfield & Luther, 2013; Shuman & Gold, 2008). The U.S. Supreme Court has recognized the death penalty is an excessive and inappropriate punishment for offenders with diminished neurocognitive capacity (Atkins v. Virginia, 2002). Consequently, FASD mitigation statutes would be an important step toward encouraging courts to take FASD into account when considering criminal sanctions.

Several studies have confirmed that a large number of youths and adults come into contact with the justice system (Fast, Conry, & Loock, 1999), yet a survey found only one out of over three million inmates across 54 corrections systems in the United States had an FASD diagnosis (Burd et al., 2004). This finding illuminates the need for greater education of law enforcement, courts, and correctional systems if persons with FASD are to be afforded fair and appropriate adjudication (Burd et al., 2004; Fast & Conry, 2004). Both the Canadian and American Bar Associations have passed resolutions acknowledging the prevalence of FASD in the juvenile and criminal justice systems, urging adoption of policies and statutes to ensure courts and corrections systems receive training on FASD, so legal professionals understand the disability's impact on behavior and are prepared to respond appropriately (American Bar Association, 2012).

1.5 Conclusion

For nearly 50 years, scientific breakthroughs have enhanced understanding of the underlying biological basis for FASD and enlightened diagnostic standards, treatment protocols, and public health advice regarding alcohol and pregnancy. However, obstacles continue to hinder dissemination of these discoveries throughout clinical practice. While limited public resources have constrained the pace of basic research, even less investment has been dedicated to translational science. Beyond insufficient public and private investment, inconsistency regarding use of terminology and diagnostic criteria in the United States substantially reduces identification and diagnosis. Internationally, widespread belief that FASD is rare and does not warrant significant attention as well as stigma surrounding birth mothers who drink have delayed progress. In contrast to the investment in autism and response to the opioid crisis, including neonatal abstinence syndrome resulting from maternal opioid addiction, FASD remains largely ignored. Just as the overdose epidemic is devastating and frightening, it is intermingled with the unnoticed tragedy of lost generations of children who were exposed to alcohol before birth, remain undiagnosed, and face lifelong impairments and suffering costly to them and society.

While these challenges persist, steady headway offers reason for optimism. An increase in scientific discoveries, clinical capacity, public health messages, policy proposals, anti-stigma awareness, and community-based initiatives are incrementally advancing the field. The Collaborative Initiative on Fetal Alcohol Spectrum Disorders (CIFASD), a research consortium of basic and clinical investigators, is informing and developing effective screening, diagnosis, intervention, and treatment approaches for FASD. Advocates are working with policymakers to boost recognition of FASD in disease classification systems, eligibility criteria for disability benefits, delivery of integrated care, and intellectual disability definitions. Women of child-bearing age who have difficulty abstaining from alcohol are finding programs such as the Circle of Hope, Recovering Mothers Anonymous (RMA), and addiction support and mentorship recovery programs. The NOFAS Affiliate Network of state and local services, support, and advocacy organizations is unifying the field, expanding resources, and giving a voice to the FASD experience. Now the aim is to ensure that ongoing expansion of strategies like these will compel systems, disciplines, and society to fulfill their obligation to accept and support children and adults with FASD, ultimately replacing the distress, grief, and injustice of living with FASD with hope, healing, and dignity.

References

American Academy of Pediatrics. (2013). *American Academy of Pediatrics AAP FASD Toolkit.* https://www.aap.org/en-us/advocacy-and-policy/aap-health-initiatives/fetal-alcohol-spectrum-disorders-toolkit/Pages/default.aspx

American Bar Association. (2012). *FASD resolution and report.* https://www.americanbar.org/groups/public_interest/child_law/resources/attorneys/fasd-resolution/

American Psychiatric Association (APA). (2013). *Diagnostic and statistical manual of mental disorders (DSM-5)* (5th ed.). Arlington, VA: American Psychiatric Association.

Astley, S. J. (2004). *Diagnostic guide for fetal alcohol spectrum disorders: The 4-digit diagnostic code* (3rd ed.). Seattle: University of Washington.

Astley, S. J. (2013). Validation of the fetal alcohol spectrum disorder (FASD) 4-digit diagnostic code. *Journal of Population Therapeutics and Clinical Pharmacology, 20*(3), e416–e467.

Atkins v. Virginia. (2002). 536 U.S. 304.

Benz, J., Rasmussen, C., & Andrew, G. (2009). Diagnosing fetal alcohol spectrum disorder: History, challenges and future directions. *Pediatrics & Child Health, 14*(4), 231–237. https://doi.org/10.1093/pch/14.4.231

Bertrand, J., Floyd, R. L., Weber, M. K., O'Connor, M. J., Riley, E. P., Johnson, K. A., … with National Task Force on Fetal Alcohol Syndrome and Fetal Alcohol Effect. (2004). *Fetal alcohol syndrome: Guidelines for referral and diagnosis.* Atlanta, GA: Centers for Disease Control and Prevention.

Breit, K. R., Zamudio, B., & Thomas, J. D. (2019). The effects of alcohol and cannabinoid exposure during the brain growth spurt on behavioral development in rats. *Birth Defects Research, 111*(12), 760–774. https://doi.org/10.1002/bdr2.1487

Brown, J. M., Haun, J., Zapf, P. A., & Novick Brown, N. (2017). Fetal alcohol spectrum disorders (FASD) and competency to stand trial (CST): Suggestions for a "best practices" approach to forensic evaluation. *International Journal of Law and Psychiatry, 52*, 19–27. https://doi.org/10.1016/j.ijlp.2017.04.002

Burd, L. (2016). Fetal alcohol spectrum disorder: Complexity from comorbidity. *Lancet, 387*, 926–927. https://doi.org/10.1016/s0140-6736(15)01346-x

Burd, L., Klug, M. G., Coumbe, M. J., & Kerbeshian, J. (2003). Children and adolescents with attention deficit-hyperactivity disorder: 1. Prevalence and cost of care. *Journal of Child Neurology, 18*(8), 555–561. https://doi.org/10.1177/08830738030180080101

Burd, L., Selfridge, R., Klug, M., & Bakko, S. (2004). Fetal alcohol syndrome in the United States corrections system. *Addiction Biology, 9*(2), 169–176. https://doi.org/10.1080/13556210410001717060

Calhoun, F., & Warren, K. R. (2007). Fetal alcohol syndrome: Historical perspectives. *Neuroscience and Biobehavioral Reviews, 31*(2), 168–171. https://doi.org/10.1016/j.neubiorev.2006.06.023

Charness, M. E., Riley, E. P., & Sowell, E. R. (2016). Drinking during pregnancy and the developing brain: Is any amount safe? *Trends in Cognitive Sciences, 20*(2), P80–P82. https://doi.org/10.1016/j.tics.2015.09.011

Chasnoff, I. J., Wells, A. M., & King, L. (2015). Misdiagnosis and missed diagnoses in foster and adopted children with prenatal alcohol exposure. *Pediatrics, 135*(2), 264–270. https://doi.org/10.1542/peds.2014-2171

Chudley, A. E., Kilgour, A. R., Cranston, M., & Edwards, M. (2007). Challenges of diagnosis in fetal alcohol syndrome and fetal alcohol spectrum disorder in the adult. *American Journal of Medical Genetics Part C: Seminars in Medical Genetics, 145C*(3), 261–272. https://doi.org/10.1002/ajmg.c.30140

Clarren, S. K., & Smith, D. W. (1978). The fetal alcohol syndrome. *New England Journal of Medicine, 298*(19), 1063–1067. https://doi.org/10.1056/nejm197805112981906

Connor, P. D., Sampson, P. D., Bookstein, F. L., Barr, H. M., & Streissguth, A. P. (2000). Direct and indirect effects of prenatal alcohol damage on executive function. *Developmental Neuropsychology, 18*(3), 331–354. https://doi.org/10.1207/S1532694204Connor

Cook, J. L., Green, C. R., Lilley, C. M., Anderson, S. M., Baldwin, M. E., Chudley, A. E., … Rosales, T. (2016). Fetal alcohol spectrum disorder: A guideline for diagnosis across the lifespan. *CMAJ: Canadian Medical Association Journal, 188*(3), 191–197. https://doi.org/10.1503/cmaj.141593

Corrigan, P. W., Lara, J. L., Shah, B. B., Mitchell, K. T., Simmes, D., & Jones, K. L. (2017). The public stigma of birth mothers of children with fetal alcohol spectrum disorders. *Alcoholism: Clinical and Experimental Research, 41*(6), 1166–1173. https://doi.org/10.1111/acer.13381

Crocker, N., Vaurio, L., Riley, E. P., & Mattson, S. N. (2009). Comparison of adaptive behavior in children with heavy prenatal alcohol exposure or attention-deficit/hyperactivity disorder. *Alcoholism: Clinical and Experimental Research, 33*(11), 2015–2023. https://doi.org/10.1111/j.1530-0277.2009.01040.x

Davis, P. J., Partridge, J. W., & Storrs, C. N. (1982). Alcohol consumption in pregnancy. How much is safe? *Archives of Disease in Childhood, 57*(12), 940–943. https://doi.org/10.1136/adc.57.12.940

Denny, C. H., Acero, C. S., Naimi, T. S., & Kim, S. Y. (2019). Consumption of alcohol beverages and binge drinking among pregnant women aged 18-44 years—United States, 2015-2017. *Morbidity and Mortality Weekly Report (MMWR), 68*(16), 365–368. https://doi.org/10.15585/mmwr.mm6816a1

Doyle, L. R., & Mattson, S. N. (2015). Neurobehavioral disorder associated with prenatal alcohol exposure (ND-PAE): Review of evidence and guidelines for assessment. *Current Developmental Disorders Reports, 2*(3), 175–186. https://doi.org/10.1007/s40474-015-0054-6

Edwards, W. J., & Greenspan, S. (2010). Adaptive behavior and fetal alcohol spectrum disorders. *Journal of Psychiatry & Law, 38*(4), 419–447. https://doi.org/10.1177/009318531003800404

Elliott, L., Haddock, C. K., Campos, S., & Benoit, E. (2019). Polysubstance use patterns and novel synthetics: A cluster analysis from three U.S. cities. *PLoS One, 14*(12), e0225273. https://doi.org/10.1371/journal.pone.0225273

Fagerlund, Å., Autti-Rämö, I., Kalland, M., Santtila, P., Hoyme, H. E., Mattson, S. N., & Korkman, M. (2012). Adaptive behaviour in children and adolescents with foetal alcohol spectrum disorders: A comparison with specific learning disability and typical development. *European Child & Adolescent Psychiatry, 21*(4), 221–231. https://doi.org/10.1007/s00787-012-0256-y

Fast, D. K., & Conry, J. (2004). The challenge of fetal alcohol syndrome in the criminal legal system. *Addiction Biology, 9*(2), 161–166. https://doi.org/10.1080/13556210410001717042

Fast, D. K., Conry, J., & Loock, C. A. (1999). Identifying fetal alcohol syndrome among youth in the criminal justice system. *Journal of Developmental & Behavioral Pediatrics, 20*(5), 370–372. https://doi.org/10.1097/00004703-199910000-00012

Fish, E. W., Murdaugh, L. B., Zhang, C., Boschen, K. E., Boa-Amponsem, O., Mendoza-Romero, H. N., … Parnell, S. E. (2019). Cannabinoids exacerbate alcohol teratogenesis by a CB1-hedgehog interaction. *Scientific Reports, 9*, 16057. https://doi.org/10.1038/s41598-019-52336-w

Food and Drug Administration (FDA). (1981). Surgeon General's advisory on alcohol and pregnancy. *FDA Drug Bulletin, 11*(2), 9–10. http://come-over.to/FAS/SurgeonGeneral.htm.

Forray, A., & Foster, D. (2015). Substance use in the perinatal period. *Current Psychiatry Reports, 17*, 91. https://doi.org/10.1007/s11920-015-0626-5

Gautam, P., Warner, T. D., Kan, E. C., & Sowell, E. R. (2015). Executive function and cortical thickness in youths prenatally exposed to cocaine, alcohol and tobacco. *Developmental Cognitive Neuroscience, 16*, 155–165. https://doi.org/10.1016/j.dcn.2015.01.010

Green, C. R., Mihic, A. M., Nikkel, S. M., Stade, B. C., Rasmussen, C., Munoz, D. P., & Reynolds, J. N. (2009). Executive function deficits in children with fetal alcohol spectrum disorders (FASD) measured using the Cambridge neuropsychological tests automated battery (CANTAB). *Journal of Child Psychology and Psychiatry, and Allied Disciplines, 50*(6), 688–697. https://doi.org/10.1111/j.1469-7610.2008.01990.x

Greenmyer, J. R., Klug, M. G., Kambeitz, C., Popova, S., & Burd, L. (2018). A multicountry updated assessment of the economic impact of fetal alcohol spectrum disorder: Costs for children and adults. *Journal of Addiction Medicine, 12*(6), 466–473. https://doi.org/10.1097/adm.0000000000000438

Greenspan, S., Novick Brown, N., & Edwards, W. (2016). FASD and the concept of "intellectual disability equivalence". In M. Nelson & M. Trussler (Eds.), *Fetal alcohol spectrum disorders in adults: Ethical and legal perspectives* (pp. 241–266). Amsterdam and New York: Springer.

Hagan, J. F., Jr., Balachova, T., Bertrand, J., Chasnoff, I., Dang, E., Fernandez-Baca, D., … on behalf of Neurobehavioral Disorder Associated with Prenatal Alcohol Exposure Workgroup and American Academy of Pediatrics. (2016). Neurobehavioral disorder associated with prenatal alcohol exposure. *Pediatrics, 138*(4), e20151553. https://doi.org/10.1542/peds.2015-1553

Hoyme, H. E., Kalberg, W. O., Elliott, A. J., Blankenship, J., Buckley, D., Marais, A. S., … May, P. A. (2016). Updated clinical guidelines for diagnosing fetal alcohol spectrum disorders. *Pediatrics, 138*(2), e20154256. https://doi.org/10.1542/peds.2015-4256

Hoyme, H. E., May, P. A., Kalberg, W. O., Kodituwakku, P., Gossage, J. P., Trujillo, P. M., Buckley,. . . Robinson, L. K. (2005). A practical clinical approach to diagnosis of fetal alcohol spectrum disorders: Clarification of the 1996 Institute of Medicine criteria. Pediatrics, 115(1), 39–47. doi:https://doi.org/10.1542/peds.2004-0259

Jarmasz, J. S., Basalah, D. A., Chudley, A. E., & Del Bigio, M. R. (2017). Human brain abnormalities associated with prenatal alcohol exposure and fetal alcohol spectrum disorder. *Journal of Neuropathology & Experimental Neurology, 76*(9), 813–833. https://doi.org/10.1093/jnen/nlx064

Johnson, S., Moyer, C. L., Klug, M. G., & Burd, L. (2018). Comparison of alcohol-related neurodevelopmental disorders and neurodevelopmental disorders associated with prenatal alcohol exposure diagnostic criteria. *Journal of Developmental & Behavioral Pediatrics, 39*(2), 163–167. https://doi.org/10.1097/dbp.0000000000000523

Jones, K. L., & Smith, D. W. (1973). Recognition of the fetal alcohol syndrome in early infancy. *Lancet, 302*(7836), 999–1001. https://doi.org/10.1016/s0140-6736(73)91092-1

Jones, K. L., Smith, D. W., Streissguth, A. P., & Myrianthopoulos, N. C. (1974). Outcome in offspring of chronic alcoholic women. *Lancet, 1*(7866), 1076–1078. https://doi.org/10.1016/s0140-6736(74)90555-8

Jones, K. L., Smith, D. W., Ulleland, C. N., & Streissguth, A. P. (1973). Pattern of malformation in offspring of chronic alcoholic mothers. *Lancet, 1*(7815), 1267–1271. https://doi.org/10.1016/s0140-6736(73)91291-9

Kable, J. A., O'Connor, M. J., Olson, H. C., Paley, B., Mattson, S. N., Anderson, S., & Riley, E. P. (2016). Neurobehavioral disorder associated with prenatal alcohol exposure (ND-PAE): Proposed DSM-5 diagnosis. *Child Psychiatry and Human Development, 47*, 335–346. https://doi.org/10.1007/s10578-015-0566-7

Kelly, S. J., Day, N., & Streissguth, A. P. (2000). Effects of prenatal alcohol exposure on social behavior in humans and other species. *Neurotoxicology and Teratology, 22*(2), 143–149. https://doi.org/10.1016/s0892-0362(99)00073-2

Lemoine, P., Harousseau, H., Borteyru, J. P., & Menuet, J. C. (1968). Les enfants des parents alcoholiques: Anomolies observees a propos de 127 cas (the children of alcoholic parents: Anomalies observed in 127 cases). *Quest Medical, 25*, 476–482.

Manning, M. A., & Hoyme, H. E. (2007). Fetal alcohol spectrum disorders: A practical clinical approach to diagnosis. *Neuroscience & Biobehavioral Reviews, 31*(2), 230–238. https://doi.org/10.1016/j.neubiorev.2006.06.016

Mansfield, M., & Luther, G. (2013). Fetal alcohol spectrum disorder: Can diminished responsibility diminish criminal behaviour? *International Journal of Law and Psychiatry, 36*(1), 46–54. https://doi.org/10.1016/j.ijlp.2012.11.007

Mattson, S. N., Bernes, G. A., & Doyle, L. R. (2019). Fetal alcohol spectrum disorders: A review of the neurobehavioral deficits associated with prenatal alcohol exposure. *Alcoholism: Clinical and Experimental Research, 43*(6), 1046–1062. https://doi.org/10.1111/acer.14040

May, P. A., Chambers, C. D., Kalberg, W. O., Zellner, J., Feldman, H., Buckley, . . . Hoyme, H. E. (2018). Prevalence of fetal alcohol spectrum disorders in 4 US communities. Journal of the American Medical Association, 319(5), 474–482. doi:https://doi.org/10.1001/jama.2017.21896

McLennan, J. D. (2015). Misattributions and potential consequences: The case of child mental health problems and fetal alcohol spectrum disorders. *Canadian Journal of Psychiatry, 60*(12), 587–590. https://doi.org/10.1177/070674371506001210

Moore, E. M., & Riley, E. P. (2015). What happens when children with fetal alcohol spectrum disorders become adults? *Current Developmental Disorders Reports, 2*(3), 219–227. https://doi.org/10.1007/s40474-015-0053-7

Olson, H. C. (2015). Advancing recognition of fetal alcohol spectrum disorders: The proposed DSM-5 diagnosis of "neurobehavioral disorder associated with prenatal alcohol exposure (ND-PAE).". *Current Developmental Disorders Report, 2*(3), 187–198. https://doi.org/10.1007/s40474-015-0056-4

Popova, S., Lange, S., Shield, K., Mihic, A., Chudley, A. E., Mukherjee, R. A. S., … Rehm, J. (2016). Comorbidity of fetal alcohol spectrum disorder: A systematic review and meta-analysis. *Lancet, 387*(10022), 978–987. https://doi.org/10.1016/s0140-6736(15)01345-8

Rosett, H. L. (1980). A clinical perspective of the fetal alcohol syndrome. *Alcoholism: Clinical and Experimental Research, 4*(2), 119–122. https://doi.org/10.1111/j.1530-0277.1980.tb05626.x

Ross, E. J., Graham, D. L., Money, K. M., & Stanwood, G. D. (2015). Developmental consequences of fetal exposure to drugs: What we know and what we still must learn. *Neuropsychopharmacology, 40*, 61–87. https://doi.org/10.1038/npp.2014.147

Scott-Goodwin, A. C., Puerto, M., & Moreno, I. (2016). Toxic effects of prenatal exposure to alcohol, tobacco and other drugs. *Reproductive Toxicology (Elmsford, NY), 61*, 120–130. https://doi.org/10.1016/j.reprotox.2016.03.043

Shuman, D. W., & Gold, L. H. (2008). Without thinking: Impulsive aggression and criminal responsibility. *Behavioral Sciences & the Law, 26*(6), 723–734. https://doi.org/10.1002/bsl.847

Stratton, K., Howe, C., & Battaglia, F. (Eds.). (1996). *Fetal alcohol syndrome: Diagnosis, epidemiology, prevention, and treatment*. Washington, DC: National Academy Press.

Streissguth, A. P. (1997). *Fetal alcohol syndrome: A guide for families and communities*. Baltimore, MD: Brookes.

Streissguth, A. P., Barr, H. M., Kogan, J., & Bookstein, F. L. (1996). *Understanding the occurrence of secondary disabilities in clients with fetal alcohol syndrome (FAS) and fetal alcohol effects (FAE): Final report*. Seattle: University of Washington. http://lib.adai.uw.edu/pubs/bk2698.pdf.

Streissguth, A. P., Bookstein, F. L., Barr, H. M., Sampson, P. D., O'Malley, K., & Young, J. K. (2004). Risk factors for adverse life outcomes in fetal alcohol syndrome and fetal alcohol effects. *Journal of Developmental and Behavioral Pediatrics (JDBP), 25*(4), 228–238. https://doi.org/10.1097/00004703-200408000-00002

U.S. Department of Health and Human Services (HHS). (2005). *U. S. Surgeon General releases advisory on alcohol use in pregnancy*. Washington, DC: US Department of Health and Human Services. https://wayback.archive-it.org/3926/20140421162517/http://www.surgeongeneral.gov/news/2005/02/sg02222005.html#

Wozniak, J. R., Riley, E. P., & Charness, M. E. (2019). Clinical presentation, diagnosis, and management of fetal alcohol spectrum disorder. *Lancet Neurology, 18*(8), 760–770. https://doi.org/10.1016/s1474-4422(19)30150-4

Chapter 2
Relevance of Fetal Alcohol Spectrum Disorder in the Forensic Context

Karen A. Steele

Abstract A person without a visible condition or disability is perceived and characterized as normal, presumed to perform according to their own autonomy or free will, and expected to perform according to societal standards. Most often, fetal alcohol spectrum disorder (FASD) is an *invisible* disorder with a range of disadvantageous structural and functional effects, many of which have implications for how (and with what information) legal determinations relative to intent, responsibility, and degree of culpability are made. Further impacting those determinations are the environmental and procedural characteristics of forensic contexts, which have predominantly negative implications in relation to the FASD population. This chapter examines civil and criminal court concepts with relevance to FASD, identifies selected FASD characteristics with relevance to those concepts, and provides a brief overview of reported cases, which reveals that thus far, forensic practice has belatedly and myopically incorporated and presented evidence of FASD. Finally, this chapter suggests an approach to integrating past, present, and future while using the science of FASD as a contextualizing framework by which the affected person's whole cloth of their life—including the charged crime—can be evaluated and analyzed. This approach largely relies on educating decision-makers with accurate and current science, using accommodations to inform as well as accommodate, emphasizing function over diagnostic labels, accentuating narratives and stories over catalogs of facts, and maintaining awareness of ever-evolving societal standards.

Keywords FASD · ND-PAE · Fitness · Competency to stand trial (CST) · Intellectual disability · Developmental disorder · Suggestibility · Confabulation · False confession · Mitigation · Sentencing

---

Never imagine yourself not to be otherwise than what it might appear to others that what you were or might have been was not otherwise than what you had been would have appeared to them to be otherwise.—Carroll (1978), *Alice's Adventures*, p. 83

K. A. Steele (✉)
Attorney at Law, Salem, OR, USA
e-mail: kasteele@karenasteele.com

N. Novick Brown (ed.), *Evaluating Fetal Alcohol Spectrum Disorders in the Forensic Context*, https://doi.org/10.1007/978-3-030-73628-6_2

2.1 Introduction

Geschwind's (1975) observation that "every behavior has an anatomy" (p. 5) holds true as it relates to fetal alcohol spectrum disorders (FASD),[1] a spectrum of disorders encompassing a range of adverse effects and deficits stemming from prenatal alcohol exposure that tend to "become more complex across the lifespan" (Kambeitz, Klug, Greenmyer, Popova, & Burd, 2019). The "anatomy" of FASD includes a range of anatomical, growth, cognitive, social, and behavioral abnormalities (Mela, Coons-Harding, & Anderson, 2019),[2] "though notable variability of relative deficits and strengths is often seen in this population" (Mullally, McLachlan, MacKillop, & Pei, 2020, p. 701). FASD often is called an invisible, brain-based disorder. Indeed, up to 90% of alcohol-affected children do not exhibit physical abnormalities associated with FASD (Kingdon, Cardoso, & McGrath, 2016). FASD involves prenatal damage to the brain, with wide-ranging neurobehavioral deficits considered to be the most debilitating impact of prenatal alcohol exposure. (Treit et al., 2013). Prenatal damage to the brain is then followed by postnatal abnormal or disrupted brain development that continues throughout life. One of the hallmark adverse effects of FASD is executive function impairment (Kingdon et al., 2016). Related abnormalities can include problems with memory, attention, impulse control, emotion regulation, linking cause and effect, generalization and contextual intelligence, confabulation, suggestibility, and adaptive functioning (Mattson, Bernes, & Doyle, 2019).

Adverse childhood experiences (ACEs) in the FASD population appear to be more common than in the broader population, and there is heightened prevalence of FASD in many vulnerable populations, including those in foster care, special education, and Indigenous populations (Kambeitz et al., 2019). Those adverse experiences and "increased prevalence of comorbid mental and developmental disorders in people with FASD" support awareness of the increasing complexity of adverse effects across the lifespan (Kambeitz et al., 2019, p. 2). In a similar vein, FASD is "significantly correlated with criminal justice involvement" (Douds, Stevens, & Sumner, 2013, p. 493; and see Mela & Luther, 2013), and there is overrepresentation of this population in the juvenile and adult criminal justice systems as compared to the broader population (McLachlan et al., 2019).[3] This overrepresentation

[1] Throughout this chapter, for simplicity, FASD is used to refer to all diagnoses within that umbrella. For a description of the diagnoses within FASD and the range of effects of the disorder, see Mattson et al. (2019), as well as other chapters within this volume.

[2] Emerging literature reflects that, by comparison to the general population, persons with FASD had health concerns at rates much higher than the general population which can include a wide range of physiological problems. "It is not unreasonable to consider these whole-body effects and realize that many behavioral, emotional and learning problems may be linked to not only the brain aspects of FASD but also to the physical complications." (Choate & Badry, 2019).

[3] McLachlan et al. (2019), also noted, "…data suggest that as many as 60% of adolescents and adults with FASD assessed through clinical settings have contact with the criminal justice system, a rate 30 times higher than the general population[.]" See also, Douds et al. (2013), p. 493 ("The effects of FASDs plague people throughout their lives, causing them to be at increased risk for delinquent and criminal behavior and for contact with criminal justice systems"); and Kambeitz et al., 2019.

is comprised of victims and witnesses as well as those accused of crime violations (Novick Brown et al., 2015). The correlation between FASDs and criminal justice involvement can be safely said to flow from the structural and functional differences stemming from FASD, comorbidities, and their consequential behaviors, rather than from a diagnostic label affixed to a person. FASD is not confined by man-made boundaries or jurisdictional lines and despite global prevention efforts, "there is reason to believe that its prevalence could increase around the globe in the coming years" (Popova, Lange, Probst, Gmel, & Rehm, 2017, p. 297).

Constitutional, statutory, regulatory, and interpretive dictates and guides, as enforced and applied by the civil and criminal courts, vary jurisdiction by jurisdiction. While generally it is assumed for purposes of this chapter that counsel's duty is to provide competent representation, applying legal knowledge, professional skill and judgment commensurate with the nature and complexity of the case (extending not only to the subject matter of the representation but also nature and complexity of the client themself[4]), counsel's legal and professional duties and responsibilities also vary depending on jurisdiction. Given jurisdictional variances, this chapter does not aim to analyze any particular forensic process but instead to identify and briefly explore broad concepts common to FASD in forensic contexts, thereby demonstrating a way of thinking about these issues that proves useful to all professionals involved as they fulfill their respective roles.

This chapter is organized as follows: Section 2.2 discusses concepts in the civil and criminal (justice) courts having particular relevance to analyzing and working with FASD in forensic contexts. Section 2.3, while not attempting to be exhaustive, identifies FASD features of particular salience to those concepts. Section 2.4 highlights the quotidian uses of FASD in forensic contexts. Section 2.5 suggests considerations and approaches in applying FASD in criminal defense cases, advocating the use of FASD science to underlie all issues in the forensic context and proposing that certain approaches be incorporated in the representation of those with FASD.

[4] See, e.g., American Bar Association (2020), providing "[c]ompetent representation requires the legal knowledge, skill, thoroughness and preparation reasonably necessary for the representation," and Rule 1.16 Declining or Terminating Representation (providing for the need to decline or withdraw if representation cannot be afforded competently); and see also Federation of Law Societies of Canada (2017), p. 15, requiring "application of appropriate skills[,]" "recognizing limitations in one's ability to handle a matter or some aspect of it and taking steps accordingly to ensure the client is appropriately served"; and "otherwise adapting to changing professional requirements, standards, techniques and practices"; United Nations Office on Drugs and Crime (UNODC) (2017), p. 7, affirming that "in all cases in which the interests of justice so require, be entitled to have a lawyer of experience and competence commensurate with the nature of the offence assigned to them in order to provide effective legal assistance"; and Eighth United Nations Congress on the Prevention of Crime and the Treatment of Offenders (1990), "Special safeguards in criminal justice matters: … 6. Any such persons who do not have a lawyer shall, in all cases in which the interests of justice so require, be entitled to have a lawyer of experience and competence commensurate with the nature of the offence…."

2.2 Relevant Civil and Criminal Court Concepts

Very generally, courts determine the existence and degree of responsibility for harms resulting from a "bad" act (or failure to take necessary action) coupled with some degree of "bad" intent, with that determination leading to the implementation of protective measures—a form of restitution, or otherwise making whole, and/or punishment (Mela & Luther, 2013). The "central thought" is an accused person must be "blameworthy in mind" before being found guilty, a concept courts have expressed over time using various terms including *mens rea*, scienter, malice aforethought, and guilty knowledge.[5] Although there are exceptions, the general rule is that a guilty mind is "a necessary element in the indictment and proof of every crime."[6] In other words, as Hart (2012) explains,

> …the general requirement of *mens rea* is an element in criminal responsibility designed to secure that those who offend without carelessness, unwittingly, or in conditions in which they lacked the bodily or mental capacity to conform to the law, should be excused. A legal system would be open to serious moral condemnation if this were not so[.] (p. 178)

Courts make determinations of responsibility and consequences pursuant to the authority granted them, subject to constitutional and common law or statutory rules and guides reflecting society's collective views and morality.[7] Described as universal and persistent in mature systems of law, "the basic principle [is] that 'wrongdoing must be conscious to be criminal.'"[8] Similarly basic is the belief in freedom of people's agency, or free will,[9] and their consequent ability and duty to choose between good and evil[10] as they make decisions to act (or resist impulse to act; Hart,

[5] Morissette v. United States (1952), 342 U.S. 246, 252, 72 S.Ct. 240, 96 L.Ed.2d 288; and see LaFave (2003), §5.1, vol. 1, pp. 332–333; Samuels (1988); Mela & Luther (2013); and P. J. Knoll, (1988).

[6] United States v. Balint (1922), 258 U.S. 250, 251, 42 S.Ct. 301, 66 L.Ed. 604.

[7] "The fundamental basis of morality is awareness of one's self over time in relation to others and the future consequences of one's actions toward others and of others' toward one's self. This daily intersection of each human's goal-directed activities among those of other goal-directed humans requires rules (ethics) for making such activities run as smoothly and peaceably as possible" (Barkley, 2012, p. 25); and see also, Kim & Gerber, 2018.

[8] *Morissette*, *supra*, 342 U.S. at 250 cited with approval in Elonis v. United States (2015) 575 U.S. ____, 135 S.Ct. 2001, 2009, 192 L.Ed.2d 1.

[9] *Elonis*, *supra*, 135 S.Ct. at 2009 (explaining that the basic principal cited in *Morissette* is "as universal and persistent in mature systems of law as belief in freedom of the human will and a consequent ability and duty of the normal individual to choose between good and evil.").

[10] *Morissette*, *supra*, 342 U.S. at 250. See also, Atiq, 2013; Blagg et al., 2018. To the extent the individual does not possess or experience agency to make decisions, complete or partial defenses to criminal accusations are made available through laws, rules, and guides (Slovenko, 1984).

2012), doing so according to societal standards (Hart, 2012)[11] and based upon an understanding of cause and consequences (Roach & Bailey, 2009).[12]

Generally, questions for the courts and parties appearing before them are whether the "bad" act qualifies as a compensable or punishable act and whether there is "bad" intent (and to what degree) such that charged persons should be held responsible for the greater good. In making these determinations, the aim is to treat like cases alike and different cases differently, employing a "shifting or varying criterion used in determining when, for any given purpose, cases are alike or different" (Hart, 2012, p. 160).[13] Whether a particular "bad" act occurred can be answered with relative ease based upon evidence presented. With few exceptions, establishing the commission of an act does not establish responsibility (Leifer, 1967). In contrast to the relative ease with which the commission of an act can be shown, whether an individual had the requisite "bad" intent at the time of the act (or failure to act) is not as easily answered because intent is inferred from the relationships between words, actions, environments and contexts, based upon generally held assumptions and expectations about what it all means.

Many believe that whether a person intends something (or not) is a straightforward question that does not require complex or sophisticated interpretation but is immediately and intuitively recognizable (Bruner, 1986, 2002; Le Guin, 2004). Thus, for many, a person's appearance of normalcy carries assumptions there also is normalcy in ability to act according to autonomous free will and according to societal standards. Within a framework of hegemony, ideology, stories, narratives, and personal experiences (Artz & Murphy, 2000; Kleinstuber, 2014; Stoddart, 2007), our own personal history and visual clues influence how we categorize the person whose intent and free will are in question. Does the person appear closer to our folk beliefs of what is normal and consistent with "how the world works" (Amsterdam & Bruner, 2000, p. 111; Artz & Murphy, 2000)[14] and according to the best possible version of ourselves (Alicke, 1985; Beauregard & Dunning, 2001; Karpen, 2018),[15] or does the person appear closer to our own myths of the disabled,

[11] Hart noted that, "[t]he social function which a criminal statute performs is that of setting up and defining certain kinds of conduct as something to be avoided or done by those to whom it applies, irrespective of their wishes." See also Amsterdam and Bruner (2000) noting the focus on "what our culture designates as *mattering*" (p. 111).

[12] Roach and Bailey (2009) note that, "the focus is on whether the accused was aware of the prohibited risks of his or her conduct and not on why he or she acted in such a manner. …[T]he law allows consideration of the accused's personal characteristics if they render him or her incapable of apprehending the prohibited risk" (p. 3).

[13] See also Bruner (2002); and Berger (2011).

[14] Amsterdam and Bruner (2000), p. 111, note that the questions and answers—matters of "fact"—"depend largely upon one's choice (considered or unconsidered) of some overall narrative as best describing *what happened* or *how the world works*".

[15] The so-called better than average effect "is one of the mechanisms by which people maintain positive views of themselves" (Silvera & Seger, 2004, p. 572), being driven by mechanisms operating below consciousness (Karpen, 2018). This is part of our own individual background information that is brought to bear in our determinations of intent and responsibility.

Steinbeck's Lenny,[16] or a "monster" (i.e., what we do not know)? Further, if a known condition or disability exists, how familiar are we with that condition? Is it congenital and immutable (Clemente, 2015)?[17] Absent specialized experiences or knowledge, the unquestioned and underlying assumptions are that a person's conduct and functioning should be in accordance with what we are familiar and know (i.e., what we deem to be "neurotypical" or "normal"). Normalcy so defined often is related to our concept of self—a perspective that operates "from outside in, based on the desired esteem of others and on the myriad expectations that we early, even mindlessly, pick up from the culture in which we are immersed" (Bruner, 2002, p. 65). Thus, a person without a visible condition or disability is perceived and characterized as normal, presumed to perform according to their own autonomy or free will and expected to perform according to societal standards.[18] Failure to do so is perceived as deviant (Munyi, 2012) or evil (J. L. Knoll, 2008). "So automatic and swift is this process of constructing reality that we are often blind to it" (Bruner, 2002, p. 8).

Upon a determination of responsibility for criminal law violations or civil wrongs, society's response (often through the courts) is sentencing or a civil judgment to address the harm that flows to victims and to society at large. In the criminal law context, sentencing principles in Australia, New Zealand, Canada, and the United States most closely resemble a *just desserts* model of criminal responsibility or proportionality, meaning a sentence must be proportionate to gravity of the offense and degree of culpability of the offender (Blagg, Tulich, Mutch, Williams, & May, 2018; P. J. Knoll, 1988; Roach & Bailey, 2009; Miller v. Alabama, 2012). Beyond this overarching principle, sentencing principles seek to achieve traditional penological objectives of retribution and deterrence and also may seek separation, rehabilitation, reparation, and/or restorative justice (Blagg et al., 2018; P. J. Knoll, 1988). Sentencing principles may be refined through consideration of aggravating and mitigating circumstances (implicating factors contributing to determinations of intent and agency), parity, evolving societal standards, and, in Canada and Australia, imposition of the least restrictive appropriate sanction and restraint in the use of imprisonment.

How, then, does this apply to persons with FASD? As is addressed in Sect. 2.3 of this chapter, the anatomy of FASD is at odds with the intuitive and societally formed assumptions of what is normal and to be expected (Roach & Bailey, 2009).[19]

---

[16] In relation to the disabled, Hahn (2000), p. 171, notes that "[t]he struggle to rebut accusations of organic inferiority is a process that other minority groups have had to sustain in order to secure eventual legal protection".

[17] Clemente (2015), p. 2778, notes that criminal law has historically distinguished between "idiocy" and "lunacy," the former providing "protect[ion] from punishment throughout life" due to its "congenital and permanent" nature while the latter was understood to be "intermittent, [thus] requir[ing] additional investigation to determine whether the defendant acted under such a disability" at the time of the crime.

[18] Citing to the historical literature, Munyi (2012) notes that, "[w]hen a stranger is encountered for the first time (by an individual or group), judgments are frequently based on physical appearance."

[19] Roach and Bailey (2009), p. 4, note that, "[t]hese assumptions unfortunately do not fit well with what is known about FASD as a permanent form of brain damage that can often leave people with

Consequently, this discrepancy calls into question inferences leading to determinations of intent, responsibility, and degree of culpability.

2.3 More about the "Anatomy" of Fetal Alcohol Spectrum Disorder and Why It Is Important in the Forensic Context

2.3.1 Importance of Accurate and Current Science

Science cannot gauge intent, responsibility, or degree of culpability. Science can, however, shed light on certain measurable attributes that the law has long treated as highly relevant to these concepts.[20] Given the role of the fact-finder in making determinations relative to intent, responsibility, and degree of culpability, relevant science should be made available to assist in those determinations. Moreover, research demonstrates that where a subject is not well-understood—as is often the case with FASD—or where reality stands in contrast with commonly held assumptions and/or misinformation—as is also the case with FASD—science can play a pivotal role in providing necessary, corrective information (Bousfield, Cook, & Roesch, 2014). That information must be accurate and current. In an intellectual disability context (equally salient to the FASD context), the U.S. Supreme Court emphasized,

> That this Court, state courts, and state legislatures consult and are informed by the work of medical experts in determining intellectual disability is unsurprising. Those professionals use their learning and skills to study and consider the consequences of the classification schemes they devise in the diagnosis of persons with mental or psychiatric disorders or disabilities. Society relies upon medical and professional expertise to define and explain how to diagnose the mental condition at issue. And the definition of intellectual disability by skilled professionals…is relevant to education, access to social programs, and medical treatment plans. In determining who qualifies as intellectually disabled, it is proper to consult the medical community's opinions. (Hall v. Florida, 2014, 572 U.S. at 710).

In other words, not only is it proper to consult the medical community's opinions, the Court has cautioned against disregarding or diminishing the force of the medical community's current standards, describing those standards as supplying one constraint on the legislating authority (i.e., the states).[21]

Fast and Conry (2009) use the mnemonic device "ALARM" to describe FASD as adversely implicating: adaptive functioning, language, attention, reasoning, and memory (p. 252). While FASD is said to be a "brain-based" disorder, it significantly

---

the basic ability to function but subject to memory loss, impulsivity, and easily led by suggestions from others."

[20] *Brief of the American Medical Association,* et al., *as Amici Curiae*, p. 3, submitted in Roper v. Simmons (2005) (citing Atkins v. Virginia (2002), 536 U.S. 304, 306, 122 S.Ct. 2242, 153 L. Ed.2d 335).

[21] Moore v. Texas (2017), 581 U.S. __, 137 S.Ct. 1039, 1053, 197 L.Ed.2d 416.

affects multiple systems and organs (Mela & Luther, 2013). Indeed, over 400 coexisting conditions have been described in persons with FASD, and comorbidities have been shown to affect a multitude of body systems, such as eyes, ears, circulatory, respiratory, digestive, skin, and musculoskeletal (Mela & Luther, 2013). Failure to accurately diagnose and properly accommodate FASD can affect allocation of resources as well as lead to inappropriate interventions and services (Mattson et al., 2019), which can result in "deficits hav[ing] an increasingly debilitating effect[,]…interfering with successful daily function" and resulting in "suffer[ing] from a broad constellation of secondary disabilities" (Douds et al., 2013, p. 493). Incorporating accurate and current science relative to FASD is crucial in forensic contexts because that science demonstrates the invalidity of the generalized inferences and assumptions that contribute to determinations of intent, responsibility, and degree of culpability (which, undisturbed, lead to distorted determinations), provides information by which fact-finders and decision-makers may revise previously held inferences and assumptions so as to accurately reflect the reality of FASD and its effect upon a person, and makes whole our understanding of the mitigating quality of FASD by providing a causal role[22] and contextualizing the framework by which the affected person's entire life functioning, including the charged crime, can be evaluated, analyzed, and appreciated.[23]

2.3.2 *Executive Dysfunction and Other Impairments*

Executive functioning is an umbrella term for "multiple, interrelated higher order cognitive processes that are responsible for purposeful, goal-directed behavior" (Davis, Gagnier, Moore, & Todorow, 2013, p. 83; see also Kingdon et al., 2016; Reynolds & Horton Jr., 2008). These processes/functions include planning and decision-making (as well as considering options, foreseeing consequences, assessing risks, and linking cause and effect), "guid[ing] adaptive responses to novel situations" (involving components of troubleshooting, novel sequences of actions, and/or overcoming poorly-learned tasks; Wyper & Pei, 2016, p. 105), and overcoming strong habitual responses or resisting temptation (including emotion regulation and modifying emotions to fit societal norms; Chan, Shum, Toulopoulou,

[22] Note that causation in a legal sense versus causation in a persuasive and contextual sense are distinct. Encouraging use of the scientific causative explanation and context—that from structure flows function—does not and should not be interpreted as surrendering to courts' and prosecutors' efforts to add to those things an accused may be held to establish as a matter of law.

[23] Greenspan and Driscoll (2016), p. 24, also advocate a contextualized approach, however, focusing on "the poor judgment (with usual predictable bad outcomes) of people with FASD[.]" As to, at least, interrogations, that context would "delve deeper, by identifying specific ploys engaged in by a manipulator, and then seeing how those ploys tie in with specific cognitive processes."

& Chen, 2008; Norman & Shallice, 1986).[24] In neurotypical or "normal" persons, executive functioning is engaged not only in awareness of "long-term self-interests but with an awareness of and in the context of other self-interested self-regulating agents with whom we interact" (Barkley, 2012, p. 25). In neurotypical functioning, this sort of memory-based decision-making entails integrating information quickly through both deliberative and intuitive processes, some of which may involve focused attention but much of which relies upon what are commonly referred to as automatic processes (Glöckner, 2009; Glöckner & Betsch, 2008; Glöckner & Hodges, 2011; Norman & Shallice, 1986).

Executive dysfunction is one of the hallmarks of FASD and is "highly related to the central clinical difficulties" in the FASD population (Kingdon et al., 2016, p. 3), with consistency of impairment increasing as complexity of the neurocognitive task increases (Davis et al., 2013; Kingdon et al., 2016; Mattson et al., 2019). In contrast with neurotypical functioning, persons with FASD have demonstrated deficits in cognitive flexibility, planning and strategy use, verbal reasoning, some aspects of inhibition, set shifting, fluency, working memory, emotion-related executive function,[25] heightened vulnerability through poor impulse control, and decreased capacity for moral judgment and rational thought (Mela & Luther, 2013).[26] Therefore, persons with FASD have particular difficulty rapidly processing relatively complex information in novel situations, including those involving aspects of social judgment, all of which require quick decisions and/or thinking on one's feet.

Contrary to common folk beliefs, executive functioning is not synonymous with intelligence or IQ. IQs in the FASD population vary widely from the intellectually disabled range to average and/or above-average ranges. Thus, executive function impairment as found in FASD does not predict IQ. Rather, "IQ-matched controls display both similarities and differences when compared to children with prenatal alcohol exposure" (Mattson et al., 2019, p. 13).

The connection between executive functioning and the kinds of information relevant to determinations of intent, responsibility, and degree of culpability is clear (Blagg et al., 2018).[27] Similarly, it also is clear that executive dysfunction in FASD is of central relevance to determinations of intent, responsibility, and degree of culpability. This is especially the case as science is able to assist in identifying structural differences that appear to be causally connected to a "biologically-driven breakdown in

---

[24] Chan et al. (2008), p. 201, define executive functioning as, "an umbrella term comprising a wide range of cognitive processes and behavioral competencies which include verbal reasoning, problem-solving, planning, sequencing, the ability to sustain attention, resistance to interference, utilization of feedback, multitasking, cognitive flexibility, and the ability to deal with novelty."

[25] See, as clarification, Davis et al. (2013) noting that executive functioning deficits in those with FASD are both cognition-based and emotion-related.

[26] See also, O'Hare et al. (2009), p. 3206, noting that working memory—representing temporary storage and manipulation of information required for concurrent cognition—"is a critical component of cognition that is affected by prenatal alcohol exposure."

[27] Blagg et al. (2018), noted that "[t]he assumptions of free will and individual responsibility [underpinning] Australian criminal law are largely incompatible with the impairments associated with FASD."

executive capacity in the context of situational complexity that directly influences adaptive behavior in most real-world situations" (Novick Brown, 2020).[28]

Executive functioning processes also are "critical for social interaction and for one to be able to successfully cope with everyday societal demands" (Davis et al., 2013, p. 83) and for self-regulation (Wyper & Pei, 2016). Thus, as might be expected, a number of studies have documented impairments in social functioning in individuals with FASD. Social impairments in this domain appear to increase with age and go "beyond what can be predicted based on deficits in intellectual functioning alone" (Davis et al., 2013, p. 85). Self-regulation and social functioning impairments associated with FASD have been described as follows:

> Many FASD sufferers exhibit impaired adaptive functioning; …essentially lack the level of social responsibility, or personal autonomy, generally expected from people in society[,]… cannot translate socially learned lessons from one situation to another, and…often have problems with externalization….[They] are likely to have difficulties with interpersonal boundaries and with identifying positive and negative peer influences. FASD sufferers [may] have normal tested IQs, but they often exhibit inferior social and adaptive skills. They may be eager to please, and they may befriend people who will take advantage of them…FASD sufferers are highly suggestible[, and] often are unlikely to consider the long-term consequences of their statements or actions, which can have profound criminal justice implications. For example, because they are socialized to respect authority figures such as police officers and court officials, they may 'confess' or testify to an untruth if they think it is what someone "wants to hear"… Language problems compound FASD sufferers' adaptive and cognitive immaturity and contribute to their difficulties with meaningful participation in criminal justice systems. In their efforts to please the authority figure posing questions, FASD sufferers may say they understand something when they do not. Because their disabilities may be 'hidden' by superficial verbal skills, they may appear to understand their rights, but cognitively they are lost. Accordingly, they may unwittingly abdicate their constitutional rights against unreasonable searches and seizures, against self-incrimination, and to assistance of counsel. (Douds et al., 2013, 494)

In addition to the characteristics noted above, people with FASD may be highly vulnerable to abuse. This population has "an overwhelming desire to have friends but, due to their social immaturity and ineptness, are often rejected by peers" (Roach & Bailey, 2009, p. 9). Thus, peer rejection often results in people with FASD either being targeted and victimized by others or used by others in criminal enterprises.

"Learning cannot take place without an adequate ability to store information in memory" (Davis et al., 2013, p. 85), and memory-based decision-making necessarily involves "working memory."[29] Persons with FASD show deficits in both learning and memory (Davis et al., 2013), negatively affecting tasks like keeping and relating

[28] Note that what the scientific and medical community considers "clear," what scientific and medical experts may testify to as "within reasonable medical certainty," and legal standards of proof that apply to admitted evidence (preponderance of the evidence, clear and convincing evidence, and beyond a reasonable doubt) are distinct issues, necessitating a teasing out among, and then integrating of, the two professions: medical and legal. See, e.g., Rappeport (1985).

[29] "Working memory" is defined as: "a psychological construct thought to represent the temporary storage and manipulation of information that is required for concurrent cognition, and neuropsychological and neuroimaging studies have implicated frontal, parietal and cerebellar regions as being crucial for performance within this cognitive domain" (O'Hare et al., 2009, p. 3201).

a timeline of events, learning and functioning according to court and forensically related processes and protocols, and doing so with awareness of individual rights that have long-term significance. Thus, in addition to the relevance of executive dysfunction in determinations of intent, responsibility, and degree of culpability, memory issues associated with FASD (e.g., poor and inconsistent memory retrieval) are similarly relevant to those fundamental legal issues.

2.4 The Quotidian Uses of Fetal Alcohol Spectrum Disorder in Forensic Contexts

2.4.1 Introduction

As to what reported cases can tell us about FASD in the forensic context, Stetler and Wendel (2013) point out that reported cases reflect attorneys' actual past conduct—conduct that led to something going wrong and/or bad case results—and in which appeal was sought for remedy. Consequently, the very nature of reported cases does not reflect best practices, practices sufficient to meet professional guidelines, or what attorneys ought to do. Similarly, reported cases focus on specific claims asserted as erroneous, thus limiting ability to evaluate how other parts of the case were handled.

Reported cases involving FASD in the civil courts include disability determinations that focus on whether a claimant's FASD is a qualifying condition/disorder according to statutes and regulations, the degree to which functioning is adversely affected, and services needed and/or allowed. Civil cases also include those involving involuntary commitment pursuant to sexually violent predator proceedings, again with a focus on whether "by acceptable cogent evidence and to a high degree of probability" a respondent has a qualifying condition, whether there is appropriate supported accommodation for that condition, and whether a supervision order can adequately protect the community.[30] Reported cases involving FASD in the criminal courts primarily involve whether an accused and/or convicted person has FASD, although a minority of cases mentioning FASD do so in quasi-criminal matters such

[30] See, e.g., Attorney-General for the State of Queensland v. Tiers [2020] QSC 135, involving the annual review of a continuing detention order finding Tiers—who had FASD and had been diagnosed with a variety of other disorders—a serious danger to the community. Upon presentation of various evaluations, the court released Tiers on a supervisory order, given the punishment he had suffered through his institutionalization for 18 years (for a sexual offense as a juvenile against a 4-year-old), and given Tiers' "complex problems and reduced cognitive functioning, which contribute to poor behavior, [such that he] should not be kept in prison for years on end under continuing detention . . . simply because the government refuses to provide the supported accommodation and resources that are required[.]"

as termination of parental rights proceedings and juvenile dispositions.[31] Few reported cases have been located in which mention is made of a crime victim or witness having FASD.[32] As to all reported cases, reference to FASD by particular diagnostic label and/or functional description varies, reflecting the evolution of scientific knowledge and parallel lack of consistent diagnostic criteria across countries—inconsistency that has contributed to the difficulty in establishing accurate prevalence rates and identifying relevant resources for affected individuals (Mattson et al., 2019).

2.4.2 *How the Scientific Literature Views the Potential Impact of Fetal Alcohol Spectrum Disorder in the Forensic Context*

Scientific literature relative to FASD in the forensic context primarily focuses on persons with FASD who are accused and/or convicted of crimes. Studies reflect that a majority of offenders with FASD show "deficits in at least one psycholegal ability relevant to the adjudicative process" (McLachlan, Roesch, Viljoen, & Douglas, 2014, pp. 18–19). More specifically, as a result of their attendant disabilities,

> …persons suffering from FASDs, and related secondary disabilities, often do not have the cognitive ability to form criminal intent, to confess or testify meaningfully, or to benefit from traditional sentencing structures. (Douds et al., 2013, p. 494)

"People with FASDs often lack the ability to comprehend abstract thought or to understand their legal rights" (Douds et al., 2013, p. 495).[33] Moreover, they often "lack the intellect necessary to understand the judicial proceedings of which they are a part" and "are unlikely to comprehend the implications of consenting to a search, plea negotiations, or sworn testimony" (Douds et al., 2013, 495). Implicated here are the rights to meaningfully assist in defense,[34] against self-incrimination

---

[31] For additional information relative to the juvenile justice context, see, *infra*, Chap. 12, "Psychological Assessment for Juvenile Courts," in this collection, regarding juvenile justice evaluations.

[32] One such case located, State v. E.S. (unpublished), No. 58637–8-I, 2007 Wash.App. LEXIS 3185, focuses on a juvenile accused of a crime, through his counsel, seeking discovery sanctions for failure to disclose the victim's educational and medical records, where the victim was suspected of having FASD. The reviewing court denied the requested discovery sanctions.

[33] A crucial distinction must be made between a person being able to simply repeat or recite their "rights" and an actual working understanding of those rights and the abstract concepts they embody (McLachlan et al., 2014). Constitutional legal principles require the latter.

[34] In the United States, a criminal defendant has a constitutional right to participate in his own defense. Medina v. California (1992), 505 U.S. 437, 445, 112 S.Ct. 2572, 120 L.Ed.2d 353 (as a matter of due process, "an indigent criminal defendant is entitled to the minimum assistance necessary to assure him a fair opportunity to present his defense and to participate meaningfully in [the] judicial proceedings") (internal quotation marks omitted). The adverse effects of FASD, including

(Douds et al., 2013),[35] and to introduce a broad range of mitigating information at sentencing.

The literature (McLachlan et al., 2019) reflects there is,

> …increasing recognition that the neurocognitive deficits, and associated behavioural and mental health comorbidities, are relevant in a range of forensic and adjudicative contexts, including arrest warning comprehension and the validity of statements provided during police interrogation, fitness to plead and stand trial, criminal responsibility, long-term and dangerous offender designations, violence risk assessment, sentencing considerations, and transition planning for discharge back to community. (p. 3)

Thus, a distinction must be made between what a person with FASD believes their level of understanding is and actual working understanding because,

> …many young offenders with FASD showed compromised understanding and appreciation of their rights (and at least some insight into these difficulties), [however,] as a group they tended to feel more confident about their decision-making abilities than was warranted. Combined, these factors may increase a young suspect's risk for making poor decisions based on limited understanding of their rights while expressing misplaced confidence to police or lawyers. (McLachlan et al., 2014, p. 19)

This issue is particularly important in the context of interrogations because people with FASD are susceptible to suggestions from authority figures of what might have happened and may incorporate those suggestions into their own retelling of the event (Roach & Bailey, 2009). Further, "[o]n repeated questioning, the individual with [fetal alcohol effects/fetal alcohol syndrome] FAS/FAE, who is often susceptible to suggestions of what might have happened, may incorporate these suggestions into his or her own retelling of the event" (Roach & Bailey, 2009, p. 17).[36] Suggestibility problems are compounded by memory problems that cause "gaps in recall and poor

---

memory and executive functioning deficits, limit the ability of the client with FASD to provide counsel with accurate historical information (about background as well as the charged offense), retain information from one representational meeting/event to the next, and follow and assimilate information produced through representational events, such that the client is able to provide context and input to counsel (Burd, Fast, Conry, & Williams, 2010 and Wyper & Pei, 2016). Those deficits also limit the client's ability to understand their rights and how those rights present themselves in the context of the representation, so they can make the decisions that are to be made by the client and the client alone, e.g., the right to proceed to trial, to testify or to remain silent, and to execute an appeal. In short, and no matter how fervent the FASD client's desire to cooperate, deficits directly associated with and/or flowing from FASD lead to the client's inability to meaningfully and substantially cooperate (i.e., participate) in their defense. See, e.g., McCoy v. Louisiana (2018) 584 U.S. __, 138 S.Ct. 1500, 200 L.Ed.2d 821.

[35] Douds et al. (2013), p. 495, note that disabilities attendant FASD may lead the person with FASD "to consent to a search, confess to a crime, or provide false testimony simply to escape the immediate discomfort of the police interrogation or court appearance. They do not understand the need to be truthful. The complexity of trials is vexing to persons of normal intellect; they can be overwhelming to persons of inferior cognitive ability, which may cause them to say or do things adverse to their interests (LaDue & Dunne, 1997; Moore & Greene, 2004)". See also, Roach and Bailey (2009), p. 13, research "demonstrating that young people have difficulties understanding right-to-counsel warnings" leads to the conclusion that "people of all ages with FASD would have even greater difficulties in understanding and exercising the right to counsel and right to silence."

[36] Similarly, "confessions," "while perhaps not oppressive in terms of an individual with a normal developmental state, did become oppressive" (Roach & Bailey, 2009, p. 16).

recollection in general" (Douds et al., 2013, p. 495). Thus, the primary neurocognitive disabilities in FASD dovetail with the "doctrinal basis for concerns about particularly vulnerable individuals [given] that part of the voluntariness rule that requires the accused to have an operating mind" (Roach & Bailey, 2009, p. 19).

Given the brain-based primary disabilities in FASD and associated functional deficits in capacities crucial to meaningful participation in the criminal justice process (including the investigatory, adjudicatory, and post-adjudicatory stages), it is clear this population is vulnerable at all levels as a direct result of their permanent physical disability. Moreover, given recognition of the relevance of FASD and its effects at various focal points in justice system processes, one would expect to find reported cases broadly covering the justice system landscape.

2.4.3 *Bias toward Mitigation*

Despite increasing recognition in the scientific community that deficits associated with FASD are relevant to a broad range of justice system processes, with the very notable exception of Pora v. The Queen (2015),[37] reported cases generally reflect failure to evaluate evidence of FASD in relation to pre-charge cautions, advisals of rights, and evidence obtained pursuant to waivers of those rights.[38] Similarly, with some exceptions in early FASD criminal litigation,[39] which tended to focus on guilty but insane and/or not criminally responsible theories,[40] and one early case seeking to use evidence of FASD as a defense to specific intent but which the reviewing court said would not have made a difference in the outcome,[41] reported cases involving FASD generally reflect failure to focus on determinations of intent and

[37] Pora v. The Queen [2015] UKPC 9 (finding that "[t]he combination of Pora's frequently contradictory and often implausible confessions and the recent diagnosis of his FASD leads to only one possible conclusion and that is that reliance on his confessions gives rise to a risk of a miscarriage of justice; on that account, his convictions must be quashed.").

[38] Note, however, at least one Australian report advocating it as "essential that we intervene, where possible, at an earlier stage of contact [between those with FASD and] the criminal justice system[,]" including at the stage during which police have "responsibility for cautioning and warning young offenders eligible for diversion" (Blagg et al., 2018).

[39] Early FASD litigation in criminal courts unsuccessfully sought to establish mental incapacity or diminished capacity in defense to charged crimes. Douds et al. (2013) found those efforts unsuccessful due to courts' adoption of strict interpretations of insanity/diminished capacity defenses. That view appears to be confirmed by Verbrugge (2003). Note that in contrast to those conditions commonly subject to guilty but insane and/or not criminally responsible theories, "[t]he cognitive abnormalities implied and implicated in disorders like fetal alcohol spectrum disorder are distinct" (Mela & Luther, 2013, p. 50).

[40] See, e.g., R. v. R.F. [2002] SKPC 137, 228 Sask R 111.

[41] See, Dillbeck v. State (1994), 643 So.2d 1027, 1029 (Fla. 1994).

responsibility.[42] Instead, a review of recent reported caselaw and published policy statements reflects a strong preference for using FASD in determining degree of culpability or mitigation of sentencing rather than in criminal responsibility determinations (Blagg et al., 2018).[43] This is so even where an accused person with FASD had limited memory of the incident(s) comprising the criminal violations that were subject to sentencing.[44]

In R v. Verdins [2007],[45] a decision that has been applied in Australia and New Zealand, the Victorian Court of Appeal stated that "an offender's mental functioning is relevant to the sentencing process" to "reduce the offender's moral culpability (but not his or her legal responsibility) for the offence" (Blagg et al., 2018).[46] In this vein, the Canadian court's decision in R v. Harper [2009][47] noted that if evidence of FASD was not taken into account in the sentencing calculus, "the offender is failed because he is being held to a standard that he cannot possibly attain, given his impairments." The court further noted the need for a different calculus relative to penological objectives in sentencing a person with FASD in that,

> Society is failed because a sentence calculated for a 'normal' offender cannot serve the same ends when imposed on an offender with FASD; it will not contribute to respect for the law, and neither will it contribute to the maintenance of a just, peaceful and safe society. The calculus of sentencing the average offender simply does not apply to an offender with FASD. Not only can traditionally calculated sentences be hopelessly ineffective when applied to FASD offenders, but the punishment itself, calibrated for a non-disabled indi-

[42] One is reminded of the issue of admissibility of evidence of quantitative electroencephalogram (qEEG) in criminal cases. Some notable early efforts to introduce qEEG evidence failed, leading to folk beliefs discounting the use of qEEG as a tool in convergent validity assessment. Notwithstanding early practice, the admissibility of qEEG evidence in criminal cases in the United States, while requiring counsel's preparation, is almost a foregone conclusion in favor of admission, with most prosecutorial actors allowing its admission without opposition. Given the state of current science relative to FASD, new efforts to challenge determinations of intent, responsibility, and degree of culpability should be mounted.

[43] The apparent preference for relying on a client's FASD in mitigation of sentencing is, in part, a function of counsel's involvement in clients with FASD pleading guilty to criminal conduct, thus putting those clients in the position of having admitted criminal responsibility and leaving nothing but the sentencing decision for the court's determination.

[44] DPP v. Slater [2020] VCC 216 (accepting Slater's guilty plea to serious offenses including aggravated carjacking in which bodily harm was threatened against one victim, reckless conduct endangering another victim, and in the context in which he was on bail for other offenses at the time of the crimes, notwithstanding Slater's inability to remember all of the events; despite Slater's high risk of re-offending, the court found that FASD and associated impaired mental functioning constituted "special reason" for not imposing the otherwise minimum prison sentence).

[45] R v. Verdins [2007] 16 VR 269.

[46] Relevance to the culpability assessment, however, appears to be restricted to instances in which a causal link exists between the condition in issue and the offending conduct. *Verdins*, [2007] 16 VR at 275. This principle was recently affirmed in Brown v. The Queen [2020] VSCA 212 (25 August 2020), noting "the informing principle of the common law is 'that there should be a close correlation between moral culpability and legal responsibility.'"

[47] R. v. Harper [2009] YKTC 18.

> vidual, can have a substantially more severe effect on someone with the impairments associated with FASD.[48]

Reported cases arising out of the United States rarely address FASD in responsibility determinations, joining the courts mentioned above in focusing instead on mitigation in sentencing. This holds true even in instances in which the court questioned whether the accused acted with the requisite mental state.[49] To the extent cases have waded into responsibility determination, those efforts have been thwarted by a failure to present evidence that was deemed sufficiently certain rather than speculative[50] or, in the case of Cyntoia Brown, where original counsel was excused from failure to identify Brown's FASD due to a focus instead on her comorbid conditions.[51] In *Brown*, original counsel's failure as to FASD led to that issue being relegated to disadvantageous post-trial procedures and presumptions. Thus, assuming FASD was established, the court did not find that,

> This evidence [of FASD] so compelling that no jury would have convicted her in light of it [but found that] the jury reasonably could have found that [Brown's FASD] did not impair her mental capacity to the extent that she could not form the requisite culpable mental state for the charged offenses. There was substantial evidence presented at trial to prove [Brown's] guilt[.][52]

---

[48] R. v. Harper [2009] YKTC 18.

[49] See, e.g., State v. Miles (2018), 243 Ariz. 511, 414 P.3d 680 (Ariz. S.Ct. 2018).

[50] See, e.g., State v. Wilson (2015), No. M2014–01487-CCA-R9-CD, 2015 Tenn. Crim. App. LEXIS 712, 2015 WL 5170970 (Tenn. Ct. of Crim. Appeals, Sept. 2, 2015), *rev. den.*, No. M2014–01487-SC-R11-CD, 2015 Tenn. LEXIS 1044 (Tenn. S.Ct., Dec. 10, 2015). Wilson, charged with murder, had FASD and sought to introduce expert testimony regarding his mental diseases, defects, and other mental conditions bearing on his guilt for the murder. The trial court excluded the proffered expert testimony, and the reviewing court upheld that exclusion because the expert testified disparately in her three instances of testimony, opining at most that "Wilson's mental diseases or defects '*could have impaired*'" his capacity to form the requisite mental state but failing to testify "conclusively that a mental disease or defect rendered Wilson incapable of acting intentionally and with premedication" (emphasis added).

[51] Brown v. State (2015), No. M2013–00825-CCA-R3-PC, 2014 Tenn. Crim. App. LEXIS 1014 (Tenn. Ct. of Crim. Appeals, Nov. 6, 2014), *rev. den.*, No. M2013–00825-SC-R11-PC, 2015 Tenn. LEXIS 400 (Tenn. S.Ct. May 15, 2015). Testimony in post-conviction proceedings was that Brown had FASD and that the "severe mental defect and disease affected, influenced, impacted, impaired her ability to appreciate the nature of her … actions and also impaired her ability to control her behavior." The reviewing court denied relief, however, because the evidence also was that Brown had been diagnosed with many disorders, and many of the symptoms of those disorders were common in FASD, such that Brown's manifestation of those symptoms "made it appear that she was having each of those distinct disorders." This possibility provided a defense against Brown's claim that she received ineffective assistance of counsel due to original counsel failing to pursue a diminished capacity defense due to FASD. Brown ultimately obtained relief through executive clemency, when the Governor of Tennessee commuted her sentence. She was released in August, 2019.

[52] Brown v. State (2013), Davidson County, Tennessee, Division II, Case No. 2005-A-215, *Order* (February 28, 2013).

In other cases, the accused (through counsel) similarly defaulted the issue of FASD's impact on ability to form the necessary intent, thus barring later challenge to a finding of guilt.

2.4.4 *Failure to Afford Mitigating Value or Distinguish from Other Mitigation*

To date, reported criminal cases involving FASD in the United States almost exclusively involve post-conviction and/or habeas litigation and therefore are subject to stringent procedural bars and rules mandating deference to lower court findings.[53] Starting from this disadvantageous procedural posture, cases generally reflect trial attorneys' failure to adequately investigate red flags suggesting the possibility clients had undiagnosed FASD or failure to recognize FASD as a diagnostic entity rather than individual symptoms that contribute to its complexity.[54] The latter ignores the significant mitigating value of FASD in providing a causal role and contextualizing framework by which an affected person's whole cloth of their life—including the charged crime—can be evaluated and analyzed.

The significant and distinct mitigating value of FASD was relied upon by the reviewing court in Williams v. Stirling (2019),[55] where original counsel's performance was found deficient for failure to follow up on red flags the defendant's mother abused alcohol during pregnancy and evidence the defendant had brain damage that included frontal lobe impairment (as well as counsel's failure to provide records and/or timely obtain testing as requested by the forensic expert).[56] As described by another reviewing court in another case involving FASD,[57] those red flags (i.e., evidence of prenatal alcohol exposure and brain damage and an expert's specific request for records and testing that would have led to a finding of FASD) were pivotal in finding Williams' counsel deficient.[58]

Not only was counsel's performance deficient in *Williams*, the reviewing court found this deficiency mattered because,

---

[53] In the United States, while there is variation among individual states, the constitutional adequacy of attorneys' past conduct cannot be legally evaluated until years after the trial, in post-conviction and/or habeas corpus proceedings. Those proceedings, while technically civil in nature, are subject to the convicted person meeting stringent burdens before relief from conviction and/or sentence can be granted.

[54] See, e.g., Anderson v. Kelley (2020), 938 F.3d 949 (8th Cir. 2019). *sub nom., Anderson v. Payne*, United States Supreme Court No. 19–8105, *cert. Den.*, 592 U.S. __, 2020 U.S. LEXIS 4018, 2020 WL 5882496 (10/05/2020).

[55] Williams v. Stirling (2019), 914 F.3d 302 (4th Cir. 2019), *cert. Den.*, 589 U.S. __, 140 S.Ct. 105, 205 L.Ed.2d 38.

[56] *Williams v. Stirling*, 914 F.3d at 315.

[57] *Anderson, supra*, 938 F.3d at 957.

[58] *Anderson, supra*, 938 F.3d at 957.

> ...[a]n investigation into FAS evidence would have been substantially different [from investigation into] other mental illnesses and behavioral issues because FAS could have established both *cause and effect* for Williams' criminal acts whereas the other mitigation evidence went more to effects on behavior.[59]

Further, availability of that evidence mattered because "FAS evidence could have provided to the jury evidence of an overarching neurological defect that *caused* Williams' criminal behavior[.]"[60] Thus, while not providing explanation and/or analysis, the court's decision spoke to the quality of FASD as mitigating evidence, implying its ability to provide information relative to a causal role and contextualizing the framework by which the whole cloth of Williams' life, including the charged crime, could be evaluated and appreciated. In other words, the *Williams* court's findings and conclusions were consistent with Geschwind's (1975) observation and in stark contrast to viewing FASD as a catalog of seemingly mitigating factors.[61]

Unlike the *Williams* court's implicit understanding of the significantly distinct mitigating value of FASD, the reviewing court in Trevino v. Davis (2018)[62] denied relief in part by diverting attention from FASD as mitigation and focusing instead on a legal standard inapplicable to that capital sentencing proceeding. Specifically, the court focused on the "know right from wrong" standard commonly applied in insanity determinations rather than determinations of culpability.[63] As the *Trevino* dissent aptly pointed out, the majority decision's focus on the "right from wrong" standard was irrelevant to capital sentencing special issues in that,

> to merely state the obvious, as Trevino did not assert an insanity defense and the same jury had already found him guilty of the offense. By focusing on (the right from wrong) statement, the majority opinion elides the much more significant part of [the testimony]: that FASD "clearly had an impact on Trevino's cognitive development, academic performance, social function, and overall adaptive functioning" and that "these deficits would have impacted his decisions to participate in or refrain from any activities that resulted in his capital murder charges."[64]

In the same vein, although relying on different means, the reviewing court in Floyd v. Filson (2020)[65] treated the diagnostic label FASD as merely one of several labels, placing it on par with and cumulative of Floyd's attention deficit hyperactivity dis-

---

[59] *Williams, supra*, 914 F.3d at 315.

[60] *Williams, supra*, 914 F.3d at 315

[61] *Williams, supra*, 914 F.3d at 315.

[62] Trevino v. Davis (2018), 861 F.3d 545, 549 (5th Cir. 2017), *cert. Den.*, U.S. __, 138 S.Ct. 1793, 201 L.Ed.2d 1014.

[63] *Trevino, supra*, 861 F.3d at 549 (underscoring that Trevino's FASD "would not have significantly interfered with his ability to know right from wrong, or to appreciate the nature and quality of his actions at the time of the capital offense."). In addition to invoking the "know right from wrong" standard, the reviewing court called the newly discovered evidence of FASD "double-edged" in nature, an approach that Justice Sotomayor termed "misguided" in her dissent from denial of certiorari (138 S.Ct. at 1798).

[64] *Trevino, supra*, 861 F.3d at 556 (Dennis, J., dissenting).

[65] Floyd v. Filson (2020), 949 F.3d 1128 (9th Cit. 2020), *sub nom., Floyd v. Gittere*, United States Supreme Court No. 19–8921, *cert. Den.*, 592 U.S. __ (November 2, 2020).

order (ADHD) diagnosis.[66] Floyd's original counsel developed information of maternal alcohol ingestion but folded that information into their mitigation presentation with a host of other mitigating information. The mitigation potpourri presented to jurors did not "use FASD terminology"[67] but included an assertion the defendant "suffered from the effects, early effects of the mother's drinking, her ingested alcohol, [and] drugs early on in her pregnancy."[68] Mitigation also included an opinion that the "mother's substance abuse might be to blame for [Floyd's] mental condition,"[69] Floyd committed the murders while under the influence of extreme mental or emotional disturbance, and he had received insufficient treatment for ADHD and had "other emotional-behavioral problems including depression."[70] While jurors "appeared to have considered [as] insufficient the existing evidence of potential ties between maternal alcohol use and [the defendant's] state of mind[,]"[71] they were not provided with a framework—FASD—that unified and made sense of the potpourri. Like the jurors who rejected Floyd's mitigation as insufficient and voted for the death penalty, the reviewing court also was unable to make sense out of the potpourri, ultimately characterizing FASD as "differ[ing] somewhat in degree, but not type, from that presented in mitigation."[72]

Similarly finding evidence of FASD fungible with other pieces of mitigating evidence presented, the reviewing court in Anderson v. Kelley (2017) agreed with the lower court's decision not to grant relief from the death penalty due to original counsel's failures, which included trial counsel's failure to investigate and learn that defendant's mother drank alcohol during pregnancy and that Anderson had FASD. According to the reviewing court, counsel's deficiencies were excused because evidence of the prevalence of alcohol in the defendant's childhood was not temporally tied to his mother's pregnancy. More fundamentally, however, the reviewing court clearly put FASD on par with other mitigators, which it categorized as "almost all related to Anderson being abused and neglected as a child."[73] Indeed, the reviewing court rejected the suggestion that adding "one more mitigating circumstance, evidence of FASD,"[74] to the "*thirty* mitigating circumstances"[75] would

[66] *Floyd, supra*, 949 F.3d at 1141. The court's consideration of FASD as one of many mitigating factors is consistent with the reported practice of criminal courts as of Douds' 2013 review, which observed that, "[v]ery few courts analyzed FASD evidence directly or independently of other evidence. Instead, the majority of the courts considered FASD evidence in conjunction with evidence of other mental health issues." (Douds et al., 2013).

[67] *Floyd, supra*, 949 F.3d at 1140.

[68] *Floyd, supra*, 949 F.3d at 1139.

[69] *Floyd, supra*, 949 F.3d at 1139.

[70] *Floyd, supra*, 949 F.3d at 1140.

[71] *Floyd, supra*, 949 F.3d at 1141 n.4.

[72] *Floyd, supra*, 949 F.3d at 1140.

[73] Anderson v. Kelley (2017), No. 5:12-cv-279-DPM, 2017 U.S. Dist. LEXIS 48268, at 9 (E.D. Ark. March 28, 2017).

[74] *Anderson, supra*, 938 F.3d at 958.

[75] *Anderson, supra*, 938 F.3d at 958.

have altered jurors' views of the balance of aggravating and mitigating factors. In other words, in the view of the reviewing court, counsel's failure to present evidence of FASD did not matter.

2.5 Applying Fetal Alcohol Spectrum Disorder in Criminal Defense Cases: The Problem and Start of a Solution

FASD is an immutable disorder that for the most part is not visible to the eye (Popova et al., 2017). Real-life behaviors resulting from FASD do not square with commonly held intuitive assumptions about intent and agency, resulting in those behaviors being characterized as deviant.[76] This disconnect, or empathic divide (Haney, 2004), implicates determinations of intent, responsibility, and degree of culpability and is exacerbated by "the public perception of FASD [being] not well informed and tend[ing] to focus on negative discourse" (Choate & Badry, 2019). The forensic context itself, with processes and procedures that further dehumanize the accused and/or implicate many deficits inherent in FASD, contributes to,

> …[fact-finders'] relative inability to perceive [those] defendants as enough like themselves to readily feel any of their pains, to appreciate the true nature of the struggles they have faced, or to genuinely understand how and why their lives have taken very different courses from the jurors' own. (Haney, 2004, p. 1558)

FASD in the forensic context will present and play out differently as a function of an individual's impairments and comorbidities, their role in the forensic context, facts and context of the issue subject to forensic determination, applicable forensic processes and procedures, and preexisting societal assumptions and perceptions relative to the aforementioned. In short, FASD must be factored into analysis of the forensic issue as well as attendant processes and procedures. No one-size-fits-all prescription will hold true for all situations. However, analysis should include recognition of the interlocking relationship of FASD vis-à-vis all pending issues, forensic processes and procedures, and roles and responsibilities of all forensic actors; recognition of the critical importance of education regarding FASD throughout the forensic process; sensitivity to evolving standards relevant to FASD (evolving as to science, societal understanding and consequent standards, and what works for a particular client at a particular time); integration of the past, present, and future

[76] "[U]ndiagnosed people [with FASD] are caught in a web where the problems arising from FASD are not seen as a disorder, but rather as a misbehaving, unregulated person" (Choate & Badry, 2019). Similarly, with respect to children who are perceived as *normal*, they "are expected to perform to academic and behavioral standards consistent with their age.…When they don't, they often are seen as unmotivated, lazy, or oppositional. Their learning problems, mood swings, social difficulties, disruptive behaviors, impulsivity, meltdowns, stealing, boundary issues, lying, running away, and occasional bizarre behaviors are viewed as willful disobedience and/or the result of deficient caregiving, even in situations where caregiving is at least adequate" (Novick Brown & Connor, 2014).

of the person into case planning, evaluation, presentation, and case determination, with reassessments and/or adjustments as needed; focus on real-life functions versus labels (diagnostic or otherwise); and integration of FASD science with real-life stories and narratives that enable a fact-finder and/or decision-maker to relate to and empathize with the affected person.

Table 2.1 provides a simplified way of looking at the interlocking nature of issues, roles, and processes in the context of FASD from the perspective of counsel representing a client accused of a crime. The case of a victim with FASD similarly can be evaluated and analyzed, incorporating an understanding of their individual presentation of FASD, how that presentation may have interacted with the actors involved in the commission of the crime against the victim as well as in law enforcement's investigation, and how particular processes and procedures within the forensic environment may burden the victim's ability to participate in the prosecutorial process.

2.5.1 *Integrating Past, Present, and Future in Forward-Thinking Mitigation*

Typical legal representation in criminal justice matters, including capital defense representation in the United States, looks retrospectively, investigating the charged offense that is the subject of the forensic proceeding. Legal representation also may require counsel (*must* require, in capital cases [American Bar Association, rev. 2003]) to investigate client background and history (e.g., factors that may frame and/or present context and informational components relative to legal and equitable issues). If we are making an FASD-informed investigation of our client's background and history, not only will we find evidence of the whole-body neurodevelopmental disorder and its associated impairments and comorbidities, we likely will find layers of trauma sewn throughout the client's life with their respective and combined effects overlaid upon the charged incident time period. Limiting representation to a backward-looking perspective puts the client in stasis, anchoring them to the problems associated with the incident time period, which often represents the worst of the worst period in their life. In addition to problems associated with so anchoring the client, to the extent the client is not well-informed regarding their own functioning and behavior (and the reason for that functioning and behavior), lack of knowledge can contribute to hopelessness and shame.

The literature confirms what we otherwise would suspect: those with FASD—whether diagnosed or not—are subject to layers of stigma that intersect with identification and provision of appropriately targeted treatments and accommodations (Morrison, Harding, & Wolfson, 2019, p. 2) :

> Due to discrimination, and negative attitudes and beliefs about FASD, individuals with FASD often experience feelings of shame regarding the problems they face in life because of their disability. In turn, the stigma associated with FASD is both external – emerging from public viewpoints – and internal – emerging from within. This dual layer of both

Table 2.1 Interlocking nature of issues, roles, and processes and FASD outlines appropriately tailored accommodations, reflecting the interlocking nature of issues, roles, and processes relative to FASD that can be developed in any number of ways. Here, one simplified example relative to the defense of a criminally charged client demonstrates how the need for those accommodations relative to certain processes and issues can be identified and lead to suggestions for the accommodations themselves

Interlocking nature of issues, roles, and processes and FASD				
Client & counsel	Case analysis	Interactions with court & court-associated actors	Court presentation	Post-court
Education & Relationship: Who is my client and how do I come to understand them and their lives? What is the best way for me to learn this information? What considerations should I keep in mind when learning information about my client from others? Are there ways to learn about my client that I should view with caution? Why? Does my client know who they are and why their lives may have unfolded in a certain way? What is the best way for my client to learn this information? Can we, together, identify my client's strengths, and learn skills and tools, that will assist my client's well-functioning?	**Case Facts & Coincident Rights & responsibilities:** How is a "standard" view and analysis of the case facts altered by FASD in general, and as to my client particularly? In view of FASD in general, and as to my client particularly, were/are there reasonably held concerns about the ability of my client to assert their rights (or fulfill their responsibilities)? In view of FASD in general, and as to my client particularly, were/are there reasonably held concerns about the ability of my client to withstand the suggestive and/or coercive words and actions of others?	**Expectations:** What are the pre-established expectations of the court and associated processes? How do they square with my client's functioning? To what extent are these processes in place for convenience? Tradition? Can the processes be broken down into mandatory components separate from other discretionary components that may be reworked to accommodate my client's functioning and needs?	**Modes of presentation:** Choose modes and manners of presenting case and FASD information that contextualizes and provides the fact-finder/decision-maker with a unified, whole-cloth life story of the client, their defense, and accurate information for purposes of assessing and making determinations of intent, culpability and ultimate criminal responsibility. Choose modes and manners of presenting case and FASD information that are memorable and easily assimilated by fact-finders.	**Expectations & responsibilities:** How can I and others effectively accommodate my client in the communication of expectations and responsibilities placed on them as a result of the court proceedings? Are others going to be involved in communicating expectations and responsibilities to my client, if so, requiring accommodations?

Interlocking nature of issues, roles, and processes and FASD

Client & counsel	Case analysis	Interactions with court & court-associated actors	Court presentation	Post-court
Competency to stand trial/aid and assist: What's needed both in and out of court for my client to assist me and make the decisions that are theirs to make?	**Case facts as to lay witnesses:** How is the view of the facts provided by lay witnesses altered by FASD in general, and in my client's expression of FASD particularly? What were/are the relational dynamics between my client and the lay witnesses? Did those relational dynamics change over time? Can precipitating factors to changes be identified and do they provide information as to patterns in the client's lifetime functioning?	**Education, generally & client-specific:** Provide notice to the court and its associated actors of the potential need for accommodations. Investigate the forensic environment on a continuing basis throughout the full course of the forensic proceedings so as to identify process, procedures, and other anticipated eventualities that can be anticipated to create problems for my client's functioning, full understanding, and meaningfully participate in the court process. Educate all involved regarding FASD in general and my client in particular, including their ability to function with full understanding and meaningfully participate in the court process. Educate all involved regarding forward-thinking mitigation and my client's incremental successes viz life plans being put into action	**Courtroom environment, process & accommodations:** Timely put into place, with my client's participation, the pre-arranged accommodations Address and modify accommodations that are not working, timely advising and educating the court and court-associated actors	**Accommodations & forward-thinking mitigation:** Do the substance and process of any post-court expectations and responsibilities on my client require accommodations? Implement the result of forward-thinking mitigation—The life plan

(continued)

Table 2.1 continued

Interlocking nature of issues, roles, and processes and FASD

Client & counsel	Case analysis	Interactions with court & court-associated actors	Court presentation	Post-court
Testing, Evaluation & Investigation: What testing and evaluation have already been done and what does it mean? What testing and evaluation should be done now, given the current forensic context? Which experts are indicated for the various testing and evaluation that should be done now? Is further investigation into my client's life history needed?	**Case facts as to law enforcement witnesses:** How is the view of the facts altered by FASD in general, and in my client's case particularly? What were the dynamics of the relationships between my client and the law enforcement witnesses? Did those relational dynamics change over time? Can precipitating factors to changes be identified and do they provide information as to patterns in the client's lifetime functioning?	**Accommodations:** Investigation into and development of, followed by education about the specific environmental factors as impacting my client in particular need for accommodations that will allow my client to function with full knowledge and meaningfully participate in the court process	**Education of the fact-finder/ decision-maker:** Educate the fact-finder about the reason for accommodations Educate the fact-finder about FASD	**Education:** Educate those forensic actors with roles and responsibility in post-court determination (e.g., probation officers) about FASD as expressed in my client
Accommodations & Forward-Thinking Mitigation: What accommodations and life plans can be constructed with my client's participation for their current and future well-being and success? What can be put into action now as an incremental demonstration to my client that their future is not hopeless, and as a similar demonstration to the court and all associated?			**Integration with the Case & Case Presentation:** Have I integrated my client's FASD into both the substance and manner of my presentation?	**Relationship & Follow-through:** Positively reinforce my client's trust in me—demonstrated by their willingness to allow me to know who they are and develop relationship with me—by continuing in the relationship and following up on monitoring the post-court determination progress.

> external and internal pressures adds to the complexity of FASD and can contribute to a perception that people with FASD are unable to care for themselves or lead positive, healthy, and successful lives. These attitudes can further decrease individuals' independence and their perceived future potential[.]

Moreover, forensic processes and procedures—fast-occurring actions and words, with multiple stimuli occurring simultaneously and having to do with stressful and/or emotionally charged subject matter that relies on memory and abstract concepts—exacerbate impairments associated with FASD. This exacerbation, expressed through a client's behavior in the forensic environment, confirms rather than dispels the basis for "discrimination and negative attitudes and beliefs about FASD" (Morrison et al., 2019, p.1) among forensic actors. Rather than bridging the empathic divide, assumptions that the affected person's actions were and/or are deviant,[77] that nothing can be done, and the client poses a future danger to all of society not only will be reinforced but widened, leaving the client, still, in a hopeless situation.

Minimally, the science of FASD involves the prenatal period through the entire lifespan. Interactions between affected clients and forensic contexts require integration of past, present, and—consistent with restorative justice (Ward, Fox, & Garber, 2014; Zehr, 1990) and good lives model principles (Ward, Yates, & Willis, 2012)—the future. This whole-cloth perspective requires developing an understanding of the client's particular FASD presentation, comorbidities, risk factors (i.e., anything that exacerbates the disadvantageous effects of FASD and/or leads to comorbid conditions), resiliency or protective factors (i.e., strengths and/or other factors that mitigate the disadvantageous effects of FASD and comorbidities), and previously attempted treatments and accommodations (and their results). Further, the past, present, and future perspective should be integrated into analysis of all legal issues: competency to stand trial in the present proceedings as well as anticipated ability to act to sufficiently preserve rights in future proceedings,[78] sufficiency of rights waivers (e.g., to make uncounseled statements, confess, and consent to searches), and factual bases for defenses (e.g., self-defense, coercion, and extreme emotional disturbance). Finally, consistent with restorative justice principles, forward-thinking mitigation should explore empathy with the victims, acceptance of responsibility where appropriate, and the need for and manners of expressing remorse.

---

[77] Note that labelling both the act committed and the identity of the offender as deviant or *evil*, in turn, fosters the formation of criminal subcultures, furthering deviant behavior (Braithwaite, 1989).

[78] Crucial to the concept of a person with FASD assisting in their defense is an examination whether that person has the capacity to integrate all information necessary to functioning in the criminal justice system *presently*. Query whether that person can reasonably be said to have the capacity to effectively participate in future review processes such as state post-conviction, in which the petitioner bears a heavy burden, and which requires retrospective integration of information generated at the time of the incident itself as well as during the investigatory and trial stages. See, e.g., McClure v. Maass (1992), 110 Or.App. 119, 821 P.2d 1105 (Or. 1991), *rev. den.*, 313 Or. 74, 828 P.2d 457 (Or. 1992) (imposing responsibility for raising claims within a post-conviction petition on the petitioner himself); and Baldwin v. Reese (2004), 541 U.S. 27, 29, 124 S.Ct. 1347, 158 L.Ed.2d 64 ("A state prisoner must exhaust all available state remedies before seeking a federal writ of habeas corpus by 'fairly presenting' his or her claims to the highest state court").

Simultaneous with FASD-and-client-informed analysis of all legal issues, whole-person assessments must be underway, with those assessments addressing factors used in culpability determinations (i.e., factors upon which judgments of future dangerousness are formed or dispelled, including deterrence and protection of society, remorse, and redemption). This perspective is of utmost importance because to the extent prognosis is assumed hopeless, perception of future dangerousness increases correspondingly. Extending the view of representation forward in time to the client's future and doing so in cooperation with the client and multidisciplinary team, reversal of what otherwise is assumed to be an inevitable hopeless process can and should begin. While one aim of the forward-thinking mitigation approach is bridging rather than widening the empathic divide, it also serves as a coda (Bruner, 2002). That is, this approach enables clients with FASD to learn about themselves and learn through treatment plan development and implementation that there is hope and they can become better versions of themselves, which not only serves their own interests but also the interests of their communities.

A forward-thinking approach requires educating team members as well as the client about how FASD has affected their functioning. For long-term success, clients must participate on equal footing with counsel and other team members rather than being subjected to top-down mandates and/or patronization. In other words, the process should embody the principle of "nothing about me without me" (Choate & Badry, 2019). This inclusive process, extending throughout the duration of representation, involves "[i]dentification of risk and resiliency factors [that] will aid in…development of targeted interventions" (Mattson et al., 2019, p. 15) as well as internal and external resources and accommodations (e.g., skills training, vocational supports, education, and social support; Walgrave, Ward, & Zinsstag, 2019). The process must include a method for evaluating and monitoring successes and failures as to all forensic actors, including the client and other team members. Additionally, all involved must be encouraged to "explore their own attitudes and beliefs regarding alcohol use, while guiding a professional response grounded in current research and best practice in FASD prevention and intervention" (Bagley & Badry, 2019, 9. 11).

As the client and team members work side by side to develop goals, identify risk and resiliency factors, select and/or create accommodations, and develop and implement monitored treatment protocols to minimize the negative effects of FASD, a meaningful, respectful, and positive outlook is created. This outlook is more than the result of *solving a problem* and represents the first steps on a path toward (and equipping for) a meaningful life. As the client progresses along steps in the process, follow-up assessments reflect progress, provide information from which modifications can be made, and provide proof of concept that in the life of the client with FASD, not only is future dangerousness not a foregone conclusion but an invalid one. Prospects for success in their life are hopeful rather than hopeless, and a new normal is established (Amsterdam & Bruner, 2000). In other words, the results of the crafting, implementation, performance, and incremental steps within a life plan demonstrate to the fact-finder and/or decision-maker that the client can and has changed for the better with the support of a proper understanding of their FASD and properly constructed plan that minimizes risks while relying on strengths and resiliency factors.

2.5.2 Education Based upon Accurate and Current Science

Mitigating evidence is information that "a fact-finder could reasonably deem to have mitigating value."[79] As has been observed by courts in various jurisdictions, it should go without saying that those suffering from "epilepsy, infancy, or senility," or victims of incest, should not be punished further on the basis of misfortune out of their control.[80] Rather, in such instances, culpability and ultimate assessment of responsibility is mitigated. The same should be held true for people with FASD, each of whom is a victim of their parent's drinking habits.

Reported decisions in criminal courts predominantly demonstrate inadequate understanding of FASD's inherent mitigation value by attorneys, courts, and jurors. Generally, results of this inadequate understanding have led to such things as the disorder and its effects being equated with other mitigating factors or unrealistic expectations imposed on the person with FASD. As to inadequate understanding of FASD's inherent mitigating value, the complexity of FASD—with both its consequential impairments as well as comorbidities—provides context and an explanation grounded in the causality of brain structure (leading to function, which leads to behavior), not only for incident conduct but also for all associated aggravating factors. Thus, to make this conceptual point clear, counsel's presentation must focus on the whole cloth of the client's life (i.e., how FASD affected every important domain of functioning across the lifespan) rather than counting a multiplicity of aggravating factors that make up and/or are scientifically correlated with FASD.[81]

As to imposition of unrealistic expectations, reviewing courts have excused counsel's deficiencies relative to FASD (thus denying relief to affected clients) due to clients not having told counsel they have the disorder.[82] Beyond the questionable logic of holding a brain-damaged person responsible for failing to advise their attorney of an undiagnosed disorder that counsel should have investigated to identify, the reasonableness of this expectation also is questionable in that it ignores societal stigma[83] associated with the disorder. Indeed, stigma is documented "on multiple

[79] Smith v. Texas (2004), 543 U.S. 37, 44, 125 S.Ct. 400, 160 L.Ed.2d 303.

[80] See, Beam v. Paskett (1993), 3 F.3d 1301, 1310 (9th Cir. 1993), *overruled on other grounds*, Lambright v. Stewart (1999), 191 F.3d 1181, 1185 (9th Cir. 1999); and *Dillbeck v. State* (1994), 643 So.2d at 1029.

[81] See, e.g., Rompilla v. Beard (2005), 545 U.S. 374, 388, 125 S.Ct. 2456, 162 L.Ed.2d 360 ("Counsel's obligation to rebut aggravating evidence extended beyond arguing it ought to be kept out.").

[82] See, e.g., United States v. Laverdure (2020), No. 19–35,466, 2020 U.S. App. LEXIS 15950 (May 19, 2020, unpublished) (reviewing court upheld the denial of relief, sanctioning trial counsel's failure to investigate and present Laverdure's FASD because client did not tell counsel that he was born with FAS, did not contend that "any debilitating condition should have been apparent to counsel[,]" told his probation officer that he "had no medical problems[,]" testified that he "was of average intelligence[,]" and he had held a steady job for several years).

[83] "A stigma is an attribute that makes a person different from others in a social category, and it reduces the person to a … discounted status … made up of a discrepancy between the virtual (or perceived) identity and the actual identity of the stigma's bearer" (Choate & Badry, 2019).

levels beginning with the issue of alcohol use and pregnancy," including the name of the disorder itself,[84] language and treatment by professionals, and extending to what has become a common narrative relative to the lives of those with FASD: lifelong dependency, prognosis of failure, susceptibility to exploitation, homelessness, widespread view that most people with FASD are unable to parent their own children, devaluation, hopelessness, and lack of agency (Choate & Badry, 2019).[85] Clearly, forensic professionals' inadequate understanding of FASD as a whole-person disorder would benefit from education about the science of FASD as well as daily and situational applications of that science specifically through requests for implementation of targeted accommodations in forensic settings, integrating past–present–future investigation data with case facts and case theory, effective communication of relevant information to the fact-finder and/or decision-maker, and planning for determinations of responsibility through integration of FASD characteristics—both strengths and deficits—into life plans that address legitimate societal goals.

2.5.3 Accommodations to Accommodate and Educate

Similar to persons with intellectual disability, the real-life needs of those within the FASD population require adjusting forensic system processes and procedures to allow them to participate in the forensic context without discrimination and the deleterious effects of stigma (Hahn, 2000). As legislative rights ensuring access to justice for those with disability become more commonplace, failure to take hold of appropriately tailored accommodations that address specific needs in specific forensic processes is without excuse.[86] In addition to accommodations that assist in leveling the forensic playing field within which people with FASD participate, the process of counsel identifying, proposing, and explaining the need for accommodations to the court/decision-maker also serves to educate forensic actors about FASD, thereby creating another opportunity to correct misperceptions and wrongly held assumptions.

The manner of evaluating need for accommodations is straightforward despite heterogeneity in FASD presentation, subjects of proceedings, and their associated processes and characteristics. Offered here is an example of how accommodations might be developed for a parent with FASD involved in family court proceedings regarding

---

[84] For a person with FASD, "The concern of FASD as a diagnosis and as a term contributes to stigma as it serves to identify the cause and nature of the condition with which the person lives" (Choate & Badry, 2019).

[85] FASD has been "connected to a series of themes in research and clinical literature about the need for the lifelong dependency on caregivers, prognosis of failure, susceptibility to exploitation, homelessness, involvement with child intervention and a belief that most people with FASD are unable to parent their own children" (Choate & Badry, 2019). The stigma associated with FASD is consistent with stigma associated with other disabilities. Specifically, "a person with a disability is seen as disabled not only with respect to the specific area of disability, but also to other characteristics, such as personality and adjustment" (Munyi, 2012).

[86] In the United States, those accommodations are available pursuant to the Americans with Disabilities Act (ADA) of 1990, (42 U.S. § 12,101), Pub. L. No. 101–336, 104 Stat. 328 (1990).

child custody. Depending upon a parent's array of strengths, impairments, and comorbidities, accommodations can be individualized to address factors that affect parenting and are relevant to the forensic issues and characteristics attendant the forensic setting. As a first step, counsel should have well-informed understanding of the client's particular deficits, vulnerabilities, and risk as well as resiliency factors and strengths.[87] Counsel also must have well-informed understanding of the emotional salience of the subject matter at issue and long-term implications of possible outcomes.

For people with FASD involved in child custody matters, the courtroom environment presents challenges. The subject matter (i.e., child custody) is a highly emotional subject, likely made more so because of problems that prevented out-of-court custody agreements. The emotionally charged nature of the subject matter likely will exacerbate FASD adaptive impairments. Given the social stigma and hopelessness narratives associated with the disorder, the parent with FASD not only may hesitate to reveal their condition but also be reluctant to seek accommodations. In addition to these considerations, the courtroom setting itself also may produce problems. Courtroom environments are formal and rely on an adversarial representational and/or inquisitorial model. They are characterized by a rapid flow of large volumes of information produced verbally by judges, lawyers, parties, victims, and witnesses, sometimes speaking simultaneously. To ask counsel a question, a party must get counsel's attention quickly, in a socially acceptable manner, and then ask the question in a volume and manner that maintains confidentiality. Judges and attorneys use legal language and terms of art, may speak in the third person, and integrate timelines and sequences of events with other information. Credibility determinations are based upon assessments of witness demeanor, clarity, social acceptability of verbal communication (including volume and content) and body language, within-testimony consistency, and consistency between testimony and out-of-court statements and actions. Courts and/or counsel may embed cues within statements that while not directly seeking a responsive answer or modification of behavior, nonetheless are so intended. Proceedings may continue for hours without breaks, requiring parties to remain seated and/or relatively still. Unwritten rules of courtroom decorum, social interaction, and procedural rules must be followed. Given the emotional salience of the child custody matter, the parties and other forensic actors may experience heightened emotions and may express those emotions with raised voices or other means. Courtroom settings often involve additional stimuli in the form of periodic interruptions, persons entering and departing during proceedings, presence of members of the public seated directly behind the parties and counsel, bright lights (often fluorescent), and either too cold or hot ambient temperature.

Targeted accommodations that address clients' specific needs within such environments can produce a more level playing field, leading to determinations based upon children's well-being rather than parental inability to function well in forensic settings. The following is a non-exhaustive list of accommodations that might be considered in relation to a client's particular FASD presentation: (a) require

[87] To the extent this information is not yet well known or understood by counsel, incremental steps can be taken, with those steps being revised and supplemented as counsel's knowledge of client's FASD and functioning continues to evolve.

pre-proceeding exchange of as much documentary evidence and exhibits as possible to give client an opportunity to review and become familiar with the content of those documents; (b) depending upon subject matter, consider holding the proceedings in a less formal room, perhaps with non-fluorescent lighting; (c) allow a person familiar with client's FASD functioning to sit at counsel's table to assist with client communication, monitor client focus and fatigue level, and facilitate confidential client–counsel communication; (d) allow more frequent breaks in proceedings to provide opportunities for client to alleviate physical and mental fatigue, "re-set" focus, and gather strength by eating a snack, while also providing additional opportunities for counsel to verify client is following the proceedings; (e) check in with client often to ensure comprehension; (f) provide a quiet place without distractions for client and counsel to retire during breaks; (g) identify issues that will require client decision-making prior to the proceedings and if that is not possible, postpone client decision-making to permit client–counsel communication; (h) ensure that proceedings are recorded, so a written record can be made available for client's later review, thereby alleviating the need for client to rely on memory; (i) if client will be required to testify, practice that testimony with client (including cross-examination) prior to the proceedings to ensure client is familiar with the process and counsel is familiar with client's word choices in response to questions; (j) object to any manner of presentation by opposing counsel that is aimed at producing (or actually results in) deleterious effects on client; (k) during client testimony, ensure questions are clear, direct, concrete (i.e., no abstract terms or double-negatives), and contain only one focus, with counsel and/or the support person at counsel table monitoring to ensure client is tracking the question (if problems are detected, intervene or request a break in the proceedings); (l) give client a written copy of any decisions, directives, or requirements imposed on them (and/or the other party) that result from the proceedings, ensuring such documents involve concrete language in simply-constructed sentences; and (m) follow up more than once after the proceedings to ensure client's understanding. Accommodations such as these should be fashioned for all persons with FASD who are subject to the forensic context.

2.5.4 *Function over Label*

The possibility of FASD in a civil or criminal justice case transforms the case into a more complex one because of the multifaceted complexity of the disorder. Best practice in health and social agencies is to look past the FASD label to understand the disorder as it manifests in a particular person, thereby enabling identification and selection of appropriate treatments. Similarly, counsel encountering FASD in forensic contexts[88] should emphasize function and behavior over any diagnostic

[88] Admittedly, many health and social agencies depend on a diagnostic label as the key to obtaining funding for services, including for FASD. Apart from the disability determination context, however, a review of reported cases demonstrates that funding for health-care services is rarely the focal issue in the civil and criminal forensic context.

label (Wayland & O'Brien, 2013).[89] This emphasis is accomplished using lay witness testimony to provide real-life examples that bridge the empathic divide while complementing such illustrations with the science of FASD so as to provide causative links and a whole-cloth contextual framework.

Does an emphasis on function mean diagnostic labels are fully cast away? The answer is "no" with respect to FASD because without the diagnostic label, the causative link (between FASD's structural brain effects with behaviors, and with events) and scientifically based contextualizing framework are lost. Further, real-life illustrations contextualized by the structural and developmental impact of FASD, with layers of comorbidity, trauma, failures to diagnose and treat (or mis-diagnosing and mis-treating),

> permit professionals to 'connect the dots' and show that history of behavioral mistakes reflects cognitively-based impairments in judgment rather than character-based knowing and intentional rejection of social norms (Novick Brown, 2020).[90]

Therefore, allowing the science of FASD to provide an anchoring framework incorporates recognition by the scientific community of the need to reject the tendency by lay and forensic actors "to ignore the cognitive weaknesses in a cognitive profile and mistakenly conclude that strengths represent real-world choice-making capacity and that bad choices are purely knowing and intentional" (Novick Brown, 2020).

In addition, the constellation of functional impairments in a client with FASD provides foundation for certain legal arguments based upon principles of parity, proportionality, and penological objectives, with the diagnostic label providing a reference point from which counsel can argue the need for like being treated alike. An appeal to the foundational legal principle 'like should be treated alike' is indicated where the structural, developmental, and behavioral characteristics of a particular category of persons are similar to those of a client with FASD and where previous judicial assessments as to the similar category have determined certain sentencing practices fail to achieve legitimate penological objectives. In short, to treat offenders with FASD otherwise would be to reject principles of parity, proportionality, and penological objectives based upon the person's characteristics. As one example, not only is it apparent that FASD is functionally equivalent to intellectual disability in many respects, there also is congruence in the analysis of penological objectives of retribution and deterrence between persons with FASD and persons with ID, who are protected by the United States Supreme Court's decision in Atkins v. Virginia (2002).[91] For more on FASD and ID equivalence, see Chaps. 8 and 10, *infra*.

---

[89] See also, Brown v. The Queen [2020] VSCA 212 (25 August 2020), a case involving a non-FASD condition, in which the reviewing court noted that "[w]hat the sentencing judge needs is not a diagnostic label but a clear, well-founded expert opinion as to the nature and extent of the offender's impairment of . . . functioning[.]"

[90] See also, Greenspan et al. (2016).

[91] Atkins v. Virginia (2002), 536 U.S. 304, 122 S.Ct. 2242, 153 L.Ed.2d 335. The Court undertook similar analysis in relation to the former practice of sentencing juveniles to death. See, Roper v. Simmons (2005), 543 U.S. 551, 125 S.Ct. 1183, 161 L.Ed.2d 1.

2.5.5 Narratives and Stories Versus Catalogs of Facts

"We are not statistical machines, and are prone to inferential errors" (Bruner, 2002, p. 29). In the absence of a visible explanation, faced with a discrepancy between how people behave versus how we expect them to behave, we almost certainly will resort to previously held assumptions, expectations, and our own individual background information as we reach conclusions. Conveying and appealing to lifelikeness with the person with FASD and bridging the empathic divide should lead to more accurate appraisals of intent, responsibility, and degree of culpability (Amsterdam & Bruner, 2000; Bruner, 2002; Olive, 2008–2009). What manner of presentation will increase likelihood that our information will be received by a fact-finder or decision-maker such that they will choose to sincerely consider and give that information meaningful effect? In addition to reliance on function versus label, it is through the telling of stories that the

> …law's actors comprehend whatever series of events they make the subject of their legal actions. It is how they try to make their actions comprehensible again within some larger series of events they take to constitute the legal system and the culture that sustains it (Amsterdam & Bruner, 2000, p. 110)

Stories and narratives require us to set the stage and provide context that allows fact-finders and/or decision-makers the information by which historical events and processes can be connected and understood. Regarding a client with FASD, this process necessarily involves pre-incident context, the incident itself, and post-incident contextual information (including forward-thinking mitigation), allowing for full comprehension of the import of FASD in the whole cloth of the client's life. Thus, the incident is positioned and presented within that whole cloth rather than as an isolated focal point, and the narrative and story extend to a new conclusion.

2.5.6 Evolving Standards

Societal standards of decency that mark the progress of a maturing society evolve over time,[92] with that evolution reflected in the law by legislative actions and constitutional interpretations by the courts. Constitutional interpretations that incorporate evolving standards of decency ensure punishment for crime is graduated in proportion to offender and offense.[93] Such a perspective—one "not fastened to the obsolete but [acquiring] meaning as public opinion becomes enlightened by a humane justice"[94]—guards against mismatches between punishment and certain defendants'

[92] Trop v. Dulles (1958), 536 U.S. 86, 101, 78 S.Ct. 590, 2 L.Ed.2d 630.

[93] See, e.g., Miller v. Alabama (2012), 567 U.S. 460, 469, 32 S.Ct. 2455, 183 L.Ed.2d 407 at 469 (quoting *Roper v. Simmons*, 543 U.S. at 560).

[94] Weems v. United States (1910), 217 U.S. 349, 378, 30 S.Ct. 544, 54 L.Ed.2d 793; and see also, and Hall v. Florida (2014), 572 U.S. 701, 708, 134 S.Ct. 1986, 188 L.Ed.2d 1007 ("[t]he Eighth Amendment's protection of dignity reflects the [n]ation we have been, the [n]ation we are, and the [n]ation we aspire to be").

culpability. In short, as society changes, knowledge accumulates.[95] Implementation of accumulated knowledge in the legal setting should be reflected in how forensic actors, including courts, use the science of FASD as contextualizing a framework by which affected persons' whole cloth of their lives, including the charged crime, can be evaluated and analyzed.

Review of the science of FASD over the past decades shows how our understanding of the disorder has evolved, and as that understanding has evolved, so too have societal standards pertinent to our understanding of the elements of statutorily defined crimes, including inferences and determinations of intent, responsibility, and degree of culpability. Finally, and consistent with evolution as to the science and societal standards relative to FASD, our understanding of accommodations and treatment likewise evolves. In short, what we knew yesterday is not what we know today, how we accommodated a particular FASD impairment yesterday is not necessarily how we should accommodate that impairment today, and how we viewed determinations of intent, responsibility, and degree of culpability yesterday is not necessarily how we should view those concepts today.

2.6 Conclusion

Research shows that where a subject is not well-understood—as has been the case with FASD—or where reality stands in contrast with commonly held assumptions and/or misinformation—as has been the case with FASD—science can play a pivotal role in providing necessary corrective information. In forensic contexts, the science of FASD demonstrates the invalidity of general commonly held assumptions and misinformation about the disorder that contribute to erroneous determinations of intent, responsibility, and degree of culpability. Incorporating accurate and current science relative to FASD, including its causative links and contextualizing framework, is crucial as it provides the means by which the whole cloth of the affected person's life can be presented. This perspective, extending from the past through to the future, appropriately places the subject of the forensic proceeding (e.g., a charged crime) within that whole cloth rather than in isolation. Given the nature of FASD, adequate and effective representation of a person with the disorder necessarily includes investigation, consideration, and analysis of the client's past, present, and future relative to all legal and factual issues, including forward-thinking mitigation. The substance, modes, and manner of presenting that information should rely heavily upon educating with accurate and current science, using accommodations to educate as well as accommodate, and emphasizing function over diagnostic labels, narratives and stories over catalogs of facts, and an awareness of ever-evolving societal standards. Doing so will equip fact-finders and/or

[95] Graham v. Florida (2010), 560 U.S. 48, 85, 130 S.Ct. 2011, 176 L.Ed.2d 825 (Stevens, J., concurring).

decision-makers to more accurately understand the reality and unique mitigating quality of FASD and empathize with how FASD has affected a particular client, leading to a more just determination of intent, responsibility, and degree of culpability while providing the client with a hopeful, new normal.

References

Alicke, M. D. (1985). Global self-evaluation as determined by the desirability and controllability of trait adjectives. *Journal of Personality and Social Psychology, 49*(6), 1621–1630. https://doi.org/10.1037/0022-3514.49.6.1621

American Bar Association. (rev. 2003). ABA guidelines for the appointment and performance of defense counsel in death penalty cases. Hofstra Law Review, 31(4), 913–1090. article 2 http://scholarlycommons.law.hofstra.edu/hlr/vol31/iss4/2

American Bar Association. (2020). Model rules of professional conduct, Rule 1.1: Competence. https://www.americanbar.org/groups/professional_responsibility/publications/model_rules_of_professional_conduct/rule_1_1_competence/

Americans with Disabilities Act (ADA) of (1990). (42 U.S. § 12101), Pub. L. No. 101–336, 104 Stat. 328 (1990).

Amsterdam, A. G., & Bruner, J. (2000). *Minding the law*. Cambridge, MA: Harvard University Press. (2nd printing 2002).

Anderson v. Kelley, No. 5:12-cv-279-DPM, 2017 U.S. Dist. LEXIS 48268, at 9 (E.D. Ark. March 28, 2017).

Anderson v. Kelley, 938 F.3d 949 (8th Cir. 2019), sub nom., *Anderson v. Payne*, U.S. Supreme Court No. 19–8105, *cert den.*, 592 U.S. __ (10/5/2020).

Artz, L., & Murphy, B. O. (2000). *Cultural hegemony in the United States*. Thousand Oaks, CA: Sage.

Atiq, E. H. (2013). How folk beliefs about free will influence sentencing: A new target for the neuro-determinist critics of criminal law. *New Criminal Law Review, 16*(3), 449–494. https://doi.org/10.1525/nclr.2013.16.3.449

Atkins v. Virginia (2002). 536 U.S. 304, 122 S.Ct. 2242, 153 L.Ed.2d 335.

Attorney-General for the State of Queensland v. Tiers, (2020). QSC 135. https://archive.sclqld.org.au/qjudgment/2020/QSC20-135.pdf

Bagley, K., & Badry, D. (2019). How personal perspectives shape health professionals' perceptions of fetal alcohol spectrum disorder and risk. *International Journal of Environmental Research and Public Health, 16*(11), 1936. https://doi.org/10.3390/ijerph16111936

Baldwin v. Reese (2004). 541 U.S. 27, 124 S.Ct. 1347, 158 L.Ed.2d 64.

Barkley, R. (2012). *Executive functions: What they are, how they work, and why they evolved*. New York: Guilford Press.

Beam v. Paskett, 3 F.3d 1301 (9th Cir. 1993), *overruled on other grounds*, *Lambright v. Stewart*, 191 F.3d 1181 (9th Cir. 1999).

Beauregard, K. S., & Dunning, D. (2001). Defining self-worth: Trait self-esteem moderates the use of self-serving trait definitions in social judgment. *Motivation and Emotion, 25*(2), 135–161. https://doi.org/10.1023/A:1010665926045

Berger, B. (2011). The abiding presence of conscience: Criminal justice against the law and the modern constitutional imagination. *Univ. of Toronto L. Journ., 61*(579–616). https://doi.org/10.3138/utlj.61.4.579

Blagg, H., Tulich, T., Mutch, R., Williams, R., & May, S. (2018). *FASD and the criminal justice system: Report to the Australian National Advisory Council on Alcohol and Drugs (ANACAD) Secretariat* (Reference ID: 6000078020). https://research-repository.uwa.edu.au/en/publications/fasd-and-the-criminal-justice-system-report-to-the-australian-nat

Bousfield, N. K., Cook, A. N., & Roesch, R. (2014). Evidence-based criminal justice policy for Canada: An exploratory study of public opinion and the perspective of mental health and legal professionals. *Canadian Psychology/Psychologie Canadienne, 55*(3), 204–215. https://doi.org/10.1037/a0036860

Braithwaite, J. (1989). *Crime, shame and reintegration*. Cambridge: Cambridge University Press.

Brief of the American Medical Association, et al. (2005). as Amici Curiae, submitted in *Roper v. Simmons*, 543 U.S. 551, 125 S.Ct. 1183, 161 L.Ed.2d 1. https://www.apa.org/about/offices/ogc/amicus/roper.pdf

Brown v. State, Davidson County, Tennessee, Division II, Case No. 2005-A-215, *Order* (February 28, 2013).

Brown v. State, No. M2013–00825-CCA-R3-PC, 2014 Tenn. Crim. App. LEXIS 1014 (Tenn. Ct. of Crim. Appeals, Nov. 6, 2014), *rev. den.*, No. M2013–00825-SC-R11-PC, 2015 Tenn. LEXIS 400 (Tenn. S.Ct. May 15, 2015).

Brown v. The Queen, [2020] VSCA 212 (25 August 2020).

Bruner, J. (1986). *Actual minds, possible worlds*. Cambridge, MA: Harvard University Press.

Bruner, J. (2002). *Making stories: Law, literature, life*. New York: Farrar, Straus and Giroux.

Burd, L., Fast, D. K., Conry, J., & Williams, A. (2010). Fetal alcohol spectrum disorder as a marker for increased risk of involvement with correction systems. *Journal of Psychiatry & Law, 38*(4), 556–583. https://doi.org/10.1177/009318531003800408

Carroll, L. (1978). *Alice's adventures in wonderland. Illus. T. Jansson* (2nd ed.). New York: Delcorte Press.

Chan, R. C. K., Shum, D., Toulopoulou, T., & Chen, E. Y. H. (2008). Assessment of executive functions: Review of instruments and identification of critical issues. *Archives of Clinical Neuropsychology, 23*(2), 201–216. https://doi.org/10.1016/j.acn.2007.08.010

Choate, P., & Badry, D. (2019). Stigma as a dominant discourse in fetal alcohol spectrum disorder. *Advances In Dual Diagnosis, 12*(1/2), 36–52. https://doi.org/10.1108/ADD-05-2018-0005

Clemente, M. (2015). A reassessment of common law protections for "idiots". *Yale Law Journal, 124*(8), 2746–2803. https://www.yalelawjournal.org/note/a-reassessment-of-common-law-protections-for-idiots

Davis, K. M., Gagnier, K. R., Moore, T. E., & Todorow, M. (2013). Cognitive aspects of fetal alcohol spectrum disorder. *Wiley Interdisciplinary Reviews, Cognitive Science, 4*(1), 81–92. https://doi.org/10.1002/wcs.1202

Dillbeck v. State, 643 So.2d 1027 (Fla. 1994).

Douds, A. S., Stevens, H. R., & Sumner, W. E. (2013). Sword or shield? A systematic review of the roles FASD evidence plays in judicial proceedings. *Criminal Justice Policy Review, 24*(4), 492–509. https://doi.org/10.1177/0887403412447809

DPP v. Slater [2020] VCC 216.

Eighth United Nations Congress on the Prevention of Crime and the Treatment of Offenders, Havana, 27 August–7 September 1990: report prepared by the Secretariat (United Nations publication, Sales No. E.91.IV.2), chap. I, sect. B.3, annex: Basic Principles on the Role of Lawyers. https://www.ohchr.org/en/professionalinterest/pages/roleoflawyers.aspx

Elonis v. United States. (2015). 575 U.S. __, 135 S.Ct. 2001, 192 L.Ed.2d 1.

Fast, D. K., & Conry, J. (2009). Fetal alcohol spectrum disorders and the criminal justice system. *Developmental Disabilities Research Reviews, 15*(3), 250–257. https://doi.org/10.1002/ddrr.66

Federation of Law Societies of Canada. (2017). *Model code of professional conduct, Rule 3.1 competence*. https://flsc.ca/wp-content/uploads/2018/03/Model-Code-as-amended-March-2017-Final.pdf

Floyd v. Filson, 949 F.3d 1128 (9th Cit. 2020), *cert. pending*, United States Supreme Court, No. 19–8921

Geschwind, N. (1975). The borderland of neurology and psychiatry: Some common misconceptions. In D. F. Benson & D. Blumer (Eds.), *Psychiatric aspects of neurologic disease* (Vol. 1, pp. 1–8). New York: Grune and Stratton.

Glöckner, A. (2009). Investigating intuition: Automatic and deliberate process in quick decisions. *Judgment and Decision making, 4*(3), 186–199. http://journal.sjdm.org/9115/jdm9115.pdf

Glöckner, A., & Betsch, T. (2008). Multiple-reason decision making based on automatic processing. *Journal of Experimental Psychology: Learning, Memory, and Cognition, 34*(5), 1055–1075. https://doi.org/10.1037/0278-7393.34.5.1055

Glöckner, A., & Hodges, S. D. (2011). Parallel constraint satisfaction in memory-based decisions. *Experimental Psychology, 58*(3), 180–195. https://doi.org/10.1027/1618-3169/a000084

Graham v. Florida, 560 U.S. 48, 130 S.Ct. 2011, 176 L.Ed.2d 825 (2010).

Greenspan, S., & Driscoll, J. H. (2016). Why people with FASD fall for manipulative ploys: Ethical limits of interrogators' use of lies. In M. Nelson & M. Trussler (Eds.), *Fetal alcohol spectrum disorders in adults: Ethical and legal perspectives* (pp. 23–38). Amsterdam: Springer.

Greenspan, S., Novick Brown, N., & Edwards, W. (2016). FASD and the concept of "intellectual disability equivalence.". In M. Nelson & M. Trussler (Eds.), *Fetal alcohol spectrum disorders in adults: Ethical and legal perspectives* (pp. 241–266). Amsterdam: Springer.

Hahn, H. (2000). Accommodations and the ADA: Unreasonable bias or biased reasoning? *Berkeley Journal of Employment and Labor Law, 21*(1), 166–192. http://www.jstor.org/stable/24051162

Hall v. Florida (2014). 572 U.S. 701, 134 S.Ct. 1986, 188 L.Ed.2d 1007.

Haney, C. (2004). Condemning the other in death penalty trials: Biographical racism, structural mitigation and the empathic divide. *DePaul Law Review, 53*(4), 1557–1590. https://via.library.depaul.edu/law-review/vol53/iss4/7

Hart, H. L. A. (2012). *The concept of law* (3rd ed.). London: Oxford University Press.

Kambeitz, C., Klug, M. G., Greenmyer, J., Popova, S., & Burd, L. (2019). Association of adverse childhood experiences and neurodevelopmental disorders in people with fetal alcohol spectrum disorders (FASD) and non-FASD controls. *BMC Pediatrics, 19*, 498. https://doi.org/10.1186/s12887-019-1878-8

Karpen, S. C. (2018). The social psychology of biased self-assessment. *American Journal of Pharmaceutical Education, 82*(5), 441–448. https://doi.org/10.5688/ajpe6299

Kim, H. J., & Gerber, J. (2018). Shaming, reintegration, and restorative justice: Braithwaite in Australia, New Zealand, and around the globe. In R. A. Triplett (Ed.), *The handbook of the history and philosophy of criminology* (pp. 289–305). Hoboken: Wiley Blackwell. https://doi.org/10.1002/9781119011385.ch17

Kingdon, D., Cardoso, C., & McGrath, J. J. (2016). Research review: Executive function deficits in fetal alcohol spectrum disorders and attention-deficit/hyperactivity disorder—A meta-analysis. *Journal of Child Psychology and Psychiatry, and Allied Disciplines, 57*(2), 116–131. https://doi.org/10.1111/jcpp.12451

Kleinstuber, R. (2014). *Hegemonic individualism and subversive stories in capital mitigation*. London: Routledge. https://doi.org/10.4324/9781315586489

Knoll, J. L. (2008). The recurrence of an illusion: The concept of "evil" in forensic psychiatry. *Journal of the American Academy of Psychiatry and the Law, 36*(1), 105–116. http://jaapl.org/content/36/1/105

Knoll, P. J. (1988). *Criminal law defences*. Toronto: Carswell.

LaDue R., & Dunne, T. (1997). Legal issues and FAS. *The challenge of fetal alcohol syndrome: Overcoming secondary disabilities*. Seattle: University of Washington Press.

LaFave, W. R. (2003). *Substantive criminal law* (Vol. 1-3, 2nd ed.). Eagan, MN: Thomson/West.

Lambright v. Stewart, 191 F.3d 1181 (9th Cir. 1999).

Le Guin, U. K. (2004). *The wave in the mind: Talk and essays on the writer, the reader, and the imagination*. Boulder, CO: Shambhala.

Leifer, R. (1967). The concept of criminal responsibility. *ETC: A Review of General Semantics, 24*(2), 177–190. https://www.jstor.org/stable/42574329

Mattson, S. N., Bernes, G. A., & Doyle, L. R. (2019). Fetal alcohol spectrum disorders: A review of the neurobehavioral deficits associated with prenatal alcohol exposure. *Alcoholism: Clinical and Experimental Research, 43*(6), 1046–1062. https://doi.org/10.1111/acer.14040

McClure v. Maass (1992). 110 Or.App. 119, 821 P.2d 1105 (1991), *rev. den.*, 313 Or. 74, 828 P.2d 457.

McCoy v. Louisiana (2018). 584 U.S. __, 138 S.Ct. 1500, 200 L.Ed.2d 821.

McLachlan, K., McNeill, A., Pei, J., Brain, U., Andrew, G., & Oberlander, T. F. (2019). Prevalence and characteristics of adults with fetal alcohol spectrum disorder in corrections: A Canadian case ascertainment study. *BMC Public Health, 19*, 43. https://doi.org/10.1186/s12889-018-6292-x

McLachlan, K., Roesch, R., Viljoen, J. L., & Douglas, K. S. (2014). Evaluating the psycholegal abilities of young offenders with fetal alcohol spectrum disorder. *Law and Human Behavior, 38*(1), 10–22. https://doi.org/10.1037/lhb0000037

Medina v. California (1992). 505 U.S. 437, 112 S.Ct. 2572, 120 L.Ed.2d 353.

Mela, M., Coons-Harding, K. D., & Anderson, T. (2019). Recent advances in fetal alcohol spectrum disorder for mental health professionals. *Current Opinion in Psychiatry, 32*(4), 328–335. https://doi.org/10.1097/YCO.0000000000000514

Mela, M., & Luther, G. (2013). Fetal alcohol spectrum disorder: Can diminished responsibility diminish criminal behavior? *International Journal of Law and Psychiatry, 36*(1), 46–54. https://doi.org/10.1016/j.ijlp.2012.11.007

Miller v. Alabama (2012). 567 U.S. 460, 32 S.Ct. 2455, 183 L.Ed.2d 407.

Moore, T. E., Green, M. (2004). Fetal alcohol spectrum disorder (FASD): A need for closer examination by the criminal justice system. *Criminal Reports, 19*, 99–108.

Moore v. Texas (2017). 581 U.S. __, 137 S.Ct. 1039, 197 L.Ed.2d 416.

Morissette v. United States (1952). 342 U.S. 246, 72 S.Ct. 240, 96 L.Ed.2d 288.

Morrison, K., Harding, K., & Wolfson, L. (2019). Individuals with fetal alcohol spectrum disorder and experiences of stigma. *CanFASD*, (August 2019), 1–7. https://canfasd.ca/wp-content/uploads/publications/Individuals-with-FASD-and-Experiences-of-Stigma-FINAL.pdf.

Mullally, K., McLachlan, K., MacKillop, E., & Pei, J. (2020). Performance validity testing in justice-involved adults with fetal alcohol spectrum disorder. *Journal of the International Neuropsychological Society, 26*(7), 701–713. https://doi.org/10.1017/S1355617720000132

Munyi, C. W. (2012). Past and present perceptions towards disability: A historical perspective. *Disability Studies Quarterly, 32*, 2. https://doi.org/10.18061/dsq.v32i2.3197

Norman, D. A., & Shallice, T. (1986). Attention to action: Willed and automatic control of behavior. In R. J. Davidson, G. E. Schwartz, & D. Shapiro (Eds.), *Consciousness and self-regulation* (pp. 1–18). Boston: Springer. https://doi.org/10.1007/978-1-4757-0629-1_1

Novick Brown, N. (2020). Fetal alcohol spectrum disorders (FASD): Intellectual disability equivalence (Fetale Alkoholspektrumstörungen. Gleichrangigkeit mit intellektuellen Beeinträchtigungen). In G. Becker, K. Hennicke, M. Klein, & M. N. Landgraff (Eds.), *Adults with fetal alcohol spectrum disorder: Diagnosis, screening, intervention, and addiction prevention (Erwachsene mit Fetalen Alkoholspektrumstörungen. Diagnostik, screening, intervention, Suchtprävention)* (2nd ed., pp. 115–132). Berlin: de Gruyter. https://doi.org/10.1515/9783110594492

Novick Brown, N., Burd, L., Grant, T., Edwards, W., Adler, R., & Streissguth, A. (2015). Prenatal alcohol exposure: An assessment strategy for the legal context. *International Journal of Law and Psychiatry, 42–43*(Special issue), 144–148. https://doi.org/10.1016/j.ijlp.2015.08.019

Novick Brown, N., & Connor, P. D. (2014). Executive dysfunction and learning in children with fetal alcohol spectrum disorders (FASD). In K. P. Bennett (Ed.), *Executive functioning: Role in early learning processes, impairments in neurological disorders and impact of cognitive behavior therapy (CBT)* (pp. 1–48). Hauppauge: Nova Science Pub.

O'Hare, E. D., Lu, L. H., Houston, S. M., Bookheimer, S. Y., Mattson, S. N., O'Connor, M. J., & Sowell, E. R. (2009). Altered frontal-parietal functioning during verbal working memory in children and adolescents with heavy prenatal alcohol exposure. *Human Brain Mapping, 30*(10), 3200–3208. https://doi.org/10.1002/hbm.20741

Olive, M. E. (2008–2009). Narrative works. UMKC Law Review, 77(4), 989–1019.

Popova, S., Lange, S., Probst, C., Gmel, G., & Rehm, J. (2017). Estimation of national, regional, and global prevalence of alcohol use during pregnancy and fetal alcohol syndrome: A systematic review and meta-analysis. *Lancet: Global Health, 5*(3), e290–e299. https://doi.org/10.1016/S2214-109X(17)30021-9

Pora v. The Queen. (2015) UKPC 9.

R v. Verdins. (2007) 16 VR 269.
R. v. Harper, (2009) YKTC 18.
R. v. R.F. (2002) SKPC 137, 228 Sask R 111.
Rappeport, J. R. (1985). Reasonable medical certainty. *Bulletin of the American Academy of Psychiatry and the Law, 13*(1), 5–15. http://jaapl.org/content/jaapl/13/1/5.full.pdf
Reynolds, C. R., & Horton, A. M., Jr. (2008). Assessing executive functions: A life-span perspective. *Psychology in the Schools, 45*(9), 875–892. https://doi.org/10.1002/pits.20332
Roach, K., & Bailey, A. (2009). The relevance of fetal alcohol spectrum disorder in Canadian criminal law from investigation to sentencing. *UBC Law Review, 42*(1), 1–68. https://www.researchgate.net/profile/Kent_Roach/publication/228263950
Rompilla v. Beard (2005). 545 U.S. 374, 125 S.Ct. 2456, 162 L.Ed.2d 360.
Roper v. Simmons (2005). 543 U.S. 551, 125 S.Ct. 1183, 161 L.Ed.2d 1.
Samuels, A. (1988). Mental condition as a defence in criminal law: A lawyer addresses medical men. *Medicine, Science and the Law, 28*(1), 21–25. https://doi.org/10.1177/002580248802800107
Silvera, D. H., & Seger, C. R. (2004). Feeling good about ourselves: Unrealistic self-evaluations and their relation to self-esteem in the United States and Norway. *Journal of Cross-Cultural Psychology, 35*(5), 571–585. https://doi.org/10.1177/0022022104268389
Slovenko, R. (1984). The meaning of mental illness in criminal responsibility. *Journal of Legal Medicine, 5*(1), 1–61. https://doi.org/10.1080/01947648409513402
Smith v. Texas (2004). 543 U.S. 37, 125 S.Ct. 400, 160 L.Ed.2d 303.
State v. E.S (unpublished). No. 58637–8-I, 2007 Wash.App. LEXIS 3185.
State v. Miles, 243 Ariz. 511, 414 P.3d 680 (Ariz. S.Ct. 2018).
State v. Wilson, No. M2014–01487-CCA-R9-CD, 2015 Tenn. Crim. App. LEXIS 712, 2015 WL 5170970 (Tenn. Ct. of Crim. Appeals, Sept. 2, 2015), *rev. den.*, No. M2014–01487-SC-R11-CD, 2015 Tenn. LEXIS 1044 (Tenn. S.Ct., Dec. 10, 2015).
Stetler, R., & Wendel, W. B. (2013). The ABA guidelines and the norms of capital defense representation. *Hofstra Law Review, 41*(3), 635–696. http://scholarlycommons.law.hofstra.edu/hlr/vol41/iss3/7
Stoddart, M. C. J. (2007). Ideology, hegemony, discourse: A critical review of theories of knowledge and power. *Social Thought & Research, 28*, 191–225. https://doi.org/10.17161/STR.1808.5226
Treit, S., Lebel, C., Baugh, L., Rasmussen, C., Andrew, G., & Beaulieu, C. (2013). Longitudinal MRI reveals altered trajectory of brain development during childhood and adolescence in fetal alcohol spectrum disorders. *Journal of Neuroscience: The Official Journal of the Society for Neuroscience, 33*(24), 10098–10109. https://doi.org/10.1523/JNEUROSCI.5004-12.2013
Trevino v. Davis (2018). 861 F.3d 545 (5th Cir. 2017), *cert. den.*, U.S. __, 138 S.Ct. 1793, 201 L.Ed.2d 1014.
Trop v. Dulles (1958). 536 U.S. 86, 78 S.Ct. 590, 2 L.Ed.2d 630.
United Nations Office on Drugs and Crime (UNODC) (2017). *Model Law on Legal Aid in Criminal Justice Systems with Commentaries*. https://www.unodc.org/documents/justice-and-prison-reform/LegalAid/Model_Law_on_Legal_Aid.pdf
United States v. Balint (1922). 258 U.S. 250, 42 S.Ct. 301, 66 L.Ed. 604.
United States v. Laverdure, No. 19–35466, 2020 U.S. App. LEXIS 15950 (May 19, 2020, unpublished).
Verbrugge, P. (2003). *Fetal alcohol spectrum disorder and the youth criminal justice system: A discussion paper*. Report prepared for Department of Justice Canada, Youth Justice Research. https://www.justice.gc.ca/eng/rp-pr/cj-jp/yj-jj/rr03_yj6-rr03_jj6/index.html
Walgrave, L., Ward, T., & Zinsstag, E. (2019). When restorative justice meets the good lives model: Contributing to a criminology of trust. *European Journal of Criminology*, 1–17. https://doi.org/10.1177/1477370819854174
Ward, T., Fox, K. J., & Garber, M. (2014). Restorative justice, offender rehabilitation and desistance. *Restorative Justice: An International Journal, 2*(1), 24–42. https://doi.org/10.5235/20504721.2.1.24

Ward, T., Yates, P. M., & Willis, G. M. (2012). The good lives model and the risk need responsivity model: A critical response to Andrews, Bonta, and Wormith (2011). *Criminal Justice and Behavior, 39*(1), 94–110. https://doi.org/10.1177/0093854811426085

Wayland, K., & O'Brien, S. D. (2013). Deconstructing antisocial personality disorder and psychopathy: A guidelines-based approach to prejudicial psychiatric labels. *Hofstra Law Review, 42*(2), 519–588. https://scholarlycommons.law.hofstra.edu/hlr/vol42/iss2/6.

Weems v. United States (1910). 217 U.S. 349, 30 S.Ct. 544, 54 L.Ed.2d 793.

Williams v. Stirling (2019). 914 F.3d 302 (4th Cir. 2019), *cert. den.*, 589 U.S. __, 140 S.Ct. 105, 205 L.Ed.2d 38.

Wyper, K., & Pei, J. (2016). Neurocognitive difficulties underlying high risk and criminal behaviour in FASD: Clinical implications. In M. Nelson & M. Trussler (Eds.), *Fetal alcohol spectrum disorders in adults: Ethical and legal perspectives* (pp. 101–120). Amsterdam: Springer.

Zehr, H. (1990). *Changing lenses: A new focus for crime and justice*. Scottdale, PA: Herald Press.

Chapter 3
Prevalence of Fetal Alcohol Spectrum Disorder and Screening in the Forensic Context

Larry Burd, Marilyn G. Klug, and Kaylee Husark

Abstract In juvenile corrections systems, 18.3% of children and adolescents (one in every six people) have a fetal alcohol spectrum disorder (FASD), and rates for adults in the criminal justice system are similar. FASD is a lifelong condition, with outcomes complicated by delayed recognition and treatment (less than 1% are ever diagnosed), which delays entry into diagnosis-informed care pathways. Rates of adverse childhood experiences (ACEs) are greatly increased in people with FASD (only 10% have 0 or 1 ACE, 35.7% have 2–6 ACES, and 54.1% have 7–10 ACEs). Delayed diagnosis and exposure to ongoing adversity increase risk of learning disorders, poor judgment, impaired socialization, substance use disorders, familial and individual mortality, chronic illness, mental disorders, incarceration, victimization, and dependent living. This chapter presents a recent validity study involving the Alcohol Related Neurodevelopmental Disorder Behavioral Checklist (ABC), a screening instrument designed to detect possible FASD in children and adolescents. Routine screening for the neurocognitive symptoms of FASD as a case-finding strategy during childhood should be a routine component in well-child visits. This process should include at least one screen for all children and three or more screens for children in out-of-home placements (e.g., foster care, special education, juvenile corrections) as well as children with attention-deficit hyperactivity disorder, intellectual disability, and anxiety disorders. Along with routine screening, increased training is urgently needed for forensic professionals (e.g., court, corrections, and

---

Screening: If you get what you want—you may not want what you get.—Burd (2015), *Screening for FASD in corrections systems*

L. Burd (✉) · K. Husark
Department of Pediatrics, North Dakota Fetal Alcohol Syndrome Center, University of North Dakota School of Medicine and Health Sciences, Grand Forks, ND, USA
e-mail: larry.burd@und.edu

M. G. Klug
Department of Population Health, University of North Dakota School of Medicine and Health Sciences, Grand Forks, ND, USA

N. Novick Brown (ed.), *Evaluating Fetal Alcohol Spectrum Disorders in the Forensic Context*, https://doi.org/10.1007/978-3-030-73628-6_3

parole and probation systems) to improve recognition of FASD and link recognition with diagnosis-specific services.

Keywords Fetal alcohol spectrum disorder · Prenatal alcohol exposure · Screening · Prevention · Services · Corrections

3.1 Introduction

This chapter describes current prevalence estimates for fetal alcohol spectrum disorders (FASD) and discusses strategies, methodologies, and a screening tool for use in forensic populations. In previous publications (e.g., Burd, 2015), we reviewed cost and prevalence estimates of FASD in the Canadian corrections system. In this chapter, we discuss these issues in the United States.

First a definition: FASD is a complex disorder with expression over the lifespan. The FASD phenotype (i.e., observable traits and characteristics) largely is exposure-dependent and comprised of increased mortality, beginning during gestation, with increased risk for multiple co-occurring neuropsychiatric disorders and increased susceptibility to chronic illness. Complexity of the phenotype is increased further by delayed recognition and accumulating effects from multiple adverse life experiences. Lack of long-term anticipatory planning with emphasis on risk reduction increases complexity of care across the lifespan. FASD is familial and generational.

The term FASD is considered a descriptor for several categorical medical entities: fetal alcohol syndrome (FAS), partial fetal alcohol syndrome (pFAS), and alcohol-related neurodevelopmental disorders (ARND). Under the 4-Digit Code (Astley, 2004), ARND is diagnosed as static encephalopathy/alcohol exposed (SE/AE) or neurobehavioral disorder/alcohol exposed (ND/AE). In the fifth edition of the *Diagnostic and Statistical Manual of Mental Disorders* (*DSM-5*; American Psychiatric Association (APA), 2013), the central nervous system (CNS) dysfunction in FASD is diagnosed as neurodevelopmental disorder associated with prenatal alcohol exposure (ND-PAE). For brevity, we will use FASD in this chapter.

Recent prevalence estimates from elementary schools in the United States found that one of every 13 first-grade students had FASD (Chambers et al., 2019; May, Hasken, Bozeman et al., 2020; May, Hasken, Stegall et al., 2020; May, Hasken, Baete et al., 2020). This prevalence is very similar to rates obtained from a longitudinal screening program we operated for nearly 20 years in a community setting (Poitra et al., 2003). What is less clearly understood by policy makers and funders who prioritize program initiatives is the societal impact of such large populations of people with FASD. A couple of examples may clarify this point. Based upon the widely accepted FASD prevalence rate of 5% of the general population (i.e., one of every 20 births in the United States), we need the capacity to identify, diagnose, and provide care plans for 547 new cases of FASD per day (Popova, Dozet, & Burd,

2020), which means we need to provide these services for 200,000 new cases per year. If 200,000 is multiplied by 18 annual birth cohorts (i.e., one birth cohort for each year of a child's life until adulthood), there are 3.6 million children and adolescents with FASD in the United States in every generation. Using this same calculation to estimate the number of adults in the United States with FASD, the bottom line is that in the United States, we have 10–15 million people with FASD who are undiagnosed.

In a recent paper (Popova et al., 2020), we discussed the implications of a disorder where less than one in every 800 people with the condition is correctly diagnosed. In addition to the obvious implications of unnecessary burdens on families as well as on those with FASD, this invisible disability has other less obvious implications. First, what is the true phenotype of FASD? Is it represented in the 1 of 800 cases diagnosed, or is it to be found in the other 799 undiagnosed cases? (See Fig. 3.1).

We have virtually no population-based data on FASD in the elderly and very little data for adults. While we know FASD is an important risk marker for entry into early intervention programs, foster care, special education, mental health treatment, and juvenile and adult corrections systems, the disorder is not part of widespread routine screening in any of these systems of care. Availability of diagnostic services for FASD is rare, and access to diagnosis-informed care is uncommon. However, a couple relevant examples offer hope for the future.

First, with very few exceptions, all infants born in the United States undergo newborn screening for hearing loss, congenital heart disease, and multiple metabolic disorders. This screening is conducted over four million times per year and repeated as needed in the event of a positive screen. Many of the metabolic conditions we routinely screen for in newborns are extremely rare, and no definitive treatment is available if cases are identified. Second, every year, several million children receive a vision or hearing screen at point of entry into Head Start, Kindergarten Roundup, or public school. So, it is clear from the routine screening we already do that we *can* screen for conditions like FASD if we develop acceptable screening tests. Currently, as depicted in Fig. 3.1, very few children, adolescents, and adults are screened for FASD in their lifetimes.

This brings us to the forensic system. Why screen for FASD before and after entry into a forensic setting? A diagnosis of FASD is a predictive risk marker associated with a 19-fold increase in risk of incarceration, beginning in adolescence (Popova, Lange, Bekmuradov, Mihic, & Rehm, 2011). Among children and adolescents in juvenile corrections settings, reported rates of FASD are 36% in Australia (Bower et al., 2018). In Canada, rates of FASD in juveniles have been found to range from 9.9% (Landgren, Svensson, Strömland, & Andersson Grönlund, 2010; Miller et al., 2006), 10.8% (Rojas & Gretton, 2007), and 11.7% (Murphy, Chittenden,, & The McCreary Centre, S., 2005) to 23.3% (Fast, Conry, & Loock, 1999).

The studies cited above show that one in every six children and adolescents in juvenile corrections has an FASD. In the United States, between 48,000 and 60,000 children and adolescents are in a juvenile corrections facility at any given time,

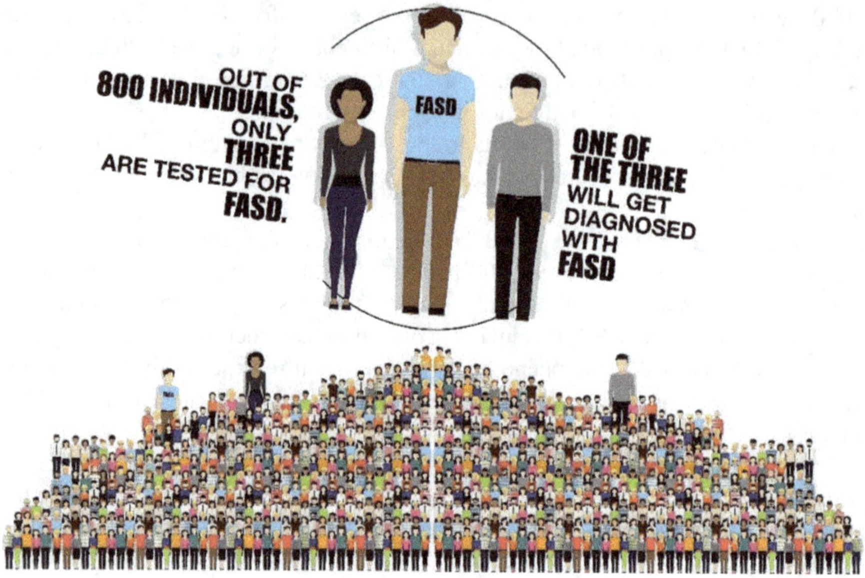

Fig. 3.1 Among people with FASD, few are ever tested, and diagnosis is rare

which suggests 8,000–10,000 of these youths have FASD. We estimate that using current FASD diagnostic systems, it would take 12–18 years to conduct diagnostic assessments on these young people. Importantly, these youths enter juvenile corrections systems after repeated involvement in other systems of care (e.g., foster care, special education, and mental health and substance use treatment programs). For example, in foster care, six studies have found FASD rates to be 25.1% (one in every four children and adolescents). This is why early screening and risk reduction programs are so sorely needed.

In adult forensic systems, the situation is far worse. In 2004, we demonstrated the number of diagnosed cases of FASD in adult corrections systems in the United States literally could be counted on one hand (Burd, Selfridge, Klug, & Bakko, 2004)! Since then, the status of FASD in these systems has changed very little. The prevalence of FASD in a Canadian prison was found to be 17.5%, but it was estimated as many as one in three inmates could have FASD if prenatal exposure status was determined (McLachlan et al., 2019). In the United States, between four and six million adults are in the corrections system. Recent prevalence estimates suggest around 17% of these adults, or 680,000 offenders, have FASD. Obtaining diagnostic evaluations for these individuals would take decades.

The diagnostic problem is made even more challenging by inadequate data about the FASD phenotype in adults, particularly in those who are middle aged and elderly, where we have virtually no data. Moreover, there are not even any preliminary efforts in the United States to identify adults with FASD in the corrections system using population-based screening. FASD screening and assessment in forensic cases is rare, despite the benefits this would yield for sentencing and parole/

probation planning. It should be noted, however, that an FASD diagnosis is quite rare in other countries as well (McLachlan et al., 2019).

3.2 Screening

Given the very high rates of FASD in incarcerated populations, what steps do we need to take to identify offenders with this disorder, so we can respond to their unique needs and reduce recidivism? In an earlier publication (Burd, 2015), we described some factors that should be considered regarding screening for FASD in forensic settings (Burd, 2015). These factors include determining an effective screening methodology and desired goal or outcome (e.g., risk stratification versus case-finding) and selecting an appropriate screening tool. One important low burden step would be to implement screening for risk stratification purposes in a given population. In Fig. 3.2, we depict a simple screening program to risk-stratify people in or entering forensic systems. This process would involve a low-cost screening strategy that could be incorporated into electronic health records or added to the intake process for people entering penal systems.

Case-finding (Fig. 3.3) is another example of a screening strategy. With this approach, offenders likely to have FASD would be screened and referred for diagnostic assessment if screening is positive. Risk stratification is an initial step in this methodology, and case-finding would be included as a follow-up to risk stratification in high-risk populations.

In previous publications, we published multiple screening tools for a screening strategy where case-finding might be the desired end point (Burd, 2015; Poitra et al., 2003).

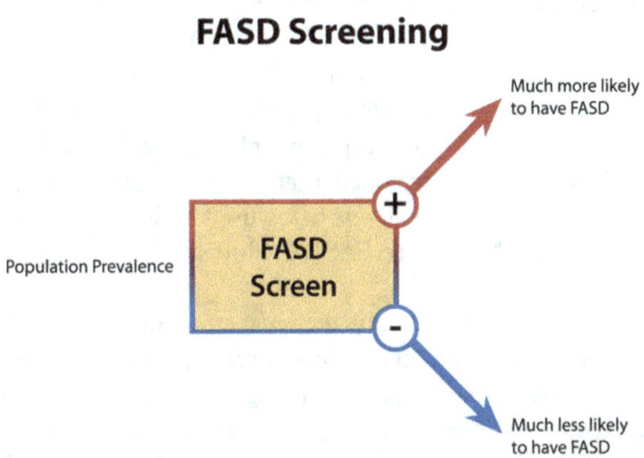

Fig. 3.2 Model of a screening methodology to identify people with high or low risk for FASD

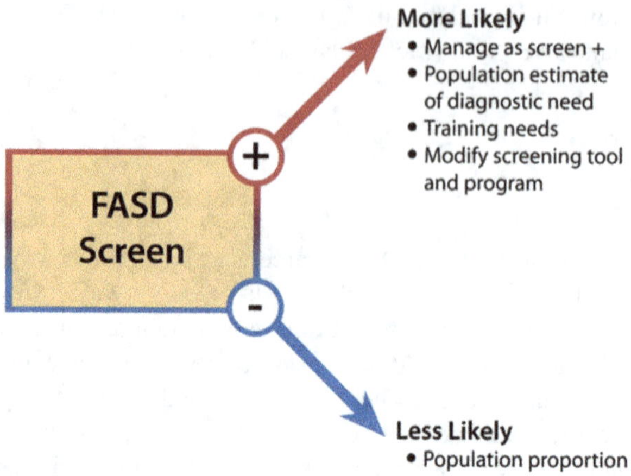

Fig. 3.3 Model of a case-finding screening methodology to identify individuals with high risk of FASD

3.2.1 What to Screen for?

Importantly, recent prevalence studies have reported consistently that the most prevalent FASD phenotype is the neurocognitive or neurobehavioral manifestation of brain damage from prenatal alcohol exposure (PAE) diagnosed as ARND (Chambers et al., 2019; May, Hasken, Baete, et al., 2020; May, Hasken, Bozeman, et al., 2020; May, Hasken, Stegall, et al., 2020; National Institute on Alcohol Abuse and Alcoholism, 2011). ARND reportedly represents about 85% of all FASDs (Weyrauch, Schwartz, Hart, Klug, & Burd, 2017). In response to this very high prevalence, a validated screening tool for ARND would be quite beneficial. Toward that end, in this chapter we update and present new validity data for an ARND screening tool, the Alcohol Related Neurodevelopmental Disorder Behavioral Checklist (ABC). In addition to screening for ARND, the ABC also screens for ND-PAE. Because the diagnostic phenotypes for ARND and ND-PAE are very similar, the ABC works well for identifying people with either diagnosis (Johnson, Moyer, Klug, & Burd, 2018). Developed as an initial screening strategy, the ABC is useful in a variety of contexts and now is being used in diagnostic settings as partial initial assessment for ARND where FASD multidisciplinary diagnostic teams are unavailable.

The consistent finding that ARND is the most common form of FASD has led to changes in the diagnostic evaluation of people referred for assessment. In Fig. 3.4, we depict these changes in an assessment strategy for FASD. In previous strategies, considerable emphasis was placed on a top-down screening approach where the first step involved determining prenatal alcohol exposure. However, if PAE could not be documented, patients were not sent on for diagnostic evaluations. Although this might be viewed as a common sense gateway for limiting access to expensive

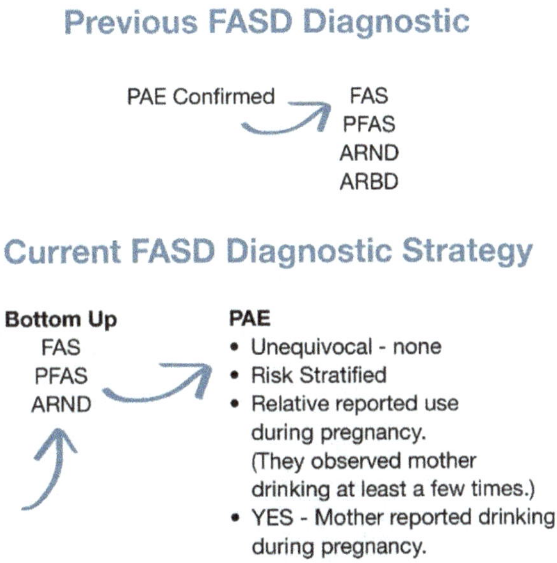

Fig. 3.4 How diagnostic philosophy has changed to emphasize finding ARND first and then confirming PAE

limited-capacity diagnostic services, the likely effect of using PAE as a pre-assessment gateway was under-ascertainment.

3.2.2 Exposure Assessment

Pre-assessment screening for PAE also tended to underestimate the complexity of exposure assessment science because it relied upon the use of a brief one-time exposure screen. These screens often are completed by phone, which probably minimizes effectiveness. Using such an approach likely precluded many people who actually had FASD from progressing to diagnostic assessment. With the recent change in screening protocol depicted in Fig. 3.4, rather than screening first for PAE, identifying people with likely ARND is the initial step. In the event of a positive screen, other categories of FASD are considered and exposure assessment is completed.

Applying the science of exposure assessment to determine PAE significantly improves detection of drinking and other substance use during pregnancy. In clinical settings, common exposure assessment constructs that require attention are exposure detection, dosimetry (i.e., quantity and frequency), and duration of exposure. In more specialized clinical or research settings, detailed systematic exposure assessment also should incorporate current knowledge of alcohol elimination kinetics (Fig. 3.5).

In general, we want data that estimate number of pregnancy days exposed, number of binge days, cumulative exposure, and days with combined exposure (especially for drinking and smoking), as depicted in Fig. 3.6.

Alcohol Elimination Kinetics

- Absorption
- Dispersion
- Metabolism
- Excretion

- First in to last out

Fig. 3.5 Four primary components in alcohol ingestion and elimination

Architecture of Exposure Episodes

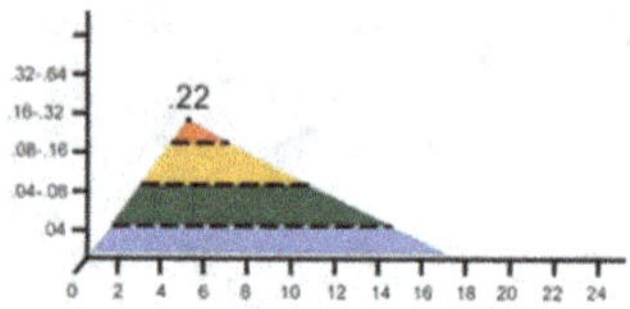

Dosimetry and cumulative exposure effects

- Drinking days
- Drinks per day
- Cumulative exposure
- Polysubstance exposure
- Multiplicative effect of combined exposure

- Smoking days
- Cigarettes per day
- Cumulative exposure

Fig. 3.6 Components of specialized exposure assessment for prenatal alcohol exposure

The goal of exposure assessment is to determine a sequential chain of potential exposure data points (Fig. 3.7). The first element in the exposure assessment chain is drinking prior to pregnancy. We determine this by using the ONE-Question Screen, "When was your last drink?" Response to this question is risk-stratified by determining if a woman drank prior to pregnancy. If her last drink occurred during pregnancy, the pregnancy is categorized as exposed, and a more detailed exposure assessment is completed. If the last drink occurred after confirmation of pregnancy, the pregnancy is categorized high risk. Figure 3.7 presents the current exposure assessment protocol we are now using in our FASD clinic.

Figure 3.8 depicts a graphic summary of an exposure assessment from our FASD clinic for a 140-pound woman who reported drinking an average of eight beers (5% alcohol content) on each drinking occasion. Based on this amount, alcohol dosimetry is 112 grams of alcohol per drinking day, with alcohol present in maternal–fetal blood for 17 h. Each drinking day constituted a binge day (four or more drinks), and

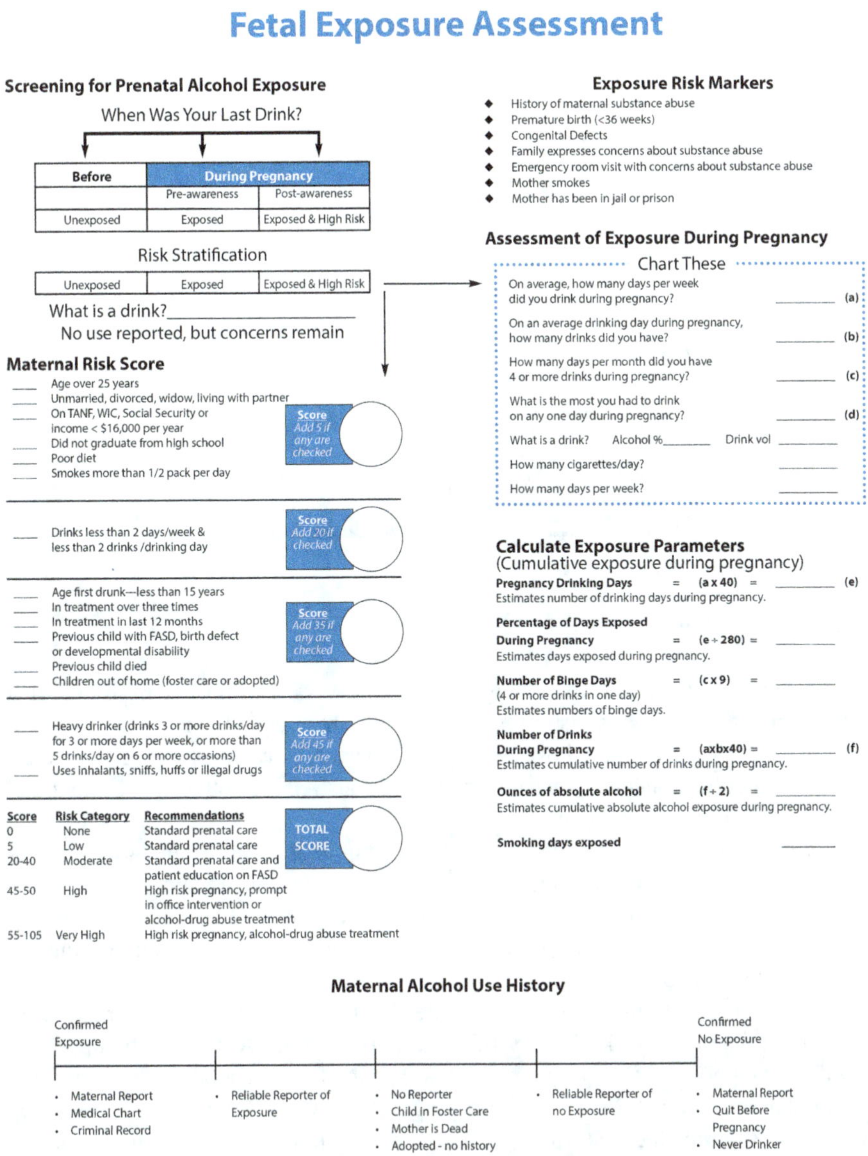

Fetal Exposure Assessment

Screening for Prenatal Alcohol Exposure

When Was Your Last Drink?

Before	During Pregnancy	
	Pre-awareness	Post-awareness
Unexposed	Exposed	Exposed & High Risk

Risk Stratification

Unexposed	Exposed	Exposed & High Risk

What is a drink?________________

No use reported, but concerns remain

Maternal Risk Score

___ Age over 25 years
___ Unmarried, divorced, widow, living with partner
___ On TANF, WIC, Social Security or income < $16,000 per year
___ Did not graduate from high school
___ Poor diet
___ Smokes more than 1/2 pack per day

Score *Add 5 if any are checked*

___ Drinks less than 2 days/week & less than 2 drinks /drinking day

Score *Add 20 if checked*

___ Age first drunk—less than 15 years
___ In treatment over three times
___ In treatment in last 12 months
___ Previous child with FASD, birth defect or developmental disability
___ Previous child died
___ Children out of home (foster care or adopted)

Score *Add 35 if any are checked*

___ Heavy drinker (drinks 3 or more drinks/day for 3 or more days per week, or more than 5 drinks/day on 6 or more occasions)
___ Uses inhalants, sniffs, huffs or illegal drugs

Score *Add 45 if any are checked*

Score	Risk Category	Recommendations
0	None	Standard prenatal care
5	Low	Standard prenatal care
20-40	Moderate	Standard prenatal care and patient education on FASD
45-50	High	High risk pregnancy, prompt in office intervention or alcohol-drug abuse treatment
55-105	Very High	High risk pregnancy, alcohol-drug abuse treatment

TOTAL SCORE

Exposure Risk Markers

- History of maternal substance abuse
- Premature birth (<36 weeks)
- Congenital Defects
- Family expresses concerns about substance abuse
- Emergency room visit with concerns about substance abuse
- Mother smokes
- Mother has been in jail or prison

Assessment of Exposure During Pregnancy

Chart These

On average, how many days per week did you drink during pregnancy? ______ (a)

On an average drinking day during pregnancy, how many drinks did you have? ______ (b)

How many days per month did you have 4 or more drinks during pregnancy? ______ (c)

What is the most you had to drink on any one day during pregnancy? ______ (d)

What is a drink? Alcohol %______ Drink vol ______

How many cigarettes/day? ______

How many days per week? ______

Calculate Exposure Parameters

(Cumulative exposure during pregnancy)

Pregnancy Drinking Days = (a x 40) = ______ (e)
Estimates number of drinking days during pregnancy.

Percentage of Days Exposed During Pregnancy = (e ÷ 280) = ______
Estimates days exposed during pregnancy.

Number of Binge Days = (c x 9) = ______
(4 or more drinks in one day)
Estimates numbers of binge days.

Number of Drinks During Pregnancy = (axbx40) = ______ (f)
Estimates cumulative number of drinks during pregnancy.

Ounces of absolute alcohol = (f ÷ 2) = ______
Estimates cumulative absolute alcohol exposure during pregnancy.

Smoking days exposed ______

Maternal Alcohol Use History

Confirmed Exposure ———— Confirmed No Exposure

- Maternal Report
- Medical Chart
- Criminal Record

- Reliable Reporter of Exposure

- No Reporter
- Child in Foster Care
- Mother is Dead
- Adopted - no history

- Reliable Reporter of no Exposure

- Maternal Report
- Quit Before Pregnancy
- Never Drinker

Fig. 3.7 Current exposure assessment used at the North Dakota FAS Center. The One Question Screen (When was your last drink?) is the initial step in risk stratification, calculation of the maternal risk score, and exposure dosimetry estimation

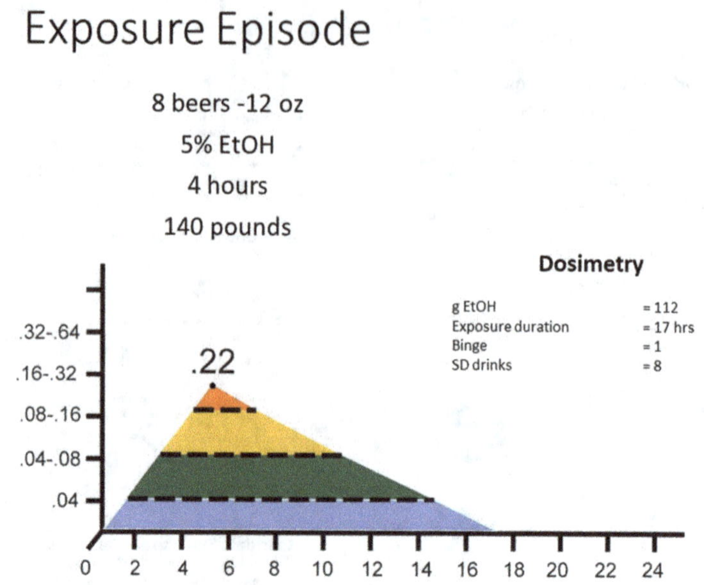

Fig. 3.8 Depiction of a prenatal exposure episode

dosimetry indicates this involved eight standard drinks. It is important to note that each exposure episode results in fetal exposure to these endpoints.

Figure 3.9 shows fetal exposure is very similar to maternal exposure. As maternal blood alcohol concentrations rise, fetal levels also rise. In other words, maternal exposure determines fetal exposure.

PAE increases risk of damage to the developing fetal brain. Brain damage manifests as cognitive impairments that increase risk of subsequent exposure to adverse events, which leads to secondary disabilities (i.e., adverse life course outcomes) such as involvement in the legal system and incarceration. This common sequence is depicted in Fig. 3.10.

We use the illustration in Fig. 3.11 to demonstrate and explain how brain-based impairments affect the day-to-day life of a person with FASD, which supports a need for diagnosis-informed interventions. In the stoplight model of impairment, initial diagnostic emphasis is on identifying ARND. Once identified, a second step can be considered: does the patient need to see a full multidisciplinary team, including a geneticist or dysmorphologist? Since many patients can be adequately assessed by individual clinicians, this limits the need for highly specialized medical professionals, who are in short supply and best used for assessing other categorical FASD phenotypes (e.g., FAS or pFAS) or when FASD is accompanied by genetic or dysmorphic disorders.

Screening for ARND before completing exposure assessment reflects the reality that confirming PAE for adolescents and adults who may have limited contact with their mothers often is a challenging process. Some birth mothers may be deceased as mortality risk in women who give birth to children with FASD is 39–42 times

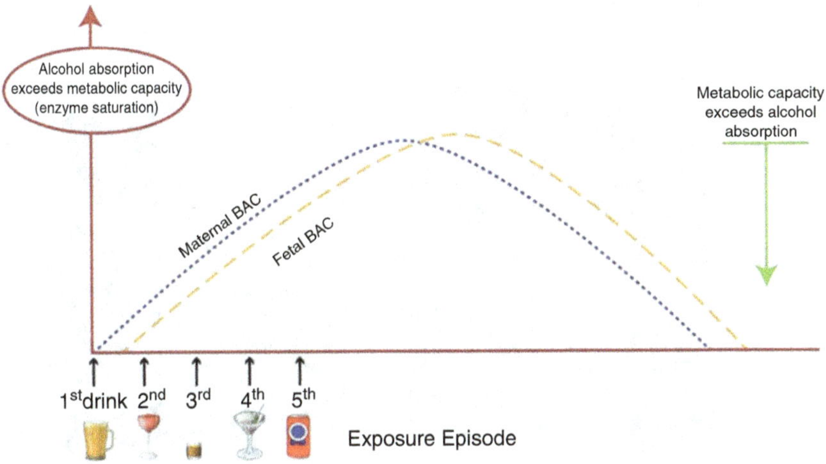

Fig. 3.9 Model of the relationship between maternal blood alcohol concentrations (BAC) and fetal BAC

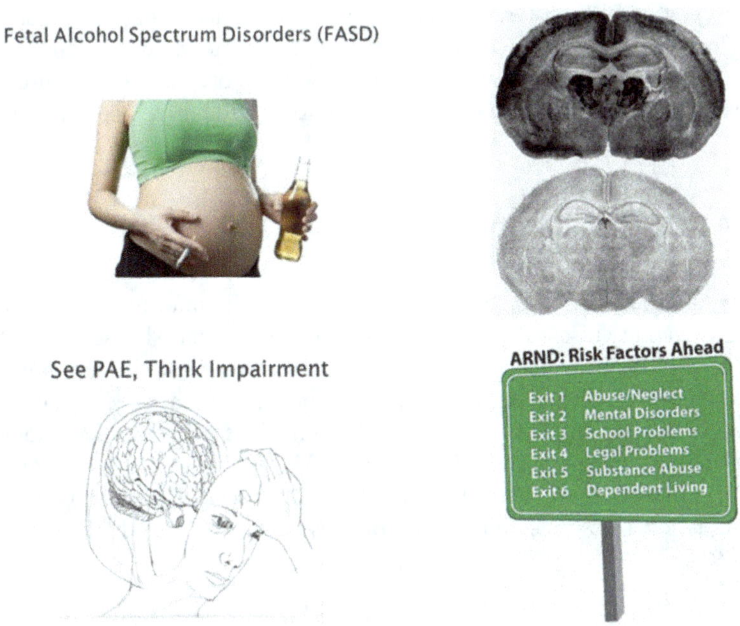

Fig. 3.10 A common sequence in FASD: exposure causes brain damage dysfunction and brain-based impairments that lead to negative long-term outcomes

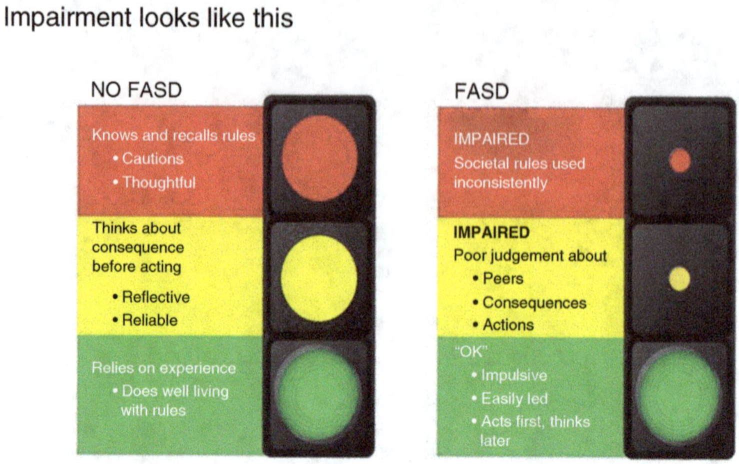

Fig. 3.11 Stoplight model of fetal alcohol spectrum disorder

higher than in the general population (Li, Fisher, Peng, Williams, & Burd, 2012; Schwartz et al., 2017). In forensic settings, access to maternal or parental data confirming maternal alcohol use during pregnancy is particularly challenging because even when birth mothers are available, their reports of low or no alcohol use during pregnancy often are unreliable (Lange, Shield, Koren, Rehm, & Popova, 2014).

3.3 ABC Screening Tool

We now turn to the ABC screening tool for ARND, with information pertaining to its updated validity assessment. Most screening tools currently in use have not been validated, which means their epidemiologic performance characteristics have not been established. In contrast, the ABC, shown in Fig. 3.12, has been validated. We present in this chapter the most recent evaluation of the ABC's epidemiologic performance characteristics. The ABC contains 33 variables. In the developmental phase of our research, we defined unique factorial constructs (domains) assessed by the ABC and then described how these domains related to each other in the diagnosis of ARND.

Alcohol Related Neurodevelopmental Disorder Behavioral Checklist

In order to complete this checklist:
1) Behaviors must be impaired for the age of the person being assessed.
2) Interviewee needs to have known the person being assessed for at least one month.
3) After the reporter fills out the form, the clinician then adds other observed behaviors not already reported.

CHECK ALL THAT APPLY FOR THE APPROPRIATE AGE RANGE:

	BEHAVIOR	**3-6 yrs.**	**7 yrs. +**
1	Hyperactive		
2	Poor attention		
3	Impulsive		
4	Disorganized		
5	Seems unaware of consequences of actions		
6	No fear		
7	Would leave with a stranger		
8	Poor social skills		
9	Few friends		
10	Will talk or interact with anyone		
11	Easily manipulated and set up by others		
12	Socially inept (inappropriate speech or touching)		
13	Difficulty staying on topic during conversation		
14	Always talking		
15	Cocktail speech - little content		
16	Too loud		
17	Can't remember from one day to the next		
18	Below average IQ (<85)		
19	Poor school performance		
20	Suspended or expelled from school		
21	Poor sleeper		
22	Can't follow routine - needs reminders to get dressed, brush teeth, etc.		
23	Temper tantrums		
24	Extreme mood swings		
25	Requires constant supervision		
26	Been in trouble with the law		
27	Inpatient treatment for mental health or substance abuse, or in jail for a crime		
28	Inappropriate sexual behavior		
29	Poor motor skills		
30	Has or needs glasses		
31	Had foster care or was adopted		
32	Medication for behavior - ever		
33	Mother used alcohol or drugs during pregnancy (OPTIONAL)		

4) Calculate total score.

TOTAL CHECKED:

16	20

(Continue assessment if score is greater than or equal to above)

Fig. 3.12 Alcohol related neurodevelopmental disorder behavior checklist (ABC)

3.3.1 Study Population

The sample for our ABC validation study involved patients seen from 2010 to 2017 at the North Dakota FASD Center. These patients had been involved in two previous studies, one where a subset of patients was used to estimate the neurocognitive outcomes of PAE (Weyrauch et al., 2017) and a second that examined prevalence and impact of adverse childhood experiences on the FASD phenotype (Kambeitz, Klug,

Greenmyer, Popova, & Burd, 2019). All patients under 22 years of age were included if they had been diagnosed with any disorder under the FASD umbrella, regardless of site or provider, or if they had been diagnosed by using the ABC. A few cases were referred with a diagnosis of FASD but were excluded from the study since PAE history was not available. Subjects also were excluded if they were not diagnosed with any neurodevelopmental disorder (e.g., people assessed for speech or language delays who did not actually have delays, children with bedtime problems; $n = 11$).

Non-FASD controls were patients under 22 years of age who did not meet criteria for any FASD and were seen in our clinic between 2010 and 2017. Of the 203 subjects used in this study, 131 (64.5%) were male, and 72 (35.5%) were female. Regarding age, 88 (43.3%) were age 6 or younger, 50 (24.6%) were ages 7–10, and 65 (32.0%) were age 11 or older. Among the 203 subjects, 98 (48.3%) were diagnosed as having FASD, and 105 were non-FASD comparison subjects. Results of the study are summarized in Table 3.1.

3.3.2 *Initial Analysis*

Of the 33 ABC variables shown in Table 3.1, poor attention (77.3%) and impulsiveness (80.3%) were the most common. Trouble with the law (19.2%), inpatient treatment (15.3%), and inappropriate sexual behavior (16.8%) were the least common. The proposed clinically derived domains were used as a starting point for the validation study.

Initially, each variable in the ABC was hypothesized to contribute to 13 domains we identified based upon our clinical experience (Table 3.1). We then used these variable groups to assess each domain by summing them to create a score for each child. CFA was used to find the set of variables that best represented a domain, which involved analyzing relations between variables and between domains. Each hypothesized set of variables was entered into a model, and adjustments were made to find the best fit for the data. Due to the large number of variables and domains, domains were grouped into four areas based upon similar concepts and tested as such. A model was considered finished if overall chi-square was not significant, root mean square error was less than 0.05, adjusted goodness of fit index was greater than 0.850, paths from the variables to the domain were significant, all error variances were significant, and covariances were significant. This analysis excluded three ABC variables (#23—temper tantrums, #29—poor motor skills, and #30—has or needs glasses) as they did not associate with any specific domain. Three proposed domains (sensory and motor, brain structure, and foster care/residential care) were excluded because there were not enough variables to clearly define these domains.

Table 3.1 Initial validation involved proposed domains (Original Domain), which then were validated by confirmatory factor analysis (CFA). Validated domains are listed in the CFA Defined Domain column

Item		*N*	%	Original domain	CFA defined domain	CFA domain area
1	Hyperactive	139	68.5	Focus/attention Juvenile justice	Focus/attention Academic skills	Basic Interaction
2	Poor attention	157	77.3	Sensory/motor Focus/attention Juvenile justice	Focus/attention Academic skills	Basic Interaction
3	Impulsive	163	80.3	Executive functioning Academic skills Focus/attention Juvenile justice	Executive functioning Focus/attention Academic skills Juvenile justice	Basic Interaction Justice
4	Disorganized	131	64.5		Executive functioning focus/attention	Basic
5	Consequences	96	47.3	Executive functioning Confabulation Juvenile justice	Executive functioning Cognition Confabulation Juvenile justice	Basic Verbal Justice
6	No fear	69	44.0	Gullibility Confabulation	Confabulation Juvenile justice	Verbal Justice
7	With stranger	77	37.9	Gullibility Confabulation	Confabulation Gullibility	Verbal
8	Social skills	116	57.1	Living/social skills Juvenile justice	Living/social skills Juvenile justice	Interaction Justice
9	Few friends	110	54.2	Living/social skills Juvenile justice	Living/social skills Juvenile justice	Interaction Justice
10	Talk anyone	90	44.3	Living/social skills Gullibility	Communication Gullibility	Verbal
11	Manipulated	86	42.4	Living/social skills Gullibility Confabulation Juvenile justice	Gullibility Juvenile justice	Verbal justice
12	Socially inept	90	44.3	Cognition Confabulation	Cognition Living/social skills	Basic Interaction
13	Topic	99	48.8	Communication Memory	Communication Living/social skills	Verbal interaction
14	Always talks	67	33.0	Communication	Communication	Verbal
15	Cocktail	57	28.1	Communication	Communication	Verbal
16	Too loud	75	37.0	Communication	Communication Living/social skills	Verbal interaction
17	Daily memory	87	42.9	Memory	Memory Academic skill	Basic Interaction
18	IQ < 85	118	58.1	Academic skills Cognition Juvenile justice	Memory Academic skill	Basic Interaction

(continued)

Table 3.1 (continued)

Item		N	%	Original domain	CFA defined domain	CFA domain area
19	School perform	109	53.7	Academic skills Cognition Juvenile justice	Academic skill Juvenile justice	Interaction Justice
20	Suspended	45	22.2	Academic skills Cognition Juvenile justice	Academic skill Juvenile justice	Interaction Justice
21	Sleep	132	65.0		Focus/attention Cognition	Basic
22	Routine	120	59.1	Sensory/motor Living/social skills Memory	Memory Communication Living/social skills	Basic Verbal Interaction
23	Temper	128	63.1	Executive functioning Cognition Juvenile justice		
24	Mood	105	51.7	Executive functioning Juvenile justice	Executive functioning	Basic
25	Supervision	109	53.7	Confabulation Juvenile justice	Memory Confabulation	Basic Verbal
26	Law trouble	39	19.2	Focus/attention Gullibility Juvenile justice	Juvenile justice	Justice
27	Inpatient	31	15.3	Juvenile justice	Juvenile justice	Justice
28	Sexual	34	16.8	Executive functioning Cognition	Cognition Juvenile justice	Basic Justice
29	Motor	72	35.5	Sensory/motor		
30	Glasses	90	44.3	Sensory/motor		
31	Foster	100	49.3	Focus/attention	Juvenile justice	Justice
32	Medication	106	52.2	Juvenile justice	Juvenile justice	Justice
33	Maternal Alc	90	44.3	Juvenile justice	Juvenile justice	Justice

3.3.3 Confirmatory Factor Analysis

Each ABC variable was identified with an original domain. CFA was performed on four domain areas with 10 unique domains. Figure 3.13 summarizes these findings by showing each proposed domain and the domains remaining after CFA. Multiple variables were categorized in more than one domain and domain area.

As shown in Fig. 3.14, CFA identified a broad range of variables in the Cognitive-Behavioral category, which consisted of four domains: executive function (four variables), cognition (three variables), attention and concentration (five variables), and memory (four variables). Some variables overlapped domains

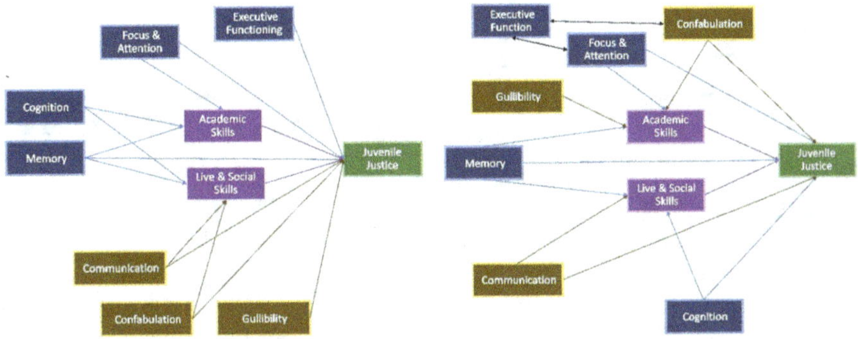

Fig. 3.13 Initial domains (left) and final factor-analysis-derived domains (right)

(e.g., #4—disorganized and #3—impulsive) and were included in both executive function and attention/concentration domains. All other domains were correlated except these two.

A second category identified by CFA involved Verbal Interactions, which was comprised of confabulation (four variables), gullibility (three variables), and impaired communication (six variables). Interestingly, multiple variables associated with impaired judgment also were included in this category. Content in the Verbal Interactions category suggests that a previously unappreciated linguistic processing impairment may underlie some of the adaptive impairment in FASD, which would imply a broad range of impairments in verbal interactions including verbal processing, memory, and expression. This linguistic impairment might manifest as naiveté, gullibility, and/or confabulation in stressful contexts or when memory problems are evident.

A third category defined by CFA was Social-Learning, which consisted of two domains: age-appropriate independent living and social skills (three variables) and academic (ten variables). No variables were associated with both domains, although both domains and eight pairs of ABC variables were correlated. ABC variables that appeared to correlate included #1—hyperactivity, #2—poor attention, #3—impulsivity, #18—low IQ, #19—poor school performance, and #20—school suspension or expulsion. These last three variables illustrate how neurocognitive impairments manifest in school settings.

Finally, CFA identified a fourth category relating to Juvenile Justice, which was comprised of one domain with 13 associated ABC variables. Ten variables were correlated with each other in two distinct groups. One group included #6—no fear, $5—unaware of consequences, #31—foster care/adopted, and #33—maternal alcohol exposure. Another group included #20—suspended or expelled, #27—inpatient or jail stays, #26—legal trouble, #28—problem sexual behavior, #9—few friends, and #8—poor social skills.

COGNITIVE AND BEHAVIOR	VERBAL INTERACTIONS	SOCIAL – LEARNING	JUVENILE JUSTICE
Executive Functioning	**Confabulation**	**Academic Skills**	**Juvenile Justice**
3 Impulsive ___ 4 Disorganized ___ 5 Consequences ___ 24 Mood Swings ___ Score ☐	5 Impulsive ___ 6 No Fear ___ 7 Leave With Stranger ___ 25 Requires Supervision ___ Score ☐	1 Hyperactive ___ 2 Poor Attention ___ 3 Impulsive ___ 8 Social Skills ___ 9 Few Friends ___ 13 Staying on Topic ___ 17 Daily Memory ___ 18 Low IQ ___ 19 Poor at School ___ 20 Suspended or Expelled ___ Score ☐	3 Impulsive ___ 5 Unaware of Consequences ___ 6 No Fear ___ 8 Social Skills ___ 9 Few Friends ___ 11 Easily Manipulated ___ 19 Poor at School ___ 20 Suspended or Expelled ___ 26 Legal Trouble ___ 27 Behavioral Inpatient ___ 28 Sexual Behavior ___ 31 Foster or Adopted ___ 33 Maternal Alcohol Use ___ Score ☐
Cognition	**Gullibility**		
5 Consequences ___ 12 Socially Inept ___ 28 Sexual Behavior ___ Score ☐	7 Leave With Stranger ___ 10 Talk With Anyone ___ 11 Easily Manipulated ___ Score ☐		
Attention & Concentration	**Communication Skills**	**Living & Social Skills**	
1 Hyperactive ___ 2 Poor Attention ___ 3 Impulsive ___ 4 Disorganized ___ 21 Poor Sleeper ___ Score ☐	10 Talk With Anyone ___ 13 Staying on Topic ___ 14 Always Talking ___ 15 Cocktail Speech ___ 16 Too Loud ___ 22 Follow Routine ___ Score ☐	12 Socially Inept ___ 16 Too Loud ___ 22 Follow Routine ___ Score ☐	
Memory			
17 Remember Daily ___ 18 Low IQ ___ 22 Routine ___ 25 Requires Supervision ___ Score ☐			

Fig. 3.14 The ABC contains four broad areas (Cognitive and Behavior, Verbal Interactions, Social-Learning, and Juvenile Justice), each with representative variables

3.3.4 Validating Domains in Fetal Alcohol Spectrum Disorder and Non-Fetal Alcohol Spectrum Disorder Controls

A central question examined in this analysis was, can the ABC discriminate children with FASD from those without FASD? Scores for each domain were created by summing the number of positive ABC variables a child had within each domain. These data then were divided into two groups, those with an FASD diagnosis ($n = 98$) and those without ($n = 105$). Means and standard deviations for the domains by group are shown in Table 3.2.

Tetrachoric correlations were estimated between the 33 items, and independent t-tests compared domain scores between 98 FASD children and 105 non-FASD children. Pearson's correlations were estimated between domain total scores, and

Table 3.2 Comparison of domains in 98 FASD and 105 non-FASD children

	Non-FASD		FASD				
Domain	Mean	SD	Mean	SD	Difference	*t*	*p*
Executive function	1.61	1.06	3.33	0.87	1.72	12.56	<0.001
Cognition	1.01	0.81	2.51	1.05	1.50	11.43	<0.001
Focus and attention	2.95	1.61	4.20	1.00	1.25	6.0.58	<0.001
Memory	1.33	1.12	3.00	0.90	1.67	11.63	<0.001
Confabulation	0.68	1.00	2.86	1.02	2.18	15.45	<0.001
Communication skills	0.93	1.13	4.18	1.40	3.25	18.25	<0.001
Gullibility	0.36	0.68	2.19	0.94	1.83	16.00	<0.001
Academic skills	3.06	1.71	5.07	1.44	2.01	9.02	<0.001
Living and social skills	1.62	1.39	4.49	1.28	2.87	15.09	<0.001
Juvenile justice	3.11	2.11	8.85	2.39	5.74	18.12	<0.001

simultaneous equations estimated predictive relationships between domains. Statistical Analysis Software (SAS) v. 14.1 was used in these analyses.

Overall, children and adolescents with FASD had significantly higher domain scores than non-FASD children for all domains ($p < 0.001$). On average, FASD children had one to six more items in each domain than non-FASD children. Nearly every domain was significantly correlated ($p < 0.01$) with other domains in non-FASD children, and 27 out of 45 pairs of domains correlated for FASD children. All domains predicted juvenile justice involvement except executive function in children with FASD, which, although correlated with attention and concentration and confabulation, was not predictive. This latter finding suggests screening strategies that emphasize only or primarily executive function deficits may not be optimal for people with FASD because executive functioning is not a unitary construct. In fact, executive function assessment typically requires multiple neuropsychological measures in FASD due to variability in individualized expression.

Interestingly, among children with FASD, gullibility and confabulation were predictors of academic skills, which was not the case for non-FASD children. In addition, cognition predicted social skills in FASD children but not for non-FASD children. Generally for non-FASD controls, there was clear delineation in how verbal interaction domains and basic behavior domains related to social and academic skills, respectively, but among children with FASD, there were less specific and more mixed differences. This latter result suggests these domains may represent FASD-specific neurocognitive impairments in children that are not present in children without FASD. Further research is needed to determine the underlying neurodevelopmental origins of this pattern of impairments.

Factor analysis of ABC data identified four distinct domain areas and 10 independent domains. Analysis also found that of the 13 original domains initially proposed based upon clinical experience, three were excluded by CFA. Importantly, all 10 domains retained after CFA were significantly different when average value of each domain score in FASD subjects was compared to non-FASD controls.

In summary, this analysis provided strong support for the validity of the ABC in discriminating between children with FASD and non-FASD controls. Although we have not conducted similar research in adults at this point, we find the ABC works well with the adults we see in our clinic. Administration time for the ABC is only 10–14 min, and it requires modest reading proficiency to complete the task. Group differences (FASD versus non-FASD) also were observed between domains. Domain differences involved common concerns for people with FASD (Weyrauch et al., 2017). Given the results described here, the ABC appears to have a useful role in screening for ARND and ND-PAE. Another important benefit of the measure is identifying discreet impairments that can inform neuropsychological assessment.

3.4 Linking Case-Finding and Services

As we mentioned earlier in this chapter, early identification is a key to timely entry into diagnosis-informed services. These services should include a risk reduction component for common problems in FASD, especially secondary disabilities. The most important aspect of risk reduction is a long-term plan. In Fig. 3.15, we graphically illustrate the difference early intervention and long-term services makes in outcomes.

The ABC may be useful in identifying youths in need of specific specialized services associated with ARND. For example, if the ABC identifies risk of confabulation and gullibility in a juvenile charged with a crime, the youth's defense attorney might use such information to address rights waiver and subsequent police statement. Relationships between variables within domain areas also identify important factors for consideration when children with FASD misbehave, and schools and residential institutions plan disciplinary action. As we found in our research, confabulation, gullibility, and communication skills are significantly different in children with FASD and correlated within the verbal domain area. As noted above, this pattern suggests a previously unappreciated neurolinguistic deficit may underlie these specific impairments, which are highly relevant in the forensic context. We elaborate on these impairments in Chap. 9 of this book, "In Fetal Alcohol Spectrum Disorder: Comorbidity Determines Complexity."

The ABC also can be an effective tool for attorneys in planning case strategy and developing referral questions for experts. For example, if a client seems to have difficulty understanding or retaining legal information about his/her case, and the ABC indicates a risk of confabulation and gullibility, such information could be used to direct a psychologist to conduct in-depth testing of domains relevant to competency (e.g., attention, auditory comprehension, receptive/expressive language, memory, executive functioning, and suggestibility). In other words, understanding relationships among ABC variables is important in appreciating a client's vulnerabilities and planning for such.

Research with the ABC shows young people with FASD have unique clusters of identifiable deficits that can inform legal professionals and medical/mental health

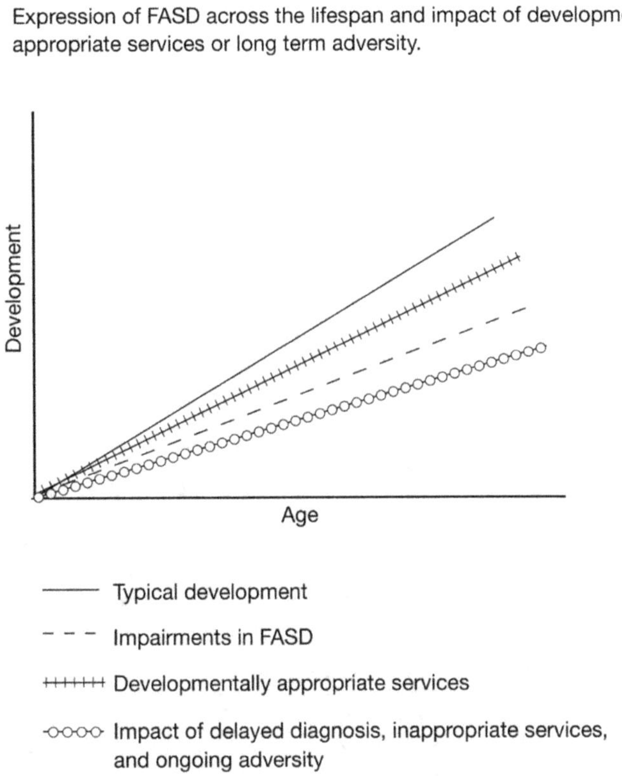

Fig. 3.15 Developmental trajectories for typically developing children and children with FASD plus differential impact of diagnosis-informed care versus inappropriate services

experts in forward-thinking case planning as well as treatment planning. Regarding the latter, knowledge of a person's specific risk profile is very important in developing a treatment plan that specifically targets risk variables that underlie secondary disabilities. We have found in our clinic that reducing the influence of such variables significantly improves quality of life, promotes educational or vocational success, and improves capacity to self-regulate.

In Figs. 3.16 and 3.17, we summarize specific components of diagnosis-informed interventions.

In our clinical care and in training, we emphasize nine basic intervention strategies that have been successful in our experience (Fig. 3.17).

We recommend the above interventions with the understanding that in most cases, FASD manifests in multiple fluctuating impairments that are permanent. Therefore, while eliminating impairments likely is not possible, these interventions assist treatment providers and caregivers in helping persons with FASD function at their highest capacity within the constraints of their brain damage. We emphasize that while early intervention is optimal, appropriate intervention at almost any point in life can yield benefits and very likely reduce future problems.

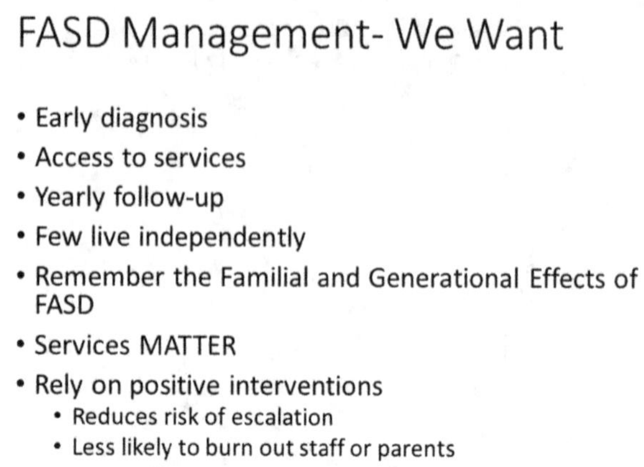

Fig. 3.16 Broad overview of interventions for people with FASD

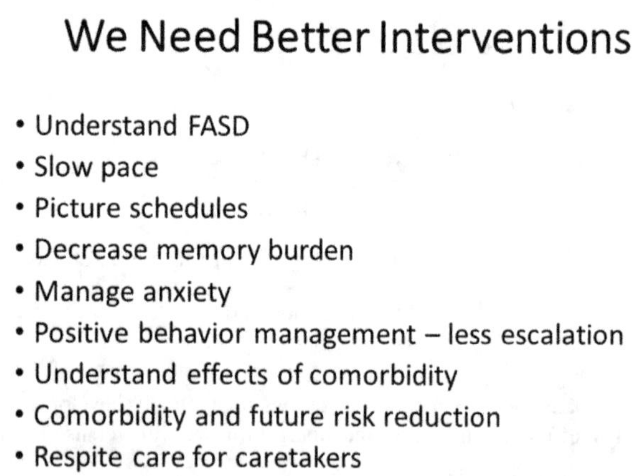

Fig. 3.17 Keys to optimal intervention for children with FASD

In our efforts to improve access to diagnostic services and increase opportunities for early intervention, we are engaged in ongoing research with a new dataset to validate ABC domains and sub-domains and determine which components best discriminate persons with FASD from non-FASD controls. This new research should enhance interpretation of variable relationships to further characterize the unique characteristics of people with FASD and enhance provider diagnostic capacity as well as inform areas of need for specific treatments and interventions.

3.5 Conclusion and Recommendations

Use of well-validated screening tools for population-based screening of FASD is an emerging science. Most current screening tools function best as strategies to improve case characterization and also add to the database on individual patients. Using such measures to screen for likelihood of FASD requires careful evaluation of tool-specific epidemiologic performance characteristics. Moreover, using a screening tool in legal settings requires a level of forensic expertise that potentially enables effective testimony regarding the relative role of the measure in assessment protocol.

We conclude this chapter with several recommendations. First, we need additional research to identify optimal screening strategies in forensic settings. This research should include efforts to incorporate a risk stratification screening system specific to FASD in correctional intake procedures. As diagnostic services become more widely available, offenders with a positive risk score would represent a priority with respect to referral and evaluation. Second, we need to continue identifying and testing screening strategies and methodologies for case identification with the goal of developing the most effective empirically based screening methodology for use in corrections systems. Such efforts should encourage multisite investigators to join in ongoing collaboration, with the goal of providing a strong evidence base to support accuracy, including sensitivity and specificity.

Finally, legal and medical/mental health professionals who use a screening measure and associated protocol should have data regarding efficacy (e.g., how well does the screening tool work within the screening methodology?), effectiveness (e.g., do the tool and methodology work within corrections settings?), and efficiency (e.g., is the screening program worthwhile in terms of financial cost and human resources)? As we have noted, ultimate responsibility for developing FASD screening programs largely depends upon advocacy by defense attorneys, medical staff in corrections settings, and perhaps most of all, judges (Burd & Edwards, 2019, Fall). Judges in particular are uniquely positioned in the legal system to understand the negative effects of FASD at all stages in the legal process—from detention, interrogation, confession, and plea agreement to trial, sentencing, and response to previous interventions, such as probation and parole.

In conclusion, it is important to emphasize that diagnostic services for FASD are not simply limited but nearly nonexistent. Most offenders, including the several hundred thousand affected adults now in correctional settings, have had *no* access to diagnostic services, much less screening. Although the largest population of offenders with FASD is adults and not children, almost all funding for FASD research and assessment resources emphasizes children. To our knowledge, no funding proposal for FASD in the elderly has ever been proposed. After a 50-year childhood for FASD in the research community, is it not time now for us to *grow FASD up*?

References

American Psychiatric Association (APA). (2013). *Diagnostic and statistical manual of mental disorders (DSM-5)* (5th ed.). Arlington, VA: American Psychiatric Association.

Astley, S. J. (2004). *Diagnostic guide for fetal alcohol spectrum disorders: The 4-digit diagnostic code* (3rd ed.). Seattle: University of Washington.

Bower, C., Watkins, R. E., Mutch, R. C., Marriott, R., Freeman, J., Kippin, N. R., … Giglia, R. (2018). Fetal alcohol spectrum disorder and youth justice: A prevalence study among young people sentenced to detention in Western Australia. *BMJ Open, 8*(2), e019605. https://doi.org/10.1136/bmjopen-2017-019605

Burd, L. (2015) *Screening for FASD in corrections systems.* Paper presented at the Legal Issues of FASD. Fetal alcohol spectrum disorder. In I. Binnie, M. Trussler, & E. Jonsson (Eds.). *Proceedings from a consensus development conference*, (pp. 47–52). Edmonton: AB. https://www.ihe.ca/download/legal_issues_fasd_proceedings.pdf

Burd, L., & Edwards, W. (2019). Fetal alcohol spectrum disorders: Implications for attroneys and the courts. *Criminal Justice, 34*(3), 21–28.

Burd, L., Selfridge, R., Klug, M. G., & Bakko, S. (2004). Fetal alcohol syndrome in the United States corrections system. *Addiction Biology, 9*(2), 169–176. https://doi.org/10.1080/13556210410001717060

Chambers, C. D., Coles, C., Kable, J., Akshoomoff, N., Xu, R., Zellner, J. A., … Jones, K. L. (2019). Fetal alcohol spectrum disorders in a Pacific Southwest City: Maternal and child characteristics. *Alcohols: Clinical and Experimental Research, 43*(12), 2578–2590. https://doi.org/10.1111/acer.14213

Fast, D. K., Conry, J., & Loock, C. A. (1999). Identifying fetal alcohol syndrome among youth in the criminal justice system. *Journal of Developmental and Behavioral Pediatrics, 20*(5), 370–372. https://doi.org/10.1097/00004703-199910000-00012

Johnson, S., Moyer, C. L., Klug, M. G., & Burd, L. (2018). Comparison of alcohol-related neurodevelopmental disorder and neurodevelopmental disorder associated with prenatal alcohol exposure diagnostic criteria. *Journal of Developmental and Behavioral Pediatrics, 39*(2), 163–167. https://doi.org/10.1097/dbp.0000000000000523

Kambeitz, C., Klug, M. G., Greenmyer, J., Popova, S., & Burd, L. (2019). Association of adverse childhood experiences and neurodevelopmental disorders in people with fetal alcohol spectrum disorders (FASD) and non-FASD controls. *BMC Pediatrics, 19*(1), 498. https://doi.org/10.1186/s12887-019-1878-8

Landgren, M., Svensson, L., Strömland, K., & Andersson Grönlund, M. (2010). Prenatal alcohol exposure and neurodevelopmental disorders in children adopted from eastern Europe. *Pediatrics, 125*(5), e1178–e1185. https://doi.org/10.1542/peds.2009-0712

Lange, S., Shield, K., Koren, G., Rehm, J., & Popova, S. (2014). A comparison of the prevalence of prenatal alcohol exposure obtained via maternal self-reports versus meconium testing: A systematic literature review and meta-analysis. *BMC Pregnancy and Childbirth, 14*, 127. https://doi.org/10.1186/1471-2393-14-127

Li, Q., Fisher, W. W., Peng, C. Z., Williams, A. D., & Burd, L. (2012). Fetal alcohol spectrum disorders: A population based study of premature mortality rates in the mothers. *Maternal and Child Health Journal, 16*(6), 1332–1337. https://doi.org/10.1007/s10995-011-0844-3

May, P. A., Hasken, J. M., Baete, A., Russo, J., Elliott, A. J., Kalberg, W. O., … Hoyme, H. E. (2020). Fetal alcohol spectrum disorders in a midwestern city: Child characteristics, maternal risk traits, and prevalence. *Alcoholism: Clinical and Experimental Ressearch, 44*(4), 919–938. https://doi.org/10.1111/acer.14314

May, P. A., Hasken, J. M., Bozeman, R., Jones, J.-V., Burns, M. K., Goodover, J., … Hoyme, H. E. (2020). Fetal alcohol spectrum disorders in a Rocky Mountain region city: Child characteristics, maternal risk rraits, and prevalence. *Alcoholism: Clinical and Experimental Ressearch, 44*(4), 900–918. https://doi.org/10.1111/acer.14315

May, P. A., Hasken, J. M., Stegall, J. M., Mastro, H. A., Kalberg, W. O., Buckley, D., … Hoyme, H. E. (2020). Fetal alcohol spectrum disorders in a southeastern county of the United States: Child characteristics and maternal risk traits. *Alcoholism: Clinical and Experimental Ressearch, 44*(4), 939–959. https://doi.org/10.1111/acer.14313

McLachlan, K., McNeil, A., Pei, J., Brain, U., Andrew, G., & Oberlander, T. F. (2019). Prevalence and characteristics of adults with fetal alcohol spectrum disorder in corrections: A Canadian case ascertainment study. *BMC Public Health, 19*(1), 43. https://doi.org/10.1186/s12889-018-6292-x

Miller, L. C., Chan, W., Litvinova, A., Rubin, A., Comfort, K., Tirella, L., … Kovalev, I. (2006). Fetal alcohol spectrum disorders in children residing in Russian orphanages: A phenotypic survey. *Alcoholism: Clinical and Experimental Ressearch, 30*(3), 531–538. https://doi.org/10.1111/j.1530-0277.2006.00059.x

Murphy, A., Chittenden, M., & The McCreary Centre, S. (2005). *Time out II: A profile of BC youth in custody*. Vancouver, BC: McCreary Centre Society.

National Institute on Alcohol Abuse and Alcoholism. (2011). *Recognizing alcohol-related neurodevelopmental disorder (ARND) in primary health care of children.* Conference, Rockville, MD, Oct. 31-Nov. 2. https://www.niaaa.nih.gov/sites/default/files/ARNDConferenceConsensusStatementBooklet_Complete.pdf

Poitra, B. A., Marion, S., Dionne, M., Wilkie, E., Dauphinais, P., Wilkie-Pepion, M., … Burd, L. (2003). A school-based screening program for fetal alcohol syndrome. *Neurotoxicology and Teratology, 25*(6), 725–729. https://doi.org/10.1016/j.ntt.2003.07.007

Popova, S., Dozet, D., & Burd, L. (2020). Fetal alcohol spectrum disorder: Can we change the future? *Alcoholism: Clinical and Experimental Research, 44*(4), 815–819. https://doi.org/10.1111/acer.14317

Popova, S., Lange, S., Bekmuradov, D., Mihic, A., & Rehm, J. (2011). Fetal alcohol spectrum disorder prevalence estimates in correctional systems: A systematic literature review. *Canadian Journal of Public Health, 102*(5), 336–340. https://doi.org/10.1007/bf03404172

Rojas, E. Y., & Gretton, H. M. (2007). Background, offence characteristics, and criminal outcomes of aboriginal youth who sexually offend: A closer look at aboriginal youth intervention needs. *Sexual Abuse: A Journal of Research and Treatment, 19*(3), 257–283. https://doi.org/10.1177/107906320701900306

Schwartz, M., Hart, B., Weyrauch, D., Benson, P., Klug, M. G., & Burd, L. (2017). The hidden face of fetal alcohol spectrum disorder. *Current Women's Health Reviews, 13*(2), 96–102. https://doi.org/10.2174/1573404813666170418114243

Weyrauch, D., Schwartz, M., Hart, B., Klug, M. G., & Burd, L. (2017). Comorbid mental disorders in fetal alcohol spectrum disorders: A systematic review. *Journal of Developmental and Behavioral Pediatrics, 38*(4), 283–291. https://doi.org/10.1097/dbp.0000000000000440

Chapter 4
Fetal Alcohol Spectrum Disorders: An Unfolding Narrative

Radhika Chimata

Abstract Fetal alcohol spectrum disorders (FASDs) encompass a range of neurodevelopmental signs and symptoms that manifest as a result of exposure to alcohol in utero. FASD leads to pervasive biopsychosocial sequelae across the lifespan and intersects with significant sociopolitical issues. However, FASD remains poorly understood as evidenced in part by multiple diagnostic guidelines, lack of FDA-approved biotechnical interventions, and no validated neuropsychological diagnostic instruments. This chapter describes an interview schedule according to proposed *DSM-5* criteria for neurobehavioral disorder associated with prenatal alcohol exposure (ND-PAE). It offers an empathic approach to collecting data from patients and their caretakers. The goal is to move toward a more comprehensive and consistent format for collecting data based upon current empirical understanding of ND-PAE.

Keywords FASD · ND-PAE · History · Interview · Prenatal alcohol exposure

4.1 Introduction

Fetal alcohol spectrum disorder (FASD) encompasses a wide range of physical and psychiatric signs and symptoms that arise in early childhood as a direct result of exposure to alcohol in utero. Because of protean influences of alcohol on the developing fetus, variability in amount/frequency/timing of exposure, and individual

---

This chapter is dedicated to Dr. Carl Compton Bell—psychiatrist, researcher, prolific writer, mentor, and warrior on behalf of the underserved. The words herein are as much his as they are mine. FASD became a part of my mission because Dr. Bell left an indelible mark on my spirit and on my practice of medicine. This chapter also is dedicated to all of the patients and mothers, grandparents, and caregivers who taught me how to speak to them about FASD. Through their painful narratives, I began to make sense of the medical and social complexity that holds this diagnosis hostage and began to search for an effective way to free patients from misdiagnosis and misinterpretation. This chapter illustrates their suffering and attempts to offer a diagnostic approach that aptly reflects their difficult life journey.

R. Chimata (✉)
Department of Psychiatry, Loretto Hospital, Chicago, IL, USA

N. Novick Brown (ed.), *Evaluating Fetal Alcohol Spectrum Disorders in the Forensic Context*, https://doi.org/10.1007/978-3-030-73628-6_4

differences in terms of nutrition and genetics, FASD carries a physiological burden that varies in terms of intensity, site, and functional impairments (Ali, Kerns, Mulligan, Olson, & Astley, 2018; Hemingway et al., 2018; Stratton, Howe, & Battaglia, 1996). According to the National Academy of Sciences, FASD is the leading cause of speech and language disorders, attention-deficit hyperactivity disorder (ADHD), specific learning disorders, and mild mental retardation (i.e., intellectual disability; Stratton et al., 1996), all of which can lead to affect dysregulation (Bell & McBride, 2010) and, in turn, to disruptive behaviors, academic failure, and psychiatric disorders in childhood. The latter often contributes to poor social and educational outcomes, including involvement in the correctional system (Popova, Lange, Bekmuradov, Mihic, & Rehm, 2011).

A person with FASD may go undiagnosed as such or, far more often, be unsuccessfully treated for a number of comorbid diagnoses that overshadow the underlying medical disorder (Chasnoff, Wells, & King, 2015). Case in point, a patient once said to me that she had been diagnosed with "bipolar, depression, schizophrenia, borderline, and posttraumatic stress disorder (PTSD)." This complex diagnostic history is a red flag as parsimony is paramount in medicine. The same patient reported no medication (e.g., antidepressants, antipsychotics, benzodiazepines, or antiepileptics) had ever helped her feel better—again, a red flag. She did not know whether she was born at full term or with a low birth weight, but she reported a history of "heart issues" at birth and exhibited notable right-sided strabismus upon examination. She reported reaching developmental milestones without delay. However, she had difficulty concentrating in school, required special education in reading and math, and continued to struggle with poor concentration throughout her adult years. She had difficulty making friends and was bullied in school, and as an adult, she was unable to maintain gainful employment due to angry outbursts that seemingly were unprovoked. She could not make sense of why she made the same mistakes repeatedly, which led to her feeling persistently demoralized. She struggled with intermittent suicidal ideation, which had prompted my emergency room evaluation. She was unsure if her mother drank alcohol while pregnant with her but noted her mother was a recovering cocaine addict.

During mental status exam, the patient was cooperative but had poor eye contact and labile affect. She was passively suicidal, without plan or intent. She reported an auditory hallucination of a male voice whispering incomprehensibly into her ear as she fell asleep at night. She had one-third word recall and reflected poor insight when asked what she would do if she found a stamped/addressed envelope on the street. Her urine toxicology was negative; complete blood count and comprehensive metabolic panel were within normal limits. While further history revealed this patient met diagnostic criteria for PTSD and persistent depressive disorder, she did not, however, meet criteria for bipolar disorder, schizophrenia, or borderline personality disorder.

4.2 Taking History: A Jigsaw Puzzle

In the fifth edition of the *Diagnostic and Statistical Manual of Mental Disorders* (*DSM-5*; American Psychiatric Association (APA), 2013), FASD was offered a place in the nomenclature under the newly coined term, neurobehavioral disorder associated with prenatal alcohol exposure (ND-PAE). Criteria for ND-PAE include a patient's biopsychosocial experience across the developmental trajectory, including perinatal status and interpersonal aptitude, with onset in childhood. Often, the key diagnostic criterion, confirmation of prenatal alcohol exposure, is the most challenging piece of history to collect. If a patient meets criteria for ND-PAE, evaluators may assign a diagnosis of "Other specified neurodevelopmental disorder," followed by ND-PAE, under ICD-10 code F88 (APA, 2013, p. 86).

Gathering history regarding ND-PAE is akin to assembling pieces of a jigsaw puzzle. An evaluator carries the burden of weaving together a history that (1) begins before the patient's conception, (2) will be forthcoming only when rapport has been established, (3) demands empirical soundness in order to be valid as a guide for treatment in the community or forensic decisions, and (4) supports a diagnosis that has been empirically validated (Johnson, Moyer, Klug, & Burd, 2018; Kable & Coles, 2018; Sanders, Hudson Breen, & Netelenbos, 2017; Sanders, Netelenbos, & Dei, 2020). Reaching a diagnosis of ND-PAE requires confirmed history of maternal alcohol use, which is difficult to obtain even in the best of circumstances. In order to assign a diagnosis that adequately explains a patient's presentation, informs treatment, and guides future research in the absence of confirmed fetal alcohol exposure, evaluators also must consider the gestalt, as the picture in total is more meaningful than the sum of the reported symptoms. There is a sense of déjà vu when interviewing patients with ND-PAE: the innocence of a child and naïveté of a teenager, sometimes ironically juxtaposed with interpersonal detachment and often disconcertingly suffused with the chaos of trauma and substance use. Pieces of the puzzle will appear disparate, but their gestalt tells a story that is pathognomonic of ND-PAE.

This section offers an empathic and non-shaming script for interviewing mothers of patients in the forensic setting and is organized according to *DSM-5* criteria for ND-PAE. These questions may be modified based upon whoever is providing the history (e.g., biological mother, caretaker, family member, patient). In community settings, a patient may present alone or with a caretaker, and questions may be modified accordingly. For example, an adult patient with ND-PAE might live alone or live with, and have many practical needs handled by, another adult; a child patient typically presents with a caregiver. Irrespective of age or level of functioning, patients may not always be reliable historians due to deficits intrinsic to FASD. Therefore, even in the case of independent adult patients with ND-PAE, it behooves evaluators to gather collateral data from family members whenever patients permit.

Depending upon the goal of an evaluation, there will be a variable threshold of suspicion and motivation to apply ND-PAE criteria. In the context of psychiatric evaluations in the community setting, evaluators should apply ND-PAE criteria whenever there is concern for alcohol exposure in utero. Moreover, suspicion should be high if a mother/caretaker presents a child patient for evaluation with a chief complaint of behavioral difficulties, social deficits, academic underachievement, failure to achieve developmental milestones, or a combination thereof. Even in the case of garden variety ADHD, due diligence requires questions about birth history, which includes exposure to substances in utero. In adult patients, whether in the community or forensic setting, there should be high suspicion when the chief complaint involves functional impairments in social adaptability, financial independence, and intellectual capacity, along with mood, anxiety, and other concomitant complaints. As illustrated in the aforementioned case example, when patients report a myriad of diagnoses over time, with no improvement in symptoms despite multiple medications, and state they have never been able to make sense of their conditions, this is a red flag for prior misdiagnosis, and evaluators should consider ND-PAE as a possibility.

Another red flag is involvement in the criminal justice system as there is growing evidence that a large number of undiagnosed offenders would meet criteria for ND-PAE, if evaluated. For example, a literature review by Popova et al. (2011) found young offenders with FASD were 19 times more likely to be incarcerated than youths without FASD. Consequently, arrest or conviction alone merit consideration of ND-PAE. While incarceration and the previous examples are by no means an exhaustive list of chief complaints that should raise suspicion for ND-PAE, they are common guises that ND-PAE wears. Unfortunately, the true culprit may not be uncovered until a keen evaluator sees through the symptoms to the underlying condition.

Generally speaking, in conducting evaluations it, helps to use conversational language and limit use of medical lingo (e.g., terms like gestational age, cardiovascular anomalies, midline defects, neurological deficits). It is imperative to create a nonjudgmental atmosphere. Interviews should not be rushed: If an interviewee seems hesitant or unable to recall details, offer to continue at the next session. Gently address issues involving the prenatal period, especially substance use, regardless of who is providing the history. Remember, a successful intake typically requires more than one session and, above all, rapport.

Of note, patients with ND-PAE generally present for evaluation after many failed attempts to succeed in life. Evaluators should allow interviewees to tell personal narratives at their own pace. A checklist approach will not build rapport, nor will it achieve the higher purpose of healing. A key to unlocking information is empathy, as trite and obvious as this may sound. Patients and birth mothers likely are on the receiving end of this eye-opening diagnosis for the first time. Most importantly, patients, mothers, and caregivers should not be shamed; their life experiences are already replete with moments of shame and regret. Therefore, interviews should serve to mitigate, not magnify, those feelings.

After allowing an interviewee to describe the chief complaint, if there is suspicion for ND-PAE, then proceed with questions subsumed under each *DSM-5* criterion. The following interview questions are only suggestions. Evaluators should glean the spirit of the phraseology and tailor guidelines presented here to their own styles. Moreover, to cover every point herein would require multiple sessions. Depending upon the purpose of an evaluation and time allotted to complete it, questions under each *DSM-5* criterion may be truncated. Refer to Table 4.1 at the end of this chapter for an interview template.

Table 4.1 Birth mother/caregiver interview template

Birth mother/caregiver interview template for neurobehavioral disorder associated with prenatal alcohol exposure (ND-PAE)
A. Exposure to alcohol during pregnancy:
1. Timeline:
When did you find out you were pregnant?
How far along were you?
2. Social determinants of health:
What was your situation like at that time?
Did you have access to prenatal care and good nutrition?
3. Prematurity:
Was your baby born premature; i.e., before 37 weeks?
Did he/she weigh less than normal, i.e., <2500 g or < 5lbs 8 oz?
4. Midline defects:
Did your baby have a heart murmur when he/she was born?
What about a deformity in his/her upper lip or a hole in the roof of his/her mouth?
5. Fetal alcohol facies:
Would you be willing to share baby pictures?
Assess for fetal alcohol facies.
Observe patient's face for residual fetal alcohol abnormalities: Epicanthal folds, flat mid-face, indistinct philtrum, thin upper lip.
6. Maternal substance use during pregnancy:
Were you drinking socially around that time?
Were you using any other substances?
Obtain frequency, amount, and duration of use, especially for alcohol binges.
7. If unable to confirm maternal alcohol use:
Was the patient's mother drinking alcohol while pregnant with the patient's siblings?
Was anyone in the house using alcohol or other substances on a regular basis?
B. Impaired neurocognitive functioning as manifested by one or more of the following:
1. Impairment in global intellect:
Did your child have difficulty in general with academics?
Has your child ever had an IQ test? If IQ <70, patient meets this sub-criterion.
2. Impairment in executive functioning:
Poor planning and organization: *Does your child generally have a tough time planning and getting organized? Can he/she set a goal and complete it?*
Inflexibility: *Does your child easily adjust to changes in the schedule or environment?*
Behavioral inhibition: *Is your child able to delay gratification?*
3. Impairment in learning:
Academic achievement: *How far did your child go in school?*
Learning disability: *Did he/she have difficulty with subjects like math or reading?*
Special education: *Was he/she in special education classes? Which subjects?*
4. Memory impairment:
Does your child generally have a tough time with his/her memory?
Is it tough for him/her to follow instructions, especially when they involve multiple steps?
Do you find that he/she makes the same mistakes over and over again?

(continued)

Table 4.1 (continued)

Birth mother/caregiver interview template for neurobehavioral disorder associated with prenatal alcohol exposure (ND-PAE)
5. Impairment in visual-spatial reasoning: *Does he/she struggle to tie his/her shoe laces or braid/comb his/her hair?* Ask the patient to tie shoelaces. Ask the patient to draw a clock with a specific time.
***Concerning performance on any of the above tasks should alert the evaluator to recommend appropriate neurocognitive evaluations.**
C. Impaired self-regulation as manifested by one or more of the following:
1. Impairment in mood or behavioral regulation: Labile/intense emotions: *Does he/she get into a bad mood easily, but come out of it quickly?* Low frustration tolerance and irritability: *Does your child become angry very easily, and about minor things?* Explosive temper and violent outbursts that may be verbal and/or physical: *Does he/she have outbursts where he/she raises his/her voice or becomes violent?* *Does your child get into fights easily?* Legal issues: *Has he/she previously had issues with the law?* Ask about jail time, prison time, and reasons for detainment.
2. Attention deficit: *Did your child have a tough time concentrating while in school? What about now?* *Can he/she complete a task once he/she starts it?*
3. Poor impulse control: *Did your child have a tough time waiting his/her turn or standing in line during childhood?* *Does he/she generally have a tough time following the rules in a given situation?*
D. Impairment in adaptive functioning as manifested by two or more of the following, one of which must be (1) or (2).
1. Communication deficit: Delay in acquisition of language: *Did your child start speaking later than other children?* Current speech impediments: Assess for current impediments. Difficulty understanding spoken language: *Does your child have a tough time understanding what people are saying to him/her?*
2. Impairment in social communication and interaction: Insight: *Does your child struggle to read social cues and understand social norms?* Foresight: *Does he/she struggle to predict how his/her choices will lead to certain consequences?* *Does he/she seem to have poor judgment?* Childish naivete: *Would you describe your child as childlike, naive, or concrete in his/her thinking?* *Is he/she quick to trust people?* *Is he/she overly friendly with strangers?* *Was he/she bullied as a child?* *Did he/she have a tough time making friends?*
3. Impairment in daily living skills: Delayed toileting, feeding, or bathing: *Did your child have a tough time being potty trained, learning how to bathe himself/herself, or feeding himself/herself as a child?* Difficulty managing daily schedule or personal finances: *Does he/she have difficulty managing a daily schedule* (e.g., *making it to appointments)?* *Does he/she manage his/her own finances* (e.g., *pay her own bills)?*

(continued)

Table 4.1 (continued)

Birth mother/caregiver interview template for neurobehavioral disorder associated with prenatal alcohol exposure (ND-PAE)
4. Impairment in motor skills: Fine motor development: *Does he/she have difficulty writing or coloring inside the lines or learning to write in cursive?* Gross motor development: *At what age did your child start crawling, walking, running?* Observe patient's gait.
When indicated, a neurological exam can help to identify ongoing deficits in gross motor function, coordination, and balance that the mother cannot identify.
E. The onset of the disturbance (symptoms in criteria B, C, D) is before age 18.
F. The disturbance causes clinically significant distress or impairment in social, academic, occupational, or other important areas of functioning. *What's your understanding of why your child has struggled with these symptoms?* *Was there ever a diagnosis that helped explain these difficulties?* *Was there ever a medication that helped him/her feel better?* *Has there ever been a time that he/she was functioning well?*
G. The disturbance is not better explained by the direct physiological effects associated with postnatal use of a substance (e.g., medication, alcohol, or other drugs), another medical condition (e.g., traumatic brain injury, delirium, dementia), another known teratogen, a genetic condition (e.g., Williams syndrome, Down's syndrome, Cornelia de Lange syndrome), or environmental neglect.
1. Traumatic brain injury: *Has your child ever been in a car accident? Did he/she hit his/her head in the accident or lose consciousness?* *Has he/she ever fallen on his/her head or been hit on the head by a hard object?*
2. Substance use: Ask about cigarettes, alcohol, marijuana, cocaine, heroin. Ask about first use, peak use, duration of use, typical use per sitting, periods of abstinence.
3. Differential diagnoses: Complete an assessment for history of depression, anxiety, mania, psychosis, trauma, ADHD, autism spectrum disorder, and genetic disorders, in addition to substance use.
4. Suicide risk assessment: Past and current suicidal ideation, plans Attempts: Near attempts, aborted attempts, completed attempts

4.3 Interview Guidelines

This section includes *DSM-5* guidelines for diagnosing ND-PAE (**bold type**), with recommendations for interviewing birth mothers following each guideline.

A. **Exposure to alcohol at any time during gestation, including prior to pregnancy recognition, and the exposure level was more than minimal (i.e., more than 13 drinks in any 1 month, with no more than two drinks on any drinking occasion). Confirmation of gestational exposure to alcohol may be obtained from any of the following sources: Maternal self-report of alcohol use in pregnancy, collateral reports, or medical or other records.**

Introduction: Begin by introducing the need for gathering information. *I'd like to start with some questions about your child's birth history. This will help me get a clearer picture of how your child may have developed the problems you've described.* Keep in mind that the patient and caretaker may have approached their primary care doctor multiple times with the same complaints. There also may have been a number of conversations with school teachers or authority figures in the workplace. Very likely, there will have been multiple prior attempts to alleviate symptoms before a patient presents for mental health evaluation, whether in the community or forensic setting. By the time a patient is seeing you for evaluation, "provider fatigue" may have set in. There also may be a sense of distrust, that no one will have a solution, and that perhaps no one is truly invested in the patient's well-being. In this vein, if an interviewee questions the pertinence of birth history, then offer a legitimate reason.

Establish a timeline: *When did you find out you were pregnant? Do you remember how far along you were? If you don't mind my asking, how old were you?* The birth mother's age is a proxy for her stage of life and level of development in terms of social responsibility. A 15-year-old pregnant adolescent is unlikely to understand, or to have been educated thoroughly about, the impact of substances, nutrition, and prenatal care on the health of her developing baby. Demographics such as the mother's educational background, employment status, and number of previous pregnancies provide information that may be relevant to her behavior during the index pregnancy.

Social determinants of health: *What was your situation like at that time? Did you feel that you had the necessary support?* These questions open the door to the mother's narrative and clarify her access to resources, both economic and emotional. It creates a picture of the patient's pre/perinatal conditions while also building rapport. This information helps the evaluator adjust remaining questions if necessary and remain respectful regarding the mother's individual circumstances.

Prenatal care: *Were you able to receive prenatal care? Were you able to get prenatal vitamins? Did you take them daily? What kind of foods did you eat—that is, what was your nutrition like during your pregnancy?* Here, the evaluator is trying to assess the presence of biochemical building blocks that could mitigate effects of alcohol on the developing fetus (Thomas, Abou, & Domiguez, 2009).

Prematurity: *Do you remember if your baby was born full term? Specifically, do you recall if you were past 37 weeks pregnant when your baby was born?* If an interviewee cannot recall the exact gestational age at which the patient was born, then the evaluator should ask, *Were you close to your due date when you delivered your baby?* Then, probe for further details that could shed light on the severity and/or timing of alcohol exposure. *How much did your baby weigh when he/she was born? Even if you don't remember the exact weight because, after all, it's hard to recall these details after so many years, do you remember if your baby was less than normal weight? Did the baby need any help breathing?* Essentially, these questions reveal whether a patient was born premature (before completing 37 of 40 weeks), had low birth weight of <2500 g or <5lbs, 8 oz. (Cutland et al., 2017), or experienced related sequelae such as immature lung development. Evaluators also could ask about "blood on the brain" or intraventricular hemorrhage, which sometimes is seen in premature neonates and can lead to a number of neurodevelopmental sequelae.

Midline defects: *Did your baby have a heart murmur when he/she was born? Were there any other issues with your baby's heart? Did the doctors do a scan of your baby's heart? Do you remember what it showed? What about any problems inside your baby's mouth, where the upper lip or roof of the mouth had a small hole in it? Was any surgery done to repair this?* These data are a proxy for the severity of exposure to alcohol and inform both psychiatric and medical treatment. Presence of a cardiac defect at birth indicates a need for cardiology follow-up. A persistent ventricular septal defect (VSD), atrial septal defect, or more significant anomaly needs to be monitored and managed medically. Presence of a significant midline defect such as a VSD in the context of confirmed alcohol exposure in utero is a harbinger of other defects that may not be easily detected or elicited on physical exam. Again, these data alert evaluators to the possible severity of physiological damage and need for medical follow-up.

Fetal alcohol facies: Ask for baby pictures to be brought to the next visit. Fetal alcohol facies may be apparent at birth but often will recede as the patient ages. Nevertheless, a trained or seasoned evaluator may be able to observe residual fetal alcohol facies (epicanthal folds, flat midface, indistinct philtrum, thin upper lip) in adult patients, and this should be duly noted. Evaluators also should request medical records from the pre/neonatal periods and adoption records, if applicable. These records, particularly adoption records, may be difficult to obtain, depending upon the age at which a patient presents for evaluation and whether it was an open or closed adoption. Especially in forensic cases requiring the burden of proof, evaluators may seek to obtain documented evidence of this criterion. Another option may be to apply the FAS Facial Photographic Screening Tool developed by Astley (2004) and colleagues at the University of Washington.

Maternal substance use during pregnancy: *You mentioned you were two months along when you found out you were pregnant. Do you remember if you were drinking socially around that time? I know it can be hard to recall, but it would really help me get to the right diagnosis so we can help your child.* Without a doubt, this is the most challenging part of this interview. Not only does confirmation of alcohol exposure rely upon an interviewee's remote memory, the topic also carries a psychological burden that can limit accuracy of reported history and potentially undermine the remainder of the interview. If an interviewee reports she was drinking alcohol to any extent, then the evaluator should attempt to determine frequency, amount, and duration of use. Ask about her "typical" drinking pattern in the weeks and months prior to pregnancy. If she cannot remember, ask if she typically drank on weekends, and if she agrees she did, ask if she likely drank most Friday and Saturday nights and—when she drank—did she usually get "buzzed." It is important to use non-pejorative terms to describe intoxication. Finally—and most importantly—ask about binge drinking (i.e., four or more alcoholic drinks per occasion) as research indicates alcohol exerts the greatest damage when given in boluses (Stratton et al., 1996).

Allow the mother to tell her narrative. Accurate history will come forth when the evaluator offers supportive body language (e.g., empathic eye contact and facial expression, body facing mother, and no note-taking if possible). Keep in mind that 40% of pregnancies worldwide are unintended (Sedgh, Singh, & Hussain, 2014). Thus, many women are unaware of their pregnancies during the critical period of organogenesis early in gestation, and even more are uninformed about alcohol's impact upon the growing fetus. In research conducted by Bell and Chimata (2015), we became aware that many mothers engaged in "social drinking" and not "alcohol abuse" in the month or two before discovering they were pregnant. Once they learned they were pregnant, these mothers abstained from alcohol, but the critical period of fetal development had already passed. It is in these moments of the interview when many mothers come to the realization that there is a connection between their actions during pregnancy and their child's lifelong suffering. Support the interviewee through the sadness such a realization likely engenders.

If an interviewee appears engaged and able to proceed, then inquire about other substances that can harm fetal brain development, such as marijuana, cocaine, heroin, methamphetamine, and nicotine. Allowing the mother to tell her story permits data to unfold gradually and, importantly, builds rapport. See below under Criterion F, Exclusionary Criteria, for a full description on characterizing use of a given substance and apply these questions to the extent that time and circumstances permit. Again, empathy is key at this critical juncture. The resulting narrative will show how the process unfolded for each mother and patient and help guide diagnosis and treatment as well as forensic conclusions.

In the event interviewees cannot recall critical information or are not forthcoming, this key criterion might remain unconfirmed. In research by Bell and Chimata (2015), maternal alcohol use was confirmed in only 87 of 224 patients (39%) who met all other criteria for ND-PAE. If an interviewee is forthcoming regarding her history of using other substances, such information may be a harbinger and veritable proxy for alcohol use but cannot serve as confirmation thereof. Therefore, if Criteria B through G are met in the absence of Criterion A, evaluators may ask for collateral information from another caretaker or reliable source: *Did you see the patient's mother drinking alcohol (using drugs) while she was pregnant with the patient or any of the patient's siblings? Was anyone in the house using alcohol or other substances on a regular basis?* Attempt to gather information about the home environment, especially if there was a partner who regularly drank alcohol. Again, these serve as proxies but do not serve as confirmation of maternal alcohol use.

B. **Impaired neurocognitive functioning as manifested by one or more of the following:**

1. **Impairment in global intellect**

An interviewee may openly describe the patient as "slow" in childhood. *Has the patient ever had an IQ test?* If reported IQ was 70 or below (actually, at or below an IQ of 75 given the 5-point margin of error), Sub-criterion #1 is met.

Otherwise, evaluators may ask patients to undergo IQ testing if evaluations require it or if treatment will be best guided by such assessment. In the case of the latter, ask the patient, *Would you be willing to take a test that helps us measure your IQ?* Then explain what IQ means and what such a test would entail.

2. **Impairment in executive functioning**

   Gather information about the patient's ability to plan, organize, and delay gratification in the service of higher goals. A simple example is grocery shopping. *Does your child know how to buy groceries for the family? Does he/she make a list before going to the grocery store?* Evaluators also might ask about waiting for a coveted item to go on sale. *Does your child think about how to save money; for example, would it be typical for your child to wait for a sale before buying an expensive item he/she wanted, or would your child buy the item at full price?* Evaluators should assess for this sub-criterion as narratives unfold, noting examples of poor planning, poor organization, inflexibility, and difficulty with behavioral inhibition.

3. **Impairment in learning**

   Ask about level of academic achievement. *How did your child do in school?* Allow interviewees to tell the story. If the following questions are not adequately answered in the process, then fill in the gaps. *Did he/she have difficulty with certain subjects, like math or reading? Was he/she ever told he/she had a learning disability? Did he/she receive professional help or special education services for it? Did he/she attend special education classes? How far did he/she go in school?* It may become evident the patient has lower academic achievement than expected for intellectual level. Attempt to confirm whether patients can read and write.

4. **Memory impairment**

   This sub-criterion requires patient involvement, irrespective of evaluation setting. *Do you find you have a hard time remembering things?* If the answer is yes, then ask, *What kinds of things – school-related information or things that come up in daily life?* Regardless of response, administer a three-word recall test to the patient for initial memory screening (Borson, Scanlan, Brush, Vitaliano, & Dokmak, 2000). *I'm going to give you three words. I'd like you to remember them for later.* An evaluator should choose three words, recite them at a rate of one word per second, have the patient repeat the three words twice, and ask the patient to repeat the words after 5 min. Hints are permitted if the patient cannot recall a word (e.g., fruit, animal, object). Duly document. Recent memory also may be assessed by asking where the patient is *right now* (i.e., name of the building, city, name of the clinic/hospital/jail/prison). Depending upon patient age, assess remote memory by asking about past presidents and/or what the patient ate for dinner. Ask caregivers: *Does your child have a tough time following instructions, especially instructions involving multiple steps? What if you asked your child to get dressed for school, pack his/her bag, and then take the trash out before catching the school bus – would your child be able to complete all of those steps, or would he/she become overwhelmed and require reminders?* Such questions highlight difficulty with multistep instructions. These quick screening questions are only rudimentary tests of memory. Therefore, any concerning results indicate a need for more thorough assessment. *Does your child make the same mistakes over and over again, and has she ever told you she wonders why?* This is a sensitive question, and it is up to an evaluator's discretion as to when/how to present this query. In my experience, every patient I have evaluated has responded affirmatively when asked this question.

5. **Impairment in visual-spatial reasoning**

   Visual-spatial or visuospatial reasoning involves ability to locate objects in space, which can extend to numbers, letters, and a patient's own body parts (Carroll, 1993). Deficiency may be reflected in disorganized or poorly planned drawings ("constructions") or difficulty differentiating left from right. Ask patients to draw a clock with a specific time. This may be less appropriate for the younger generation as they are more accustomed to digital clocks. If appropriate, this task can be repeated serially to assess improvement with treatment. Inquire about a patient's fine motor skills. *Can your child tie shoelaces or braid/comb his/her hair without a problem?* If circumstances are conducive, actually ask the patient to tie his/her shoelaces as you observe. Then, ask the patient to draw a picture with the patient on the right side of the picture and his/her family on the left, placing his/her signature on the bottom center of the drawing. Needless to say, the above tasks merely scratch the surface of visuospatial skills but may inform a need for further assessment.

   DSM-5 notes that neurodevelopmental disorders frequently co-occur with ND-PAE (APA, 2013). Significant comorbidity occurs because fetal alcohol exposure damages the brain in myriad ways, leading to symptoms that resemble other neurodevelopmental disorders. While fetal alcohol exposure may well be the primary etiology for these symptoms, extended intake should aim to gather history that adequately explores whether patients have other neurodevelopmental disorders comorbid with ND-PAE.

C. **Impaired self-regulation as manifested by one or more of the following:**

1. **Impairment in mood or behavioral regulation**

   Patients may report and/or be observed with labile emotionality (e.g., low frustration tolerance, explosive temper, irritability), including violent verbal and/or physical outbursts. These affective states generally are short-lived and do not meet criteria for a mood episode; rather, they are more accurately defined as labile mood. Try to characterize these shifts in mood and affect in order to rule out/in bipolar disorder. *Does your child become angry very easily and about minor things? Does your child have outbursts where he/she raises his/her voice or becomes violent? Has this affected his/her relationships or job situation? Does he/she get into a bad mood easily but come out of it pretty quickly? Does he/she get into fights more than most people? What's the usual reason for the fighting? Has he/she previously had issues with the law?* Ask about detention, jail, or prison time and reasons for incarceration. Ask if the patient was ever committed by the juvenile court to a treatment program.

2. **Attention deficit**

   Look for difficulties with shifting attention or sustaining mental effort. *Did your child have a tough time concentrating while in school? What about now? Can he/she complete a task once he/she starts it?*

3. **Poor impulse control**

   In childhood, did your child have difficulty waiting his/her turn or standing in line? Does he/she have difficulty following rules in general? Did this lead to any problems, socially or otherwise? Sub-criterion 1 (emotional dysregulation) and Sub-criterion 3 (poor impulse control) may overlap, but this does not affect whether or not a patient meets Criterion C.

D. **Impairment in adaptive functioning as manifested by two or more of the following, one of which must be (1) or (2)**

   DSM-5 describes impairment in adaptive functioning as failure to meet standards of "personal independence and social responsibility in one or more aspects of daily life, including communication, social participation, academic or occupational functioning, and personal independence at home or in community settings" (APA, 2013, p. 31).

1. **Communication deficit**

   Delayed acquisition of language: *How old was your child when he/she started speaking?* If the interviewee does not know, then ask, *Did anyone in the family or your friends ever mention your child started speaking later than expected?* Assess patients for this developmental milestone and then observe for current speech impediments. For example, there may be a notable lisp or inability to enunciate certain phonemes. Patients may have chronic difficulty understanding spoken language: *Does your child find it difficult to make sense of what people are saying?* With age, patients may find ways to compensate for the latter, but interviewees likely will offer examples of this point if they are relevant and memorable.

2. **Impairment in social communication and interaction**

   Look for insight and foresight. *Is your child quick to trust people? Is he/she overly friendly with strangers? Has this led to any problems?* Patients may report and/or be observed to be childlike, naïve, or concrete in thinking. They may have had difficulty reading social cues and understanding social consequences and as such will report or exhibit poor judgment and limited ability to foresee the consequences of their choices. *Was your child bullied as a child? Did your child have a tough time making or keeping friends?* Patients may pointedly state they really want people to like them and do not know why they have been ostracized for much of their lives.

3. **Impairment in daily living skills**

   Look for delayed toileting, feeding, or bathing in early childhood and difficulties managing daily schedule or personal finances later in life. *Did your child have any issues with being potty trained, learning how to bathe, or feeding himself/herself as a child? During your child's teen and adult years, did he/she have difficulty managing a daily schedule? Does he/she manage his/her own finances?*

4. **Impairment in motor skills**

   Fine motor development: *Did your child have difficulty writing or coloring inside the lines?* Delayed attainment of gross motor milestones: *How old was your child when he/she started crawling, walking, running?* If interviewees cannot recall, then ask, *Did anyone in the family ever say your child crawled/walked a little later than expected? Does your child have any difficulty throwing or catching a ball? Did your child have difficulty learning to write cursive? Does your child have "butter fingers" or spill things often?* Observe the patient's gait. If circumstances permit, have patients throw and catch a ball. When indicated, a neurological exam may help to identify ongoing deficits in gross motor function, coordination, and balance that patients are unable to articulate.

E. **Onset of the disturbance (symptoms in Criteria B, C, D) is before the age of 18 years**

F. **The disturbance causes clinically significant distress or impairment in social, academic, occupational, or other important areas of functioning**

   Criteria E and F should be clear by the time Criteria A–D have been addressed. Still, if an interviewee has not clarified level of functional impairment and distress by this point, the evaluator should elicit the patient's personal sense about his/her symptoms, such as: *What's your understanding of why you've struggled with these symptoms? Was there ever a diagnosis that helped explain your difficulties? Was there ever a medication that helped you feel better or helped you function the way you wanted to in your life?*

G. **The disturbance is not better explained by the direct physiological effects associated with postnatal use of a substance (e.g., medication, alcohol, or other drugs), another medical condition (e.g., traumatic brain injury, delirium, dementia), another known teratogen (e.g., Fetal Hydantoin Syndrome), a genetic condition (e.g., Williams Syndrome, Down's syndrome, Cornelia de Lange syndrome), or environmental neglect**

   This exclusionary criterion demands that evaluators have (a) acquired sufficient evidence that exposure to alcohol in utero was the proximal cause of presenting symptoms, and (b) ruled out all other possible explanations for patient symptoms in the service of parsimony. This diagnostic criterion also serves to remind evaluators that there may be multiple comorbid factors contributing to the patient's presentation. For example, individuals with ND-PAE may place themselves unwittingly in high-risk situations due to poor insight. Therefore, it is important to ask about traumatic brain injury (TBI), as such injury may exacerbate existing symptoms and/or lead to new symptoms affecting cognition and adaptive functioning. *Has your child ever been in a car accident? Did he/she hit his/her head? Did he/she lose consciousness? For how long? Did a doctor examine him/her? Has your child ever fallen on his/her head or been hit on the head with a hard object? Did he/she lose consciousness? Did he/she go to the emergency room? Did he/she ever get a brain scan or picture of his/her brain? Did a doctor ever say there was blood on his/her brain or that his/her brain was injured?* History of TBI does not preclude an ND-PAE diagnosis; rather, a history of risk-taking behavior in ND-PAE may inadvertently lead to TBI.

Approximately 50% of individuals with mental illness will have a comorbid substance use disorder in their lifetime (National Institute on Drug Abuse (NIDA), 2020). Individuals with ND-PAE are at even greater risk of substance abuse. Consequently, obtaining substance use history is imperative in treatment planning and forensic contexts, as it sheds light on factors that may have contributed to behavior. *I need to ask you a few questions about substance use, because using substances like alcohol can make your child's current symptoms worse in the long run. Do you know if your child smokes cigarettes? Has he/she ever tried alcohol, marijuana, cocaine, methamphetamine, or heroin?* After asking about a given substance, pause for interviewees to reply, then ask about the next substance. Finally, ask if there are any other substances: *Has your child ever tried anything else, maybe Ecstasy or PCP or huffing inhalants?* Next, characterize use of each substance across the patient's lifespan. *Let's talk more about XX. How old was your child when he/she first tried it? Since then, how often has he/she used it? How much did he/she use each time?* Alcohol may be quantified according to milliliters or ounces of hard liquor/wine/beer, while other substances will be measured according to grams, bags, or cost. Gather history regarding typical parameters: first use, peak use, duration of use, and periods of abstinence around each substance. Asking about attempts to abstain and past treatments can open up a conversation about healing. Once again, the presence of a substance use disorder does not preclude a primary diagnosis of ND-PAE, but differential diagnosis is essential for appropriate treatment planning that includes limiting further injury to already damaged organ systems and neuronal circuitry.

As is necessary in any valid psychiatric or psychological intake, basic diagnostic categories must be covered: depression, anxiety, mania, psychosis, and substances. PTSD also should be included, especially in the case of putative ND-PAE. In addition, evaluators should touch upon basic neurodevelopmental diagnoses such as ADHD, learning disability, and autism spectrum disorder. Even when fetal alcohol exposure is confirmed, patients may meet bona fide criteria for another *DSM-5* diagnosis and may benefit from related interventions. In sum, a complete psychiatric or psychological evaluation involves questions about major/persistent depressive disorder, bipolar disorder, generalized anxiety/panic disorder, posttraumatic stress disorder, substance use disorders, schizophrenia, psychotic symptoms in the context of all of the aforementioned, as well as other neurodevelopmental disorders such as ADHD.

History offers numerous examples of misdiagnosis. For example, individuals with autism spectrum disorder have been misdiagnosed with schizophrenia (Gama Marques & Pires, 2019), and African-Americans with bipolar disorder have been misdiagnosed with undifferentiated schizophrenia and prescribed antipsychotics instead of lithium, the gold standard treatment (Bell & Mehta, 1980). Adult patients with ND-PAE often present with a prior diagnosis of bipolar disorder based upon persistent emotional dysregulation, which, as delineated above, needs to be accurately characterized for valid differential diagnosis. Anecdotally, individuals with ND-PAE also may report late-onset auditory hallucinations that began in their 30s (as described in the case example). On further characterization, hallucination content often does not comport with symptoms in schizophrenia where patients may hear either a running commentary, one or more voices arguing, or one's own thoughts out loud. Adult patients with ND-PAE also have more interpersonal skills than schizophrenics, albeit impaired, and do not manifest the negative symptoms seen in schizophrenia. Child patients with ND-PAE may present with some combination of reactive attachment disorder, disruptive mood dysregulation disorder, intermittent explosive disorder, and/or ADHD in addition to other neurodevelopmental disorders. Adolescents with ND-PAE often present with oppositional defiant disorder or conduct disorder. While a patient may meet criteria for one or more of these diagnoses, an etiological explanation of fetal alcohol exposure can support the more parsimonious diagnosis of ND-PAE.

Lastly, evaluators should conduct a suicide risk assessment. This involves inquiry into past and current suicidal ideation, plans, near attempts, aborted attempts, and completed attempts. According to research by Thanh and Jonsson (2016), life expectancy for persons with fetal alcohol syndrome is 34 years on average, with "external causes" accounting for 44% of deaths. Suicide was responsible for 15% of deaths, followed by accidents at 14%, and poisoning by recreational substances at 7%. In one of Bell's commentaries, he wanted to call attention to "a biologic etiology of suicidal behavior" in FASD (Bell, 2017), which posits that affect dysregulation leads patients to engage in risky behaviors such as substance use, violence, unsafe sexual practices, and suicide. Therefore, suicide risk assessment is extremely important in the context of ND-PAE. It behooves an evaluator to obtain a complete narrative of suicidal history rather than simply going through a checklist, not only to determine patient risk profile in the context of affect dysregulation and impulsivity but also to understand how the patient typically copes with stress (i.e., adaptive behavior).

4.4 Concluding Remarks

Recent research finds that FASD is far more prevalent (May et al., 2018) and at the root of more extensive psychopathology (Popova et al., 2016) than previously realized. As such, *DSM-5* has proposed a set of criteria under the diagnosis ND-PAE to facilitate mental health assessment of the central nervous system dysfunction in FASD. Accurate diagnosis requires a comprehensive assessment that includes neonatal and neurodevelopmental status, childhood educational trajectory, mood/affect regulation, and adaptive functioning across the lifespan. The assembled pieces of this jigsaw puzzle reveal a picture in bas relief that goes beyond individual criteria to portray an individual who struggles to comprehend and self-regulate yet persistently experiences a sense of underachievement without the means to reroute. Like intellectual disability and autism, ND-PAE impacts patients across all areas of functioning throughout life. A supportive interview process can move a patient one step forward toward a better understanding of symptoms. Similarly, using *DSM-5* criteria in a systematic manner can move the field one step forward within a validated framework for understanding ND-PAE. Such understanding should remain couched in each patient's rich narrative, and our medical understanding of ND-PAE should be refracted through a sociopolitical lens that informs larger shifts that are needed to prevent this multifaceted and debilitating disorder in future generations.

References

Ali, S., Kerns, K. A., Mulligan, B. P., Olson, H. C., & Astley, S. J. (2018). An investigation of intra-individual variability in children with fetal alcohol spectrum disorder (FASD). *Child Neuropsychology, 24*(5), 617–637. https://doi.org/10.1080/09297049.2017.1302579

American Psychiatric Association (APA). (2013). *Diagnostic and statistical manual of mental disorders (DSM-5)* (5th ed.). Arlington, VA: American Psychiatric Association.

Astley, S. J. (2004). *Diagnostic guide for fetal alcohol spectrum disorders: The 4-digit diagnostic code* (3rd ed.). Seattle, WA: University of Washington.

Bell, C. C. (2017). Fetal alcohol spectrum disorders and suicidality. *Clinical Psychiatry News (Commentary)*.. https://www.mdedge.com/psychiatry/article/155222/addiction-medicine/fetal-alcohol-spectrum-disorders-and-suicidality

Bell, C. C., & Chimata, R. (2015). Prevalence of neurodevelopmental disorders in low-income African-Americans at a clinic on Chicago's south side. *Psychiatric Services, 66*(5), 539–542. https://doi.org/10.1176/appi.ps.201400162

Bell, C. C., & McBride, D. F. (2010). Affect regulation and the prevention of risky behaviors. *JAMA: Journal of the American Medical Association, 304*(5), 565–566. https://psycnet.apa.org/doi/10.1001/jama.2010.1058

Bell, C. C., & Mehta, H. (1980). The misdiagnosis of black patients with manic depressive illness. *Journal of the National Medical Association, 72*(2), 141–145. https://www.ncbi.nlm.nih.gov/pmc/articles/PMC2552475/pdf/jnma00034-0059.pdf

Borson, S., Scanlan, J., Brush, M., Vitaliano, P., & Dokmak, A. (2000). The mini-cog: A cognitive "vital signs" measure for dementia screening in multilingual elderly. *International Journal of Geriatric Psychiatry, 15*(11), 1021–1027. https://doi.org/10.1002/1099-1166(200011)15:11<1021::AID-GPS234>3.0.CO;2-6

Carroll, J. B. (1993). Abilities in the domain of visual perception. In J. B. Carroll (Ed.), *Human cognitive abilities: A survey of factor-analytic studies* (pp. 304–363). Cambridge: Cambridge University Press. https://doi.org/10.1017/CBO9780511571312

Chasnoff, I. J., Wells, A. M., & King, L. (2015). Misdiagnosis and missed diagnoses in foster and adopted children with prenatal alcohol exposure. *Pediatrics, 135*(2), 264–270. https://doi.org/10.1542/peds.2014-2171

Cutland, C. L., Lackritz, E. M., Mallett-Moore, T., Bardají, A., Chandrasekaran, R., Lahariya, … Muñoz, F. M. (2017). Low birth weight: Case definition & guidelines for data collection, analysis, and presentation of maternal immunization safety data. *Vaccine, 35*(48) part A, 6492–6500. https://doi.org/10.1016/j.vaccine.2017.01.049

Gama Marques, J., & Pires, S. (2019). Psychosis in autistic patients with splinter skills (savant syndrome) presenting abnormal cerebellar anatomy misdiagnosed as disorganized (hebephrenic) schizophrenia. *Primary Care Companion: CNS Disorders, 21*(5), 18l02421. https://doi.org/10.4088/PCC.18l02421

Hemingway, S. J. A., Bledsoe, J. M., Davies, J. K., Brooks, A., Jirikowic, T., Olson, E. M., & Thorne, J. C. (2018). Twin study confirms virtually identical prenatal alcohol exposures can lead to markedly different fetal alcohol spectrum disorder outcomes-fetal genetics influences fetal vulnerability. *Advances in Pediatric Research, 5*(3), 1–19. https://doi.org/10.24105/apr.2019.5.23

Johnson, S., Moyer, C. L., Klug, M. G., & Burd, L. (2018). Comparison of alcohol-related neurodevelopmental disorders and neurodevelopmental disorders associated with prenatal alcohol exposure diagnostic criteria. *Journal of Developmental & Behavioral Pediatrics, 39*(2), 163–167. https://doi.org/10.1097/dbp.0000000000000523

Kable, J. A., & Coles, C. D. (2018). Evidence supporting the internal validity of the proposed ND-PAE disorder. *Child Psychiatry and Human Development, 49*(2), 163–175. https://doi.org/10.1007/s10578-017-0738-8

May, P. A., Chambers, C. D., Kalberg, W. O., Zellner, J., Feldman, H., Buckley, D., … Hoyme, H. E. (2018). Prevalence of fetal alcohol spectrum disorders in 4 US communities. *Journal of the American Medical Association, 319*(5), 474–483. https://doi.org/10.1001/jama.2017.21896

National Institute on Drug Abuse (NIDA). (2020). Part 1: The connection between substance use disorders and mental illness. https://www.drugabuse.gov/publications/research-reports/common-comorbidities-substance-use-disorders/part-1-connection-between-substance-use-disorders-mental-illness. Accessed 2 Sept. 2020.

Popova, S., Lange, S., Bekmuradov, D., Mihic, A., & Rehm, J. (2011). Fetal alcohol spectrum disorder prevalence estimates in correctional systems: A systematic literature review. *Canadian Journal of Public Health, 102*(5), 336–340. https://doi.org/10.1007/BF03404172

Popova, S., Lange, S., Shield, K., Mihic, A., Chudley, A. E., Mukherjee, R. A. S., … Rehm, J. (2016). Comorbidity of fetal alcohol spectrum disorder: A systematic review and meta-analysis. *Lancet, 387*(10022), 978–987. https://doi.org/10.1016/s0140-6736(15)01345-8

Sanders, J. L., Hudson Breen, R. E., & Netelenbos, N. (2017). Comparing diagnostic classification of neurobehavioral disorder associated with prenatal alcohol exposure with the Canadian fetal alcohol spectrum disorder guidelines: A cohort study. *CMAJ: Canadian Medical Association Journal, 5*(1), e178–e183. https://doi.org/10.9778/cmajo.20160137

Sanders, J. L., Netelenbos, N., & Dei, S. O. (2020). Construct and factorial validity of neurobehavioral disorder associated with prenatal alcohol disorder (ND-PAE). *BMC Psychology, 8*, 53. https://doi.org/10.1186/s40359-020-00405-5

Sedgh, G., Singh, S., & Hussain, R. (2014). Intended and unintended pregnancies worldwide in 2012 and recent trends. *Studies in Family Planning, 45*(3), 301–314. https://doi.org/10.1111/j.1728-4465.2014.00393.x

Stratton, K., Howe, C., & Battaglia, F. C. (Eds.). (1996). *Fetal alcohol syndrome: Diagnosis, epidemiology, prevention, and treatment*. Institute of Medicine, Committee to Study Fetal Alcohol Syndrome. Washington, DC: National Academy Press.

Thanh, N. X., & Jonsson, E. (2016). Life expectancy of people with fetal alcohol syndrome. *Journal of Population Therapeutics & Clinical Pharmacology, 23*(1), e53–e59. https://jptcp.com/index.php/jptcp/article/view/240/196

Thomas, J. D., Abou, E. J., & Domiguez, H. D. (2009). Prenatal choline supplementation mitigates the adverse effects of prenatal alcohol exposure on development in rats. *Neurotoxicology and Teratology, 31*(5), 303–311. https://doi.org/10.1016/j.ntt.2009.07.002

Chapter 5
Neuropsychological Assessment of Fetal Alcohol Spectrum Disorder in Adults

Paul D. Connor

Abstract Assessment of current neuropsychological status is an essential component in the fetal alcohol spectrum disorders (FASD) diagnostic process. Because assessment and diagnosis of children with FASD has been occurring routinely for nearly 50 years now, psychometric measures that address this disability in children are fairly well established. By contrast, testing protocols for adults with possible FASD are less well described. The following chapter addresses the body of neuropsychological research in adults with FASD. Based upon this research and formal training in FASD as well as neuropsychology, I describe specific tests found to be sensitive to the effects of prenatal alcohol exposure. The chapter includes specific suggestions for presenting neuropsychological data in reports and testimony in order to make findings more understandable to legal professionals, which includes comparing individual performance to diagnostic guidelines and the FASD empirical literature.

Keywords Fetal alcohol spectrum disorder, FASD · Neurodevelopmental disorder associated with prenatal alcohol exposure, ND-PAE · Neuropsychological assessment

5.1 Introduction

Since fetal alcohol syndrome (FAS) was first identified and described in the United States in 1973 (Jones & Smith, 1973; Jones, Smith, Ulleland, & Streissguth, 1973), a large body of research has been published on the neuropsychological effects of prenatal alcohol exposure. Most of that research focuses on children and early adolescents with relatively little attention to adults with FASD, although it is clear FASD is a lifelong condition caused by permanent brain damage (Bookstein,

P. D. Connor (✉)
University of Washington, Seattle, WA, USA
e-mail: paul@connornp.com

N. Novick Brown (ed.), *Evaluating Fetal Alcohol Spectrum Disorders in the Forensic Context*, https://doi.org/10.1007/978-3-030-73628-6_5

Streissguth, Sampson, Connor, & Barr, 2002; Landgren et al., 2019), and cognitive impairments observed in children persist throughout life. In clinical settings, FASD conditions are diagnosed as fetal alcohol syndrome (FAS), partial FAS (pFAS), or conditions that have no outward physical manifestations: alcohol-related neurodevelopmental disorder (ARND), static encephalopathy/alcohol-exposed (SE/AE), or neurobehavioral disorder/alcohol-exposed (ND/AE). Under the *Diagnostic and Statistical Manual of Mental Disorders*, fifth edition (*DSM-5*; American Psychiatric Association (APA), 2013), central nervous system (CNS) dysfunction in FASD is diagnosed as neurodevelopmental disorder associated with prenatal alcohol exposure (ND-PAE). Like all conditions under the FASD umbrella except FAS, ND-PAE requires confirmation of prenatal alcohol exposure.

With varying levels of FASD awareness and limited access to diagnostic services, it is not at all uncommon for individuals who are exposed to alcohol prenatally to "fall through the cracks" and not be diagnosed in childhood. Because FASD was unknown in the United States prior to 1973 and not generally known even in the 1980s, most alcohol-exposed children born in the 1970s and 1980s were never diagnosed. In other words, most children seriously damaged by prenatal alcohol exposure entered adulthood with undiagnosed FASD, often with the condition misattributed to other cognitive or mental health conditions. This under-identification problem has direct implications for adults in the criminal justice system, where it is estimated 17% to perhaps a third of all prison inmates in the United States have FASD (see Chap. 3). Studies examining criminal behavior in FASD find as many as 60% of adults with FASD experience trouble with the law (Forrester et al., 2015; MacPherson, Chudley, & Grant, 2011; Streissguth et al., 2004). A significant risk factor for secondary disabilities (i.e., adverse developmental outcomes) in individuals with FASD is age of diagnosis (Streissguth et al., 2004; Streissguth, Barr, Kogan, & Bookstein, 1996). In fact, diagnosis after age 6 was identified as one of the greatest risk factors for developing secondary disabilities associated with FASD, including mental health disorders, alcohol and drug use problems, trouble with the law, and confinement.

Much of my professional forensic practice has involved adult evaluees suspected of having FASD because maternal alcohol use was either confirmed or likely. During multidisciplinary evaluation, the "gold standard" process for diagnosing FASD (Novick Brown, Wartnik, Connor, & Adler, 2010), neuropsychological assessment typically is the first step. Because of the high-stakes nature of many forensic cases, an empirically based test protocol during neuropsychological assessment is the standard of practice, as described over a decade ago in the peer-reviewed literature (Novick Brown et al., 2010). Since 2010, the forensic assessment protocol for FASD has been updated periodically to remain consistent with the evolving science in FASD. This chapter describes the current forensic protocol for neuropsychological assessment in adults with FASD, along with suggestions for presenting test results in reports and testimony to assist triers of fact in making legal decisions.

5.2 Current Neuropsychological Assessment in the Multidisciplinary Diagnostic Process

In the diagnostic guidelines that have been developed for diagnosing FASD in the clinical context (i.e., American Psychiatric Association (APA), 2013; Astley, 2004; Astley & Clarren, 1999; Bertrand et al., 2004; Chudley et al., 2005; Hoyme et al., 2016; Stratton, Howe, & Battaglia, 1996), neuropsychological impairments are a necessary central component. In the forensic context, if current impairments are found during initial neuropsychological assessment, it then is important to confirm prenatal exposure to alcohol and assess whether cognitive, behavioral, and adaptive impairments manifested across the lifespan. In the case of possible FAS or pFAS, a third step involves medical examination to determine if there are visible physical indicia (i.e., characteristic facial anomalies and growth deficit).

Diagnostic guidelines use neuropsychological assessment protocols that vary in specificity. For example, guidelines for cognitive functioning published by the Institute of Medicine (IOM) note "evidence of a complex pattern of behavior or cognitive abnormalities that are inconsistent with the developmental level and cannot be explained by familial background or environment alone, such as learning difficulties; deficits in school performance; poor impulse control; problems in social perception; deficits in higher-level receptive and expressive language; poor capacity for abstraction or metacognition; specific deficits in mathematical skills; or problems in memory, attention, or judgment" (Stratton et al., 1996, p. 76). Proposed diagnostic guidelines for ND-PAE in *DSM-5* (American Psychiatric Association (APA), 2013) refer only to "impairments" in neurocognitive, self-regulation, and adaptive functioning. However, what constitutes an "impairment" is not defined. It is preferable to have diagnostic criteria that are specific and can be consistently and reliably applied across cases.

Some diagnostic guidelines (Astley, 2004; Bertrand et al., 2004; Chudley et al., 2005) set specific test result cut-points to quantify level of impairment as well as a minimum number of neuropsychological domains that must be impaired to constitute an FASD (typically three). However, cut-points vary among these guidelines. Nonetheless, an advantage of using these diagnostic guidelines is they are more highly structured and thus are amenable to being applied consistently and reliably across cases. For example, if an individual demonstrates deficits in only two functional domains (even if impairments are severe), such a presentation would not be consistent with FASD. By contrast, an individual with mild impairments in seven or eight domains would meet criteria. Although an actuarial method of identifying levels and extent of impairments across domains allows for greater diagnostic consistency, given the disparity in guidelines, clinical judgment and experience in recognizing cognitive-behavioral characteristics associated with FASD are critical.

Diagnostic guidelines from Astley and Clarren (1999), Astley's (2004) updated guidelines, and guidelines from Chudley et al. (2005) set cut-points at 2 or more standard deviations below the mean (≤−2 SD). Several studies have concluded the −2 SD cut-point is too restrictive because it results in an unacceptably high number of false-negative conclusions (Sanders, Hudson Breen, & Netelenbos, 2017; Sanders, Netelenbos, & Dei, 2020). In contrast, using the −1 SD cut-point in the CDC guidelines (Bertrand et al., 2004) allows for detection of FASD in persons with mild as well as moderate and severe levels of cognitive impairment, thereby reducing false-negative error. In such cases, the multidisciplinary protocol described in Novick Brown et al. (2010) as well as this and other chapters of this book (see Chaps. 6, 7, and 8) reduces false-positive error. In forensic practice, limiting both types of error increases trustworthiness of the findings (Du, 2017).

In our earlier FASD multidisciplinary assessment protocol for the forensic context (Novick Brown et al., 2010), we proposed a hybrid model incorporating the IOM diagnostic framework and terminology (Stratton et al., 1996; FAS, pFAS, and ARND) and CDC's more structured diagnostic guidelines (Bertrand et al., 2004) in order to quantify IOM's requirement for a "complex pattern of behavior or cognitive abnormalities…" This hybrid approach has been used in hundreds of forensic cases and described in state, federal, and local testimony across the United States with no legal challenge. Since publication of *DSM-5* (American Psychiatric Association (APA), 2013), I have used a similar approach to operationalize diagnostic criteria for ND-PAE, again without legal challenge.

5.3 Neuropsychological Assessment by Domain

Thorough neuropsychological assessment of possible FASD requires testing in multiple domains of cognitive functioning. Widespread testing is necessary because patterns and profiles of FASD expression are largely dependent upon amount of alcohol consumed (Alvik, Aalen, & Lindemann, 2013; Flak et al., 2014) *and* timing of that exposure (Guerri, Bazinet, & Riley, 2009; Maier & West, 2001). Although some types of cognitive impairment are seen very commonly in individuals with FASD (e.g., deficits in math, attention, and executive functioning), not all individuals with diagnosable FASD have deficits in all of these areas. The following sections review the research on neuropsychological functioning in individuals with FASD by functional domain. Where possible, emphasis is on research with adolescents or adults. Each section concludes with recommendations for tests that can be used to assess the domain.

5.3.1 Intellectual Functioning

FASD often is identified as one of the leading preventable causes of intellectual disability (ID; e.g., Williams & Smith, 2015). Despite this description, only a minority of individuals with FASD actually have intellectual functioning within the ID range. In a large study that included many adolescents and adults with FASD, Streissguth et al. (2004) found an average IQ of 80 (borderline to low-average range) in persons with FAS, only 24% of whom had IQs below 70, historically the cut-point for identifying ID. Those with the equivalent of ARND had an average IQ of 88 (low-average range), and only 7% of this group had IQ scores below 70. In an earlier study involving an even larger sample of children, adolescents, and adults (Streissguth et al., 1996), IQ scores ranged from a low of 29 to a high of 142. Thus, full-scale IQ is not the best predictor of FASD.

Although full-scale IQ is not a predictive measure of FASD, performance variability across domains of intellectual functioning appears to be informative. Connor, Sampson, Bookstein, Barr, and Streissguth (2000) found that for individuals with FAS, Verbal IQ was more than 11 points lower than Performance IQ. For those with fetal alcohol effects (FAE), an outdated term for non-dysmorphic FASD, Verbal IQ was 9 points lower than Performance IQ. In contrast, control subjects demonstrated no such between-domain "split." In a longitudinal Swedish study that followed a group of adoptees diagnosed in childhood with FASD (Landgren et al., 2019), median IQ was 86 in childhood but 71 in early adulthood (median age 22 years), which represented a significant decline in functioning over the years.

The most frequently used IQ measures in studies of individuals with FASD are the Wechsler scales. The current edition of this test for adults is the Wechsler Adult Intelligence Scale, Fourth Edition (WAIS-IV; Wechsler, 2008). In forensic matters, group and abbreviated IQ tests are contraindicated.

5.3.2 *Academic Functioning*

Disruptions in schooling (suspension, expulsion, dropping out) are extremely common in children with FASD (Popova, Lange, Burd, Nam, & Rehm, 2016; Streissguth et al., 1996; Streissguth et al., 2004). Additionally, people with FASD often need academic assistance. In one study, 42% of individuals with FASD had received special education services, and approximately two-thirds had received some form of remedial assistance with reading and arithmetic (Streissguth et al., 2004). Mathematical abilities appear particularly impacted in FASD (Jacobson, Dodge, Burden, Klorman, & Jacobson, 2011; Kopera-Frye, Dehaene, & Streissguth, 1996; Streissguth et al., 1996) and may be a hallmark indicator of the diagnosis. In one study (Streissguth et al., 1996), people with FAS performed two-thirds of a standard deviation lower than IQ on a test of math calculation, and those with FAE performed nearly one standard deviation below IQ.

There are several tests of academic functioning that are appropriate for using with adults. These tests include the (Woodcock, McGrew, & Mather, 2001); Wechsler Individual Achievement Test, Fourth Edition (WRAT-4; Wilkinson & Robertson, 2006); and Wide Range Achievement Test, Fifth Edition (WRAT-4; Wilkinson & Robertson, 2006). All of these measures assess word pronunciation, reading comprehension, spelling, and math calculation. Because earlier editions of the WRAT were used in research on adults with FASD (Streissguth et al., 1996, 2004), I use the WRAT in my FASD assessment battery.

5.3.3 Attention

Attention deficits often are the earliest noticeable mental health symptoms in children with FASD. For example, in one study (Streissguth et al., 1996), 51% of children age five and under had attention impairments, and attention problems were the most frequent reason for obtaining therapeutic services. Indeed, 61% of children and adolescents and over 40% of adults had histories of attention impairments. A relatively recent study (Mukherjee, Cook, Norgate, & Price, 2019) found high rates of attention-deficit/hyperactivity disorder (ADHD) symptoms in children and adolescents with FASD, 74% of whom had been diagnosed with ADHD. The Swedish longitudinal study referenced earlier found 62% of children with FASD also were diagnosed with ADHD (Landgren et al., 2019), and when the same individuals were assessed again in adulthood, 70% were identified with ADHD, with nearly a quarter of the sample prescribed medication for the condition.

A number of studies have measured visual and/or auditory sustained attention in children and adolescents with FASD (Coles, Platzman, Lynch, & Freides, 2002; Mattson, Calarco, & Lang, 2006; Nanson & Hiscock, 1990), with fewer studies examining these skills in adults (Bookstein et al., 2002; Connor, Streissguth, Sampson, Bookstein, & Barr, 1999; Kerns, Don, Mateer, & Streissguth, 1997). In a study that compared attention in persons with FASD and controls, those with FASD were less efficient and made more omission errors (failing to respond to a stimuli; Coles et al., 2002). In a similar study, Mattson et al. (2006) found poor accuracy and slower reaction times. Variability in reaction time for both visual and auditory stimuli has been found in both adolescents (Coles et al., 2002) and adults (Connor et al., 1999) with FASD.

With respect to test instruments, most of the research on attention control in FASD has focused on sustained attention. Relatively short tasks, such as Digit Span from the WAIS-IV (Wechsler, 2008) and Digit Vigilance Test (Heaton, Grant, & Matthews, 1991; Lewis & Rennick, 1979) may not be long enough to assess effectively for ability to sustain attention. Furthermore, these tests do not include assessment of response time speed or variability, key features found in the research to be affected by prenatal alcohol exposure. In contrast, computerized measures such as the Conners Continuous Performance Test, now in its third edition (CPT-3; Conners, 2014), the Conners Auditory Test of Attention (CATA; Conners, 2014), or Test of Variables of Attention (TOVA; Leark, Greenberg, Kindschi, Dupuy, & Hughes, 2007) are preferable, as these tests measure for multiple types of error as well as timing and pattern of responding over the course of the task.

5.3.4 Visuospatial Construction

Impairments in visuospatial perception and construction usually are found in FASD (Connor, Baldwin, Barr, Huggins, & Streissguth, 2004; Mattson, Gramling, Riley, Delis, & Jones, 1996; Uecker & Nadel, 1996). For example, one study (Uecker &

Nadel, 1996) found children with FASD were able to remember objects they had been shown but could not identify where the objects had been placed, indicating impairment in spatial awareness. Similarly, Kaemingk and Halverson (2000) found that once visuospatial perceptual abilities were taken into account, there was no difference between control subjects and those with FASD in spatial memory performance. In a third study (Mattson, Gramling, Riley, et al., 1996), children with FASD had greater difficulty reproducing and remembering small details relative to larger components. In a study of adults (Connor et al., 2004) who were administered the Rey Complex Figure Test (RCFT; Meyers & Meyers, 1995), participants with FASD were significantly less able than controls to accurately draw a complex figure. Results of this study indicated good sensitivity and specificity at differentiating adults with FASD from those without FASD.

Several measures assess visuospatial construction abilities. Some of these instruments, including the Brief Visuospatial Memory Test-Revised (BVMT-R; Benedict, 1997) and Beery Visual-Motor Integration Test (VMI; Beery, Buktenica, & Beery, 2010) assess visuospatial construction skills by having examinees draw relatively simple geometric designs. Other measures such as Repeatable Battery for Neuropsychological Status (RBANS; Randolph, 1998) and RCFT (Meyers & Meyers, 1995) use relatively complex designs with smaller details, which requires more organization skills. Simple measures may produce more false-negative results than more complex measures. For this reason and because the measure has proven itself in research on adults with FASD, the RCFT measure is recommended in forensic settings.

5.3.5 Learning and Memory

Many studies of individuals with FASD have found impairments in language-based learning and memory. In one such study of children with FASD, researchers found impairments in learning lists of words, although study participants were able to retain what they had learned (Mattson, Riley, Delis, Stern, & Jones, 1996). Studies have found that children with FASD have particular difficulty with perseveration (repeating the same word multiple times) and intrusions (adding words not included on the target list; Gibbard, Wass, & Clarke, 2003; Mattson, Riley, Delis, et al., 1996; Pei, Rinaldi, Rasmussen, Massey, & Massey, 2008). In adults, a similar pattern of impairments in learning and memory was found on a list learning task (Bookstein et al., 2002). Contextual or story-based learning also has been identified as an area of impairment for adults with FASD (Novick Brown, Gudjonsson, & Connor, 2011). In this latter study, adults with FASD demonstrated significantly poor immediate and delayed recall of a simple story compared to control subjects.

Visuospatial learning and memory problems also have been found in research on individuals with prenatal exposure and FASD (Gray & Streissguth, 1990; Streissguth, Barr, Sampson, & Bookstein, 1994). For example, children with FAS performed less well than control subjects on a maze learning task (Gray & Streissguth, 1990).

The same test was found to be more sensitive than other short-term memory tasks in individuals with high levels of prenatal alcohol exposure (Streissguth et al., 1994). Another study using the same maze learning task found that in addition to impairments in learning and memory, persons with FAS made many perseverative errors and took longer to learn the maze pattern than control subjects (Olson, Feldman, Streissguth, Sampson, & Bookstein, 1998). Uecker and Nadel (1996) found that while children with FAS were able to remember familiar objects, they showed impairment in ability to recall the spatial arrangement of those objects.

With respect to test instruments, child and adult versions of the California Verbal Learning Test (CVLT; Delis, Kramer, Kaplan, & Ober, 2017) have been used extensively in research on individuals with FASD. Therefore, CVLT-3 is a good test to use with adults when assessing language-based list learning abilities. The Gudjonsson Suggestibility Scale (GSS; Gudjonsson, 1997) is effective for assessing contextual learning and memory and has the added advantage of also assessing suggestibility, which often is impaired in FASD (see more discussion below). Visuospatial memory can be assessed by using either the BVMT-R (Benedict, 1997) or memory components of the RCFT (Meyers & Meyers, 1995). Since the RCFT is the recommended task for assessing visuospatial construction (see previous discussion), adding the memory components of this test would be appropriate and efficient.

5.3.6 *Motor Coordination*

Motor coordination impairments in children and adults are found in the FASD literature. Although generally, motor coordination may not be a particularly important issue to address in criminal proceedings, it is a very important domain in FASD assessment. In their review of the FASD literature, Doney et al. (2014) found complex fine motor skills were impaired more often than basic fine motor skills, especially in individuals exposed in utero to moderate-to-high levels of alcohol. Gross motor impairments also have been found in a study of children with FASD (Lucas et al., 2016), as have difficulties with postural balance (Roebuck, Simmons, Mattson, & Riley, 1998). Landgren et al. (2019) found 47% of the young adults they had been following since childhood exhibited dysdiadochokinesis (difficulty making rapidly alternating movements, particularly with the limbs), and 16% showed disturbances in balance. Similar deficits have been observed in adults (Connor, Sampson, Streissguth, Bookstein, & Barr, 2006). In this latter study, adults with FASD exhibited greater difficulty with fine motor control, diadochokinesis, finger tapping and sequencing, and balance than neurotypical individuals. Notably, impairments in motor coordination in this study were associated with significant thinning of the corpus callosum (Bookstein et al., 2002).

Many measures of fine and gross motor coordination described in the FASD literature are research instruments that have not been developed or marketed for neuropsychological assessment purposes. However, there are some clinically available tests that address some of the motor control problems found in the research. For example, Finger Tapping (FT) and Grooved Pegboard (GP) (Heaton et al., 1991) are two well-established and clinically available tests of fine motor coordination and as such are recommended as components in an FASD test battery.

5.3.7 *Processing Speed*

Processing speed impairment is associated with many neurological conditions as well as FASD, including traumatic brain injury, stroke, and multiple sclerosis. For example, Burden, Jacobson, and Jacobson (2005) found children exposed to prenatal alcohol demonstrated slower processing speed and efficiency. Slow processing speed was particularly evident on tasks requiring pronounced mental effort but were less prominent on tasks requiring more automatic responding. In a neurological study, children with FASD showed slower event-related potential latencies than control subjects (Burden et al., 2009). In a study of adolescents with FASD, researchers found poorer processing speed and accuracy in adolescents with FAS compared to healthy controls (Olson et al., 1998).

Several tasks embedded in measures comprising the proposed neuropsychological assessment battery for FASD address processing speed. Such tasks include the reaction time score from CPT-3 (Conners, 2014), Trails A (Heaton et al., 1991) and word-reading and color-naming tasks in the Stroop Color Word Test (STROOP; Golden & Freshwater, 2002). In addition, processing speed index on the WAIS-IV (Wechsler, 2008) is a proxy measure.

5.3.8 *Executive Functioning and Suggestibility*

Executive functions are described as future-oriented integrative abilities (Denckla, 1996). Eslinger (1996) described executive functions as a group of cognitive abilities that include self-regulation, sequencing, cognitive flexibility, inhibition, planning, and organization. Rather than a solitary construct, executive functioning embodies a group of skills that rely on more basic abilities in order to achieve goals.

One aspect of executive functioning is idea generation. Compared to control subjects, both children and adults with FASD generate fewer words based on letter cues (Connor et al., 2000; Kodituwakku et al., 2006; Kodituwakku, Handmaker, Cutler, Weathersby, & Handmaker, 1995). Research also has found that compared with controls, people with FASD demonstrate poorer visuospatial idea generation when asked to create as many unique designs as possible (Connor et al., 2000; Kerns et al., 1997). Working memory, which involves holding bits of information in mind while manipulating that information, is a specific executive function skill that often is impaired in children with FASD (Kodituwakku et al., 1995) as well as adults (Connor et al., 2000). Response inhibition impairments also have been documented in individuals with FASD (Connor et al., 2000; Mattson, Goodman, Caine, Delis, &

Riley, 1999). Impairments in cognitive flexibility and set shifting, ability to quickly and easily switch focus of attention, have been documented in individuals with FASD. In particular, research finds that when adults are asked to alternate rules on a task of visual scanning, those with FASD perform more slowly and make more errors than control subjects (Connor et al., 2000). Planning, problem-solving, reasoning, and perseveration are core areas of executive functioning that tend to be impaired in children and adults with FASD (Astley et al., 2009; Bookstein et al., 2002; Connor et al., 2000; Kodituwakku et al., 1995; Mattson et al., 1999; Rangmar, Dahlgren Sandberg, Aronson, & Fahlke, 2015). Compared to control subjects, those with FASD tend to do less preplanning, break rules more often, get stuck on an unsuccessful strategy (perseveration), and employ less efficient problem-solving than controls (Connor et al., 2000; Kodituwakku et al., 1995; Mattson et al., 1999). Notably, those with FASD also demonstrate significantly more impairment as tasks increase in difficulty (Green et al., 2009).

One aspect of executive functioning that has not been well researched is suggestibility, despite research indicating people with FASD are quite gullible and easily led by others (Clark, Lutke, Minnes, & Ouellette-Kuntz, 2004; Streissguth, Bookstein, Barr, Press, & Sampson, 1998). Thought to contribute to the high rate of trouble with the law found in FASD (Streissguth et al., 1996; Streissguth et al., 2004), interrogative suggestibility has direct implications regarding case outcomes when suspects with FASD are interviewed by police officers, as described by Gudjonsson and Clark (1986). In fact, there is considerable concern about the potential for false or exaggerated confessions in this population (Conry & Fast, 2000; Fast & Conry, 2004; Pollard et al., 2004). Novick Brown et al. (2011) assessed these issues in a pilot study. Upon initial questioning, adults with FASD were not more likely to endorse misleading information compared to normative data. However, when told they had made errors and questioning would need to be repeated, they were significantly more likely to change their responses, indicating a tendency to acquiesce to this mild pressure. Overall, adults with FASD in the sample exhibited a significant level of suggestibility.

Because of the many aspects of executive functioning, multiple tests are recommended. Language-based idea generation can be assessed with the Controlled Oral Word Association Test (COWAT; Heaton et al., 1991), and visuospatial idea generation can be investigated with Ruff's Figural Fluency Test (RFF; Ruff, 1996). A clinically available working memory test is the Paced Auditory Serial Addition Test (PASAT; Gronwall, 1977). However, this test requires considerable math ability, an area of particular difficulty for individuals with FASD (Streissguth et al., 1996). Therefore, Auditory Consonant Trigrams Test (ACT) is a better measure (Stuss, Stethem, & Pelchat, 1988; Stuss, Stethem, & Poirier, 1987). To assess set shifting, Trails B (Heaton et al., 1991) is recommended. The Test of General Reasoning Abilities (TOGRA; Reynolds, 2014) also assesses switching in the context of reasoning and problem-solving, as the test requires quickly changing focus among language-based, visuospatial, and mathematical tasks. Many FASD studies use the STROOP (Golden & Freshwater, 2002) to assess response inhibition. Because planning and problem-solving skills are critical executive function skills that are particularly difficult for persons with FASD, several tests are recommended. Wisconsin Card Sorting Test (WCST) (Heaton, 2005) is used frequently in FASD to measure planning, problem-solving, adaptability, and perseveration. Also recommended are the Delis-Kaplan Executive Function System (D-KEFS) Proverbs task for verbal abstract reasoning and Tower task for visuospatial sequential planning (Delis, Kaplan, & Kramer, 2001). As noted, the previously mentioned TOGRA not only is helpful in assessing facile shifting of attention in problem-solving but also can detect problems with processing speed. Finally, the GSS (Gudjonsson, 1997) is recommended to assess for suggestibility.

5.3.9 Adaptive Functioning

Adaptive functioning, or ability to independently apply knowledge on a day-to-day basis, is crucial for successful independent living. Typically, adaptive functioning is assessed with structured interviews of collateral respondents (e.g., parents, caregivers, or others) regarding evaluee behavior. One such assessment is the Vineland Adaptive Behavior Scales, now in the third edition (Vineland-3; Sparrow, Cicchetti, & Saulnier, 2016). Many studies using the Vineland have found adaptive impairments in FASD (Jirikowic, Kartin, & Olson, 2008; Streissguth et al., 1991; Streissguth et al., 1996; Streissguth et al., 2004). In addition to respondent reports of impairments in adaptive functioning, several measures directly test various aspects of adaptive functioning, such as social cognition and recognition of emotion, prosody (tone of voice), and facial expression (Greenbaum, Stevens, Nash, Koren, & Rovet, 2009; Kerns, Siklos, Baker, & Müller, 2016; Monnot, Lovallo, Nixon, & Ross, 2002).

Vineland-3 (Sparrow et al., 2016), an adaptive measure that has been used extensively in FASD research, can be administered to respondents who have observed evaluee behavior on a regular basis. Items on the Vineland consist of behaviors in three adaptive domains (communications, daily living skills, and socialization). Respondents rate how often they have observed the evaluee performing the behavior (i.e., often/always, sometimes, or never). In the case of retrospective assessment, the Vineland-3 manual (Sparrow et al., 2016) recommends administering the measure to two or more respondents to determine consistency. In addition to multiple respondents, directly testing primary adaptive domains in an evaluee at the time of cognitive assessment provides another way to cross-check consistency with Vineland results. For example, the Neuropsychological Assessment Battery: Auditory Comprehension test (NAB:AC; Stern & White, 2003) could be used to directly measure receptive communication skills, instruction following, and ability to understand and properly respond to convoluted questions. Expressive and receptive communication skills can be assessed directly with the Vocabulary Assessment Scales (VAS; Gerhardstein Nader, 2013). The Texas Functional Living Scale (TFLS; Cullum, Weiner, & Saine, 2009) or Independent Living Scales (ILS; Persel, 2012) are recommended for directly measuring day-to-day practical skills, although both instruments are slightly dated. Finally, in order to assess social functioning including emotion regulation, facial expression, and prosody, Advanced Clinical Solutions' Social Cognition test (ACS:SC; Pearson, 2009) is recommended.

5.4 Recommended Test Battery

As noted, many of the tests described in this chapter are recommended in a neuropsychological test battery because versions of the specific tests were used in research on adults with FASD. These tests include WAIS, WRAT, CVLT, GSS, RCFT, WCST, COWAT, RFF, STROOP, ACT, and Vineland. Although the other tests in the proposed battery (Table 5.1) have not been included in FASD research studies, they are included because they address skills and abilities known to be affected in FASD. The battery of tests below is recommended for use in forensic evaluations that address whether evaluees exhibit cognitive and adaptive functioning characteristic of FASD.

5.5 Presenting Test Results

When presenting complicated data, it often is helpful to triers of fact to receive information in more than one modality. For example, one way to present test data in a report is to list standardized scores, with mean and standard deviation for each test (e.g., reporting an evaluee's Full-Scale IQ score and noting that the mean or average score for the test is 100 with a standard deviation of 15). This allows readers of neuropsychological evaluation reports to calculate how far from the mean a particular score is, which is fine for psychologists or others familiar with test score normative data and varying scales of normative data (e.g., T-scores, z-scores, scaled scores). However, as the target audience for neuropsychological reports in forensic assessments is triers of fact with varying levels of statistical knowledge, normative data should be described in lay terms, so it is easily understandable. For example, a T-score of 29 (mean = 50, standard deviation = 10) might be described as performance within the "moderately impaired range." Deviations from the mean and percentiles also could be provided, with interpretations regarding direction of strength or weakness. It is important in such cases to present "cut-points" or thresholds used in making interpretive statements to help readers contextualize levels of functioning, such as the guide in Table 5.2:

A third, and arguably the best, way to present test data so it is easy for legal professionals and juries to understand is visual representations in graph or table format. For example, Fig. 5.1 is a graphical representation of an evaluee's pattern of performance on a forensic test battery. In creating the graph, all test scores are converted to standardized scores (z-scores) wherein mean or average score on each test is 0 with a standard deviation of 1. By doing such a conversion, results from tests with

Table 5.1 Test battery recommended in neuropsychological assessment for possible FASD

Domain	Instrument	Developer
Intellectual functioning	Wechsler Adult Intelligence Scale—Fourth Edition (WAIS-IV)	Wechsler, (2008)
Academic achievement	Wide Range Achievement Test—Fifth Edition (WRAT-5)	Wilkinson & Robertson (2006)
Memory	California Verbal Learning Test—Third Edition (CVLT-3)	Delis et al. (2017)
	Gudjonsson Suggestibility Scale–2 (Gss-2)—Story Learning	Gudjonsson (1997)
	Rey Complex Figure Test (RCFT)	Meyers & Meyers (1995)
Attention	Conners' Continuous Performance Test—Third Edition (CPT-3)	Conners (2014)
Motor coordination	Grooved Pegboard Test (GP)	Heaton et al. (1991)
	Finger Tapping Test (FT)	Heaton et al. (1991)
Executive functioning	Wisconsin Card Sorting Test—Fourth Edition (WCST-4)	Heaton, (2005)
	Delis-Kaplan Executive Function System (D-KEFS) Tower Test & Proverbs Test	Delis et al. (2001)
	Test of General Reasoning Abilities (TOGRA)	Reynolds (2014)
	Controlled Oral Word Association Test (COWAT)	Heaton et al. (1991)
	Ruff's Figural Fluency Test (RFF)	Ruff (1996)
	Stroop Color and Word Test (STROOP)	Golden & Freshwater (2002)
	Trail Making Test (TMT)	Heaton et al. (1991)
	Auditory Consonant Trigrams Test (ACT)	Stuss et al. (1988) Stuss et al. (1987)
	Gudjonsson Suggestibility Scale—2 (GSS-2)	Gudjonsson, (1997)
Adaptive functioning	Vineland Adaptive Behavior Scales—Third Ed. (Vineland-3)	Sparrow et al. (2016)
	NAB: Auditory Comprehension (NAB:AC)	Stern & White (2003)
	ACS: Social Cognition (ACS:SC)	Pearson, (2009)
	Texas Functional Living Scale (TFLS)	Cullum et al., (2009)
Effort & malingering	Combination of Several Tests, Both Stand Alone and Embedded within Other Tests	

different normative scales can be compared easily to each other on an apples-to-apples basis that is further adjusted by making the direction of deficit consistent for all of the tests (i.e., lower scores = poorer performance). The graph is subdivided by functional domains listed across the top of the graph, with individual tests listed across the bottom. In order to help readers orient to the z-scale, the horizontal green line represents average performance on all of the tests. Consistent with CDC guidelines (Bertrand et al., 2004) described earlier in this chapter, the horizontal red line depicts impaired functioning (i.e., −2 SD for intellectual testing and −1 SD for all other tests). The evaluee's performance on each test is shown by a blue dot above

Table 5.2 A descriptive guide to performance level

Performance range	Context
Superior	At least 97% of the population did more poorly
High average	At least 84% of the population did more poorly
Average	Approximately 50% of the population performed above/below
Low average	At least 73% of the population performed better
Borderline	At least 84% of the population performed better
Mildly impaired	At least 86% of the population performed better
Mildly-to-moderately impaired	At least 95% of the population performed better
Moderately impaired	At least 98% of the population performed better
Moderately-to-severely impaired	At least 99.5% of the population performed better
Severely impaired	At least 99.9% of the population performed better

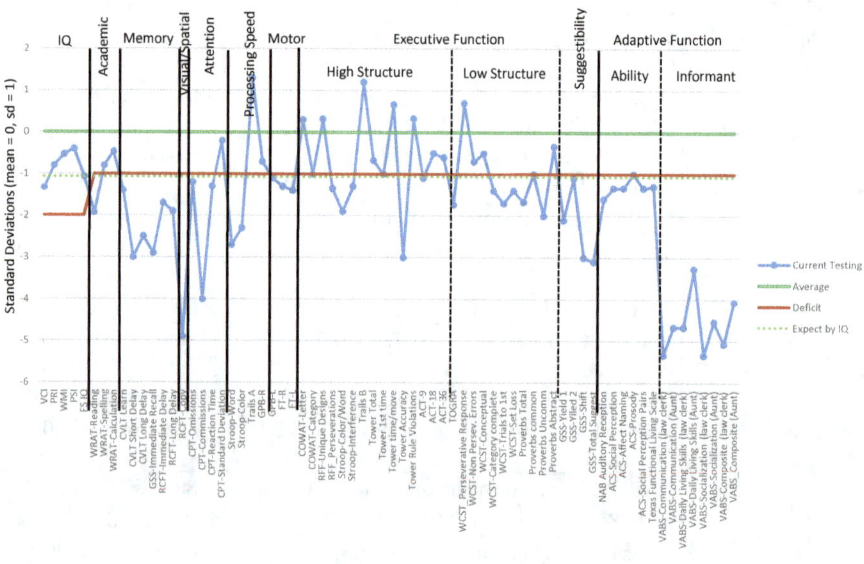

Fig. 5.1 Scores on a neuropsychological test battery shown in graphical format

the test, with connecting lines to show overall performance pattern. Finally, the horizontal dotted green line represents Full-Scale IQ, so performance on other tests can be compared to it.

Graphical presentation of test results makes it easy to understand an evaluee's relative strengths and weaknesses. For example, in Fig. 5.1, the evaluee's test performance reflects significant deficits in 10 domains (academics, memory, visuospatial construction, attention, motor coordination, processing speed, executive functioning, and all three aspects of adaptive functioning). Visuospatial construction performance is particularly deficient (i.e., −5 SD), as can be seen by comparing the test result to the z-scale on the left. Using a graphical presentation of test data such as Fig. 5.1 also clarifies variable performance across tests, which is a hallmark finding in FASD (Sheliza, Kerns, Mulligan, Olson, & Astley, 2018). Additional graphs can be used to demonstrate test performance patterns often seen in FASD. One such pattern is variability across domains of intellectual functioning (Connor et al., 2000), which is depicted in Fig. 5.2.

Research has shown that children, adolescents, and adults with FASD tend to perform worse than expected on academic achievement tests in relation to level of intellectual functioning. Furthermore, day-to-day adaptive functioning often is even more impacted (Streissguth et al., 1996). This downward decline in functioning from intellectual to academic skills and then to adaptive functioning is a rather consistent pattern in FASD. Indeed, in many cases, even when IQ is in the average range, persons with FASD typically exhibit adaptive behavior that falls within the intellectually disabled range (Greenspan, Novick Brown, & Edwards, 2016). Figure 5.3 graphically represents this characteristic downward slope.

The left side of Fig. 5.3 shows average test scores for IQ, Academic, and Adaptive Functioning in research with a large FASD sample (Streissguth et al., 1996). The right side of Fig. 5.3 shows an evaluee's performance on the same tests. This side-by-side juxtaposition allows for comparison of an evaluee's test pattern with the characteristic FASD pattern. In this case, the downward pattern of test results in this individual (i.e., performing much worse than predicted by IQ) is consistent with the research.

Apart from determining whether evaluees exhibit the characteristic downward sloping pattern found in the FASD research, graphical representations of test data also can be illustrative (and therefore helpful to triers of fact) in showing consistency or inconsistency when multiple similar assessments have been administered over time (Fig. 5.4).

Generally, graphical representations of test data help judges and juries "see" the patterns of relative strengths and impairments in evaluees. Once oriented to the

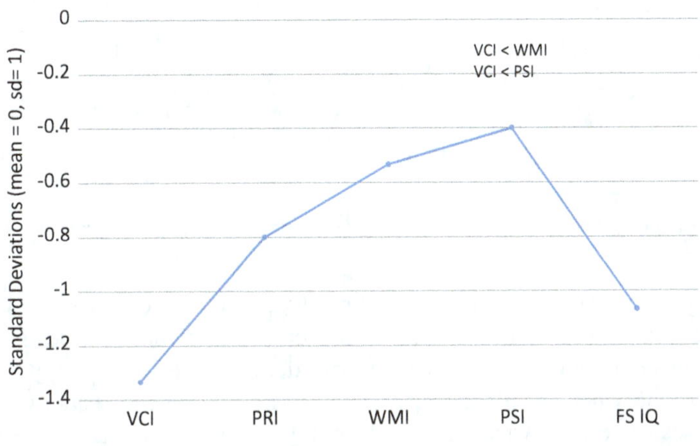

Fig. 5.2 Graphical representation of an evaluee's performance across domains of intellectual functioning

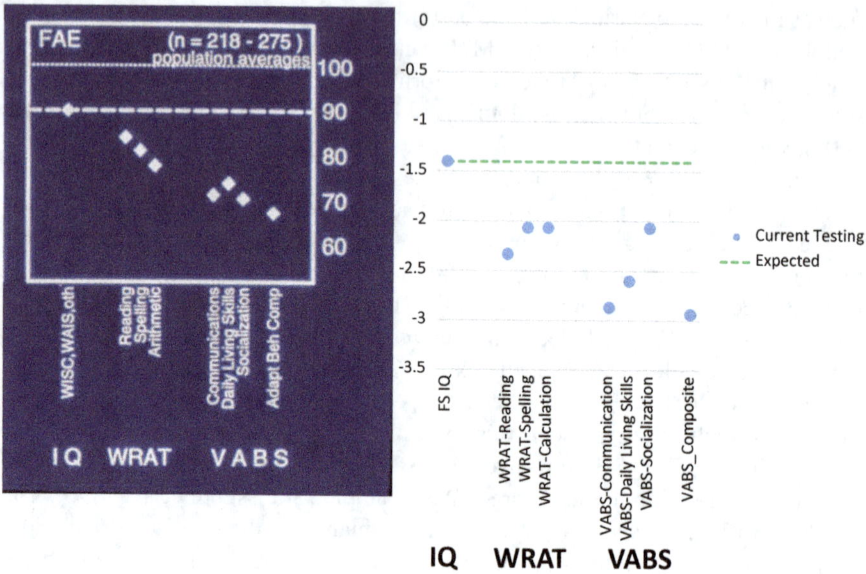

Fig. 5.3 Downward sloping test results (IQ, achievement, adaptive) in an evaluee with a low-average IQ

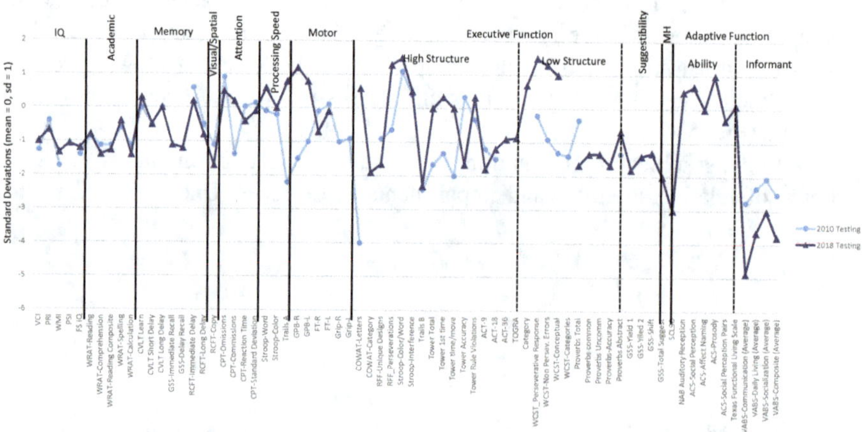

Fig. 5.4 Similarity (and change) in an evaluee's performance on many of the same tests over time

scale (e.g., z-score transformation of test results), triers of fact can appreciate visually whether evaluee test performance reflects the variability typically seen in FASD, immediately detect which functional domains are significantly impacted, and determine whether an evaluee's test performance matches patterns found in FASD research (e.g., downward slope from IQ to academics to adaptive functioning). In other words, a picture is worth a thousand words when it comes to explaining a complex subject.

5.6 Conclusion

This chapter has described how comprehensive neuropsychological evaluation is a vital first step in the adult FASD diagnostic process. Importantly, psychometric testing can identify if an evaluee's current pattern of cognitive functioning not only is consistent with diagnostic guidelines for FASD but also is consistent with characteristic empirical patterns. In diagnostic multidisciplinary assessments, test information is combined with information from other specialists (e.g., evidence of prenatal exposure to alcohol; documentation of a lifelong history of cognitive, behavioral and adaptive difficulties; evaluation of facial and other physical features; neuroimaging) to reach diagnostic conclusions. Patterns of cognitive strengths and weaknesses shed light on an evaluee's day-to-day functioning, explaining how brain functioning has affected behavior. Importantly, illustrating an evaluee's current neuropsychological functioning in graphic form to visually show its relation to underlying neurological damage caused by prenatal alcohol exposure provides functional capacity information that is directly relevant to case data such as alleged offense conduct. Documenting and describing this linkage or "nexus" during testimony can assist judges and juries in understanding offense conduct in a broader perspective, potentially assisting triers of fact in making decisions.

References

Alvik, A., Aalen, O. O., & Lindemann, R. (2013). Early fetal binge alcohol exposure predicts high behavioral symptom scores in 5.5-year-old children. *Alcoholism: Clinical and Experimental Research, 37*(11), 1954–1962. https://doi.org/10.1111/acer.12182

American Psychiatric Association (APA). (2013). *Diagnostic and statistical manual of mental disorders (DSM-5)* (5th ed.). Arlington, VA: American Psychiatric Association.

Astley, S. J. (2004). *Diagnostic guide for fetal alcohol spectrum disorders: The 4-digit diagnostic code* (3rd ed.). Seattle: University of Washington.

Astley, S. J., & Clarren, S. K. (1999). *Diagnostic guide for fetal alcohol syndrome and related conditions: The 4-digit diagnostic code* (2nd ed.). Seattle: University of Washington Press.

Astley, S. J., Olson, H. C., Kerns, K., Brooks, A., Aylward, E. H., Coggins, T. E., … Richards, T. (2009). Neuropsychological and behavioral outcomes from a comprehensive magnetic resonance study of children with fetal alcohol spectrum disorders. *Canadian Journal of Clinical Pharmacology, 16*(1), e178–e201.

Beery, K. E., Buktenica, N. A., & Beery, N. A. (2010). *The Beery–Buktenica developmental test of visual-motor integration: Administration, scoring, and teaching manual* (6th ed.). Minneapolis, MN: Pearson.

Benedict, R. H. B. (1997). *Brief visuospatial memory test (rev. ed.)*. Odessa, FL: Psychological Assessment Resources.

Bertrand, J., Floyd, L. L., Weber, M. K., O'Connor, M., Johnson, K. A., Riley, E., & Cohen, D. (2004). *Fetal alcohol syndrome: Guidelines for referral and diagnosis*. Atlanta, GA: Centers for Disease Control and Prevention. https://www.cdc.gov/ncbddd/fasd/documents/fas_guidelines_accessible.pdf.

Bookstein, F. L., Streissguth, A. P., Sampson, P. D., Connor, P. D., & Barr, H. M. (2002). Corpus callosum shape and neuropsychological deficits in adult males with heavy fetal alcohol exposure. *NeuroImage, 15*(1), 233–251. https://doi.org/10.1006/nimg.2001.0977

Burden, M. J., Andrew, C., Saint-Amour, D., Meintjes, E. M., Molteno, C. D., Hoyme, H. E., … Jacobson, S. W. (2009). The effects of fetal alcohol syndrome on response execution and inhibition: An event-related potential study. *Alcoholism: Clinical and Experimental Research, 33*(11), 1994–2004. https://doi.org/10.1111/j.1530-0277.2009.01038.x

Burden, M. J., Jacobson, S. W., & Jacobson, J. L. (2005). Relation of prenatal alcohol exposure to cognitive processing speed and efficiency in childhood. *Alcoholism: Clinical and Experimental Research, 29*(8), 1473–1483. https://doi.org/10.1097/01.alc.0000175036.34076.a0

Chudley, A. E., Conry, J., Cook, J. L., Loock, C., Rosales, T., & LeBlanc, N. (2005). Fetal alcohol spectrum disorder: Canadian guidelines for diagnosis. *CMAJ: Canadian Medical Association Journal, 172*(Suppl. 5), S1–S21. https://doi.org/10.1503/cmaj.1040302

Clark, E., Lutke, J., Minnes, P., & Ouellette-Kuntz, H. (2004). Secondary disabilities among adults with fetal alcohol spectrum disorder in British Columbia. *Journal of FAS International, 2*(e13), 1–12. https://citeseerx.ist.psu.edu/viewdoc/download?doi=10.1.1.510.9908&rep=rep1&type=pdf.

Coles, C. D., Platzman, K. A., Lynch, M. E., & Freides, D. (2002). Auditory and visual sustained attention in adolescents prenatally exposed to alcohol. *Alcoholism: Clinical and Experimental Research, 26*(2), 263–271. https://doi.org/10.1097/00000374-200202000-00015

Conners, C. K. (2014). *Conners continuous performance test* (3rd ed.). Toronto, ON: Multi-Health Systems.

Connor, P. D., Baldwin, K. D., Barr, H. M., Huggins, J. E., & Streissguth, A. P. (2004). Visuoconstructional impairment in patients with fetal alcohol spectrum disorders. *Alcoholism: Clinical and Experimental Research, 28*, 45A.

Connor, P. D., Sampson, P. D., Bookstein, F. L., Barr, H. M., & Streissguth, A. P. (2000). Direct and indirect effects of prenatal alcohol damage on executive function. *Developmental Neuropsychology, 18*(3), 331–354. https://doi.org/10.1207/S15326942O4Connor

Connor, P. D., Sampson, P. D., Streissguth, A. P., Bookstein, F. L., & Barr, H. M. (2006). Effects of prenatal alcohol exposure on fine motor coordination and balance: A study of two adult samples. *Neuropsychologia, 44*(5), 744–751. https://doi.org/10.1016/j.neuropsychologia.2005.07.016

Connor, P. D., Streissguth, A. P., Sampson, P. D., Bookstein, F. L., & Barr, H. M. (1999). Individual differences in auditory and visual attention among fetal alcohol-affected adults. *Alcoholism: Clinical and Experimental Research, 23*(8), 1395–1402. https://doi.org/10.1111/j.1530-0277.1999.tb04362.x

Conry, J. L., & Fast, D. K. (2000). *Fetal alcohol syndrome and the criminal justice system*. Vancouver, BC: British Columbia Fetal Alcohol Syndrome Resource Society.

Cullum, C. M., Weiner, M. F., & Saine, K. C. (2009). *Texas functional living scale examiner's manual*. San Antonio, TX: Pearson.

Delis, D. C., Kaplan, E., & Kramer, J. H. (2001). *The Delis-Kaplan executive function system (D-KEFS)*. San Antonio, TX: Psychological.

Delis, D. C., Kramer, J. H., Kaplan, E., & Ober, B. A. (2017). *California Verbal Learning Test (CVLT-3)* (3rd ed.). San Antonio, TX: Pearson.

Denckla, M. B. (1996). A theory and model of executive function: A neuropsychological perspective. In G. R. Lyon & N. A. Krasnegor (Eds.), *Attention, memory, and executive function* (pp. 263–278). Baltimore, MD: Brookes.

Doney, R., Lucas, B. R., Jones, T., Howat, P., Sauer, K., & Elliott, E. J. (2014). Fine motor skills in children with prenatal alcohol exposure or fetal alcohol spectrum disorder. *Journal of Developmental and Behavioral Pediatrics, 35*(9), 598–609. https://doi.org/10.1097/dbp.0000000000000107

Du, M. (2017). Analysis of errors in forensic science. *Journal of Forensic Science and Medicine, 3*(3), 139–143. https://doi.org/10.4103/jfsm.jfsm_8_17

Eslinger, P. J. (1996). Conceptualizing, describing, and measuring components of executive function: A summary. In G. R. Lyon & N. A. Krasnegor (Eds.), *Attention, memory, and executive function* (pp. 367–395). Baltimore, MD: Brookes.

Fast, D. K., & Conry, J. L. (2004). The challenge of fetal alcohol syndrome in the criminal legal system. *Addiction Biology, 9*(2), 161–166. https://doi.org/10.1080/13556210410001717042

Flak, A. L., Su, S., Bertrand, J., Denny, C. H., Kesmodel, U. S., & Cogswell, M. E. (2014). The association of mild, moderate, and binge prenatal alcohol exposure and child neuropsychological outcomes: A meta-analysis. *Alcoholism: Clinical and Experimental Research, 38*(1), 214–226. https://doi.org/10.1111/acer.12214

Forrester, P., Davis, C. G., Moser, A., MacPherson, P., Gobeil, R., & Chudley, A. E. (2015). *Assessing fetal alcohol spectrum disorder in women offenders. Research report R-346*. Ottawa, ON: Correctional Service of Canada.

Gerhardstein Nader, R. (2013). *Vocabulary assessment scales—Expressive and receptive*. Lutz, FL: Psychological Assessment Resources.

Gibbard, W. B., Wass, P., & Clarke, M. E. (2003). The neuropsychological implications of prenatal alcohol exposure. *Canadian Academy of Child and Adolescent Psychiatry, 12*(3), 72–76.

Golden, C. J., & Freshwater, S. M. (2002). *The stroop color and word test: A manual for clinical and experimental uses*. Wood Dale, IL: Stoelting.

Gray, J., & Streissguth, A. P. (1990). Memory deficits and life adjustment in adults with fetal alcohol syndrome: A case control study. *Alcoholism: Clinical and Experimental Research, 14*(2), 294. https://doi.org/10.1111/j.1530-0277.1990.tb00486.x

Green, C. R., Mihic, A. M., Nikkel, S. M., Stade, B. C., Rasmussen, C., Munoz, D. P., & Reynolds, J. N. (2009). Executive function deficits in children with fetal alcohol spectrum disorders (FASD) measured using the Cambridge neuropsychological tests automated battery (CANTAB). *Journal of Child Psychology and Psychiatry, 50*(6), 688–697. https://doi.org/10.1111/j.1469-7610.2008.01990.x

Greenbaum, R. L., Stevens, S. A., Nash, K., Koren, G., & Rovet, J. (2009). Social cognitive and emotional processing abilities of children with fetal alcohol spectrum disorders: A comparison with attention deficit hyperactivity disorder. *Alcoholism: Clinical and Experimental Research, 33*(10), 1656–1670. https://doi.org/10.1111/j.1530-0277.2009.01003.x

Greenspan, S., Novick Brown, N., & Edwards, W. (2016). FASD and the concept of "intellectual disability equivalence.". In M. Nelson & M. Trussler (Eds.), *Fetal alcohol spectrum disorders in adults: Ethical and legal perspectives* (pp. 241–266). Amsterdam and New York: Springer.

Gronwall, D. M. A. (1977). Paced auditory serial-addition task: A measure of recovery from concussion. *Perceptual and Motor Skills, 44*(2), 367–373. https://doi.org/10.2466/pms.1977.44.2.367

Gudjonsson, G. H. (1997). *The Gudjonsson suggestibility scales manual*. Hove: Psychology Press.

Gudjonsson, G. H., & Clark, N. K. (1986). Suggestibility in police interrogation: A social psychological model. *Social Behaviour, 1*(2), 83–104.

Guerri, C., Bazinet, A., & Riley, E. P. (2009). Foetal alcohol spectrum disorders and alterations in brain and behaviour. *Alcohol and Alcoholism, 44*(2), 108–114. https://doi.org/10.1093/alcalc/agn105

Heaton, R. K. (2005). *Wisconsin card sorting test: Computer version 4–research edition (WCST: CV4)*. Lutz, FL: Psychological Assessment Resources.

Heaton, R. K., Grant, I., & Matthews, C. G. (1991). *Comprehensive norms for an extended Halstead-Reitan battery: Demographic corrections, research findings, and clinical applications*. Odessa, FL: Psychological Assessment Resources.

Hoyme, H. E., Kalberg, W. O., Elliott, A. J., Blankenship, J., Buckley, D., Marais, A.-S., … May, P. A. (2016). Updated clinical guidelines for diagnosing fetal alcohol spectrum disorders. *Pediatrics, 138*(2), e20154256. https://doi.org/10.1542/peds.2015-4256

Jacobson, J. L., Dodge, N. C., Burden, M. J., Klorman, R., & Jacobson, S. W. (2011). Number processing in adolescents with prenatal alcohol exposure and ADHD: Differences in the neurobehavioral phenotype. *Alcoholism: Clinical and Experimental Research, 35*(3), 431–442. https://doi.org/10.1111/j.1530-0277.2010.01360.x

Jirikowic, T., Kartin, D., & Olson, H. C. (2008). Children with fetal alcohol spectrum disorders: A descriptive profile of adaptive function. *Canadian Journal of Occupational Therapy, 75*(4), 238–248. https://doi.org/10.1177/000841740807500411

Jones, K. L., & Smith, D. W. (1973). Recognition of the fetal alcohol syndrome in early infancy. *Lancet, 302*(7836), 999–1001. https://doi.org/10.1016/s0140-6736(73)91092-1

Jones, K. L., Smith, D. W., Ulleland, C. N., & Streissguth, A. P. (1973). Pattern of malformation in offspring of chronic alcoholic mothers. *Lancet, 301*(7815), 1267–1271. https://doi.org/10.1016/s0140-6736(73)91291-9

Kaemingk, K. L., & Halverson, P. T. (2000). Spatial memory following prenatal alcohol exposure: More than a material specific memory deficit. *Child Neuropsychology, 6*(2), 115–128. https://doi.org/10.1076/chin.6.2.115.7058

Kerns, K. A., Don, A., Mateer, C. A., & Streissguth, A. P. (1997). Cognitive deficits in nonretarded adults with fetal alcohol syndrome. *Journal of Learning Disabilities, 30*(6), 685–693. https://doi.org/10.1177/002221949703000612

Kerns, K. A., Siklos, S., Baker, L., & Müller, U. (2016). Emotion recognition in children with fetal alcohol spectrum disorders. *Child Neuropsychology, 22*(3), 255–275. https://doi.org/10.1080/09297049.2014.993310

Kodituwakku, P. W., Adnams, C. M., Hay, A., Kitching, A. E., Burger, E., Kalberg, W. O., … May, P. A. (2006). Letter and category fluency in children with fetal alcohol syndrome from a community in South Africa. *Journal of Studies on Alcohol, 67*(4), 502–509. https://doi.org/10.15288/jsa.2006.67.502

Kodituwakku, P. W., Handmaker, N. S., Cutler, S. K., Weathersby, E. K., & Handmaker, S. D. (1995). Specific impairments in self-regulation in children exposed to alcohol prenatally. *Alcoholism: Clinical and Experimental Research, 19*(6), 1558–1564. https://doi.org/10.1111/j.1530-0277.1995.tb01024.x

Kopera-Frye, K., Dehaene, S., & Streissguth, A. P. (1996). Impairments of number processing induced by prenatal alcohol exposure. *Neuropsychologia, 34*(12), 1187–1196. https://doi.org/10.1016/0028-3932(96)00043-7

Landgren, V., Svensson, L., Gyllencreutz, E., Aring, E., Grönlund, M. A., & Landgren, M. (2019). Fetal alcohol spectrum disorders from childhood to adulthood: A Swedish population-based naturalistic cohort study of adoptees from Eastern Europe. *BMJ Open, 9*(10), e032407. https://doi.org/10.1136/bmjopen-2019-032407

Leark, R. A., Greenberg, L. K., Kindschi, C. L., Dupuy, T. R., & Hughes, S. J. (2007). *Test of variables of attention: Professional manual*. Los Alamitos: TOVA.

Lewis, R., & Rennick, P. M. (1979). *Manual for the repeatable cognitive-perceptual-motor battery*. Grosse Point, MI: Axon.

Lucas, B. R., Latimer, J., Doney, R., Watkins, R. E., Tsang, T. W., Hawkes, G., … Elliott, E. J. (2016). Gross motor performance in children prenatally exposed to alcohol and living in remote Australia. *Journal of Paediatrics and Child Health, 52*(8), 814–824. https://doi.org/10.1111/jpc.13240

MacPherson, P. H., Chudley, A. E., & Grant, B. A. (2011). *Fetal alcohol spectrum disorder (FASD) in a correctional population: Prevalence, screening and characteristics. Research report R-247*. Ottawa, ON: Correctional Service Canada.

Maier, S. E., & West, J. R. (2001). Drinking patterns and alcohol-related birth defects. *Alcohol Research and Health, 25*(3), 168–174.

Mattson, S. N., Calarco, K. E., & Lang, A. R. (2006). Focused and shifting attention in children with heavy prenatal alcohol exposure. *Neuropsychology, 20*(3), 361–369. https://doi.org/10.1037/0894-4105.20.3.361

Mattson, S. N., Goodman, A. M., Caine, C., Delis, D. C., & Riley, E. P. (1999). Executive functioning in children with heavy prenatal alcohol exposure. *Alcoholism: Clinical and Experimental Reseach, 23*(11), 1808–1815. https://doi.org/10.1111/J.1530-0277.1999.TB04077.X

Mattson, S. N., Gramling, L., Riley, E. P., Delis, D. C., & Jones, K. L. (1996). Global-local processing in children prenatally exposed to alcohol. *Child Neuropsychology, 2*(3), 16–175. https://doi.org/10.1080/09297049608402249

Mattson, S. N., Riley, E. P., Delis, D. C., Stern, C., & Jones, K. L. (1996). Verbal learning and memory in children with fetal alcohol syndrome. *Alcoholism: Clinical and Experimental Research, 20*(5), 810–816. https://doi.org/10.1111/j.1530-0277.1996.tb05256.x

Meyers, J. E., & Meyers, K. R. (1995). *Rey complex figure test and recognition trial*. Lutz, FL: Psychological Assessment Resources.

Monnot, M., Lovallo, W. R., Nixon, S. J., & Ross, E. (2002). Neurological basis of deficits in affective prosody comprehension among alcoholics and fetal alcohol-exposed adults. *Journal of Neuropsychiatry and Clinical Neurosciences, 14*(3), 321–328. https://doi.org/10.1176/appi.neuropsych.14.3.321

Mukherjee, R. A. S., Cook, P. A., Norgate, S. H., & Price, A. D. (2019). Neurodevelopmental outcomes in individuals with fetal alcohol spectrum disorder (FASD) with and without exposure to neglect: Clinical cohort data from a national FASD diagnostic clinic. *Alcohol, 76*, 23–28. https://doi.org/10.1016/j.alcohol.2018.06.002

Nanson, J. L., & Hiscock, M. (1990). Attention deficits in children exposed to alcohol prenatally. *Alcoholism: Clinical and Experimental Research, 14*(5), 656–661. https://doi.org/10.1111/j.1530-0277.1990.tb01223.x

Novick Brown, N., Gudjonsson, G., & Connor, P. (2011). Suggestibility and fetal alcohol spectrum disorders: I'll tell you anything you want to hear. *Journal of Psychiatry and Law, 39*(1), 39–71. https://doi.org/10.1177/009318531103900103

Novick Brown, N., Wartnik, A. P., Connor, P. D., & Adler, R. S. (2010). A proposed model standard for forensic assessment of fetal alcohol spectrum disorders. *Journal of Psychiatry & Law, 38*(4), 383–418. https://doi.org/10.1177/009318531003800403

Olson, H. C., Feldman, J. J., Streissguth, A. P., Sampson, P. D., & Bookstein, F. L. (1998). Neuropsychological deficits in adolescents with fetal alcohol syndrome: Clinical findings. *Alcoholism: Clinical and Experimental Research, 22*(9), 1998–2012. https://doi.org/10.1111/j.1530-0277.1998.tb05909.x

Pearson. (2009). *Advanced clinical solutions for WAIS-IV and WMS-IV*. San Antonio, TX: Pearson.

Pei, J. R., Rinaldi, C. M., Rasmussen, C., Massey, V., & Massey, D. (2008). Memory patterns of acquisition and retention of verbal and nonverbal information in children with fetal alcohol spectrum disorders. *Canadian Journal of Clinical Pharmacology, 15*(1), e44–e56.

Persel, C. (2012). The independent living scale. *The Center for Outcome Measurement in Brain Injury*. http://tbims.org/combi/ils/

Pollard, R., Trowbridge, B., Slade, P. D., Streissguth, A. P., Laktonen, A., & Townes, B. D. (2004). Interrogative suggestibility in a U.S. context: Some preliminary data on normal and FAS/FAE subjects. *Personality and Individual Differences, 37*(5), 1101–1108. https://doi.org/10.1016/j.paid.2003.12.004

Popova, S., Lange, S., Burd, L., Nam, S., & Rehm, J. (2016). Special education of children with fetal alcohol spectrum disorder. *Exceptionality, 24*(3), 165–175. https://doi.org/10.1080/09362835.2015.1064415

Randolph, C. (1998). *Repeatable battery for the assessment of neuropsychological status*. San Antonio, TX: Psychological.

Rangmar, J., Dahlgren Sandberg, A., Aronson, M., & Fahlke, C. (2015). Cognitive and executive functions, social cognition and sense of coherence in adults with fetal alcohol syndrome. *Nordic Journal of Psychiatry, 69*(6), 472–478. https://doi.org/10.3109/08039488.2015.1009487

Reynolds, C. R. (2014). *Test of general reasoning ability professional manual*. Lutz, FL: Psychological Assessment Resources.

Roebuck, T. M., Simmons, R. W., Mattson, S. N., & Riley, E. P. (1998). Prenatal exposure to alcohol affects the ability to maintain postural balance. *Alcoholism: Clinical and Experimental Research, 22*(1), 252–258. https://doi.org/10.1111/j.1530-0277.1998.tb03646.x

Ruff, R. M. (1996). *Ruff figural fluency test*. Lutz, FL: Psychological Assessment Resources.

Sanders, J. L., Hudson Breen, R. E., & Netelenbos, N. (2017). Comparing diagnostic classification of neurobehavioral disorder associated with prenatal alcohol exposure with Canadian fetal alcohol spectrum disorder guidelines: A cohort study. *CMAJ: Canadian Medical Association Journal, 5*(1), e178–e183. https://doi.org/10.9778/cmajo.20160137

Sanders, J. L., Netelenbos, N., & Dei, S. O. (2020). Construct and factorial validity of neurobehavioral disorder associated with prenatal alcohol exposure (ND-PAE). *BMC Psychology, 8*(53), 1–10. https://doi.org/10.1186/s40359-020-00405-5

Sheliza, A., Kerns, K., Mulligan, B., Olson, H. C., & Astley, S. J. (2018). An investigation of intra-individual variability in children with fetal alcohol spectrum disorder (FASD). *Child Neuropsychology, 24*(5), 617–637. https://doi.org/10.1080/09297049.2017.1302579

Sparrow, S. S., Cicchetti, D. V., & Saulnier, C. A. (2016). *Vineland adaptive behavior scales (Vineland-3)* (3rd ed.). Bloomington, MN: NCS Pearson.

Stern, R. A., & White, T. (2003). *Neuropsychological assessment battery: Auditory comprehension test professional manual*. Lutz, FL: Psychological Assessment Resources.

Stratton, K., Howe, C., & Battaglia, F. (Eds.). (1996). *Fetal alcohol syndrome: Diagnosis, epidemiology, prevention, and treatment*. Washington, DC: National Academy Press.

Streissguth, A., Barr, H., Kogan, J., & Bookstein, F. (1996). *Understanding the occurrence of secondary disabilities in clients with fetal alcohol syndrome (FAS) and fetal alcohol effects (FAE)*. Final Report: Centers for Disease Control and Prevention, Grant No. R04/CCR008515. http://lib.adai.uw.edu/pubs/bk2698.pdf

Streissguth, A. P., Aase, J. M., Clarren, S. K., Randels, S. P., LaDue, R. A., & Smith, D. F. (1991). Fetal alcohol syndrome in adolescents and adults. *JAMA: Journal of the American Medical Association, 265*(15), 1961–1967. https://doi.org/10.1001/jama.1991.03460150065025

Streissguth, A. P., Barr, H. M., Sampson, P. D., & Bookstein, F. L. (1994). Prenatal alcohol and offspring development: The first fourteen years. *Drug and Alcohol Dependence, 36*(2), 89–99. https://doi.org/10.1016/0376-8716(94)90090-6

Streissguth, A. P., Bookstein, F. L., Barr, H. M., Press, S., & Sampson, P. D. (1998). A fetal alcohol behavior scale. *Alcoholism: Clinical and Experimental Research, 22*(2), 325–333. https://doi.org/10.1111/j.1530-0277.1998.tb03656.x

Streissguth, A. P., Bookstein, F. L., Barr, H. M., Sampson, P. D., O'Malley, K., & Young, J. K. (2004). Risk factors for adverse life outcomes in fetal alcohol syndrome and fetal alcohol effects. *Journal of Developmental and Behavioral Pediatrics, 25*(4), 228–238. https://doi.org/10.1097/00004703-200408000-00002

Stuss, D. T., Stethem, L. L., & Pelchat, G. (1988). Three tests of attention and rapid information processing: An extension. *The Clinical Neuropsychologist, 2*(3), 246–250. https://doi.org/10.1080/13854048808520107

Stuss, D. T., Stethem, L. L., & Poirier, C. A. (1987). Comparison of three tests of attention and rapid information processing across six age groups. *The Clinical Neuropsychologist, 1*(2), 139–152. https://doi.org/10.1080/13854048708520046

Uecker, A., & Nadel, L. (1996). Spatial locations gone awry: Object and spatial memory deficits in children with fetal alcohol syndrome. *Neuropsychologia, 34*(3), 209–223. https://doi.org/10.1016/0028-3932(95)00096-8

Wechsler, D. (2008). *Wechsler Adult Intelligence Scale® (WAIS–IV®)* (4th ed.). San Antonio, TX: Pearson.

Wilkinson, G. S., & Robertson, G. J. (2006). *Wide Range Achievement Test® (WRAT4®)* (4th ed.). Lutz, FL: Psychological Assessment Resources.

Williams, J. F., & Smith, V. C. (2015). Fetal alcohol spectrum disorders. *Pediatrics, 136*(5), e1395–e1406. https://doi.org/10.1542/peds.2015-3113

Woodcock, R. W., McGrew, K. S., & Mather, N. (2001). *Woodcock-Johnson® III tests of achievement*. Itasca, IL: Riverside.

Chapter 6
Forensic Medical Evaluation and Differential Diagnosis of Fetal Alcohol Spectrum Disorder

Julian K. Davies

Abstract This chapter briefly describes the history of fetal alcohol spectrum disorders (FASD), from references in antiquity to the modern understanding that prenatal alcohol exposure (PAE) can lead to birth defects including growth deficiency, a unique cluster of minor facial anomalies, and central nervous system (CNS) abnormalities. Diagnoses under the FASD umbrella include fetal alcohol syndrome (FAS), partial fetal alcohol syndrome (pFAS, in which "partial" refers to incomplete physical manifestations), and various diagnostic terms for individuals impacted by PAE who lack sentinel physical features but do have evidence of CNS damage. Areas of consensus and divergence in modern diagnostic criteria are explored, with attention to nomenclature, the problematic nature of alcohol thresholds, the importance of growth as a sentinel physical feature, the specificity of facial features of FAS, other congenital anomalies associated with PAE, structural criteria for CNS damage including imaging approaches, and differing definitions of CNS dysfunction. Recommendations are provided for guidelines to use in forensic practice. The extensive differential diagnosis of FASD is described, including genetic etiologies, other prenatal influences, perinatal risks, adverse childhood experiences, head injuries, substance use disorders, and mental health disorders. Practical suggestions for FASD evaluations in forensic practice are offered, from pre-detention screening through evaluations, reports, and testimony. The intended audience for this chapter includes legal and mental health professionals learning about medical diagnosis of FASDs, medical FASD experts new to forensic evaluations, and forensic-experienced physicians seeking training in FASD diagnosis.

Keywords Prenatal alcohol exposure · Fetal alcohol syndrome · FAS · Fetal alcohol spectrum disorders · FASD · Forensic medical evaluation

---

J. K. Davies, M.D. (✉)
University of Washington, Seattle, WA, USA
e-mail: joolian@uw.edu

N. Novick Brown (ed.), *Evaluating Fetal Alcohol Spectrum Disorders in the Forensic Context*, https://doi.org/10.1007/978-3-030-73628-6_6

6.1 Introduction

Death row is not a typical place to find a pediatrician. But fetal alcohol spectrum disorders (FASD) are pediatric conditions with lifelong impacts, and there are few adult doctors with fetal alcohol expertise. So, there I was, an FASD expert on my first capital appeals case, pulling a rubber reflex hammer shaped like a friendly giraffe out of my bag. I had left the standard reflex hammer at home, as it was metal and a bit pointy—I had watched enough shows to know how such things sharpen right up in prison. Turns out, it is possible to simultaneously over-think and under-think a packing decision. Since that first evaluation, I have learned a few things about forensic FASD evaluations for people who are not "kiddos" and do not get a sugar-free lollipop at the end of the visit.

The intended audience for this chapter is legal and mental health professionals learning about medical diagnosis of FASDs, FASD experts new to forensic evaluations (like me, back when), and forensic-experienced physicians seeking training in FASD diagnosis. After briefly describing the history of FASD to provide context, I examine areas of consensus and divergence in current diagnostic criteria, emerging from the weeds with a recommendation of which diagnostic approach to use. I explore the differential diagnosis process and finish with practical suggestions for FASD evaluations in forensic practice.

In forensic practice, an FASD diagnostic evaluation may be sought to better understand competency, inform alternative processes (e.g., diversion, restorative justice, conditional sentences), provide support and direction to prevent recidivism, assist with probation planning, explain functioning for mitigation purposes, support an intellectual disability (ID) diagnosis or provide ID-equivalent diagnosis in capital cases, or demonstrate ineffective assistance of counsel in post-conviction relief. In an adversarial justice system, these are more typical defense counsel goals. Prosecutors may be interested in an FASD diagnosis to emphasize a victim's vulnerable status. Ideally, FASD education and evaluations inform all members of the criminal justice system (Fast & Conry, 2009).

6.2 The Fetal Alcohol Spectrum

Fetal alcohol spectrum disorder (FASD) is an umbrella term for a spectrum of diagnoses resulting from in utero alcohol exposure. Fetal alcohol syndrome (FAS) was the original diagnosis on the fetal alcohol spectrum. FAS is a permanent birth defect syndrome caused by prenatal alcohol exposure (PAE), which is characterized by prenatal and/or postnatal growth deficiency, unique cluster of minor facial anomalies, and central nervous system (CNS) abnormalities. A diagnosis of FAS requires confirmation of all three features (abnormal growth, face, brain). For alcohol-exposed individuals who lack one or more of the criteria for FAS, diagnoses on the broader fetal alcohol spectrum may be appropriate. One such diagnosis is partial fetal alcohol syndrome (pFAS), wherein "partial" refers to incomplete physical manifestations (such as absence of growth impairments or moderate facial features). Effects on the brain in pFAS are considered equivalent to FAS. In contrast to FAS and pFAS, the majority of individuals impacted by PAE lack sentinel physical features but do have CNS damage. Various diagnostic terms exist for this outcome, such as alcohol-related neurodevelopmental disorder (ARND), static encephalopathy/alcohol-exposed (SE/AE), neurobehavioral disorder/alcohol-exposed (ND/AE), and neurodevelopmental disorder associated with prenatal alcohol exposure (ND-PAE).

6.3 Diagnostic History

Biblical, Talmudic, Sumerian, and Greco-Roman texts revealed early concerns about the impact of parental drinking on pregnancy outcomes but lacked modern understanding that maternal consumption of alcohol could lead to a birth defect syndrome (Abel, 1997, 1999). English physicians in the nineteenth century had more specific observations about children of alcoholic mothers exhibiting "a starved, shriveled, and imperfect look," as well as stillbirths and epilepsy in surviving offspring (Jones & Smith, 1973, p. 999). In the United States, medical attitudes about alcohol during pregnancy prior to the discovery of FAS ranged from concerns about adverse fetal outcomes to the use of high-dose intravenous alcohol in pregnant women at risk for preterm delivery (Warren, 2015).

Modern understanding that drinking in pregnancy could cause growth problems, a distinct pattern of facial features, and neurodevelopmental disabilities arose in the late 1950s to 1970s from two independent studies in France by Rouquette and Lemoine (2012) and subsequent studies by a group of researchers at the University of Washington in Seattle. Lemoine's description was comprehensive but unfortunately neglected at the time (Lemoine, Harousseau, Borteyru, & Menuet, 1968). In Seattle, pediatric resident Christy Ulleland (1972) noted a triad of intrauterine growth failure, poor growth in infancy, and mothers with relatively severe chronic alcoholism. This observation led to the involvement of dysmorphologists, who identified a pattern of related malformations (Jones, Smith, Ulleland, & Streissguth, 1973) and named this condition *Fetal Alcohol Syndrome* in 1973 (Jones & Smith, 1973).

In the half-century since 1973, various definitions and diagnostic criteria for fetal alcohol diagnoses have been developed by researchers and expert committees around the world. Much progress has been made in defining how maternal drinking affects growth, facial features, and the CNS. It now is clear that PAE causes a spectrum of effects throughout a fetus. FAS is just the most visible of those outcomes.

In the 1970s and 1980s, FAS and suspected *fetal alcohol effects* (referred to as FAE at the time) were further described by Clarren and Smith (1978), as well as the Research Society on Alcoholism (Rosett, 1980; Sokol & Clarren, 1989), which developed early guidelines for diagnosing FAS. At the behest of the U.S. Congress, the Institute of Medicine (IOM) published a report in 1996 on FAS diagnosis, epidemiology, prevention, and treatment (Stratton, Howe, & Battaglia, 1996). This report included a chapter with specific diagnostic criteria for FAS, pFAS, ARND, and alcohol-related birth defects (ARBD). Soon thereafter, the first edition of the University of Washington 4-Digit Diagnostic Code was published (Astley & Clarren, 1997), with a second edition in 1999 and third edition in 2004 (Astley, 2004).

The IOM criteria and 4-Digit Code introduced an interdisciplinary approach to diagnosis, with the latter guided by rigorously and empirically case-defined criteria to overcome limitations of gestalt diagnosis and better capture the fetal alcohol spectrum (Astley & Clarren, 2000). Under the 4-Digit Code, the spectrum is defined as FAS, pFAS, static encephalopathy/alcohol-exposed (SE/AE), which involves structural evidence of brain damage and/or severe dysfunction, and neurobehavioral disorder/alcohol-exposed (ND/AE), which involves mild–moderate dysfunction. In 2004, the Centers for Disease Control (CDC) published diagnostic criteria for FAS (Bertrand et al., 2004). New guidelines based on IOM criteria were published in 2005 (Hoyme et al., 2005) and updated in 2016 (Hoyme et al., 2016).

In 2013, the fifth edition of the *Diagnostic and Statistical Manual of Mental Disorders* (*DSM-5*; American Psychiatric Association (APA), 2013) addressed the CNS dysfunction in FASD with a specified condition under Other Specified Neurodevelopmental Disorder: *Neurodevelopmental disorder associated with prenatal alcohol exposure* (ND-PAE, F88), placing diagnostic criteria for ND-PAE in a section entitled "Conditions for Future Study." These proposed *DSM-5* guidelines have been promoted by the American Academy of Pediatrics Neurobehavioral Disorder–Prenatal Alcohol Exposed (ND-PAE) Work Group (Hagan et al., 2016) and are currently in wide clinical use in the United States. In the forensic context in the United States, it now is common to diagnose ND-PAE for the CNS dysfunction in FASD along with the appropriate FASD medical condition.

Other countries have also published FASD guidelines, including Canada, which in 2005 adopted a system based on the 4-Digit-Code with IOM terminology (Chudley et al., 2005). In 2015, Canada went in another direction by dropping the growth criterion and collapsing all diagnoses into two categories: *FASD with sentinel facial features* and *FASD without sentinel facial features* (Cook et al., 2015). Australian guidelines (Bower & Elliott, 2016) are similar to the 2015 Canadian criteria in many ways. Canadian guidelines have been criticized (Kable & Coles, 2018; Sanders, Hudson Breen, & Netelenbos, 2017) for having overly restrictive criterion levels for CNS dysfunction (i.e., −2 standard deviations [SDs] below the mean in three neurodevelopmental domains).

It is unclear why the world needed so many FASD diagnostic systems. FASDs do not present so differently in the United States, Canada, Germany, and Australia as to require multiple country-specific guidelines. As our scientific and clinical understanding of FASD advances, so too should our diagnostic guidelines. A requisite for introducing another set of guidelines ought to be empirical evidence confirming superior performance of the new guidelines over the old. The 4-Digit Code is the only set of guidelines that were introduced as an empirical study confirming superior performance over the preceding gestalt method (Astley & Clarren, 2000). All guidelines subsequent to the 4-Digit Code have been introduced in the absence of empirical evidence of superior performance. Since publication in 2013, ND-PAE has engendered multiple validation studies (Johnson, Moyer, Klug, & Burd, 2017; Kable & Coles, 2018; Sanders et al., 2017; Sanders, Netelenbos, & Dei, 2020). Although as set forth below, my preferred method for clinical and forensic use is the 4-Digit Code, FASD criteria developed by the IOM, Hoyme et al., CDC (for FAS only), and *DSM-5* are all professionally acceptable for evaluations conducted in the United States.

6.4 Areas of Consensus and Divergence

It is generally agreed in the scientific community that intrauterine alcohol exposure:

- is the leading preventable cause of developmental disabilities/intellectual disability in the developed world;
- can lead to prenatal and postnatal growth deficiency;
- may cause a cluster of facial features in the midline of the face, an area embryologically linked to brain development;
- is associated with a range of potential cardiac, renal, ocular, auditory, endocrine, and orthopedic anomalies;
- causes a wide variety of structural brain impacts and functional impairments, which are often more apparent in school-age and beyond;
- is frequently missed by clinicians—both the exposure and the outcomes; and,
- is ideally evaluated with a multidisciplinary approach.

There remains some debate about the following topics. Prepare to enter the weeds. As there are several currently used diagnostic criteria, it seems important to carefully compare and contrast them at a level of detail that may give the misleading impression that FASD diagnosis is controversial or impractical. It is neither of those things. There is substantial scientific agreement about how alcohol impacts a developing fetus in the key diagnostic areas of growth deficiency, facial phenotype, and brain structural and functional outcomes. Current differences in criteria are more about how to specifically define these impacts and what to call the outcomes.

6.4.1 Nomenclature

The decision to name a new disorder "the fetal alcohol syndrome" (Jones & Smith, 1973, p. 999) after its asserted cause rather than something traditionally eponymous was controversial at the time but is no longer, as decades of animal and human research have confirmed PAE is the cause of FAS. However, terminology that explicitly assigns blame to maternal drinking for clinical outcome *when the facial features uniquely caused by alcohol are not present* has long been a key area of difference in FASD guidelines. This can be seen in the contrast between FAE, ARND, ARBD, and FASD, which assert outcome is an "alcohol effect" or "alcohol-related," and SE/AE, ND/AE, and ND-PAE, which observe that outcome occurs in the presence of PAE but does not assert alcohol caused the outcome.

Advocates for the former approach claim one can use clinical judgment to avoid assigning an "alcohol-related" diagnosis when outcome is unlikely to have been caused by PAE. Advocates for the "associated with PAE" approach argue that in the absence of specific biomarkers (i.e., the face of FAS), it is more accurate to use terminology that reports outcome and exposure without reference to causation. With the latter approach, a provider or team may still use clinical judgment to arrive at a medical opinion that does implicate PAE.

6.4.2 Alcohol Threshold

Alcohol is a known teratogen, and perennial popular media reports notwithstanding, there is no clear "safe" amount of drinking during pregnancy. Studies that have failed to find negative outcomes from "low-to-moderate" prenatal alcohol consumption generally have not looked at appropriate outcomes (e.g., over-emphasis on perinatal outcomes; Henderson, Gray, & Brocklehurst, 2007) or time frames (e.g., non-comprehensive assessments at young ages; Skogerbø et al., 2013) to support a conclusion that it is safe to drink during pregnancy (Kesmodel et al., 2019). Notably, studies *have* found adverse effects associated with low–moderate levels of PAE (Flak et al., 2013; Lees et al., 2020; Sood et al., 2001).

Perhaps most importantly, risk of FASD is not based solely upon timing and level of PAE. Research has demonstrated significant maternal variability in risk of damage to offspring from drinking (McLachlan et al., 2019). Effects of teratogens also can be modified by genetic differences in fetal susceptibility and resistance. Among twins with identical exposure, monozygotic twins experience identical adverse outcomes while dizygotic twins experience strikingly discordant outcomes (Astley Hemingway et al., 2018). For these reasons, CDC and the U.S. Surgeon General continue to advise, "No amount of alcohol consumption can be considered safe during pregnancy" (U.S. Public Health Service, Office of the Surgeon General, 2005). Nonetheless, some diagnostic criteria set a bar for amount/frequency of alcohol exposure to avoid misattributing clinical presentation to "minimal" alcohol exposure. Using nomenclature that assigns responsibility to alcohol when specific biomarkers (e.g., the face of FAS) are not present accentuates this concern in the absence of meticulous differential diagnosis.

From a public health perspective, exposure thresholds in diagnostic guidelines carry a hard-to-avoid implication that drinking below the threshold is safe. From a clinical practice perspective, it is uncommon to have precise amounts and frequencies of PAE. Several factors potentially limit ability to document whether exposure meets such thresholds, such as stigma, denial, up to 70% of patients no longer in the care of biological parents (Astley, 2010), time elapsed since pregnancy (especially for older evaluees), and the fact that "one drink" may mean very different things to a researcher versus a birth mother. A recent comparison of diagnostic criteria found the new Hoyme and Canadian alcohol exposure thresholds prevented 47–59% of patients with confirmed PAE from receiving an FASD diagnosis. Moreover, over half of individuals with the most severe outcome (FAS) had reportedly low to moderate PAE (Astley Hemingway et al., 2019). In another analysis (appropriately titled, "Prenatal alcohol history – setting a threshold for diagnosis requires a level of detail and accuracy that does not exist"), the new Canadian prenatal alcohol threshold prevented 71% of individuals from receiving an FASD diagnosis compared to the previous guidelines (Petryk, Siddiqui, Ekeh, & Pandey, 2019).

IOM criteria require "a pattern of excessive intake" but allow for this threshold to be lowered, "As further research is completed and as, or if, lower quantities or variable patterns of alcohol use are associated with ARBD or ARND, these patterns of alcohol use should be incorporated into the diagnostic criteria" (p. 78). Such research *has* been completed, and such patterns *should* be incorporated into diagnostic criteria. Unfortunately, *DSM-5*'s ND-PAE also has an alcohol threshold. Rather than requiring evidence of "excessive" alcohol consumption, these guidelines might have considered using reliable evidence of minimal consumption to exclude diagnosis. However, this still would not address the public health messaging muddle or the fact that for certain vulnerable pregnancies, sub-threshold drinking can have significant teratogenic effects.

6.4.3 Growth

Prenatal alcohol exposure may lead to prenatal and/or postnatal growth deficiency. Postnatal short stature is the most common form of growth deficiency in our FASD clinic at the University of Washington. We also have found that over time, height percentiles tend to decrease while weight percentiles increase (Astley, Bledsoe, & Davies, 2016). Other researchers have described low weight-for-height in FASD populations (del Campo & Jones, 2017).

Why is growth important in an FASD evaluation? Growth impairment has been shown to be a "sentinel physical feature" of FASD. About one-fifth of individuals seen in our FASD clinic have moderate to severe growth deficiency (≤third percentile), and one-third have mild growth deficiency (≤tenth percentile). Alcohol-exposed children with significant growth deficiency are two to three times more likely to have severe brain dysfunction than those with normal growth (Astley et al., 2016). Another study found alcohol-exposed children born small for gestational age who remain small tend to have been more heavily exposed and show more impact on neurocognition. Those born small who catch up tend to have more intermediate prenatal exposure and moderate neurocognitive effects. Those without growth restriction in childhood tend to have lowest exposure and weakest effects (Carter et al., 2016).

Canadian and Australian guidelines removed pre- and postnatal growth deficiency from their criteria, citing concerns that growth deficiency was neither sensitive nor specific to FASD diagnosis (Cook et al., 2015). However, two subsequent independent analyses demonstrated that growth should remain a part of FASD diagnosis by showing that growth deficiency was as prevalent as other core diagnostic features (face and brain), highly correlated with prenatal alcohol exposure, and highly correlated with and predictive of severe brain dysfunction (Astley et al., 2016; Carter et al., 2016). Current diagnostic guidelines that include growth deficiency differ somewhat in how such deficiency is defined but generally agree growth percentiles should be adjusted for prematurity, age, and gender. If both birth parents' heights are known, adjustment for mid-parent stature can be performed (Himes, Roche, Thissen, & Moore, 1985). Other explanations for poor growth should also be considered, such as acute illness or other postnatal environmental influences.

6.4.4 Facial Features

The "face of FAS" is a constellation of three facial features unique to prenatal alcohol damage—so much so in fact that one can make a diagnosis of FAS when prenatal alcohol exposure is unconfirmed. Research suggests the facial features of FAS require alcohol exposure during a very narrow window of time early in pregnancy. Thus, the majority of alcohol-affected individuals do not have the facial features; in fact, only 9% of patients in our FAS clinic have "the face" of FAS (Astley, 2010) (Fig. 6.1).

It generally is agreed that the "face of FAS" involves a thin upper lip, smooth/flat philtrum (groove between nose and lip), and short palpebral fissures (horizontal eye openings). How those features are defined and how many are required vary among guidelines. This variability has a marked impact on the specificity of the facial features to prenatal alcohol exposure. The 4-Digit Code Rank 4 facial phenotype ("severe facial features of FAS"), which requires all three features with palpebral fissures at a third percentile cutoff, has a specificity and positive predictive value (PPV) that are both 100%, according to a recent study (Astley Hemingway, 2020). The 4-Digit Rank 3 facial phenotype, with essentially 2.5 of the 3 facial features, has a specificity of 89% and PPV of 35%.

The Hoyme criteria (which require only two facial features, with a relaxed tenth percentile eye width cutoff and relaxed upper lip thinness threshold if using the Hoyme lip-philtrum guides) have a specificity of only 77% and PPV of 18% with the Hoyme lip threshold, and a specificity of 91% and PPV of 30% using the 4-Digit lip guide. This means that over 80% of individuals with the Hoyme face of FAS did not have documented PAE. Even if you add growth deficiency and head circumference less than tenth percentile to the Hoyme facial phenotype, the PPV does not increase beyond chance (52%) (Astley Hemingway, 2020). In another study, 25% of high-functioning, non-alcohol-exposed control subjects met Hoyme criteria for the

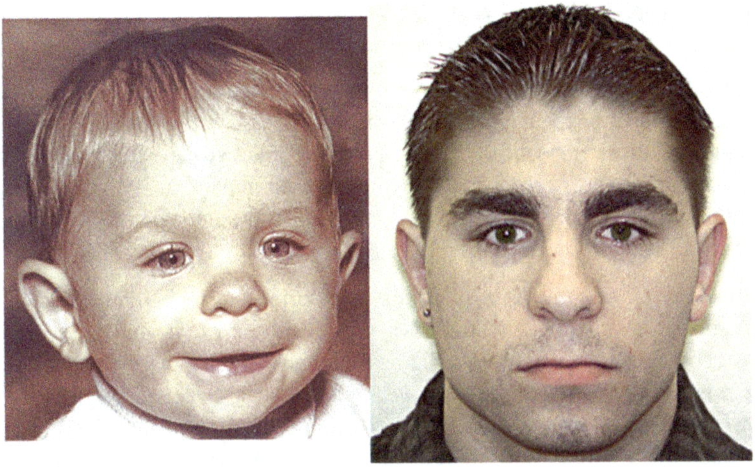

Fig. 6.1 Young man presenting with the three facial features of FAS (small eyes, smooth philtrum, and thin upper lip) at 2 years of age and 20 years of age. Copyright 2020, Susan Astley Hemingway, PhD, University of Washington

face of FAS (Astley, 2006). In both clinical and forensic contexts, it is important to use facial feature criteria that are unique to PAE, especially when the face of FAS can be used to assume PAE when it is unknown. If the face of FAS is not specific to (i.e., caused only by) prenatal alcohol exposure, then diagnoses such as "FAS, alcohol exposure unknown" are rendered invalid.

It is possible PAE may create other facial phenotypes influenced by timing of exposure and a fetus's genetic vulnerability to the exposure. This possibility has been suggested in animal models (Lipinski et al., 2012) but has not been replicated in humans as yet (Suttie et al., 2013). The 4-Digit Code clearly documents how the FAS facial phenotype presents on a clinically meaningful continuum: the higher the PAE, the more severe the expression of the FAS facial phenotype. Moreover, the more severe the FAS facial phenotype, the more severe the growth deficiency and structural/functional CNS abnormalities. The 4-Digit Code is the only diagnostic system that captures the FAS facial phenotype on such a continuum (Astley, 2013).

6.4.5 *Value of Sentinel Physical Findings*

DSM-5's proposed criteria for ND-PAE do not include physical features, such as growth deficiency, facial features, or microcephaly. If the intended users are non-physicians, this is understandable and serves to broaden access to an FASD diagnosis. However, for medical professionals diagnosing FASDs who have or can develop expertise in physical feature analysis, ignoring physical features is a significant omission. Sentinel physical findings can both increase confidence in PAE as the primary etiology and predict brain dysfunction.

6.4.6 *Minor Dysmorphic Features*

Since the discovery of FAS, many other dysmorphic features, while not themselves diagnostic of an FASD, have been described in the context of PAE. Many of these features are related to age and ethnicity or may be "background noise" in that minor physical anomalies are more frequently encountered in patients with developmental disabilities (Myers et al., 2017). Some examples follow, and a helpful review is also available (del Campo & Jones, 2017):

- midface hypoplasia/retrusion: frequently described in FASD but challenging to both measure and adjust for familial, age, and ethnic variation;
- ptosis (lid lag) and strabismus (eye misalignment): ocular anomalies, also including refractive errors and optic nerve hypoplasia, are seen more frequently in FASD (Gyllencreutz et al., 2020) but are not specific;
- epicanthal folds (redundant skin at inner eye): this feature is normal in infants and many ethnicities;
- low/flat nasal bridge: a common, normal feature in younger children and certain ethnicities, although depressed nasal bridge can be diagnosed when the bridge is more posterior than is typical for age and ethnic background;
- long philtrum: may represent more of an abnormal philtrum to nose ratio, although small noses are more common in infancy and show familial/ethnic variability;
- ear anomalies: "railroad track ears" (prominent horizontal crus of the helix in combination with prominent and parallel inferior crus of the antihelix) are a somewhat subjective finding described in FASD, and hearing or middle ear problems (fluid, infections) also are common in this population;
- abnormal palmar creases (e.g., "hockey stick crease"): this feature, reported in FASD but also seen in other syndromes, may be linked to atypical hand movements during gestation; and,
- orthopedic anomalies, including fifth digit brachy/clinodactyly (short/curved pinkies), and limited elbow supination (possible radioulnar synostosis) are worth looking for but also are not unique to FASD.

The Hoyme 2016 criteria outline a dysmorphology score used in their research, which they have found useful in differentiating children with FASD from other genetic and teratogenic syndromes but is not used in assigning FASD diagnosis (Hoyme et al., 2016). A morphology reference sponsored by the National Institutes of Health (NIH, 2020) represents an important attempt to standardize dysmorphology terms and has helpful case definitions for medical providers (Allanson, Biesecker, Carey, & Hennekam, 2009).

6.4.7 More Significant Congenital Anomalies

Prenatal alcohol exposure can damage multiple fetal organ systems in a dose- and timing-dependent fashion, with the brain typically most severely impacted. However, prenatal alcohol exposure is associated with a spectrum of other significant congenital anomalies (Caputo, Wood, & Jabbour, 2016) that may include the following:

- Eye (refractive errors, strabismus, optic nerve hypoplasia; Gyllencreutz et al., 2020);
- Ear/Nose/Throat (cleft, ear anomalies, recurrent/chronic ear infections, hearing impairments, central auditory processing challenges; Church & Kaltenbach, 1997; McLaughlin et al., 2019);
- Heart (septal and conotruncal/outflow tract defects; Chen, Li, Guo, Peng, & Liu, 2020);
- Kidney (renal or ureteral malformations; Hofer & Burd, 2009);
- Skeletal (limited range of motion of digits, elbows, or other joints; vertebral anomalies; Spiegel et al., 1979); and.
- Endocrine (possible effects on stress hormones, growth hormone, testes/testosterone; Gabriel, Hofmann, Glavas, & Weinberg, 1998).

However, none of these anomalies is unique to prenatal alcohol damage.

6.4.8 Structural Brain Impacts

The developing CNS is highly vulnerable to teratogens like alcohol. PAE can damage the CNS through direct toxic effects of ethanol and its metabolites on developing nerve and supporting cells, by deranging nerve cell migration, affecting the size and functionality of brain structures, disrupting connectivity between brain regions, altering neurotransmitter systems, causing damaging patterns of inflammation, and affecting gene expression through lasting epigenetic alterations. PAE can cause structural abnormalities in both gray and white matter throughout the CNS, including microcephaly, midline defects, changes in size and shape of brain structures, altered patterns of brain maturation during childhood, and disordered connectivity. Brain imaging studies have documented PAE impacts on brain structures including frontal lobes, corpus callosum, caudate nucleus, hippocampus, diencephalon, and cerebellum (Nguyen et al., 2017).

Current FASD diagnostic systems used in the United States differ in what constitutes evidence of structural brain impacts, whether structural anomalies are allowed for or required in an FASD diagnosis, and if structural criteria suffice in the absence of functional impairments (a common clinical scenario in young children):

- IOM *requires* at least one of the following for FAS: decreased cranial size at birth, abnormal structure (e.g., microcephaly, partial/complete agenesis of the corpus callosum, cerebellar hypoplasia), or neurological hard or soft signs. IOM *allows* these structural features to meet brain criteria in pFAS and ARND, which also can be met with functional evidence.
- 4-Digit Code *allows* the following structural criteria to meet CNS criteria for FAS, pFAS, and SE/AE: head circumference ≤ third percentile, abnormal structure on brain imaging, seizure disorder, or hard neurological signs. 4-Digit Code CNS criteria for those diagnoses also can be met by evidence of severe brain dysfunction.
- CDC criteria for FAS are similar to 4-Digit Code for structural criteria but relax head circumference to ≤tenth percentile (unless height and weight are below tenth percentile, in which case head size cutoff is third percentile) and broaden neurological signs to include "soft neurological signs outside normal limits." CDC criteria can also be met by functional CNS evidence.
- *DSM-5* does not include structural brain criteria.
- Hoyme 2016 criteria *require* at least one of the following for FAS: head circumference ≤ tenth percentile, structural brain anomalies, or recurrent nonfebrile seizures (with other causes of seizures having been ruled out). These features *can* play a role in Hoyme et al. (2016) "partial FAS without documented prenatal alcohol exposure" but are *not allowed* to meet brain criteria for Hoyme et al. (2016) ARND.

6.4.9 Use of Neurodiagnostic Testing and Imaging

In clinical FASD evaluations, it currently is unusual to have extensive neurodiagnostic testing available. This is due to many factors, including cost, feasibility for a typically younger and wriggly clinic population, evolving standards of what constitutes a clinical versus research tool (doctors and insurers can be quite conservative in this regard), and the plain fact that for the majority of FASD clinical evaluations, neuropsychometric testing data are sufficient and more relevant to a patient's clinical recommendations. In forensic practice where it is common to have concerns regarding malingering (it is hard to fake magnetic resonance imaging [MRI]) and there is desire for additional evidence to support a diagnosis in an adversarial process, such neurodiagnostic testing is more common. This testing may include brain MRI, volumetric analysis of brain structures, diffusion tensor imaging (DTI) to evaluate brain connectivity, and functional measures such as quantitative electroencephalogram (qEEG), functional MRI (fMRI), and positron emission tomography (PET) scans, which measure brain electrical or metabolic activity.

Neurofunctional modalities such as qEEG and functional imaging studies are akin to "electronic soft signs" that may serve as convergent evidence of dysfunction. Post-processing imaging approaches, such as automated volumetric brain region analysis and DTI, are closer to "hard signs" of structural anomalies, provided there is an adequate normative database to determine normal versus abnormal. To date, research has not found a pattern of brain damage as unique to PAE as the face of FAS, but as in much of medicine, pattern recognition and differential diagnosis (weighing possible etiologies) play important roles in diagnosis. Choice of neurodiagnostic modalities involves methods currently used in clinical practice, with published reference norms and empirical support. In the forensic context, which has different goals and different end users, neuroimaging may augment clinical diagnosis by providing ancillary, malinger-proof evidence of structural brain damage. How do current FASD guidelines address neuroimaging? As usual, criteria differ but seem to suggest neuroimaging is helpful:

- IOM criteria seem self-contradictory regarding use of ancillary imaging measures. The authors perceived in 1996 that since normative criteria and requisite evidentiary base were limited, the utility of imaging in making a diagnosis of FAS was "yet to be established" (Stratton et al., 1996; p. 69). Nonetheless, IOM criteria include intracranial features (corpus callosum and cerebellum abnormalities), which would require the use of imaging to diagnose in living patients.
- 4-Digit Code (Astley, 2004) allows, "Significant brain abnormalities of presumed prenatal origin observable through imaging techniques. Abnormalities may include but are not limited to hydrocephaly, heterotopias, and change in shape and/or size of brain regions. These abnormalities should be determined by appropriately trained medical professionals" (p. 36).
- CDC (Bertrand et al., 2004) allows for, "Clinically significant brain abnormalities observable through imaging techniques (e.g. reduction in size, or change in shape of the corpus callosum, cerebellum, or basal ganglia) as assessed by an appropriately trained professional" (p. 3).
- Hoyme 2016 guidelines for FAS and pFAS (Hoyme et al., 2016; p. 3) include "deficient brain growth, abnormal morphogenesis or neurophysiology," including "structural brain anomalies."

6.4.10 Functional Evidence of Brain Impacts

Brain injuries caused by drinking during pregnancy are variable but can include such functional outcomes as lower IQ, attention-deficit/hyperactivity disorder (ADHD), language and social difficulties, learning disabilities, visuospatial deficits, motor and coordination challenges, memory problems, and impairments in executive functioning—"higher-level" cognitive skills like flexibility, planning, organization, impulse control, judgment, and novel problem-solving. Persons with FASDs have daily functioning skills and life outcomes that typically are more impaired than IQ alone would predict (Streissguth et al., 2004). While research has not yet found a unique neurobehavioral profile in FASD, there are empirically supported neurodevelopmental hallmarks, including individual variability in cognitive testing (e.g., variability between domains of functioning and within-test variability) as well as a generalized deficit in the processing and integration of complex information (Kodituwakku, 2009). Effects of FASD may be quite subtle in early childhood but are often more apparent during elementary school, with widening gaps as demands for more abstract/complex thought and independence increase. Children with FASD often fail to keep up with peers in academics and adaptive functioning at developmental "turning points" like second to fourth grade, transition to middle school, and extended transition to young adulthood (Olson, Oti, Gelo, & Beck, 2009).

As might be expected, current guidelines show significant variability in functional criteria for CNS impairments:

- IOM criteria for pFAS and ARND include the following definition for brain functional impairment (Stratton et al., 1996, p. 76): "Evidence of a complex pattern of behavior or cognitive abnormalities that are inconsistent with developmental level and cannot be explained by familial background or environment alone, such as learning difficulties; deficits in school performance; poor impulse control; problems in social perception; deficits in higher level receptive and expressive language; poor capacity for abstraction or metacognition; specific deficits in mathematical skills; or problems in memory, attention, or judgment."
- 4-Digit Code contains two levels of dysfunction and specific cut points for severe dysfunction: SE/AE (severe impairment) reflects probable CNS damage and requires "significant" impairment—performance that falls 2 or more SDs below the mean on a standardized test—in three or more domains of brain function. ND/AE (mild-moderate impairment) is quite broad, encompassing a range of delays and/or dysfunction that suggests the possibility of CNS damage. Evidence for this level of dysfunction can come from standardized psychometric tests, observational data, and/or caregiver interview. "Moderate dysfunction" in ND/AE has been viewed in research comparisons of criteria as "one to two domains ≤ -2 SDs and/or one or more domains ≤ 1.5 SDs" (Astley Hemingway et al., 2019).
- *DSM-5* criteria for ND-PAE introduce three new "superordinate" categories of dysfunction that lack specific cutoffs for standardized testing, relying more on clinical judgment (Olson, 2015). Criteria require at least one neurocognitive deficit (e.g., full-scale IQ ≤ 70, impaired executive functioning, learning, memory, or visual-spatial reasoning), at least one self-regulation deficit (mood or behavioral dysregulation, attention deficit, or impulse control impairment), and at least two adaptive deficits (communication, social communication/interaction, daily living skills, motor skills). IQ is the only deficit where a cutoff point is specified.
- Hoyme 2016 criteria (Hoyme et al., 2016) for functional impairments are complex, varying based on age and diagnosis. For an FAS or pFAS diagnosis in children under three, there must be evidence of developmental delay that falls at least 1.5 SD below the mean. In children of age 3 or older, neurobehavioral impairment in FAS and pFAS is defined as follows (a or b):

(a) WITH COGNITIVE IMPAIRMENT:

- Evidence of global impairment (general conceptual ability at least 1.5 SD below the mean, or performance IQ or verbal IQ or spatial IQ at least 1.5 SD below the mean), *OR*
- Cognitive deficit in at least 1 neurobehavioral domain at least 1.5 SD below the mean (e.g., impairments in executive function, specific learning skill, memory, visual-spatial functioning).

(b) WITH BEHAVIORAL IMPAIRMENT (but) WITHOUT COGNITIVE IMPAIRMENT:

- Evidence of behavioral deficiency (at least 1.5 SD below the mean) in at least one self-regulation domain (e.g., mood or behavioral regulation, attention deficit, impulse control).

• For a diagnosis of ARND, neurobehavioral impairment is defined as follows for children of age 3 and older (note there are no ARND criteria for children under age 3, not even those with severe microcephaly):

(a) WITH COGNITIVE IMPAIRMENT:

- Evidence of global impairment (general conceptual ability at least 1.5 SD below the mean, or performance IQ or verbal IQ or spatial IQ at least 1.5 SD below the mean), *OR*
- Cognitive deficits in at least two neurobehavioral domains that fall at least 1.5 SD below the mean (e.g., impairments in executive function, specific learning skill, memory, visual-spatial functioning).

(b) WITH BEHAVIORAL IMPAIRMENT (but) WITHOUT COGNITIVE IMPAIRMENT:

- Evidence of behavioral deficits in at least two self-regulation domains (e.g., mood or behavioral regulation, attention deficit, impulse control) that fall at least 1.5 SD below the mean.

6.5 Choice of Diagnostic System

While consensus on a single diagnostic approach has not been achieved to date, this is hardly unusual in the practice of medicine. For a practicing clinician, choice of diagnostic criteria may be determined by the clinic, medical system, or country in which he/she works. For a forensic medical expert, one's clinical experience certainly plays a role in choice of criteria. It should be noted that I was trained in and practice at the clinic where the 4-Digit Code was created.

With respect to legal precedence and published forensic protocols, IOM has a significant history in forensic practice. However, as noted, IOM criteria limitations include publication date in relation to empirical findings after 1996 and reliance on relatively vague gestalt criteria. A proposed forensic protocol that addresses such concerns (Novick Brown, Wartnik, Connor, & Adler, 2010) uses IOM criteria as a framework in conjunction with CDC guidelines to quantify neurocognitive deficits (i.e., either IQ below 70 and/or impairments in at least three functional domains that fall 1 or more SDs below the mean) and 4-Digit Code techniques to measure facial features. This forensic protocol has been used extensively and effectively in the United States over the past decade, typically in tandem with neuroimaging that provides supplemental information.

Because of my training and practice, my bias is toward the 4-Digit Code, which was developed at the same time as IOM but has several relative strengths, including more specific case-defined criteria; more accurate facial feature measurements and analysis; capacity to capture the spectrum of growth deficiency, facial features, and level of brain dysfunction; diagnostic terminology that strives to be as accurate as possible in assigning responsibility to alcohol; and strong history of validation research (Astley, 2013). Another 4-Digit Code advantage for a provider new to the FASD field is availability of a detailed manual, lip-philtrum guides, facial feature analysis software, and low-cost online training course in the 4-Digit diagnostic process (FAS Diagnostic and Prevention Network, 2020). A perceived disadvantage of the 4-Digit Code is that it is too complex. I would argue rather that it accurately captures the fetal alcohol spectrum and is actually straightforward to use in clinical practice. The 4-Digit Codes that fall broadly under the umbrella of FASD cluster easily into four clinically meaningful FASD diagnostic subcategories: FAS, pFAS, SE/AE which describes structural evidence of brain damage and/or severe dysfunction, and ND/AE which includes mild–moderate dysfunction (see Fig. 6.2). SE/AE and ND/AE are considered equivalent to IOM's ARND.

There is no other FASD diagnostic system other than 4-Digit Code that accommodates both moderate and severe brain dysfunction. Research is clear that PAE may cause mild–moderate CNS dysfunction, which nonetheless can cause significant behavioral dysfunction. In fact, mild–moderate CNS dysfunction is the most common result. For example, in a primate study where the only risk variable was prenatal alcohol exposure, the spectrum of outcomes included 5% FAS/PFAS, 31% SE/AE, 59% ND/AE, and 5% not FASD/AE (Astley Hemingway et al., 2019). The 4-Digit Code is the only system that produces near-identical distribution of diagnoses across the full spectrum.

In contrast to 4-Digit Code, CDC criteria are limited by an exclusive focus on FAS, although an argument could be made that presumably these criteria are at least as stringent as they would be for other FASD diagnoses. Hoyme et al. (2016) criteria have been used in many FASD research projects but have significant limitations: lack of facial criteria specificity, lip-philtrum guides that perform poorly, terminology that assigns blame to alcohol more loosely than other criteria, and use of an alcohol threshold that prevents FASD diagnosis in many individuals with confirmed exposure (Astley, Bledsoe, Davies, & Thorne, 2017). Australian criteria are limited by excluding individuals with moderate dysfunction and eliminating one of the key sentinel physical features (growth deficiency) that is highly predictive of brain dysfunction. Canadian criteria present with the same limitations and, in addition,

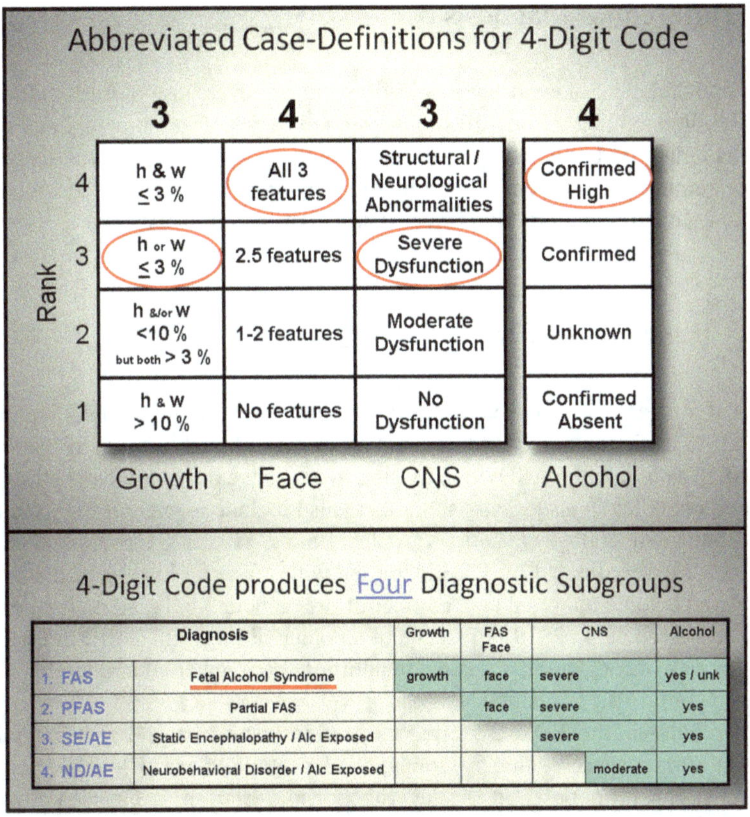

Fig. 6.2 Abbreviated case definitions of the FASD 4-Digit Code. The 4-Digit Code produces four diagnostic subgroups under the umbrella of FASD: FAS, pFAS, SE/AE, and ND/AE. Copyright 2020, Susan Astley Hemingway, PhD, University of Washington

require a threshold of exposure. While *DSM-5* criteria for ND-PAE permit mental health providers to diagnose the CNS dysfunction in FASD (a very important goal), ND-PAE presents limitations for medical providers by only addressing brain dysfunction. In so doing, *DSM-5* guidelines fail to identify or rule out the most severe end of the spectrum (FAS and pFAS) and are not able to document sentinel physical features (growth, face, brain structure) that are key predictors of alcohol-related CNS dysfunction.

In summary, medical providers working in the forensic context are encouraged to use validated criteria that include evaluation of sentinel physical features, but one also can assign a *DSM-5* diagnosis to capture CNS dysfunction. In my forensic work, I have mapped 4-Digit Code diagnoses onto both IOM and *DSM-5* terminology when appropriate to reduce confusion, describing the consistency of conclusions across diagnostic criteria.

6.6 Differential Diagnosis

While prenatal alcohol exposure is a leading preventable cause of birth defects and neurodevelopmental abnormalities in the United States, developmental and behavioral challenges certainly have other causes, both known and unknown. Diagnostic practice requires a comprehensive differential diagnosis process to consider other possible competing or comorbid issues that may have led to current presentation.

6.6.1 Prior Probability

Who is at greatest risk to have an FASD? Mothers of children with FAS are diverse in racial, educational, and economic backgrounds. Although women at risk of giving birth to a child with FASD often live in poverty, have been victims of abuse, and/or have mental health issues, at-risk mothers also include women of high socioeconomic status with college educations (Astley, Bailey, Talbot, & Clarren, 2000). Risk of having a child affected by PAE increases with maternal history of alcohol use disorder, advancing maternal age, number of pregnancies, and maternal undernutrition (McLachlan et al., 2019). Presence of an older sibling with FASD dramatically increases risk of FASD (Abel, 1988). In addition, both maternal and fetal genotype appear to confer risk or resilience.

Individuals with FASD are overrepresented in foster care and correctional systems. In a foster care screening program, prevalence of FAS was 10–15 times greater than in the general population (Astley, Stachowiak, Clarren, & Clausen, 2002). In North America, FASD prevalence estimates in correctional systems are scant but range from 0.9% to 23%. According to Canadian data, youths with FASD are 19 times more likely to be incarcerated than youths without FASD (Popova, Lange, Bekmuradov, Mihic, & Rehm, 2011). At this time, we lack accurate prevalence data regarding FASD in the U.S. criminal justice system (Flannigan, Pei, Stewart, & Johnson, 2018), but it is abundantly clear FASD has been underdiagnosed in correctional systems. In one 2004 survey of U.S. corrections systems with over three million inmates, only one inmate had been diagnosed with FAS, and there were high unmet needs to screen, identify, and treat offenders with FASD (Burd, Selfridge, Klug, & Bakko, 2004).

6.6.2 Competing Versus Co-Occuring?

It is vanishingly rare to see a patient in FASD clinic who does not have some combination of at-risk family history, prenatal alcohol exposure, other prenatal adverse influences, and adverse childhood experiences. In fact, over half of our clinic patients have parents with learning disabilities, 93% experienced other prenatal substance exposures, one-third had no prenatal care, and a similar number had prenatal complications (Astley, 2010). Half of our patients had perinatal difficulties, and 70% no longer were in the care of birth parents, with an average of three out-of-home placements. At least 34% were physically abused, 24% were sexually abused, and 64% were neglected. In addition, three-quarters of our patients had one or more mental health disorders.

Research involving adults as well as children and adolescents has found similar results. For example, a study commissioned by CDC in the mid-1990s (Streissguth et al., 2004; Streissguth, Barr, Kogan, & Bookstein, 1996) found that as children with FASD mature with what often are "invisible disabilities," they are at high risk for secondary impacts ("secondary disabilities") in adolescence and adulthood, with lifespan prevalence rates of:

- 90% for Mental Health Problems,
- 61% for Disrupted School Experiences,
- 60% for Trouble with the Law,
- 50% for Confinement (in detention, jail, prison, or psychiatric or alcohol/drug inpatient settings),
- 49% for Inappropriate Sexual Behaviors,
- 35% for Alcohol/Drug Problems,
- 80% for Dependent Living in adulthood, and
- 80% for Employment Problems in adulthood.

Odds of escaping these adverse life outcomes are increased two- to four-fold by receiving an FASD diagnosis at an earlier age and being raised in good stable environments (Streissguth et al., 2004). In my forensic experience, such protective factors are very rare.

It is impossible to tease apart the negative influences of all of these risks with precision, particularly in forensic evaluations involving adults who often abused multiple substances from a young age, dropped out of school, and suffered significant head injuries as well as multiple environmental adversities. However, careful clinical analysis during differential diagnosis allows for weighting of risk factors. Of course, diagnoses of FAS clearly implicate PAE as the primary etiology; pFAS also describes prenatal alcohol as a primary risk factor. For FASD diagnoses without sentinel physical features, when onset of neurobehavioral symptoms predates other etiological possibilities (e.g., substance use, head injuries, school dropout), FASD carries more weight with respect to clinical diagnostic judgment. Neuroimaging results consistent with diffuse prenatal injury as opposed to later head trauma may provide confirmatory data.

Assigning blame to individual risk factors in forensic analysis may feel circular at times. For example, is a head injury a competing explanation for a particular functional impairment, or was the head injury itself made more likely by impulsivity and poor judgment from underlying FASD? Is adolescent polysubstance use disorder the primary risk factor, or was that substance use itself a consequence of PAE (which multiplies any genetic risk for substance use disorder) and adverse childhood experiences? For adults with FASD diagnoses (especially with physical features or earlier-onset challenges), it often seems more appropriate to consider later risk factors as co-occurring rather than competing risk factors, which certainly can worsen outcomes in an additive, cumulative manner although not the primary etiology.

Some support for the above approach comes from a recent study that investigated what proportion of the brain structural and functional abnormalities observed in children with FASD was explained by PAE and other prenatal and postnatal risk factors. As expected, other risk factors were quite common: three- to seven-fold more prevalent than in the general population. PAE was found to be *the dominant risk factor* explaining the largest proportion of variance in regional brain size and brain function. Individually, each non-alcohol risk factor explained a statistically significant, but smaller, proportion of variance in brain outcomes. It only was in combination that the proportion of variance explained by the presence of multiple prenatal and postnatal risks rivaled that of PAE (Astley Hemingway, Davies, Jirikowic, & Olson, 2020).

6.6.3 Birth Family History

Growth and CNS features in FASD certainly can be influenced by family history. During medical assessment, we attempt to adjust for parental heights when both are known, which may be found in records. It also is important to explore records for family histories of developmental disabilities, learning challenges, ADHD, and mental health disorders. That said, it is very difficult to differentiate risk from genetic loading versus multigenerational impacts of substance abuse, mental health challenges, poverty, and developmental adversity.

6.6.4 Other Prenatal Exposures

Prenatal exposure to other drugs and substances is common. In a survey of children with FAS, 40% of birth mothers reported illicit drug use during pregnancy; 84% had smoked tobacco (Astley et al., 2000). Regarding the latter, prenatal nicotine exposure is associated with low birthweight and later risks for ADHD and antisocial behavior/delinquency. Prenatal cannabis exposure is not associated with significant growth deficits but may affect executive functioning, behavior, mental health, and achievement. Prenatal opiate exposure carries a risk of fetal, but not long-term, growth impairments as well as neonatal abstinence syndrome and moderate neurobehavioral risks. Prenatal cocaine exposure may affect fetal growth and specific domains of functioning such as language but does not appear to have significant effects on broad measures such as IQ. We lack adequate evidence regarding long-term effects of prenatal methamphetamine exposure. Alcohol remains the most widely studied prenatal substance, with the strongest evidence for lifelong impacts on neurodevelopment (Behnke et al., 2013).

6.6.5 Prematurity

Prematurity alone carries increased risks for hearing and vision impairments, cerebral palsy, hydrocephalus, neurodevelopmental disabilities, academic underachievement, and behavioral challenges that are influenced by degree of prematurity, birthweight, and perinatal and neonatal intensive care unit (NICU) complications (Aylward, 2005). PAE may increase risk for preterm birth (O'Leary, Nassar, Kurinczuk, & Bower, 2009). In contrast to typical FASD trajectories of functioning, long-term outcomes of prematurity show better adult functioning than might have been expected based on childhood neurodevelopmental assessments (Moster, Lie, & Markestad, 2008).

6.6.6 Perinatal Risks

In forensic "family lore," perinatal complications often are blamed incorrectly for developmental outcomes. This may be due to stigma and other factors affecting willingness to share PAE information. To ensure accuracy, it is important to examine birth records carefully for evidence of actual perinatal adversity, such as prolonged low Apgar scores (i.e., <7 at 5 min, which still has low absolute risk for neurologic disability; Ehrenstein, 2009), need for NICU care or prolonged hospital stay, and neurological evidence of perinatal asphyxia.

6.6.7 Postnatal Toxins

While it is rare to find specific blood lead levels in records, environmental lead exposure may be a neurodevelopmental risk for some clients, especially older clients who grew up prior to awareness of risks associated with lead in gasoline and paint. Older housing and industrial exposures continue to be a concern in this respect. Early childhood lead exposure has been found to lower IQ but not typically by more than 5–10 points for low–moderate exposure (Lanphear et al., 2005).

6.6.8 Adverse Childhood Experiences

Childhood maltreatment (also known as complex or developmental trauma) is nearly universal in my forensic experience and has significant overlap with FASD in terms of brain structural and functional outcomes. The developing brain is vulnerable to "toxic stress" (extreme, repetitive, or abnormal patterns of stress), which can impair major neuroregulatory systems with profound and durable neurobehavioral consequences (Anda et al., 2005). Maltreatment-related childhood adversity may be the leading preventable risk factor for mental illness and substance abuse. In particular, maltreatment appears to specifically affect sensory systems, network architecture and circuits involved in threat detection, emotional regulation, and reward anticipation (Teicher, Samson, Anderson, & Ohashi, 2016). However, a study examining neurodevelopmental outcomes in FASD with and without childhood neglect concluded, "behavioral difficulties are likely to be related to prenatal alcohol exposure and not necessarily reflective of parenting quality" (Mukherjee, Cook, Norgate, & Price, 2019; p. 23).

6.6.9 Academic Neglect

Histories of school absenteeism and dropout are common in forensic evaluations. Frequently, there is evidence of school challenges despite adequate attendance that precedes school dropout. Keep in mind that the majority of children with FASD have disrupted school experiences. Without an early diagnosis of FASD and extensive special education supports, it can be very challenging for adolescents with FASD to succeed academically (and socially) in middle and high school.

6.6.10 Head Injury

Traumatic brain injury (TBI) is a prominent risk factor in many forensic evaluations. Generally, prognosis for children with TBI is better than that for adults with comparable TBI. A recent systematic review of pediatric mild TBI found that most studies showed post-concussion symptoms and cognitive deficits resolved over time, with limited evidence suggesting post-concussion symptoms persisted in those with lower cognitive ability and pathology on neuroimaging at time of injury (Hung et al., 2014).

6.6.11 Substance Use

Unfortunately, substance use during the adolescent developmental period and adulthood is common in forensic FASD evaluations. Literature on long-term impacts of substance use during the developmental period is emerging and as yet poorly controlled for other risk factors (such as preexisting impairments like FASD), but substance abuse in adolescence has been implicated in cognitive deficits and brain structural impacts. Nonetheless, there also is evidence of at least partial recovery from deficits after a period of abstinence. Onset of use before age 18 has been linked with the most significant neurocognitive deficits, for alcohol and marijuana at least (Lisdahl, Gilbart, Wright, & Shollenbarger, 2013). Long-term cocaine use may cause general cognitive impairment across functions rather than specific cognitive deficits (Spronk, van Wel, Ramaekers, & Verkes, 2013). Research on methamphetamine abuse and cognitive decline is mixed, but meth appears to cause mild (on average) cognitive decline of unknown duration in at least some users of the drug (Dean, Groman, Morales, & London, 2013).

6.6.12 Mental Health

Comorbid mental health challenges are expected in FASD. In one study of adults with FASD, 92% met criteria for disorders such as alcohol or drug dependence (60%), depression (44%), psychotic symptoms (40%), and anxiety or bipolar disorder (20% each). In addition, 48% met criteria for at least one personality disorder, which included 19% with antisocial personality disorder (Famy, Streissguth, & Unis, 1998). A large meta-analysis of 127 studies found conduct disorder (91% prevalence in FAS), alcohol dependence (55%), and drug dependence (55%) were the mental health conditions with the highest pooled prevalence in FASD (Popova et al., 2016).

6.6.13 Other Malformation Syndromes

In addition to FASD, other syndromes caused by genetic variations and teratogenic exposures should be considered. None is a perfect phenocopy of FAS, but some could be confused with broader diagnoses on the fetal alcohol spectrum. Malformation syndromes with similarities to FASD are well-addressed in the CDC criteria (Bertrand et al., 2004), a publication by Manning and Hoyme (2007), and a review by Leibson, Neuman, Chudley, and Koren (2014). Table 6.1 synthesizes shared and contrasting features between FASD and other selected malformation syndromes. If you suspect an alternate or comorbid syndrome, inform counsel and

Table 6.1 Shared and contrasting features between FASD and selected malformation syndromes

Syndrome	Possibly shared features	Contrasting features
Fetal anticonvulsant (phenytoin, valproate) effects	Midface hypoplasia, long and thin lip, shallow philtrum, microcephaly, developmental delays	Trigonocephaly, medial eyebrow deficiency, maternal anticonvulsant exposure during pregnancy
Toluene embryopathy (from "huffing" during pregnancy, which frequently includes comorbid PAE)	Midface hypoplasia, short palpebral fissures, smooth philtrum, thin vermilion, microcephaly, developmental delay	Abnormal scalp hair pattern, large fontanelle, low set ears, micrognathia, and history of maternal inhaled solvent use during pregnancy
Maternal phenylketonuria (PKU) effects	Short palpebral fissures, thin lip, intrauterine growth restriction (IUGR), intellectual disability	Prominent glabella, round face, and mother with poorly controlled PKU
22q11.2 deletion syndrome, also known as velocardiofacial syndrome and DiGeorge syndrome	Short palpebral fissures, microcephaly, cardiac defects, learning and behavioral issues	Tubular nasal shape, history of hypocalcemia, and 22q11 microdeletions
Cornelia de Lange syndrome	Midface hypoplasia, long smooth philtrum, thin upper lip, IUGR, intellectual disability	Low anterior hairline, synophrys, downturned mouth angles, upper limb anomalies, molecular defects
Dubowitz syndrome	Short palpebral fissures, IUGR, microcephaly, intellectual disability	Rounded nasal tip, eczematous skin, bleeding disorders, limb and urogenital anomalies, genetic mutation
Noonan syndrome	Appearance of hypertelorism, short stature, congenital heart disease	Down-slanting palpebral fissures, short neck with webbing or skin redundancy and low posterior hairline, molecular deletion
Williams syndrome	Short palpebral fissures, long philtrum, growth deficiency, microcephaly, learning and behavioral problems	Broad forehead, stellate irises, periorbital fullness, wide mouth, full lips, connective tissue disorders, 7q11 microdeletion

discuss involving a genetics expert and possibly genetic testing. Keep in mind that patients may be impacted by a genetic disorder *and* exposure to prenatal substances.

6.6.14 Genetic Testing

Developments in genetic testing have transformed the approach to diagnosing developmental delays and intellectual disabilities (DD/ID). At least 30% of neurodevelopmental disorders now are thought to have a genetic basis, and this number is increasing as next-generation genetic testing becomes more widespread (Retterer et al., 2016). As genetic testing becomes more accessible and comprehensive, it appears genetic screening will become a more routine part of both clinical and forensic FASD evaluations. Older options for testing include karyotype, fragile X testing, and single-gene analyses. Currently, these approaches are more appropriate in evaluations where a specific syndrome is suspected. Chromosomal microarray (CMA) and targeted gene panels designed to look at known causes of developmental disabilities are a current mid-level approach to testing with respect to cost and comprehensiveness. In a 2010 practice guideline (Manning et al., 2010), CMA was recommended as first-line testing for multiple anomalies not specific to a suspected syndrome, apparently non-syndromic DD/ID, and autism spectrum disorders. The current next-level approach is whole exome or whole genome sequencing (WES/WGS), which is more expensive and cumbersome (especially if using family-based trio testing) but has a higher diagnostic yield of 16–45% (Han & Lee, 2020).

Current FASD guidelines do not mandate genetic testing, but genetic referral and/or testing should be strongly considered when dysmorphic features are present that are inconsistent with FASD. Small studies of genetic testing (primarily CMA) with FASD evaluations have shown significant copy number variations in 9–14% of the samples; prenatal alcohol exposure also could have contributed to the phenotype in these patients (Douzgou et al., 2012; Jamuar, Picker, & Stoler, 2018; Zarrei et al., 2018). Genetic screening likely will become a more routine part of FASD evaluations, especially when sentinel FASD features are lacking. The presence of structural malformations also may increase yield of genetic testing in suspected FASD.

Genetic testing results can be challenging to interpret as "variants of uncertain significance" are common. Even when a gene variant with known developmental consequences is present, this does not exclude FASD. Our clinical and my forensic experience has found several patients with evidence of both a genetic syndrome and fetal alcohol impacts.

6.7 Practical Tips for Forensic Evaluations

For detailed diagnostic procedures, readers are referred to the guidelines of their choice. What follows is intended to address specific issues that arise in forensic practice.

6.7.1 Focus of Evaluation

When evaluating for an FASD, keep in mind there are four main areas to explore: (1) presence of PAE, (2) history of prenatal and/or postnatal growth deficiency, (3) degree of FAS facial features, and (4) evidence of brain damage/dysfunction. The process of differential diagnosis is also very important, which includes consideration of other potential explanations (e.g., genetic, prenatal, postnatal, medical, psychiatric) for a patient's presentation.

6.7.2 Staffing

It can be challenging to adapt typically interdisciplinary FASD clinic workflows to a forensic evaluation. At minimum, legal teams will typically want evaluations from at least one psychologist with FASD experience (for neuropsychological testing as well as examining the evaluee's developmental history and deficits in the context of the instant offense) and a medical professional trained in diagnosing FASDs. There also may be ancillary experts with specific tasks (e.g., psychologists who examine a particular specialty area like childhood adversity or substance abuse, medical specialists in neuroimaging or genetics).

6.7.3 Screening

When initially contacted by counsel (i.e., before retention), providers should screen the possible case for any known evidence of growth deficiency, facial features (historical and "mugshot" photos), evidence of brain damage/dysfunction (historical evidence such as special education, "neuropsych" testing, and neuroimaging), and evidence of prenatal alcohol exposure. If legal teams are unable to obtain information about alcohol use *during the index pregnancy*, FASD diagnosis will be quite challenging unless the person has the face of FAS. Other matters to discuss and consider prior to retention include budget, timeline, potential conflicts of interest, billing and "outside work" policies in your workplace, and medical licensing restrictions in the state where the evaluation will occur.

6.7.4 Record Review

At the beginning of any engagement, request all available family history, pregnancy and prenatal exposure history, birth and perinatal records, childhood and adult medical records, social history, school and developmental records, occupational history, criminal justice history, mental health records, results of any neurologic or neuropsychological testing, and reports from other experts. Additional information can be requested as the legal team may have investigators or mitigation specialists that are adept at obtaining older school and medical records. If neurofunctional testing is inadequate, inform counsel that broad neuropsychological testing is required and suggest a psychological colleague experienced in FASD evaluations. At minimum, testing should address the following functional domains: intellectual, memory, attention/hyperactivity, academic achievement/learning, speech and language, visuospatial reasoning, sensory-motor, adaptive/social functioning, and executive skills (Novick Brown et al., 2010). For an empirically based adult neuropsychological test battery to assess for FASD, see Chap. 5 in this book.

It is essential for neuropsychologists to know about prenatal alcohol exposure as standard adult batteries for competency, dementia, or TBI may be too superficial to capture FASD effects or insensitive to the functional effects of PAE, which sometimes are subtle. Some tests are not designed to capture evidence of injuries below assumed floors it is presumed neurotypical adults will have reached. Psychologists' clinical judgment will be important in choosing and interpreting standardized tests, *if* they know FASD is suspected.

Early growth measures are often difficult to find but may be tucked away in school files as well as medical records. It is worth the time to wade through old records, as growth impairments in FAS are typically most evident in the newborn and early childhood periods; children with early growth deficits often "catch up" in adolescence (Carter, Jacobson, Sokol, Avison, & Jacobson, 2013). A finding of microcephaly in early childhood records can provide important evidence of structural brain damage.

Nonclinical historical photographs may be available for review. One myth in the FASD field is that the face of FAS only presents in middle childhood. In our clinical experience, facial features may change somewhat with time, but the face of FAS can be seen from infancy to adulthood (Astley, 2010). A reliable thin lip and/or smooth philtrum in retrospective photos can be used as evidence of the facial features of FAS. If facial photographs are of adequate quality (frontal and non-rotated, with relaxed facial expression), one can measure the lip and philtrum from past photos and measure the current palpebral fissure length (PFL) in person or from a clinical photo with an internal measure of scale. In our clinic's experience at the University of Washington, PFL percentile does not change appreciably across the lifespan. If current PFL is significantly small in an adult, it was small in childhood. If PFL is currently large, it is unlikely it was significantly small in childhood.

It is uncommon to find a prior diagnosis of FASD in record review. Despite FASD prevalence as high as 5% in the general US population (May et al., 2018) and as high as 23% in correctional populations (Popova et al., 2011), FASD is all-too-often missed in routine medical and mental health care. One clinical sample of foster or adopted youths showed an 80% missed FASD diagnosis rate (Chasnoff, Wells, & King, 2015).

6.7.5 Interview and Examination

Well in advance of your scheduled examination of the evaluee, provide counsel with a list of materials you will need for the evaluation and type of setting you will need. This list includes the evaluee having a clean-shaven upper lip. The camera for taking clinical photographs ideally is your own, but sometimes a facility will insist you use theirs. Access to a facility's medical room is optimal for physical examination and measurements, but often your evaluation will be limited to a semi-private "legal visit" room. Request unshackled access with appropriate supervision for physical examination and mental status testing.

At the outset of the examination, inform the evaluee and document consent regarding the purpose of your evaluation and lack of typical medical confidentiality expectations. A structured interview form can help ensure you address necessary aspects of the history. Review records prior to evaluation to help guide questions and check accuracy of responses.

A formal mental status examination such as the Montreal Cognitive Assessment (Nasreddine et al., 2005) or Mini-Mental State Exam (Folstein, Folstein, & McHugh, 1975) does not replace neuropsychological assessment but can provide a primarily qualitative impression of performance in various functional domains.

Perform the physical examination to the extent you can in the facility provided. Undressed or even gowned exams typically are not possible. Prison stadiometers are frequently miscalibrated, so you may want to check your own height to provide correction or use weight and height from medical records. Measure head circumference carefully. Typically, your measurements will be the only available occipital frontal circumference (OFC) since records usually lack such information. While Nellhaus (1968) head circumference norms have traditionally been used, the more modern Rollins OFC charts are based on larger sample sizes and are more racially representative of US adults (Rollins, Collins, & Holden, 2010).

Take manual measurements of key FAS facial features. Two lip-philtrum guides are available from the University of Washington, one for Caucasians and one for African Americans. The guide that best matches the phenotypic profile of the evaluee's race should be used. The mean of lip circularity norms for Black/White mixed-race individuals can be used when appropriate. Measure PFLs to the nearest mm with a clear plastic ruler, held as close as possible to the eye without touching the eye or eyelashes. Take ample photographs as below. Document other dysmorphic features that potentially could be caused by prenatal alcohol exposure or another syndrome (Fig. 6.3).

Take note of the following tips when obtaining and analyzing facial photographs:

- Take facial photographs with an internal measure of scale (e.g., 3/4-inch round sticker between eyebrows) in frontal, profile, and 3/4 view (halfway between frontal and profile, best for philtrum depth).
- For the frontal photo, you should be able to see the evaluee's ears equally on both sides. Improper rotation may result in erroneous right and left palpebral fissure length (PFL) measures.
- For the frontal photo, ensure that a line drawn between the ear canals intersects the bony ridge under the eyes (Frankfort horizontal plane) in order to produce accurate lip measurements.
- Ask the evaluee to relax facial expression: lips gently together without smiling, breathing through the nose. If an evaluee has a dental appliance, he/she should be wearing it, if possible.
- Ask the evaluee to open eyes widely with a "surprised" look and gaze upwards (without tilting head upwards), to help with PFL measurements.

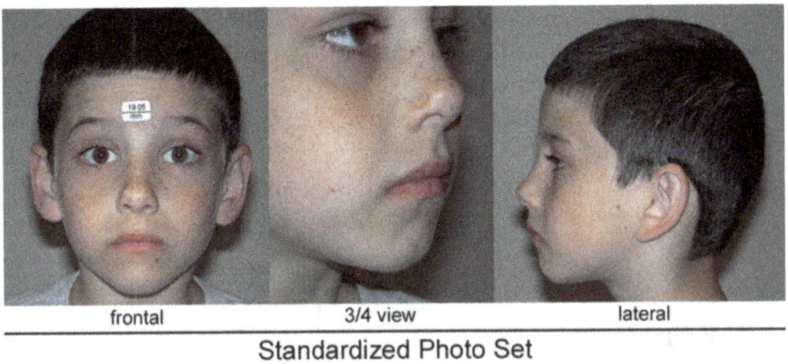

Fig. 6.3 Standardized FAS Photographs and Analysis: Three standardized digital facial photographs are obtained to measure the three facial features of FAS (short palpebral fissure lengths, smooth philtrum, and thin upper lip) using the FAS Facial Photographic Analysis Software (Astley Hemingway, 2020) and University of Washington Lip-Philtrum Guides. The evaluee should have eyes fully open, no glasses, no smile, and lips gently closed. The frontal photo should not be turned to the left or right, or tipped up or down. A 3/4-inch adhesive sticker is placed between the eyebrows as an internal measure of scale. Copyright 2020, Susan Astley Hemingway, PhD, University of Washington

- To prevent distortion of PFLs, the camera should be held 3–4 feet from the face, with the zoom feature used to increase size of the face to fill the photo frame.
- Ensure adequate resolution; photos should be at least one megabyte in size.
- Take photos with and without flash, which can help gauge philtrum depth.
- Review photographs on the camera before leaving to verify quality.

The benefit of using software to analyze facial features is that it allows measurement of lip circularity to aid in upper lip thickness ranking and provides a more accurate PFL measurement (Astley, 2015). The 4-Digit facial analysis software has built-in PFL norms. An online z-score calculator is also available (FAS Diagnostic & Prevention Network, 2020). Our clinic currently uses the Scandinavian PFL charts for Caucasians (Strömland, Chen, Norberg, Wennerström, & Michael, 1999) and the Iosub PFL charts for African Americans (Iosub et al., 1985). In addition to analyzing facial photographs for FAS features, diagnostic assistance programs that use facial images such as Face2Gene may be helpful in identifying candidate dysmorphic syndromes.

6.7.6 Genetic Testing and Brain Imaging

If you think you may want genetic testing, bring a kit from the lab you intend to use, so you can get consent from the client and obtain an environmentally stable buccal swab sample pending your decision with counsel. Imaging recommendations should go through counsel as they may require a court order and involvement of another expert. Standard clinical head computerized tomography (CT) or MRI can occasionally be grossly abnormal in FASD but generally are insensitive to the more common subtle brain injury and dysmorphology patterns revealed in FASD imaging studies (Wozniak, Riley, & Charness, 2019). The radiologist and/or imaging expert should be informed that FASD is suspected so more attention can be paid to midline brain structures (which are especially vulnerable to PAE), subtle alterations in cortical thickness, volumetric differences in distinct brain structures, and alterations in white matter and connectivity (Nguyen et al., 2017).

6.7.7 Diagnosis

See above for discussions of FASD diagnosis and the differential diagnosis process. To briefly review, the fundamentals are as follows: (1) documentation of prenatal alcohol exposure; (2) growth measurement, both historical and current; (3) clinical facial photograph analysis and physical evaluation; (4) record review; (5) analysis of childhood school and developmental reports, with adult neuropsychological assessment and any available imaging; and (6) differential diagnosis process. If you are using 4-Digit Code, a few straight-forward algorithms (with the help of the manual and/or software) will generate a code that reflects the magnitude of expression in four areas: growth, face, brain, and alcohol. As noted previously, 4-Digit Code analysis may fall into one of the four FASD diagnostic outcomes: FAS, pFAS, SE/AE, or ND/AE.

6.7.8 Report

Your report should educate the trier of fact about FASD and how you arrived at your diagnostic conclusions. It is important to document enough of your findings from record review, interview, and examination to support detailed testimony months or years after your evaluation. Expect to submit notes and other work products in the discovery process.

6.7.9 Testimony

Medicine is typically a collegial field, especially in pediatrics. It can be unsettling to encounter adversarial questioning that does not just attempt to overturn your findings but also may try to undermine your qualifications and the field of FASD generally. Prepare a testimony binder that includes your CV, report, and key materials from records review. You may wish to use a slide presentation to help illustrate a complex diagnosis and your findings, especially if physical features of FAS are present. Your role as a medical expert witness is to educate the finder of fact (judge or jury) about FASD, the specific facts in the case that support diagnosis, and your findings. You have a responsibility to explain your conclusions without being partisan or getting drawn into snippy exchanges.

6.7.10 *Common Areas of Discussion*

In addition to the basis for your diagnostic opinions, there are a number of other areas that may be relevant to your testimony:

- your training and expertise: keep in mind your specific expertise in FASD as well as more general medical training and experience;
- reliance on others' reports: in an interdisciplinary field such as FASD, this is typical in both clinical and forensic contexts;
- your ability to incorporate neuropsychological and imaging evaluations in diagnosis: you have relevant experience as a consumer of other specialists' work products;
- FASD as established science: while DSM has been slow to address FASD (FAS was mentioned in prior DSM editions but without diagnostic criteria; Sanders, 2013), other guidelines like 4-Digit Code have been establishing diagnostic criteria for many years—essentially, FASD is a medical diagnosis with over 50 years of research showing considerable consensus despite differences in diagnostic systems noted previously;
- concerns about malingering: "effort" tests are typically administered by psychologists in forensic evaluations, but they are not well-normed for individuals with developmental disabilities, and justice-involved adults with FASD in particular are more likely to fail performance validity tests (Mullally, McLachlan, MacKillop, & Pei, 2020);
- emphasis on life "choices" in differential diagnosis (poor school attendance, substance abuse, head injuries from risky behaviors, etc.): the concept of primary and secondary disabilities in FASDs (Streissguth et al., 2004) is generally illuminating here, as well as any sentinel physical features or neurobehavioral concerns that predate adolescent-adult risk factors;
- mental health and personality disorders: mental health comorbidities are expected, and personality disorder diagnoses are suspect if better explained by an underlying medical diagnosis; and,
- a corrections officer who thinks the defendant actually is quite functional: people with FASD often presently superficially as more capable than they are; in fact, significantly higher adaptive functioning (to the level of adequacy) in structured environments is expected in FASD.

6.8 Future Directions

As of this writing, clinical and forensic evaluations are impacted significantly by the coronavirus pandemic. Our local FASD diagnostic clinics in 2020-21 have used either a hybrid approach with in-person (for clinicians who must perform face-to-face testing) plus telehealth evaluations, or an entirely telehealth protocol (for team evaluations when there is adequate neuropsychological testing, using remote interviewing and photographic facial feature analysis). Forensic evaluations currently are limited by travel and visitation restrictions. Thus, it appears that telehealth may play a role in this arena as well. Relevant areas of active investigation in FASD diagnosis include formal screening for FASDs in correctional populations, postnatal markers of in utero alcohol exposure, use of 3D facial feature analysis, artificial intelligence (AI)-assisted dysmorphology evaluations, attempts to develop neurobehavioral screening tools that are more specific to FASD, and advanced neuroimaging techniques.

6.9 Conclusion

For a medical professional, FASD evaluations in forensic settings add some challenges to an already complex diagnostic process. Diagnostic criteria continue to evolve and proliferate. For example, a workgroup is currently developing consensus criteria for a research definition of FASDs, but it remains to be seen whether they can resolve the differences enumerated above. I have suggested in this chapter that medical professionals entering the forensic arena consider using the 4-Digit Diagnostic Code—it has stood the test of time since 1997, has strong empirical validation, uses specific case definitions of the sentinel physical features and possible brain impacts, addresses the full spectrum of outcomes caused by PAE, and includes easily accessible training and diagnostic tools. In my forensic experience evaluating adolescents and adults for possible FASD, the rigor of the 4-Digit Code has served me well. This highly structured approach to diagnosis is practical, reproducible, and defensible in court. With a careful differential diagnosis process, one can also weigh possible etiologies for a client's outcomes.

However, the combined diagnostic protocol used in the forensic context (Novick Brown et al., 2010) is another appropriate option as it incorporates the framework for three widely used FASD diagnostic categories (i.e., FAS, pFAS, and ARND) that have received robust research support since 1996, uses specific case definitions of CNS damage (i.e., CDC guidelines), and includes 4-Digit Code analysis for facial features and growth deficits. This combined approach has also stood the test of time and acceptance in the forensic context.

FASD expertise and education in the justice system are badly needed. Forensic practitioners are encouraged to develop expertise in FASD diagnosis as there are too few of us. My clinical colleagues with FASD experience also may find forensic evaluations to be a valuable extension of their work. Just leave your giraffe hammers at home.

References

Abel, E. L. (1988). Fetal alcohol syndrome in families. *Neurotoxicology and Teratology, 10*(1), 1–2. https://doi.org/10.1016/0892-0362(88)90060-8

Abel, E. L. (1997). Was the fetal alcohol syndrome recognized in the ancient Near East? *Alcohol and Alcoholism, 32*(1), 3–7. https://doi.org/10.1093/oxfordjournals.alcalc.a008231

Abel, E. L. (1999). Was the fetal alcohol syndrome recognized by the Greeks and Romans? *Alcohol and Alcoholism, 34*(6), 868–872. https://doi.org/10.1093/alcalc/34.6.868

Allanson, J. E., Biesecker, L. G., Carey, J. C., & Hennekam, R. C. M. (2009). Elements of morphology: Introduction. *American Journal of Medical Genetics, Part A, 149A*(1), 2–5. https://doi.org/10.1002/Fajmg.a.32601

American Psychiatric Association (APA). (2013). *Diagnostic and statistical manual of mental disorders (DSM-5)* (5th ed.). Arlington, VA: American Psychiatric Association.

Anda, R. F., Felitti, V. J., Bremner, J. D., Walker, J. D., Whitfield, C., Perry, B. D., … Giles, W. H. (2005). The enduring effects of abuse and related adverse experiences in childhood. *European Archives of Psychiatry and Clinical Neuroscience, 256*(3), 174–186. https://doi.org/10.1007/s00406-005-0624-4

Astley Hemingway S. J. (2020). High facial specificity and positive predictive value are required to diagnose fetal alcohol syndrome when prenatal alcohol exposure is unknown. *Advances in Pediatric Research, 7*(44), 1–11. https://doi.org/10.35248/2385-4529.20.7.44

Astley Hemingway, S. J., Bledsoe, J. M., Brooks, A., Davies, J. K., Jirikowic, T., Olson, E. M., & Thorne, J. C. (2019). Comparison of the 4-digit code, Canadian 2015, Australian 2016 and Hoyme 2016 fetal alcohol spectrum disorder diagnostic guidelines. *Advances in Pediatric Research, 6*(2), 31. https://doi.org/10.35248/2385-4529.19.6.31

Astley Hemingway, S. J., Bledsoe, J. M., Davies, J. K., Brooks, A., Jirikowic, T., & Olson, E. M. (2018). Twin study confirms virtually identical prenatal alcohol exposures can lead to markedly different fetal alcohol spectrum disorder outcomes-fetal genetics influences fetal vulnerability. *Advances in Pediatric Research, 5*(3), 23. https://doi.org/10.24105/apr.2019.5.23

Astley Hemingway, S. J., Davies, J. K., Jirikowic, T., & Olson, E. M. (2020). What proportion of the brain structural and functional abnormalities observed among children with fetal alcohol spectrum disorder is explained by their prenatal alcohol exposure and their other prenatal and postnatal risks? *Advances in Pediatric Research, 7*(41), 1–16. https://www.longdom.org/articles/what-proportion-of-the-brain-structural-and-functional-abnormalities-observed-among-children-with-fetal-alcohol-spectrum.pdf

Astley, S. J. (2004). *Diagnostic guide for fetal alcohol spectrum disorders: The 4-digit diagnostic code* (3rd ed.). Seattle: University of Washington.

Astley, S. J. (2006). Comparison of the 4-digit diagnostic code and the Hoyme diagnostic guidelines for fetal alcohol spectrum disorders. *Pediatrics, 118*(4), 1532–1545. https://doi.org/10.1542/peds.2006-0577

Astley, S. J. (2010). Profile of the first 1,400 patients receiving diagnostic evaluations for fetal alcohol spectrum disorder at the Washington State fetal alcohol syndrome diagnostic & prevention network. *Canadian Journal of Clinical Pharmacology, 17*(1), e132–e164.

Astley, S. J. (2013). Validation of the fetal alcohol spectrum disorder (FASD) 4-digit diagnostic code. *Journal of Population Therapeutics and Clinical Pharmacology, 20*(3), e416–e467.

Astley, S. J. (2015). Palpebral fissure length measurement: Accuracy of the FAS facial photographic analysis software and inaccuracy of the ruler. *Journal of Population Therapeutics and Clinical Pharmacology, 22*(1), e9–e26.

Astley, S. J., Bailey, D., Talbot, C., & Clarren, S. K. (2000). Fetal alcohol syndrome (FAS) primary prevention through FAS diagnosis: II. A comprehensive profile of 80 birth mothers of children with FAS. *Alcohol and Alcoholism (Oxford, Oxfordshire), 35*(5), 509–519. https://doi.org/10.1093/alcalc/35.5.509

Astley, S. J., Bledsoe, J. M., & Davies, J. K. (2016). The essential role of growth deficiency in the diagnosis of fetal alcohol spectrum disorder. *Advances in Pediatric Research, 3*(9), 1–20. https://depts.washington.edu/fasdpn/pdfs/Astley-Growth2016Abstract.pdf.

Astley, S. J., Bledsoe, J. M., Davies, J. K., & Thorne, J. C. (2017). Comparison of the FASD 4-digit code and Hoyme et al. 2016 FASD diagnostic guidelines. *Advances in Pediatric Research, 4*(13), 1–26. https://depts.washington.edu/fasdpn/pdfs/APR-84363.pdf.

Astley, S. J., & Clarren, S. K. (1997). *Diagnostic guide for fetal alcohol syndrome and related conditions: The 4-digit diagnostic code* (1st ed.). Seattle: University of Washington Press.

Astley, S. J., & Clarren, S. K. (2000). Diagnosing the full spectrum of fetal alcohol-exposed individuals: Introducing the 4-digit diagnostic code. *Alcohol and Alcoholism, 35*(4), 400–410. https://doi.org/10.1093/alcalc/35.4.400

Astley, S. J., Stachowiak, J., Clarren, S. K., & Clausen, C. (2002). Application of the fetal alcohol syndrome facial photographic screening tool in a foster care population. *Journal of Pediatrics, 141*(5), 712–717. https://doi.org/10.1067/mpd.2002.129030

Aylward, G. P. (2005). Neurodevelopmental outcomes of infants born prematurely. *JDBP: Journal of Developmental and Behavioral Pediatrics, 26*(6), 427–440. https://doi.org/10.1097/00004703-200512000-00008

Behnke, M., Smith, V. C., & Committee on Substance Abuse, & Committee on Fetus and Newborn. (2013). Prenatal substance abuse: Short- and long-term effects on the exposed fetus. *Pediatrics, 131*(3), e1009–e1024. https://doi.org/10.1542/peds.2012-3931

Bertrand, J., Floyd, R. L., Weber, M. K., O'Connor, M., Johnson, K. A., .Riley, E. P., & Cohen, D. E. (2004). Fetal alcohol syndrome: Guidelines for referral and diagnosis. Atlanta, GA: Centers for Disease Control and Prevention. https://www.cdc.gov/ncbddd/fasd/documents/fas_guidelines_accessible.pdf

Bower, C., & Elliott, E. J. (2016). Australian guide to the diagnosis of fetal alcohol spectrum disorder (FASD). Report to Australian Government Department of Health, 2–105. https://www.fasdhub.org.au/siteassets/pdfs/australian-guide-to-diagnosis-of-fasd_all-appendices.pdf

Burd, L., Selfridge, R., Klug, M., & Bakko, S. (2004). Fetal alcohol syndrome in the United States corrections system. *Addiction Biology, 9*(2), 169–176. https://doi.org/10.1080/13556210410001717060

Caputo, C., Wood, E., & Jabbour, L. (2016). Impact of fetal alcohol exposure on body systems: A systematic review. *Birth Defects Research, Part C, Embryo Today, 108*(2), 174–180. https://doi.org/10.1002/bdrc.21129

Carter, R. C., Jacobson, J. L., Molteno, C. D., Dodge, N. C., Meintjes, E. M., & Jacobson, S. W. (2016). Fetal alcohol growth restriction and cognitive impairment. *Pediatrics, 138*(2), e20160775. https://doi.org/10.1542/peds.2016-0775

Carter, R. C., Jacobson, J. L., Sokol, R. J., Avison, M. J., & Jacobson, S. W. (2013). Fetal alcohol-related growth restriction from birth through young adulthood and moderating effects of maternal prepregnancy weight. *Alcoholism: Clinical and Experimental Research, 37*(3), 452–462. https://doi.org/10.1111/j.1530-0277.2012.01940.x

FAS Diagnostic & Prevention Network (2020). FAS DPN website. http://depts.washington.edu/fasdpn/

Chasnoff, I. J., Wells, A. M., & King, L. (2015). Misdiagnosis and missed diagnoses in foster and adopted children with prenatal alcohol exposure. *Pediatrics, 135*(2), 264–270. https://doi.org/10.1542/peds.2014-2171

Chen, Z., Li, S., Guo, L., Peng, X., & Liu, Y. (2020). Prenatal alcohol exposure induced congenital heart diseases: From bench to bedside. *Birth Defects Research*. https://doi.org/10.1002/bdr2.1743

Chudley, A. E., Conry, J., Cook, J. L., Loock, C., Rosales, T., LeBlanc, N., & Public Health Agency of Canada's National Advisory Committee on Fetal Alcohol Spectrum Disorder. (2005). Fetal alcohol spectrum disorder: Canadian guidelines for diagnosis. *CMAJ: Canadian Medical Association Journal, 172*(Suppl. 5), S1–S21. https://doi.org/10.1503/cmaj.1040302

Church, M. W., & Kaltenbach, J. A. (1997). Hearing, speech, language, and vestibular disorders in the fetal alcohol syndrome: A literature review. *Alcoholism: Clinical and Experimental Research, 21*(3), 495–512. https://doi.org/10.1111/j.1530-0277.1997.tb03796.x

Clarren, S. K., & Smith, D. W. (1978). The fetal alcohol syndrome. *New England Journal of Medicine, 298*, 1063–1067. https://doi.org/10.1056/NEJM197805112981906

Cook, J. L., Green, C. R., Lilley, C. M., Anderson, S. M., Baldwin, M. E., Chudley, A. E., … Rosales, T. (2015). Fetal alcohol spectrum disorder: A guideline for diagnosis across the lifespan. *CMAJ: Canadian Medical Association Journal, 188*(3), 191–197. https://doi.org/10.1503/cmaj.141593

Dean, A. C., Groman, S. M., Morales, A. M., & London, E. D. (2013). An evaluation of the evidence that methamphetamine abuse causes cognitive decline in humans. *Neuropsychopharmacology, 38*(2), 259–274. https://doi.org/10.1038/npp.2012.179

del Campo, M., & Jones, K. L. (2017). A review of the physical features of the fetal alcohol spectrum disorders. *European Journal of Medical Genetics, 60*(1), 55–64. https://doi.org/10.1016/j.ejmg.2016.10.004

Douzgou, S., Breen, C., Crow, Y. J., Chandler, K., Metcalfe, K., Jones, E., … Clayton-Smith, J. (2012). Diagnosing fetal alcohol syndrome: New insights from newer genetic technologies. *Archives of Disease in Childhood, 97*(9), 812–817. https://doi.org/10.1136/archdischild-2012-302125

Ehrenstein, V. (2009). Association of Apgar scores with death and neurologic disability. *Clinical Epidemiology, 1*, 45–53.

Famy, C., Streissguth, A. P., & Unis, A. S. (1998). Mental illness in adults with fetal alcohol syndrome or fetal alcohol effects. *American Journal of Psychiatry, 155*(4), 552–554. https://doi.org/10.1176/ajp.155.4.552

FAS Diagnostic & Prevention Network. (2020). Palpebral fissure length Z-score calculator. http://depts.washington.edu/fasdpn/htmls/diagnostic-tools.htm#pfl

Fast, D. K., & Conry, J. (2009). Fetal alcohol spectrum disorders and the criminal justice system. *Developmental Disabilities Research Reviews, 15*(3), 250–257. https://doi.org/10.1002/ddrr.66

Flak, A. L., Su, S., Bertrand, J., Denny, C. H., Kesmodel, U. S., & Cogswell, M. E. (2013). The association of mild, moderate, and binge prenatal alcohol exposure and child neuropsychological outcomes: A meta-analysis. *Alcoholism: Clinical and Experimental Research, 38*(1), 214–226. https://doi.org/10.1111/acer.12214

Flannigan, K., Pei, J., Stewart, M., & Johnson, A. (2018). Fetal alcohol spectrum disorder and the criminal justice system: A systematic literature review. *International Journal of Law and Psychiatry, 57*, 42–52. https://doi.org/10.1016/j.ijlp.2017.12.008

Folstein, M. F., Folstein, S. E., & McHugh, P. R. (1975). "Mini-mental state." A practical method for grading the cognitive state of patients for the clinician. *Journal of Psychiatric Research, 12*(3), 189–198. https://doi.org/10.1016/0022-3956(75)90026-6

Gabriel, K., Hofmann, C., Glavas, M., & Weinberg, J. (1998). The hormonal effects of alcohol use on the mother and fetus. *Alcohol Health & Research World, 22*(3), 170–177.

Gyllencreutz, E., Aring, E., Landgren, V., Svensson, L., Landgren, M., & Grönlund, M. A. (2020). Ophthalmological findings in fetal alcohol spectrum disorders – A cohort study from childhood to adulthood. *American Journal of Ophthalmology, 214*, 14–20. https://doi.org/10.1016/j.ajo.2019.12.016

Hagan, J. F., Balachova, T., Bertrand, J., Chasnoff, I., Dang, E., Fernandez-Baca, D., … Zubler, J. (2016). Neurobehavioral disorder associated with prenatal alcohol exposure. *Pediatrics, 138*(4), e20151553. https://doi.org/10.1542/peds.2015-1553

Han, J. Y., & Lee, I. G. (2020). Genetic tests by next-generation sequencing in children with developmental delay and/or intellectual disability. *Clinical and Experimental Pediatrics, 63*(6), 195–202. https://doi.org/10.3345/kjp.2019.00808

Henderson, J., Gray, R., & Brocklehurst, P. (2007). Systematic review of effects of low-moderate prenatal alcohol exposure on pregnancy outcome. *BJOG : An International Journal of Obstetrics and Gynaecology, 114*(3), 243–252. https://doi.org/10.1111/j.1471-0528.2006.01163.x

Himes, J. H., Roche, A. F., Thissen, D., & Moore, W. M. (1985). Parent-specific adjustments for evaluation of recumbent length and stature of children. *Pediatrics, 75*(2), 304–313.

Hofer, R., & Burd, L. (2009). Review of published studies of kidney, liver, and gastrointestinal birth defects in fetal alcohol spectrum disorders. *Birth Defects Research, Part A: Clinical and Molecular Teratology, 85*(3), 179–183. https://doi.org/10.1002/bdra.20562

Hoyme, H. E., Kalberg, W. O., Elliott, A. J., Blankenship, J., Buckley, D., Marais, A.-S., … May, P. A. (2016). Updated clinical guidelines for diagnosing fetal alcohol spectrum disorders. *Pediatrics, 138*(2), e20154256. https://doi.org/10.1542/peds.2015-4256

Hoyme, H. E., May, P. A., Kalberg, W. O., Kodituwakku, P., Gossage, J. P., Trujillo, P. M., … Robinson, L. K. (2005). A practical clinical approach to diagnosis of fetal alcohol spectrum disorders: Clarification of the 1996 institute of medicine criteria. *Pediatrics, 115*(1), 39–47. https://doi.org/10.1542/peds.2004-0259

Hung, R., Carroll, L. J., Cancelliere, C., Côté, P., Rumney, P., Keightley, M., … Cassidy, J. D. (2014). Systematic review of the clinical course, natural history, and prognosis for pediatric mild traumatic brain injury: Results of the international collaboration on mild traumatic brain injury prognosis. *Archives of Physical Medicine and Rehabilitation, 95*(Suppl. 3), S174–S191. https://doi.org/10.1016/j.apmr.2013.08.301

Iosub, S., Fuchs, M., Bingol, N., Stone, R. K., Gromisch, D. S., & Wasserman, E. (1985). Palpebral fissure length in black and Hispanic children: Correlation with head circumference. *Pediatrics, 75*(2), 318–320.

Jamuar, S. S., Picker, J. D., & Stoler, J. M. (2018). Utility of genetic testing in fetal alcohol spectrum disorder. *Journal of Pediatrics, 196*, 270–274.e1. https://doi.org/10.1016/j.jpeds.2017.12.046

Johnson, S., Moyer, C. L., Klug, M. G., & Burd, L. (2017). Comparison of alcohol-related neurodevelopmental disorders and neurodevelopmental disorders associated with prenatal alcohol exposure diagnostic criteria. *Journal of Developmental and Behavioral Pediatrics, 39*, 163–167. https://doi.org/10.1097/dbp.0000000000000523

Jones, K. L., & Smith, D. W. (1973). Recognition of the fetal alcohol syndrome in early infancy. *Lancet, 302*(7836), 999–1001. https://doi.org/10.1016/s0140-6736(73)91092-1

Jones, K. L., Smith, D. W., Ulleland, C. N., & Streissguth, A. P. (1973). Pattern of malformation in offspring of chronic alcoholic mothers. *Lancet, 301*(7815), 1267–1271. https://doi.org/10.1016/s0140-6736(73)91291-9

Kable, J. A., & Coles, C. D. (2018). Evidence supporting the internal validity of the proposed ND-PAE disorder. *Child Psychiatry and Human Development, 49*(2), 163–175. https://doi.org/10.1007/s10578-017-0738-8

Kesmodel, U. S., Nygaard, S. S., Mortensen, E. L., Bertrand, J., Denny, C. H., Glidewell, A., & Astley Hemingway, S. (2019). Are low-to-moderate average alcohol consumption and isolated episodes of binge drinking in early pregnancy associated with facial features related to fetal alcohol syndrome in 5-year-old children? *Alcoholism: Clinical and Experimental Research, 43*(6), 1199–1212. https://doi.org/10.1111/acer.14047

Kodituwakku, P. W. (2009). Neurocognitive profile in children with fetal alcohol spectrum disorders. *Developmental Disabilities Research Reviews, 15*(3), 218–224. https://doi.org/10.1002/ddrr.73

Lanphear, B. P., Hornung, R., Khoury, J., Yolton, K., Baghurst, P., Bellinger, D. C., … Roberts, R. (2005). Low-level environmental lead exposure and children's intellectual function: An international pooled analysis. *Environmental Health Perspectives, 113*(7), 894–899. https://doi.org/10.1289/ehp.7688

Lees, B., Mewton, L., Jacobus, J., Valadez, E. A., Stapinski, L. A., Teesson, M., … Squeglia, L. M. (2020). Association of prenatal alcohol exposure with psychological, behavioral, and neurodevelopmental outcomes in children from the adolescent brain cognitive development study. *American Journal of Psychiatry, 177*(11), 1060–1072. https://doi.org/10.1176/appi.ajp.2020.20010086

Leibson, T., Neuman, G., Chudley, A. E., & Koren, G. (2014). The differential diagnosis of fetal alcohol spectrum disorder. *Journal of Population Therapeutics & Clinical Pharmacology, 21*(1), e1–e30.

Lemoine, P. (2012). The history of alcoholic fetopathies. 1997. *Journal of Population Therapeutics & Clinical Pharmacology, 19*(2), e224–e226.

Lemoine, P., Harousseau, H., Borteyru, J. P., & Menuet, J. C. (1968). Les enfants de parents alcooliques: Anomalies observees a propos de 127 cas. *Ouest méd, 21*, 476–482.

Lipinski, R. J., Hammond, P., O'Leary-Moore, S. K., Ament, J. J., Pecevich, S. J., Jiang, Y., … Sulik, K. K. (2012). Ethanol-induced face-brain dysmorphology patterns are correlative and exposure-stage dependent. *PLoS One, 7*(8), e43067. https://doi.org/10.1371/journal.pone.0043067

Lisdahl, K. M., Gilbart, E. R., Wright, N. E., & Shollenbarger, S. (2013). Dare to delay? The impacts of adolescent alcohol and marijuana use onset on cognition, brain structure, and function. *Frontiers in Psychiatry, 4*, 53. https://doi.org/10.3389/fpsyt.2013.00053

Manning, M., Hudgins, L., & Professional Practice and Guidelines Committee. (2010). Array-based technology and recommendations for utilization in medical genetics practice for detection of chromosomal abnormalities. *Genetics in Medicine, 12*(11), 742–745.

Manning, M. A., & Hoyme, E. (2007). Fetal alcohol spectrum disorders: A practical clinical approach to diagnosis. *Neuroscience & Biobehavioral Reviews, 31*(2), 230–238. https://doi.org/10.1016/j.neubiorev.2006.06.016

May, P. A., Chambers, C. D., Kalberg, W. O., Zellner, J., Feldman, H., Buckley, D., … Hoyme, H. E. (2018). Prevalence of fetal alcohol spectrum disorders in 4 US communities. *JAMA: Journal of the American Medical Association, 319*(5), 474–482. https://doi.org/10.1001/jama.2017.21896

McLachlan, K., McNeil, A., Pei, J., Brain, U., Andrew, G., & Oberlander, T. F. (2019). Prevalence and characteristics of adults with fetal alcohol spectrum disorder in corrections: A Canadian case ascertainment study. *BMC Public Health, 19*(1), 43. https://doi.org/10.1186/s12889-018-6292-x

McLaughlin, S. A., Thorne, J. C., Jirikowic, T., Waddington, T., Lee, A. K. C., & Astley Hemingway, S. J. (2019). Listening difficulties in children with fetal alcohol spectrum disorders: More than a problem of audibility. *Journal of Speech, Language, and Hearing Research, 62*(5), 1532–1548. https://doi.org/10.1044/2018_JSLHR-H-18-0359

Moster, D., Lie, R. T., & Markestad, T. (2008). Long-term medical and social consequences of preterm birth. *New England Journal of Medicine, 359*(3), 262–273. https://doi.org/10.1056/nejmoa0706475

Mukherjee, R. A. S., Cook, P. A., Norgate, S. H., & Price, A. D. (2019). Neurodevelopmental outcomes in individuals with fetal alcohol spectrum disorder (FASD) with and without exposure to neglect: Clinical cohort data from a national FASD diagnostic clinic. *Alcohol, 76*, 23–28. https://doi.org/10.1016/j.alcohol.2018.06.002

Mullally, K., McLachlan, K., MacKillop, E., & Pei, J. (2020). Performance validity testing in justice-involved adults with fetal alcohol spectrum disorder. *Journal of International Neuropsychological Society, 7*, 701–713. https://doi.org/10.1017/s1355617720000132

Myers, L., Anderlid, B. M., Nordgren, A., Willfors, C., Kuja-Halkola, R., Tammimies, K., & Bölte, S. (2017). Minor physical anomalies in neurodevelopmental disorders: A twin study. *Child and Adolescent Psychiatry and Mental Health, 11*, 57. https://doi.org/10.1186/s13034-017-0195-y

Nasreddine, Z. S., Phillips, N. A., Bédirian, V., Charbonneau, S., Whitehead, V., Collin, I., … Chertkow, H. (2005). The Montreal Cognitive Assessment, MoCA: A brief screening tool for mild cognitive impairment. *Journal of the American Geriatrics Society, 53*(4), 695–699. https://doi.org/10.1111/j.1532-5415.2005.53221.x

National Institutes of Health (NIH). (2020). National Human Genome Research Institute. Elements of morphology: Human malformation terminology. https://elementsofmorphology.nih.gov

Nellhaus, G. (1968). Head circumference from birth to eighteen years. Practical composite international and interracial graphs. *Pediatrics, 41*(1), 106–114.

Nguyen, V. T., Chong, S., Tieng, Q. M., Mardon, K., Galloway, G. J., & Kurniawan, N. D. (2017). Radiological studies of fetal alcohol spectrum disorders in humans and animal models: An updated comprehensive review. *Magnetic Resonance Imaging, 43*, 10–26. https://doi.org/10.1016/j.mri.2017.06.012

Novick Brown, N., Wartnik, A. P., Connor, P. D., & Adler, R. S. (2010). A proposed model standard for forensic assessment of fetal alcohol spectrum disorders. *Journal of Psychiatry & Law, 38*(4), 383–418. https://doi.org/10.1177/009318531003800403

O'Leary, C. M., Nassar, N., Kurinczuk, J. J., & Bower, C. (2009). The effect of maternal alcohol consumption on fetal growth and preterm birth. *BJOG : An International Journal of Obstetrics and Gynaecology, 116*(3), 390–400. https://doi.org/10.1111/j.1471-0528.2008.02058.x

Olson, H. C. (2015). Advancing recognition of fetal alcohol spectrum disorders: The proposed DSM-5 diagnosis of "neurobehavioral disorder associated with prenatal alcohol exposure (ND-PAE).". *Current Developmental Disorders Reports, 2*(3), 187–198. https://doi.org/10.1007/s40474-015-0056-4

Olson, H. C., Oti, R., Gelo, J., & Beck, S. (2009). "Family matters": Fetal alcohol spectrum disorders and the family. *Developmental Disabilities Research Reviews, 15*(3), 235–249. https://doi.org/10.1002/ddrr.65

Petryk, S., Siddiqui, M. A., Ekeh, J., & Pandey, M. (2019). Prenatal alcohol history - setting a threshold for diagnosis requires a level of detail and accuracy that does not exist. *BMC Pediatrics, 19*(1), 372. https://doi.org/10.1186/s12887-019-1759-1

Popova, S., Lange, S., Bekmuradov, D., Mihic, A., & Rehm, J. (2011). Fetal alcohol spectrum disorder prevalence estimates in correctional systems: A systematic literature review. *Canadian Journal of Public Health, 102*(5), 336–340. https://doi.org/10.1007/bf03404172

Popova, S., Lange, S., Shield, K., Mihic, A., Chudley, A. E., Mukherjee, R. A. S., … Rehm, J. (2016). Comorbidity of fetal alcohol spectrum disorder: A systematic review and meta-analysis. *Lancet, 387*(10022), 978–987. https://doi.org/10.1016/s0140-6736(15)01345-8

Retterer, K., Juusola, J., Cho, M. T., Vitazka, P., Millan, F., Gibellini, F., … Bale, S. (2016). Clinical application of whole-exome sequencing across clinical indications. *Genetics in Medicine, 18*(7), 696–704. https://doi.org/10.1038/gim.2015.148

Rollins, J. D., Collins, J. S., & Holden, K. R. (2010). United States head circumference growth reference charts: Birth to 21 years. *Journal of Pediatrics, 156*(6), 907–913. https://doi.org/10.1016/j.jpeds.2010.01.009

Rosett, H. L. (1980). A clinical perspective of the fetal alcohol syndrome. *Alcoholism: Clinical and Experimental Research, 4*(2), 119–122. https://doi.org/10.1111/j.1530-0277.1980.tb05626.x

Sanders, J. (2013). "A window of opportunity": The proposed inclusion of fetal alcohol spectrum disorder in the DSM-5. *Journal on Developmental Disabilities, 19*(3), 7–14. https://oadd.org/wp-content/uploads/2013/01/41014_JoDD_19-3_FASD_7-14_Sanders.pdf

Sanders, J. L., Hudson Breen, R. E., & Netelenbos, N. (2017). Comparing diagnostic classification of neurobehavioral disorder associated with prenatal alcohol exposure with the Canadian fetal alcohol spectrum disorder guidelines: A cohort study. *CMAJ: Canadian Medical Association Journal, 5*(1), e178–e183. https://doi.org/10.9778/cmajo.20160137

Sanders, J. L., Netelenbos, N., & Dei, S. O. (2020). Construct and factorial validity of neurobehavioral disorder associated with prenatal alcohol disorder (ND-PAE). *BMC Psychology, 8*, 53. https://doi.org/10.1186/s40359-020-00405-5

Skogerbø, A., Kesmodel, U. S., Denny, C. H., Kjaersgaard, M. I. S., Wimberley, T., Landrø, N. I., & Mortensen, E. L. (2013). The effects of low to moderate alcohol consumption and binge drinking in early pregnancy on behaviour in 5-year-old children: A prospective cohort study on 1628 children. *BJOG : An International Journal of Obstetrics and Gynaecology, 120*(9), 1042–1050. https://doi.org/10.1111/1471-0528.12208

Sokol, R. J., & Clarren, S. K. (1989). Guidelines for use of terminology describing the impact of prenatal alcohol on the offspring. *Alcoholism: Clinical and Experimental Research, 13*(4), 597–598. https://doi.org/10.1111/j.1530-0277.1989.tb00384.x

Sood, B., Delaney-Black, V., Covington, C., Nordstrom-Klee, B., Ager, J., Templin, T., … Sokol, R. J. (2001). Prenatal alcohol exposure and childhood behavior at age 6 to 7 years: I. dose-response effect. *Pediatrics, 108*(2), E34. https://doi.org/10.1542/peds.108.2.e34

Spiegel, P. G., Pekman, W. M., Rich, B. H., Versteeg, C. N., Nelson, V., & Dudnikov, M. (1979). The orthopedic aspects of the fetal alcohol syndrome. *Clinical Orthopaedics and Related Research, 139*, 58–63.

Spronk, D. B., van Wel, J. H. P., Ramaekers, J. G., & Verkes, R. J. (2013). Characterizing the cognitive effects of cocaine: A comprehensive review. *Neuroscience & Biobehavioral Reviews, 37*(8), 1838–1859. https://doi.org/10.1016/j.neubiorev.2013.07.003

Stratton, K. R., Howe, C. J., Battaglia, F. C. (1996). (Eds.), Institute of Medicine (U.S.). Division of Biobehavioral Sciences and Mental Disorders. Committee to Study Fetal Alcohol Syndrome, & National Institute on Alcohol Abuse and Alcoholism (U.S.). *Fetal alcohol syndrome: Diagnosis, epidemiology, prevention, and treatment*. Washington, DC: National Academies Press.

Streissguth, A. P., Barr, H. M., Kogan, J., & Bookstein, F. L. (1996). *Final report: Understanding the occurrence of secondary disabilities in clients with fetal alcohol syndrome (FAS) and fetal alcohol effects (FAE)*. Seattle, WA: University of Washington Publication Services.

Streissguth, A. P., Bookstein, F. L., Barr, H. M., Sampson, P. D., O'Malley, K., & Young, J. K. (2004). Risk factors for adverse life outcomes in fetal alcohol syndrome and fetal alcohol effects. *Journal of Developmental & Behavioral Pediatrics, 25*(4), 228–238. https://doi.org/10.1097/00004703-200408000-00002

Strömland, K., Chen, Y., Norberg, T., Wennerström, K., & Michael, G. (1999). Reference values of facial features in Scandinavian children measured with a range-camera technique. *Scandinavian Journal of Plastic and Reconstructive Surgery and Hand Surgery, 33*(1), 59–65. https://doi.org/10.1080/02844319950159631

Suttie, M., Foroud, T., Wetherill, L., Jacobson, J. L., Molteno, C. D., Meintjes, E. M., … Hammond, P. (2013). Facial dysmorphism across the fetal alcohol spectrum. *Pediatrics, 131*(3), e779–e788. https://doi.org/10.1542/peds.2012-1371

Teicher, M. H., Samson, J. A., Anderson, C. M., & Ohashi, K. (2016). The effects of childhood maltreatment on brain structure, function and connectivity. *Nature Reviews Neuroscience, 17*(10), 652–666. https://doi.org/10.1038/nrn.2016.111

U.S. Public Health Service, Office of the Surgeon General. (2005). *A 2005 message to women from the U.S. surgeon general*. Washington, DC: US Department of Health and Human Services. https://www.cdc.gov/ncbddd/fasd/documents/surgeongenbookmark.pdf.

Ulleland, C. N. (1972). The offspring of alcoholic mothers. *Annals of the New York Academy of Sciences, 197*(1), 167–169. https://doi.org/10.1111/j.1749-6632.1972.tb28142.x

Warren, K. R. (2015). A review of the history of attitudes toward drinking in pregnancy. *Alcoholism: Clinical and Experimental Research, 39*(7), 1110–1117. https://doi.org/10.1111/acer.12757

Wozniak, J. R., Riley, E. P., & Charness, M. E. (2019). Clinical presentation, diagnosis, and management of fetal alcohol spectrum disorder. *Lancet Neurology, 18*(8), 760–770. https://doi.org/10.1016/s1474-4422(19)30150-4

Zarrei, M., Hicks, G. G., Reynolds, J. N., Thiruvahindrapuram, B., Engchuan, W., Pind, M., … Scherer, S. W. (2018). Copy number variation in fetal alcohol spectrum disorder. *Biochemistry and Cell Biology, 96*(2), 161–166. https://doi.org/10.1139/bcb-2017-0241

Chapter 7
Neuroimaging in Fetal Alcohol Spectrum Disorder

Richard S. Adler

Abstract This chapter describes the important role of neuroimaging in forensic evaluation of fetal alcohol spectrum disorder (FASD). Beginning with an historical context for neuroimaging, the chapter emphasizes the not uncommon circumstance in which prenatal alcohol exposure (PAE) cannot be established definitively and the important role neuroimaging can play in establishing an FASD diagnosis. The chapter surveys specific neuroimaging techniques used presently in forensic FASD assessment, often in the capital murder context, with an emphasis on quantitative electroencephalography (QEEG), brain magnetic resonance imaging (MRI), and diffusion tensor imaging (DTI). Following this, the chapter addresses theoretical and practical issues (e.g., evidentiary admissibility) that are highly pertinent to using neuroimaging in the medico-legal setting. The chapter ends with a proposed protocol for optimizing the use of neuroimaging data in forensic cases involving FASD, with an illustrative case example.

Keywords Neuroimaging · Fetal alcohol spectrum disorder · FASD · Quantitative encephalography · EEG · QEEG · Magnetic resonance imaging · MRI · Diffusion tensor imaging · DTI · Differential diagnosis

7.1 Introduction

Several of the first infants identified in the United States as having fetal alcohol syndrome (FAS), one of several medical conditions included under the fetal alcohol spectrum disorder (FASD) umbrella, had died in the perinatal period (Jones &

The original version of this chapter was revised. The correction to this chapter is available at https://doi.org/10.1007/978-3-030-73628-6_19

R. S. Adler (✉)
University of Washington, Seattle, WA, USA
e-mail: richadler@fcpsych.com

N. Novick Brown (ed.), *Evaluating Fetal Alcohol Spectrum Disorders in the Forensic Context*, https://doi.org/10.1007/978-3-030-73628-6_7

Smith, 1973).[1] Later, central nervous system (CNS) abnormalities (i.e., brain damage) found at autopsy in these and other infants were described in the professional literature (Jarmasz, Basalah, Chudley, & Del Bigio, 2017). Neuroimaging performed on persons living with FASD also reported various CNS abnormalities (Moore, Migliorini, Infante, & Riley, 2014; Riley et al., 1995).

As explained in detail in this chapter, the role of neuroimaging in diagnosis was unequivocally established by two of the most important FASD diagnostic systems: Institute of Medicine, 1996 (IOM) guidelines published in 1996 (Stratton et al., 1996) and Centers for Disease Control and Prevention (CDC) guidelines published in 2004 (Bertrand et al., 2004). IOM criteria, still in use and highly relevant today, were generated pursuant to a directive from Congress (U.S. Congress, 1992, Public Law 102–321, Section 705). Per IOM diagnostic schema, CNS abnormalities are a diagnostic element for both FAS and alcohol-related neurodevelopmental disorder (ARND) and may be used to satisfy the diagnostic criterion for partial FAS (pFAS).

Apropos of the FASD diagnoses we encounter most often in the forensic context, confirmation of prenatal alcohol exposure (PAE) generally is required by IOM criteria (Criterion A). The only exception here pertains to FAS, which has a full complement of diagnostic features that together are not seen in other known disorders. Highly relevant to this chapter is our forensic experience, which is comprised mostly of felony murder defendants. It is *only rarely* among this group that we encounter examinees who end up being diagnosed with FAS. This situation resembles prevalence studies that find FAS in only a very small percentage of persons with FASD (Fast, Conry, & Loock, 1999).

Taking the issue further, the majority of evaluees seen in our forensic cases are as follows: (1) adults, (2) who had not been diagnosed previously with an FASD, and for whom (3) definitively establishing PAE often was not possible. On this last point, factors that complicate PAE verification include the simple passage of time or birth mothers and other reliable historians who are deceased or not able to be located. In such circumstances, it often is the case that ancillary neuroimaging permits a forensic expert to diagnose an FASD nonetheless. This process will be discussed in detail in the following. According to the IOM, the prime age for diagnosing an FASD in the clinical context is between 2 and 11 years. For adults presenting for evaluation, whether clinically or forensically, the utility of ancillary data such as neuroimaging can be particularly important. This chapter will address the details of how such efforts are undertaken, including "clinical pearls" and other insights.

7.2 More about Neuroimaging and Diagnostic Criteria

Per IOM criteria, neuroimaging data reflecting CNS abnormalities constitute an element that can be used to establish a diagnosis. As the IOM stated explicitly (Stratton et al., 1996, p. 69): "Other indicators of the effects of alcohol on the brain may be

[1] The author wishes to acknowledge Natalie Novick Brown, Ph.D., for her important suggestions and insights during the development of this material. Additionally, the assistance of my intern, Ms. Andrea Candalla, in researching and organizing the references cited here is much appreciated.

provided through neuroimaging techniques such as computed tomography (CT) or magnetic resonance imaging (MRI)." Insightfully, well over 20 years ago, the IOM also stated: "No single expression of structural or functional brain damage is universal or pathognomonic" (p. 72). Focusing more deeply on the fine points of diagnosis, IOM diagnostic criteria for partial FAS with confirmed maternal alcohol exposure (a.k.a., Category 3 or pFAS) requires *only one* of three elements (i.e., Criterion C, Criterion D, or Criterion E) to establish the diagnosis. Criterion C relates to growth retardation, and Criterion E relates to "evidence of a complex pattern of behavior or cognitive abnormalities," which usually is addressed by psychological and/or neuropsychological testing.

For the present purpose, I will be focusing on Criterion D, which concerns itself with CNS neurodevelopmental abnormalities. This criterion pertains to structural brain abnormalities such as microcephaly, partial or complete agenesis of the corpus callosum, cerebellar hypoplasia, and neurological hard or soft signs (e.g., impairment of fine motor skills). Importantly, IOM notes (p. 73): "Neurologic evidence for brain damage may include seizures…" In the context of evaluating neurological indicia of FASD, IOM also emphasizes consideration of what is age appropriate (Table 4.1, p. 76). As for a diagnosis of ARND—in which the presence of facial abnormalities is not a requirement—only Criterion D or E is required (i.e., CNS abnormalities *or* a complex pattern of behavior or cognitive abnormalities). Simply put, the complex pattern of behavior or cognitive abnormalities in FASD often is established by specialized neuropsychological testing (especially in the forensic context). It should be noted that in no forensic case in which our forensic group has participated has neuroimaging been used alone to establish a diagnosis, that is, *in the absence* of evidence establishing cognitive and behavioral abnormalities (Criterion E). Although theoretically, making a diagnosis of pFAS based upon evidence satisfying Criterion D alone (i.e., without evidence satisfying Criterion E) *can* be done, from a practical perspective the reader is strongly cautioned against doing so.

In addition to IOM, the CDC (Bertrand et al., 2004) published another centrally important set of diagnostic criteria for FASD. However, unlike IOM criteria, CDC guidelines *quantify* criterion severity. Although the U.S. Congress directed a working group to "develop guidelines for the diagnosis of FAS [Fetal Alcohol Syndrome] and other negative birth outcomes resulting from prenatal exposure to alcohol" (p. vii), ultimately only diagnostic criteria for FAS were generated. Nonetheless, it is worthwhile in the forensic context to apply the CDC quantification system to other conditions under the FASD umbrella involving CNS impairment (Novick Brown, Wartnik, Connor, & Adler, 2010).

Generally, with respect to IOM criteria, the CDC guidelines represent "variations on a theme." For a diagnosis of FAS, CDC requires: (1) the presence of specific facial dysmorphic features, (2) confirmed growth deficits either prenatally or postnatally, and (3) CNS abnormalities that can be demonstrated in one or more of the following ways: structural, neurological, or functional. Of special relevance for this chapter is the statement that in terms of evidence satisfying the presence of CNS abnormalities, one can rely upon "(c)linically significant brain abnormalities observable through imaging" (p. vii). The following examples are provided: reduction in size or change in shape of the corpus callosum, cerebellum, or basal ganglia "as assessed by an appropriately trained professional" (p. 14). A citation noted by CDC mentions electroencephalography (EEG) explicitly (Mattson et al., 1992).

Echoing the IOM, the CDC emphasized the importance of "up-to-date scientific evidence" as being "urgently needed to advance the field of FAS diagnosis…" (p. 3). Furthermore, it was acknowledged that "a number of structures of the brain are affected versus a single, isolated structure" (p. 7). Accordingly, "it was decided that rather than creating strict criteria …. more general guidelines should be described" (p. 7). CDC criteria also mention "(n)eurological problems…or other soft neurological signs…" (pp. vii–viii). Seizures, when not due to postnatal insult or fevers, are identified specifically as being relevant. Soft neurological signs also are applicable. It is emphasized in the CDC guidelines that to be meaningful, such findings should be "outside normal limits" (p. viii). Going a step further, the CDC also emphasized: "The use of norm-referenced measures of neurological functioning is recommended" (p. 14).

CDC concurs with IOM in its statement that: "An individual could meet the CNS abnormality criteria for the FAS diagnosis through a structural abnormality, yet not demonstrate detectable functional deficits" (p. 14). However, as mentioned previously, judicious forensic practice argues against proceeding accordingly. Our group developed a proposed model standard for the forensic assessment of FASD (Novick Brown et al., 2010). Although structural and neurological assessment was mentioned, we noted: "The team's diagnostician *may want to refer* the defendant for structural brain imaging… [which] can sometimes be helpful in illustrating the impact of FASD within the courtroom setting" (p. 409; italics added for emphasis). Over the course of time, neuroimaging has become a routine element in our evaluation protocol, in part because neuropsychological tests do not assess all functional areas of the brain and also because visual depiction of brain damage appears to have a compelling impact on legal decision makers. Consequently, failure of counsel to pursue recommended neuroimaging may support appeal based on a claim of ineffective assistance of counsel (IAC).

In 2013, the American Psychiatric Association (APA) published the fifth edition of the *Diagnostic and Statistical Manual of Mental Disorders* (*DSM-5*; APA, 2013). *DSM-5* included two elements of particular relevance to FASD. The first was explicit inclusion of the diagnosis *neurodevelopmental disorder associated with prenatal alcohol exposure* (ND-PAE), which has the *DSM-5* diagnostic code 315.8 and ICD-10 code F88 (APA, 2013, p. 86). In fact, ND-PAE is the only specific example provided under the diagnostic entity Other Specified Neurodevelopmental Disorder. No specific diagnostic criteria are provided in this section of *DSM-5* and instead, ND-PAE is simply described as "characterized by a range of developmental disabilities following exposure to alcohol in utero" (p. 86).

The second relevant element in *DSM-5* is a detailed section on Neurobehavioral Disorder Associated with Prenatal Alcohol Exposure, which contains diagnostic criteria. These criteria are contained in a subsection of Section III ("Emerging Measures and Models"), specifically "Conditions for Further Study" (pp. 798–801). To complicate matters, both the established diagnosis in Section II and Section III's Neurobehavioral Disorder Associated with Prenatal Alcohol Exposure often are abbreviated as ND-PAE. Proposed diagnostic criteria for Section III ND-PAE include the *neurobehavioral features* of the condition as well as the neurocognitive, self-regulatory, and adaptive features, which are reflected in criteria elements A to F. Importantly, although *DSM-5* characterizes this disorder as "proposed," mental health providers quickly began using Section III ND-PAE criteria to diagnose the CNS dysfunction in FASD (Doyle & Mattson, 2015; Hagan et al., 2016; Kable et al., 2016; Olson, 2015). The final element in Section III ND-PAE criteria (item G) is specifically relevant to neuroimaging and reads: "The disorder is not better explained by the direct physiological effects associated with postnatal use of a substance (e.g., a medication, alcohol or other drugs), a general medical condition (e.g., traumatic brain injury [TBI], delirium, dementia), another known teratogen (e.g., fetal hydantoin syndrome), a genetic condition (e.g., Williams syndrome, Down syndrome, Cornelia de Lange syndrome), or environmental neglect" (p. 799).

Although nowhere in these ND-PAE criteria is neuroimaging mentioned explicitly, neuroimaging may play an important role in differentiating the impact of prenatal alcohol from other causes of the clinical presentation. Differential diagnosis is especially poignant since persons with PAE are known to have an increased incidence of postnatal substance abuse, TBI, and a variety of other comorbid conditions. More often than not, the circumstance confronting experts is not one of "either—or" but carefully sorting out "how much from which?"

Having considered relevant IOM, CDC, and *DSM-5* diagnostic criteria, it is important to mention that there are additional diagnostic schema for FASD. However, these other guidelines were developed in samples that primarily involved children (e.g., Hemingway et al., 2019; Hoyme et al., 2005). For forensic (as opposed to academic or research) purposes in the United States, IOM and CDC diagnostic criteria have been of primary interest, likely in large part because forensic contexts typically involve a large percentage of adults.

7.2.1 So Then, How does Neuroimaging Help in Bridging a Potential Shortfall in Terms of Elements Needed to Establish a Diagnosis?

It is important to begin answering this question by pointing out that all opinions offered by a physician expert witness (e.g., making a diagnosis) must be offered with "reasonable medical certainty." Reasonable medical certainty is the kind of certainty a medical professional would use in making clinical decisions. At a minimum, this level of certainty must be on a "more likely than not basis." A prudent practitioner engages in a reasoning process called "differential diagnosis." In this process, the expert considers, "what diagnostic possibilities can reasonably explain the data in this case?" What is the evidence that argues for and against each diagnostic possibility, and why is one particular diagnosis being made among the various possibilities? In the absence of firm information about PAE, neuroimaging data may provide a plethora of data consistent with FASD, establishing the diagnosis.

7.3 Neuroimaging Methods Frequently Used

IOM encouraged "research to identify potential structural or functional brain abnormalities and other neurobiological indices that may be associated with, or distinguish FAS, ARBD, or ARND, and to relate these abnormalities and indices to cognitive and behavioral correlates" (Stratton et al., 1996, pp. 80–81). IOM also encouraged the development of "more specific biological markers for diagnosis" (p. 81). Along similar lines, CDC anticipated developments in this arena and set no limitations on what neuroimaging methods could be utilized. Although neuroimaging research in FASD certainly extends beyond the methods listed below, those currently most relevant to evaluating the effects of PAE on the brain in FASD are as follows: (1) quantitative electroencephalography (QEEG), (2) magnetic resonance imaging (MRI), (3) diffusion tensor imaging (DTI) and (4) positron emission tomography (PET). This "short list" of methods is informed by a number of factors relevant to the forensic context, including general availability of equipment needed, cost of the test, "turnaround time" involved, track record of a test's evidentiary admissibility, ease with which the tests can be explained and understood by the decider, and depth of the research database (i.e., not only as it relates to FASD itself but more specifically to *adults* with FASD). It generally is a good idea to be mindful of the number of tests included in testimony. Be judicious and avoid presenting multiple graphics from multiple scans—less is more.

The proposed model forensic standard for diagnosing FASD (Novick Brown et al., 2010) emphasized the important role of convergent validity. As shown graphically in Fig. 7.1, convergent validity remains unchanged (not surprisingly) as an essential, and organizing, principle. In providing testimony accompanied by visual aids (e.g., PowerPoint) to assist the court in understanding scientific information, Fig. 7.1 is introduced to the jury early on. That is, the slide is shown prior to any discussion of specific test results. "Clinical interview," which includes a full physical and neurologic examination (shown in Fig. 7.1 at the 4 o'clock position), is especially important. In our experience, the trier of fact is impressed by: (1) the physical stigmata of FASD and (2) demonstration of correlations between different "channels" of data, such as the severity of volume reduction in brain anatomic structures and their relationship to neurobehavioral impairments (Fryer et al., 2012).

Fig. 7.1 The many data sources contributing to convergent validity

7.4 The Groundbreaking Role of Quantitative Electroencephalography

Clinical application of brain wave testing (a.k.a., electroencephalography or EEG) is credited to the German neuropsychiatrist Hans Berger, who presented the first human EEG study in 1929. The "Q" in QEEG stands for "quantitative" and reflects the application of digitization (via computerized software) to EEG, making "the enormous amount of data contained in a typical electrophysiological recording more accessible" (Boutros, Thatcher, & Galderisi, 2008, p. 196). Over the past 50 years, there has been a steady explosion in QEEG research. A significant breakthrough in evidentiary admissibility of QEEG occurred in 2010 during the capital murder resentencing of Grady Nelson in Dade County, Florida (State of Florida v. Grady Nelson, 2010, No. F05–846 [11th Fla. Cir. Ct. Dec. 2, 2010]; Thatcher, Biver, & North, 2003). Florida used the Frye evidentiary admissibility standard (Frye v.

United States, 1923, 293 F. 1013 [D.C. Cir 1923]), considered by many to be more "conservative" and restrictive than the Daubert standard (Daubert v. Merrell Dow Pharmaceuticals Inc., 1993, 509 U.S. 579 [1993]). In the matter of Nelson, QEEG was admitted after a fraught evidentiary challenge and ultimately was perceived to be highly impactful in obtaining a jury verdict for a life sentence.

Around the time of the Nelson resentencing, researchers (Bell et al., 2010) reported a "remarkably high" rate (i.e., 17.7%) of epilepsy and seizure history in FASD. The authors noted such prevalence was more than 10 times the rate in the general population. The second most common type of seizures reported in the study (among those with or without FASD) was the "unclassified" type. This finding shone a spotlight on atypical presentations of EEG abnormalities. Quite importantly, the authors found it was *a history of PAE*—independent of other risk factors—that was most closely associated with epilepsy and seizures in individuals with FASD.

The Bell et al. study (2010) engendered in us a focus on atypical electrical activity in FASD rather than epilepsy per se. Their findings suggested that indicia of abnormal electrical activity could be expected on (Q)EEG. We also found encouragement in the forward-thinking IOM, which stated insightfully in 1996: "No single expression of structural or functional brain damage is universal or pathognomonic…" (Stratton et al., 1996, p. 72). Our group's first use of QEEG occurred in 2012. In 2015, we presented our initial findings at the International Association of Law and Mental Health in Vienna, Austria (Adler, Novick Brown, Connor, & Wartnik, 2015). We started by using QEEG only in "special cases," such as when neuropsychological test findings were considered atypical for any number of reasons. Early on in our experience with QEEG, "naked eye" analysis of the studies suggested that the presence of bilateral, symmetric abnormalities of LORETA (i.e., low resolution electromagnetic tomographic analysis) in anatomically midline structures was associated with FASD. See Fig. 7.2 showing the statistically

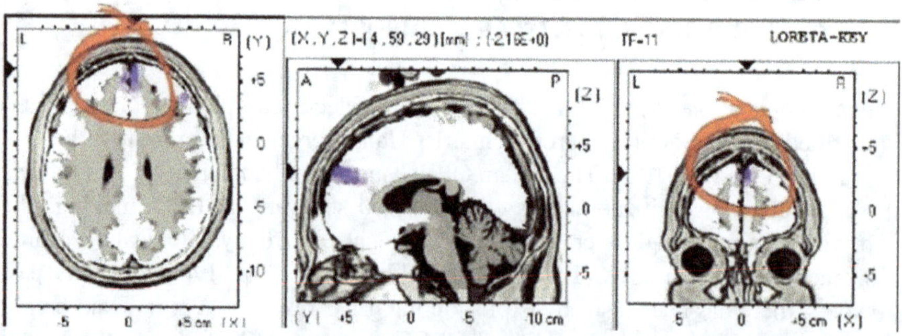

Fig. 7.2 An example of a bilateral, symmetrical midline abnormality of electrical activity on LORETA in a defendant with FASD

significant decrease in electrical activity (shown in blue and circled in red) on the axial, sagittal, and coronal views (left to right). This finding became an a priori hypothesis in our forensic evaluations going forward.

Over the course of time, QEEG has become a routine part of our evaluative protocol. QEEG's many positive attributes are worth stating explicitly, so the reader can understand the reasons for its somewhat rapid "ascendancy." What follows, incidentally, only focuses on the main features/benefits. First, availability of portable EEG equipment permits acquisition of QEEG tracings within correctional settings. Second, the cost of QEEG compares favorably with other neuroimaging methods. Third, QEEG results in a myriad of highly impactful, easily understood graphic displays (as shown above and Fig. 7.3 below), which with some frequency have prompted successful stipulated plea agreements. Fourth, certification for QEEG technicians (i.e., board certification in neurofeedback (BCN); www.BCIA.org) is valid on a national level, so worries regarding state-by-state licensing requirements do not pertain. Fifth, a "doctor's order" is not required to obtain a QEEG. In fact, any attorney can request a QEEG directly. As attorney-client work product, a QEEG can be confidential until counsel elects otherwise. Sixth, recent findings have resulted in the development of testable hypotheses specific to FASD (see immediately below). Seventh, QEEG (and other neuroimaging tests) help circumvent concerns about malingering and response style, which are routinely raised about neuropsychological test results. Eighth, unlike neuropsychological testing, QEEG is able to assess the functional status of deep anatomical structures (e.g., non-surface, subcortical, limbic, cerebellar regions). Access to such data is especially pertinent to forensic issues such as mental state at the time of the offense, legal culpability, mitigation, recommendations for remediation/rehabilitation, and risk of future dangerousness (Fig. 7.3).

In Rome, Italy (Adler, Center, Connor, & Steele, 2019), we reported an analysis of 21 QEEGs obtained from male felony defendants 16—62 years old (average age = 38). Each subject had been diagnosed by our team with an FASD, established independent of the QEEG findings. Utilizing voxel-based analysis of LORETA Z-scores, we found 17 of the 21 subjects had bilateral LORETA Coherence abnormalities at Brodmann Area 24. Applying the TBI discriminant analysis from each QEEG tracing, we found a Probability Index average of 75%, with average TBI Severity Score in the mild range. Of greatest interest and importance was the fact that average TBI discriminant score was *notably negative* (−0.49). This suggested that per the TBI discriminant analysis, features of the QEEG reflected brain injury functionally but had an appearance that was divergent from impairment caused by documented postnatal brain trauma. Figure 7.4 is the TBI discriminant analysis from one of the persons in our FASD study cohort.

QEEG findings in this analysis were incorporated into our updated, and more specific, testable a priori hypotheses following confirmation that the data correlated with neuropsychological test data. On average, the FASD cohort in our study exhibited deficits in seven domains of cognitive and adaptive functioning (i.e., academics, memory, visuospatial construction, executive functioning, communication, daily

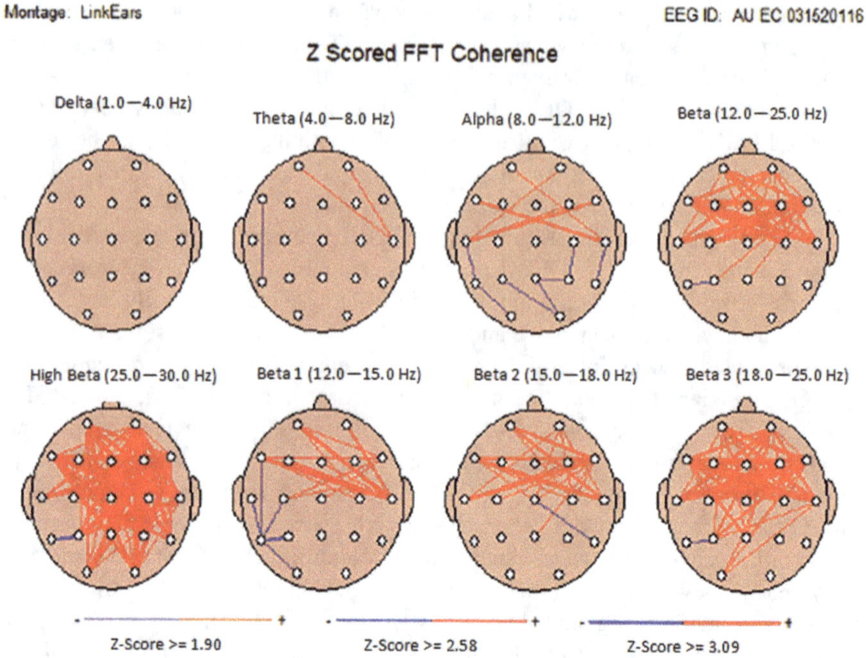

Fig. 7.3 Prominent and widespread abnormalities in Coherence (same evaluee as in Fig. 7.2), which is one of several specific measures of brain electrical activity. The presence of any line in this figure is indicative of an abnormality of $Z > 1.96$ between brain areas as defined by standard placement of electrodes

living skills, and socialization). Furthermore, statistically significant correlations were observed between neuropsychological functioning and the QEEG TBI discriminant score, specifically in intellectual/academic functioning, executive functioning, and socialization. Fig. 7.5 reflects how the results of an individual's TBI discriminant QEEG data (i.e., Fig. 7.4) is reported in tabular form in a forensic report.

There may be lingering concern regarding the evidentiary admissibility of QEEG, particularly in the State of Florida. However, in the 2020 case of *Florida v. Timothy Hurst* (State of Florida v. Timothy Hurst, 2020, 147 So. 3d 435), QEEG was admitted without being contested. A pre-trial informational interview seemingly dismissed any notion of contesting the QEEG. By following proper scientific discipline and restraint, drawing only appropriate inferences and conclusions from the data, it generally has been our recent experience nationwide (i.e., in both state and federal venues) that QEEG has been accepted into testimony without any challenge. Our current neuroimaging protocol is to recommend QEEG as early as possible in the evaluation process.

Montage: LinkEars EEG ID: AU EC 031520116

Traumatic Brain Injury Discriminant Analysis*

TBI DISCRIMINANT SCORE = -0.62 TBI PROBABILITY INDEX = 75.0%

The TBI Probability Index is the subject's probability of membership in the mild traumatic brain injury population. (see Thatcher et al, EEG and Clin. Neurophysiol., 73: 93-106, 1989.)

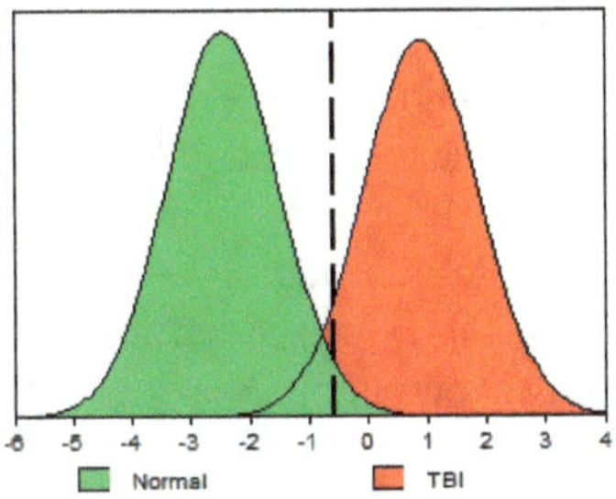

			RAW	Z
FP1-F3	COH	Theta	81.78	-0.19
T3-T5	COH	Beta	42.68	-0.64
C3-P3	COH	Beta	77.41	-0.36
FP2-F4	PHA	Beta	0.45	0.19
F3-F4	PHA	Beta	0.26	-0.33
F4-T6	AMP	Alpha	19.27	0.89
F8-T6	AMP	Alpha	-23.90	1.01
F4-T6	AMP	Beta	19.37	0.37
F8-T6	AMP	Beta	-15.80	0.69
F3-O1	AMP	Alpha	21.75	1.62
F4-O2	AMP	Alpha	-19.74	0.75
F7-O1	AMP	Alpha	30.29	-1.76
F4-O2	AMP	Beta	11.58	0.91
P3	RP	Alpha	41.58	-0.84
P4	RP	Alpha	46.21	-0.55
O1	RP	Alpha	42.57	-1.09
O2	RP	Alpha	52.82	-0.56
T4	RP	Alpha	29.79	-1.10
T5	RP	Alpha	41.68	-0.88
T6	RP	Alpha	45.06	-0.79

Fig. 7.4 Traumatic Brain Injury Discriminant Analysis of one of the FASD subjects reported on in Rome, Italy (Adler, 2019)

SCORE	MR. EVALUEE'S SCORES	COHORT MEAN SCORES (Standard Deviation)
TBI Discriminant	-0.628	-0.46 (1.27)
TBI Probability Index	75%	71% (39)
TBI Severity Index	3.654.60	2.63 (1.83)

Fig. 7.5 An illustrative example of how Mild TBI Discriminant Analysis is used in the forensic evaluation of persons with FASD (Adler, 2019)

In addition to administering an EEG, whenever possible the technician also administers a computer-based neuropsychological screening test, the CNS-VS (www.cnsvs.com), around the time of acquiring the QEEG tracing. The CNS-VS (see Fig. 7.10 in the case example) screens for cognitive deficits and provides compelling and readily understandable information for the trier of fact. Although the CNS-VS serves as an external validity indicator in terms of "effort" and alertness/attention, it should be noted that the QEEG is scientifically valid regardless of any external measures of "effort" and alertness (Thatcher et al., 2003). Consequently, the CNS-VS actually is scientifically unnecessary. That said, we find that administering the CNS-VS very capably addresses the nagging "old chestnut" about malingering, which invariably gets raised by opposing counsel. As an additional side benefit, the CNS-VS generates standardized neuropsychological data at a separate point in time from other similar data. Comparing CNS-VS test results and those from the formal neuropsychological test battery typically adds to test–retest reliability (and convergent validity) of the database. On occasions where it has become relevant, the CNS-VS developer (CNS Vital Signs) has been quite willing to microanalyze and document an examinee's responses "keystroke-by-keystroke." The availability of such in-depth analysis, when needed, can be very useful.

It also is part of our protocol that QEEG test results are not provided to the team's forensic neuropsychologist until after the neuropsychological report has been finalized. At that point, QEEG data are reviewed by the neuropsychologist, integrated into test findings, and documented as an addendum. Clinical pearl: at trial, the original QEEG tracing and the edited, artifact-free digital file are placed on a USB drive and taken to the witness stand to be close at hand should opposing counsel raise any sort of detailed challenge. Without exception, raw QEEG data have never been requested as part of a request for production by opposing experts. Such an omission, in itself, detracts from the credibility of an opposing expert impugning the proffered QEEG data.

7.5 Brain Magnetic Resonance Imaging

CDC criteria properly placed a spotlight on neuroradiological structures that had been identified in the early FASD literature as affected by PAE. Among such findings was the decreased size of the corpus callosum as well as "focal defects" (Riley et al., 1995). Occasionally in our forensic work, we have found both types of damage (see Fig. 7.6, "notch" shown in the red circle). A recent research study (Schneble et al., 2020) focused on notches in the corpus callosum and reported a notably high incidence on the dorsal callosal surface in their non-FASD control group (63.3%). The authors reported that the FASD cohort had an incidence of 55.9%, which represented no significant difference. For both groups, this appears to be a rather high incidence of abnormalities, entirely inconsistent with both the literature and our own experience. The authors acknowledged various limitations of their study but failed to highlight that they identified the FASD cohort as those in electronic records with an ICD-10 code of "an FASD diagnosis." It is unclear what actual code or codes were used in this study. Also, 37 of 96 FASD subjects (i.e., 38%) had structural abnormalities such as dysgenesis of the corpus callosum, cortical migration abnormalities, Chiari 1 malformations, or periventricular leukomalacia. Cortical migration abnormalities (i.e., heterotopias) have been present in some of our cases. As already articulated here, Schneble et al. are far from alone in pointing out that: "A single anatomic feature … is unlikely to be a suitable marker of FASD" (p. 727).

Without exception, the abnormalities we have found in MRI scans had not been appreciated originally by the scanning/reading facility. As first reported by Bookstein, Streissguth, Sampson, Connor, and Barr (2002), radiologists routinely fail to properly assess the corpus callosum—one of the brain's (and FASD's) most important structures. Our own forensic experience confirmed Bookstein et al.'s observation and became the basis for a number of practices that have become

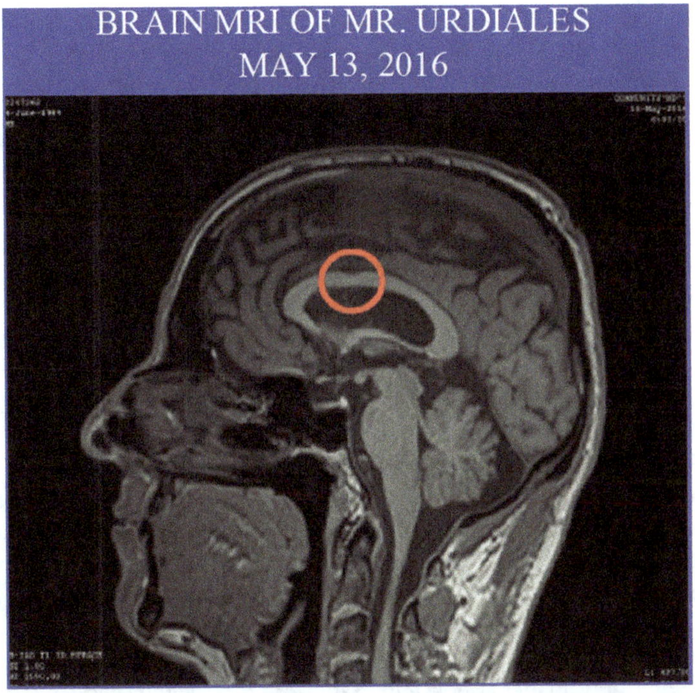

Fig. 7.6 A focal defect (a.k.a., "notch") in the outline of the Corpus Callosum

routine: (1) using standard physician's orders to document PAE and/or FASD in differential diagnosis, requesting a review of the shape and size of the corpus callosum; (2) distributing a "boilerplate" declaration to support a request for funding, which should indicate that although neuroradiologic abnormalities may be found in FASD, absence of the same does not rule out the diagnosis; (3) using an independent neuroradiological consultant, initially blinded to the circumstances of the case, to independently review the MRI in the presence of the testifying expert; (4) documenting this independent review; (5) obtaining the neuroradiologist's written confirmation of the findings; and (6) notifying the original "reading" radiologist of any discrepant findings, inviting input from them.

The advent of brain MRI quantification is another significant advance in neuroimaging technology that now is employed routinely in our work. The published literature serves as the a priori hypothesis for what might be expected in FASD (Moore et al., 2014). It is a powerful fact that quantification provides a level of exactitude that the "naked eye" is simply incapable of achieving (Ross, Ochs, DeSmit, Seabaugh, & Havranek, 2015). All too often, a brain MRI is read as being "within normal limits" when later results of volumetric quantification demonstrate otherwise. Thus, although there is no legally applicable "ineffective assistance of expert," it is our opinion that an expert's failure to recommend brain MRI quantification in cases involving possible FASD represents suboptimal practice. Quantification provides information about many important issues such as intracranial volume (ICV), total cerebral volume, total gray matter, total white matter, total cerebral ventricular volume, and volume of the frontal, parietal, temporal, and occipital lobes as well as the cerebellum and numerous sub-lobal structures, each reported with their total, right- and left-sided volumes. Sophisticated understanding of such data can provide deep insights directly relevant to differential diagnosis. For example, ICV is related to the *size* of the skull, which largely is determined during the prenatal period. However, decreased total cerebral volume in the context of a normal ICV might be indicative of cerebral atrophy from such things as chronic alcoholism during adulthood. Additionally, data regarding asymmetry of structures is especially important since FASD often is found with TBI as a comorbid condition. Volumetric quantification can vividly demonstrate such asymmetries.

At the present time, there are no "bright line" diagnostic indicia of FASD on brain MRI. That is, there are no findings that can definitively rule in or rule out FASD. Regardless, published studies support an approach of methodically looking at regions of interest (ROI) that have been reported in the literature as being impacted by PAE. First and foremost, research has demonstrated that PAE is associated with reduction in total brain size, specifically the size of the posterior corpus callosum, pars opercularis, caudate nuclei and lingual gyri, and cerebellum, all in a bilateral manner, as would be expected, given the generalized nature of alcohol as a teratogen. In addition to decreased volumes, *increased* volume has been encountered both for white and gray matter. Bookstein, Sampson, Streissguth, and Connor (2001) noted increased thickness in areas of the corpus callosum, and abnormalities in the process of pruning have been considered to explain the significant increases in volume found (personal communication, R. Adler & P. Connor, January 6, 2021). However, neither the animal nor the human scientific literature has reported on this phenomenon. Adverse developmental experiences (e.g., trauma, malnutrition) themselves are known to impact brain development and must be properly taken into account when analyzing neuroimaging data (Puetz et al., 2017).

There is an FDA-approved, "cloud-based," and widely used MRI quantification methodology that is relatively low in cost and capable of providing results within minutes of uploading brain MRI data. Although various levels of analyses are available, we have found that the most in-depth and detailed of the offerings is particularly useful. Results provided may define statistical significance at a z-score of ±1.65. Decreased volume is shown in one color and increased volume in another. Close inspection of results is warranted, however, since abnormalities not highlighted in color may be still be important and notable at the "trend" level.

Generally, we have found that there is great complementarity in using a widely used "commercial" method along with analyses provided by highly specialized experts and/or firms. A rationale for using both in tandem is the proprietary nature of the underlying database for commercial methodologies. Such status means that the scientific underpinnings of the commercial method may be fiercely guarded. This situation can lead to an evidentiary quandary when, per Daubert criteria, a

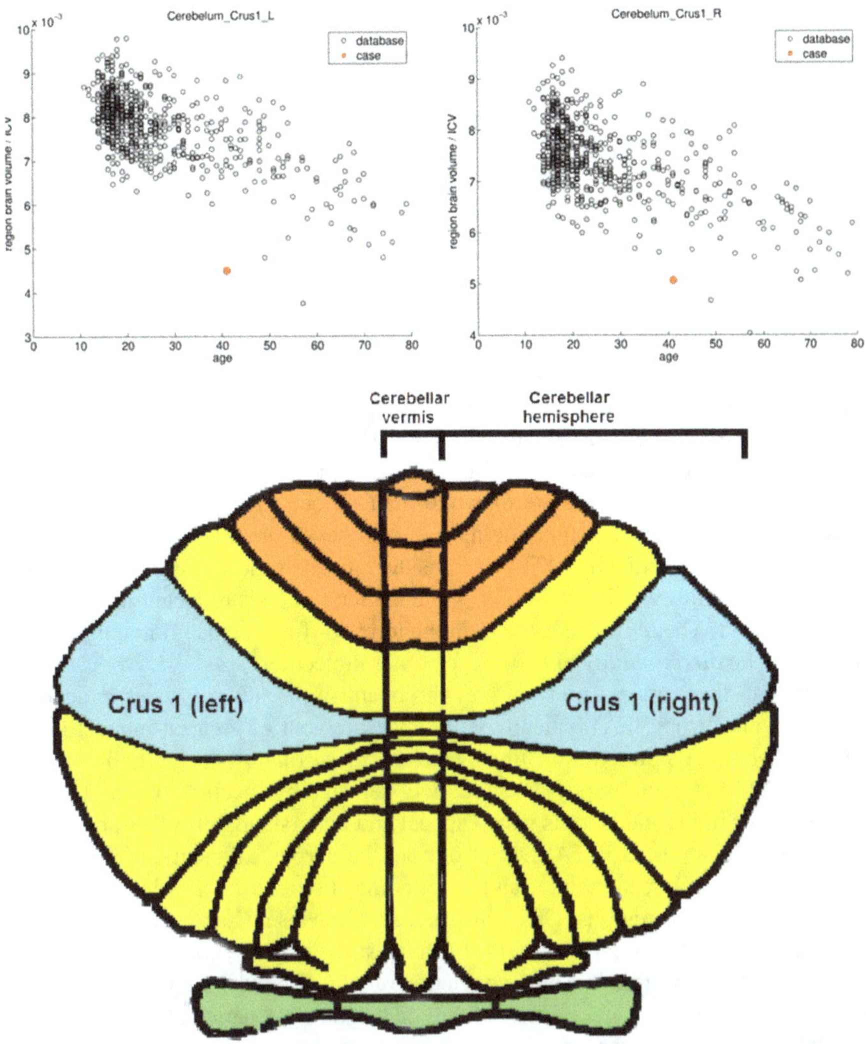

Fig. 7.7 A specially requested analysis of volumetric data in a subsection of the cerebellum (Crus 1), produced by Mindset in New Mexico

"look under the hood" at the underlying methodology is needed. In contrast, recognized specialists (e.g., Mindset in New Mexico, Dr. Ruben Gur at the University of Pennsylvania, and Dr. Joseph Wu at the University of California, Irvine) not only have an "open book policy" regarding their analyses, but they also can analyze a wider set of structures than the "plug and play" commercial providers. Specialty providers are well-suited to respond to special requests, including those for customized graphic displays (see Fig. 7.7). The evidentiary advantage of obtaining results from *both* kinds of sources cannot be overemphasized.

Above and beyond analysis of brain and sub-structure volume, morphometric (i.e., shape) analysis of the corpus callosum, bilateral caudate, and hippocampal nuclei also are available. Abnormalities of shape have been reported in FASD, but technical issues may limit their usefulness at present. Apropos of the Daubert standard, no standardized a priori method for analysis has been published, and the database used for comparison is not generally available.

7.6 Diffusion Tensor Imaging

Diffusion tensor imaging (DTI) is performed on an MRI scanner. A separate, additional scanning sequence is performed using specialized software. DTI produces valuable and important data that are complementary to data obtained from MRI. This is because MRI reflects *brain structure*, while DTI provides information about both the number *and* functional state of white matter fibers. In DTI, measurement of these two aspects of neural functioning (i.e., number of fibers and functional state) are interwoven. Specifically, DTI measures the rate and orderliness of the diffusion of water molecules within the brain's white matter, which is reflected in the terminology of DTI. The *tensor* referred to in the term "diffusion tensor imaging (DTI)" alludes to the *directionality* of the flow of water molecules.

Although there are a variety of ways to quantify the flow of water molecules, fractional anisotropy (FA) typically is the measurement of greatest interest in our forensic work. The direction of fibers, such as those running anterior to posterior (a.k.a., DTI fiber tractography), are routinely depicted by specific colors. The presence of color in DTI adds to its visual appeal and understandability. FA abnormalities have been reported in FASD, not only in the corpus callosum but also in the cerebellar peduncles, cingulum, and longitudinal fasciculi connecting the frontal and temporoparietal regions (Ghazi Sherbaf, Aarabi, Hosein Yazdi, & Haghshomar, 2019; see Fig. 7.8). As early as 2014, FA analysis of both the corpus callosum and other structures was used in a post-conviction relief matter wherein the issue of PAE could not be definitively confirmed (State of Arizona v. Charles D. Ellison, 2006, CR-04-0073-AP). Decreased FA values between z-scores of −5.56 and −12.95 were found at the body of the corpus callosum, genu of the corpus callosum, middle cerebellar peduncle, deep cerebellar nuclei, and the superior cerebellar nuclei. Although TBI also may cause abnormalities of the corpus callosum on DTI (Aoki, Inokuchi, Gunshin, Yahagi, & Suwa, 2012), concurrent abnormalities of the cerebellum are not reported. The presence of abnormalities at both the corpus callosum and cerebellum on DTI argues in favor of FASD with co-occurring TBI. Furthermore, the magnitude of FA abnormalities in the corpus callosum can be markedly greater in TBI than FASD (Treit et al., 2017), which can inform the use of DTI for differential diagnosis.

Technical issues preclude comparing FA measurements between scanners. Thus, in some circumstances it may be necessary to have a technician travel and have a DTI performed on the technician at the same facility (i.e., "human phantom

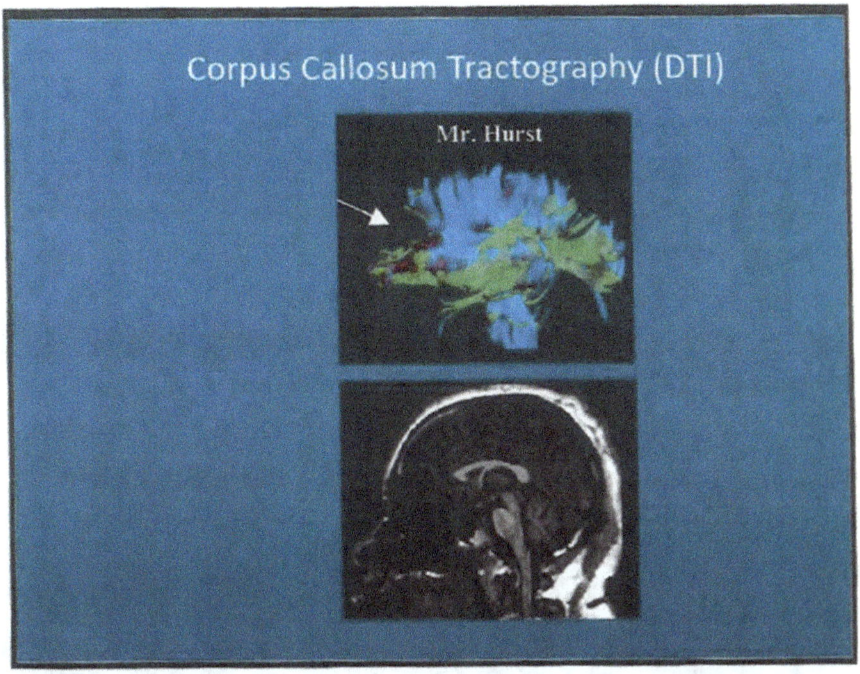

Fig. 7.8 DTI Tractography of the corpus callosum. The arrow brings attention to a prominent defect in the corpus callosum not obvious in the thinned corpus callosum on the mid-sagittal MRI (below).

phenomenon") (Palacios et al., 2017). By doing this, FA values at both of the relevant scanners can be compared, and the normative database being used can be relied upon with confidence (and adjusted if necessary for any differences). In this way, the FA values are compared properly and represent an "apples to apples" approach.

7.7 Positron Emission Tomography

PET scan is an assessment method that provides information about brain activity at rest. The assessment is accomplished by using an intravenous injection of radiolabeled glucose (F-FDG), followed by a period of 30 minutes in which the examinee rests in a quiet, nominally illuminated setting. The scan is then performed. Although there is a limited body of PET scan research in adults with FASD, obtaining PET scans has been a fairly routine matter for defense attorneys in capital cases, especially in certain venues. It is not uncommon to have FASD raised in the course of post-conviction relief (i.e., appellate) proceedings, especially if it was not raised at trial. In such circumstances, the neuroimaging expert may "inherit" previously obtained test data (e.g., a PET scan).

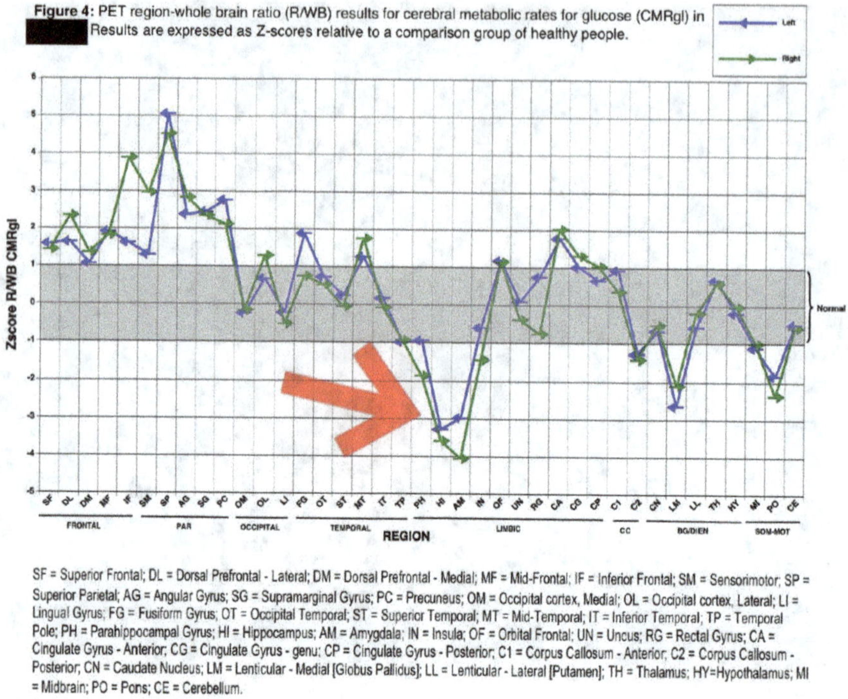

Fig. 7.9 A graphic display of PET scan data used in a forensic case (the red arrow highlights markedly decreased metabolic activity in the amygdala and hippocampi bilaterally)

One of the benefits of PET scan data involves their potential to provide additional convergent validity. PET results, like QEEG results, reflect brain *activity*. In the case of PET, brain activity is reflected in cumulative uptake of radio-labeled glucose. In the case of QEEG, brain activity is reflected in electrical current. Although it is not always the case, there is a general tendency for anatomic brain structures that are decreased in volume (on quantitative MRI) to show decreased metabolic activity on PET and decreased electrical activity on QEEG. Furthermore, given the co-morbidity of traumatic experiences and posttraumatic stress disorder (PTSD) in those with FASD, PET scans reflect in part the brain's resting state (a.k.a., default mode network), which can be important in differential diagnosis. Just as in brain MRI, PET data can be quantified and displayed graphically (see Fig. 7.9). The study here reflects marked decrease of at-rest metabolic activity in various limbic lobe structures (e.g., hippocampi, amygdala).

7.8 Practical Advice

When considered within a forensic evaluation of FASD, neuroimaging is inherently linked to established diagnostic criteria (e.g., IOM, CDC) and informed by constantly emerging progress in our scientific understanding of FASD. It is essential to state clearly in reports and testimony that the role of neuroimaging—practically speaking—is only *ancillary* in nature. In the forensic context, neuroimaging may be effective as "the cherry on the sundae," but neuroimaging never should be mistaken for the sundae itself. Sometimes derisively referred to as "eye candy," such studies should never be used as a substitute for subpar attention to the essentials of diagnosis (e.g., addressing PAE, comprehensive neuropsychological testing and adaptive assessment, assiduous efforts by counsel to obtain relevant records) and meticulous review of all relevant data with respect to life functioning. Also, scientific conservatism and caution must be the watchword. At no time should the expert over-extrapolate or make claims or assumptions about the meaning and/or implications of the data. Similarly, success in having slides accepted into evidence and testimony proceeding smoothly can be aided by proffering the images as illustrative exhibits rather than proof of the matter in and of itself. This represents a subtle but important distinction.

Unless a state's particular medical licensing provisions preclude it, it is highly advisable to have the neuroimaging expert perform a comprehensive evaluation that includes (1) review of pertinent discovery material; (2) evaluee interview, with a formal mental status examination; (3) physical examination, including assessment of FASD facial features and other physical indicia associated with FASD; and (4) thorough and detailed neurological examination. All of these diagnostic elements help put neuroimaging into a larger perspective. Moreover, having a "hands-on" and "up close and personal" interaction with an evaluee not only is consistent with current standards and recommended practice (Woods, Freedman, & Greenspan, 2012) but also adds to the credibility and gravitas of the expert.

It is entirely inappropriate to render a diagnosis about someone a physician has not personally examined. Therefore, in order to make a medical diagnosis, in-person examination of the evaluee is required. When an examination is simply not possible—for any number of reasons—the expert must limit opinions to whether data are consistent or inconsistent with FASD. It must be emphasized that even in the face of various limitations, an expert nonetheless can provide important and compelling testimony. As the adage goes, "the perfect should not be the enemy of the good."

The highest degree of vigilance must be paid to the issue of medical licensing. In each and every out-of-state matter, our office makes (and fully documents) de novo inquiry with the pertinent state medical licensing authority. Licensing board rules can change without formal notice. It also is not uncommon for such offices to be unresponsive to contact, whether by phone, fax, email, or by other methods. Medical licensing missteps are "low hanging fruit" for cross-examination, and even the *appearance of impropriety* can do serious damage to an expert's credibility. At times, it has been necessary for me to obtain assistance from my professional liability insurance carrier. In fact, on more than one occasion, my insurer has provided local counsel who reviewed applicable state law and authored formal opinions.

Another important caveat involves writing medical orders. It should not be presumed that having a temporary medical license in a state conveys with it privileges to prescribe medication or order tests (e.g., laboratory, neuroimaging). Since the latter may be a "gray zone" that cannot be adequately clarified, the better part of valor may be to have the defense team hire a local physician to order tests and provide/document proper informed consent for any procedures. It is important at the outset to inform counsel (and for counsel to inform the court) that arranging for neuroimaging and post-processing/analysis to follow takes a lot of time and that mishaps (and associated delays) should be anticipated. Making sure scanning facilities fully understand the orders (including specifications) is essential.

Typically, the neuroimaging expert testifies following one or more other expert witnesses (e.g., forensic neuropsychologist). Ideally, the neuroimaging expert is part of a multidisciplinary evaluative team that has some experience working collaboratively. Testimony should be reasonably streamlined, but repetition of some important material can be useful, such as pointing out the generalized toxic effects of prenatal alcohol. Juries must be informed that since alcohol is a generalized toxin, the a priori hypothesis is that the location of alcohol-induced brain damage is expected to be *bilateral and symmetrical* in nature. Given the embryogenesis of the brain, it also is expected that at least some of the damage will be located in midline, deeper (i.e., early forming) structures. Testimony should be organized along important foundational themes, such as the *scientific method* and relatedly, on the generation and testing of hypotheses. What are the key questions? How can those questions be answered? What was discovered? A glossary of important terms and concepts (e.g., statistical significance, z-scores) should be provided up front. Tests to be presented should include some mention of their reliability, validity, and general acceptability among professionals. These are, of course, the underlying elements upon which *Frye* and *Daubert* standards of evidentiary admissibility are based. Accordingly, if a standardized approach or procedure is being used, that fact should be noted and emphasized.

Now is as good a time as any to convey an important dictum to the reader: it is much better to *show* people what you mean than *tell* them what you mean. Toward that goal, it is best to err on the side of using an abundance of bold, clear graphics and to avoid an undue amount of accompanying text. The essential and focal source of whatever explanation(s) may be required is to be found within the expert witness, not on any slide. All eyes (and ears) on the expert!

7.9 Proposed Neuroimaging Protocol

The following list summarizes a proposed neuroimaging protocol that has been useful in my forensic work:

1. QEEG is recommended ideally as the first neuroimaging test to be performed.
2. CNS-VS or similar testing is done concurrently with the QEEG.
3. The forensic neuropsychologist sees the QEEG results only after documenting the formal neuropsychological test data and its interpretation. When QEEG results are provided, an addendum is produced that integrates the QEEG data.
4. A priori hypotheses and plan for analysis of QEEG data are identified in advance.
5. Brain MRI, DTI, and PET are routinely recommended, including quantification of each, for a comprehensive evaluation.

6. The brain MRI is reviewed by the FASD neuroimaging expert, along with a qualified neuroradiologist. This review is documented.
7. If the review produces findings discrepant from those of the scanning facility, the original "reading radiologist" is informed, and input is requested.
8. Results of the studies are integrated. Both convergent and inconsistent data are addressed.
9. If at all possible, the FASD neuroimaging expert should examine the evaluee in person. Depending on medical licensing issues, the expert might alternately observe a local physician conducting an examination. This could be attended virtually, if necessary.

7.10 Case Example

A young man was facing several charges for violent offenses. Counsel retained an initial psychologist, who was unable to obtain valid and interpretable results on cognitive testing. However, the psychologist raised a concern about possible FASD since PAE was contained in records she had reviewed. The psychologist recommended to counsel that specialty FASD consultation be obtained. The second psychologist, a recognized expert in FASD, obtained confirmation of PAE directly from the defendant's mother. The FASD expert then recommended a QEEG. Counsel not only succeeded in getting publicly authorized funds for the QEEG but also (due to my technician's COVID-19 health-related concerns) arranged for the examinee to be brought to my office from jail. During the visit, the examinee completed computerized neuropsychological testing (i.e., CNS-VS) (see Fig. 7.10), but technical issues made the initial QEEG tracing unusable.

Fortuitously, our QEEG expert had been scheduled to travel to Seattle from Texas. Given the importance of the QEEG to the overall evaluation and in the face of a court deadline, our QEEG expert submitted the paperwork needed for approval to enter the jail. Necessary logistical arrangements were made by the facility, and a second QEEG was administered successfully with counsel observing. By being present, counsel acquired poignant familiarity with the test, particularly the conditions of its administration. I reviewed QEEG results and concluded they were consistent with FASD. Among relevant findings were bilateral and symmetrical abnormalities of BA24 (see Fig. 7.11), a brain area where we repeatedly find abnormalities in felony defendants independently diagnosed with FASD.

During my debrief with the consulting QEEG expert, he raised concerns about indicia of trauma sequelae. This possibility was suggested by marked abnormalities in functional connectivity of the limbic and frontal lobes. Furthermore, there were widespread abnormalities of connectivity in the amygdala bilaterally (i.e., on the 2-D LORETA Coherence map; see Fig. 7.12). I circled back to the FASD expert psychologist and inquired about any known history of trauma. Interestingly, the initial psychologist documented in her report that the examinee had experienced at least nine of ten potential adverse childhood experiences (ACEs; Felitti et al., 1998).

CNS Vital Signs Report		Test Date: October 14, 2020 09:29:28
Patient ID: DOE, John		Administrator: Richard Adler
Age: 22		Language: English (United States)
Total Test Time: 34:34 (min:secs)	CNSVS Duration: 34:30 (min:secs)	Online Version 1.1.13

Patient Profile	Percentile Range				> 74	25 - 74	9 - 24	2 - 8	< 2
	Standard Score Range				> 109	90 - 109	80 - 89	70 - 79	< 70
Domain Scores	Patient Score	Standard Score	Percentile	Valid Score**	Above	Average	Low Average	Low	Very Low
Neurocognitive Index (NCI)	NA	79	8	Yes				X	
Composite Memory	71	44	1	Yes					X
Verbal Memory	36	39	1	Yes					X
Visual Memory	35	66	1	Yes					X
Psychomotor Speed	222	124	95	Yes	X				
Reaction Time*	628	94	34	Yes		X			
Complex Attention*	17	68	2	Yes					X
Cognitive Flexibility	26	63	1	Yes					X
Processing Speed	40	69	2	Yes					X
Executive Function	31	70	2	Yes				X	
Reasoning	3	84	14	Yes			X		
Simple Attention	40	108	70	Yes		X			
Motor Speed	175	149	99	Yes	X				

Fig. 7.10 CNS-VS results in the case example, "John Doe"

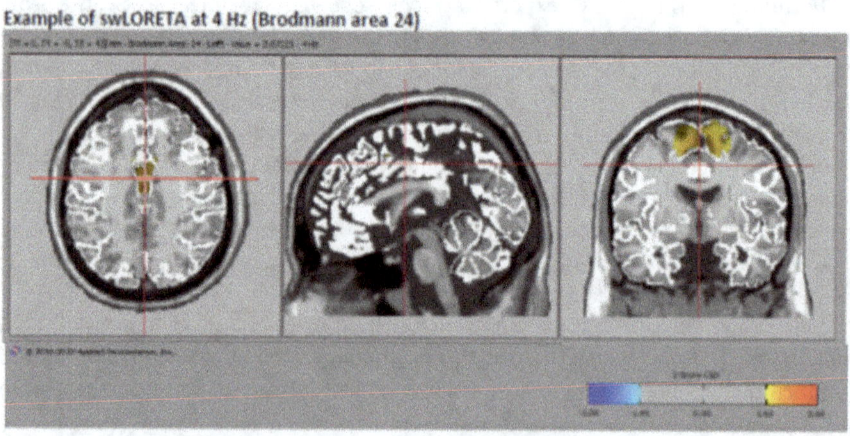

Fig. 7.11 swLORETA of Brodmann Area 24

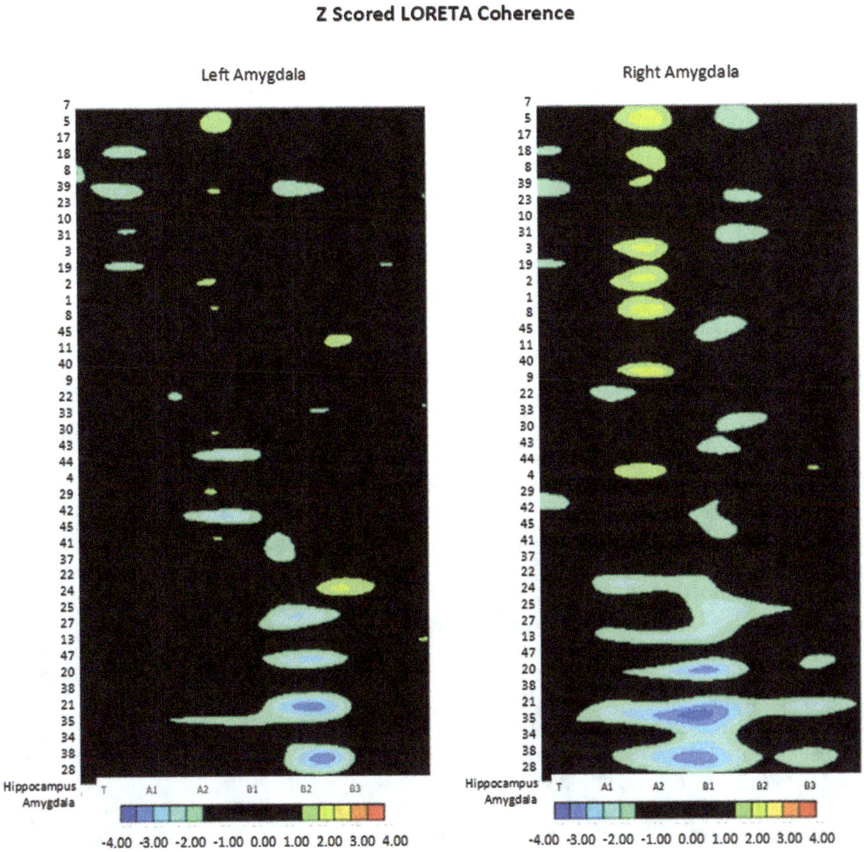

Fig. 7.12 LORETA Coherence map of the amygdala

Furthermore, on a specialized trauma inventory, the examinee scored at the 90th percentile.

As another fortuitous turn of events, the QEEG expert elected to include in his report a section addressing recommendations for neurofeedback (NFB). The QEEG report graphically showed abnormalities in the Default Mode Network and Salience Network, both of which have been identified as being impaired in persons with PTSD. These networks, and PTSD by extension, have been shown to be highly amenable to NFB. CNS-VS results indicated a relative strength in the domain of Simple Attention, with no evidence of neuropsychiatric impulsivity on the CNS-VS Continuous Performance Test. Taken together, neuroimaging/testing results not only supported a diagnosis of both FASD and PTSD, providing meaningful mitigation in terms of the prenatal and childhood etiologies of the evaluee's criminal behavior, but perhaps most important of all, data also provided helpful and hopeful options regarding remediation of future offense risk.

References

Adler, R. S. (2019). *The Emerging Role of Quantitative Electroencephalography (QEEG) in the Forensic Assessment of Fetal Alcohol Spectrum Disorders (FASDs): Current and Long-term Implications*. 36th International Congress on Law and Mental Health, Rome, Italy. https://netorg199010-my.sharepoint.com/:p:/g/personal/richadler_fcpsych_com/EcybcmQwZr5EoGIFpAbsZ0AB6_IoF_wTTVR8y97E_pt2sw?rtime=bxzBwQZD2Eg

Adler, R. S., Center, W. D., Connor, P. D., & Steele, K. A. (2019). *Quantitative electroencephalography: Forensic assessment of FASD*. 36th International Congress on Law and Mental Health, Rome, Italy.

Adler, R. S., Novick Brown, N., Connor, P. C., & Wartnik, A. P. (2015). *FASD in the Courtroom: FASD experts approaches its eighth year*. 34th International Congress on Law and Mental Health, Vienna, Austria.

American Psychiatric Association (APA). (2013). *Diagnostic and statistical manual of mental disorders (DSM-5)* (5th ed.). Arlington, VA: American Psychiatric Association.

Aoki, Y., Inokuchi, R., Gunshin, M., Yahagi, N., & Suwa, H. (2012). Diffusion tensor imaging studies of mild traumatic brain injury: A meta-analysis. *Journal of Neurology, Neurosurgery, and Psychiatry, 83*(9), 870–876. https://doi.org/10.1136/jnnp-2012-302742

Bell, S. H., Stade, B., Reynolds, J. N., Rasmussen, C., Andrew, G., Hwang, P. A., & Carlen, P. L. (2010). The remarkably high prevalence of epilepsy and seizure history in fetal alcohol spectrum disorders. *Alcoholism: Clinical and Experimental Research, 34*(6), 1084–1089. https://doi.org/10.1111/j.1530-0277.2010.01184.x

Bertrand, J., Floyd, L. L., Weber, M. K., O'Connor, M., Johnson, K. A., Riley, E., … National Task Force on FAS/FAE. (2004). *Fetal alcohol syndrome: Guidelines for referral and diagnosis*. Atlanta, GA: Centers for Disease Control and Prevention. https://www.cdc.gov/ncbddd/fasd/documents/fas_guidelines_accessible.pdf.

Bookstein, F. L., Sampson, P. D., Streissguth, A. P., & Connor, P. D. (2001). Geometric morphometrics of corpus callosum and subcortical structures in the fetal-alcohol-affected brain. *Teratology, 64*(1), 4–32. https://doi.org/10.1002/tera.1044

Bookstein, F. L., Streissguth, A. P., Sampson, P. D., Connor, P. D., & Barr, H. M. (2002). Corpus callosum shape and neuropsychological deficits in adult males with heavy fetal alcohol exposure. *NeuroImage, 15*(1), 233–251. https://doi.org/10.1006/nimg.2001.0977

Boutros, N. N., Thatcher, R. W., & Galderisi, S. (2008). Electrodiagnostic techniques in neuropsychiatry. In S. D. Yudofsky & R. E. Hales (Eds.), *Textbook of neuropsychiatry and behavioral neurosciences: Electrodiagnostic techniques in neuropsychiatry* (5th ed., pp. 189–213). Washington, DC: American Psychiatric Publishing.

Daubert v. Merrell Dow Pharmaceuticals Inc., 509 U.S. 579 (Supreme Court of the United States 1993). https://supreme.justia.com/cases/federal/us/509/579/

Doyle, L. R., & Mattson, S. N. (2015). Neurobehavioral disorder associated with prenatal alcohol exposure (ND-PAE): Review of evidence and guidelines for assessment. *Current Developmental Disorders Reports, 2*(3), 175–186. https://doi.org/10.1007/s40474-015-0054-6

Fast, D. K., Conry, J., & Loock, C. A. (1999). Identifying fetal alcohol syndrome among youth in the criminal justice system. *Journal of Developmental and Behavioral Pediatrics: JDBP, 20*(5), 370–372. https://doi.org/10.1097/00004703-199910000-00012

Felitti, V. J., Anda, R. F., Nordenberg, D., Williamson, D. F., Spitz, A. M., Edwards, V., … Marks, J. S. (1998). Relationship of childhood abuse and household dysfunction to many of the leading causes of death in adults: The adverse childhood experiences (ACE) study. *American Journal of Preventive Medicine, 14*(4), 245–258. https://doi.org/10.1016/S0749-3797(98)00017-8

Frye v. United States, *Frye v. United States*, 293 F. 1013 (Court of Appeals of the District of Columbia December 3, 1923). https://www.law.ufl.edu/_pdf/faculty/little/topic8.pdf

Fryer, S. L., Mattson, S. N., Jernigan, T. L., Archibald, S. L., Jones, K. L., & Riley, E. P. (2012). Caudate volume predicts neurocognitive performance in youth with heavy prenatal alcohol exposure. *Alcoholism, Clinical and Experimental Research, 36*(11), 1932–1941. https://doi.org/10.1111/j.1530-0277.2012.01811.x

Ghazi Sherbaf, F., Aarabi, M. H., Hosein Yazdi, M., & Haghshomar, M. (2019). White matter microstructure in fetal alcohol spectrum disorders: A systematic review of diffusion tensor imaging studies. *Human Brain Mapping, 40*(3), 1017–1036. https://doi.org/10.1002/hbm.24409

Hagan, J. F., Balachova, T., Bertrand, J., Chasnoff, I., Dang, E., Fernandez-Baca, D., … Zubler, J. (2016). Neurobehavioral disorder associated with prenatal alcohol exposure. *Pediatrics, 138*(4), e20151553. https://doi.org/10.1542/peds.2015-1553

Hemingway, S. J. A., Bledsoe, J. M., Brooks, A., Davies, J. K., Jirikowic, T., Olson, E., & Thorne, J. C. (2019). Comparison of the 4-digit code, Canadian 2015, Australian 2016 and Hoyme 2016 fetal alcohol spectrum disorder diagnostic guidelines. *Advances in Pediatric Research, 6*(2), 1–31. https://doi.org/10.35248/2385-4529.19.6.31

Hoyme, H. E., May, P. A., Kalberg, W. O., Kodituwakku, P., Gossage, J. P., Trujillo, . . . Robinson, L. K. (2005). A practical clinical approach to diagnosis of fetal alcohol spectrum disorders: Clarification of the 1996 Institute of Medicine criteria. Pediatrics, 115(1), 39–47. doi:https://doi.org/10.1542/peds.2004-0259

Institute of Medicine. (1996). *Institute of Medicine 1996 Report on FAS*. http://www.come-over.to/FAS/IOMsummary.htm

Jarmasz, J. S., Basalah, D. A., Chudley, A. E., & Del Bigio, M. R. (2017). Human brain abnormalities associated with prenatal alcohol exposure and fetal alcohol spectrum disorder. *Journal of Neuropathology and Experimental Neurology, 76*(9), 813–833. https://doi.org/10.1093/jnen/nlx064

Jones, K. L., & Smith, D. W. (1973). Recognition of the fetal alcohol syndrome in early infancy. *Lancet (London, England), 302*(7836), P999–P1001. https://doi.org/10.1016/s0140-6736(73)91092-1

Kable, J. A., O'Connor, M. J., Olson, H. C., Paley, B., Mattson, S. N., Anderson, S. M., & Riley, E. P. (2016). Neurobehavioral disorder associated with prenatal alcohol exposure (ND-PAE): Proposed DSM-5 Diagnosis. *Child Psychiatry & Human Development, 47*(2), 335–346. https://doi.org/10.1007/s10578-015-0566-7

Mattson, S. N., Riley, E. P., Jernigan, T. L., Ehlers, C. L., Delis, D. C., Jones, K. L., … Bellugi, U. (1992). Fetal alcohol syndrome: A case report of neuropsychological, MRI, and EEG assessment of two children. *Alcoholism: Clinical and Experimental Research, 16*(5), 1001–1003. https://doi.org/10.1111/j.1530-0277.1992.tb01909.x

Moore, E. M., Migliorini, R., Infante, M. A., & Riley, E. P. (2014). Fetal alcohol spectrum disorders: Recent neuroimaging findings. *Current Developmental Disorders Reports, 1*(3), 161–172.

Novick Brown, N., Wartnik, A. P., Connor, P. D., & Adler, R. S. (2010). A proposed model standard for forensic assessment of FASD. *Journal of Psychiatry and Law, 38*(4), 383–418. https://doi.org/10.1177/009318531003800403

Olson, H. C. (2015). Advancing recognition of fetal alcohol spectrum disorders: The proposed DSM-5 diagnosis of "neurobehavioral disorder associated with prenatal alcohol exposure (ND-PAE).". *Current Developmental Disorders Reports, 2*(3), 187–198. https://doi.org/10.1007/s40474-015-0056-4

Palacios, E. M., Martin, A. J., Boss, M. A., Ezekiel, F., Chang, Y. S., Yuh, E. L., … Mukherjee, P. (2017). Towards precision and reproducibility of diffusion tensor imaging: A multicenter diffusion phantom and traveling volunteer study. *AJNR. American Journal of Neuroradiology, 38*(3), 537–545. https://doi.org/10.3174/ajnr.A5025

Puetz, V. B., Parker, D., Kohn, N., Dahmen, B., Verma, R., & Konrad, K. (2017). Altered brain network integrity after childhood maltreatment: A structural connectomic DTI-study. *Human Brain Mapping, 38*(2), 855–868. https://doi.org/10.1002/hbm.23423

Riley, E. P., Mattson, S. N., Sowell, E. R., Jernigan, T. L., Sobel, D. F., & Jones, K. L. (1995). Abnormalities of the corpus callosum in children prenatally exposed to alcohol. *Alcoholism, Clinical and Experimental Research, 19*(5), 1198–1202. https://doi.org/10.1111/j.1530-0277.1995.tb01600.x

Ross, D. E., Ochs, A. L., DeSmit, M. E., Seabaugh, J. M., & Havranek, M. D. (2015). Man versus machine part 2: Comparison of radiologists' interpretations and NeuroQuant measures of brain asymmetry and progressive atrophy in patients with traumatic brain injury. *Journal of Neuropsychiatry and Clinical Neurosciences, 27*(2), 147–152. https://doi.org/10.1176/appi.neuropsych.13040088

Schneble, E., Lack, C., Zapadka, M., Pfeifer, C. M., Bardo, C. M. E., Cagley, J., … Pollock, J. M. (2020). Increased notching of the corpus callosum in fetal alcohol spectrum disorder: A callosal misunderstanding? *American Journal of Neuroradiology, 41*(4), 725–728. https://doi.org/10.3174/ajnr.A6475

State of Arizona v. Charles D. Ellison, No. CR-04-0073-AP (Mojave County Superior Court August 9, 2006).

State of Florida v. Grady Nelson, No. F05–846 (11th Fla. Cir. Ct. Dec. 2, 2010).

State of Florida v. Timothy Hurst, No.17–1998-CF-001795 (Escambia County Superior Court, March 2020).

Stratton, K., Howe, C., & Battaglia, F. C. (1996). *Fetal alcohol syndrome: Diagnosis, epidemiology, prevention, and treatment*. Washington, DC: National Academies Press. https://doi.org/10.17226/4991

Thatcher, R. W., Biver, C. J., & North, D. M. (2003). Quantitative EEG and the Frye and Daubert standards of admissibility. *Clinical EEG (Electroencephalography), 34*(2), 39–53. https://doi.org/10.1177/155005940303400203

Treit, S., Chen, Z., Zhou, D., Baugh, L., Rasmussen, C., Andrew, G., … Beaulieu, C. (2017). Sexual dimorphism of volume reduction but not cognitive deficit in fetal alcohol spectrum disorders: A combined diffusion tensor imaging, cortical thickness and brain volume study. *NeuroImage: Clinical, 15*, 284–297. https://doi.org/10.1016/j.nicl.2017.05.006

U.S. Congress. (1992). (Public Law 102–321, 106 STAT. 323, 102nd cong.) *The Alcohol, Drug Abuse, and Mental Health Services Administration Reorganization Act*. https://www.govinfo.gov/content/pkg/STATUTE-106/pdf/STATUTE-106-Pg323.pdf

Woods, G. W., Freedman, D., & Greenspan, S. (2012). Neurobehavioral assessment in forensic practice. *International Journal of Law and Psychiatry, 35*(5–6), 432–439. https://doi.org/10.1016/j.ijlp.2012.09.014

Chapter 8
Connecting the Dots: Functional Behavior Evaluation in Fetal Alcohol Spectrum Disorder

Natalie Novick Brown and Cecil R. Reynolds

Abstract This chapter describes a practical and forensically tested approach to conducting adaptive behavior assessments, also known as functional behavior evaluations (FBAs), in the FASD context. From stand-alone FBAs in contexts such as disabilities determination, where mental health evaluators conduct neuropsychological testing as well as adaptive assessments, to "gold standard" multidisciplinary assessments in high-stakes criminal matters involving multiple mental health and medical experts, the ultimate role of the FBA expert is to synthesize and analyze data from multiple sources and methods across the lifespan, integrating neurocognitive/adaptive assessment data with behavioral data to explain brain–behavior connections. The chapter highlights empirically based patterns expected in psychometric testing and adaptive assessment of those with FASD as well as behaviors that typically stem from such patterns, linking that information with neurobehavioral disorder associated with fetal alcohol exposure (ND-PAE), the *DSM-5* diagnosis for the central nervous system (CNS) impairment in FASD medical conditions. The chapter concludes with suggestions for mental health professionals on how to present relevant data in reports or testimony in order to describe how the behavior at issue is consistent with developmental trajectory.

Keywords Adaptive dysfunction · Central nervous system dysfunction · Executive dysfunction · Neurocognitive profile · Arrested development · Brain–behavior · Nexus analysis

---

The original version of this chapter was revised. The correction to this chapter is available at https://doi.org/10.1007/978-3-030-73628-6_19

N. N. Brown (✉)
University of Washington, Seattle, WA, USA

C. R. Reynolds
Texas A&M University, College Station, TX, USA

N. Novick Brown (ed.), *Evaluating Fetal Alcohol Spectrum Disorders in the Forensic Context*, https://doi.org/10.1007/978-3-030-73628-6_8

Adaptive dysfunction is a signature deficit in fetal alcohol spectrum disorders (FASD) and a central focus in functional behavior evaluations (FBAs) that address cognitive and adaptive functioning and associated behavior across the lifespan. Neurodevelopmental disorder associated with prenatal alcohol exposure (ND-PAE), a mental health diagnosis in the fifth edition of the *Diagnostic and Statistical Manual of Mental Disorders* (*DSM-5*; American Psychiatric Association [APA], 2013), encompasses the central nervous system (CNS) dysfunction in FASD. ND-PAE requires impairment in at least two adaptive domains as well as at least one impairment each in neurocognitive and self-regulatory domains. Although *DSM-5* does not quantify the *level* of impairment required in ND-PAE, official guidelines for fetal alcohol syndrome (FAS; Bertrand et al., 2004), the most severe disorder under the FASD umbrella, specify at least 1 standard deviation below the mean (−1 SD) on norm-referenced psychometric instruments in at least three cognitive/adaptive domains. Consequently, in forensic matters in the United States, −1 SD has become the standard of practice (Brown, Haun, Zapf, & Novick Brown, 2017; Doyle & Mattson, 2015; Hagan et al., 2016; Kable et al., 2016; Novick Brown, 2020; Novick Brown et al., 2015; Olson, 2015). In contrast, Canadian guidelines for FASD define a deficit as −2 SD from the mean in three domains of cognitive and/or adaptive functioning (Chudley et al., 2005; Cook et al., 2015)—a criterion level that has been called too restrictive as it results in a large number of false-negative findings (Kable & Coles, 2018; Sanders, Hudson Breen, & Netelenbos, 2017).

For adolescent and adult evaluees in the forensic context, FBAs that address adaptive behavior across the lifespan and explain criminal behavior in the context of neurocognitive dysfunction are an integral component in multidisciplinary investigations that often involve neuropsychological testing, medical examination, and—in high-stakes forensic matters—neuroimaging. [See other chapters in this book for detailed descriptions of these components.] Multidisciplinary team assessment by several specialists, the standard of care in clinical FASD assessment since at least 1996 (e.g., Bertrand et al., 2004; Chudley et al., 2005; Cook et al., 2015; Coons-Harding, Flannigan, Burns, Rajani, & Symes, 2019; Novick Brown, Wartnik, Connor, & Adler, 2010; Stratton, Howe, & Battaglia, 1996), is the gold standard in general forensic assessment (Glancy et al., 2015; Heilbrun, DeMatteo, Marczyk, & Goldstein, 2008; Woods, Freedman, & Greenspan, 2012; Ziegler, 2016). Similar in some respects to multidisciplinary assessments (MDAs) in the school setting that rely on standardized psychometric testing, adaptive assessment, direct observation, interviews, and relevant psychometric data in the records to determine if a student has a learning disability, FBAs go beyond MDAs in several respects, such as (a) assessing behavior in the home and community as well as the school with standardized psychometric measures; (b) examining pre- as well as postnatal history across the lifespan; (c) analyzing developmental trajectory in the context of relevant empirical findings; (d) comparing competing etiologies to the diagnostic hypothesis at issue to determine which possibility carries the most explanatory power; and (e) addressing the nexus with respect to the specific behavior(s) of interest (e.g., offense conduct). Unlike MDAs, FBAs explain cause-and-effect: how prenatal alcohol exposure caused brain dysfunction, which in turn caused deficient adaptive/social functioning that directly influenced offense conduct (APA, 2013; Freedman & Woods, 2018; Novick Brown et al., 2010). Since FBAs in the FASD context require evaluators to compare and contrast evaluee characteristics with expected functioning seen in the FASD literature (i.e., differential diagnosis), it is necessary for evaluators to have a foundational understanding of how this population functions neurocognitively and neurodevelopmentally across the developmental years.

8.1 Underlying Neurocognitive Impairment

Adaptive behavior has been defined as the performance of daily activities required for personal and social self-sufficiency or the ability to respond successfully to everyday demands (Sparrow, Balla, & Cicchetti, 1984). More simply put, adaptive behavior is *typical everyday behavior*. Largely based upon Greenspan's (1979) formulation over four decades ago, adaptive behavior is conceptualized by the American Association on Intellectual and Developmental Disabilities (AAIDD) as a tripartite construct composed of conceptual, practical, and social domains. Adaptive *dysfunction* is defined in *DSM-5* (APA, 2013, p. 31) as failure to meet "standards of personal independence and social responsibility in one or more aspects of daily life, including communication, social participation, academic or occupational functioning, and personal independence at home or in community settings." Adaptive assessment in the FASD context must be comprehensive enough to find such impairments if they exist and sensitive enough to appreciate that adaptive behavior likely will vary based upon task complexity as well as personal and environmental factors that differentially influence need for independent decision-making.

Since alcohol was first identified as a teratogen in the peer-reviewed literature half a century ago (Jones & Smith, 1973; Jones, Smith, Ulleland, & Streissguth, 1973; Lemoine, Harousseau, Borteyru, & Menuet, 1968), an extensive amount of animal and human research has investigated the effects of prenatal alcohol exposure on cognition and behavior. As reviewed by Jones (2011), a woman's drinking at any time in pregnancy may damage the central nervous system of a fetus, especially early in pregnancy before many women know they are pregnant (Maier & West, 2001). Regular or binge episodes of alcohol exposure in utero are especially harmful, causing pervasive but often subtle brain damage that manifests as cognitive deficits in a range of affected functional domains, including global and subglobal intellectual skills (e.g., Adnams et al., 2001; Mattson & Riley, 1998; Mattson, Riley, Gramling, Delis, & Jones, 1997; Streissguth, Barr, Kogan, & Bookstein, 1996; Streissguth, Bookstein, Sampson, & Barr, 1989), attention and activity level (Bertrand et al., 2004; Kodituwakku, Handmaker, Cutler, Weathersby, & Handmaker, 1995; Lee, Mattson, & Riley, 2004; Nanson & Hiscock, 1990; Streissguth et al., 1986; Streissguth, Barr, Sampson, & Bookstein, 1994), rate of information processing

(Burden, Jacobson, & Jacobson, 2005; Jacobson, 1998), auditory comprehension (Franklin, Deitz, Jirikowic, & Astley, 2008; Rasmussen et al., 2013; Stephen et al., 2012), visual perception and construction (Coles, Platzman, Lynch, & Freides, 2002; Connor, Streissguth, Sampson, Bookstein, & Barr, 1999; Mattson, Calarco, & Lang, 2006; Rasmussen et al., 2013), learning and memory (Aragon et al., 2008; Kaemingk & Halverson, 2000; Mattson & Riley, 1999; Uecker & Nadel, 1996, 1998; Willford, Richardson, Leech, & Day, 2004), motor skills (Connor, Sampson, Streissguth, Bookstein, & Barr, 2006; Doney et al., 2014), social communication (Abkarian, 1992; Adnams et al., 2001; Becker, Warr-Leeper, & Leeper Jr., 1990; Coggins, Timler, & Olswang, 2007), and executive functioning (Kodituwakku, Kalberg, & May, 2001; Mattson, Goodman, Caine, Delis, & Riley, 1999; Rasmussen, 2005).

As *DSM-5* (APA, 2013) now recognizes, it is higher-level executive functioning rather than IQ that most determines how information is processed in the brain and ultimately manifests as adaptive behavior. Executive functioning (EF) is an umbrella term for a set of interrelated higher-order cognitive processes that involve conscious effort or supervisory attention and guide purposeful goal-directed behavior (Anderson, 2002; Shallice & Burgess, 1998; Stuss & Knight, 2002; Welsh & Pennington, 1998). Intact executive skills are necessary for successful developmental progress, competent performance of daily life activities, socially appropriate behavior, and academic functioning (Anderson, 2002). Executive functions are analogous to an air traffic controller in the brain that organizes and directs thoughts, modulates emotional responses, and regulates behavior (Gioia, Isquith, & Guy, 2001). Among other things, executive skills include planning, set-shifting (shifting attention from one task to another), working memory (limited-capacity information storage while performing mental operations on that information), fluency (retrieving task-related information from memory), response inhibition (i.e., impulse control), and attentional vigilance (maintaining focus and concentration over a period of time necessary to accomplish a task).

As in intellectual disability (ID), EF typically is impaired in FASD but unlike ID, EF impairment in FASD occurs regardless of IQ (Doyle et al., 2018; Rasmussen, 2005) or medical diagnosis on the FASD continuum (Astley et al., 2009; Green et al., 2009; Kingdon, Cardoso, & McGrath, 2016; Nash et al., 2014). For example, children with FASD consistently perform worse than controls on complex EF measures of cognitive planning (Green et al., 2009; Kodituwakku et al., 1995; Mattson et al., 1999), conceptual set-shifting (Coles et al., 1997; Olson, Feldman, Streissguth, Sampson, & Bookstein, 1998), affective set-shifting (Kodituwakku, May, Clericuzio, & Weers, 2001), nonverbal and verbal fluency (Kodituwakku et al., 2006; Schonfeld, Mattson, Lang, Delis, & Riley, 2001), working memory (Green et al., 2009; Rasmussen, 2005; Rasmussen, Soleimani, & Pei, 2011), response inhibition (Green, Munoz, Nikkel, & Reynolds, 2007; Noland et al., 2003), and measures of concept formation (McGee, Schonfeld, Roebuck-Spencer, Riley, & Mattson, 2008). Since the executive system processes lower-level (i.e., unconscious) neural information from other brain regions, if lower-level input is distorted due to brain damage outside the frontal lobes, this situation further impairs mental control and subsequent behavior (Kodituwakku, 2009).

Intellectual testing can be quite misleading in FASD as scores range from extremely low to superior but typically fall in the average to borderline ranges (Adnams et al., 2001; Streissguth et al., 1996). Rather than IQ, it is EF that directly predicts adaptive behavior in FASD. Notably, Schonfeld, Paley, Frankel, and O'Connor (2006) found that executive function ratings on the Behavior Rating Inventory of Executive Function (BRIEF; Gioia, Isquith, Guy, & Kenworthy, 2000) predicted social behavior in children, and more generally, Ware et al. (2012) found that EF predicted adaptive behavior on the Vineland Adaptive Behavior Scales (Vineland; Sparrow, Balla, & Cicchetti, 1984) in children with prenatal alcohol exposure. Thus, there is a direct causative link between executive dysfunction and adaptive dysfunction in FASD.

Systematic reviews of the FASD literature have identified a prototypical cognitive profile in ND-PAE that involves generalized executive deficits in the processing and integration of *complex* information (Kodituwakku, 2009; Kodituwakku et al., 1995; Kodituwakku, Kalberg, & May, 2001). Task complexity increases in direct proportion to intrinsic mental challenge, defined as complex cognitive processing that requires multiple neural circuits and/or interhemispheric transfer of neural information (Kodituwakku & Kodituwakku, 2014). Task complexity not only is a function of mental challenge but also involves contextual factors such as novelty, ambiguity, environmental structure, external guidance, distraction, unpredictability, simultaneous task demands, abstract/compound social demands, and time and/or performance pressure. Of course, additional personal factors such as stress, frustration, anger, boredom, acute intoxication, and/or fatigue increase situational complexity and further erode executive control.

Time pressure and novelty are particularly important in the context of FASD. While generally, this population seems to have relatively little difficulty with automatic information processing based on procedural motor memory or highly structured tasks involving considerable external guidance, persons with FASD have significant difficulty with rapidly processing information that is novel and complex (Burden et al., 2005; Kodituwakku, 2009; Roebuck-Spencer, Mattson, & Riley, 2002). Generally, it follows from Kodituwakku's (2009) elegant analysis of the EF literature in FASD that the more elements of complexity in a task, the more mental effort required and the more impaired mental processing will be (Jacobson, Jacobson, Stanton, Meintjes, & Molteno, 2011; Kodituwakku & Kodituwakku, 2014). Moreover, because of the causal link between executive and adaptive functioning in FASD (Schonfeld et al., 2006; Ware et al., 2012), if higher-level thinking is impaired, adaptive behavior likewise will be impaired, with level of impairment increasing in the context of situational complexity. Since the everyday world is a very complex place full of unpredictable events, it is not surprising that a deficient adaptive profile is a robust finding in the FASD literature.

The complexity-based deficit in FASD manifests in neuropsychological testing as deficits in multiple cognitive domains, with significant within- and between-task variability (Ali, Kerns, Mulligan, Olson, & Astley, 2018), as well as impaired adaptive behavior that tends to vary in level of deficiency based on degree of task-related complexity (Adubato & Cohen, 2011; Ali et al., 2018; Kodituwakku et al., 1995; Olson et al., 1998). In particular, comprehensive neuropsychological assessment of adults in the forensic context generally finds cognitive profiles that reflect this variability, expressed as: (a) *Between-test Variability* (i.e., variable test scores reflecting relative strengths and weaknesses across the entire test battery as well as variability in scores for the same test administered at two different times), (b) *Within-test Variability* (e.g., significant domain-level discrepancies or "splits" in an IQ test), and (c) *Context-Dependent Thinking and Behavior* (i.e., poorer results on tests with minimal structure that require more independent thinking; Novick Brown, 2020; Novick Brown, Connor, & Adler, 2012).

Figures 8.1, 8.2, and 8.3 illustrate these variable test patterns in a typical forensic case involving cognitive testing and adaptive assessment. The young adult male defendant whose test results are depicted in the figures underwent multidisciplinary assessment and ultimately was diagnosed with ND-PAE. Prior to diagnosis, neuropsychological testing was administered to him in a private institutional conference room with no distractions or interruptions. The assessment battery included standardized tests in a number of cognitive domains that involved varying degrees of task and examiner guidance and, in some cases, opportunities to practice. To be consistent with Centers for Disease Control (CDC) diagnostic protocol

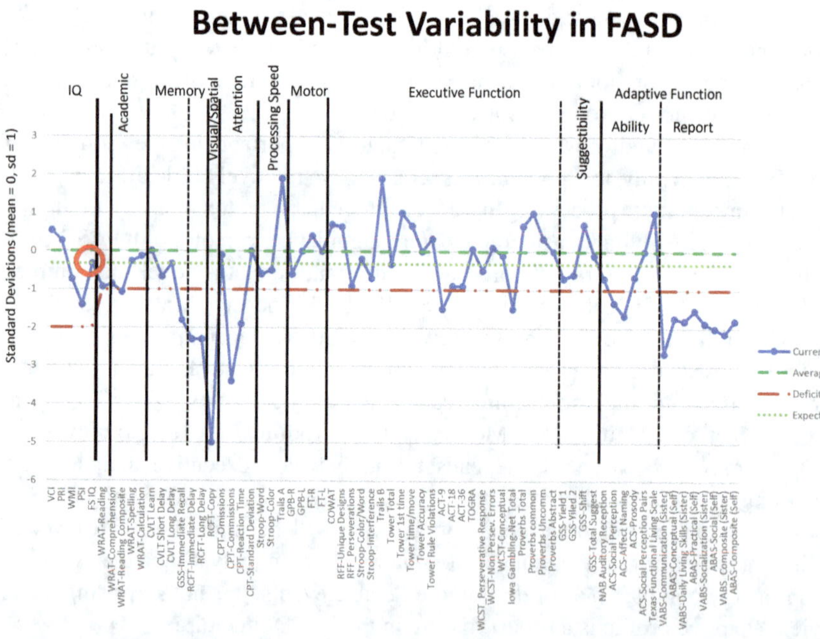

Fig. 8.1 Between-test variability in the test battery of a young adult male forensic evaluee with an average full-scale IQ (96) and diagnosis of ND-PAE. Figure provided by and with permission of Paul Connor, PhD

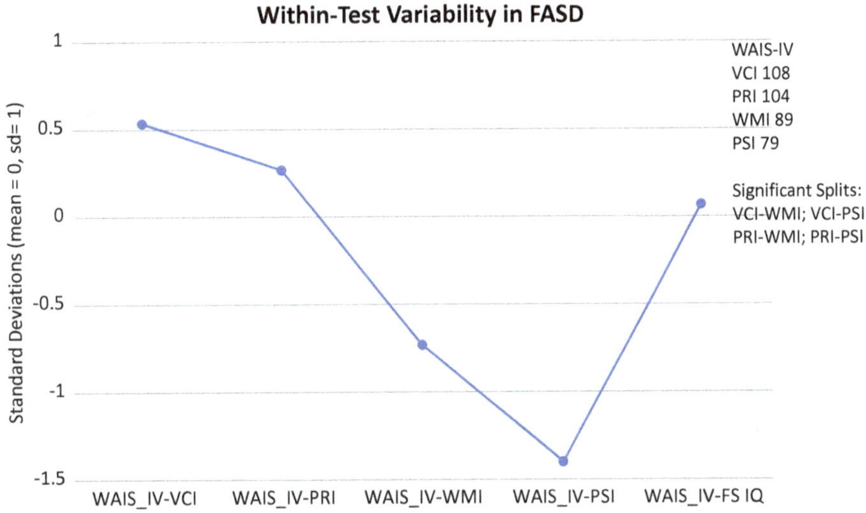

Fig. 8.2 Within-test variability in the test battery of a young adult male forensic evaluee with an average full-scale IQ (96) and diagnosis of ND-PAE. Figure provided by and with permission of Paul Connor, PhD

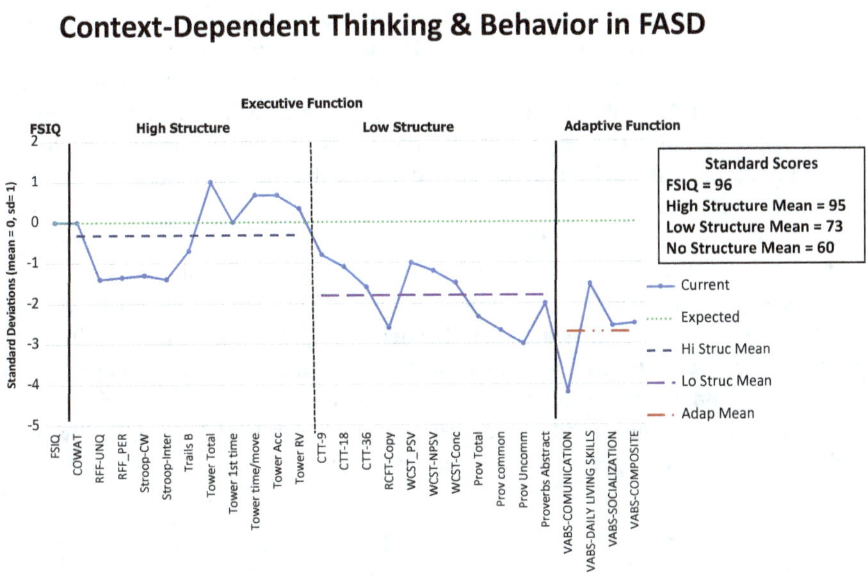

Fig. 8.3 Context-dependent thinking and behavior in FASD. Figure provided by and with permission of Paul Connor, PhD

(Bertrand et al., 2004) and permit an "apples-to-apples" comparison to enhance understanding, test scores and adaptive assessment results are converted to z-scores (i.e., standard deviations from a mean or average score of "0"), with the direction of deficit made constant (i.e., lower scores reflecting poorer performance and higher scores reflecting better performance).

8.1.1 Between-Test Variability

Figure 8.1 illustrates test results across the entire neuropsychological battery as well as adaptive assessment results on the Vineland. Overall, the pattern reflects considerable variability in scores among the different tests administered, with relative strengths as well as weaknesses that on average fall well below the evaluee's full-scale standard score (SS) of 96 (circled in red in Fig. 8.1). Such variability likely reflects intermittent exposure to alcohol during gestation as well as differences in mental effort required by the tests. The "Adaptive Function" column on the right side of the Figure shows scores on the third edition of the Vineland Adaptive Behavior Scales (Vineland-3; Sparrow, Saulnier, Cicchetti, & Doll, 2016). The horizontal green line in Fig. 8.1 depicts z-score mean or average score (i.e., "0") for each test, and the horizontal red line depicts the cut-point for a "deficit" finding. CDC guidelines define "deficit" as −1 SD except for IQ, which requires −2 SD.

As can be seen in Fig. 8.1, although full-scale IQ (96) falls in the average range with a couple other scores (Trails A and B) nearly 2 SDs above average, many test scores and adaptive assessment results fall well below average and full-scale IQ (FSIQ). In neurotypical individuals, most test scores within a comprehensive neuropsychological test battery are expected to fall within normal limits (i.e., cluster around a score of "0"), although in test batteries with at least 20 measures that use −1 SD as a criterion, it is not unusual to see two or three abnormal test scores (Binder, Iverson, & Brooks, 2009; Iverson, Brooks, & Holdnack, 2008). In contrast, test profiles in forensically involved persons with FASD involve at least three deficient cognitive *domains* (i.e., cognitive categories where the prevailing functional level among multiple tasks is deficient; Novick Brown et al., 2010). While it might be possible for an individual to compensate for mild damage in a focal area of the brain as in traumatic brain injury, compensation is impossible when such damage involves multiple domains and includes EF (Greenspan, Novick Brown, & Edwards, 2016; Livingston & Happe, 2017; Novick Brown et al., 2015).

8.1.2 Within-Test Variability

Test profiles in FASD also may show significant discrepancies among tasks within the same test (i.e., within-test variability). Figure 8.2 illustrates within-test variability on the Wechsler Adult Intelligence Scale, fourth edition (WAIS-IV), for the same young man whose full test battery is displayed in Fig. 8.1.

As can be seen in Fig. 8.2, verbal comprehension and perceptual reasoning, relative strengths, are significantly higher than working memory and processing speed, relative weaknesses. In cases such as this, FSIQ is not a reliable representation of intellectual functioning, which should be noted in reports.

8.1.3 Context-Dependent Thinking and Behavior

The same between- and within-test variability seen in comprehensive test batteries in FASD also characterizes EF and adaptive behavior in this population. Figure 8.3 depicts test results based on test and task complexity. "High Structure" executive function tests involve considerable external guidance and consequently are less challenging than "Low Structure" tests where external guidance is minimal and evaluees must problem-solve independently. In contrast to both, "Adaptive Functioning" tasks involve typical everyday performance in the unstructured real world, measured in this case by the Vineland-3.

Figure 8.3 illustrates a profile often seen in FASD: higher scores on straightforward tasks involving a high degree of external structure and relatively little mental effort (average = 95 SS), with decreased performance on less-structured executive tasks requiring some mental challenge (average = 73 SS), and an even greater drop in performance on everyday adaptive tasks (average adaptive score = 60 SS). In the context of ND-PAE and an average IQ, the context-dependent adaptive dysfunction seen in this young defendant's test profile explains why his adaptive functioning is so much lower than IQ-based expectations.

In FASD, executive thinking and adaptive behavior are direct reflections of task and environmental complexity and the corresponding mental challenge required to problem-solve and cope. Consequently, addressing referral questions in FBAs that involve thinking and behavior during a particular moment in time (e.g., mental state in a felony context) requires nuanced analysis of factors that affect task and environmental complexity as well as personal state. Nuanced task/environment/state analysis can answer questions such as why a person with an average IQ but ND-PAE needed special education services in school and could not function successfully in any adult domain but nonetheless could master a skill involving hands-on training and repetition. Nuanced analysis also can explain why a person with ND-PAE and average IQ could perform adequately in structured and supervised environments but consistently failed in unstructured real-world settings.

8.2 Developmental Trajectory

Organic brain damage in FASD directly impairs the executive skills needed to function adequately and deal effectively with the stresses of everyday living. When children exhibit chronic learning, social, and self-regulation problems in the relatively structured school years, such a pattern predicts that later in life, they will have even greater difficulties in the unstructured real world. Adaptive functioning reflects everyday capacity to deal with tasks and challenges in contexts that range from semi-structured school environments to completely unstructured community settings. Compared to typically developing peers, deficient adaptive functioning appears to be universal in FASD, regardless of stage of development or instrument used to measure behavior (Olson et al., 1998; Carr, Agnihotri, & Keightley, 2010; Crocker, Vaurio, Riley, & Mattson, 2009; Fagerlund et al., 2012; Jirikowic, Kartin, & Olson, 2008; Mattson, Bernes, & Doyle, 2019; Panczakiewicz et al., 2016; Steinhausen & Spohr, 1998; Streissguth et al., 1996; Streissguth et al., 1991, 2004).

In an early study that examined adaptive behavior in adolescents and adults (mean age 17) with dysmorphic and non-dysmorphic FASD (70% diagnosed with FAS), average global age-equivalence on the Vineland fell at a 7-year-old level, with communication skills at an 8-year-old level, daily living skills at a 9-year-old level, and socialization skills at a 6-year-old level (Streissguth et al., 1991). Several years later, a major study commissioned by the Centers for Disease Control (Streissguth et al., 1996) investigated developmental trajectories in 415 individuals with FASD, who ranged in age from 6 to 51. Although mean IQs fell in the low-average to borderline ranges for all three age groups in the study (children, adolescents, and adults), Vineland standard scores in these age groups ranged from 58 to 73 for communication, from 68 to 74 for daily living skills, and from 61 to 72 for socialization. On average, Vineland global composite scores tended to fall approximately 1.0 to 1.5 standard deviations below mean IQ (79 for those with FAS and 90 for those with non-dysmorphic FASD), with adaptive scores inversely related to age. A life history interview administered to caregivers in the study found 76% of the entire sample had experienced sexual or physical abuse, and most had lived in unstable homes. The study identified protective factors (a stable nurturing home for much of childhood, FASD diagnosis before age 6, developmental disabilities services across the school years) and risk factors (history of physical or sexual abuse in childhood and witnessing domestic violence). Eight adverse life course outcomes, identified as "secondary disabilities," were found:

- Mental Health Problems (experienced by 90% of the entire study sample);
- Disrupted School Experience, defined as having been suspended or expelled from school or having dropped out before graduating (experienced by 60% of adolescents and adults);
- Trouble with the Law, defined as arrests, charges, or convictions (experienced by 60% of adolescents and adults);

- Confinement, which included inpatient treatment for mental health or substance abuse problems as well as incarceration (experienced by approximately 50% of adolescents and adults);
- Inappropriate Sexual Behavior (50% of adolescents and adults);
- Dependent Living (80% of adults); and
- Employment Problems (80% of adults).

Of adult females in the study who were parents, 40% had consumed alcohol during pregnancy, and 17–30% had given birth to children with FASD. Nearly 40% of adult females had had children removed by Child Protective Service (CPS), and over 30% had relinquished parenting responsibility.

Since the secondary disabilities study, subsequent research has found similar results with regard to adverse developmental outcomes (e.g., Burd, Carlson, & Kerbeshian, 2007; Clark, Lutke, Minnes, & Ouellette-Kuntz, 2004; Popova, Lange, Bekmuradov, Mihic, & Rehm, 2011; Steinhausen & Spohr, 1998). Studies that address adaptive functioning in FASD also find results consistent with the secondary disabilities study (e.g., Carr et al., 2010; Crocker et al., 2009; Fagerlund et al., 2012; Streissguth et al., 2004; Thomas, Kelly, Mattson & Riley, 1998; Whaley, O'Connor, & Gunderson, 2001). An exception was an early study that examined adaptive functioning in very young alcohol-exposed children (mean age 5:10), which failed to find adaptive deficits (Coles et al., 1991). As later research has found and *DSM-5* (APA, 2013) now notes, adaptive deficits may not be evident in very young children with FASD.

Based upon research that compares adaptive functioning in alcohol-exposed and nonexposed children, there is general agreement that adaptive development in FASD is arrested rather than simply delayed, with socialization the most impaired domain, followed by communication (Crocker et al., 2009; Mattson, Crocker, & Nguyen, 2011; McGee, Bjorkquist, Price, Mattson, & Riley, 2009; McGee, Fryer, Bjorkquist, Mattson, & Riley, 2008; Thomas et al., 1998; Whaley et al., 2001). In the first IQ-controlled study to examine the rate of social development in FASD (Thomas et al., 1998), the Vineland was used to compare social functioning between a group of children with FAS and an age-/IQ-matched group of nonexposed controls (mean age and verbal IQ in the FAS group were 10.3 and 76.8, respectively; mean age and verbal IQ in the nonexposed group were 9.2 and 77.7, respectively). Results of the study indicated children with FAS had significantly lower socialization scores on the Vineland compared to nonexposed children with similar IQs (i.e., mean socialization scores were 61 and 81, respectively), with increasingly greater differences between the two groups in older children, suggesting arrested development. Subsequent research in children with prenatal alcohol exposure found similar arrested development in socialization and communication (Crocker et al., 2009; Jirikowic et al., 2008; Mattson et al., 2011).

Studies of EF in FASD are consistent with the arrested adaptive development seen in this population, which is not surprising, given the causal link between executive and adaptive functioning (Schonfeld et al., 2006; Ware et al., 2012). In a meta-analysis of 51 studies that compared EF in groups of children with FASD and typically developing controls, Kingdon et al. (2016) found EF declined as age increased in FASD, with group differences peaking at age 12 and stabilizing in the teen years. Similarly, neuroimaging studies have found delayed white matter development in children and adolescents with FASD (Robertson et al., 2016; Treit et al., 2013) as well as reduced global network efficiency (Moore, Migliorini, Infante, & Riley, 2014), which is thought to underlie the age-related decline in cognitive and adaptive functioning as children with FASD move into the adolescent and adult years (Treit et al., 2013).

Arrested adaptive development has broad implications for those with FASD, particularly in the context of childhood adversity, which is a common experience for children with FASD (Olson, Oti, Gelo, & Beck, 2009; Rasmussen, Andrew, Zwaigenbaum, & Tough, 2008; Streissguth et al., 1996). In fact, maladaptive behaviors seen in nearly all children with FASD are thought to reflect broad coping failure (Coggins et al., 2007; Novick Brown et al., 2012; Olson et al., 2009; Paley & O'Connor, 2011). Coping, a sub-domain under Socialization in the Vineland, is defined in psychology as thoughts or action(s) used to deal with stressful or unpleasant situations (American Psychological Association, 2020, Coping strategy) that involve either conscious direct approaches or unconscious defensive reactions (Folkman, Lazarus, Dunkel-Schetter, DeLongis, & Gruen, 1986). Multiple studies have found increasingly deficient coping skills with increasing age in people with FASD (e.g., Coles et al., 1991; Thomas et al., 1998), suggesting this population tends to respond to stress with unconscious defensive reactions rather than direct problem-solving approaches. Related research has found that deficient affect regulation (i.e., inability to modulate emotional arousal) is an executive skill that not only plays a major role in behavioral reactivity but also contributes significantly to deficient coping and high levels of psychiatric dysfunction in FASD. For example, a study that examined the role of affect regulation in adults and children with FASD found those with impaired affect regulation were significantly more likely than those without such impairment to be diagnosed with conduct disorder (odds ratio 4.8), attachment disorder (odds ratio 6.1), and posttraumatic stress disorder (odds ratio 8.1), as well as suicidality (odds ratio 8.6; Temple, Cook, Unsworth, Rajani, & Mela, 2019). Research using functional magnetic resonance imaging (fMRI) indicates affect regulation is controlled largely by the prefrontal cortex (e.g., dorsolateral, dorsal medial, orbitofrontal lobes) as well as neurological circuitry (anterior cingulate) between the frontal lobes and amygdala (Banks, Eddy, Angstadt, Nathan, & Phan, 2007).

In addition to coping impairment, a growing body of research suggests persons with FASD are hyperreactive to stress. For example, in a study using diurnal cortisol levels in the saliva of alcohol-exposed and nonexposed youths to measure functioning of the hypothalamic-pituitary-adrenal (HPA) axis (i.e., the neuroendocrine system that handles stress), children and adolescents in the alcohol-exposed sample exhibited HPA dysregulation (McLachlan et al., 2016), which was consistent with previous research and thought to underlie behavior problems in FASD (Jacobson, Bihun, & Chiodo, 1999; Keiver, Bertram, Orr, & Clarren, 2015; Oberlander et al., 2010; Ouellet-Morin et al., 2011; Ramsay, Bendersky, & Lewis, 1996). The HPA axis is shaped and programmed during prenatal (Haley, Handmaker, & Lowe, 2006; Jacobson et al., 1999; Oberlander et al., 2010; Ramsay et al., 1996) and neonatal development (Kapoor, Dunn, Kostaki, Andrews, & Matthews, 2006; Smith & Vale, 2006), and alcohol exposure in utero apparently programs the system such that HPA tone is increased (i.e., overactive) throughout life, which impairs responsiveness to and regulation of stress (Weinberg, Sliwowska, Lan, & Hellemans, 2008). In fact, HPA dysregulation may explain the relatively high rates of posttraumatic stress disorder (PTSD) and other anxiety-related mental health conditions in FASD (Famy, Streissguth, & Unis, 1998; Hellemans, Sliwowska, Verma, & Weinberg, 2010).

8.3 Data Collection

Consistent with best practices in forensic mental health assessment (Heilbrun et al., 2003; Heilbrun et al., 2008; Heilbrun, Grisso, & Goldstein, 2013), data collection in FBAs should involve multiple sources of information and preferably, multiple modalities.

8.3.1 Record Review

Meticulous review of contemporaneous records across the lifespan is the starting point in a mental health evaluation to determine whether an evaluee's life history is consistent or inconsistent with ND-PAE. While reading records, it is helpful to develop a chronological log of pertinent functional information and life events (including tables of all test results), which will provide perspective on life functioning prior to a face-to-face interview. It is particularly important to note data relevant to adaptive functioning. For example, if records document a significant accomplishment that involved persistence (e.g., completing a college degree program), such events should be included in the chronology along with detailed contextual information (e.g., extent to which the accomplishment reflected independent effort). Conversely, if records contain chronic behavior problems, variable test results with relative strengths and weaknesses, and multiple secondary disabilities, these types of data also should be included in the chronology. At the end of the record review process, the chronology should contain all documented functional and adaptive data—positive or negative—that are relevant to diagnosis and the referral matter as well as significant postnatal events that may have impacted brain maturation during the developmental years (e.g., head injuries, traumatic childhood events, evaluee substance abuse).

From a forensic standpoint, contemporaneous records prior to the instant matter tend to contain some of the most reliable data about behavior, especially standardized cognitive testing and adaptive assessments during the school years as well as behavioral observations or ratings from teachers and other professionals. On the other hand, unless corroborated by third-party data, be cautious about accepting documented self-reports as reliable. For example, documented self-reports may reflect inaccuracies due to memory problems or perceptual and interpretive distortions as well as secondary gain influences. Notably, documented reports from birth mothers may minimize or conceal information that reflects poor parenting (e.g., denial of substance use during pregnancy or developmental delays and behavior problems in offspring).

The following records should be requested from referring parties at the outset of FBAs: birth, medical, school, adoption, child protective services, Social Security disability or state rehabilitation agency, and juvenile court/justice. Also very important in terms of potentially relevant information are sibling records as well as the biological mother's medical, treatment, and legal records. Birth records often are unavailable in cases involving adult evaluees. However, if such records are available, unless a mother presents at time of delivery with obvious signs of intoxication or drug use, birth records rarely contain evidence of maternal substance use, although they may contain evidence of complications and birth defects associated with FASD. It is important to know that known drug use by birth mothers often overshadows or conceals alcohol use. Birth and ongoing pediatric records can be excellent sources of information regarding early life problems associated with FASD (e.g., prematurity, microcephaly, failure to thrive, growth deficit, facial and other physical abnormalities, heart murmur, and other birth defects). Pediatric records may contain information about preschool behaviors associated with FASD such as poor state and behavior regulation (e.g., constant crying, tantrums, sleep disturbance, developmental delays, attachment problems, hyperactivity, attention problems, difficulty understanding and following directions, chronic disobedience). Relevant behaviors that may be documented in pediatric records during the elementary school years include learning problems, speech and language services, immaturity, externalizing behaviors, peer relationship problems, risk unawareness, and suggestibility. Although children with FASD often are bullied due to their cognitive and behavioral differences, they also may become bullies in response to peer rejection.

Regarding birth mother records, it is relatively rare in obstetrical records to see doctors asking pregnant patients about their drinking and drug use habits, although records in the last 20 years are beginning to contain such information. If a birth mother had alcohol and drug problems at any time in her life, such history significantly increases the likelihood she drank and/or used drugs during the index pregnancy. Alcohol use almost always accompanies drug use, although as noted, drug use is far more likely to be the focus of attention in medical records. Maternal medical records (including death certificates, if applicable) may contain evidence of alcohol-related medical conditions such as cirrhosis. Sometimes, maternal medical and treatment records contain information pertaining directly to alcohol and drug use around the time of the pregnancy. Of course, substance abuse diagnoses and/or substance abuse treatment at any point in life are maternal red flags for risk of FASD in offspring. Other red flags in maternal records include alcohol- or drug-related arrests.

Risk of delivering a child with FASD increases in direct proportion to maternal age, gravidity, and parity (May et al., 2005, 2006; Jacobson, Jacobson, & Sokol, 1996; Jacobson, Jacobson, Sokol, & Ager, 1998). Older women with histories of episodic drinking, multiple pregnancies (gravidity), and multiple children (parity) are at increased risk of bearing children with an FASD (May et al., 2013). Because alcohol metabolism appears to be affected by body size and maternal nutrition (Abel, 1998; Badger et al., 2005; Khaole, Ramchandani, Viljoen, & Li, 2004; Shankar et al., 2006; Shankar, Ronis, & Badger, 2007; Sokol et al., 1986), short women with a low body mass index are more likely than larger women to give birth to a child with FASD (May et al., 2005, 2008). Risk of FASD in an evaluee is extremely high in the case of an evaluee who has a sibling diagnosed with an FASD (Abel, 1988, 1998; Kvigne, Leonardson, Borzelleca, Neff-Smith, & Welty, 2009; McQuire, Daniel, Hurt, Kemp, & Paranjothy, 2020).

The importance of elementary school records cannot be overstated as such data often provide contemporaneous evidence of functioning associated with FASD in standardized assessments of academic achievement and related cognitive functioning. School records also may contain data relevant to differential diagnosis, such as events that could have affected brain development during adolescence. Many children with FASDs receive special education services at some point during their school years, and triennial school evaluations for Individual Educational Plans (IEPs) tend to be rich repositories of relevant data such as IQ testing and adaptive assessments by teachers. According to the secondary disabilities study (Streissguth et al., 2004), 42% of the large FASD sample had been in a self-contained classroom, 66% had received special education services in a "resource" room, 65% had received remedial help in either reading or arithmetic, and 29% had received life skills training (i.e., a special education service in high school). In a Canadian study (Brownell et al., 2013), children with FASD were more than nine times as likely to receive special education services compared to children without FASD. Although speech and language services were not specifically assessed in the secondary disabilities study, subsequent studies found that a very high percentage of children with FASD received special education services for speech and language disability (Church, Eldis, Blakley, & Bawle, 1997; Egeland et al., 1998; Elliott, Payne, Morris, Haan, & Bower, 2008; Kvigne et al., 2004; Spohr, Willms, & Steinhausen, 1994). Speech and language services in the early school years are evidence of delayed development in communication.

For evaluees with FASD who did not receive special education supports, school records typically reflect academic decline over time as schoolwork becomes more complex and external structure diminishes. When reviewing school records, it is important to look carefully for regular progression to the next grade at the end of each academic year because retention often is not mentioned directly in records and can only be determined by carefully charting academic progression from year to year. When children with FASD enter middle school/junior high, where coursework increases in complexity and external structure decreases, academic performance and social behavior often decline. If students with FASD reach high school, many give up and drop out of school due to the mental challenge and persistence required to succeed. Although a large minority (40%) of adults with FASD in the secondary disabilities study (Streissguth et al., 1996) had graduated from high school, nearly all had special education supports at some point in their school years. Some (30%) even attempted college.

Other records that may be available during the childhood years include adoption, CPS, and juvenile records. Such records often contain contemporaneous data about the birth mother as well as the evaluee. According to the literature (Olson et al., 2009; Streissguth et al., 2004), only 10–20% of children with FASD are raised by their biological mothers. Among the environmental circumstances often seen in this population are early maternal death, child abuse and neglect, removal from the home by authorities, repetitive periods of foster care and other transient home placements, and being raised by adoptive or extended family caregivers. In fact, foster care and adoption are common experiences for children with FASD as studies find FASD prevalence rates in these groups ranging from 23.7% to 73.3% (Astley, 2010; Greenbaum, Stevens, Nash, Koren, & Rovet, 2009; May, Hymbaugh, Aase, & Samet, 1983), and meta-analysis indicates as many as 17% of children in adoptive and foster placements have FASD (Lange, Shield, Rehm, & Popova, 2013). If school records are unavailable, juvenile records may contain historical academic information as well as evaluations, testing, and relevant behavioral data. Notably, juveniles with FASD are 19 times more likely than typically developing youths to be incarcerated in juvenile facilities (Popova et al., 2011).

In addition to discovery in criminal cases, other adult records that should be examined include Social Security earnings statements, employment records, police and legal records pertaining to prior arrests, Department of Corrections (DOC) records (medical, mental health, behavioral) if applicable, and all previous mental health evaluations—forensic and clinical. If previous evaluations contain test data, such information should be tabulated and compared to present testing as well as test results during the childhood years. If DOC records contain test results based upon group testing, reliability is questionable due to administration format among other things, which should be noted. Regarding employment-related records, Social Security earnings statements provide annual summaries of wages; records from employers may contain details about work performance or behavior and interpersonal problems.

8.3.2 Interviewing the Evaluee

At the outset of initial interviews with evaluees, it is important to ensure they understand the purpose of the evaluation and limits on confidentiality. Regardless of presentation, a useful technique in the case of possible FASD is to have evaluees repeat disclosure information in their own words to ensure understanding. Although it is necessary to interview evaluees to obtain firsthand information relevant to diagnostic impressions and forensic questions, self-reports may be compromised by deliberate over- or under-reporting and/or unintentional inaccuracies (e.g., confabulation) due to cognitive impairments (e.g., memory problems, impaired communication skills). Consequently, administering objective measures of response style is recommended. Of course, relevant information provided by evaluees should not be relied on for conclusions or opinions unless corroborated by objective testing and reliable third-party information, either from records or collateral interviews.

As is the case for persons with ID (Emerson, Felce, & Stancliffe, 2013; Fujiura, 2012), the extent to which accurate self-reported information can be obtained from people with FASD requires careful consideration. For example, evaluees may camouflage cognitive deficits with superficial chattiness, joking around, or indifference, and they may mask low-esteem with bravado, boasting, and self-aggrandizement, all of which serve as defensive coping strategies in FASD (Carpenter, Blackburn, & Egerton, 2014; Edgerton, 1993; Hull et al., 2017; Moore & Green, 2004; Novick Brown, Gudjonsson, & Connor, 2011; Streissguth, Bookstein, Barr, Press, & Sampson, 1998). People with FASD tend to be easily led and eager to please authority figures (Brown, Reichel, & Quinlan, 2011), which may influence self-reports as well as responses to personality inventories and mental health questionnaires. To our knowledge, no personality tests have been developed and normed on FASD samples, a caveat that also applies to commonly used behavioral self-assessments and physiological measures such as the polygraph and penile plethysmograph, which calls into question results on such measures in the context of prenatal alcohol exposure.

Questions during interviews or on questionnaires regarding frequencies and time frames are especially problematic for those with FASD (Finlay & Lyons, 2001; Fujiura, 2012; Stancliffe, Wilson, Bigby, Balandin, & Craig, 2013). For instance, rating scales that require nuanced self-rating (e.g., 5- or even 3-point Likert scales) may overwhelm cognitive capacity (Fang et al., 2011). Compared to normally constituted persons, response bias may be more common in those with significant cognitive limitations (Finlay & Lyons, 2001; Stancliffe, 2000), which includes acquiescence bias (i.e., tendency to endorse questions, regardless of content) and recency bias (i.e., tendency to endorse the last alternative in multiple-choice or either/or questions, regardless of content). See Emerson et al. (2013) for a review of self-report problems in ID, which apply equally to FASD, and suggestions for addressing some of the challenges.

8.3.3 Collateral Interviews

Interviews with collateral witnesses are essential in order to (a) fill in gaps left in the chronology following record review, and (b) corroborate important information. Potential collateral witnesses include the birth mother if available as well as others who have firsthand information about the evaluee (e.g., family members, neighbors, friends, professionals who interacted with the family). The latter might include former teachers, probation officers, therapists, or treatment providers. Although in-person interviews are preferred whenever possible, telephonic interviews do not diminish reliability (Limperopoulos, Majnemer, Steinbach, & Shevell, 2006). For example, one study found that telephonic interviews obtained rich narrative data on sensitive subjects such as alcohol use (Drabble, Trocki, Salcedo, Walker, & Korche, 2016), and a systematic review comparing qualitative telephonic to in-person interviews concluded there was little evidence of data loss/distortion or compromised quality of findings when interview data were collected by telephone (Novick, 2008).

As other authors in this collection have noted, confirming prenatal alcohol exposure in ND-PAE can be quite challenging, especially if interviews are telephonic. Women who have used alcohol and/or drugs in pregnancy may be reluctant to report such use for various reasons, not the least of which is stigma (Corrigan et al., 2017; Stone, 2015). If birth mothers have children who are under age 18, reluctance may stem from fear of losing their children due to CPS intervention (Ostrea, Brady, Gause, Raymundo, & Stevens, 1992). Often, birth mothers minimize or conceal substance use during pregnancy due to concern they might be blamed for their children's problematic behavior (Kushner & Sher, 1991; Yang, Wong, Griver, & Hasin, 2017). Chapter 4 in this book addresses techniques found effective for interviewing birth mothers.

8.3.4 Structured Behavior Assessment

According to *DSM-5* (APA, 2013), adaptive behavior should be assessed with clinical evaluation and individualized, culturally appropriate, psychometrically sound measures that are administered to knowledgeable informants (e.g., parent, caregiver or other family member, teacher, counselor) as well as to evaluees to the extent possible. Regarding direct adaptive assessment of evaluees, there are multiple instruments available that can be administered alongside neurocognitive measures. Additional sources of information relevant to adaptive behavior include previous educational, developmental, medical, and mental health records. *DSM-5* notes that when adaptive functioning is difficult to assess for evaluees in controlled settings (e.g., prisons, detention centers), information regarding functioning outside those settings should be obtained.

Rather than adaptive measures that require self-assessment, structured third-party behavior rating instruments such as the Vineland-3 (Sparrow et al., 2016) or Adaptive Behavior Assessment System (ABAS), also in its third edition (ABAS-III; Harrison & Oakland, 2015), are the most reliable way to quantify evaluee adaptive functioning. The focus in these adaptive measures is on typical independent behavior in the real world rather than what the person is capable of doing if prompted or directed. Behavioral items on these measures are categorized into the tripartite factor structure of adaptive behavior found in research dating back to 1959 (Tassé et al., 2012), which is consistent with AAIDD (Schalock et al., 2010) and *DSM-5* (APA, 2013): (a) Practical skills (activities of daily living and personal care, occupational skills, use of money, safety, health care, travel and transportation, schedules/routines, and use of the telephone); (b) Conceptual skills (e.g., language, reading and writing, and money, time, and number concepts); and (c) Social skills (e.g., interpersonal skills, social responsibility, self-esteem, gullibility, naiveté, following rules and obeying laws, avoiding being victimized, and social problem-solving). Scores are generated for each of the three domains and subdomains, with a composite score that summarizes global adaptive functioning.

Test manuals for adaptive measures like the Vineland-3 and ABAS-3 recommend that family members or individuals who know an evaluee well function as raters. Although face-to-face administration of adaptive instruments is recommended, telephonic interviews are permitted when in-person interviews are impractical or cost-prohibitive. Research has found that telephonic administration of the Vineland does not diminish reliability (Limperopoulos et al., 2006). Using structured adaptive instruments like the Vineland to measure adaptive behavior has become the standard of practice in the forensic as well as the mental health, education, and research fields (Greenspan & Switzky, 2006; Tassé, 2009). Unlike other adaptive instruments, the Vineland has the advantage of being the measure most often used in FASD research, which facilitates comparison between evaluation findings and the empirical literature.

Retrospective adaptive assessment is necessary in forensic contexts involving those who have been incarcerated for long periods of time (Tassé, 2009). In private communication with one of the authors of this chapter, a developer of the Vineland-3 (Celine Saulnier) endorsed retrospective assessment for individuals who have been out of the community for some time, provided the measure was administered to at least two individuals to ensure consistency. The accuracy of retrospective adaptive ratings has been endorsed by AAIDD (Schalock et al., 2010). Another way to verify accuracy in adaptive ratings is to administer an ancillary measure that includes validity scales. The Behavior Rating Instrument of Executive Function, Second Edition (BRIEF-2; Gioia, Isquith, Guy, & Kenworthy, 2015), is a good example of such a measure and also has the added advantage of including third-party ratings of executive skills, which often correlate with adaptive scores. The adult version of the BRIEF-2 (i.e., BRIEF-A; Roth, Isquith, & Gioia, 2005) takes relatively little time to administer (approximately 15 min) and contains three validity scales that screen for significant Negativity, Inconsistency, and Infrequency in third-party behavior ratings. Other ways to verify Vineland-3 or ABAS-3 results include consistency with (a) childhood adaptive ratings documented in school records, (b) neuropsychological testing (especially EF), (c) documented anecdotal information, and (d) secondary disabilities analysis.

The Fetal Alcohol Behavior Scale (FABS; Streissguth et al., 1998) is an efficient way to screen specifically for behaviors consistent with FASD. [The FABS is included at the end of chapter.] Developed by researchers at the University of Washington to capture the behavioral essence of FASD, the FABS was based on a large reference sample of 472 FASD patients (ages 2–51). Imbedded within a larger measure called the Personal Behaviors Checklist to make it less transparent, the FABS demonstrated high item-to-scale reliability and good test–retest reliability over an average interval of 5 years, accurately identifying subjects with known or presumed prenatal alcohol exposure in multiple detection studies. The 36 behavioral items comprising the FABS are organized into seven categories (Communication and Speech, Personal Manner, Emotions, Motor Skills and Activities, Academic/Work Performance, Social Skills/Interactions, and Bodily/Physiologic Functions). Endorsement of 15 or more items on the FABS reliably differentiates people with FASD from those without FASD. Median scores on the FABS were 20 for persons with FASD and 5 for those without FASD.

8.4 Diagnosis

As previously noted, the central nervous system (CNS) abnormality central to the medical conditions under the FASD umbrella is diagnosed in *DSM-5* (APA, 2013) as *neurodevelopmental disorder associated with prenatal alcohol exposure* (ND-PAE). Prior to *DSM-5*, the mental health defect in FASDs was diagnosed in *DSM-IV-TR* (American Psychiatric Association, 2000) and *DSM-IV* (American Psychiatric Association, 1994) as cognitive disorder not otherwise specified (NOS; code 294.9), which generally covered CNS dysfunction due to an underlying general medical condition, as in mild neurocognitive disorder due to prenatal alcohol exposure. Since 2013, ND-PAE has been used to diagnose the cognitive and adaptive dysfunction in all medical conditions under the FASD umbrella (i.e., FAS, partial fetal alcohol syndrome (pFAS), alcohol-related neurodevelopmental disorder (ARND), static encephalopathy/alcohol-exposed (SE/AE), and neurobehavioral disorder/alcohol-exposed (ND/AE) (Astley et al., 2009; Carr et al., 2010; Kingdon et al., 2016; Mattson et al., 1997; Riley & McGee, 2005). ND-PAE is listed under the general category, Other Specified Neurodevelopmental Disorder, and coded 315.8.

Primary diagnostic criteria in ND-PAE are (a) "more than minimal" alcohol exposure during gestation, defined as more than 13 alcoholic beverages per month, with no more than two drinks consumed on any single drinking occasion; (b) impaired neurocognitive functioning in one or more of the following domains: global intellectual deficit (i.e., IQ of 70 or below, or a standard score of 70 on a comprehensive developmental assessment); impaired EF (e.g., poor planning and organization, inflexibility, difficulty with behavioral inhibition); impaired learning (e.g., lower academic achievement than expected for intellectual level, specific learning disability); memory impairment (e.g., problems remembering information learned recently, repeatedly making the same mistakes, difficulty remembering lengthy verbal instructions); or impaired visuospatial reasoning (e.g., disorganized or poorly planned drawings or constructions, problems differentiating left from right); (c) impaired self-regulation in one or more of the following: mood or behavioral dysregulation, attention deficit, or impaired impulse control; and (d) impaired adaptive functioning in two or more of the following domains: communication, social communication/interaction, daily living skills, or motor skills (APA, 2013, pp. 798–801). As in all neurodevelopmental disorders, symptoms in ND-PAE must manifest during the developmental period. Consistent with the robust findings in FASD that executive function deficits increase with age, peaking around age 12 and stagnating from that point on (Kingdon et al., 2016), *DSM-5* (APA, 2013) acknowledges ND-PAE is not easy to diagnose in young children but is better detected later in childhood. ND-PAE diagnostic criteria require clinically significant distress or impairment in important functional domains and also require differential diagnosis.

Unlike other neurodevelopmental disorders, diagnostic criteria for ND-PAE are found in a chapter near the end of the *DSM-5* (APA, 2013, pp. 798–801) called "Conditions for Further Study," which makes it appear the criteria are in process. Initially, bifurcating the diagnosis and criteria created confusion in the mental health field, although ND-PAE criteria were consistent with FASD guidelines published by CDC (Bertrand et al., 2004) and Institute of Medicine (IOM; Stratton et al., 1996). Likely because of this consistency, diagnostic criteria for ND-PAE quickly became widely accepted in the mental health field and now are generally accepted as the standard of practice for diagnosing the CNS impairment in FASD (Doyle & Mattson, 2015; Hagan et al., 2016; Kable et al., 2016; Olson, 2015). National organizations relevant to FASD have adopted ND-PAE diagnostic guidelines. For example, the National Organization on Fetal Alcohol Syndrome (NOFAS) recommended that mental health clinicians diagnose patients with ND-PAE by recording "Other specified neurodevelopmental disorder" and coding 315.8, followed by the specific reason for the condition (e.g., neurobehavioral disorder associated with prenatal alcohol exposure) (NOFAS, 2020). The National Institute on Alcohol Abuse and Alcoholism (NIAAA) states that those who meet criteria for a medical FASD diagnosis under IOM guidelines likely meet mental health criteria for ND-PAE in *DSM-5* as the two essential features common to both sets of guidelines are prenatal alcohol exposure and CNS abnormality (NIAAA, 2015). In conjunction with multidisciplinary assessment in high-stakes forensic contexts (Novick Brown et al., 2010), forensic experts routinely rely on ND-PAE criteria to determine whether evaluees exhibit the mental defect in FASD (Brown et al., 2017; Grant et al., 2013; Novick Brown et al., 2015).

Research supports the validity of ND-PAE diagnostic criteria. For example, using "deficit" criterion levels of 1.5 and 1.0 SD below the mean on norm-referenced measures and symptom descriptions, Kable and Coles (2018) found internal validity in ND-PAE symptoms across childhood in a sample of children with FAS and pFAS, independent of environmental factors, although criterion levels were thought to be too restrictive for adaptive functioning in younger children. In another study (Sanders et al., 2017), retrospective multidisciplinary chart diagnosis in children, adolescent, and adult patients found that ND-PAE correlated moderately with medical conditions under the FASD umbrella. In that study, the conservative deficit threshold of −2.0 SD also was thought to be too restrictive. A third study involving chart review of children and adolescents found concordance (95% sensitivity and 75% specificity) between ND-PAE criteria and an ARND checklist, with ND-PAE correctly classifying 89.5% of cases meeting criteria for ARND (Johnson, Moyer, Klug, & Burd, 2018).

In a recent prospective study of children ages 7–15 (mean age 10.79 years) with confirmed prenatal alcohol exposure (Sanders, Netelenbos, & Dei, 2020), multidisciplinary assessment using Canadian diagnostic criteria for FASD (i.e., −2 SD) found that the majority (70.7%) received an FASD medical diagnosis, but fewer (41.4%) received an ND-PAE diagnosis. Although medical diagnoses and ND-PAE were highly correlated, ND-PAE was the more conservative system (i.e., 94.1% specificity and 56.1% sensitivity). With respect to ND-PAE diagnostic criteria, 91.4% of this research sample met criteria for neurocognitive impairment, and 87.9% met criteria for impaired self-regulation, with no overlap between the two domains. However, only 41.5% met criteria for adaptive impairment, although this domain correlated with both the neurocognitive and self-regulation domains. Consistent with prior research, the researchers concluded that while adaptive impairment was relatively common in children with ND-PAE, requiring two domains of adaptive impairment (defined as −2 SD) in young children was too restrictive.

8.5 Comorbidity and Differential Diagnosis

Documenting the results of a multimethod-multisource FBA evaluation in a report is a meticulous process. The report should contain all relevant data as well as referral source, reason for the evaluation, referral questions, list of procedures, and notifications. The body of the report should summarize relevant data from the following sources: documented life history from records reviewed in the evaluation, evaluee self-report, collateral interviews with (or reports from) individuals who interacted with the evaluee in various contexts, results of current psychometric testing and adaptive behavior assessment in the context of all prior testing/assessments across the lifespan, neuroimaging (if available), relevant results from prior evaluations, contemporaneous observations, information regarding prenatal alcohol and drug exposure, and a conclusion section that synthesizes and transparently analyzes data relevant to opinions (e.g., diagnostic impressions, differential diagnosis, responses to referral questions). Generally, there is a direct relation between the number of data sources and methods and the reliability of conclusions and opinions in a mental health evaluation (Heilbrun et al., 2003; Heilbrun et al., 2008; Heilbrun et al., 2013).

Differential diagnosis is an integral element in the analysis portion of a report. Required in *DSM-5*, differential diagnosis involves comparing ND-PAE to other possible etiologies (e.g., postnatal substance use, general medical conditions other than FASD such as traumatic brain injury [TBI], other known teratogens, genetic conditions, environmental neglect, mental health and personality disorders) in order to determine which etiology best explains *all* behavior across the entire lifespan. With respect to environmental neglect, it should be noted that a recent study found childhood neglect did not worsen developmental outcomes in children with FASD (Mukherjee, Cook, Norgate, & Price, 2019). Regarding comorbidity, since ND-PAE is comorbid with numerous mental health conditions (as well as many medical problems), it is important to designate ND-PAE as the primary mental health diagnosis due to its prenatal origins and direct link to the underlying medical condition (e.g., FAS, pFAS, ARND).

ND-PAE may co-occur with other neurodevelopmental conditions such as attention deficit hyperactivity disorder (ADHD) and ID. Comorbidity, the norm in FASD, often overshadows and conceals the underlying medical condition (Clarke & Gibbard, 2003; Famy et al., 1998; Nash & Davies, 2017; Popova et al., 2016; Streissguth et al., 1996). In a meta-analysis that examined comorbidity in FAS, Popova et al. (2016) found that the most common co-occurring mental disorders in FAS included conduct disorder (90.7% pooled prevalence) and alcohol or drug dependence (54.5% pooled prevalence). In addition, mood disorders (e.g., bipolar disorder, severe depressive episode with or without psychotic symptoms, dysthymia) were seen in a large minority of persons with FAS as were psychotic disorders (approximately 44% pooled prevalence). In a systematic review of children with diagnoses across the FASD continuum (Weyrauch, Schwartz, Hart, Klug, & Burd, 2017), rates of oppositional defiant disorder were higher than expected (i.e., 16.3% in FASD versus 3.3% in the general population) as were rates of depression (14.1% versus 3.5%), psychotic disorder (12.3% versus 0.5%), bipolar disorder (8.6% versus 2.7%), anxiety disorder (7.8% versus 0.7%), and PTSD (6.0% versus 4.0%). Regarding behavioral disorder comorbidity such as oppositional defiant disorder and conduct disorder, *DSM-5* (APA, 2013) urges caution, noting such diagnoses need to be weighed in the context of significant cognitive impairments.

Rates of comorbidity between FASD and other neurodevelopmental disorders also are quite high. A meta-analysis of FAS studies found comorbidity (pooled prevalence) between FASD and receptive and expressive language disorders (81.8% and 76.2%, respectively), ID (69.2%), speech and language disorder (67.2%), and ADHD (51.2%) (Popova, Lange, Shield, Burd, & Rehm, 2019). Similarly, systematic review of diagnoses in children with dysmorphic and non-dysmorphic FASD (Weyrauch et al., 2017) found ADHD in 50.2% of children with FASD compared to 5% in the general population, ID in 23% of FASD children compared to 1% in the general population, and specific learning disorder in 19.9% of those with FASD compared to 10% in the general population. As noted, this overlap in clinical presentation often obscures accurate diagnosis in affected individuals (Coles, 2011; Coles et al., 1997; Jacobson, Dodge, Burden, Klorman, & Jacobson, 2011; Mattson et al., 2011), particularly when information about maternal drinking is unavailable, not sought, or falsely denied (Peadon & Elliott, 2010).

While IQ distinguishes between ID and FASD in the majority of individuals with FASD who have IQs above 75 (70 +/− 5 points margin of error), executive and adaptive functioning in both conditions tends to be similar (Greenspan et al., 2016). Significant discrepancies among IQ domains are seen frequently in persons with FASD (Bertrand et al., 2004), making FSIQ an inaccurate way to classify IQ in this population (Greenspan et al., 2016; Novick Brown, 2020). In *DSM-5* (APA, 2013), FSIQ also is less important in ID because "intellectual" deficiency now is defined as a broad array of mixed impairments that mostly involve EF (i.e., reasoning, problem-solving, planning, abstract thinking, judgment, learning from instruction and experience, and practical understanding). Level of impairment is specified for ID as approximately 2 SDs below the population mean on norm-referenced tests with means of 100 (i.e., 70 +/− 5 points). As both ID and FASD involve considerable executive dysfunction as well as adaptive impairment (at least one deficient adaptive domain is required in ID, and two or more deficient domains are required in FASD), people with ID or FASD are indistinguishable from each other in terms of everyday behavior (Greenspan et al., 2016).

Thus, ND-PAE represents the cognitive-behavioral expression of an underlying FASD medical condition, of which ADHD and perhaps other neurodevelopmental disorders may be components. ND-PAE is qualitatively different from ADHD in many ways:

- Unlike ADHD, FASD is functionally equivalent to ID (Greenspan et al., 2016).
- Meta-analyses have found persons with ADHD have FSIQs that are 9 points lower than neurotypical controls (Barkley, DuPaul, & McMurray, 1990; Frazier, Demaree, & Youngstrom, 2004). A meta-analysis found FSIQ was 16 points lower in FASD than in ADHD (Kingdon et al., 2016).
- Although both ADHD and FASD involve executive dysfunction, not all children with ADHD exhibit impairments in EF (Nigg, Willcutt, Doyle, & Sonuga-Barke, 2005; Willcutt, Doyle, Nigg, Faraone, and Pennington, 2005).
- There is robust empirical evidence that IQ does not explain EF deficits in FASD (e.g., Kodituwakku, 2009; Streissguth et al., 1991; Streissguth et al., 1996; Thomas et al., 1998; Whaley et al., 2001); research is mixed whether IQ influences EF deficits in ADHD (e.g., Brown et al., 2011; Mahone et al., 2002).
- There is a fundamental difference in the attention deficit that may be seen in both conditions: children with FASD have greater difficulty with *encoding* (i.e., capacity to hold information temporarily in working memory while performing mental operations) and *set-shifting* (i.e., ability to flexibly shift attention from one stimulus facet to another when appropriate), while children with ADHD have greater difficulty with *focusing* (i.e., concentrating attention on a particular task) and *sustaining attention* (i.e., staying on task; Coles et al., 1997; Mirsky, Anthony, Duncan, Ahearn, & Kellam, 1991; Peadon & Elliott, 2010).
- A 15-study meta-analysis that compared EF in FASD and ADHD found persons with FASD performed significantly worse on neuropsychological measures of EF than those with ADHD (Khoury & Milligan, 2019).
- A 51-study meta-analysis found more extensive executive dysfunction in FASD compared to ADHD, particularly in executive skills requiring complex mental effort (Kingdon et al., 2016).
- Symptoms of ADHD often are eliminated or significantly reduced with medication; in contrast, ND-PAE symptoms are permanent and relatively resistant to medication (Oesterheld et al., 1998; Peadon & Elliott, 2010).
- Children with FASD display more severe adaptive dysfunction than children with ADHD (Crocker et al., 2009; Greene et al., 1996; Mikami, Huang-Pollock, Pfiffner, McBurnett, & Hangai, 2007; Roizen, Blondis, Irwin, & Stein, 1994;

Stein, Szumowski, Blondis, & Roizen, 1995; Thomas et al., 1998; Ware et al., 2012; Whaley et al., 2001).

- ADHD symptoms often diminish in severity across the developmental years; ND-PAE symptoms become more severe and complex with age (Crocker et al., 2009; Mattson et al., 2011; McGee et al., 2009; McGee, Fryer, et al., 2008; Thomas et al., 1998; Whaley et al., 2001).
- Adaptive delays in children with ADHD gradually improve with age and typically disappear by adulthood; adaptive deficits in FASD worsen with age, with adolescents showing arrested development that endures well into the adult years (Crocker et al., 2009; Fagerlund, Autti-Ramo, Hoyme, Mattson, & Korkman, 2011; Mattson et al., 2019).
- Unlike ADHD, FASD has extremely high rates of comorbidity. For example, a systematic review of prevalence studies that compared rates of comorbid mental disorders and neurodevelopmental disorders in FASD versus normally constituted age-peers found those with FASD were 45 times more likely to be diagnosed with ADHD, 22 times more likely to be diagnosed with ID, 13 times more likely to be diagnosed with oppositional defiant disorder, nearly 12 times more likely to be diagnosed with a psychotic disorder, 10.6 times more likely to be diagnosed with depression, and 10 times more likely to be diagnosed with a learning disorder (Weyrauch et al., 2017).
- Most people with ADHD are able to support themselves and live independently in their adult years; only a very small percentage of adults with ND-PAE can do both (Burd & Popova, 2019; Streissguth et al., 1996).

In short, ND-PAE/FASD is a significantly more severe disability than ADHD, with broad ramifications that affect all important functional domains. [See Chapter 10 for additional analysis of this topic.] Unlike ADHD, ND-PAE/FASD is a cause-and-effect disorder with clear etiology informed by decades of science: prenatal alcohol exposure causes brain damage, which causes cognitive and adaptive dysfunction. In sum, while a diagnosis of ADHD may explain attention deficits, impulsivity, and hyperactive behavior during childhood; a diagnosis of ND-PAE/FASD explains all behavior across the lifespan.

8.6 Data Synthesis and Analysis

If investigative data in an FBA support a diagnosis of ND-PAE, the concluding section of the evaluation report describes all information relevant to diagnostic decision-making. For example, this section contains alternative hypotheses considered in the evaluation, summaries of relevant information from interviews and record review, and characteristic patterns in psychometric testing. Relevant data from other examiners (e.g., medical findings and diagnosis, neuropsychological testing, neuroimaging results) are integrated into the analysis. Pertinent behavior and functioning during the school and adult years are described as well as developmental outcomes in important adaptive domains. If data are organized chronologically, beginning with the birth mother's consumption of alcohol (and perhaps other substances) and ending with the instant matter, this sequence can show how ND-PAE manifested across the developmental years.

Cognitive testing requires meticulous analysis. Current test results are compared to all prior testing and also compared to empirically based expectations. In FASD, not only do we expect adaptive functioning to be considerably lower than FSIQ, we also expect adaptive functioning to reflect *decreasing* age-indexed capacity over time (i.e., arrested development) such that during the adult years, functioning is equivalent to levels seen in young children (Jirikowic et al., 2008; Whaley et al., 2001). Current test results should be compared to test profiles found in the research (e.g., inter-test and intra-test variability based upon mental effort, with functionality generally dependent upon amount of external structure and guidance). Test result variability should be explained and reconciled, as should behaviors that are inconsistent with the diagnosis. All reasonable conditions that might explain behavior should be considered and described, ultimately ruling out interpretations that do not explain or only partially explain functioning and leaving in only the explanation that best accounts for all behavior across the lifespan as the ultimate opinion (i.e., differential diagnosis). Opinions regarding referral questions should be based upon convergent data from multiple sources and methods to increase reliability. In summary, the overall role of the FBA evaluator in an FASD investigation is to connect the dots (i.e., synthesize the relevant data) to explain how the underlying brain damage in ND-PAE affected cognitive functioning across the lifespan, which in turn affected adaptive functioning and ultimately, where relevant, offense conduct.

Personal Behaviors Checklist (PBCL-FABS)

Your Name: ______________________ **Subject's Name:** ______________________

Your Relationship to Subject: ____

Subject's age when you had frequent/regular contact with him/her:___________________

Today's Date: ____________________

Instructions: Please complete this questionnaire regarding the individual I am evaluating (the "subject"). The descriptions below contain statements about people's behaviors. For each statement, please circle "yes," "no," or "don't know" regarding whether the statement describes the person. These statements describe people of all ages, but if the statement does not currently apply to this person because he/she is now an adult, please write "no" on the line but **note if the statement *used to apply* to the person when he/she was a child.** If you haven't seen the person for many years, please rate his/her behavior during the period you had the most contact with him/her. Please respond to ALL of the statements, giving examples wherever possible.

Communication and Speech:

1	Yes	No	Don't know	Loud, deep, or unusual sounding voice
2	Yes	No	Don't know	Talks too much and too fast
3	Yes	No	Don't know	Interrupts; talks with poor timing in terms of the listener
4	Yes	No	Don't know	Unusual conversational topics; dwells on one or two particular subjects or speaks about unrealistic or unusual topics
5	Yes	No	Don't know	Can be very opinionated; at times, seems almost incapable of examining the other side of an argument or of considering an idea from a different point of view
6	Yes	No	Don't know	Speaks indistinctly; either speaks very rapidly or mumbles or has poor pronunciation
7	Yes	No	Don't know	Likes to talk; talking seems more important than the content
8	Yes	No	Don't know	Repeats certain words or phrases often
9	Yes	No	Don't know	Makes "off the wall" comments; sometimes says things that seem completely out of context
10	Yes	No	Don't know	Talks a lot but says little; is chatty but with shallow content
11	Yes	No	Don't know	Any phrases/questions this person says frequently? ____________
12	Yes	No	Don't know	Other unusual speech or communication patterns? ____________

Personal Manner:

13	Yes	No	Don't know	Cute and pixie-ish as a child; very charming or likable
14	Yes	No	Don't know	Impulsive; often acts before considering consequences
15	Yes	No	Don't know	Klutzy; tasks often unintentionally end up in a mess; tends to upset/spill things more than normal
16	Yes	No	Don't know	Messy; paperwork is smudgy/rumpled; makes more of a mess eating than others the same age; unconcerned about personal cleanliness (e.g., hands, face, clothes are often dirty)
17	Yes	No	Don't know	Touches things and people frequently; seems to need to touch or be touched more than others; needs lots of hugs
18	Yes	No	Don't know	Loves to be the center of attention; draws attention to self
19	Yes	No	Don't know	Tends to lose or misplace things a lot
20	Yes	No	Don't know	Any other special characteristics? ________

Emotions:

21	Yes	No	Don't know	Unusually happy and carefree; laughs readily
22	Yes	No	Don't know	Has rapid mood swings; can be happy one moment and made/upset the next, with mood swings triggered by seemingly small things
23	Yes	No	Don't know	Very sensitive; often takes things too personally; especially sensitive to being teased
24	Yes	No	Don't know	Over-reacts to situations; emotional reactions are often stronger than you would expect
25	Yes	No	Don't know	Fearless; does not usually foresee potential danger
26	Yes	No	Don't know	Depressed; feels very unhappy at times; has thoughts of suicide (please describe and give age when this began) ________
27	Yes	No	Don't know	Low self-esteem; not satisfied with his/her own performance (please describe and give age when this began) ________
28	Yes	No	Don't know	Can be very stubborn
29	Yes	No	Don't know	Sometimes has tantrums or outbursts of excessive anger
30	Yes	No	Don't know	Any other special characteristics? ________

Motor Skills and Activities:

31	Yes	No	Don't know	Very active; always on the go; runs around a lot
32	Yes	No	Don't know	Had difficulty learning new motor skills (e.g., riding a bicycle, throwing a ball, skating, swimming) but may eventually master them
33	Yes	No	Don't know	Had difficulty performing precise tasks or difficulty learning tasks (e.g., writing with a pencil, gluing models, cutting out cookies or measuring ingredients)
34	Yes	No	Don't know	Finds team sports like soccer or football difficult or has had trouble playing on a team
35	Yes	No	Don't know	Loves to climb (as a child) and sometimes climbed without concern for safety; reckless in moving about
36	Yes	No	Don't know	Enjoys taking apart or trying to fix things such as radios or hair dryers (please describe) ________
37	Yes	No	Don't know	Any other motor characteristics? ________

Social Skills and Interactions:

38	Yes	No	Don't know	Very people-oriented; "reaches out" to people; starts lots of conversations
39	Yes	No	Don't know	Overly friendly with strangers (give example) ________
40	Yes	No	Don't know	Often demands attention or monopolizes a conversation
41	Yes	No	Don't know	Establishes superficial friendships easily but has no close friends
42	Yes	No	Don't know	Seems unaware of the consequences of his/her behavior, particularly the social consequences
43	Yes	No	Don't know	Seems unaware of or ignores "good manners" (e.g., may pass gas or burp in public)
44	Yes	No	Don't know	Can't take a hint; needs strong, clear commands because the fine points escape him/her
45	Yes	No	Don't know	Is physically loving/demonstrative; enjoys bodily contact more than most people his/her age; sometimes touches peers more than they prefer
46	Yes	No	Don't know	Gets over-stimulated in social situations, especially in a crowded room or when strangers are present
47	Yes	No	Don't know	Is a flirt; social manner has sexual overtones
48	Yes	No	Don't know	Too easily led by others
49	Yes	No	Don't know	Shows poor judgment in the people he/she trusts
50	Yes	No	Don't know	Engages in inappropriate behaviors at home with family or pets (give example) ________
51	Yes	No	Don't know	Engages in inappropriate behaviors outside the home, such as at school with teachers/students, in the neighborhood, at work (give example) ________
52	Yes	No	Don't know	Any other social problems? ________

Academics / Work Performance:

53	Yes	No	Don't know	Appears brighter and more alert than tests show (please describe)
54	Yes	No	Don't know	Seems as if he/she should have done better than he/she did in school; gives the impression of being more capable than he/she really is (please describe)
55	Yes	No	Don't know	If still in school and in special education, does better than other children in class (please describe)
56	Yes	No	Don't know	Has poor attention span
57	Yes	No	Don't know	Tries hard and wants to please, but the end result is often disappointing
58	Yes	No	Don't know	Has trouble completing tasks
59	Yes	No	Don't know	Has/had problems with school attendance (please describe)
60	Yes	No	Don't know	Has difficulty keeping a job (please describe)
61	Yes	No	Don't know	What areas/subjects does he/she do best in?

Bodily or Physiologic Functions:

62	Yes	No	Don't know	Seems very sensitive to bright lights (e.g., squints more than others in the sun; blinks to flash cameras; turns away from bright lights)
63	Yes	No	Don't know	Seems very sensitive to loud noises (e.g., startles easily, doesn't tune out repetitive noises, seems bothered by certain sounds)
64	Yes	No	Don't know	Attracted to things like CD players, radios, sprinklers, electric gadgets, etc.(give examples)
65	Yes	No	Don't know	Rocks or swings rhythmically when going to sleep, when unhappy, or when alone
66	Yes	No	Don't know	Bangs head; hits or bits self
67	Yes	No	Don't know	Has dry or flaky skin
68	Yes	No	Don't know	Is fidgety; can't sit still
69	Yes	No	Don't know	Has an unusual smell or his/her room has a particular odor (please describe)
70	Yes	No	Don't know	Has feeding problems (e.g., poor suck as a baby and took very long to finish bottles; late in accepting solid foods readily; seemed to choke more than other children while eating; sometimes vomited while eating) (if yes to any of these, at what age did the problem stop)
71	Yes	No	Don't know	Had lots of stomach aches

72	Yes	No	Don't know	Has had sleep problems (e.g., unpredictable sleep/wake patterns, difficulty falling asleep, walking very early in the morning, irregular naps)
73	Yes	No	Don't know	Had vision problems (please describe) ______
74	Yes	No	Don't know	Had hearing problems (please describe) ______
75	Yes	No	Don't know	Had difficulty with toilet training, wetting the bed, or soiling pants (at what age did these problems stop?) ______
76	Yes	No	Don't know	Had problems with personal hygiene (e.g., forgets to bathe, wash hands, brush teeth)
77	Yes	No	Don't know	Had difficulty with onset of puberty (e.g., unusual fears or concerns, problems with independence in managing personal hygiene, irregular or painful periods (please describe) ______
78	Yes	No	Don't know	Has had problems with sexual functioning (e.g., inappropriate masturbation, inappropriate touching of others, other unusual sexual activity)
79	Yes	No	Don't know	Any other problems with bodily functions? (please describe) ______

References

Abel, E. L. (1988). Fetal alcohol syndrome in families. *Neurotoxicology and Teratology, 10*(1), 1–2. https://doi.org/10.1016/0892-0362(88)90060-8

Abel, E. L. (1998). *Fetal alcohol abuse syndrome*. New York: Plenum Press.

Abkarian, G. G. (1992). Communication effects of prenatal alcohol exposure: An investigation of intra-individual variability in children with fetal alcohol spectrum disorder (FASD). *Journal of Communication Disorders, 25*(4), 221–240. https://doi.org/10.1016/0021-9924(92)90017-q

Adnams, C. M., Kodituwakku, P. W., Hay, A., Molteno, C. D., Viljoen, D., & May, P. A. (2001). Patterns of cognitive-motor development in children with fetal alcohol syndrome from a community in South Africa. *Alcoholism: Clinical and Experimental Research, 25*(4), 557–562. https://doi.org/10.1111/j.1530-0277.2001.tb02250.x

Adubato, S. A., & Cohen, D. E. (Eds.). (2011). *Prenatal alcohol use and fetal alcohol spectrum disorders: Diagnosis, assessment and new directions in research and multimodal treatment*. Sharjah: Bentham Science.

Ali, S., Kerns, K. A., Mulligan, B. P., Olson, H. C., & Astley, S. J. (2018). An investigation of intra-individual variability in children with fetal alcohol spectrum disorder (FASD). *Child Neuropsychology, 24*(5), 617–637. https://doi.org/10.1080/09297049.2017.1302579

American Psychiatric Association (APA). (1994). *Diagnostic and statistical manual of mental disorders (DSM-IV)* (4th ed.). Washington, DC: American Psychiatric Association.

American Psychiatric Association (APA). (2000). *Diagnostic and statistical manual of mental disorders (DSM-IV-TR)* (4th ed., Text Revision ed.). Washington, DC: American Psychiatric Association.

American Psychiatric Association (APA). (2013). *Diagnostic and statistical manual of mental disorders (DSM-5)* (5th ed.). Arlington, VA: American Psychiatric Association.

American Psychological Association. (2020). Coping strategy. In *APA Dictionary*. https://dictionary.apa.org/coping-strategy

Anderson, P. (2002). Assessment and development of executive function (EF) during childhood. *Child Neuropsychology, 8*(2), 71–82. https://doi.org/10.1076/chin.8.2.71.8724

Aragon, A. S., Kalberg, W. O., Buckley, D., Barela-Scott, L. M., Tabachnick, B. G., & May, P. A. (2008). Neuropsychological study of FASD in a sample of American Indian children: Processing simple versus complex information. *Alcoholism: Clinical and Experimental Research, 32*(12), 2136–2148. https://doi.org/10.1111/j.1530-0277.2008.00802.x

Astley, S. J. (2010). Profile of the first 1,400 patients receiving diagnostic evaluations for fetal alcohol spectrum disorder at the Washington state fetal alcohol syndrome diagnostic & prevention network. *Canadian Journal of Clinical Pharmacology (Journal canadien de pharmacologie clinique), 17*(1), e132–e164.

Astley, S. J., Olson, H. C., Kerns, K., Brooks, A., Aylward, E. H., Coggins, T. E., … Richards, T. (2009). Neuropsychological and behavioral outcomes from a comprehensive magnetic resonance study of children with fetal alcohol spectrum disorders. *Canadian Journal of Clinical Pharmacology, 16*(1), e178–e201.

Badger, T. M., Hidestrand, M., Shankar, K., McGuinn, W. D., Ronis, J. J., et al. (2005). The effects of pregnancy on ethanol clearance. *Life Sciences, 77*(17), 2111–2126. https://doi.org/10.1016/j.lfs.2005.02.019

Banks, S. J., Eddy, K. T., Angstadt, M., Nathan, P. J., & Phan, K. L. (2007). Amygdala-frontal connectivity during emotion regulation. *Social Cognitive and Affective Neuroscience, 2*(4), 303–312. https://doi.org/10.1093/scan/nsm029

Barkley, R. A., DuPaul, G. J., & McMurray, M. B. (1990). Comprehensive evaluation of attention deficit disorder with and without hyperactivity as defined by research criteria. *Journal of Consulting and Clinical Psychology, 58*(6), 775–789. https://doi.org/10.1037/0022-006x.58.6.775

Becker, M., Warr-Leeper, G. A., & Leeper, H. A., Jr. (1990). Fetal alcohol syndrome: A description of oral motor, articulatory, short-term memory, grammatical, and semantic abilities. *Journal of Communication Disorders, 23*(2), 97–124. https://doi.org/10.1016/0021-9924(90)90016-r

Bertrand, J., Floyd, L. L., Weber, M. K., O'Connor, M., Johnson, K. A., Riley, E., & Cohen, D. (2004). *National task force on FAS/FAE. Fetal alcohol syndrome: Guidelines for referral and diagnosis*. Atlanta, GA: Centers for Disease Control and Prevention. https://www.cdc.gov/ncbddd/fasd/documents/fas_guidelines_accessible.pdf

Binder, L. M., Iverson, G. L., & Brooks, B. L. (2009). To err is human: "Abnormal" neuropsychological scores and variability are common in healthy adults. *Archives of Clinical Neuropsychology, 24*(1), 31–46. https://doi.org/10.1093/arclin/acn001

Brown, J. M., Haun, J., Zapf, P. A., & Novick Brown, N. (2017). Fetal alcohol spectrum disorder (FASD) and competency to stand trial (CST): Suggestions for a "best practices" approach to forensic evaluation. *International Journal of Law and Psychiatry, 52*, 19–27. https://doi.org/10.1016/j.ijlp.2017.04.002

Brown, T. E., Reichel, P. C., & Quinlan, D. M. (2011). Executive function impairments in high IQ children and adolescents with ADHD. *Open Journal of Psychiatry, 1*, 56–65. https://caddac.ca/adhd/wp-content/uploads/2017/06/Brown.Reichel.Quinlan_Executive-Function-Impairments-in-High-IQ-Children-and-Adolescents-with-ADHD.pdf

Brownell, M. D., Hanlon-Dearman, A. C. B., MacWilliam, L. R., Chudley, A. E., Roos, N. P., Yallop, L. P., & Longstaffe, S. E. A. (2013). Use of health, education, and social services by individuals with fetal alcohol spectrum disorder. *Journal of Population Therapeutics and Clinical Pharmacology, 20*(2), e95–e106.

Burd, L., Carlson, C., & Kerbeshian, J. (2007). Fetal alcohol spectrum disorders and mental illness. *International Journal on Disability and Human Development, 6*(4), 383–396. https://doi.org/10.1515/IJDHD.2007.6.4.383

Burd, L., & Popova, S. (2019). Fetal alcohol spectrum disorders: Fixing our aim to aim for the fix. *International Journal of Environmental Resources and Public Health, 16*(2), 3978. https://doi.org/10.3390ijerph16203978

Burden, M. J., Jacobson, S. W., & Jacobson, J. L. (2005). Relation of prenatal alcohol exposure to cognitive processing speed and efficiency in childhood. *Alcoholism: Clinical and Experimental Research, 29*(3), 1473–1483. https://doi.org/10.1097/01.alc.0000175036.34076.a0

Carpenter, B., Blackburn, C., & Egerton, J. (Eds.). (2014). *Fetal alcohol spectrum disorders: Interdisciplinary perspectives*. New York: Routledge.

Carr, J. L., Agnihotri, S., & Keightley, M. (2010). Sensory processing and adaptive behavior deficits of children across the fetal alcohol spectrum disorder continuum. *Alcoholism: Clinical and Experimental Research, 34*(6), 1022–1032. https://doi.org/10.1111/j.1530-0277.2010.01177.x

Chudley, A. E., Conry, J., Cook, J. L., Loock, C., Rosales, T., & LeBlanc, N. (2005). Fetal alcohol spectrum disorder: Canadian guidelines for diagnosis. *Canadian Medical Association Journal, 172*(Suppl. 5), S1–S21. https://doi.org/10.1503/cmaj.1040302

Church, M. W., Eldis, F., Blakley, B. W., & Bawle, E. V. (1997). Hearing, language, speech, vestibular, and dentofacial disorders in fetal alcohol syndrome. *Alcoholism: Clinical and Experimental Research, 21*(2), 227–237.

Clark, E., Lutke, J., Minnes, P., & Ouellette-Kuntz, H. (2004). Secondary disabilities among adults with fetal alcohol spectrum disorder in British Columbia. *Journal of FAS International, 2*, 1–12.

Clarke, M. E., & Gibbard, W. B. (2003). Overview of fetal alcohol spectrum disorders for mental health professionals. *Canadian Child and Adolescent Psychiatric Reviews, 12*(3), 57–63.

Coggins, T. E., Timler, G. R., & Olswang, L. B. (2007). A state of double jeopardy: Impact of prenatal alcohol exposure and maltreatment on social communicative abilities in school-age children with fetal alcohol Spectrum disorders. *Language, Speech, and Hearing Services in Schools, 38*(2), 117–127. https://doi.org/10.1044/0161-1461(2007/012)

Coles, C. D. (2011). Discriminating the effects of prenatal alcohol exposure from other behavioral and learning disorders. *Alcohol Research and Health, 34*(1), 42–50.

Coles, C. D., Brown, R. T., Smith, I. E., Platzman, K. A., Erickson, S., & Falek, A. (1991). Effects of prenatal alcohol exposure at school age: Physical and cognitive development. *Neurotoxicology and Teratology, 13*(4), 357–367. https://doi.org/10.1016/0892-0362(91)90084-a

Coles, C. D., Platzman, K. A., Lynch, M. E., & Freides, D. (2002). Auditory and visual sustained attention in adolescents prenatally exposed to alcohol. *Alcoholism: Clinical and Experimental Research, 26*(2), 263–271. https://doi.org/10.1097/00000374-200202000-00015

Coles, C. D., Platzman, K. A., Raskind-Hood, C. L., Brown, R. T., Falek, A., & Smith, I. E. (1997). A comparison of children affected by prenatal alcohol exposure and attention deficit, hyperactivity disorder. *Alcoholism: Clinical and Experimental Research, 21*(1), 150–161. https://doi.org/10.1111/j.1530-0277.1997.tb03743.x

Connor, P. D., Sampson, P. D., Streissguth, A. P., Bookstein, F. L., & Barr, H. M. (2006). Effects of prenatal alcohol exposure on fine motor coordination and balance: A study of two adult samples. *Neuropsychologia, 44*(5), 744–751. https://doi.org/10.1016/j.neuropsychologia.2005.07.016

Connor, P. D., Streissguth, A. P., Sampson, P. D., Bookstein, F. L., & Barr, H. M. (1999). Individual differences in auditory and visual attention among fetal alcohol-affected adults. *Alcoholism: Clinical and Experimental Research, 23*(8), 1395–1402. https://doi.org/10.1097/00000374-199908000-00014

Cook, J. L., Green, C. R., Lilley, C. M. N., Anderson, S. M., Baldwin, M. E., Chudley, A. E., … Rosales, T. (2015). Fetal alcohol spectrum disorder: A guideline for diagnosis across the lifespan. *CMAJ: Canadian Medical Association Journal (Journal de L'association Medicale Canadienne), 188*(3), 191–197. https://doi.org/10.1503/cmaj.141593

Coons-Harding, K. D., Flannigan, K., Burns, C., Rajani, H., & Symes, B. (2019). Assessing for fetal alcohol spectrum disorders: A survey of assessment measures used in Alberta, Canada. *Journal of Population Therapeutics and Clinical Pharmacology, 26*(1), e39–e55. https://doi.org/10.22374/1710-6222.26.1.4

Corrigan, P. W., Lara, J. L., Shah, B. B., Mitchell, K. T., Simmes, D., & Jones, K. L. (2017). The public stigma of birth mothers of children with fetal alcohol spectrum disorders. *Alcoholism: Clinical and Experimental Research, 41*(6), 1166–1173. https://doi.org/10.1111/acer.13381

Crocker, N., Vaurio, L., Riley, E. P., & Mattson, S. N. (2009). Comparison of adaptive behavior in children with heavy prenatal alcohol exposure or attention-deficit/hyperactivity disorder. *Alcoholism: Clinical and Experimental Research, 33*(11), 2015–2023. https://doi.org/10.1111 j.1530-0277.2009.01040.x

Doney, R., Lucas, B. R., Jones, T., Howat, P., Sauer, K., & Elliott, E. J. (2014). Fine motor skills in children with prenatal alcohol exposure or fetal alcohol Spectrum disorder. *Journal of Developmental and Behavioral Pediatrics, 35*(9), 598–609. https://doi.org/10.1097/dbp.0000000000000107

Doyle, L. R., & Mattson, S. N. (2015). Neurobehavioral disorder associated with prenatal alcohol exposure (ND-PAE): Review of evidence and guidelines for assessment. *Current Developmental Disorders Reports, 2*(3), 175–186. https://doi.org/10.1007/s40474-015-0054-6

Doyle, L. R., Moore, E. M., Coles, C. D., Kable, J. A., Sowell, E. R., Wozniak, J. R., … Mattson, S. N. (2018). Executive functioning correlates with communication ability in youth with histories of heavy prenatal alcohol exposure. *Journal of the International Neuropsychological Society, 24*(10), 1026–1037. https://doi.org/10.1017S1355617718000772

Drabble, L., Trocki, K. F., Salcedo, B., Walker, P. C., & Korche, R. A. (2016). Conducting qualitative interviews by telephone: Lessons learned from a study of alcohol use among sexual minority and heterosexual women. *Qualitative Social Work, 15*(1), 118–133. https://doi.org/10.1177/1473325015585613

Edgerton, R. B. (1993). *The cloak of competence: Revised and updated*. Berkeley, CA: University of California Press.

Egeland, G. M., Perhain-Hestet, K. A., Gessnet, B. D., Ingle, D., Berne, J. E., & Miclcldalgh, J. P. (1998). Fetal alcohol syndrome in Alaska, 1977 through 1992: An administrative prevalence derived from multiple data sources. *American Journal of Public Health, 88*(5), 781–786. https://doi.org/10.2105/ajph.88.5.781

Elliott, E., Payne, J. M., Morris, A., Haan, E., & Bower, C. (2008). Fetal alcohol syndrome: A prospective national surveillance study. *Archives of Disease in Childhood, 93*(9), 732–737. https://doi.org/10.1136/adc.2007.120220

Emerson, E., Felce, D., & Stancliffe, R. J. (2013). Issues concerning self-report data and population-based data sets involving people with intellectual disabilities. *Intellectual and Developmental Disabilities, 51*(5), 333–348. https://doi.org/10.1352/1934-9556-51.5.333

Fagerlund, A., Autti-Ramo, I., Hoyme, H. E., Mattson, S. N., & Korkman, M. (2011). Risk factors for behavioural problems in foetal alcohol spectrum disorders. *Acta Paediatrica, 100*(11), 1481–1488. https://doi.org/10.1111j.1651-2227.2011.02354.x

Fagerlund, A., Autti-Ramo, I., Kalland, M., Santtila, P., Hoyme, H. E., Mattson, S. N., & Korkman, M. (2012). Adaptive behavior in children and adolescents with foetal alcohol spectrum disorders: A comparison with specific learning disability and typical development. *European Child and Adolescent Psychiatry, 21*(4), 221–231. https://doi.org/10.1007s00787-012-0256-y

Famy, C., Streissguth, A. P., & Unis, A. S. (1998). Mental illness in adults with fetal alcohol syndrome or fetal alcohol effects. *American Journal of Psychiatry, 155*(4), 552–554. https://doi.org/10.1176/ajp.155.4.552

Fang, J., Fleck, M. P., Green, A., McVilly, K., Hao, Y., Tan, W., … Power, M. (2011). The response scale for the intellectual disability module of the WHOQOL: 5-point or 3-point? *Journal of Intellectual Disability Research, 55*(6), 537–549. https://doi.org/10.1111/j.1365-2788.2011.01401.x

Finlay, W. M. L., & Lyons, E. (2001). Methodological issues in interviewing and using self-report questionnaires with people with mental retardation. *Psychological Assessment, 13*(3), 319–335. https://doi.org/10.1037//1040-3590.13.3.319

Folkman, S., Lazarus, R. S., Dunkel-Schetter, C., DeLongis, A., & Gruen, R. J. (1986). Dynamics of a stressful encounter: Cognitive appraisal, coping and encounter outcomes. *Journal of Personality and Social Psychology, 50*(5), 992–1003. https://doi.org/10.1037//0022-3514.50.5.992

Franklin, L., Deitz, J., Jirikowic, T., & Astley, S. (2008). Children with fetal alcohol spectrum disorders: Problem behaviors and sensory processing. *American Journal of Occupational Therapy, 62*(3), 265–273. https://doi.org/10.5014/ajot.62.3.265

Frazier, T. W., Demaree, H. A., & Youngstrom, E. A. (2004). Meta-analysis of intellectual and neuropsychological test performance in attention-deficit/hyperactivity disorder. *Neuropsychology, 18*(3), 543–555. https://doi.org/10.1037/0894-4105.18.3.543

Freedman, D., & Woods, G. W. (2018). The developing significance of context and function: Neuroscience and law. *Behavioral Sciences & the Law, 36*(4), 411–425. https://doi.org/10.1002/bsl.2351

Fujiura, G. T. (2012). Self-reported health of people with intellectual disability. *Intellectual and Developmental Disabilities, 50*(4), 352–369. https://doi.org/10.1352/1934-9556-50.4.352

Gioia, G. A., Isquith, P. K., & Guy, S. C. (2001). Assessment of executive functions in children with neurological impairment. In R. J. Simeonsson & S. L. Rosenthal (Eds.), *Psychological and developmental assessment: Children with disabilities and chronic conditions* (pp. 317–356). New York: Guilford Press.

Gioia, G. A., Isquith, P. K., Guy, S. C., & Kenworthy, L. (2000). *Behavior rating inventory of executive function (BRIEF)*. Lutz, FL: Psychological Assessment Resources.

Gioia, G. A., Isquith, P. K., Guy, S. C., & Kenworthy, L. (2015). *Behavior rating inventory of executive function, second edition (BRIEF-2)*. Lutz, FL: Psychological Assessment Resources.

Glancy, G. D., Ash, P., Bath, E. P. J., Buchanan, A., Fedoroff, P., Frierson, R. L., … Zonana, H. V. (2015). AAPL practice guidelines for the forensic assessment. *Journal of the American Academy of Psychiatry and the Law, 43*(Suppl. 2), S3–S53.

Grant, T. M., Novick Brown, N., Graham, J. C., Whitney, N., Dubovsky, D., & Nelson, L. A. (2013). Screening in treatment programs for fetal alcohol spectrum disorders that could affect therapeutic progress. *International Journal of Alcohol and Drug Research, 2*(3), 37–49. https://doi.org/10.7895/ijadr.v2i3.116

Green, C. R., Mihic, A. M., Nikkel, S. M., Stade, B. C., Rasmussen, C., Munoz, D. P., & Reynolds, J. N. (2009). Executive function deficits in children with fetal alcohol spectrum disorders (FASD) measured using the Cambridge Neuropsychological Tests Automated Battery (CANTAB). *Journal of Child Psychology and Psychiatry, 50*(6), 688–697. https://doi.org/10.1111/j.1469-7610.2008.01990.x

Green, C. R., Munoz, D. P., Nikkel, S. M., & Reynolds, J. N. (2007). Deficits in eye movement control in children with fetal alcohol spectrum disorders. *Alcoholism: Clinical and Experimental Research, 31*(3), 500–511. https://doi.org/10.1111/j.1530-0277.2006.00335.x

Greenbaum, R. L., Stevens, S. A., Nash, K., Koren, G., & Rovet, J. (2009). Social cognitive and emotion processing abilities of children with fetal alcohol spectrum disorders: A comparison with attention deficit hyperactivity disorder. *Alcoholism: Clinical and Experimental Research, 33*(10), 1656–1670. https://doi.org/10.1111/j.1530-0277.2009.01003.x

Greene, R. W., Biederman, J., Faraone, S. V., Ouellette, C. A., Penn, C., & Griffin, S. M. (1996). Toward a new psychometric definition of social disability in children with attention-deficit hyperactivity disorder. *Journal of the American Academy of Child and Adolescent Psychiatry, 35*(5), 571–578. https://doi.org/10.1097/00004583-199605000-00011

Greenspan, S. (1979). Social intelligence in the retarded. In N. R. Ellis (Ed.), *Handbook of mental deficiency: Psychological theory and research* (2nd ed., pp. 483–531). Hillsdale, NJ: Erlbaum.

Greenspan, S., Novick Brown, N., & Edwards, W. (2016). FASD and the concept of "intellectual disability equivalence". In M. Nelson & M. Trussler (Eds.), *Law and ethics in fetal alcohol spectrum disorder* (pp. 241–266). Amsterdam: Springer.

Greenspan, S., & Switzky, H. N. (2006). Forty-four years of AAMR manuals. In H. N. Switzky & S. Greenspan (Eds.), *What is mental retardation: Ideas for an evolving disability in the 21st century* (pp. 3–28). Washington, DC: American Association on Mental Retardation.

Hagan, J. F., Balachova, T., Bertrand, J., Chasnoff, I., Dang, E., Fernandez-Baca, D., … Zubler, J. (2016). Neurobehavioral disorder associated with prenatal alcohol exposure. *Pediatrics, 138*(4), e2011553. https://doi.org/10.1542/peds.2015-1553

Haley, D. W., Handmaker, N. S., & Lowe, J. (2006). Infant stress reactivity and pre-natal alcohol exposure. *Alcoholism: Clinical and Experimental Research, 30*(12), 2055–2064. https://doi.org/10.1111/j.1530-0277.2006.00251.x

Harrison, P. L., & Oakland, T. (2015). *Adaptive behavior assessment system (ABAS-3)* (3rd ed.). Torrance, CA: Western Psychological Services.

Heilbrun, K., DeMatteo, D., Marczyk, G., & Goldstein, A. M. (2008). Standards of practice and care in forensic mental health assessment: Legal, professional, and principles-based considerations. *Psychology, Public Policy, and Law, 14*(1), 1–26. https://doi.org/10.1037/1076-8971.14.1.1

Heilbrun, K., Grisso, T., & Goldstein, A. M. (2013). Foundations of forensic mental health assessment. *American Journal of Forensic Psychology, 31*, 80–82.

Heilbrun, K., Marczyk, G. R., DeMatteo, D., Zillmer, E. A., Harris, J., & Jennings, T. (2003). Principles of forensic mental health assessment: Implications for neuropsychological assessment in forensic contexts. *Assessment, 10*(4), 329–343. https://doi.org/10.1177/1073191103258591

Hellemans, K. G. C., Sliwowska, J. H., Verma, P., & Weinberg, J. (2010). Prenatal alcohol exposure: Fetal programming and later life vulnerability to stress, depression, and anxiety disorders. *Neuroscience and Biobehavioral Reviews, 34*(6), 791–807. https://doi.org/10.1016/j.neubiorev.2009.06.004

Hull, L., Petrides, K. V., Allison, C., Smith, P., Baron-Cohen, S., Lai, M.-C., & Mandy, W. (2017). "Putting on my best normal": Social camouflaging in adults with autism spectrum conditions. *Journal of Autism and Developmental Disorders, 47*(8), 2519–2534. https://doi.org/10.1007/s10803-017-3166-5

Iverson, G. L., Brooks, B. L., & Holdnack, J. A. (2008). Misdiagnosis of cognitive impairment in forensic neuropsychology. In R. L. Heilbronner (Ed.), *Neuropsychology in the courtroom: Expert analysis of reports and testimony* (pp. 243–266). New York: Guilford Press.

Jacobson, J. L., Dodge, N. C., Burden, M. J., Klorman, R., & Jacobson, S. W. (2011). Number processing in adolescents with prenatal alcohol exposure and ADHD: Differences in the neurobehavioral phenotype. *Alcoholism: Clinical and Experimental Research, 35*(3), 431–442. https://doi.org/10.1111/j.1530-0277.2010.01360.x

Jacobson, J. L., Jacobson, S. W., & Sokol, R. J. (1996). Increased vulnerability to alcohol-related birth defects in the offspring of mothers over 30. *Alcoholism: Clinical and Experimental Research, 20*(2), 359–363. https://doi.org/10.1111/j.1530-0277.1996.tb01653.x

Jacobson, J. L., Jacobson, S. W., Sokol, R. J., & Ager, J. W. (1998). Relation of maternal age and pattern of pregnancy drinking to functionally significant cognitive deficit in infancy. *Alcoholism: Clinical and Experimental Research, 22*(2), 345–351. https://doi.org/10.1111/j.1530-0277.1998.tb03659.x

Jacobson, S. W. (1998). Specificity of neurobehavioral outcomes associated with prenatal alcohol exposure. *Alcoholism: Clinical and Experimental Research, 22*(2), 313–320. https://doi.org/10.1111/j.1530-0277.1998.tb03654.x

Jacobson, S. W., Bihun, J. T., & Chiodo, L. M. (1999). Effects of prenatal alcohol and cocaine exposure on infant cortisol levels. *Development and Psychopathology, 11*(2), 195–208. https://doi.org/10.1017/s0954579499002011

Jacobson, S. W., Jacobson, J. L., Stanton, M. E., Meintjes, E. M., & Molteno, C. D. (2011). Biobehavioral markers of adverse effect in fetal alcohol spectrum disorders. *Neuropsychological Reviews, 21*(2), 148–166. https://doi.org/10.1007/s11065-011-9169-7

Jirikowic, T., Kartin, D., & Olson, H. C. (2008). Children with fetal alcohol spectrum disorders: A descriptive profile of adaptive function. *Canadian Journal of Occupational Therapy, 75*(4), 238–248. https://doi.org/10.1177/000841740807500411

Johnson, S., Moyer, C. L., Klug, M. G., & Burd, L. (2018). Comparison of alcohol-related neurodevelopmental disorders and neurodevelopmental disorders associated with prenatal alcohol exposure diagnostic criteria. *Journal of Developmental and Behavioral Pediatrics, 39*(2), 163–167. https://doi.org/10.1097/dbp.0000000000000523

Jones, K. L. (2011). The effects of alcohol on fetal development. *Birth Defects Research, 93*(Pt. C, 1), 3–11. https://doi.org/10.1002/bdrc.20200

Jones, K. L., & Smith, D. W. (1973). Recognition of the fetal alcohol syndrome in early infancy. *Lancet, 302*(7836), 999–1001. https://doi.org/10.1016/s0140-6736(73)91092-1

Jones, K. L., Smith, D. W., Ulleland, C. N., & Streissguth, A. P. (1973). Pattern of malformation in offspring of chronic alcoholic mothers. *Lancet, 301*(7815), 1267–1271. https://doi.org/10.1016/s0140-6736(73)91291-9

Kable, J. A., & Coles, C. D. (2018). Evidence supporting the internal validity of the proposed ND-PAE disorder. *Child Psychiatry and Human Development, 49*(2), 163–175. https://doi.org/10.1007/s10578-017-0738-8

Kable, J. A., O'Connor, M. J., Olson, H. C., Paley, B., Mattson, S. N., Anderson, S. M., & Riley, E. P. (2016). Neurobehavioral disorder associated with prenatal alcohol exposure (ND-PAE): Proposed DSM-5 diagnosis. *Child Psychiatry and Human Development, 47*(2), 335–346. https://doi.org/10.1007/s10578-015-0566-7

Kaemingk, K. L., & Halverson, P. T. (2000). Spatial memory following prenatal alcohol exposure: More than a material specific memory deficit. *Child Neuropsychology, 6*(2), 115–128. https://doi.org/10.1076/chin.6.2.115.7058

Kapoor, A., Dunn, E., Kostaki, A., Andrews, M. H., & Matthews, S. G. (2006). Fetal programming of hypothalamo-pituitary-adrenal function: Prenatal stress and glucocorticoids. *Journal of Physiology, 572*(Pt. 1), 31–44. https://doi.org/10.1113/jphysiol.2006.105254

Keiver, K., Bertram, C. P., Orr, A. P., & Clarren, S. (2015). Salivary cortisol levels are elevated in the afternoon and at bedtime in children with prenatal alcohol exposure. *Alcohol, 49*(1), 79–87. https://doi.org/10.1016/j.alcohol.2014.11.004

Khaole, N. C., Ramchandani, V. A., Viljoen, D. L., & Li, T.-K. (2004). A pilot study of alcohol exposure and pharmacokinetics in women with or without children with fetal alcohol syndrome. *Alcohol and Alcoholism, 39*(6), 503–508. https://doi.org/10.1093/alcalc/agh089

Khoury, J. E., & Milligan, K. (2019). Comparing executive functioning in children and adolescents with fetal alcohol spectrum disorders and ADHD: A meta-analysis. *Journal of Attention Disorders, 23*(14), 1801–1815. https://doi.org/10.1177/1087054715622016

Kingdon, D., Cardoso, C., & McGrath, J. J. (2016). Research review: Executive function deficits in fetal alcohol spectrum disorders and attention-deficit/hyperactivity disorder – a meta-analysis. *Journal of Child Psychology and Psychiatry, 57*(2), 116–131. https://doi.org/10.1111/jcpp.12451

Kodituwakku, P., & Kodituwakku, E. (2014). Cognitive and behavioral profiles of children with fetal alcohol spectrum disorders. *Current Developmental Disorders Reports, 1*(3), 149–160. https://doi.org/10.1007/s40474-014-0022-6

Kodituwakku, P. W. (2009). Neurocognitive profile in children with fetal alcohol spectrum disorders. *Developmental Disabilities Research Review, 15*(3), 218–224. https://doi.org/10.1002/ddrr.73

Kodituwakku, P. W., Adnams, C. M., Hay, A., Kitching, A. E., Burger, E., Kalberg, W. O., … May, P. A. (2006). Letter and category fluency in children with fetal alcohol syndrome from a community in South Africa. *Journal of Studies on Alcohol, 67*(4), 502–509. https://doi.org/10.15288/jsa.2006.67.502

Kodituwakku, P. W., Handmaker, N. S., Cutler, S. K., Weathersby, E. K., & Handmaker, S. D. (1995). Specific impairments in self-regulation in children exposed to alcohol prenatally. *Alcohol: Clinical and Experimental Research, 19*(6), 1558–1564. https://doi.org/10.1111/j.1530-0277.1995.tb01024.x

Kodituwakku, P. W., Kalberg, W., & May, P. A. (2001). The effects of prenatal alcohol exposure on executive functioning. *Alcohol Research and Health, 25*(3), 192–198.

Kodituwakku, P. W., May, P. A., Clericuzio, C. L., & Weers, D. (2001). Emotion-related learning in individuals prenatally exposed to alcohol: An investigation of the relation between set shifting, extinction of responses, and behavior. *Neuropsychologia, 39*(7), 699–708. https://doi.org/10.1016/s0028-3932(01)00002-1

Kushner, M. G., & Sher, K. J. (1991). The relation of treatment fearfulness and psychological service utilization: An overview. *Professional Psychology: Research and Practice, 22*(3), 196–203. https://doi.org/10.1037/0735-7028.22.3.196

Kvigne, V. L., Leonardson, G. R., Borzelleca, J., Neff-Smith, M., & Welty, T. K. (2009). Characteristics of children whose siblings have fetal alcohol syndrome or incomplete fetal alcohol syndrome. *Pediatrics, 123*(3), e526–e533. https://doi.org/10.1542/peds.2008-2423

Kvigne, V. L., Leonardson, G. R., Neff-Smith, M., Brock, E., Borzelleca, J., & Welty, T. K. (2004). Characteristics of children who have full or incomplete fetal alcohol syndrome. *Journal of Pediatrics, 145*(5), 635–640. https://doi.org/10.1016/j.jpeds.2004.07.015

Lange, S., Shield, K., Rehm, J., & Popova, S. (2013). Prevalence of fetal alcohol spectrum disorders in a child care settings: A meta-analysis. *Pediatrics, 132*(4), e980–e995. https://doi.org/10.1542/peds.2013-0066

Lee, K. T., Mattson, S. N., & Riley, E. P. (2004). Classifying children with heavy prenatal alcohol exposure using measures of attention. *Journal of the International Neuropsychological Society, 10*(2), 271–277. https://doi.org/10.1017/S1355617704102142

Lemoine, P., Harousseau, H., Borteyru, J. P., & Menuet, J. C. (1968). Les enfants de parents alcooliques: Anomalies observees a propos de 127 cas. *Ouest méd, 21*, 476–482.

Limperopoulos, C., Majnemer, A., Steinbach, C., & Shevell, M. (2006). Equivalence reliability of the Vineland adaptive behavior scale between in-person and telephone administration. *Physical and Occupational Therapy in Pediatrics, 26*(1–2), 115–127. https://doi.org/10.1080/J006v26n01_08

Livingston, L. A., & Happe, F. (2017). Conceptualising compensation in neurodevelopmental disorders: Reflections from autism spectrum disorder. *Neuroscience and Biobehavioral Reviews, 80*, 729–742. https://doi.org/10.1016/j.neubiorev.2017.06.005

Mahone, E. M., Hagelthorn, K. M., Cutting, L. E., Schuerholz, L. J., Pelletier, S. F., Rawlins, C., … Denckla, M. B. (2002). Effects of IQ on executive function measures in children with ADHD. *Child Neuropsychology, 8*(1), 52–65. https://doi.org/10.1076/chin.8.1.52.8719

Maier, S. E., & West, J. R. (2001). Drinking patterns and alcohol-related birth defects. *Alcohol Research and Health, 25*(3), 168–169.

Mattson, S. N., Bernes, G. A., & Doyle, L. R. (2019). Fetal alcohol spectrum disorders: A review of the neurobehavioral deficits associated with prenatal alcohol exposure. *Alcoholism: Clinical and Experimental Research, 43*(6), 1046–1062. https://doi.org/10.1111/acer.14040

Mattson, S. N., Calarco, K. E., & Lang, A. R. (2006). Focused and shifting attention in children with heavy prenatal alcohol exposure. *Neuropsychology, 20*(3), 361–369. https://doi.org/10.1037/0894-4105.20.3.361

Mattson, S. N., Crocker, N., & Nguyen, T. T. (2011). Fetal alcohol spectrum disorders: Neuropsychological and behavioral features. *Neuropsychology Review, 21*(2), 81–101. https://doi.org/10.1007/s11065-011-9167-9

Mattson, S. N., Goodman, A. M., Caine, C., Delis, D. C., & Riley, E. P. (1999). Executive functioning in children with heavy prenatal alcohol exposure. *Alcoholism: Clinical and Experimental Research, 23*(11), 1808–1815. https://doi.org/10.1111/j.1530-0277.1999.tb04077.x

Mattson, S. N., & Riley, E. P. (1998). A review of the neurobehavioral deficits in children with fetal alcohol syndrome or prenatal exposure to alcohol. *Alcoholism: Clinical and Experimental Research, 22*(2), 279–294. https://doi.org/10.1111/j.1530-0277.1998.tb03651.x

Mattson, S. N., & Riley, E. P. (1999). Implicit and explicit memory functioning in children with heavy prenatal alcohol exposure. *Journal of the International Neuropsychological Society, 5*(5), 462–471. https://doi.org/10.1017/S1355617799555082

Mattson, S. N., Riley, E. P., Gramling, L., Delis, D. C., & Jones, K. L. (1997). Heavy prenatal alcohol exposure with or without physical features of fetal alcohol syndrome leads to IQ deficits. *Journal of Pediatrics, 131*(5), 718–721. https://doi.org/10.1016/s0022-3476(97)70099-4

May, P. A., Fiorentino, D., Gossage, J. P., Kalberg, W. O., Hoyme, H. E., Robinson, L. K., … Ceccanti, M. (2006). The epidemiology of FASD in a province in Italy: Prevalence and characteristics of children in a random sample of schools. *Alcoholism: Clinical and Experimental Research, 30*(9), 1562–1575. https://doi.org/10.1111/j.1530-0277.2006.00188.x

May, P. A., Gossage, J. P., Brooke, L. E., Snell, C. L., Marais, A. S., Hendricks, L. S., … Viljoen, D. L. (2005). Maternal risk factors for fetal alcohol syndrome in the Western Cape Province of South Africa: A population-based study. *American Journal of Public Health, 95*(7), 1190–1199. https://doi.org/10.2105/AJPH.2003.037093

May, P. A., Gossage, J. P., Marais, A. S., Hendricks, L. S., Snell, C. L., Tabachnick, B. G., … Viljoen, D. L. (2008). Maternal risk factors for fetal alcohol syndrome and partial fetal alcohol syndrome in South Africa: A third study. *Alcoholism: Clinical and Experimental Research, 32*(5), 738–753. https://doi.org/10.1111/j.1530-0277.2008.00634.x

May, P. A., Hymbaugh, K. J., Aase, J. M., & Samet, J. M. (1983). Epidemiology of fetal alcohol syndrome among American Indians of the Southwest. *Social Biology, 30*(4), 374–387. https://doi.org/10.1080/19485565.1983.9988551

May, P. A., Tabachnick, B. G., Gossage, J. P., Kalberg, W. O., Marais, A.-S., Robinson, L. K., … Adnams, C. M. (2013). Maternal factors predicting cognitive and behavioral characteristics of children with fetal alcohol spectrum disorders. *Journal of Developmental and Behavioral Pediatrics, 34*(5), 314–325. https://doi.org/10.1097/DBP.0b013e3182905587

McGee, C. L., Bjorkquist, O. A., Price, J. M., Mattson, S. N., & Riley, E. P. (2009). Social information processing skills in children with histories of heavy prenatal alcohol exposure. *Journal of Abnormal Child Psychology, 37*(6), 817–830. https://doi.org/10.1007/s10802-009-9313-5

McGee, C. L., Fryer, S. L., Bjorkquist, O. A., Mattson, S. N., & Riley, E. P. (2008). Deficits in social problem solving in adolescents with prenatal exposure to alcohol. *American Journal of Drug and Alcohol Abuse, 34*(4), 423–431. https://doi.org/10.1080/00952990802122630

McGee, C. L., Schonfeld, A. M., Roebuck-Spencer, T. M., Riley, E. P., & Mattson, S. N. (2008). Children with heavy prenatal alcohol exposure demonstrate deficits on multiple measures of concept formation. *Alcoholism: Clinical and Experimental Research, 32*(8), 1388–1397. https://doi.org/10.1111/j.1530-0277.2008.00707.x

McLachlan, K., Rasmussen, C., Oberlander, T. F., Loock, C., Pei, J., Andrew, G., … Weinberg, J. (2016). Dysregulation of the cortisol diurnal rhythm following prenatal alcohol exposure and early life adversity. *Alcohol, 53*, 9–18. https://doi.org/10.1016/j.alcohol.2016.03.003

McQuire, C., Daniel, R., Hurt, L., Kemp, A., & Paranjothy, S. (2020). The causal web of foetal alcohol spectrum disorders: A review and causal diagram. *European Child and Adolescent Psychiatry, 29*(5), 575–594. https://doi.org/10.1007/s00787-018-1264-3

Mikami, A. Y., Huang-Pollock, C. L., Pfiffner, L. J., McBurnett, K., & Hangai, D. (2007). Social skills differences among attention-deficit/hyperactivity disorder types in a chat room assessment task. *Journal of Abnormal Child Psychology, 35*(4), 509–521. https://doi.org/10.1007/s10802-007-9108-5

Mirsky, A. F., Anthony, B. J., Duncan, C. C., Ahearn, M. B., & Kellam, S. G. (1991). Analysis of the elements of attention: A neuropsychological approach. *Neuropsychology Review, 2*(2), 109–145. https://doi.org/10.1007/bf01109051

Moore, E. M., & Green, M. (2004). Fetal alcohol spectrum disorder (FASD): A need for closer examination by the criminal justice system. *Criminal Reports, 19*(Pt. 1), 99–108.

Moore, E. M., Migliorini, R., Infante, M. A., & Riley, E. P. (2014). Fetal alcohol spectrum disorders: Recent neuroimaging findings. *Current Developmental Disorders Reports, 1*(3), 161–172. https://doi.org/10.1007/s40474-014-0020-8

Mukherjee, R. A. S., Cook, P. A., Norgate, S. H., & Price, A. D. (2019). Neurodevelopmental outcomes in individuals with fetal alcohol spectrum disorder (FASD) with and without exposure to neglect: Clinical cohort data from a national FASD diagnostic clinic. *Alcohol, 76*, 23–28. https://doi.org/10.1016/j.alcohol.2018.06.002

Nanson, J. L., & Hiscock, M. (1990). Attention deficits in children exposed to alcohol prenatally. *Alcoholism: Clinical and Experimental Research, 14*(5), 656–661. https://doi.org/10.1111/j.1530-0277.1990.tb01223.x

Nash, A., & Davies, L. (2017). Fetal alcohol spectrum disorders: What pediatric providers need to know. *Journal of Pediatric Health Care, 31*(5), 594–606. https://doi.org/10.1016/j.pedhc.2017.04.002

Nash, K., Stevens, S., Greenbaum, R., Weiner, J., Koren, G., & Rovet, J. (2014). Improving executive functioning in children with fetal alcohol spectrum disorders. *Child Neuropsychology, 21*(2), 191–201. https://doi.org/10.1080/09297049.2014.889110

National Institute on Alcohol Abuse and Alcoholism (NIAAA). (2015). Fetal alcohol exposure. https://pubs.niaaa.nih.gov/publications/fasdfactsheet/fasd.pdf. Retrieved 15 Jan 2020.

National Organization on Fetal Alcohol Syndrome (NOFAS). (2020). Recognizing FASD. https://www.nofas.org/recognizing-fasd/. Retrieved 15 Jan 2020.

Nigg, J. T., Willcutt, E. G., Doyle, A. E., & Sonuga-Barke, E. J. S. (2005). Causal heterogeneity in attention-deficit/hyperactivity disorder: Do we need neuropsychologically impaired subtypes? *Biological Psychiatry, 57*(11), 1224–1230. https://doi.org/10.1016/j.biopsych.2004.08.025

Noland, J. S., Singer, L. T., Arendt, R. E., Minnes, S., Short, E. J., & Bearer, C. F. (2003). Executive functioning in preschool-age children prenatally exposed to alcohol, cocaine, and marijuana. *Alcoholism: Clinical and Experimental Research, 27*(4), 647–656. https://doi.org/10.1097/01.ALC.0000060525.10536.F6

Novick Brown, N. (2020). Fetal alcohol spectrum disorders (FASD): Intellectual disability equivalence (Fetale Alkoholspektrumstörungen. Gleichrangigkeit mit intellektuellen Beeinträchtigungen). In G. Becker, K. Hennicke, M. Klein, & M. N. Landgraff (Eds.), *Adults with fetal alcohol spectrum disorder: Diagnosis, screening, intervention, and addiction prevention (Erwachsene mit Fetalen Alkoholspektrumstörungen. Diagnostik, Screening, Intervention, Suchtprävention)* (2nd ed., pp. 115–132). Berlin: de Gruyter. https://doi.org/10.1515/9783110594492

Novick Brown, N., Burd, L., Grant, T., Edwards, W., Adler, R., & Streissguth, A. (2015). Prenatal alcohol exposure: An assessment strategy for the legal context. *International Journal of Law and Psychiatry, 42–43*(Special issue), 144–148. https://doi.org/10.1016/j.ijlp.2015.08.019

Novick Brown, N., Connor, P. D., & Adler, R. S. (2012). Conduct-disordered adolescents with fetal alcohol spectrum disorder: Intervention in secure treatment settings. *Criminal Justice and Behavior, 39*(6), 770–793. https://doi.org/10.1177/0093854812437919

Novick Brown, N., Gudjonsson, G., & Connor, P. (2011). Suggestibility and fetal alcohol spectrum disorders: I'll tell you anything you want to hear. *Journal of Psychiatry and Law, 39*(1), 39–71. https://doi.org/10.1177/009318531103900103

Novick Brown, N., Wartnik, A. P., Connor, P. D., & Adler, R. S. (2010). A proposed model standard for forensic assessment of FASD. *Journal of Psychiatry and Law, 38*(4), 383–418. https://doi.org/10.1177/009318531003800403

Novick, G. (2008). Is there a bias against telephone interviews in qualitative research? *Research in Nursing and Health, 31*(4), 391–398. https://doi.org/10.1002/nur.20259

Oberlander, T. F., Jacobson, S. W., Weinberg, J., Grunau, R. E., Molteno, C. D., & Jacobson, J. L. (2010). Prenatal alcohol exposure alters biobehavioral reactivity to pain in newborns. *Alcoholism: Clinical and Experimental Research, 34*(4), 681–692. https://doi.org/10.1111/j.1530-0277.2009.01137.x

Oesterheld, J. R., Kofoed, L., Tervo, R., Fogas, B., Wilson, A., & Fiechtner, H. (1998). Effectiveness of methylphenidate in native American children with fetal alcohol syndrome and attention deficit/hyperactivity disorder: A controlled pilot study. *Journal of Child and Adolescent Psychopharmacology, 8*(1), 39–48. https://doi.org/10.1089/cap.1998.8.39

Olson, H. C. (2015). Advancing recognition of fetal alcohol spectrum disorders: The proposed DSM-5 diagnosis of "neurobehavioral disorder associated with prenatal alcohol exposure (ND-PAE)". *Current Developmental Disorders Reports, 2*(3), 187–198. https://doi.org/10.1007/s40474-015-0056-4

Olson, H. C., Feldman, J. J., Streissguth, A. P., Sampson, P. D., & Bookstein, F. L. (1998). Neuropsychological deficits in adolescents with fetal alcohol syndrome: Clinical findings. *Alcoholism: Clinical and Experimental Research, 22*(9), 1998–2012. https://doi.org/10.1023/A:1019969503528

Olson, H. C., Oti, R., Gelo, J., & Beck, J. (2009). "Family matters": Fetal alcohol spectrum disorders and the family. *Developmental Disabilities Research Reviews, 15*(3), 235–249. https://doi.org/10.1002/ddrr.65

Ostrea, E. M., Brady, M., Gause, S., Raymundo, A. L., & Stevens, M. (1992). Drug screening of newborns by meconium analysis: A large-scale, prospective, epidemiologic study. *Pediatrics, 89*(1), 107–113. https://doi.org/10.1016/s0022-3476(89)80860-1

Ouellet-Morin, I., Dionne, G., Lupien, S. J., Muckle, G., Côté, S., Pérusse, D., ... Boivin, M. (2011). Prenatal alcohol exposure and cortisol activity in 19-month-old toddlers: An investigation of the moderating effects of sex and testosterone. *Psychopharmacology, 214*(1), 297–307. https://doi.org/10.1007/s00213-010-1955-z

Paley, B., & O'Connor, M. J. (2011). Behavioral interventions for children and adolescents with fetal alcohol spectrum disorders. *Alcohol Research and Health, 34*(1), 64–75.

Panczakiewicz, A. L., Glass, L., Coles, C. D., Kable, J. A., Sowell, E. R., Wozniak, J. R., ... Mattson, S. N. (2016). Neurobehavioral deficits consistent across age and sex in youth with prenatal alcohol exposure. *Alcoholism: Clinical and Experimental Research, 40*(9), 1971–1981. https://doi.org/10.1111/acer.13153

Peadon, E., & Elliott, E. J. (2010). Distinguishing between attention-deficit hyperactivity and fetal alcohol spectrum disorders in children: Clinical guidelines. *Neuropsychiatric Disorders and Treatment, 6*(1), 509–515. https://doi.org/10.2147/ndt.s7256

Popova, S., Lange, S., Bekmuradov, D., Mihic, A., & Rehm, J. (2011). Fetal alcohol spectrum disorder prevalence estimates in correctional systems: A systematic literature review. *Canadian Journal of Public Health, 102*(5), 336–340. https://doi.org/10.1007/bf03404172

Popova, S., Lange, S., Shield, K., Burd, L., & Rehm, J. (2019). Prevalence of fetal alcohol spectrum disorder among special subpopulations: A systematic review and meta-analysis. *Addiction, 114*(7), 1150–1172. https://doi.org/10.1111/add.14598

Popova, S., Lange, S., Shield, K., Mihic, A., Chudley, A. E., Mukherjee, R. A. S., ... Rehm, J. (2016). Comorbidity of fetal alcohol spectrum disorder: A systematic review and meta-analysis. *Lancet, 387*(10022), 978–987. https://doi.org/10.1016/s0140-6736(15)01345-8

Ramsay, D. S., Bendersky, M. I., & Lewis, M. (1996). Effect of prenatal alcohol and cigarette exposure on two- and six-month-old infants' adrenocortical reactivity to stress. *Journal of Pediatric Psychology, 21*(6), 833–840. https://doi.org/10.1093/jpepsy/21.6.833

Rasmussen, C. (2005). Executive functioning and working memory in fetal alcohol spectrum disorder. *Alcoholism: Clinical and Experimental Research, 29*(8), 1359–1367. https://doi.org/10.1097/01.alc.0000175040.91007.d0

Rasmussen, C., Andrew, G., Zwaigenbaum, L., & Tough, S. (2008). Neurobehavioural outcomes of children with fetal alcohol spectrum disorders: A Canadian perspective. *Paediatrics and Child Health, 13*(3), 185–191.

Rasmussen, C., Tamana, S., Baugh, L., Andrew, G., Tough, S., & Zwaigenbaum, L. (2013). Neuropsychological impairments on the NEPSY-II among children with FASD. *Child Neuropsychology, 19*(4), 337–349. https://doi.org/10.1080/09297049.2012.658768

Rasmussen, C. R., Soleimani, M., & Pei, J. (2011). Executive functioning and working memory deficits on the CANTAB among children with prenatal alcohol exposure. *Journal of Population Therapeutics and Clinical Pharmacology, 18*(1), e44–e53.

Riley, E. P., & McGee, C. L. (2005). Fetal alcohol spectrum disorders: An overview with emphasis on changes in brain and behavior. *Experimental Biology and Medicine, 230*(6), 357–365. https://doi.org/10.1177/15353702-0323006-03

Robertson, F. C., Narr, K. L., Molteno, C. D., Jacobson, J. L., Jacobson, S. W., & Meintjes, E. M. (2016). Prenatal alcohol exposure is associated with regionally thinner cortex during the preadolescent period. *Cerebral Cortex, 26*(7), 3083–3095. https://doi.org/10.1093/cercor/bhv131

Roebuck-Spencer, T., Mattson, S., & Riley, E. (2002). Interhemispheric transfer in children with heavy prenatal alcohol exposure. *Alcoholism: Clinical & Experimental Research, 26*(12), 1863–1871. https://doi.org/10.1097/01.ALC.0000042219.73648.46

Roizen, N. J., Blondis, T. A., Irwin, M., & Stein, M. (1994). Adaptive functioning in children with attention-deficit hyperactivity disorder. *Archives of Pediatrics and Adolescent Medicine, 148*(11), 1137–1142. https://doi.org/10.1001/archpedi.1994.02170110023004

Roth, R. M., Isquith, P. K., & Gioia, G. A. (2005). *Behavior rating inventory of executive function – Adult version (BRIEF-A)*. Lutz, FL: Psychological Assessment Resources.

Sanders, J. L., Hudson Breen, R. E., & Netelenbos, N. (2017). Comparing diagnostic classification of neurobehavioral disorder associated with prenatal alcohol exposure with the Canadian fetal alcohol spectrum disorder guidelines: A cohort study. *CMAJ: Canadian Medical Association Journal, 5*(1), e178–e183.

Sanders, J. L., Netelenbos, N., & Dei, S. O. (2020). Construct and factorial validity of neurobehavioral disorder associated with prenatal alcohol disorder (ND-PAE). *BMC Psychology, 8*, 53. https://doi.org/10.1186/s40359-020-00405-5

Schalock, R. L., Borthwick-Duffy, S. A., Bradley, V. J., Buntinx, W. H. E., Coulter, D. L., Craig, E. M., … Yeager, M. H. (2010). *Intellectual disability: Diagnosis, classification, and systems of supports* (11th ed.). Washington, DC: American Association on Intellectual and Developmental Disabilities.

Schonfeld, A. M., Mattson, S. N., Lang, A. R., Delis, D. C., & Riley, E. P. (2001). Verbal and nonverbal fluency in children with heavy prenatal alcohol exposure. *Journal of Studies on Alcohol, 62*(2), 239–246. https://doi.org/10.15288/jsa.2001.62.239

Schonfeld, A. M., Paley, B., Frankel, F., & O'Connor, M. J. (2006). Executive functioning predicts social skills following prenatal alcohol exposure. *Child Neuropsychology, 12*(6), 439–452. https://doi.org/10.1080/09297040600611338

Shallice, T., & Burgess, P. (1998). The domain of supervisory processes and the temporal organization of behaviour. In A. C. Roberts, T. W. Robbins, & L. Weiskrantz (Eds.), *The prefrontal cortex: Executive and cognitive functions* (pp. 22–35). New York: Oxford University Press.

Shankar, K., Hidestrand, M., Liu, X., Xiao, R., Skinner, C. M., Simmen, F. A., … Ronis, M. J. J. (2006). Physiologic and genomic analyses of nutrition-ethanol interactions during gestation: Implications for fetal ethanol toxicity. *Experimental Biology and Medicine, 231*(8), 1379–1397. https://doi.org/10.1177/153537020623100812

Shankar, K., Ronis, M. J., & Badger, T. M. (2007). Effects of pregnancy and nutritional status on alcohol metabolism. *Alcohol Research and Health, 30*(1), 55–59.

Smith, S. M., & Vale, W. W. (2006). The role of the hypothalamic-pituitary-adrenal axis in neuroendocrine responses to stress. *Dialogues in Clinical Neuroscience, 8*(4), 383–395. https://doi.org/10.31887/DCNS.2006.8.4/ssmith

Sokol, R. J., Ager, J., Martier, S., Debanne, S. M., Ernhart, C. B., Kuzma, J. A., & Miller, S. I. (1986). Significant determinants of susceptibility to alcohol teratogenicity. *Annals of the New York Academy of Sciences, 477*, 87–102. https://doi.org/10.1111/j.1749-6632.1986.tb40323.x

Sparrow, S. S., Balla, D. A., & Cicchetti, D. V. (1984). *Vineland adaptive behavior scales*. Circle Pines, MN: American Guidance Service.

Sparrow, S. S., Saulnier, C. A., Cicchetti, D. V., & Doll, E. A. (2016). *Vineland adaptive behavior scales: Vineland-3 manual* (3rd ed.). San Antonio, TX: Pearson.

Spohr, H. L., Willms, J., & Steinhausen, H. C. (1994). The fetal alcohol syndrome in adolescence. *Acta Paediatrica, 83*(s404), 19–26. https://doi.org/10.1111/j.1651-2227.1994.tb13379.x

Stancliffe, R. J. (2000). Proxy respondents and quality of life. *Evaluation and Program Planning, 23*(1), 89–93. https://doi.org/10.1016/S0149-7189(99)00042-7

Stancliffe, R. J., Wilson, N. J., Bigby, C., Balandin, S., & Craig, D. (2013). Responsiveness to self-report questions about loneliness: A comparison of mainstream and intellectual-disability-specific instruments. *Journal of Intellectual Disability Research, 58*(5), 399–405. https://doi.org/10.1111/jir.12024

Stein, M. A., Szumowski, E., Blondis, T. A., & Roizen, N. J. (1995). Adaptive skills dysfunction in ADD and ADHD children. *Journal of Child Psychology and Psychiatry and Allied Disciplines, 36*(4), 663–670. https://doi.org/10.1111/j.1469-7610.1995.tb01317.x

Steinhausen, H.-C., & Spohr, H.-L. (1998). Long-term outcome of children with fetal alcohol syndrome: Psychopathology, behavior, and intelligence. *Alcoholism: Clinical and Experimental Research, 22*(2), 334–338. https://doi.org/10.1111/j.1530-0277.1998.tb03657.x

Stephen, J. M., Kodituwakku, P. W., Kodituwakku, E. L., Romero, L., Peters, A. M., Sharadamma, N. M., … Coffman, B. A. (2012). Delays in auditory processing identified in preschool children with FASD. *Alcoholism: Clinical and Experimental Research, 36*(10), 1720–1727. https://doi.org/10.1111/j.1530-0277.2012.01769.x

Stone, R. (2015). Pregnant women and substance use: Fear, sigma, and barriers to care. *Health and Justice, 3*, 1–15. https://doi.org/10.1186/s40352-015-0015-5

Stratton, K. R., Howe, C. J., & Battaglia, F. C. (Eds.). (1996). *Fetal alcohol syndrome: Diagnosis, epidemiology, prevention, and treatment*. Washington, DC: National Academy Press.

Streissguth, A. P., Aase, J. M., Clarren, S. K., Randels, S. P., LaDue, R. A., & Smith, D. F. (1991). Fetal alcohol syndrome in adolescents and adults. *JAMA: Journal of the American Medical Association, 265*(15), 1961–1967. https://doi.org/10.1001/jama.1991.03460150065025

Streissguth, A. P., Barr, H. M., Kogan, J., & Bookstein, F. L. (1996). *Understanding the occurrence of secondary disabilities in clients with fetal alcohol syndrome (FAS) and fetal alcohol effects (FAE). Final Report to the Centers for Disease Control and Prevention (CDC)*. Seattle, WA: University of Washington Publication Services.

Streissguth, A. P., Barr, H. M., Sampson, P. D., & Bookstein, F. L. (1994). Prenatal alcohol and offspring development: The first fourteen years. *Drug and Alcohol Dependence, 36*(2), 89–99. https://doi.org/10.1016/0376-8716(94)90090-6

Streissguth, A. P., Barr, H. M., Sampson, P. D., Parrish-Johnson, J. C., Kirchner, G. L., & Martin, D. C. (1986). Attention, distraction and reaction time at age 7 years and prenatal alcohol exposure. *Neurobehavioral Toxicology and Teratology, 8*(6), 717–725.

Streissguth, A. P., Bookstein, F. L., Barr, H. M., Press, S., & Sampson, P. D. (1998). A fetal alcohol behavior scale. *Alcoholism: Clinical and Experimental Research, 22*(2), 325–333. https://doi.org/10.1111/j.1530-0277.1998.tb03656.x

Streissguth, A. P., Bookstein, F. L., Barr, H. M., Sampson, P. D., O'Malley, K., & Kogan Young, J. (2004). Risk factors for adverse life outcomes in fetal alcohol syndrome and fetal alcohol effects. *Developmental and Behavioral Pediatrics, 25*(4), 228–238. https://doi.org/10.1097/00004703-200408000-00002

Streissguth, A. P., Bookstein, F. L., Sampson, P. D., & Barr, H. M. (1989). Neurobehavioral effects of prenatal alcohol: Part III. PLS analyses of neuropsychologic tests. *Neurotoxicology and Teratology, 11*(5), 493–507. https://doi.org/10.1016/0892-0362(89)90026-3

Stuss, D. T., & Knight, R. T. (Eds.). (2002). *Principles of frontal lobe functioning*. New York: Oxford University Press.

Tassé, M. J. (2009). Adaptive behavior assessment and the diagnosis of mental retardation in capital cases. *Applied Neuropsychology, 16*(2), 114–123. https://doi.org/10.1080/09084280902864451

Tassé, M. J., Schalock, R. L., Balbon, G., Bersani, H., Jr., Borthwick-Duffy, S. A., Spreat, S., … Zhang, D. (2012). The construct of adaptive behavior: Its conceptualization, measurement, and use in the field of intellectual disability. *American Journal of Developmental Disabilities, 117*(4), 291–303. https://doi.org/10.1352/1944-7558-117.4.291

Temple, V. K., Cook, J. L., Unsworth, K., Rajani, H., & Mela, M. (2019). Mental health and affect regulation in fetal alcohol spectrum disorder (FASD): Results from the Canadian national FASD database. *Alcohol and Alcoholism, 54*(5), 545–550. https://doi.org/10.1093/alcalc/agz049

Thomas, S. E., Kelly, S. J., Mattson, S. N., & Riley, E. P. (1998). Comparison of social abilities of children with fetal alcohol syndrome to those of children with similar IQ scores and normal controls. *Alcoholism: Clinical and Experimental Research, 22*(2), 528–533. https://doi.org/10.1097/00000374-199804000-00034

Treit, S., Lebel, C., Baugh, L., Rasmussen, C., Andrew, G., & Beaulieu, C. (2013). Longitudinal MRI reveals altered trajectory of brain development during childhood and adolescence in fetal alcohl spectrum disorders. *Journal of Neuroscience, 33*(24), 10098–10109. https://doi.org/10.1523/JNEUROSCI.5004-12.2013

Uecker, A., & Nadel, L. (1996). Spatial locations gone awry: Object and spatial memory deficits in children with fetal alcohol syndrome. *Neuropsychologia, 34*(3), 209–223. https://doi.org/10.1016/0028-3932(95)00096-8

Uecker, A., & Nadel, L. (1998). Spatial but not object memory impairments in children with fetal alcohol syndrome. *American Journal of Mental Retardation, 103*(1), 12–18. https://doi.org/10.1352/0895-8017(1998)103<0012:SBNOMI>2.0.CO;2

Ware, A. L., Crocker, N., O'Brien, J. W., Deweese, B. N., Roesch, S. C., … Mattson, S. N. (2012). Executive function predicts adaptive behavior in children with histories of heavy prenatal alcohol exposure and attention deficit/hyperactivity disorder. *Alcoholism: Clinical and Experimental Research, 36*(8), 1431–1441. https://doi.org/10.1111/j.1530-0277.2011.01718.x

Weinberg, J., Sliwowska, J. H., Lan, N., & Hellemans, K. G. C. (2008). Prenatal alcohol exposure: Foetal programming, the hypothalamic-pituitary-adrenal axis and sex differences in outcome. *Journal of Neuroendrocrinology, 20*(4), 470–488. https://doi.org/10.1111/j.1365-2826.2008.01669.x

Welsh, M. C., & Pennington, B. F. (1998). Assessing frontal lobe functioning in children: Views from developmental psychology. *Developmental Neuropsychology, 4*(3), 199–230. https://doi.org/10.1080/87565648809540405

Weyrauch, D., Schwartz, M., Hart, B., Klug, M. G., & Burd, L. (2017). Comorbid mental disorders in fetal alcohol spectrum disorders: A systematic review. *Journal of Developmental and Behavioral Pediatrics, 38*(4), 283–291. https://doi.org/10.1097/dbp.0000000000000440

Whaley, S. E., O'Connor, M. J., & Gunderson, B. (2001). Comparison of the adaptive functioning of children prenatally exposed to alcohol to a nonexposed clinical sample. *Alcoholism: Clinical and Experimental Research, 25*(7), 1018–1024. https://doi.org/10.1111/j.1530-0277.2001.tb02311.x

Willcutt, E. G., Doyle, A. E., Nigg, J. T., Faraone, S. V., & Pennington, B. F. (2005). Validity of the executive function theory of attention-deficit/hyperactivity disorder: A meta-analytic review. *Biological Psychiatry, 57*(11), 1336–1346. https://doi.org/10.1016/j.biopsych.2005.02.006

Willford, J. A., Richardson, G. A., Leech, S. L., & Day, N. L. (2004). Verbal and visuospatial learning and memory function in children with moderate prenatal alcohol exposure. *Alcoholism: Clinical and Experimental Research, 28*(3), 497–507. https://doi.org/10.1097/01.ALC.0000117868.97486.2D

Woods, G. W., Freedman, D., & Greenspan, S. (2012). Neurobehavioral assessment in forensic practice. *International Journal of Law and Psychiatry, 35*, 432–439. https://doi.org/10.1016/j.ijlp.2012.09.014

Yang, L., Wong, L. Y., Griver, M. M., & Hasin, D. S. (2017). Stigma and substance use disorders: An international phenomenon. *Current Opinion in Psychiatry, 30*(5), 378–388. https://doi.org/10.1097/YCO.0000000000000351

Ziegler, R. S. (2016). Principles and practice of a neuropsychological approach to conducting independent educational evaluations. *Pediatric Neuropsychology, 2*(1–2), 70–77. https://doi.org/10.1007/s40817-016-0012-1

Chapter 9
In Fetal Alcohol Spectrum Disorder: Comorbidity Determines Complexity

Larry Burd, Marilyn G. Klug, Ann Marie O'Connell, Amanda Palme, and Anne L. Sandstrom

Abstract In the forensic context, fetal alcohol spectrum disorder (FASD) affects one of every six people. Seldom is FASD diagnosed correctly, which can have serious consequences for people in forensic systems whose impairments are unrecognized. Impairments in FASD increase risk of exploitation and manipulation while in police custody (e.g., rights waivers and false/exaggerated confessions) and risk of making uninformed and impulsive decisions prior to trial (e.g., plea bargaining) and at sentencing (e.g., allocutions). Forensic systems should improve screening for FASD, and defense attorneys and prosecutors need increased awareness of FASD. Due to multiple cognitive and adaptive impairments and high rates of comorbid mental health and neurodevelopmental disorders, the negative impact of this disorder on capacity to assist at trial, understand plea options, and exercise appropriate caution at all phases of the legal system is substantial. Judges need to exercise judicial leadership in improving recognition of FASD and its effects across the legal system. This is especially important with respect to closely related (comorbid) issues of gullibility, confabulation, impaired comprehension, and attention deficits.

Keywords Comorbidity · Fetal alcohol spectrum disorder · Alcohol-related neurodevelopmental disorder · Severity · Phenotype · Cost of care · Utilization

L. Burd (✉)
North Dakota Fetal Alcohol Syndrome Center, University of North Dakota School of Medicine and Health Sciences, Grand Forks, ND, USA

Department of Pediatrics, University of North Dakota School of Medicine and Health Sciences, Grand Forks, ND, USA
e-mail: larry.burd@und.edu

M. G. Klug
Department of Population Health, University of North Dakota School of Medicine and Health Sciences, Grand Forks, ND, USA
e-mail: marilyn.klug@und.edu

A. M. O'Connell · A. Palme · A. L. Sandstrom
University of North Dakota School of Medicine and Health Sciences, Grand Forks, ND, USA
e-mail: annmarie.oconnell@und.edu; amanda.palme@und.edu; anne.l.sandstrom@und.edu

N. Novick Brown (ed.), *Evaluating Fetal Alcohol Spectrum Disorders in the Forensic Context*, https://doi.org/10.1007/978-3-030-73628-6_9

9.1 Introduction

Substance use disorders are a global concern (Popova, Lange, Probst, Gmel, & Rehm, 2018). Over the last 20 years, the United States has experienced a national crisis from prenatal exposure to alcohol, opioids, amphetamines, cigarette smoking, and marijuana. The public health magnitude of this slowly increasing wave of alcohol and other substance overuse/abuse is amplified by increasing use among women of childbearing age (Popova, Dozet, & Burd, 2020). In part, this problem is attributable to inadequate national, state, and local responses to these now decades-long epidemics, which are dependent upon news coverage. New problems are presented in the media with urgency, sensationalism, and without context compared to enduring problems such as substance use disorders, especially alcohol use during pregnancy. Prenatal alcohol exposure is a useful example of this problem (Chang, 2020). In the United States, research among non-pregnant women of childbearing age found more than half reported alcohol use in the previous month. One in seven women reported drinking four or more drinks on a single occasion (Substance Abuse & Mental Health Data Archive [SAMHDA], 2011). In other words, alcohol use during pregnancy has not decreased in the past two decades despite well-known risks to unborn children.

Substance use among pregnant women is a major public health concern due to high potential for maternal/fetal mortality and morbidity. Drinking during pregnancy is most prevalent in the early weeks of gestation prior to pregnancy recognition (Popova et al., 2020; Williams & Smith, 2015). Since 50% of pregnancies in the United States are unplanned, large numbers of unborn children are potentially exposed to alcohol in early pregnancy (Paintner, Williams, & Burd, 2012). In a large national survey, one of every nine *pregnant* women reported alcohol use in the previous month, and one of every five reported binge drinking (SAMHDA, 2011; Paintner et al., 2012). More than 3 of every 10 women self-report drinking during pregnancy, with 1 of every 13 women reporting at least one episode of binge drinking (Williams & Smith, 2015).

In fact, alcohol use in the first trimester of pregnancy may be as high as 56% for all women and 78.9% for women with recent alcohol dependence (Stratton, Howe, & Battaglia, 1996). Response by public health and medical systems to the increasing prevalence of alcohol use during pregnancy has been underwhelming to say the least. In particular, response within the public health sector has been minimal and characterized by acceptance, lack of sustained attention, and high likelihood the issue will be overrun by the next big problem in substance use/abuse. For example, after alcohol, it was cocaine, then crack cocaine, then opioids, and then methamphetamine epidemics. Within this sequence, there was a heroin epidemic that now has returned as an opioid epidemic.

One example of our inadequate response is failure to screen women entering hospital emergency departments. Pregnant women are screened for substance use about 50% less often than non-pregnant women (Greenmyer et al., 2020; Moyer, Johnson, Klug, & Burd, 2018). Even more concerning is the finding that in the context of over four million births in the United States each year, scientific reports of positive blood alcohol concentration (BAC) in women during labor or delivery occur only once every few years (Schaff, Moreno, Foster, Klug, & Burd, 2019). In a recent review of global publications, we were able to identify only 16 women and infants who had BAC assessments reported in the scientific literature (Schaff et al., 2019). Recognition of drinking at the end of pregnancy also is rare and appears to occur at a rate of one case in every 4–8 million births (Schaff et al., 2019).

These statistics reflect the closely held belief among prenatal care providers we so often hear, "I have no doubt that a lot of pregnant women drink and have substance use disorders, but these are just not the women I see in my practice." Such perceptions are in sharp contrast to recent publications where biomarkers of alcohol use in late pregnancy show 1 in 12 women (333,000 each year) are still drinking at the end of pregnancy (Burd, 2020). Such statistics clearly demonstrate a need for more training in cooperation with professional organizations that represent medical providers.

Prenatal alcohol exposure increases risk of adverse outcomes for a fetus, including development of a fetal alcohol spectrum disorder (FASD; Astley, Bailey, Talbot, & Clarren, 2000; Stratton et al., 1996). FASD is a common neurodevelopmental disorder with prevalence estimates in recent studies using active case ascertainment methodologies of 3.1–9.9% of the population (Chambers et al., 2019; May, Hasken, Baete, et al., 2020; May, Hasken, Bozeman, et al., 2020; May, Hasken, Stegall, et al., 2020). With a midpoint prevalence rate of 5% and four million annual pregnancies in the United States, it is likely 200,000 infants with FASD are born each year, or about 550 affected newborns each day. Annual cost of care for children with FASD is $22,810 and for adults is $24,308 (Greenmyer, Klug, Kambeitz, Popova, & Burd, 2018).

9.2 Diagnosis

Diagnosing FASD is somewhat complex and not simply a matter of exposure, central nervous system effects, and possible physical characteristics (e.g., facial abnormalities and growth deficit). In Fig. 9.1, we depict four broad areas that affect diagnostic thresholds in FASD.

Diagnosis is complicated further by the use of multiple categorical conditions ("phenotypes"), with varying diagnostic criteria. Medical diagnoses in the United States include fetal alcohol syndrome (FAS), partial fetal alcohol syndrome (pFAS), alcohol-related birth defects (ARBD), and alcohol-related neurodevelopmental disorder (ARND; Burd, Martsolf, Klug, & Kerbeshian, 2003). ARND, which accounts for about 85% of all FASDs, requires evidence of confirmed prenatal alcohol exposure plus cognitive deficits and neurobehavioral impairments (Burd, Martsolf, et al., 2003; Chambers et al., 2019; May, Hasken, Baete, et al., 2020; Stratton et al., 1996).

In a very positive step, some countries and diagnostic centers have elected to use "FASD" as a primary diagnostic category (Chudley et al., 2005). An important

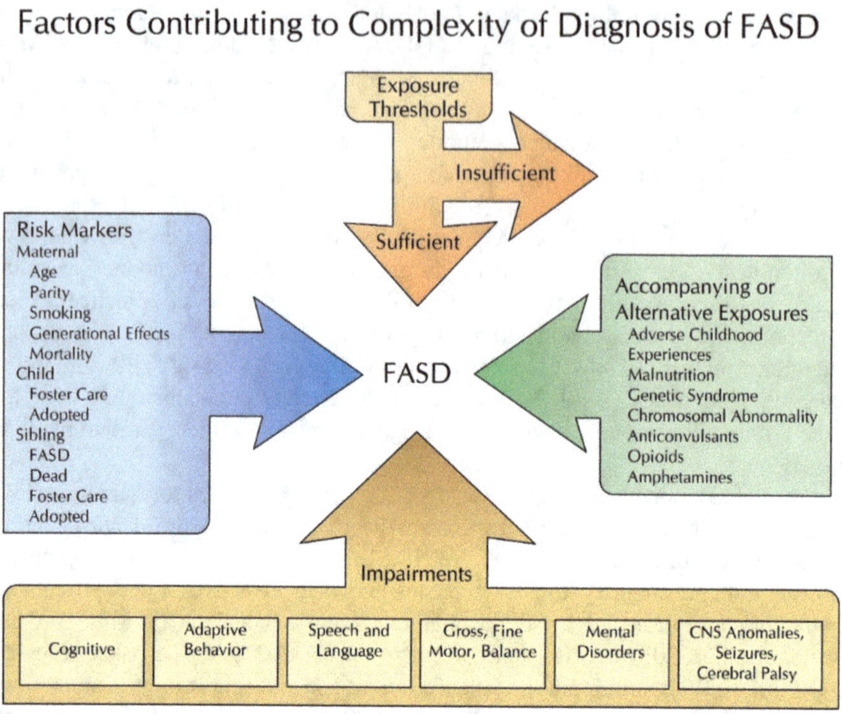

Fig. 9.1 Factors affecting diagnostic thresholds in FASD

diagnostic development in the future would be an international classification of diseases (ICD) code for FASD. At present, there only is an ICD code for FAS. ICD codes allow for easier comparison of data across centers and geographic settings and also allow for enhanced use of administrative data (e.g., health claims and utilization databases for prevalence and cost studies).

Currently, diagnosing FASD in the clinical setting typically involves a multidisciplinary team that includes a neuropsychologist (Burd, Klug, Li, Kerbeshian, & Martsolf, 2010; Burd, Martsolf, et al., 2003; Coles et al., 2016) and, in children, a pediatrician or dysmorphologist. Limited availability in community settings of such specialists significantly restricts diagnostic capacity. Specialized clinics often rely on referrals from many sources, but inadequate frontline clinical recognition of individuals who warrant evaluation has resulted in very low referral rates. Even with relatively few referrals, high rates of undiagnosed or misdiagnosed patients are ongoing concerns (Chasnoff et al., 2005; Kable & Mukherjee, 2017; May et al., 2014). Many factors account for lack of frontline recognition, including infrequent FASD training, limited use of screening measures and protocols, barriers to reporting maternal alcohol use, legal concerns, and the presence of comorbid health conditions (Burd et al., 2010; Kable & Mukherjee, 2017).

9.3 Diagnostic Capacity in Forensic Settings

Currently, diagnostic capacity in the United States is about 200–300 new patients per day. As a result, less than 1% of people affected by prenatal alcohol exposure ever obtain an FASD diagnosis, and nearly all experience long delays accessing diagnostic centers (Popova et al., 2020). In forensic settings, need for diagnosis is greater than in the general population. Although one study found children and adolescents with FASD were 19 times more likely to be incarcerated (Popova, Lange, Bekmuradov, Mihic, & Rehm, 2011), capacity for forensic evaluations in the United States is less than 30 per day. In highly secure settings, it seems doubtful diagnostic capacity would be more than 10–15 people per day. Consequently, if screening programs are developed but diagnostic criteria for FASD remain unchanged, the waiting list will be in the tens of thousands, which means very few people with FASD will ever be diagnosed.

Delays in diagnosis also delay entry into FASD-informed treatments, which often increases exposure to multiple adverse life experiences that are avoidable, such as childhood adversity (Kambeitz, Klug, Greenmyer, Popova, & Burd, 2019; Popova et al., 2016; Price, Cook, Norgate, & Mukherjee, 2017). Foreseeable and potentially preventable postnatal adversities have a large impact on cost of care and service systems that serve this population. Thus, it seems likely diagnostic criteria for FASD will have to be modified for forensic application if diagnostic capacity is to increase enough to meet even 10% of the need.

The most important need in forensic settings is to identify people with specific patterns of impairments that could be addressed with evidence-based interventions. In particular, we need to begin now to identify people with an FASD phenotype, estimate the prevalence of that population in forensic settings, and then begin to identify effective treatments for these individuals. It would be extremely useful to be able to agree on a broad phenotype for FASD that could be applied in forensic as well as community settings, which would involve a set of criteria that could be applied several thousand times a year rather than a few dozen times a year, as is the current situation. Underdiagnosis is of greatest concern for ARND, the most common but most invisible category of FASD in terms of physical appearance. In part, underdiagnosis in forensic settings largely is due to difficulty in accessing accurate information about prenatal care, dosimetry (quantity and frequency of exposure), and duration of exposure. In most cases, such information simply is not available.

9.4 Developmental Course and Changing Phenotype

Phenotypic complexity in FASD begins with exposure, and polysubstance exposure (e.g., nicotine, marijuana, prescription medications, illegal drugs, and/or a wide array of alternative treatments as well as alcohol) is the norm. In Fig. 9.2, we present a graphic image of reciprocal links between polysubstance exposure, brain changes,

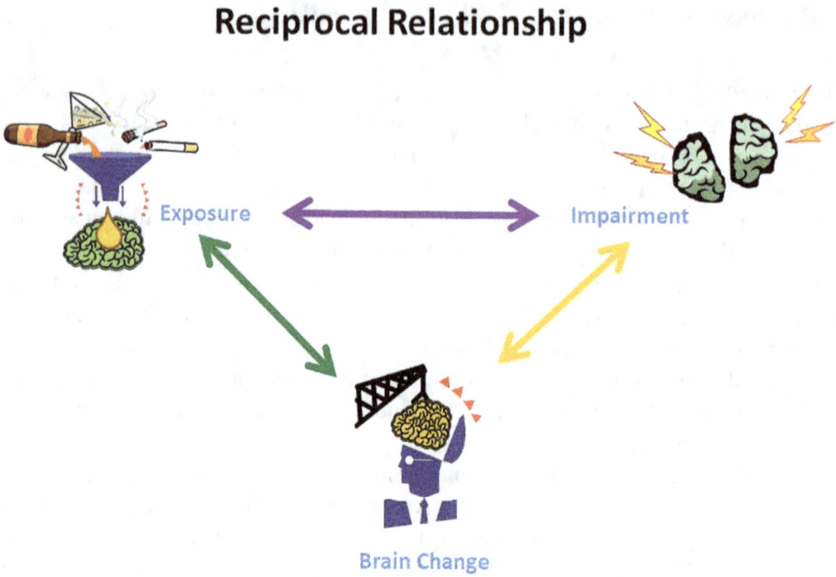

Fig. 9.2 Reciprocal relationships in FASD between exposure elements, brain changes, and functional impairments

and impairment. Science regarding the consequences of polysubstance exposure remains an emerging area.

Another concern is FASD is both multigenerational and familial. Prevalence of FASD often is higher in families of parents who have children with FASD. Within a single family, younger siblings tend to have increased risk of FASD and greater severity.

Developmental outcomes from prenatal alcohol/polysubstance exposure are profound and enduring. In Table 9.1, we summarize nearly 30 years of ongoing research in people with FASD and their families:

The first six variables in Table 9.1 estimate mortality risk. For example, stillbirth rate in FASD is four times the rate in the general population. Indeed, increased mortality risk—a lifelong risk—is a much underappreciated aspect of FASD that often is ignored in the phenotype for this population, which is heavily biased toward morbidity. The six postnatal variables in Table 9.1 illustrate changes in the FASD phenotype over time. Such experiences increase diagnostic complexity and phenotype severity, and people with a high degree of FASD severity pose complex diagnostic challenges. In fact, much of the complexity and severity in FASD is the result of increasing comorbidity over time. While the FAS phenotype tends to attenuate over time, the ARND phenotype very often becomes more severe over time, as shown in Fig. 9.3.

Adaptive behavior impairments due to neurocognitive deficits and comorbidity increase with age in both FAS and ARND, which gradually increases likelihood of

Table 9.1 Risk ratios: mortality and postnatal adversity in FASD

Mortality	Risk Ratio
Stillbirth	4.0
SIDS	10.2
Infectious illness	13.7
Mortality risk	5.3
Sibling risk	5.0
Maternal mortality	(33–44)
Postnatal adversity	
Adverse childhood experiences (four or more)	61%
Head injury	15%
Juvenile corrections	×19
Foster care	×25
Residential care	×6
Independent living	15%

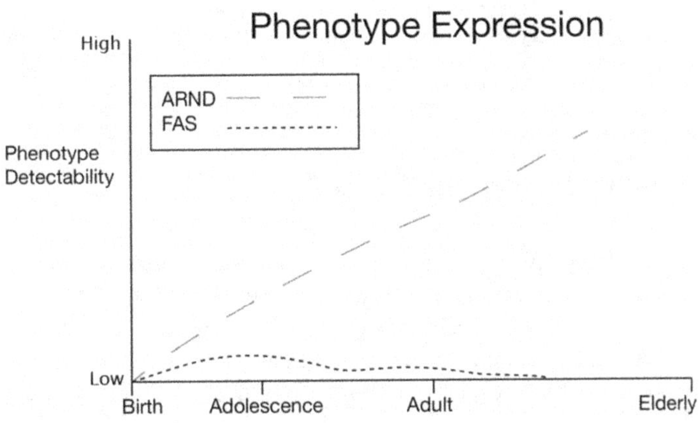

Fig. 9.3 Change over time in phenotype expression: FAS versus ARND

diagnosis in childhood. In FAS, this process continues until about age 18 when age and diagnosis become negatively correlated.

Figure 9.4 illustrates the complexity of diagnosis for people with ARND, which may present as classic ARND, severe ARND, or ARND complicated by high rates of comorbidity. Many factors influence severity of FASD, such as misdiagnosis, no diagnosis, or diagnosis but no access to FASD-informed services. As can be seen in Fig. 9.4, ARND is mostly undiagnosed.

In part, low rates of diagnosis in ARND also are due to complex behaviors that often are misinterpreted as oppositional and manipulative, with inadequate remorse and repetition of the same behaviors over and over despite negative consequences.

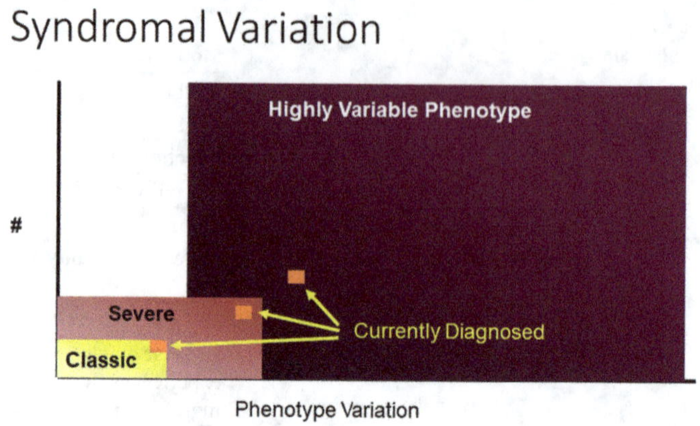

Fig. 9.4 Syndromal variation significantly reduces likelihood of diagnosis

Misunderstanding such behaviors and effects of impairments on offense conduct (characterized as an interaction between brain damage and postnatal adversity) was appreciated by the legal system in a 1994 case before the Florida Supreme Court, *Dillbeck v. State of Florida* (1994). Justices in *Dillbeck* opined, "we can envision few things more certainly beyond one's control than the drinking habits of a parent prior to one's birth."

9.5 Neurodevelopmental Disability

Much of the challenge in caring for people with FASD is difficulty in navigating a poorly defined system of care where even basic knowledge of FASD may be absent. FASD is a significant neurodevelopmental disability and therefore should be eligible for developmental disability services just like intellectual disability and autism spectrum disorder. FASD is present at birth, lasts a lifetime, closely resembles the functional elements of other developmental disabilities, requires similar services, and involves a similar response to interventions. People with FASD currently do not have dedicated service providers. In contrast, those with intellectual disability and autism spectrum disorder have unique access to special education services and developmental disabilities services. In our experience, developmental disability services have been among the most useful and effective interventions for FASD.

FASD should not be considered as one of many options for diagnostic convenience. That is, FASD is not attention-deficit/hyperactivity disorder (ADHD), autism spectrum disorder (ASD), or intellectual disability (ID), although it may share attention and self-regulation symptoms with ADHD, share communication and social behavior symptoms with ASD, and can be functionally equivalent to ID except for IQ. ADHD, ASD, and ID do not replace a diagnosis of FASD, although there may be comorbidity because neurodevelopmental conditions are not identical and interchangeable disorders. The unique aspects of FASD are especially important in forensic settings.

Like ADHD, ASD, and ID, FASD co-occurs with hundreds of other conditions, including birth defects, mental disorders, neurological deficits, vision and hearing loss, growth failure, organ defects, and the list goes on (Popova et al., 2016; Weyrauch, Schwartz, Hart, Klug, & Burd, 2017). Almost all patients diagnosed with FASD also have at least one additional diagnosis, with most patients having several comorbid conditions (Olson, 2015; Weyrauch et al., 2017). A young child with abnormal facial features, growth impairment, and intellectual disability is not typical of FASD; such patients are only typical of published research. In fact, the number of people who have the most well-known or classic type of FASD (i.e., FAS) is quite small, comprising only about 1–5% of cases (Chambers et al., 2019; May, Hasken, Baete, et al., 2020; May, Hasken, Bozeman, et al., 2020; May, Hasken, Stegall, et al., 2020; Popova et al., 2020). By far, the most common category of FASD is ARND (Popova et al., 2020; see also Chap. 3 in this book).

9.6 Mechanisms and Forensic Implications of Comorbidity

Comorbidity is the co-occurrence of two conditions with greater than chance frequency. In most cases, comorbidity also could be considered multimorbidity. We discussed previously several key concepts in the conceptualization of comorbidity. The wide-ranging impact of comorbidity in FASD is summarized by the empirically based findings in Table 9.2 (Burd, Burd, Klug, Kerbeshian, & Popova, 2019). In FASD, comorbidity significantly affects phenotypic variability and severity.

Neurobehavioral and cognitive challenges faced by patients with ARND are the most prevalent source of impairment across the lifespan (Burd, Klug, Martsolf, & Kerbeshian, 2003; Chasnoff, Wells, & King, 2015). Prenatal alcohol exposure damages the developing brain in FASD (Burd, Martsolf, et al., 2003), which manifests as an array of cognitive and neurobehavioral impairments. Many neurodevelopmental and mental health disorders (e.g., ID, ADHD, language disorder, learning disorder, anxiety disorder, depression) have much higher prevalence in FASD compared

Table 9.2 Empirically-based consequences of comorbidity in FASD

Comorbidity in FASD	
1.	Prevalence of comorbidity increases with age
2.	Exposure to adversity increases risk for comorbidity
3.	Comorbidity increases risk for additional comorbidity (the complexity principle)
4.	Increasing comorbidity increases diagnostic uncertainty
5.	Increasing comorbidity increases phenotype severity
6.	Comorbidity increases the complexity of care
7.	Increasing comorbidity increases service utilization and cost of care
8.	Comorbidity decreases access to evidence-based treatments
9.	Comorbidity decreases likelihood of optimal outcomes

to the general population (Burd, Klug, et al., 2003; Olson, 2015; Weyrauch et al., 2017). Regarding service needs, FASD patients with comorbid conditions likely have increased phenotypic severity, which requires multiple services to effectively address. Much broader and more frequent than in the general population (Doyle & Mattson, 2015), service needs in FASD include such things as educational supports if not special education, developmental therapies, medication management, foster home placement, residential treatment for mental health and substance abuse problems, and supportive services within juvenile correctional systems.

Exposure to adverse childhood experiences (ACEs; Kambeitz et al., 2019) in infancy and childhood contributes to much of the comorbidity in FASD. Recently, it has become apparent that ACEs are not equal-impact exposures in the context of FASD. That is, children with FASD appear to be more affected by ACEs than their typically developing peers, likely because children with this disability have impaired capacity to cope with such trauma. In the ACEs context, prenatal alcohol exposure seems to account for most of the adversity-attributable variance in development when children with FASD are compared to neurotypical children exposed to ACEs (Price et al., 2017).

In a mega review, Popova et al. (2016) demonstrated FASD was a condition with very high rates of co-occurring conditions across multiple organ systems. In a previous publication, we presented a model for examining the relative prevalence of neurodevelopmental comorbidity in FASD (Weyrauch et al., 2017). An example of this model is shown in Fig. 9.5.

In FASD, phenotypic complexity appears to increase with age, due in large part to the impact of increasing comorbidity (Fig. 9.6). Ongoing exposure to

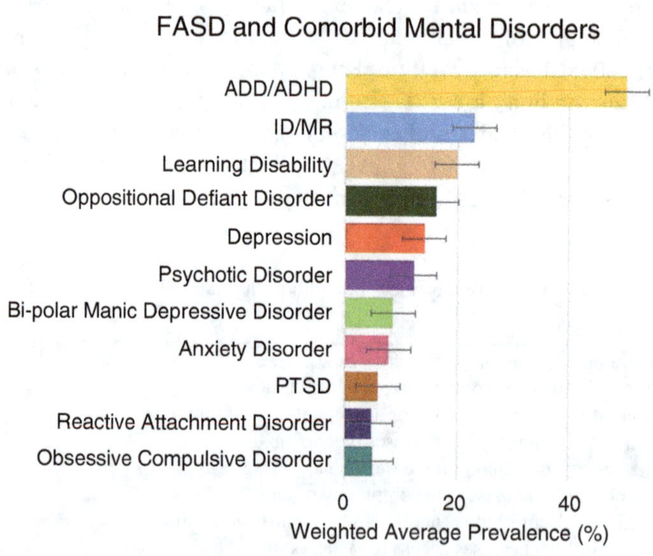

Fig. 9.5 Relative prevalence of common comorbid conditions in FASD

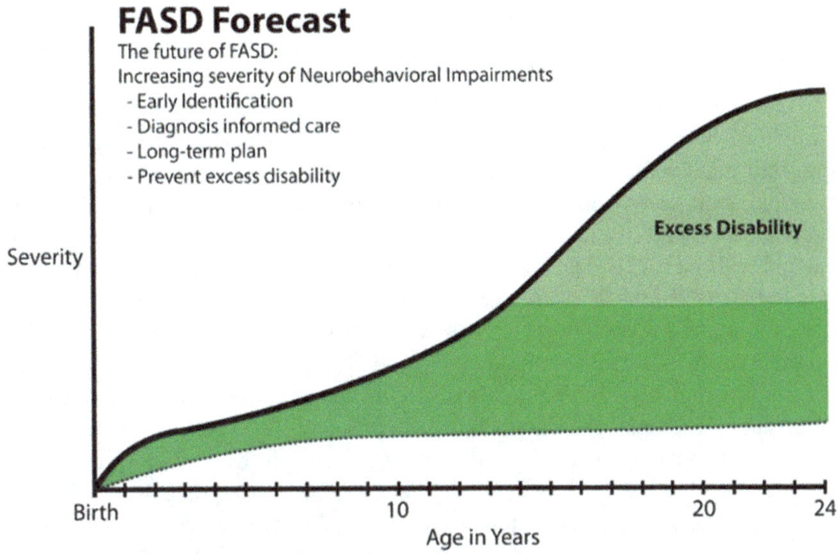

Fig. 9.6 Increasing phenotypic severity over time in FASD

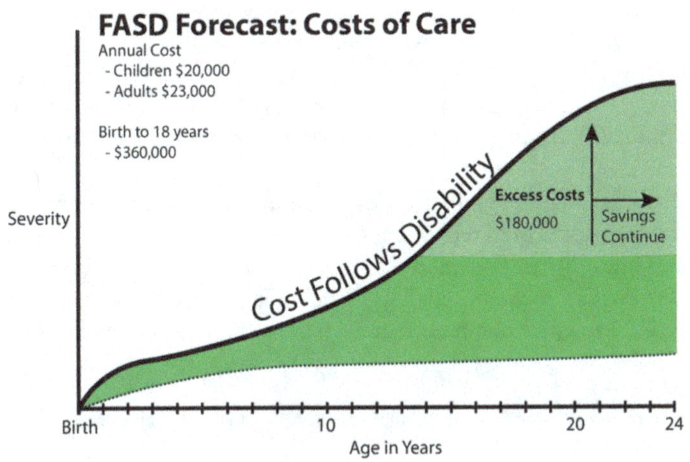

Fig. 9.7 Cost of care increases with comorbidity and phenotypic severity

environmental adversity is a major cause of secondary disabilities and excess disability, which are largely preventable. In addition, high comorbidity rates increase phenotypical severity and complexity of care, which results in large increases in cost of care, as illustrated in Fig. 9.7.

Although the term "comorbidity" typically is used to describe co-occurrence of two diagnostic conditions, it also is a useful concept when considering interactions across developmental domains in FASD. Neurocognitive deficits are an important component of the comorbidity in FASD, especially in forensic settings. Neurodevelopmental disorders often seen in FASD include ID, ADHD, and learning disabilities (Table 9.1 and Fig. 9.5), which persist over the lifespan.

In forensic settings, cognitive and adaptive impairments often are accompanied by impaired insight, which leads to difficulty in or resistance to changing behavior. Comorbidity outcomes in Table 9.2 were identified from an analysis of a population of people with and without FASD. In the study, we used the Alcohol Related Neurodevelopmental Behavioral Checklist (ABC) to distinguish between persons with and without FASD. Data from using this validated assessment are presented in detail in Chap. 3 of this book. Generally, analysis of ABC data identified four broad areas of impairment, each of which was comprised of one or more discreet domains of impairments that can be used as independent measures for FASD (Table 9.3). Importantly, total ABC score reliably distinguished people with and without FASD as did each of the four broad domains.

Like comorbid mental health conditions, specific cognitive impairments in FASD also increase phenotypic severity, which tends to be underappreciated in forensic settings. For example, capacity for insight, a developmentally regulated executive skill that involves accurately and deeply understanding something like one's own behavior, often is impaired in FASD. Without insight, people lack capacity to appreciate the negative effects of their actions on others (i.e., regret or remorse) as well as themselves. Impaired insight increases risk of adverse outcomes, especially as developmental demands increase with age. In FASD, impaired insight interacts with other cognitive impairments, such as poor comprehension, gullibility, confabulation, or anxiety—each contributing to the everyday adaptive impairments that are so prevalent in FASD, resulting in increasing levels of cumulative impairment across the lifespan.

In forensic settings, cognitive deficits interact with marked implications. For example, poor insight could reduce capacity to appreciate the consequences of illegal actions. Gullibility might reduce appropriate skepticism and caution when interacting with law enforcement, leading to defendants readily believing everything they are told. Impaired comprehension could reduce accurate understanding of

Table 9.3 Domains of impairment in the Alcohol Related Neurodevelopmental Behavioral Checklist (ABC)

Broad domains of impairment	Discrete domains of impairment
Cognitive-behavioral	Executive functioning
	Cognition
	Attention and concentration
Verbal interactions	Confabulation
	Gullibility
	Communication skills
Social learning	Academic skills
	Living and social skills
Juvenile justice	Juvenile-specific impairments

verbal and written material and increase automatic acquiescence. Unintentional confabulation to cope with spotty memory gaps could be viewed by others as deliberate lying. Impaired executive functioning could increase impulsive responding. The interaction of such deficits impacts important legal capacities, such as understanding risks in waiving Miranda rights, appreciating the consequences of criminal conviction, making independent decisions in plea agreements and confessions, and complying with probation orders.

When cognitive impairments are not identified and understood as impairments stemming from brain damage, they typically are viewed negatively. Since such impairments do not improve with experience or with age, legal professionals often conclude that affected individuals either do not care or deliberately intend to cause trouble. Cognitive impairments often are synergistic contributors to overall phenotypic severity. When construed as willful behavior or lack of concern for societal norms, punishment seems like the appropriate response. However, when identified and appreciated as brain-based impairments, diagnosis-informed intervention is possible. Essentially, appropriate intervention involves risk reduction.

Appreciating cognitive deficits and associated impairments in FASD as disabilities rather than misconduct is essential if this population is to receive true justice under our legal system. Just as we do not use punishment to improve eyesight in a person with visual impairment, we should not use punishment to improve behavior in people with cognitive deficits. Instead, just as we provide supports and appropriate accommodations for those with vision impairment in order to maximize their functional capacity, we need to do the same for those with FASD, appreciating their cognitive impairments as consequences of brain damage and providing the diagnosis and supports they need to perform adequately.

9.7 Managing Comorbidity

Comorbidity and associated impairments almost always increase across the lifespan. Interaction between static or slowly developing cognitive skills and increasing societal demands due to developmental expectations results in increasing phenotypic severity across the developmental years. Severity is modified by comorbidity and developmental expectations. In FASD, severity can be minimized by diagnosis-informed social and family support systems. For example, a child diagnosed with FASD who lives with a knowledgeable family and attends a school with a diagnosis-informed individual education program (IEP) may function relatively well. However, as that same child matures and environmental structure gradually decreases over the developmental years, he or she likely will have problems making independent decisions. In fact, adolescence often reveals impairments that were present but masked during early childhood years when informed caregivers and providers handled the child's needs within structured environments. It is important to note it is not the child or his/her impairments that change in adolescence but rather societal expectations and demands. Consequently, for adolescents and adults with FASD, anything that increases structure in their lives is key to diagnosis-informed interventions and treatment. For example, a job can add structure, predictability, and accountability to daily life while reducing free time and opportunities for completely independent decision-making.

Evidence suggests the professionals most likely to encounter persons with FASD are not adequately prepared to identify or treat this population (Burd & Edwards, 2019). This problem also holds true for service systems. As previously noted, many states that view ID and ASD as developmental disabilities do not include FASD, despite functional similarities. Mental health system providers often do not appreciate the need to distinguish between impairments and behavior. Substance abuse treatment providers usually do not modify programs to accommodate patients with FASD. Such accommodations might include supports for reading impairments, deficient auditory comprehension, language impairments, memory deficits that may vary widely day to day, and executive function deficits such as poor insight.

In Fig. 9.8, we present a stoplight model of impairment-based behaviors and situations. Red light situations (e.g., aggression, stealing) stem from impairments that require rule-governed behavior, and yellow light situations (e.g., peer influence, sexual encounters, chat rooms, internet meetings, or in-person meetings) require

Name____________________ Date________________

"No, I won't." → Jack____________________

"Let's wait; I want to talk this over..." → Friends____________________

"OK!"

Our plan:

1) Place to live Who________ #________
2) Treatment Who________ #________
3) Parenting Class Who________ #________
4) Treatment Who________ #________

Fig. 9.8 Translating FASD impairments into intervention plans

Name________________________________ Date________________________________

Green Light problems in the last year

1)____________________________
2)____________________________
3)____________________________
4)____________________________
5)____________________________

The plan:

1)____________________________
2)____________________________
3)____________________________

Fig. 9.9 Depiction of FASD-related deficits and plan to manage impulsive actions

some forethought to evaluate appropriate courses of action. Lastly, green light situations involve rapid decision-making and impulsive behavior. The worksheet is used to help clients identify and link problems to desirable responses and available resources.

Figure 9.9 is another programmatic worksheet that matches common recurring behaviors with actions to change those behaviors. Yellow light problems are similar and serve as reminders for problems we want to avoid. These planning worksheets can be used with the checklist we have developed (Fig. 9.10) to summarize areas needing attention when planning services for people with FASD in forensic settings. In Fig. 9.11, we summarize some of our experiences in forensic settings. It is important to emphasize the very high prevalence of neurocognitive limitations in reading, understanding what has been read, listening to and understanding others' communication, and problems with memory (short-term, intermediate, and long-term memory).

Finally, we encourage some critical thinking about the effectiveness of available programs. For instance, if a substance use treatment program is only 10% effective, why would we view it as a lack of commitment if someone with FASD tries but is unable to complete the program? The entire legal system, including prosecutors, defense and the judiciary, should have concerns about the effectiveness of standard treatment programs for such things as substance use disorders, anger management, and parenting skills for persons with FASD.

FASD Checklist for Legal System

Check all that apply.

___ Cognitive deficits
___ Intellectual disability
___ Adaptive behavior scores are often lower than IQ scores
___ Impaired listening
___ Impaired understanding
___ Reading deficits
___ Reading comprehension deficits

___ Attention deficit
___ Hyperactivity disorder
___ Does not exercise appropriate judgment
___ Does not make well thought out choices
___ Anxiety
___ Cannot adequately assist in their defense
___ Imipaired insight
___ Confabulation
___ Imipaired insight
___ Problem Peers
___ Does not understand sentencing options
___ Will need assistance to follow the conditions of parole
___ Gullibility
___ Will need assistance to meet the conditions of probation
___ Will need assistance and modification to complete court ordered treatments
___ Financial assistance
___ Shared decision making

FASD may affect behavior in court

___ May look disinterested
___ May appear fidgety
___ May speak out inappropriately on unrelated topics
___ May agree too much
___ May indicate they understand when they do not
___ May have a version of temper tantrums
___ May have limited understanding of court proceedings. Examples:
  ___ "I could ask questions."
  ___ "I can talk during court - if it is important."
  ___ "I can explain things to the judge or jury."
  ___ "The judge will look out for me."

Services which may need adaptation

___ Substance use disorder treatment
___ Anger management
___ Parent training
___ Getting and keeping a job
___ Finding housing
___ Taking medications as prescribed

Fig. 9.10 Brief checklist of typical FASD concerns in legal settings

9.8 Conclusion

In summary, FASD is a brain-based disorder that is present at birth. It is not caused by mental illness but increases risk for and is exacerbated by mental illness. FASD resembles ASD in that it involves significant social dysfunction and high rates of comorbidity. FASD resembles ID in that it involves significant cognitive deficits including executive functioning and associated functional impairments. Persons with FASD have service needs similar to those with ID and ASD. Nonetheless, despite the important similarities among these three neurodevelopmental disorders, persons with FASD often are excluded from developmental disability programs that accept people with ID and ASD.

We now know that FASD is quite prevalent in forensic settings yet almost always is undiagnosed or misdiagnosed. As a result, persons with FASD often are blamed for impairments that are misconstrued as deliberate actions. In order to reduce this unfair treatment, neurocognitive deficits that produce the behavioral impairments in FASD need to be identified and considered in all stages of the forensic process.

FASD: Implications for the Legal System

Children, adolescents, and adults with FASD are much more likely to have contact with legal systems.

Key point:

- People with FASD often have cognitive limitations and neurobehavioral disorders.
- Basic Cognitive Skills in Adolescents and Adults with FASD

Characteristics	**Grade Level**
Reading	5.0
Reading Comprehension	4.5
Oral Comprehension	5.0
	Percent with Impairment
Memory	80%
Attention (ADHD)	75%
Executive Function Disorder	80%

An Important Consideration: Don't Utilize Interventions which Increase Severity!

- Use of level systems
- This program works for people who are motivated to change.
- No outcome data, but we are sure this is an effective intervention
- Treatment failure is not our problem, it's their choice.

Impairments may limit the ability of people with FASD to exercise caution during interviews or in court

Fig. 9.11 FASD: Important considerations in FASD intervention planning

Screening, diagnostic staff training, and funding for research should be increased, especially with respect to newer and more useful screening strategies, biomarkers of expression, and specialized diagnostic strategies that adapt well to the forensic setting. Most important, FASD needs to be recognized as a severe neurodevelopmental disorder in the same category as ID and ASD.

References

Astley, S. J., Bailey, D., Talbot, C., & Clarren, S. K. (2000). Fetal alcohol syndrome (FAS) primary prevention through FAS diagnosis: I. Identification of high-risk birth mothers through the diagnosis of their children. *Alcohol and Alcoholism, 35*(5), 499–508. https://doi.org/10.1093/alcalc/35.5.499

Burd, L. (2020). Drinking at the end of pregnancy: Why don't we see it? *Pediatric Research, 88*, 142. https://doi.org/10.1038/s41390-020-0846-1

Burd, L., Burd, M., Klug, M. G., Kerbeshian, J., & Popova, S. (2019). Comorbidity and intellectual disability. In J. Matson (Ed.), *Handbook of intellectual disabilities: Integrating theory, research, and practice* (pp. 121–139). Cham: Springer.

Burd, L., & Edwards, W. (2019, Fall). Fetal alcohol spectrum disorders: Implications for attroneys and the courts. *Criminal Justice, 34*(3), 21–28.

Burd, L., Klug, M. G., Li, Q., Kerbeshian, J., & Martsolf, J. T. (2010). Diagnosis of fetal alcohol spectrum disorders: A validity study of the fetal alcohol syndrome checklist. *Alcohol, 44*(7–8), 605–614. https://doi.org/10.1016/j.alcohol.2009.08.010

Burd, L., Klug, M. G., Martsolf, J. T., & Kerbeshian, J. (2003). Fetal alcohol syndrome: Neuropsychiatric phenomics. *Neurotoxicology and Teratology, 25*(6), 697–705. https://doi.org/10.1016/j.ntt.2003.07.014

Burd, L., Martsolf, J. T., Klug, M. G., & Kerbeshian, J. (2003). Diagnosis of FAS: A comparison of the fetal alcohol syndrome diagnostic checklist and the Institute of Medicine criteria for fetal alcohol syndrome. *Neurotoxicology and Teratology, 25*(6), 719–724. https://doi.org/10.1016/j.ntt.2003.07.015

Chambers, C. D., Coles, C., Kable, J., Akshoomoff, N., Xu, R., Zellner, J. A., … Jones, K. L. (2019). Fetal alcohol spectrum disorders in a Pacific southwest city: Maternal and child characteristics. *Alcoholism: Clinical and Experimental Research, 43*(12), 2578–2590. https://doi.org/10.1111/acer.14213

Chang, G. (2020). Maternal substance use: Consequences, identification, and interventions. *Alcohol Research, 40*(2), 06. https://doi.org/10.35946/arcr.v40.2.06

Chasnoff, I. J., McGourty, R. F., Bailey, G. W., Hutchins, E., Lightfoot, S. O., Pawson, L. L., … Campbell, J. (2005). The 4's plus screen for substance use in pregnancy: Clinical application and outcomes. *Journal of Perinatology, 25*(6), 368–374. https://doi.org/10.1038/sj.jp.7211266

Chasnoff, I. J., Wells, A. M., & King, L. (2015). Misdiagnosis and missed diagnoses in foster and adopted children with prenatal alcohol exposure. *Pediatrics, 135*(2), 264–270. https://doi.org/10.1542/peds.2014-2171

Chudley, A. E., Conry, J., Cook, J. L., Loock, C., Rosales, T., LeBlanc, N., & Public Health Agency of Canada's National Advisory Committee on Fetal Alcohol Spectrum Disorder. (2005). Fetal alcohol spectrum disorder: Canadian guidelines for diagnosis. *CMAJ: Canadian Medical Association Journal (Journal de l'Association medicale canadienne), 172*(Suppl. 5), S1–S21. https://doi.org/10.1503/cmaj.1040302

Coles, C. D., Gailey, A. R., Mulle, J. G., Kable, J. A., Lynch, M. E., & Jones, K. L. (2016). A comparison among 5 methods for the clinical diagnosis of fetal alcohol spectrum disorders. *Alcoholism: Clinical and Experimental Research, 40*(5), 1000–1009. https://doi.org/10.1111/acer.13032

Dillbeck v. State of Florida. 643 So. 2d 1027. (Fl. 1994). (1994, April 21).

Doyle, L. R., & Mattson, S. N. (2015). Neurobehavioral disorder associated with prenatal alcohol exposure (ND-PAE): Review of evidence and guidelines for assessment. *Current Developmental Disorders Report, 2*(3), 175–186. https://doi.org/10.1007/s40474-015-0054-6

Greenmyer, J. R., Klug, M. G., Kambeitz, C., Popova, S., & Burd, L. (2018). A multicountry updated assessment of the economic impact of fetal alcohol spectrum disorder: Costs for children and adults. *Journal of Addiction Medicine, 12*(6), 466–473. https://doi.org/10.1097/adm.0000000000000438

Greenmyer, J. R., Stacy, J. M., Klug, M. G., Foster, K., Tiongson, C., & Burd, L. (2020). Pregnancy status is associated with screening for alcohol and other substance use in the emergency department. *Journal of Addiction Medicine, 14*(4), e64–e69. https://doi.org/10.1097/adm.0000000000000616

Kable, J. A., & Mukherjee, R. A. (2017). Neurodevelopmental disorder associated with prenatal exposure to alcohol (ND-PAE): A proposed diagnostic method of capturing the neurocognitive phenotype of FASD. *European Journal of Medical Genetics, 60*(1), 49–54. https://doi.org/10.1016/j.ejmg.2016.09.013

Kambeitz, C., Klug, M. G., Greenmyer, J., Popova, S., & Burd, L. (2019). Association of adverse childhood experiences and neurodevelopmental disorders in people with fetal alcohol spectrum disorders (FASD) and non-FASD controls. *BMC Pediatrics, 19*(1), 498. https://doi.org/10.1186/s12887-019-1878-8

May, P. A., Baete, A., Russo, J., Elliott, A. J., Blankenship, J., Kalberg, W. O., … Hoyme, H. E. (2014). Prevalence and characteristics of fetal alcohol spectrum disorders. *Pediatrics, 134*(5), 855–866. https://doi.org/10.1542/peds.2013-3319

May, P. A., Hasken, J. M., Baete, A., Russo, J., Elliott, A. J., Kalberg, W. O., … Hoyme, H. E. (2020). Fetal alcohol spectrum disorders in a Midwestern city: Child characteristics, maternal risk traits, and prevalence. *Alcoholism: Clinical and Experimental Research, 44*(4), 919–938. https://doi.org/10.1111/acer.14314

May, P. A., Hasken, J. M., Bozeman, R., Jones, J. V., Burns, M. K., Goodover, J., … Hoyme, H. E. (2020). Fetal alcohol spectrum disorders in a Rocky Mountain region city: Child characteristics, maternal risk traits, and prevalence. *Alcoholism: Clinical and Experimental Research, 44*(4), 900–918. https://doi.org/10.1111/acer.14315

May, P. A., Hasken, J. M., Stegall, J. M., Mastro, H. A., Kalberg, W. O., Buckley, D., … Hoyme, H. E. (2020). Fetal alcohol spectrum disorders in a southeastern county of the United States: Child characteristics and maternal risk traits. *Alcoholism: Clinical and Experimental Research, 44*(4), 939–959. https://doi.org/10.1111/acer.14313

Moyer, C. L., Johnson, S., Klug, M. G., & Burd, L. (2018). Substance use in pregnant women using the emergency department: Undertested and overlooked? *Western Journal of Emergency Medicine, 19*(3), 579–584. https://doi.org/10.5811/westjem.2018.1.35630

Olson, H. C. (2015). Advancing recognition of fetal alcohol spectrum disorders: The proposed DSM-5 diagnosis of "neurobehavioral disorder associated with prenatal alcohol exposure (ND-PAE)". *Current Developmental Disorders Reports, 2*(3), 187–198. https://doi.org/10.1007/s40474-015-0056-4

Paintner, A., Williams, A. D., & Burd, L. (2012). Fetal alcohol spectrum disorders – Implications for child neurology, Part 1: Prenatal exposure and dosimetry. *Journal of Child Neurology, 27*(2), 258–263. https://doi.org/10.1177/0883073811428376

Popova, S., Dozet, D., & Burd, L. (2020). Fetal alcohol spectrum disorder: Can we change the future? *Alcoholism, Clinical and Experimental Research, 44*(4), 815–819. https://doi.org/10.1111/acer.14317

Popova, S., Lange, S., Bekmuradov, D., Mihic, A., & Rehm, J. (2011). Fetal alcohol spectrum disorder prevalence estimates in correctional systems: A systematic literature review. *Canadian Journal of Public Health, 102*(5), 336–340. https://doi.org/10.1007/bf03404172

Popova, S., Lange, S., Probst, C., Gmel, G., & Rehm, J. (2018). Global prevalence of alcohol use and binge drinking during pregnancy, and fetal alcohol spectrum disorder. *Biochemistry and Cell Biology, 96*(2), 237–240. https://doi.org/10.1139/bcb-2017-0077

Popova, S., Lange, S., Shield, K., Mihic, A., Chudley, A. E., Mukherjee, R. A. S., … Rehm, J. (2016). Comorbidity of fetal alcohol spectrum disorder: A systematic review and meta-analysis. *Lancet, 387*(10022), 978–987. https://doi.org/10.1016/S0140-6736(15)01345-8

Price, A., Cook, P. A., Norgate, S., & Mukherjee, R. (2017). Prenatal alcohol exposure and traumatic childhood experiences: A systematic review. *Neuroscience and Biobehavioral Reviews, 80*, 89–98. https://doi.org/10.1016/j.neubiorev.2017.05.018

Schaff, E., Moreno, M., Foster, K., Klug, M. G., & Burd, L. (2019). What do we know about prevalence and management of intoxicated women during labor and delivery? *Global Pedicatric Health, 6*, 2333794X1989479. https://doi.org/10.1177/2333794X19894799

Stratton, K. R., Howe, C. J., & Battaglia, F. C. (1996). *Fetal alcohol syndrome: Diagnosis, epidemiology, prevention, and treatment*. Washington, DC: National Academy Press.

Substance Abuse & Mental Health Data Archive (SAMHDA). (2011). National survey on drug use and heath: 10 year substrate R-DAS (NSDUH-2002-2011-DS0001). https://www.datafiles.samhsa.gov/study-dataset/national-survey-drug-use-and-health-10-year-substate-r-das-nsduh-2002-2011-ds0001. Retrieved 27 Sept 2020.

Weyrauch, D., Schwartz, M., Hart, B., Klug, M. G., & Burd, L. (2017). Comorbid mental disorders in fetal alcohol spectrum disorders: A systematic review. *Journal of Developmental and Behavioral Pediatrics, 38*(4), 283–291. https://doi.org/10.1097/dbp.0000000000000440

Williams, J. F., & Smith, V. C. (2015). Fetal alcohol Spectrum disorders. *Pediatrics, 136*(5), e1395–e1406. https://doi.org/10.1542/peds.2015-3113

Chapter 10
Determining Disability Severity Level for Fetal Alcohol Spectrum Disorder: Assessing the Extent of Impairment

Stephen Greenspan, Natalie Novick Brown, and William J. Edwards Billy

Abstract Fetal alcohol spectrum disorder (FASD) is a biomedical disorder that places an individual at high risk for intellectual disability (ID) or developmental disability (DD). Yet in some legal settings, people with FASD are denied legal protections or entitlements because of a mistaken belief that the disorder has low severity. Commonly, this misunderstanding reflects a view of FASD as the functional equivalent of attention-deficit/hyperactivity disorder (ADHD). This view also reflects the fact that FASD typically is not diagnosed in childhood and because of the near-universal co-occurrence of attentional problems, affected individuals commonly are diagnosed with ADHD, which masks the underlying FASD. In this chapter, we develop a model for establishing disability severity and compare the relative severity of FASD with other disorders, concluding that FASD is much more severe than ADHD and comparable in severity to ID. We also use this model to assess individual disability severity, finding that while ADHD as a whole is a low-severity disorder, there are a minority of people within that category who have a high-severity disability and very possibly have undiagnosed FASD. Implications of these findings for forensic practice are explored, with emphasis on the importance of basing severity determination on an evaluee's competence profile and support needs rather than diagnostic label history.

Keywords Fetal alcohol · FASD · Intellectual disability · ID-equivalence · Attention-deficit/hyperactivity disorder · ADHD

S. Greenspan
Educational Psychology, University of Connecticut, Storrs, CT, USA

N. N. Brown (✉)
University of Washington, Seattle, WA, USA

W. J. Edwards Billy
Los Angeles County Office of the Public Defender, Los Angeles, CA, USA

N. Novick Brown (ed.), *Evaluating Fetal Alcohol Spectrum Disorders in the Forensic Context*, https://doi.org/10.1007/978-3-030-73628-6_10

10.1 Introduction

A major obstacle in securing services and protections for people with fetal alcohol spectrum disorder (FASD) is the frequent assumption that FASD does not meet the severity threshold for a developmental disability. The basis for this misconception often confounds FASD with attention-deficit/hyperactivity disorder (ADHD). This misconception reflects the fact that attentional problems are almost always found in people with FASD, and since FASD typically is not diagnosed in children even when facial signs are evident (May et al., 2018), ADHD is the diagnosis most evaluators are familiar with and consequently assign to many individuals who later are diagnosed with FASD (Popova, Lange, Shield, Burd, & Rehm, 2019). It is understandable, therefore, that FASD would come to be seen incorrectly as the functional equivalent of ADHD. The problem with such an assumption is that ADHD is a bifurcated disorder, containing many individuals who do not have a severe disability as well as some (many of whom actually have FASD) who have a fairly severe disorder comparable to intellectual disability (ID), for which prenatal alcohol exposure is in fact the largest known cause in the Western world (Abel & Sokol, 1986).

To best navigate this confusion, it helps to keep in mind that FASD is a medical disorder while disability is a social and bureaucratic concept, and the two are not perfectly aligned (Salvador-Carulla et al., 2011). In other words, within FASD and other disorder categories, individual disability severity varies substantially. A related issue is that severity is measured differently in a disorder (where it refers mainly to depth of impairment on a single defining ability) than it is for a disability, where it refers to the number of abilities that are impaired and their effect on overall functioning (Wehmeyer, 2013). Using both of these criteria (depth of disorder impairment and breadth of disability needs), it is argued that: (a) FASD is a very severe disorder, comparable to ID, while ADHD is a much less severe disorder, and (b) even within ADHD, there are individuals (likely, many with undiagnosed FASD) who have a very severe disability. Evidence for these assertions, both clinical and empirical, is presented in this chapter. Practical implications of this severity exploration for forensic determinations in bureaucratic criminal (but also civil) proceedings are explored. While some of these implications incorporate existing methodology (such as intelligence quotient [IQ] and adaptive behavior instruments), some lead to the development of new methods (such as qualitative and quantitative considerations in personal competence profiles). Pervading this paper is an exploration of the concept of severity, a topic with major implications for ameliorating the arbitrariness of forensic and human services diagnosis and classification.

10.2 Court Case that Inspired this Chapter

The legal case motivating us to address the severity of FASD involves Zane Floyd, a former U.S. Marine who around 5 a.m. on the third of June 1999 entered a Las Vegas supermarket with a shotgun and hunted down several store employees, killing four and critically injuring a fifth (Floyd v. Filson, 2019). In the 2000 trial, there was testimony that Floyd (a) was born to a mother who abused alcohol, (b) had been diagnosed with ADHD as a child and placed on Ritalin, (c) qualified for a diagnosis of FASD, and (d) suffered from extreme mental disturbance at the time of the crimes.

The state did not dispute the fact that Floyd had FASD but argued FASD was in the same severity ballpark as ADHD and therefore should not be given substantial weight as a mitigating factor when considered against so many aggravating factors. The jury voted to impose the death penalty, apparently buying the state's argument about the low-severity nature of FASD. In Floyd v. Baker (2019), the U.S. Court of Appeals for the Ninth Circuit agreed with the state's position.

In our opinion, the court rulings regarding the supposed equivalence of FASD and ADHD invalidly minimized the severity of FASD as a mitigating factor in a capital case. Despite nearly 50 years of research documenting the severity of FASD as a brain-based medical condition that occurs in utero and manifests in infancy and early childhood as a developmental disability, the court failed to recognize FASD as a congenital disorder that (unlike ADHD) was permanent and became worse and more complex over time (see Burd & Edwards, 2019). In 2020, the United States Supreme court denied certiorari and refused to hear an appeal from the Ninth Circuit Court of Appeals.

This judicial decision basically encouraged courts (along with prosecutors and disability organizations) to minimize the severity of this organic disorder. Not only does this ruling affect the future of FASD as a mitigating factor in sentencing and capital cases, but it also allows other entities such as state disability agencies and possibly the federal government to deny benefits, treatment, and services to people with an FASD diagnosis (e.g., fetal alcohol syndrome, partial fetal alcohol syndrome, alcohol related neurodevelopmental disorder, and static encephalopathy-alcohol exposed).

After the Ninth Circuit denied a rehearing in Floyd v. Filson (2019), the National Organization on Fetal Alcohol Syndrome issued a position statement describing how experts in the FASD field have noted the following significant differences between FASD and ADHD (e.g., Peadon & Elliott, 2010), differences that refute the court's concept of equivalency: (a) etiology and course of the two conditions are very different; FASD has a single etiology that is known, while ADHD is etiologically multifactorial (and typically unknown); (b) FASD has greatly increased mortality risk when compared to ADHD; (c) FASD typically is far more complex and severe and requires much higher levels of care than ADHD; (d) annual cost of care is over 10 times higher for FASD compared to ADHD; (e) expression of the two conditions is dissimilar in that FASD has a similar male to female ratio, while ADHD is three times more prevalent among males; (f) although FASD is a causal factor for ADHD, there is no evidence ADHD is a causal factor for FASD; (g) ADHD gradually decreases in severity across childhood and adolescence, while FASD becomes more complex, resulting in more deficits and greater adversity across the lifespan; and (h) FASD is equivalent to ID in terms of executive dysfunction and everyday adaptive behavior, which is not the case for ADHD. It is not our intention in this chapter to repeat the above arguments, although some repetition is unavoidable. Rather, we intend to address the nature of disability severity, using three conditions—FASD, ADHD, and ID—for illustrative purposes. Such an exercise is essential, we believe, in validating the above assertions as well as developing mechanisms for establishing the disability severity of FASD in individual defendants in future cases.

10.3 Definition of Key Terms

Four terms used throughout this chapter need definition. These terms are "disability," "severity," "impairment," and "disorder." The definitions below are kept brief for the simple reason that the balance of this chapter is an extended elaboration on these definitions, especially the first two.

10.3.1 Meaning of Disability

A disability can be defined (Cambridge University Press, 2019, *Cambridge English Dictionary*) as "an illness, injury, or condition that makes it difficult for someone to do the things that other people do." Here is a more jargon-laden version from the U.S. Centers for Disease Control and Prevention (CDC, 2020), which essentially says the same thing: "any condition of the body or mind (impairment) that makes it more difficult for the person with the condition to do certain activities (activity limitation) and interact with the world around them (participation restrictions)." In this last definition, there is a distinction between the contributing medical or other condition (described as an impairment) and the participation restriction (disability) that results. The three terms in parentheses were developed by the World Health Organization (WHO, 2001) in its *International Classification of Functioning, Disability and Health.*

In line with the sociological orientation that dominates the field of disability studies, the intervening variable here (activity limitation, described in earlier WHO documents by the now politically incorrect term "handicap") was viewed as the degree to which society facilitates, or places obstacles in the way of, full participation in various social roles. Undoubtedly, there is some truth to the idea that social values and biases contribute to an impairment becoming a disability, but this view fails to give sufficient weight to personal qualities (e.g., perseverance, emotionality, etc.) that also contribute to participation. Such a more balanced "personological" perspective undergirds this chapter.

One thing that should be kept in mind when considering the term "disability" is that it is a bureaucratic and socio-legal concept and not a medical concept. The term is believed to have originated within the vocational rehabilitation field, where it referred to someone's inability to work without short- or long-term supports or services. Today, disability is a concept assigned and used by many gatekeeper bureaucracies (schools, residential companies, treatment agencies, etc.) to determine eligibility for disorder-based special services,

10.3.2 Meaning of Impairment

The term "impairment" refers to a state of being diminished, weakened, or damaged, especially mentally or physically. One way of comparing "impairment" to "disability" is the former is an input variable, while the latter is an outcome variable. An example of such an input is having a visual impairment, with the disability outcome involving the supports that a visually impaired person needs in order to function in a real-world social role, such as holding a job. Severity as it relates to impairment typically is viewed narrowly. For example, in the case of a visual impairment, severity refers to the relative absence or distortion of vision. Disability, almost by definition, is much broader as it incorporates both number and depth of individual impairments on more than the one defining ability domain and also incorporates personality and situational factors contributing to bad outcomes.

10.3.3 Meaning of Severity

The term "severe" refers to something bad or undesirable, and "severity" therefore refers to the degree of badness or undesirability of the thing being described. We realize that under the current value system in the disability field, many would take exception to the description of a disability as undesirable, but most affected individuals, not to mention their parents, would gratefully give up their impairments if offered the chance. Thus, one does not use the word "severe" to refer to something good or desirable. For instance, in the sentence, "John received a severe sentence for his offense," it is unlikely John would be happy to be given such news.

Severity can be applied to an almost endless number of things (from plant ill health to boat hull decay to a child's delayed language) for which bad or undesirable outcomes can be envisioned. The concept of severity is related to "risk" (or danger) and also to "seriousness," but in different ways. In the case of risk, the danger involves a possibility things could get much worse (a plant with a few brown spots could suddenly become brown all over and be on the verge of dying). With regard to seriousness, the thought to always keep in mind is someone with a *mild* impairment may in fact be quite disabled, which is why the subcategory "mild ID" is so misleading, as people with that designation often receive extensive supports and would be in danger of dying if living on their own. Conversely, it often is the case that someone with relatively severe impairments may be functioning in the world in a manner far more competent than one might have thought possible. It is for this reason, along with ethical considerations, that the infantilizing over-protectiveness, which at one time characterized ID services for adults, is no longer considered acceptable (Bannerman, Sheldon, Sherman, & Harchik, 1990). This lack of predictive fit between severity subcategory and expected functional outcome (e.g., a child with Down syndrome considered "trainable" who despite expectation learns how to read) is perhaps the strongest argument against intra-diagnostic category severity classification (Hughes, 2006) as it reduces opportunities for individual growth.

10.3.4 Meaning of Disorder

Another term used throughout this chapter that also needs defining is "disorder." This term refers to "a state of being diminished, weakened, or damaged, especially mentally or physically" (Spitzer, Endicott, & Franchic, 2018). In contrast to the bureaucratic/legalistic construct of disability, a disorder is a biomedical construct and therefore is an input variable that increases (in part because many gatekeeper bureaucrats are concrete) the likelihood an individual will qualify for a disability designation. A disorder is related to an impairment, except the latter is dimensional (e.g., degree of visual acuity), while the former is categorical (e.g., a particular vision disease, such as *retinitis pigmentosa*).

10.4 Severity in Medicine

Severity has widespread applicability in medical and human services, even apart from the practical matter of cost estimation. Some of the relevant literature will be discussed before heading into the heart of this chapter, which is devising a method for addressing the relative severity of FASD.

10.4.1 Severity of Illness

The severity concept has attracted much interest in the health services literature, with the driving force being the need to come up with better mechanisms for validating the individualized cost of hospital and medical care. This situation reflects the fact that a medical diagnosis is not always a reliable predictor of cost and within any given diagnostic category, there often is considerable variability in need for services. As similar funding concerns also arise in the disability field, some lessons may be gleaned from a brief look at the medical severity concept.

In medicine, severity plays a role in efforts to control costs by basing insurance reimbursement on the particular procedures needed rather than on whatever a clinician or medical group asks for. An interim method was developed for the U.S. Medicare/Medicaid system termed diagnostic-related group (DRG), which combined primary and secondary diagnoses plus required procedures to come up with a severity number. This method proved inadequate because it did not take into account such individual factors as demands on staff, recovery rate, complications, and residual impairment. An improved version, termed the severity of illness (SOI) index (Horn, Horn, & Sharkey, 1984), was constructed by looking at seven factors, each with four severity levels: state of principal diagnosis, complications, interactions (with other disorders), dependency (staff utilization), procedures (non-operative), rate of response to intervention, and residual impairment. Within-factor severity scores were assigned to each factor, with ratings of severity ranging from mild to catastrophic. The result of considering all of these ratings (with synthesis handled by highly trained persons rather than computer algorithm) was to place each patient in one of four overall severity categories: minor, moderate, major, and extreme. Considerable reliability and validity were obtained for this method, although push-back from health service providers (who preferred being reimbursed for individual services) caused it to remain more of a localized than universally adopted system.

The SOI methodology was used mainly to determine individual severity rather than to compare the severity of diseases, but it seems to us that within the developmental disability (DD) field, a comparable methodology could be used for both purposes. That is, different disorders could receive severity scores on two scales: overall comparison to other disorders (e.g., FASD compared to ADHD) but also to capture individual severity variation within each category. Such a modified use of the SOI system is, in fact, what is proposed later in this chapter for calculating severity between and within developmental conditions.

10.4.2 Risk of Death

One of the controversies in the medical severity literature is whether risk of mortality can be considered an index of illness severity. Tasker and Randolph (2016) consider mortality risk to be an indicator of illness severity, but Pollack (2016) disputes that view. Pollack's position is that severity of illness refers to "extent of physiological decompensation or organ system loss of function" (p. 583) and is a predictor of both mortality and morbidity (becoming ill), while risk of death reflects many things other than bodily health, such as the training of doctors and competence of hospitals. To us, this disagreement seems a little too much of a technical argument in that risk of a bad outcome is central to severity, and dying is the ultimate bad outcome in medicine.

In a later section, wherein we attempt to develop a severity method for evaluating people with FASD and other disorders, risk is one of the concepts utilized, and while mortality is not an outcome associated with a chronic neurodevelopmental disorder such as FASD, it does enter indirectly into the mix. This view is because, when asking what services an individual with DD needs, one question that must be asked is, "what type and level of support is needed to keep the person from potentially fatal outcomes (e.g., starving, being assaulted, getting run over) as a result of their inability in order to anticipate or avoid physical and social risks?" A relevant statistic is people with FAS (the least prevalent subtype of FASD) live only to the age of 34 years on average (Thanh & Jonsson, 2016). The reason for this shockingly low mortality rate is primarily attributable to socially and emotionally mediated behavioral factors (especially impulsivity), such as accidents, poisoning, drug overdoses, suicide, crime victimization, and poor health maintenance rather than physiological vulnerability although that, too, can be a factor due to alcohol-related birth defects (ARBD).

10.5 Severity of Core Symptom(s)

While the severity concept is applied most meaningfully to overall degree of functional impairments or risk, a very common approach in medicine, and to a somewhat lesser extent in the DD field, is to look at severity more narrowly as it relates to depth of impairment on a core symptom. Often, such an approach is used to devise a subclassification system, which in the *Diagnostic and Statistical Manual of Mental Disorders, Fifth Edition* (*DSM-5*; American Psychiatric Association [APA], 2013), generally is covered by the term "specifier." A controversy in the severity literature (Mehlman & Neuhauser, 1999) has to do with whether it makes sense to convert continuous severity sum scores into discontinuous severity categories as opposed to just leaving individuals on a continuum. We are somewhat on the fence regarding this matter, recognizing the artificiality of qualitative severity subcategories but at the same time understanding the widespread preference for such categories. Part of this preference reflects the historical fact that subcategories for some disorders may in fact predate the existence of a unified disorder. This is the case with ID, as there was some historical evidence (Clemente, 2015) that what today would be considered severity score-based subtypes such as "mild," "moderate," and "severe" ID previously were considered distinct disorders with such (today, repugnant) names as "Idiocy" and "Imbecility."

10.5.1 Upper Extremity as a Medical Example

An example of a core symptom viewed as the basis for severity-level determination can be found in the Fugl-Meyer Upper Extremity (FM-UE) Scale of Motor Impairment (Woytowicz, Rietschel, Goodman, Whitall, & McCombe Waller, 2013), the most widely used method for measuring arm use limitations in chronic stroke patients. The FM-UE has four subsections with 33 items scored on an ordinal impairment scale of 0 (absent), 1 (partial impairment), and 2 (no impairment), resulting in a range of possible scores from 0 to 66. Patients are placed into four severity groups: mild, mild–moderate, moderate–severe, and severe, depending on where their total scores fall in the range of possible scores. It is understood that FM-UE does not measure global functional disability, but nonetheless there is a use for such a narrow severity instrument. However, where such a rating system becomes a problem is when a narrow core symptom severity index becomes the sole basis for a global disability severity index. In fact, this is exactly what has been the historic practice in the field of ID.

10.5.2 Severity Subcategorization in Intellectual Disability

When the current three-prong definition of ID was developed six decades ago (Heber, 1961), severity subclassification was barely mentioned. In fact, the only mention of it was in a single footnote in a single table (Greenspan & Switzky, 2006). In subsequent American Association on Intellectual and Developmental Disabilities (AAIDD) (formerly American Association on Mental Retardation [AAMR]) classification manuals, severity classification became far more emphasized. The initial basis for categorical subgrouping (mild, moderate, etc.) was full-scale IQ, with groupings determined by number of standard deviation (SD) points (arbitrarily set by test publishers at 15 points) below the population mean (arbitrarily set at 100). In the earliest manual, there actually were five subcategories, with the least impaired termed, "Borderline Mental Retardation," which was set at −1 SD (for a full-scale IQ range of 71–85). As an IQ score of 85 placed someone at the 16th percentile of the population, the bar obviously was set too high for a disorder estimated to take in the bottom 3% of the population (Mercer, 1973). Adaptive behavior (AB) was supposed to bring the incidence down, but the initial absence of a standardized AB measure meant IQ was the only basis for diagnosis for a long time. Subsequently, the "borderline" subcategory was eliminated in the 1970s, an act that has proven controversial as it prevented many deserving individuals from receiving educational or developmental services (Greenspan, 2017; MacMillan, Siperstein, & Gresham, 1996).

Setting the IQ cut-score too high (and in a subsequent rebound action, too low) reflected the impossibility of identifying an IQ cut-off that adequately captured the inflection point at which someone with a global disability was included or excluded.

This kind of approach reflects three basic problems: (a) the arbitrariness of establishing a quantitative cut-off for a qualitative category, (b) the "scientistic" (illusory use of a scientific concept to justify what basically is a policy decision) nature of using standard deviation units in the first place, and (c) the limited content coverage of IQ, which mainly taps into academic potential (Anastasi, 1983) and fails to capture the full range of intellectual and other impairments and needs. For this reason, both AAIDD and *DSM* later came to devise subcategorization severity subtype mechanisms based upon indices other than IQ.

The alternative approach now is used in *DSM-5* to substitute adaptive functioning for IQ as the basis for ID severity subgroupings. This makes some sense as adaptive functioning is closer to the concept of real-world functioning in multiple contexts, which is what disability is all about. However, a problem is that adaptive functioning, as reflected in the most-used instruments, has little cognitive content (e.g., social adaptive functioning has few social judgment items). One possible way around this problem would be to combine IQ and adaptive functioning into a single index, but such an approach has never been seriously considered to our knowledge.

In AAIDD manuals, beginning in the ninth edition (Luckasson et al., 1992), the basis for severity subgrouping was to substitute "support needs" for IQ ranges. This approach continues to be used today. The proposed mechanism for operationalizing the approach is an instrument published by AAIDD termed the "Supports Intensity Scale" or SIS (Wehmeyer et al., 2009). A problem with the SIS, which reflects a general tendency in the ID field—including the behavior instruments used to measure adaptive functioning, such as the third edition of *Vineland Adaptive Behavior Scales* (*Vineland-3*) (Sparrow, Saulnier, Cicchetti, & Doll, 2016) and the third edition of *Adaptive Behavior Assessment System* (ABAS-3) (Harrison & Oakland, 2015)—is that social aspects of competence are grossly under-emphasized, despite the fact people with ID are most at risk because of limited ability to make friends or deal with interpersonal challenges and situations (Guralnick, 1989), a characteristic well known to most family members.

10.5.3 Lack of Severity Subcategorization in Fetal Alcohol Spectrum Disorder and Attention-Deficit Hyperactivity Disorder

Unlike ID where severity subclassification is a central (even if somewhat controversial) part of the diagnostic process, such is not the case for either FASD or ADHD. FASD obviously does have a subclassification scheme, but the main subcategories (e.g., fetal alcohol syndrome [FAS], partial fetal alcohol syndrome [pFAS], alcohol-related neurodevelopmental disorder [ARND]) are based on the presence of physical signs (FAS with three facial anomalies, pFAS with one or two, ARND with none) and are not formulated in terms of disability severity, even if it is empirically the case that individuals with full-blown FAS have somewhat lower mean IQ scores than is seen in the other two subcategories (Kodituwakku & Kodituwakku, 2014). In fact, one challenge in seeking to have people with the pFAS and ARND subtypes receive DD classification and related accommodations is getting across the idea that people in all three FASD subcategories are equally disabled academically, socially, and adaptively.

Recent efforts to find early childhood biomarkers for FASD (considered essential for developing more reliable diagnostic procedures) may contribute inadvertently to an impairment severity protocol. An example is multinational research in Ukraine (where heavy drinking by pregnant women is commonplace), which found that plasma micro ribonucleic acid (miRNA) profiles in second and third trimester pregnant women were predictive of the severity of alcohol-induced infant impairment outcomes (Balaraman et al., 2016).

With regard to ADHD, there is no official subcategorization scheme to our knowledge. However, on occasions when someone is described as having "severe ADHD," it likely is the case that they have co-occurring problems in addition to impulsivity or inattention and also is likely, in fact, that they have undiagnosed FASD. This latter situation tends to confound much of the research on ADHD, which rarely accounts for the possibility of prenatal alcohol exposure in subject samples.

10.6 Severity as the Implicit Basis for Developmental Disability

The concept of developmental disability (DD) was invented in the 1970s (see Gettings, 2011, for an historic overview) to identify conditions similar to ID that may not qualify for that designation because full-scale IQ was above the arbitrary ceiling score (approximately 2 SDs below the population mean, or a standard score of 70–75, which generally is used as the cut-off for ID). This term owes its origins to pioneering Kennedy-era legislation in the United States that authorized various government-funded disability-related human rights, research, training, and facility-building initiatives. The term "DD," now widely used in many state and provincial eligibility statutes, was first used in the Developmental Disabilities Services and Facilities Construction Amendments of 1970. In that law, DD was defined categorically as in this expanded list: "mental retardation, epilepsy, cerebral palsy, and other neurological conditions originating before the age of 18." In 1975, the legislation was revised again as the *Developmentally Disabled Assistance and Bill of Rights Act*, and DD remained defined categorically to include mental retardation plus conditions "closely related to mental retardation: cerebral palsy, epilepsy, autism and dyslexia" (this last item a curious inclusion, as it was not globally disabling) with a pre-18 age of onset, which were expected to "continue indefinitely" and "constitute a substantial handicap." The term "other neurological conditions" probably was dropped because of an overly concrete tendency to equate it with Traumatic Brain

Injury. This deletion was a mistake in our opinion as it would have reinforced the idea that DD conditions are brain-based and would have left the door open for a wide range of conditions not yet known (i.e., FAS was a brand-new concept at that time) or were able to be contained in a list that did not go on for pages.

A major revision in 1978 to the Developmentally Disabled Assistance and Bill of Rights Act (1975) raised the age-of-onset ceiling from 18 to 22 years old and switched from a categorical to functional definition of DD as a "severe, chronic disability … attributable to a physical or mental impairment…likely to continue indefinitely" that resulted in "substantial functional limitations in three or more areas of major life activity." A final revision in 2000 (Roman numerals dropped here) defined DD as "a severe, chronic disability of an individual that is attributable to a mental or physical impairment or combination of mental and physical impairments; is manifested before the individual attains age 22 years; is likely to continue indefinitely; results in substantial functional limitations in three or more of the following seven areas of major life activity: self-care, receptive and expressive language, learning, mobility, self-direction, capacity for independent living, [and] economic self-sufficiency." The term also included: "reflects the individual's need for a combination and sequence of special, interdisciplinary, or generic services, individualized supports, or other forms of assistance that are of lifelong or extended duration and are individually planned and coordinated."

Pervading the language used in the above-cited DD legislation is the idea these DD conditions are similar to ID in terms of also being brain-based, involving impaired cognition, having lifelong duration, and being very severe with respect to multiple impairments and having support needs similar to ID that are "of lifelong or extended duration and are individually planned and coordinated." Notably, the list of seven areas of impairment in DD is (without using the term) somewhat analogous to adaptive behavior/functioning (Crocker, Vaurio, Riley, & Mattson, 2009), although it is a rather inadequate list. For example, as is often the case, there is no mention of the critical area of social functioning. In addition, the requirement for a minimum of three areas of impairment is arbitrary. The original purpose of the list was to categorize programs in terms of the population they served and was not intended for the purpose of diagnosing individuals. However, and unfortunately, this list has become an official service eligibility-determining diagnostic framework in many jurisdictions.

In an earlier publication, the three of us (Greenspan, Novick Brown, & Edwards, 2016) coined the term "ID Equivalence" to refer to various mechanisms devised to get around the barrier that rigid reliance on IQ ceilings has created for providing services, supports, and protections to severely impacted individuals otherwise deserving of being served. The DD mechanism is the most widely used such framework, but it is not the only one, nor is FASD the only disorder deserving ID Equivalence status as there are many brain-based disorders (e.g., Dandy Walker Malformation or Prader-Willi syndrome) where phenotype is similar to ID in terms of impairment pattern and overall severity, despite a mean IQ that straddles the IQ cut-point. In states that still use a categorical path to DD services, FASD generally is not mentioned by name except in Alaska and Minnesota where statutes note several "related conditions," defined as: "a condition … that is found to be closely related to a developmental disability, including but not limited to, cerebral palsy, epilepsy, autism, fetal alcohol spectrum disorder, and Prader-Willi syndrome" (Minnesota, 2012).

In states that have a more functional approach to DD eligibility, people with FASD are increasingly being found eligible on an individual basis, but it remains a case-by-case struggle (often involving wrangles over whether IQ is low enough), in part because FASD is a rather hidden disorder when it is overshadowed by symptoms resembling better-known conditions (with most cases not diagnosed until right before service eligibility is requested) and also because of the persistent belief that FASD is a low-severity disorder analogous to ADHD. This belief is challenged in the next three sections, which compare FASD to ADHD and ID in terms of (a) definitional elements, (b) competence profiles, and (c) risk of bad outcomes.

10.7 Definitional Elements as Severity Indicators

Although a severity judgment typically is made as an add-on classification to a diagnosis, it is possible to gather some comparative information about severity from the elements in a condition's definition. Following is a brief statement defining the three conditions being compared: FASD, ADHD, and ID. We include the last of these conditions, ID, because it is the yardstick against which all conditions included under the umbrella "Developmental Disability" (i.e., severe brain-based conditions comparable to ID except for not meeting an arbitrary IQ cut-off) are measured. Following a brief summary of each definition, we comment on implicit severity distinctions touched upon in the definitions.

10.7.1 Intellectual Disability

ID has three definitional criteria: significant deficits in intellectual functioning, impaired adaptive functioning, and onset within the developmental period (typically interpreted to mean before age 18). Prong One (intellectual impairment) is measured by a full-scale IQ score of 70–75 or below, although other measures such as executive functions can be cited. Adaptive functioning, typically measured through a rating instrument such as the ABAS or *Vineland*, has three components: Conceptual/Communication, Practical, and Social, summarized into a composite Adaptive Index. Qualitative evidence, such as for gullibility and poor risk awareness, also is important. Significant deficiency (below 2 SDs) has to be shown on standardized instruments for only one of these four indices. As a rule, ID is a lifelong status, although individuals can acquire improved adaptive skills during adulthood.

10.7.2 Attention-Deficit Hyperactivity Disorder

In *DSM-5*, ADHD is described as "a persistent pattern of inattention and/or hyperactivity-impulsivity that interferes with functioning or development." Three subtypes are identified: (a) inattention, (b) hyperactivity—impulsivity, and (c) mixed. Most individuals fall into the third, mixed, subcategory. For the first two subtypes, six or more symptoms from a list of behaviors must have persisted "for at least six months (five months for older adolescents and adults) to a degree that is inconsistent with developmental level and that negatively impacts directly on social and academic/occupational activities," and are "not solely a manifestation of oppositional behavior, defiance, hostility, or failure to understand tasks or instructions" (for type 1) and "do not occur exclusively during the course of schizophrenia or another psychotic disorder" (for type 2). These symptoms must be evident before age 12. Although ADHD can be diagnosed in adults, most individuals diagnosed with the disorder in childhood cease to manifest the disorder as they enter adulthood (Newton-Howes, 2004). Although people with ADHD often do poorly in school because of inattention and interpersonal insensitivity due to impulsivity, there is no cognitive or adaptive functioning criterion for the diagnosis.

10.7.3 Fetal Alcohol Spectrum Disorder

The defining features of FASD have remained essentially the same since FAS was first described in the United States in 1973: (a) selected facial malformations, (b) growth retardation, (c) central nervous system (CNS) abnormality, and (d) evidence of drinking during pregnancy (for full-fledged FAS, this can be established solely by facial anomalies). CNS abnormality typically is established by cognitive impairments (executive dysfunction and other cognitive impairments) and impairments in adaptive functioning. For the latter, *DSM-5* requires impairments in at least two of the three domains usually included in standardized instruments (communication, daily living or practical skills, and socialization), which actually is a more stringent requirement than in ID (where only one impaired adaptive domain is required). The CNS dysfunction in FASD is diagnosed under the category "Other Specified Neurodevelopmental Disorder" in *DSM-5* as *neurodevelopmental disorder associated with prenatal alcohol exposure* (*ND-PAE*). However, the diagnostic criteria are included as a "condition for further study" under the rubric "Neurobehavioral Disorder Associated with Prenatal Alcohol Exposure." Despite *DSM-5*'s odd bifurcation of the name of the diagnosis with its criteria, diagnosing ND-PAE for the CNS dysfunction in FASD has become the standard of practice in the mental health field.

10.7.4 Comparison of Required Definitional Elements (Diagnostic Complexity)

One of several ways to compare disability severity in competing conditions is to add the number of required or nearly universal elements in their official definitions. In Table 10.1, we do this for the three conditions being compared. The furthest right column in the table is labeled "Number of elements," which is calculated simply by adding the items that are checked off for each of the three conditions. FASD and ID both have many elements, while ADHD has only two, indicating ADHD is less complex a condition than either ID (which has four) or FASD (which has six). The ND-PAE definition (for what essentially is the ARND subtype of FASD) includes self-regulatory deficits as a criterion, so it is possible that if anything, we have understated the broad-based complexity of FASD.

The two elements that separate ID from FASD are physical signs and causal evidence, which are both required for a diagnosis of FASD (the physical features being growth restriction and facial anomalies) but not for ID (where both are commonplace but not required). If one drops those two rows, then FASD and ID are tied for severity, with four required elements apiece. The two columns required for ADHD are "self-regulatory deficits" and "interferes with functioning." In fact, the first item often is present in people with FASD and ID and is required in ND-PAE, while ADHD at its core is defined by two aspects of self-regulation: attention and impulse control. For all three conditions, interference with functioning is a requirement (as is the case for almost all *DSM* categories), although the interference typically is more narrow (e.g., primarily academic learning) for ADHD. In sum, if one looks only at the definitional elements, FASD is tied or even exceeds complexity scores for ID, and both are much more complex and thus more severe than ADHD. This finding is confirmed and amplified in the following pages, where we look at severity in two other ways: competence profiles and outcome risks with concomitant need for protections.

10.8 Competence Profiles as Severity Indicators

When both *DSM-IV* (American Psychiatric Association [APA], 1994) and *DSM-5* were being developed, there was some sentiment (Blashfield, 1993) in favor of shifting from categorical classification to a non-categorical "dimensional" system in which individuals were classified not by placement into distinct categories but by profiling on a number of dimensions. Such a proposal never went anywhere because of the absence of an agreed-upon dimensional taxonomy. In a book on contemporary approaches to intelligence, Greenspan and Driscoll (1997) proposed a classificatory taxonomy derived from the first author's model of personal competence. The taxonomy (see Fig. 10.1) has not been explored previously as a severity indicator, except in one study that found it a better predictor of mainstreaming readiness than

Table 10.1 Required definitional elements for FASD, ADHD, and ID. (Source: chapter authors)

Definition elements			Neurocognitive deficits						
Conditions	Physical signs	Casual evidence	Intelligence	Executive functions	Adaptive functioning deficits	Self-regulatory deficits	Interferes with functioning	Lifelong condition	Number of elements
FASD	YES	YES	NO	YES	YES	YES	YES	YES	7
ADHD	NO	NO	NO	NO	NO	YES	YES	NO	2
ID	NO	NO	YES	NO	YES	NO	YES	YES	4

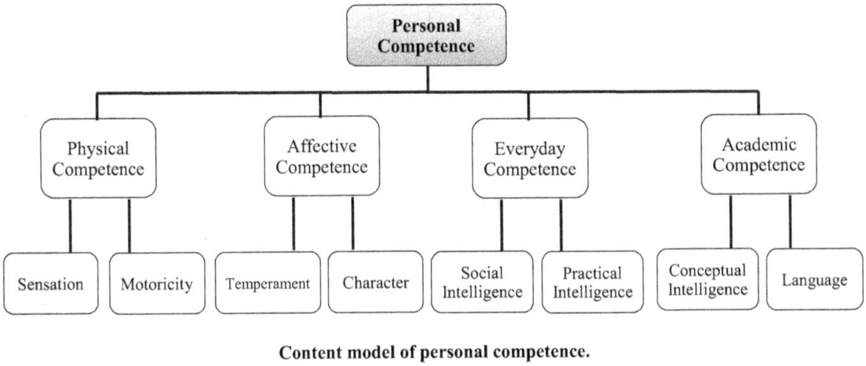

Fig. 10.1 Content model of personal competence. (*Source*: Greenspan & Driscoll, 1997)

a special education label (Javel & Greenspan, 1983). In the balance of this chapter, we illustrate how the taxonomy might be used along with other information to rank disorders in terms of where they fall on a severity continuum. In a later section, the taxonomy is used as part of a proposed method for evaluating the disability severity of individuals.

10.8.1 Model of Personal Competence Taxonomy

The taxonomy has four competence domains, each divided into two sub-domains: Physical Competence (divided into Sensation and Motoricity), Affective Competence (divided into Temperament and Character); Everyday Competence (divided into Social Intelligence and Practical Intelligence); and Academic Competence (divided into Conceptual Intelligence and Language). Two cross-domain constructs are Social Competence (a combination of Temperament, Character, and Social Intelligence) and Intellectual Competence (a combination of Social Intelligence, Practical Intelligence, and Conceptual Intelligence). We use such a model of personal competence as our severity framework because brain-based disorders are fundamentally characterized by relative incompetence in playing various age-relevant roles. The same thing is true to some extent of physical disabilities but not so much for purely psychiatric disorders, where persons are characterized more by behavioral deviance than incompetence (e.g., one can have a marked character or emotional disorder and still attain superior financial or political success). However, this distinction is not absolute as people with psychotic disorders such as schizophrenia (where a brain-lesion probably is involved) are differentiated from those with neurotic or character disorders primarily by inability to play most age-relevant social roles.

Sensation. This element refers to relative abnormality in sensory modalities and perceptions, such as touch, taste, sight, hearing, and smell. In contrast to more conventional forms in physical disorders (e.g., lack of vision and hearing), in some developmental disorders, this element can take the form of unusual sensory symptoms, such as appearing to be deaf, being very sensitive to (and avoidant of) touch, having a very highly developed sense of smell, or finding certain visual stimuli aversive (e.g., wallpaper with busy patterns).

Motoricity. This element has to do with coordination as well as effectiveness and normality of gross and fine motor functioning. Motor movements are neurologically controlled, and as DD conditions are brain-based, it often is the case that motoricity is affected. In some developmental disorders (e.g., autism), motoricity symptoms are less in the realm of impaired limbs or motoric ability and more in the self-regulatory realm of bizarre or unusual movements.

Temperament. This element involves self-regulatory competence. The two main aspects of temperament are attention focus and emotion regulation. Attention is somewhat impaired in all brain-based disorders, but it is especially impaired (and is the defining feature) in ADHD.

Character. This element refers primarily to how empathic one is toward others. People with DD generally are not lacking in empathy, but it often appears they have no empathy because they lack role-taking ability (i.e., social intelligence). That is, it is difficult to be moved by the plight of another person if you are unable to know how they might be feeling.

Social Intelligence. This element refers to the ability to "read" people and social contexts and, consequently, exhibit adequate judgment in addressing problematic or routine social situations. As brain-based conditions often involve impairments in intelligence, broadly defined, failure in social judgment is commonplace.

Practical Intelligence. This element refers to the ability to understand and cope with physical and mechanical tasks and challenges. Examples include finding one's way within a region or neighborhood, operating a machine, or dealing with daily living challenges such as cooking and making purchases.

Conceptual Intelligence. This element involves the ability to understand and cope with academic tasks and challenges. Examples include abstract reasoning, use of logic, doing math calculations, and problem-solving. Generally, IQ is a good measure of this ability, but there are other indicators, such as cause–effect tests of executive function and performance on school learning instruments.

Language. This element involves ability to communicate expressively and receptively. As with motoricity, language impairments in people with developmental disorders can be found in psycholinguistic inability to make speech sounds or use symbols as well as in sociolinguistic oddness or language atypicality (e.g., echolalia, nonsense, failure to understand or communicate clearly, and delays in acquiring literacy).

In Table 10.2, we repeat the severity comparison for the three conditions under consideration, with one change: we now list two subtypes for ID: Mild and Moderate–Severe. The reason we do not do this in Table 10.1 is the definitions upon which Table 10.1 is based do not discriminate between levels of ID, while the competence elements definitely do. For each of the eight competence domains, a score from 0 to 3 is assigned for each of four conditions: 0 = no incompetence is found,

Table 10.2 Personal incompetence as a basis for severity of developmental disorders. (*Source:* chapter authors)

Competence domains	Physical incompetence		Affective incompetence		Everyday incompetence		Academic incompetence			
Conditions	Sensation	Motoricity	Temperament	Character	Social intelligence	Practical intelligence	Conceptual intelligence	Language	Total severity	Disability severity category
FASD	0	0	2	2	2	1	2	0	9	Serious
ADHD	0	0	3	0	1	0	0	0	4	Mild
ID (mild)	0	0	0	0	2	2	3	1	8	Serious
ID (moderate to severe)	0	1	2	0	3	3	3	2	14	Pervasive

Domain severity ratings: None = 0; Substantial = 1; Major = 2; Extreme = 3
Total severity: 0–3 Non-disabled; 4–6 Mild disability; 7–13 Serious disability; 14–24 Pervasive disability

1 = significant incompetence, 2 = severe incompetence, and 3 = extreme incompetence. As in Table 10.1, ADHD (with a score of 4) is characterized as a mild disability, while FASD (with a score of 9) and Mild ID (with a score of 8) are serious disabilities. As might be expected, Moderate–Severe ID is a profound disability, with a score of 14. Such an analysis constitutes more support for the contention that FASD is a substantial disability comparable to Mild ID, in contrast to ADHD, which is a disorder with a much lower level of severity.

10.9 Risky Outcomes as Severity Indicators

A third way to view disability severity is in terms of outcomes, specifically the level of supports needed to enable an individual to function adequately and safely. Persons with FASD often are unable to improve adaptive functioning over time and frequently cannot live independently in society as adults (Burd & Kerbeshian, 2013). This situation is because adaptive development in FASD becomes increasingly delayed as age-related societal expectations increase, resulting in adaptive behavior that diminishes over time compared to age peers (Kambeitz, Klug, Greenmyer, Popova, & Burd, 2019).

This outcome-oriented way of looking at the matter actually is very close to the original meaning of disability in the vocational rehabilitation field, where DD referred to people who usually were unable to work without temporary supports or training. As a variation on the supports theme, we are conceptualizing outcomes in terms of risks that supports are intended to prevent or ameliorate. This is a somewhat contrarian exercise, as during the current zeitgeist, it generally is considered a sign of poor values to even mention the possibility of failure or deficiencies when discussing people with disabilities.

The outcome risk model in Fig. 10.2 is divided into four types of risk: Physical, Daily Living, Social, and Duty. These categories are further subdivided into two

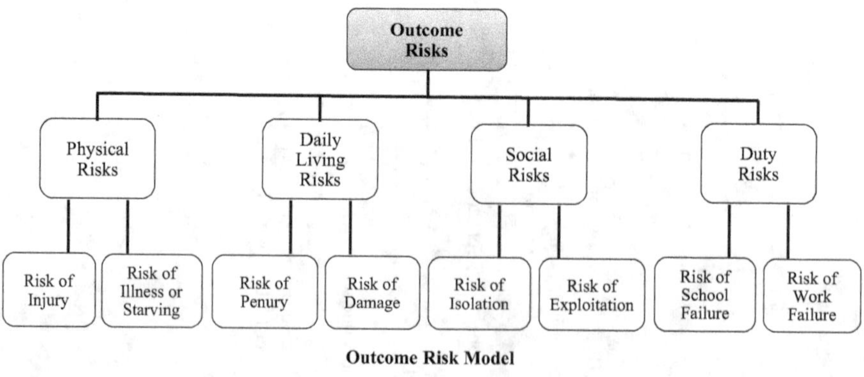

Fig. 10.2 Outcome risk model. (*Source*: chapter authors)

domains each, for a total of eight risk domains: Physical risk is divided into risk of injury and risk of illness or starving; Daily Living risk is divided into risk of penury and risk of damage; Social risk is divided into risk of isolation and risk of exploitation; and Duty risk is divided into risk of school failure and risk of work failure. These constructs are now described briefly:

Risk of Injury. People with cognitive disabilities tend to show poor judgment when addressing social and practical challenges. Lack of practical skill can put one at risk of injury and is one of the reasons why supported living arrangements may be indicated.

Risk of Illness or Starving. Securing food, cooking, and eating adequately also can be a challenge. The same is true for things like taking prescribed medications appropriately or getting treated for illness when necessary.

Risk of Penury. Because of inability to secure or keep a job, people with cognitive disabilities often have no financial support and are in need of financial assistance.

Risk of Damage. Living autonomously exposes one to many situations that could take a destructive turn, such as starting a fire when using a microwave oven incorrectly, leaving water running in a bathtub, and failing to close the front door.

Risk of Isolation. Making or keeping friends is difficult for many people with cognitive disorders, which can result in isolation that requires social and recreational supports.

Risk of Exploitation. Because of social isolation and impaired interpersonal skills, people with cognitive disorders are easily exploited by malign individuals who portray friendliness in order to manipulate them sexually, financially, or criminally.

Risk of School Failure. People with cognitive disorders usually have sad histories of school failure. In fact, the purpose of special education is to make it possible for those who otherwise would fail academically to feel some sense of efficacy.

Risk of Work Failure. Succeeding in work, even of a menial nature, requires some modicum of skill, along with attentional, social, and self-regulatory skills that often are missing in people with cognitive disorders.

10.9.1 Calculating Severity of Three Conditions Using the Outcome Risk Model

As we did previously with competence impairments in Table 10.2, we now depict the typical profile of outcome risks for FASD, ADHD, and ID, with this last category divided into Mild and Moderate–Severe subgroups. These profiles are depicted in Table 10.3:

Overall, the risk outcome pattern in Table 10.3 is very similar to the competence impairment pattern in Table 10.2. Again, ADHD emerges as a mild severity disability, with very few areas of support needs, and with these mainly manifesting in academic contexts. FASD and Mild ID are, again, essentially tied, with many areas

Table 10.3 Outcome risk as a basis for severity of developmental disorders. (Source: chapter authors)

	Physical outcomes		Daily living outcomes		Social outcomes		Duty outcomes			
Conditions	Risk of injury	Rick of illness or starving	Risk of Penury	Risk of damage	Risk of isolation	Risk of exploitation	Risk of school failure	Risk of work failure	Total severity	Severity category
FASD	1	1	2	1	1	2	2	2	12	Serious
ADHD	0	0	0	1	0	0	2	1	4	Mild
ID (mild)	1	2	2	1	1	2	2	2	13	Serious
ID (moderate)	3	3	3	3	3	3	3	3	24	Pervasive

Risk Outcome Ratings: Minor = 0; Substantial = 1; Major = 2; Extreme = 3
Total Severity: 0-3 Non-disabled; 4-6 Mild disability; 7-13 Serious disability; 14-24 Pervasive disability

of risk-minimizing support needs and with a total score in the Serious Disability category. Finally, Moderate–Severe ID is rated as having very pervasive support needs, with maximum scores in every outcome risk category.

10.10 Assessing Individual Disability Severity

Thus far, we have demonstrated that FASD is a much more severe disorder than ADHD and is well-deserving of being considered a developmental disability under the rubric "ID Equivalence." The reasons for this equivalency are that FASD is brain-based, manifests congenitally or in early childhood, is of lifelong duration, and in terms of its definitional elements, has an incompetence pattern and risk-based support needs that are essentially identical to those in Mild ID. The consequence of so many people with FASD not having their conditions diagnosed and then being misdiagnosed with ADHD is that they are prevented from qualifying as DD and becoming eligible for services and protections to which they are entitled.

But we would be remiss if we stopped with just demonstrating the underappreciated severity of FASD. It also is important to note categorical classification is an inherently unreliable process (Aboraya, 2007) because it results in people being misdiagnosed, with incorrect labels following them throughout life. In terms of severity, this situation has the unfortunate consequence that people with high-severity needs are incorrectly assigned a lower severity label and mistakenly assumed to have few needs. With respect to a large number of people with FASD, this situation means double jeopardy: (a) people with a high-severity disorder (i.e., FASD) are given a lower severity label such as ADHD, and even in the minority of cases where FASD is correctly diagnosed, (b) they are handicapped by the incorrect belief (as in the Floyd v. Filson [2019] ruling or DD regulations in Illinois) that FASD is itself a low-severity condition.

One solution to the above problem would be to do away with categorical classification altogether, but we are not naïve enough to think this is likely to happen in our lifetimes. An alternative would be to develop a method for assigning all labeled individuals to a disability severity category, analogous to the "specifiers" used in *DSM-5*. Then, one could make decisions about eligibility for DD bureaucratic purposes based upon a person's severity specifier rather than label, assuming certain basic requirements (e.g., developmental and brain-based) were met. The main challenge in devising such a system is to avoid falling into the conventional trap of relying on full-scale IQ or some other arbitrary indictor of a single dimension of impairment, one that does not translate adequately to the broad-based concept of disability.

It is our opinion that the basis for an individualized developmental disability specifier index might be obtained by summing the eight incompetence ("input") variables in Table 10.2 with the eight outcome risk ("outcome") variables in Table 10.3. The utility of this proposed framework is demonstrated in Table 10.4. The *y*-axis contains 16 factors, the first eight of which are incompetence inputs, and

Table 10.4 Individual severity ratings for six young adults. (Source: chapter authors)

	Individual Characteristics	John (FASD 1)	Amy (FASD 2)	Stan (ID 1)	June (ID 2)	Alan (ADHD 1)	Mary (ADHD 2)
Input factors	Sensation	0	0	0	0	0	0
	Motoricity	0	0	0	1	0	0
	Temperament	1	1	1	3	3	3
	Character	0	1	1	1	0	1
	Social intelligence	2	2	2	3	0	2
	Practical intelligence	1	1	1	3	1	1
	Conceptual intelligence	2	2	2	3	1	2
	Language	0	0	0	2	0	0
Outcome factors	Risk of injury	1	1	1	3	1	1
	Risk of illness or starving	1	1	1	3	0	1
	Risk of penury	1	1	2	3	0	1
	Risk of damage	2	2	2	3	0	1
	Risk of isolation	1	1	1	3	0	1
	Risk of exploitation	2	2	2	3	0	1
	Risk of school failure	2	2	2	3	2	3
	Risk of work failure	2	2	2	3	1	2
Total severity		**18**	**19**	**20**	**40**	**9**	**20**

Impairment Ratings: Minor = 0; Substantial = 1; Major = 2; Extreme = 3

the next eight are risk outcomes. On the *x*-axis are six individuals who are rated on this proposed instrument, with four impairment ratings for each variable: 0 = no impairment, 1 = low impairment, 2 = high impairment, and 3 = very high impairment. Thus, individual scores can vary from 0 (score of 0 on all 16 variables) to 48 (score of 3 on the 16 variables). Two people each in the example have been given the labels, FASD, ID, or ADHD. First names are listed, with diagnosis placed in parentheses along with the number 1 or 2, indicating their order in the table. Their names are John (FASD 1), Amy (FASD 2), Stan (ID 1), June (ID 2), Alan (ADHD 1), and Mary (ADHD 2). All of these individuals are young adults between ages 21 and 28. Each person's scores on the 16 variables, as well as the sum (disability severity) index obtained by summing across the 16 variables, are shown in Table 10.4.

At this point, we do not have an empirically derived basis for categorizing the disability severity numbers but have done so intuitively, using the ranges we proposed in Table 10.2 and then summing across them. Scores between 6 and 13 are in the "Mild Disability" category, scores between 14 and 30 are in the "Serious

Disability" category, and scores between 31 and 48 are in the "Pervasive Disability" category. Scores for all six rated individuals are depicted in Fig. 10.3.

Scores (18 and 19) for the two people with FASD (John and Amy) are comparable to the score (20) for Stan (ID 1), suggesting the three of them have "Serious Disability." The score (40) for June (ID 2) is extremely high, in the range of "Pervasive Disability," and shows ratings of 3 nearly across the board. June's score indicates Moderate–Severe ID in contrast to the score Stan (ID 1) received. Thus, the severity of Stan's ID, while substantial, is in line with the less pervasive nature of Mild ID. The severity score (9) for Alan (ADHD 1) is quite low and labeled "Mild Disability." Alan's score is consistent with most people with ADHD and very much in line with the demonstrations in Tables 10.1, 10.2, and 10.3, indicating the low-severity nature of ADHD.

Thus far, results for the individuals in Table 10.4 are very much in line with what one might expect from the earlier findings we have noted, specifically the equivalency of FASD with Mild ID and the much lower severity findings for ADHD. However, the sixth person in our example, Mary (ADHD 2), illustrates why automatically equating individual disability severity with the severity of the label is a mistake that could result in an unfair eligibility decision. Mary's score (20) is very much in line with those of the three individuals who have Serious Disability stemming from FASD and Mild ID but substantially different from the low-severity score (9) obtained by Alan (ADHD 1). This situation reflects the bifurcated nature of ADHD, with basically two subgroups: one with low severity and one with high severity. A viable hypothesis concerning Mary's high-severity score is the likelihood she has undiagnosed FASD.

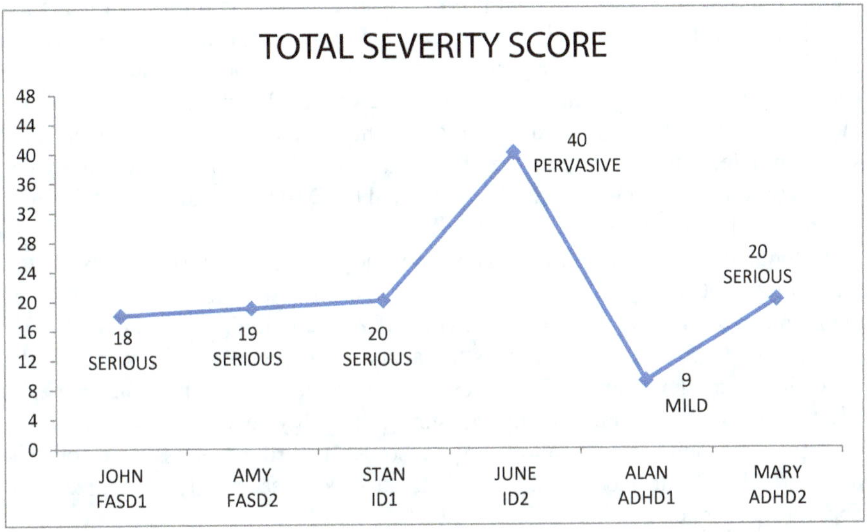

Fig. 10.3 Individual severity total scores chart. (*Source:* chapter authors)

10.11 Conclusion

In this chapter, we have explored the construct of disability severity and argued, as have many others, that FASD is a lifelong, globally impactful, developmental disorder deserving of the rubric "ID Equivalence." The functional real-world implications of FASD are in stark contrast to ADHD, which is a more narrowly focused form of impairment that typically becomes less problematic after the school years and does not qualify as an ID-Equivalence disorder. Using the competence and outcome criteria we have described to evaluate and compare the relative severity of the two disorders, it is possible to apply such a system to individuals as well as categories. When one does this individualized assessment, some ADHD-labeled individuals—perhaps because they have undiagnosed FASD—manifest disabilities that are more in line with an ID-Equivalence disorder. Given this, and the fact FASD typically goes undiagnosed, it seems prudent and just to develop and apply an individual severity metric—not only for persons applying for disability benefits but also for those facing criminal charges as part of a mitigation assessment.

While a primary focus of this chapter, and of this book, is on criminal adjudication, the widespread myth that FASD is a low-severity disorder on par with ADHD rears its misleading head in the human services realm as well. As an example, consider the following statement in the manual used by the state DD agency, Illinois Department of Human Services (IDHS) (2019) to determine whether an individual "has mental retardation or a related condition … and whether he or she requires active treatment." Section 500.20 of that document states, "most diagnosable syndromes, such as Fetal Alcohol Syndrome, are not related conditions." The document does not specifically equate FASD with ADHD, but it is likely such a view played a role in this inaccurate statement. The practical effect of such language is to make it almost impossible for someone with FASD to become eligible for developmental services unless they also qualify as having ID. In so doing, provisions such as this support the continued hegemony of "King IQ" (Castles, 2007) as the reason why people with FASD fail to qualify as ID when they have IQ scores a few points above the ID cut-score of 70–75 but adaptive functioning well within the ID range. This situation defeats the entire purpose of a "related condition" option in DD regulations, given there are few disorders more related to ID (both in causing that disorder and resembling it functionally) than FASD.

Without legislative changes and grass roots advocacy, other jurisdictions around the United States may follow the lead of the Ninth Circuit in *Floyd* and Illinois Department of Human Services (IDHS) (2019) by continuing to conflate ADHD with FASD. If this mistake continues to happen, many people will not receive the educational and developmental services or legal protections to which they are entitled. Further work in defining and measuring disability severity may be a key to ensuring everyone with a developmental disorder, regardless of assigned (or misassigned) diagnostic label, will have their conditions accurately recognized and appropriately treated.

References

Abel, E. L., & Sokol, R. J. (1986). Fetal alcohol syndrome is now the leading cause of mental retardation. *Lancet, 328*(8517), P1222. https://doi.org/10.1016/S0140-6736(86)92234-8

Aboraya, A. (2007). The reliability of psychiatric diagnoses: Our psychiatric diagnoses are still unreliable. *Psychiatry (Edgmont), 4*(1), 22–25. https://www.ncbi.nlm.nih.gov/pmc/articles/PMC2922387/pdf/PE_4_1_22.pdf.

American Psychiatric Association (APA). (1994). *Diagnostic and statistical manual of mental disorders (DSM-IV)* (4th ed.). Washington, DC: American Psychiatric Association.

American Psychiatric Association (APA). (2013). *Diagnostic and statistical manual of mental disorders (DSM-5)* (5th ed.). Arlington, VA: American Psychiatric Association.

Anastasi, A. (1983). What do intelligence tests measure? In S. B. Anderson & J. S. Hemlick (Eds.), *On educational testing: Intelligence, performance standards, test anxiety, and latent traits* (pp. 5–28). San Francisco, CA: Jossey-Bass.

Balaraman, S., Schafer, J. J., Tseng, A. M., Wertelecki, W., Yevtushok, L., Zymak-Zakutnya, N., ... Miranda, R. C. (2016). Plasma miRNA profiles in pregnant women predict infant outcomes following prenatal alcohol exposure. *PLoS One, 11*(11), e0165081. https://doi.org/10.1371/journal.pone.0165081

Bannerman, D. J., Sheldon, J. B., Sherman, J. A., & Harchik, A. E. (1990). Balancing the right to habilitation with the right to personal liberties: The rights of people with developmental disabilities to eat too many doughnuts and take a nap. *Journal of Applied Behavioral Analysis, 23*(1), 79–89. https://doi.org/10.1901/jaba.1990.23-79

Blashfield, R. K. (1993). Variants of categorical and dimensional models. *Psychological Inquiry, 4*(2), 95–98. https://doi.org/10.1207/s15327965pli0402_3

Burd, L., & Edwards, W. (2019). Fetal alcohol Spectrum disorders: Implications for attorneys and the courts. *Criminal Justice, 34*, 3. https://www.americanbar.org/groups/criminal_justice/publications/criminal-justice-magazine/2019/fall/fetal-alcohol-spectrum-disorders-implications-attorneys-courts/.

Burd, L., & Kerbeshian, J. (2013). Commentary: Fetal alcohol spectrum disorders. *International Journal of Alcohol and Drug Research, 2*(3), 3–6. https://doi.org/10.7895/ijadr.v2i3.173

Cambridge University Press. (2019). *Cambridge english dictionary* (4th ed.). Cambridge: Cambridge University Press. http://www.dictionary.cambridge.org/us/dictionary/.

Castles, E. E. (2007). *Inventing intelligence: How America came to worship IQ*. Santa Barbara, CA: ABC- CLIO.

Centers for Disease Control and Prevention (CDC). (2020). Impairments, activity limitations, and participation restrictions. *Disability and Health Overview*. https://www.cdc.gov/ncbddd/disabilityandhealth/disability.html

Clemente, M. (2015). A reassessment of common law protections for "idiots.". *Yale Law Journal, 124*(8), 2746–2803. https://www.yalelawjournal.org/pdf/c.2746.Clemente.2803_u6x66sv8.pdf

Crocker, N., Vaurio, L., Riley, E. P., & Mattson, S. N. (2009). Comparison of adaptive behavior in children with heavy prenatal alcohol exposure or attention-deficit/hyperactivity disorder. *Alcoholism: Clinical and Experimental Research, 33*(11), 2015–2023. https://doi.org/10.1111/j.1530-0277.2009.01040.x

Developmental Disabilities Services and Facilities Construction Amendments. (1970). P.L. 91-517.

Developmentally Disabled Assistance and bill of Rights Act. (1975). P.L. 94-103.

Floyd v. Baker, (2019). U.S. Court of Appeals for the Ninth Circuit, Case No. 14-99012, Opinion (940 F.3d 1082 (Oct. 11, 2019) and amended 949 F.3d 1128 (Feb. 2, 2020).

Floyd v. Filson, 940 F.3d 1082 (9th Cir. 2019).

Gettings, R. M. (2011). *Forging a federal-state partnership: A history of state and federal developmental disabilities policy*. Silver Springs, MD: American Association on Intellectual and Developmental Disabilities (AAIDD).

Greenspan, S. (2017). Borderline intellectual functioning: An update. *Current Opinion in Psychiatry, 30*(2), 113–122. https://doi.org/10.1097/yco.0000000000000317

Greenspan, S., & Driscoll, J. (1997). The role of intelligence in a broad model of personal competence. In D. P. Flanagan, J. L. Genshaft, & P. L. Harrison (Eds.), *Contemporary intellectual assessment: Theories, tests and issues* (pp. 131–150). New York, NY: Guilford.

Greenspan, S., Novick Brown, N., & Edwards, W. (2016). FASD and the concept of "intellectual disability equivalence". In M. Nelson & M. Trussler (Eds.), *Fetal alcohol spectrum disorders in adults: Ethical and legal perspectives* (pp. 241–266). Amsterdam and New York, NY: Springer.

Greenspan, S., & Switzky, H. N. (2006). Forty-four years of AAMR manuals. In H. N. Switzky & S. Greenspan (Eds.), *What is mental retardation?: Ideas for an evolving disability in the 21st century (rev. ed.)* (pp. 2–28). Washington, DC: American Association on Mental Retardation.

Guralnick, M. J. (1989). Social competence as a future direction for early intervention programs. *Journal of Mental Deficiency Research, 33*(4), 275–281. https://depts.washington.edu/chdd/guralnick/pdfs/Guralnick_SocialCompetenceFuture_JMDR-1989.pdf

Harrison, P., & Oakland, T. (2015). *Adaptive behavior assessment system (ABAS-3)* (3rd ed.). Toronto, ON: Pearson Assessment.

Heber, R. A. (1961). *A manual on terminology and classification in mental retardation. Monograph supplement to the American Journal of Mental Deficiency* (2nd ed.). Springfield, IL: American Association on Mental Deficiency.

Horn, S. D., Horn, R. A., & Sharkey, P. D. (1984). The severity of illness index as a severity adjustment to diagnosis-related groups. *Health Care Financing Review*, (Suppl), 33–45.

Hughes, J. (2006). Teaching reading skills to children with down syndrome. *Down Syndrome News and Update, 6*(2), 62–65. https://doi.org/10.3104/practice.349

Illinois Department of Human Services (IDHS). (2019). *Developmental disabilities program manual*. Chicago, IL: IDHS.

Javel, M. E., & Greenspan, S. (1983). Influence of personal competence profiles on mainstreaming recommendations of school psychologists. *Psychology in the Schools, 20*(4), 459–465. https://doi.org/10.1002/1520-6807(198310)20:4<459::AID-PITS2310200413>3.0.CO;2-2

Kambeitz, C., Klug, M. G., Greenmyer, J., Popova, S., & Burd, L. (2019). Association of adverse children experioences and neurodevelopmental disorders in people with fetal alcohol spectrum disorders (FASD) and non-FASD controls. *BMC Pediatrics, 19*, 498. https://doi.org/10.1186/s12887-019-1878-8

Kodituwakku, P., & Kodituwakku, E. (2014). Cognitive and behavioral profiles of children with fetal alcohol spectrum disorders. *Current Developmental Disorders Reports, 1*(3), 149–160. https://doi.org/10.1007/s40474-014-0022-6

Luckasson, R., Coulter, D. L., Polloway, E. A., Reiss, S., Schalock, R. L., Snell, M. E., et al. (1992). *Mental retardation: Definition, classification and systems of support* (Vol. 2, 9th ed.). Washington, DC: American Association on Mental Retardation.

MacMillan, D. L., Siperstein, G. N., & Gresham, F. M. (1996). A challenge to the viability of mild mental retardation as a diagnostic category. *Exceptional Children, 62*(4), 356–371.

May, P. A., Chambers, C. D., Kalberg, W. O., Zellner, J., Feldman, H., Buckley, . . . Hoyme, H. E. (2018). Prevalence of fetal alcohol spectrum disorders in 4 US communities. Journal of the American Medical Association, 319(5), 474-482. doi:https://doi.org/10.1001/jama.2017.21896

Mehlman, M. J., & Neuhauser, D. (1999). Alternative definitions of disability: Changes in a dichotomous v continuous system. *Disability and Rehabilitation, 21*(8), 385–387.

Mercer, J. R. (1973). *Labeling the mentally retarded: Clinical and social system perspectives on mental retardation*. Berkeley: University of California Press.

Minnesota. (2012). 252.27. Children's Services; Parental contribution. In Chapter 252. Services for persons with developmental disabilities. https://www.revisor.mn.gov/statutes/cite/252.27

Newton-Howes, G. (2004). What happens when children with attention deficit/hyperactivity disorder grow up? *Journal of the Royal Society of Medicine, 97*(11), 531–535. https://www.ncbi.nlm.nih.gov/pmc/articles/PMC1079646/

Peadon, E., & Elliott, E. J. (2010). Distinguishing between attention-deficit hyperactivity and fetal alcohol spectrum disorders in children: Clinical guidelines. *Neuropsychiatric Disorders and Treatment, 6*(1), 509–515. https://doi.org/10.2147/ndt.s7256

Pollack, M. M. (2016). Severity of illness confusion. *Pediatric Critical Care Medicine, 17*(6), 583. https://doi.org/10.1097/PCC.0000000000000732

Popova, S., Lange, S., Shield, K., Burd, L., & Rehm, J. (2019). Prevalence of fetal alcohol spectrum disorders among special sub-populations: A systematic review and met-analysis. *Addiction, 114*(7), 1150–1172. https://doi.org/10.1111/add.14598

Salvador-Carulla, L., Reed, G. M., Vaez-Azizi, L. M., Cooper, S.-A., Martinez-Leal, R., Bertelli, M., … Saxena, S. (2011). Intellectual developmental disorders: Towards a name, definition and framework for "mental retardation/intellectual disability" in ICD-11. *World Psychiatry, 10*(3), 175–180. https://doi.org/10.1002/j.2051-5545.2011.tb00045.x

Sparrow, S. S., Saulnier, C. A., Cicchetti, D. V., & Doll, E. A. (2016). *Vineland adaptive behavior scales: Vineland-3 manual* (3rd ed.). San Antonio, TX: Pearson.

Spitzer, R. L., Endicott, J., & Franchic, J.-A. M. (2018). Medical and mental disorder: Proposed definition and criteria. *Annales Médico-psychologiques, revue psychiatrique, 176*(7), 656–665. https://doi.org/10.1016/j.amp.2018.07.004

Tasker, R. C., & Randolph, A. G. (2016). Severity-of-illness scoring in pediatric critical care: Quo vadis? *Pediatric Critical Care Medicine, 17*(1), 83–85. https://doi.org/10.1097/PCC.0000000000000559

Thanh, N. X., & Jonsson, E. (2016). Life expectancy of people with fetal alcohol syndrome. *Journal of Population Therapeutics and Clinical Pharmacology, 23*(1), e53–e59. https://jptcp.com/index.php/jptcp/article/view/240/196

Wehmeyer, M., Chapman, T. E., Little, T. D., Thompson, J. R., Schalock, R., Tassé, M. J., & MacLean, W. E., Jr. (2009). Efficacy of the supports intensity scale (SIS) to predict extraordinary support needs. *American Journal of Intellectual Developmental Disabilities, 114*(1), 3–14. https://doi.org/10.1352/2009.114:3-1

Wehmeyer, M. L. (2013). Disability, disorder and identity. *Intellectual Developmental Disability, 51*(2), 122–126. https://doi.org/10.1352/1934-9556-51.2.122

World Health Organization (WHO). (2001). *International classification of functioning, disability and health. WHO.* https://www.who.int/standards/classifications/international-classification-of-functioning-disability-and-health

Woytowicz, E. J., Rietschel, J., Goodman, R. N., Whitall, J., & McCombe Waller, S. (2013). Cluster analysis of upper extremity Fugl-Meyer Assessment defines levels of motor impairment severity. Combined Sections Meeting Neurology Section Poster Presentations; San Diego, CA.

Chapter 11
Psychological Assessment for Juvenile Courts

Dilys Haner, Valerie McGinn, and Kimberly Harris

Abstract The authors of this chapter, two clinical-forensic psychologists and one neuropsychologist, are dedicated to conducting and promoting fetal alcohol spectrum disorder (FASD)-specific assessments for juvenile courts in Canada and New Zealand. Our two countries share similar legal structures, and FASD is overrepresented in both justice systems. Both countries have large city centers with large populations that are spread out rurally, creating unique challenges for resourcing justice and mental health work. Our countries also have similar issues regarding our Indigenous populations, who are potentially at increased risk for the effects of FASD due to the unique generational effects of colonization, mistrust in government organizations, and dearth of Indigenous psychologists to create trusting relationships between FASD-informed professionals and their communities. We strive to properly identify offenders with FASD and educate the courts in order to reduce involvement of youths with FASD, both as perpetrators of crime and as victims. This chapter describes the process we use to evaluate young people who have committed crimes that were influenced by the neurodevelopmental deficits associated with FASD. With our evaluations, we seek to increase awareness of the unique needs and supports for such youths in the juvenile justice systems.

Keywords Fetal alcohol spectrum disorder (FASD) · Juvenile justice · Forensic assessment · Neurodevelopmental disorder · Recidivism

---

D. Haner (✉) · K. Harris
London Family Court Clinic, London, ON, Canada
e-mail: dilys.haner@lfcc.on.ca

V. McGinn
The Fetal Alcohol Spectrum Disorder Centre, Aotearoa, New Zealand

N. Novick Brown (ed.), *Evaluating Fetal Alcohol Spectrum Disorders in the Forensic Context*, https://doi.org/10.1007/978-3-030-73628-6_11

11.1 Introduction

Fetal alcohol spectrum disorder (FASD) is a lifelong disability that creates special risks, needs, and responsivity challenges for those involved with the justice system.[1] Unlike youths with other neurodevelopmental disabilities (e.g., autism), those with FASD typically are social and want to participate in activities with peers, leaving them vulnerable to antisocial influences. Suggestibility, impulsivity, poor perspective taking, and difficulty understanding cause and effect not only put youths with FASD at risk of trouble, these and other impairments also affect their ability to respond to treatment. Problems with learning, memory, attention, emotional regulation, motor skills, and social skills may escape the notice of judges, lawyers, and case managers because FASD is largely an invisible disability that is unlikely to be considered unless a diagnosis is suspected and assessment is formally ordered.

Although youths with FASD are overrepresented in our justice systems, research suggests that when provided with appropriate support, people with FASD offend no more than those in the general population (Landgren et al., 2019). Unfortunately, in the absence of FASD-informed communities, youths with FASD are at increased risk of being harmed as well as causing harm (McLachlan & Cook, 2020). Although more inclined to be victims rather than perpetrators of crime (Streissguth, Barr, Kogan, & Bookstein, 1996), it is the inappropriate behaviors of youths who offend that most often come to the attention of police. Because of our understanding of the benefits of a tailored neurobehavioral approach to supporting youths with FASD who have justice involvement, we are committed to accurate assessment, diagnosis, and court-supported interventions for this population.

11.2 Guidelines for Diagnosis

Canada and New Zealand have adopted the Canadian guidelines for diagnosing FASD across the lifespan (Cook et al., 2016). *FASD with or without sentinel facial features* is the diagnostic term used. Assessment of adolescents involves a multidisciplinary team (e.g., occupational therapist, physician, psychologist, and speech-language pathologist) as well as physical and neurodevelopmental assessment. It is helpful to reflect on the difference between a full *diagnostic assessment* and *meeting diagnostic criteria*. Although a physician or psychologist can diagnose FASD in our countries, full multidisciplinary assessment is recommended to pinpoint strengths and weaknesses that guide future case management to ensure specific needs are met to reduce recidivism. Thus, nuanced understanding is necessary to apply the risk–needs–responsivity (RNR) model that guides assessment and intervention in our youths justice systems.

[1] The authors of Chap. 12, Dilys Haner, Valerie McGinn, and Kimberly Harris, wish to thank Ms. Alynne Holness, a dedicated caregiver to two youths with FASD, for her review and feedback on our work.

A full team of specialists may not be available in all jurisdictions. Nonetheless, comprehensive understanding of the severity and pervasiveness of a youth's FASD often can be provided to inform a court's response to alleged offending. Prenatal alcohol exposure (PAE) above the threshold outlined in the guidelines must be confirmed either through the presence of all three sentinel facial features (short palpebral fissures, flat philtrum, and thin upper lip) or through confirmation of prenatal alcohol exposure (by birth mother's report, clinical documentation, or a reliable source) and neurodevelopmental impairments.

Regarding neurodevelopmental impairment, the following brain domains are assessed by a neuropsychologist:

1. Motor skills,
2. Cognition,
3. Language,
4. Academic achievement,
5. Memory,
6. Attention,
7. Executive function,
8. Affect regulation,
9. Adaptive behavior, social skills, or social communication,
10. Neuroanatomy/neurophysiology (whenever possible).

An FASD diagnosis is made when there are impairments (≥2 standard deviations below the mean) in three or more brain domains. Multiple convergent sources of evidence also are considered, which includes developmental history, diagnoses in the Diagnostic and Statistical Manual, Fifth Edition (*DSM-5*; American Psychiatric Association (APA), 2013), psychometric testing, and clinical judgment. Recommendations must address each individual's basic and immediate needs and provide direction for accessing required resources. This latter consideration is particularly important when making recommendations to Youth Courts where there may be unmet disability, care, protection, and criminogenic needs.

11.3 Risk–Need–Responsivity Model

Although the concept was in development for decades, the RNR model was first articulated by Canadian forensic researchers Andrews, Bonta, and Hoge (1990). Risk–Need–Responsivity (RNR) is the dominant model for recommending sentencing and treatment in Canadian Youth Courts and involves the most widely used assessment tools based on this framework.[2] RNR is considered particularly important in working with FASD-impaired youths who exhibit broad variation in

[2] Although the RNR model appears to support youths with FASD in Canada by conceptualizing the disorder as a responsivity factor, our clinical experience suggests it is more likely to highlight risk and contribute to harsher penalties for youths with FASD in New Zealand.

functioning. Learning principles and consequences that tend to work for neurotypical youths frequently do not work for youths with FASD due to significant differences in brain functioning. Yet youths with FASD, particularly those who do not have sentinel facial features, often look and behave like neurotypical youths in many environments and circumstances.

Based upon cognitive profiles, the RNR model can highlight specific vulnerabilities and strengths that can be considered and integrated into sentencing and treatment so intervention is individually tailored and effective. Although the justice systems in New Zealand and Canada still function to punish the guilty and protect society, they also have developed to rehabilitate offenders. Consequently, the RNR model, when properly applied to FASD youths who offend, increases the likelihood of preventing recidivism to safeguard both society and the youths who have offended.

The RNR model was well articulated by Bonta and Andrews (2016) and Bonta and Wormith (2013). The *risk principle* postulates that offenders differ in likelihood to reoffend (recidivism) and that likelihood can be estimated using standardized tools based on scientific knowledge of empirically established risk factors. This principle leads to the maxim that the levels of service provided to youths should match their risk levels. For example, when risk is low, complicated and costly interventions are not required and may be iatrogenic by exposing offenders to the influence of antisocial peers. As level of risk increases, so does the intensity of required supports.

The *needs principle* assists in determinating and differentiating offenders' criminogenic and non-criminogenic needs. Andrews and Bonta (2010) specify eight primary domains that should be addressed (parenting/family relationships, education/employment, substance use, leisure/recreation, peer relationships, emotional stability/mental health, criminal orientation/thinking, and residential stability), noting that changes in these needs are associated with changes in recidivism. Needs factors are further broken down into static (unchangeable) and dynamic (changeable) types. Dynamic needs should be targeted for successful intervention.

The *responsivity principle* suggests the importance of using interventions that are evidence-based to reduce risk. Generally, there is considerable evidence for cognitive behavioral, behavioral, and social-learning interventions for neurotypically developing youths. Thus, effective risk assessment for adolescents not only involves comprehensive evaluation of each youths but also assessment of the multiple systems they inhabit (see Borum & Verhaagen, 2006). Information should be triangulated from multiple sources whenever possible and used to identify RNR factors as well as any protective factors (e.g., prosocial peers, positive parental influence) that could positively impact intervention and improve overall functioning (Campbell, Schmidt, & Wershler, 2016).

Campbell et al. (2016) provide an overview of three frequently used RNR-informed assessment tools for adolescents who offend: *Youth Level of Service/Case Management Inventory (YLS/CMI)*, *Structured Assessment for Violence Risk in Youth (SAVRY)*, and *Psychopathy Checklist: Youth Version (PCL-YV)*. Although there is suitable research to guide the use of these tools with gender-based and ethnically diverse groups, there is little forensic research that guides the use of these instruments with adolescents who have neurodevelopmental disabilities. Given the prevalence of youths with FASD in the justice systems in Canada and New Zealand, it is possible and even likely they are accurately represented within the norming samples for these tools. However, this supposition has not been verified.

McLachlan, Gray, Roesch, Douglas, and Viljoen (2018) have started to examine the issue of applicability for youths with FASD. For example, in their study of 100 justice-involved youths (50 with diagnosed FASD and 50 without FASD or PAE) using the YLS/CMI and SAVRY, adolescents with FASD had higher rates of historical offending and custody experiences and a greater likelihood of reoffending within the next 12 months. Those with FASD also tended to reoffend more quickly than youths without FASD and had higher ratings across domains in both tools. That is, significantly more youths with FASD were rated "high-risk" on these tools. Overall, this study found preliminary support for the validity of both tools in predicting recidivism in youths with FASD. The study highlighted the importance of forensic assessment and treatment to both buffer recidivism risk and address the specific needs of young offenders with FASD, emphasizing that this population presents with complex profiles that include lifetime adversity and strong clinical needs. Importantly, high recidivism rates in the FASD group suggested that risk-management strategies to mitigate risk may not have been effective or not effectively implemented, suggesting a "next step" for researchers would involve investigation of the responsivity principle for justice-involved youths with FASD.

11.4 Assessment and Diagnosis in Youth Justice Systems

In Canada, youths can be charged with criminal offenses as early as age 12, and Youth Courts typically process those who offend up until the age of 18. At any point in court proceedings, a judge may order an assessment under *Section 34* of the *Criminal Youth Justice Act* in Canada and *Section 333* of the *Oranga Tamariki Act* in New Zealand. The young person or the prosecutor also may request such an order. As psychologists, we often are asked to assess individuals for emotional disturbance, psychological disorder, mental health problems, and neurodevelopmental disorders. Although a single assessor is appointed in Canada, evaluators may use a team approach. In New Zealand, two assessors usually are appointed. The Canadian system gives considerable weight to reports produced by psychologists, and findings typically stand on their own merits. However, in New Zealand, it is common for two professionals to produce reports that conflict with each other, with only one assessor being FASD-informed, and both psychologists are required to give testimony as expert witnesses.

Whether the assessment process involves single or dual reports, timelines for evaluation often are 6–8 weeks. In addition to assessing criminogenic risks and needs, assessing FASD as a responsivity factor adds considerable complexity to an already tight time schedule. In addition, it may be difficult for young offenders with FASD to attend appointments due to the memory and executive functioning deficits that are common in this disorder. Assessors must quickly gather collateral information from families, schools, child welfare, child support services, and medical and paramedical practitioners as well as organize formal testing to ensure all brain domains are assessed. It is a fast-paced process that requires coordination and flexibility to respond to the youths and adults in their support systems.

When youths who offend also are from Indigenous or immigrant cultures, services may need to be coordinated with language translators or cultural liaisons, such as the Indigenous Services Worker at our Family Court Clinic in London, Ontario, or a Maori Advisor in New Zealand. In some jurisdictions in Canada and New Zealand, formalized courts exist that are designed to incorporate the values of Indigenous peoples and consider the negative influences of colonization on Indigenous people who become involved in Western legal systems (e.g., Rangitahi Courts in New Zealand; Gladue Courts in Canada). However, these courts are not necessarily FASD-informed, and the responsibility to educate the court on neurodevelopmental disabilities lies with the assessors.

A further complexity in assessment is the need for confirming prenatal alcohol exposure (PAE). Assessors may find relevant information in prenatal medical files, child protection records, or through reports from reliable informants (though what constitutes "reliable" is left to clinician discretion). If PAE is confirmed through the presence of all three sentinel facial features, assessors may be spared a difficult task. However, all three facial features are present in only about 10% of individuals with FASD (Popova et al., 2019). The team at London Family Court Clinic recognizes the need for sensitive, non-judgmental, and culturally appropriate inquiry into the matter of PAE, and so assessors undergo special training in interviewing designed to reduce stigma and blame.

In Canada, a diagnosis of FASD typically is accepted and integrated into sentencing and rehabilitation plans (e.g., probation, Youth Mental Health Court) for affected youths. In New Zealand, there often are additional hurdles to be overcome before courts accept the diagnosis. If one court-appointed assessor provides an FASD diagnosis, it may be contested in High Court or challenged by the other assessor. In our experience, such challenges typically are from professionals who are not yet FASD-informed. Judges in both countries are increasingly aware of FASD's effects on youths' thoughts, feelings, and behaviors that may lead them to break the law. Both court systems are becoming increasingly creative and accommodating in providing tailored structure, support, and supervision for youths with FASD who have offended.

Before coming to the attention of the courts, it usually is the case that young offenders with FASD already have faced considerable disadvantages, thereby increasing risk for adverse outcomes. Although developmental environments range widely as they are influenced by multiple factors (e.g., amount of accurate FASD knowledge, access to services, caretaker capacity, healthy attachment to primary caregivers, family resources, level of stigma, child welfare involvement), FASD and developmental trauma often are fellow travelers (Pei, Leung, Jampolsky, & Alsbury, 2016; Price, Cook, Norgate, & Mukherjee, 2017). Even for the most attuned caregivers, it is difficult to understand and appropriately respond to children with FASD because they learn and experience cause and effect differently than neurotypically developing children. There also is increased risk of removal from biological parents and placement in foster and adoption homes (Lange, Shield, Rehm, & Popova, 2013). In addition, Indigenous youths in Canada and New Zealand have experienced the unique detrimental effects of colonization and intergenerational trauma. Even when raised in attuned and adequately resourced homes, children and adolescents with FASD often struggle in school. In particular, they may have had chronic difficulty trying to focus, learn, retain, follow instructions, and inhibit impulsivity in classrooms (Crawford et al., 2020). These youths tend to work hard initially, until it becomes demoralizing to experience repetitive failures at school. Young offenders with FASD often tell us about their experiences of being treated as inferior to neurotypical peers, who do not need as much effort to learn.

Non-FASD-informed school staff often see these problems as intentional, oppositional or conduct-disordered behavior rather than limitations due to brain damage. With unrecognized attention, memory, organizational, and reasoning impairments, children with FASD tend to slip further behind as academic curricula increase in complexity over the school years. Because this population typically has limited capacity to recognize how their behavior affects others, they are at increased risk of breaking school rules and facing discipline. Some are excluded from school in early grades due to lack of awareness and inability to manage their behavior by school staff. Many youths with FASD experience frequent school changes, further reducing their sense of belonging and security. Young people with FASD who are facing charges likely have experienced considerable underachievement and criticism at school, which stems from the education system's current inability to effectively support them. Consequently, it is common for affected youths facing such challenges to drop out of school if they are not already suspended or expelled, which introduces a clear risk factor for involvement in the justice system. When routinely faced with demands that exceed their capacities to learn while also managing their emotions and behavior, many youths with FASD become frustrated and give up, adopting oppositional and defiant stances at school and at home (Novick Brown, Connor, & Adler, 2012).

Prior to committing an offense, youths with FASD may have become increasingly irritable and dysregulated. They may have had sleep disturbance or struggled to maintain regular day–night routines. Self-medication with cannabis or alcohol may have been attempted, which further reduces ability to learn, evaluate choices, and consider consequences while at the same time increasing exposure to antisocial peers. Emotional dysregulation and impulsivity magnify poor social reasoning and judgment, which leads to impulsive or coerced responses during stressful or exciting situations that constitute crime in the eyes of the law. Standing before the court for the first time typically reflects the culmination of deteriorating behavior over many months or years. Generally, families do not understand either the underlying source of the problem or the resources their children need in order to divert them from potential negative outcomes. The initial appearance in court often is the first opportunity to bring FASD into the conversation. In Canada and New Zealand, when a Youth Court judge orders an assessment, this is an excellent opportunity for an FASD-informed assessor to collect, review, and synthesize a youth's medical, child protection, school, family, and community involvement information and then provide formalized testing to summarize and synthesize a history that may indicate FASD.

When considering FASD within a forensic setting, it is important that guidelines for diagnosis have been rigorously applied with a detailed report explaining the findings and conclusions (Novick Brown et al., 2012). Doing so ensures an individualized analysis of how a particular youths has been affected by FASD across the developmental years and describes the relationship between the prenatal brain damage and offending behavior so degree of culpability and appropriate responses can be formulated. When a diagnosis of FASD is made, safeguards are required to ensure vulnerable youths who have offended are protected from further disadvantage and supported appropriately, so they may participate adequately in the legal process (Hand, Pickering, Kedge, & McCann, 2016). In the context of FASD, additional safeguards are needed to meet internationally recognized treaties for both children and the disabled (for specific information, see United Nations Conventions on the Rights of the Child and on the Rights of Persons with Disabilities). While many in the judiciary increasingly strive to construct orders that provide young offenders with FASD the structure and supervision they need, there is considerable work to be done to bring supports and funding in line with the needs of this population.

In many New Zealand and Canadian provinces and territories, FASD-informed supports and interventions remain largely at a grass-roots stage. The provinces of British Columbia and Manitoba are furthest along in terms of providing specialized supports. For example, Winnipeg, Manitoba, piloted the FASD Youth Justice Pilot Project in 2004–2006, which resulted in recommendations for increasing capacity for FASD assessment outside of the justice system, reducing the amount of time spent in the system and improving coordination among community services to tailor supports and interventions. In addition, Manitoba boasts Canada's only specialized FASD Court, which is designed to prevent youths and adults with this disorder from getting caught in the "revolving door" of the justice system by means of identification and diagnosis, appropriate assessment of ability to stand trial, and creation of meaningful supportive rehabilitation with a neurobehavioral approach. Generally, the rehabilitation prospects for young people who offend are considerably better than for adults whose antisocial attitudes and behavior patterns may have become entrenched. Young people, especially those with FASD, are malleable psychologically and developmentally and therefore tend to mirror prosocial thinking when they are exposed to it (Klinger, 2007).

11.5 Response of the Justice System to Youths with Fetal Alcohol Spectrum Disorder

Currently in Canada and New Zealand, most people with FASD have not been diagnosed with the disorder, which contributes to its status as an invisible disability. Youths with FASD often are diagnosed with attention-deficit hyperactivity disorder

(ADHD), conduct disorder, attachment disorder, and/or a learning disability—overlooking the underlying neurodevelopmental brain damage that best explains all of the symptoms (Chasnoff, Wells, & King, 2015). In Canada, young people with FASD are 19 times more likely than those without FASD to be incarcerated (Popova, Lange, Bekmuradov, Mihic, & Rehm, 2011). In an analysis for the Canadian National FASD Database, approximately 30% of youths with PAE aged 12–17 years had legal problems related to offending, and this result was found to be well in excess of the approximately 1.8% rate in the general Canadian population (McLachlan & Cook, 2020). In a Western Australian study, 36% of youths sentenced at Banksia Hill Detention Centre were diagnosed with FASD (Bower et al., 2018), far in excess of the 11–23% predicted from previous youths justice studies (Fast, Conry, & Loock, 1999; Hughes, Williams, Chitsabean, Davies, & Mounce, 2012). Thus, FASD is well-established as a neurodevelopmental disability that is substantially overrepresented in Youth Courts. Moreover, we strongly suspect the known cases make up only a small proportion of the number of defendants with FASD that have not been diagnosed.

Fast et al. (1999) documented cognitive deficits associated with FASD that impact an individual's capacity to participate effectively in the criminal justice system at all stages from arrest to trial. Although not an exhaustive list, these researchers indicated that relevant impairments included impulsivity, poor judgment, inability to foresee consequences and understand cause and effect, difficulty learning and generalizing from past mistakes, poor and fluctuating memory, deficient social skills, and impaired abstract reasoning. A multidisciplinary FASD assessment not only provides a definitive diagnosis (or lack thereof), but it also informs courts how affected youths may have reduced capacity to participate in legal processes and the extent to which they should be held accountable (and therefore sanctioned) for their criminal actions (Novick Brown, Wartnik, Connor, & Adler, 2010). Knowledge of how PAE has affected functioning, including relative strengths as well as weaknesses, enables psychologists to inform courts on how young offenders' cognitive profiles impacted their actions at the time of offending and, as well, during legal processes.

There are cases wherein severity of brain impairment and complexity of the charges may render young defendants incapable of standing trial (Brown, Carter, Haun, Wartnik, & Zapf, 2019). Individuals with FASD are known to easily waive their rights without understanding the implications and to give inconsistent and unreliable statements to police without knowing the consequences (McLachlan, Roesch, Viljoen, & Douglas, 2014). These are crucial functional deficiencies for police, counsel, and courts to understand and appreciate so as to not unwittingly solicit inaccurate information in interview; incorrectly assume affected defendants understand charges, consequences, and rights; and produce judgments that may punish neurotypical youths appropriately but disadvantage youths with FASD and lead to iatrogenic effects.

A founding principle in our legal systems is proportionality. Defendants who have admitted or been found guilty of crimes are to be punished in proportion to the severity of their crimes and degrees of culpability. FASD reduces culpability when affected individuals have impaired capacity to inhibit impulsive actions, think through consequences, and realize how their actions may impact others. Therefore, to provide fair and effective sanctions, courts need to be well-informed about FASD, including knowing the disorder usually is not evident at first glance. It is important for legal and forensic professionals to understand punishment cannot change behavior that is a symptom of brain damage. Therefore, youths with FASD require a different approach to sanctions, which involves awareness they respond well to *support* as well as structure (Wartnik & Carlson, 2011). Youth Courts are in an ideal position to tailor orders to target the specific needs of young offenders with FASD when assessment evidence is available to inform decision-making.

11.6 Working with Youths in the Justice System

When working with young offenders who have FASD, a paradigm shift is required: instead of viewing their difficult behaviors as intentional, conduct should be understood as symptoms of brain damage for which these youths were not responsible. The focus then could shift from blaming these youths to adapting their environments to facilitate success. Extending this paradigm shift to the disability needs of young offenders in the justice system, a similar societal and judicial paradigm shift is required (Wartnik & Carlson, 2011). Rather than applying a fundamental principle of law that all individuals are rational and autonomous agents, able to reason and choose right from wrong, it is important to understand that young offenders with FASD often are *not* rational and autonomous agents able to successfully reason and choose right from wrong. All those involved with this population in the legal process should learn how to adapt the way they communicate with, understand, and respond to young people with FASD. It also is important to understand these youths have differing profiles of strengths and weaknesses as they have varying patterns of brain damage. Under Canadian diagnostic guidelines (Cook et al., 2016), many will be impaired in five or more domains, which increases risk of adverse outcomes (McLachlan & Cook, 2020). Comprehensive multidisciplinary assessment is the key to understanding how each individual is affected by PAE and providing that information to the court along with how identified areas of brain impairment are expected to impact on the legal process (Freckelton, 2016).

Although effective participation in legal processes may be reduced by impairments in any functional domain, executive function deficits appear most limiting. While it may be possible to compensate somewhat for one or two minor impairments in attention, memory, language, or literacy (academic achievement), impairments in reasoning, abstract thinking, judgment, consequential thinking, and perspective taking cannot be rectified. There is substantial risk that decision-making for youths with FASD will be taken over by family members, counsel, social workers, communication assistants, or even the court-appointed assessor, essentially eliminating self-determination for these youths. Symptoms of executive dysfunction, such as confabulation, suggestibility, inability to appreciate when one is wrong, perseveration, and lack of insight into one's limitations, can have a devastating impact on the integrity of the legal process.

Interrogation techniques commonly used by police may easily elicit false confessions or other inaccurate information from youths with FASD (Greenspan & Driscoll, 2016). Such practices have led to wrongful convictions when information about FASD has not been available to the court to challenge the veracity of statements made to police by young people charged with murder (Freckelton, 2016). For example, the murder conviction of Teina Pora was quashed by the Privy Council in New Zealand due to FASD evidence that described his making a false confession when he was 17 years old. Following this judicial decision, Pora was released and subsequently found innocent. He received an apology from the New Zealand government and was compensated for the 21 years he had been wrongly imprisoned. The Court's decision stated, "The combination of Pora's frequently contradictory and often implausible confessions and the recent diagnosis of his FASD leads to only one possible conclusion and that is that reliance on his confessions gives rise to a risk of a miscarriage of justice. On that account, his conviction must be quashed."[3]

In another case, a 15-year-old New Zealand youths named Sam (not his real name) was facing 18 charges in Youth Court, which included aggravated robbery, unlawfully taking motor vehicles, burglary, and dangerous driving. Soon after release from custody, Sam reoffended and was assessed for FASD upon return to custody. During psychological assessment, he presented as a disinhibited, sociable, and pleasant youths who insisted he would never offend again if released but would continue to commit crimes if kept in custody. Because the birth mother had disclosed heavy drinking during pregnancy, the pediatrician who had assessed Sam in childhood suggested he may have FASD; however, no formal testing had been done to provide a firm diagnosis. When the judge in Sam's case ordered a neuropsychological assessment, Sam was found to have extremely impaired ability to regulate and inhibit incorrect responding on a measure of regulatory control. He demonstrated impairments in seven of ten brain domains, with an overall cognitive functioning score only marginally above the threshold for impairment. Daily living skills fell well below the threshold. While in custody, Sam was reported to tell fanciful stories, perseverate intensely with staff to get things he wanted, and to talk incessantly with a childlike quality. During formal memory testing, Sam fabricated information and easily accepted new (but false) information suggested to him as "memories."

Sam's test results indicated a propensity to confabulate. When interviewed about the events that constituted his crimes, Sam told wild stories. For example, he described stealing a sports car, being chased by police, flipping the car 360 degrees, and driving off while skillfully evading police! His narrative certainly did not coincide with events documented in the Police Summary of Facts. The defense lawyer, who faced a similar difficulty with Sam not being able to tell fact from fiction,

---

[3] *Pora v R* [2015] UKPC 9, para. 58.

reported there was no reasoning with Sam about his stories not making sense. Surprisingly, Sam had adequate basic understanding of the legal process. Confabulation in defendants such as Sam raises a dilemma in terms of whether it is fair to accept a guilty plea from young suspects who are unable to provide accurate accounts of events. Ultimately, Sam admitted responsibility—not only for his charges but also for other uncharged crimes that clearly were fictitious. Formal testing indicated a high-risk Sam had made a false confession.

The Gudjonsson Suggestibility Scale—Second Edition (GSS-2; Gudjonsson, 1997) is a widely used measure that evaluates interrogative suggestibility by putting youths into a testing situation where they may confabulate, yield to suggestive questioning, and/or change their answers in the face of negative feedback if they are so inclined. After listening to a short story, evaluees are immediately asked to retell the story. After a delay, they are asked again to retell the story. A measure of confabulation is derived from fabricated and distorted information that is inaccurately reported as part of the story. After recalling the story, 20 questions are asked, 15 of which are misleading. At the conclusion of the 20 questions, evaluees are told that because they have made several errors, it will be necessary to repeat the questions again. The assessor applies modest interpersonal pressure by requesting that the second time around with the questions, evaluees should try to be more accurate with their responses. Although this level of coercion is minor compared with the pressure applied in typical police interviews, the GSS nonetheless permits psychologists to see firsthand how youths with FASD respond to suggestive situations. Ultimately, results of the GSS may form part of the evidence upon which psychologists rely when providing opinions to the court about the possibility of unreliable statements made by young suspects with FASD and whether such statements should be used in evidence.

11.7 Case Management

The RNR model stipulates that the best legal outcomes occur when justice system response is titrated to the needs of the individual. In the context of community sentences, this titration is done through case management by a probation officer (PO). FASD carries clear implications for case management. For example, executive functioning deficits affect ability to comply with reporting requirements and conditions. Unless there is a functional support system, which is rare, missed appointments and lack of follow-though are the norm. Level of case management should match responsivity needs. In other words, a low-risk youths with FASD may need disproportionately high levels of case management. A developmental lens is helpful in illustrating this point. FASD is characterized by dysmaturity (i.e., varying social/emotional functioning in different contexts), and those with FASD often present as much younger than their chronological ages. Therefore, the case management approach in working with 13-year-olds may need to be applied to a 19-year-old with FASD. POs may need to take a proactive approach, such as reaching out to an affected youths for check-ins rather than waiting for the youths to show up at the office at the appointed time. Successful outcomes are far more likely when professionals work collaboratively to reduce brain-based (and thus irreversible) barriers to meeting expectations.

A high level of case management does not mean other justice system responses also should intensify for youths with FASD—more is not always better. A significant consideration for case managers is confabulation (discussed earlier). In such cases, multiple courses of cognitive behavior therapy and group treatments will be contraindicated. As is typical in individuals with brain injury, those with FASD struggle on a daily basis to make sense of their world due to memory and information processing deficits and may "borrow" information they have heard from others and apply it to themselves to fill in memory gaps. At best, young persons with FASD are at high risk of relaying false information; at worst, they are at risk of falsely implicating themselves. Thus, POs may not be able to rely on reports from those with FASD. To obtain an accurate assessment of a youth's circumstances at each reporting period, a PO will need to have amassed a network of collateral sources to ensure a valid and reliable narrative of the youth's achievements, challenges, and day-to-day functioning. Without accurate assessment, case management decisions are unlikely to adequately support youths with FASD.

Emerging evidence about suggestibility in individuals with FASD (Brown, Spiller, Carter, & Asp, 2019; Novick Brown, Gudjonsson, & Connor, 2011) highlights a need for structured case management, using sound interviewing techniques (Davis, 2019). Case managers will find they get the most valid and reliable information when they set an agenda of topics to be addressed in appointments, share written versions of agendas, and keep agendas consistent across appointments. The best questions to ask young people with FASD are concrete, open-ended, void of judgment and accusation, and one query at a time, using a slow pace. It should be remembered that these youths may say things to please those in their circles of support and accountability. Confrontational approaches are likely to confuse, create anxiety, and either provoke inaccurate responses or aggressive (fight) responses. Injection of information or misinformation into questions likely will influence responses.

Although prevalence of FASD in the youths justice system is estimated to be 23% (Popova et al., 2011), inadequate diagnostic capacity in most mental health systems around the world means most young offenders with FASD will not be identified or diagnosed. Therefore, case managers are encouraged to routinely screen all justice-involved youths[4] and apply a brain-based approach to service recommendations for those suspected of having FASD. Everyone within a youth's circle of support and accountability needs to understand FASD so as not to overestimate ability. For these youths, the root cause of their impaired judgment and impulsivity is FASD and irreversible brain damage. Case managers will find they obtain better results if they take the time to build strong rapport, provide calm environments, break down tasks into smaller steps, use a multisensory approach in teaching, and build sustainable community support networks for their young clients with FASD.

[4] Using measures such as the FASD Screening and Referral Tool for Youth Probation Officers, available at www.asantecentre.org (Conry & Asante, 2010).

11.8 Considerations for Psychometric Testing

The Canadian guidelines offer an appendix containing over 100 pages prescribing specific domains and assessment tools. While such guidelines are critical for establishing consistency and common understanding among professionals, in practice they can be difficult to implement for youths with FASD due to the very deficits associated with the disorder. Consequently, we have found it is important to be flexible as professionals. Youths with FASD have difficulty remembering assessment appointments just as they do with PO appointments, and these difficulties are exacerbated by precarious living arrangements and lack of supports. Not only do we often have youths who "no-show," but these youths also may present on the wrong day or at the wrong time. To the extent possible, we endeavor to not send these clients away as we know they are unlikely to return. Instead, we create an infrastructure where we can shuffle our schedules and draw in colleagues to assist with assessment components whenever those with FASD present themselves.

In our view, it is critical to choose assessment tools to not only inform diagnosis but also allow for clinical observations that may inform formulation and recommendations. For example, while the Canadian guidelines suggest tools for measuring verbal memory, we have found that assessing memory for the sake of diagnosis alone does not help professionals in the justice system address an individual's specific needs and responsivity factors. For example, because people with FASD often confabulate, this often is mistaken as deliberate lying. Both phenomena have similar and significant social implications with friends, family, and teachers/employers when confabulation is interpreted as lying when in fact it is an adaptive behavior to compensate for memory deficits.

Although some individuals with FASD may do well on list-learning tests and story memory tests because they can remember key words and details, performance on more complex narrative tasks may be significantly impaired. Through observation, assessors can evaluate whether details are well-sequenced, whether additional details are inserted, and whether those inserted details are distorted and similar to actual facts or completely fabricated. This clinically relevant information may help those working with this population appreciate that what appears to be lying is a neurobehavioral symptom of brain damage rather than manipulative and deliberate behavior. We recommend assessors obtain corroborating information whenever possible to better understand an evaluee's narrative but *not* to discredit or undermine the narrative. Care must be taken in testing and interviewing so as to not trap individuals with FASD in their own narratives, which is a common police interviewing technique. To reduce cognitive load on those with FASD and to increase likelihood they will be able to rise to the challenge of formal testing, we have found frequent brief testing sessions are better than fewer long sessions.

A final consideration with respect to formal testing involves variability in test results. It is not uncommon for testing to show broadly average cognitive functioning (Greenspan, Brown, & Edwards, 2016) with scattered mild impairment in a few domains yet at the same time show significant difficulties with day-to-day living (adaptive functioning). A profile with average cognitive functioning (IQ) may act as a barrier for accessing support services, such as developmental disability services. Clinically, we have found that a robust and well-planned assessment of executive functioning has had practical utility in helping those in the justice system understand and meet the needs of youths with FASD as well as advocate for them in qualifying for support services. Once professionals are supported in their understanding of how executive functioning deficits affect planning, organizing, focusing, shifting and maintaining attention, initiating tasks, generalizing, regulating emotions, and self-monitoring—seeing these abilities as separate from IQ—they may be more likely to facilitate access to support services specific to youths' needs.

Diagnosing FASD requires analyzing the findings of medical assessment and psychological testing, with a formulation that takes into account other pre- and postnatal adversities. The investigation requires differential diagnosis, with FASD only one of many possible disorders that may enter consideration. An open and nonjudgmental discussion with the family is vital to developing an understanding of how their child has developed and what struggles have been encountered along the way to fully understand how the young person has come to appear before the court. FASD is a neurodevelopmental condition. Therefore, the difficulties found in adolescence would have been evident at a much younger age. A developmental history that involves neurotypical behavior, learning, and social functioning prior to adolescence contraindicates FASD, even when impairment criteria are met. For example, there may have been a head injury, traumatic experience, emerging mental health condition, or substance abuse disorder that better explains the problems. All of these other factors, if relevant to the individual being assessed, are information of use to the court in meeting the needs of the young person, whether or not an FASD diagnosis is assigned. Discovering what has and has not been helpful in the past will also guide the court in responding most effectively to the needs of youths with FASD.

11.9 Special Considerations for Non-Dominant Cultural Groups

Assessments with non-dominant cultural groups are most accessible and recommendations most practical when accomplished through collaboration. For youths from non-dominant cultures, it is very important to include in both the assessment and intervention-planning process all relevant individuals, families, communities, and organizations serving the relevant cultural group. This collaboration involves appropriate operationalization of four key principles: (1) non-dominant cultural groups may have different worldviews, (2) adoption of a transdiagnostic approach, (3) implementation of a trauma-informed approach, and (4) ensuring a strengths-based focus.

Non-dominant cultural groups may have a different worldview. Mainstream practitioners should be aware that their clients' worldviews may be vastly different than their own. For example, collectivist perspectives may view culture and spirituality as the foundation for well-being. Newcomers to a country and Indigenous populations may have pre-migration or historical trauma that impact their trust in government institutions and foster an unstable sense of safety with respect to mainstream authority figures, which may affect level of cooperation to their detriment in Western justice systems (Baobaid & Ashbourne, 2016). We have found that including a person from the relevant culture on the assessment team and/or seeking cultural consultation increases evaluees' comfort with the process as well as our confidence in the validity of assessment outcomes.

Adoption of a transdiagnostic approach. A transdiagnostic approach presumes poor functioning results from only a few core underlying mechanisms, and trauma is the primary underlying phenomenon that explains a range of internalizing symptoms, externalizing symptoms, and substance use (Ehrenreich-May & Chu, 2014; Kruse, Tippin, & Mushquash, 2014). A transdiagnostic event may involve interpersonal, cognitive, emotional, community, spiritual, and physiological aspects, with each aspect divided into smaller components. For example, cognitive aspects of trauma may include problems with attention and memory; emotional aspects may include poor emotion regulation; and interpersonal aspects may include conflict in peer relationships, parent–child relations, and other family systems. Community components may include school climate and neighborhood risk and resources. With a transdiagnostic approach, underlying causes of mental health problems such as poverty or trauma can provide context to clinical diagnoses. Based upon an assumption of comorbidity, a transdiagnostic approach to assessment may account for subclinical symptoms that nonetheless are associated with significant distress and dysfunction. In addition, using a transdiagnostic approach in assessment may offer clues about systemic barriers faced by those in the non-dominant culture.

Be trauma-informed. A trauma-informed approach to service delivery incorporates several ideals. The primary objective is to promote the physical and psychological safety of youths with FASD as well as their families and communities. A trauma-informed approach requires recognition that trauma is pervasive and can take many forms, such as a single event or chronic, historical, and intergenerational trauma experiences. In Canada, children with FASD are disproportionately represented in the child protection system (Popova, Lange, Burd, & Rehm, 2014) and may be members of Indigenous cultural groups where the Truth and Reconciliation Commission of Canada has identified a history of cultural genocide (See Canada, Truth and Reconciliation Commission, 2015). Because trust in others and in systems is compromised when people have been the victims of violence and intergenerational trauma, trustworthiness and transparency in service provision are pillars of the trauma-informed approach. Other important factors in this approach include ensuring an informed and ongoing consent process, meaningful participation of youths in decision-making about their own care in a developmentally appropriate manner, and consistency and predictability in service provision. Well-meaning efforts to help sometimes reinforce disempowerment. Therefore, the collaborative and mutuality aspects of a trauma-informed approach also include efforts to equalize power imbalances, ensure clients have a voice in intervention planning, and strengths-based connections to supports and services. Overall, clearly stating and working toward a goal of eliminating barriers that discriminate, prevent, or inhibit access to services is a fundamental aspect of a trauma-informed approach.

Focus on strengths. Mainstream forensic assessment models typically focus on illness, risk, and individual characteristics. Yet, many cultural groups have endured despite civil wars, colonization, and genocide. For example, government efforts to eradicate First Nations, Inuit, and Métis cultures in Canada over the last 200 years show non-Indigenous people often underestimate the level to which Indigenous communities are able to maintain their cultures. Opportunities to take part in celebrations and ceremonies and keep traditions alive are seen as ways to contribute to individual and community wellness. There are many strengths and survival skills within families and communities that can be leveraged to support wellness for youths who find themselves involved in the justice system. Therefore, it is essential that these buffers be elicited throughout the assessment process and subsequently highlighted for the court.

11.10 Special Considerations for Reports

Once we have determined an FASD diagnosis is appropriate, we turn our attention to report writing, with the aim of creating a document that is clear, concise, and tailored to the Youth Court. Once submitted, reports become the property of the Court; however, they typically are reviewed by the involved youths, caregivers, and counsel. Reports also are likely to be shared in whole or part (with the Court's permission) among staff in group homes or detention facilities, involved child protection agencies, and educational services. If probation takes over case management, reports also will be shared with POs. Although reports contain analysis and synthesis of all relevant information that led assessors to their diagnostic conclusions, readers tend to be most interested in the recommendations section. Recall that youths with FASD can present in quite different ways based upon individual profiles of strengths and weaknesses. Although there are commonalities in terms of educating readers about the disorder and key generalities among youths with FASD, it is important to individualize recommendations by basing each recommendation on clinical findings.

We emphasize the neurodevelopmental approach of providing youths with supports and environmental management that will support their success by decreasing or removing the need to rely on specific executive skills that are not working well for them. We provide a thorough explanation of the neurodevelopmental approach, along with links to resources for caregivers and family members, education professionals, and any other adults in youths' circles of care. In Canada, we recommend as a starting point that these adults receive psychoeducation about FASD as a brain disorder through the CanFASD website. We also recommend persons involved in the youths' care access support for their own mental health and well-being in order to mitigate the unique stresses they experience in caring for someone with a largely misunderstood and invisible neurodevelopmental disability and to cope with stigma they likely encounter from community members who are not FASD-informed.

Children and adolescents with FASD do better when they understand their disability and when the people around them are informed about the disorder and work together to promote awareness, understanding, and empathy. We write highly specific recommendations regarding case management, school and education, peers and socialization, community involvement, and links to supports that include financial resources and transition to adult services. By doing so, we carefully outline how FASD influenced law-breaking behavior and the specific supports required to prevent future trouble. Recommendations represent ideal conditions we would put in place for youths with FASD; therefore, they must be balanced with our knowledge regarding services and opportunities that actually are available within the relevant geographical area as well as barriers to services. As such, we clearly outline hierarchical options and specific pathways to various supports and services. At the conclusion of this chapter, we provide examples of such FASD-informed recommendations.

Before writing recommendations, we consider the FASD diagnosis along with a youth's clinical profile, recalling that FASD is an important RNR factor. How FASD is related to each individual's ability to respond to the recommendations must be carefully considered. Consequently, we suggest that assessors may want to consider the following points when developing recommendations:

- Clearly label the FASD diagnosis as a neurodevelopmental disorder and explain it involves a brain difference caused by PAE. As such, the youth's behavior must be considered within the context of brain damage.
- Outline how FASD should be considered a mitigating factor in the youth's offense behavior as well as in sentencing and rehabilitation.
- Highlight the importance of FASD education for all those involved in the youth's care. Link caregivers to specific training appropriate to their roles with the youths, such as tiered trainings available at www.canfasd.ca/onlinelearners/. Alcohol Healthwatch and Fetal Alcohol Network New Zealand at www.ahw.org.nz also direct readers to resources.
- Highlight the importance of a paradigm shift away from thinking of the youth's behavior as oppositional and deliberate toward seeing the behavior as the result of a neurodevelopmental difference.
- Link recommendations to clinical findings regarding the youth's specific profile of strengths and weaknesses.
- Comment on the youth's ability to participate actively and effectively in court proceedings.
- Provide information on how secondary disabilities (e.g., comorbid physical or mental health conditions) stem from an interaction between PAE and environmental factors and tailor recommendations to address these considerations.
- Provide specific examples of literature that will be useful to adults involved in the youth's care.
- Discuss the importance of structure, routine, and consistency at home and in the school and community.
- Discuss the importance for all adults who interact with the youths to use simple, concrete, and specific language when communicating.

- Emphasize the importance of the FASD diagnosis following the youths throughout life. Clearly name individuals and systems who should be informed of the diagnosis, particularly as the youths transitions to adult services. Offer to appropriately redact the report to provide relevant information to school and community systems. Note the necessity of placing the report in the youth's ongoing medical file.
- Discuss the importance of not just preventing future trouble with the law but also protecting the youths from those who would take advantage of their vulnerability.
- Address identity factors such as culture, language, financial resources, and sexual identity that may impact the ability of the youths and caregivers to navigate various systems and benefit from supports.
- Direct the reader of the report to specific resources for funding and support and clearly outline pathways to access those resources.

11.11 Summary and Future Directions

As awareness of FASD increases in our countries and justice systems, it is vital that accurate and timely identification and education occur in Juvenile Court. FASD is a lifelong disability with implications for executive functioning that put youths at risk of recidivism. Problems with learning, memory, attention, emotional regulation, motor skills, and social skills may escape the notice of judges, lawyers, and case managers. FASD-informed psychologists have the knowledge to provide an important service to youths who are brain damaged through no fault of their own. We are in a position to assist courts in understanding FASD and tailoring meaningful and feasible supports into sentencing and diversion decisions. It is our hope that with increased FASD awareness, stigma will diminish as our courts and communities continue to build strong, coordinated responses that highlight the strengths of youths with FASD and their families.

11.12 Fetal Alcohol Spectrum Disorder Informed Recommendations

The deficits related to FASD stem from brain damage and therefore are lifelong. The following are *key developmental problems*[5] for youths with FASD:

- Executive functioning is a primary deficit in a youths with FASD. Executive functioning includes organization, planning, working memory, social thinking,

[5] We thank Dr. Kimberly Harris (C Psych) and Dr. Esther Goldberg (C Psych) for permission to share this list of recommendations.

emotional processing, and impulse control. Most youths with FASD have *significant difficulties with self-regulation*, which is the foundation of executive functioning. A youths with FASD needs direct instruction on self-regulation and requires ongoing lifelong support to engage coping skills and de-escalate in the face of stress/frustration. Monitoring and prevention of distress is the most effective way to manage self-regulation deficits.

- Youths with FASD have *difficulty transferring learning* from one situation to another. They require more repetition than others to learn from experience. Be prepared and anticipate problems in this area. Rules learned in one setting may not move with them when the environment changes.
- Youths with FASD *require constant reminders* for basic activities at home and school. This is not because they do not *want* to remember but because they *cannot* remember, organize, or plan properly. Be patient, even when a very familiar routine does not go smoothly. Provide only one direction at a time. Routines need to be clear and consistent, with little variation from day-to-day.
- Youths with FASD often demonstrate problem behaviors that resemble lying. Memory and processing deficits lead to "filling in the blanks" when information is forgotten, which can result in *confabulation* (fabricated or distorted details to fill in memory gaps). Confabulation is not lying. However, both have similar and significant social implications with peers, teachers, and parents because youths with FASD often are perceived to be lying rather than compensating for memory deficits. Be understanding and help youths develop a coherent story about relevant events in their life. Seek corroborating information if available.
- Youths with FASD demonstrate "flow-through" *phenomena*, wherein information is learned and retained for a while and then lost (e.g., losing previously learned skills). This can give the impression of inconsistent skills, which often is misconstrued as deliberate. Try to not fall into the trap of getting upset with youths because they could do a task yesterday but cannot do the task today.
- Youths with FASD have difficulties with social skills and interpersonal relationships because they *function much below chronological age*. They may be unable to share or wait their turn. They may be inappropriately intrusive or engage in behaviors that are more common in much younger children. They often have superficially friendly social skills. Many youths are easily influenced by peers and struggle to find where they fit in. They need coaching to develop appropriate social skills and should participate in adult-guided prosocial activities with peers.
- Youths with FASD demonstrate *dysmaturity*, which involves widely varying levels of maturity in different areas of development. Therefore, youths may present as much more capable than they actually are. Given that FASD usually is not outwardly visible, effects of dysmaturity can be confusing and frustrating to both affected youths and those around them. Youths with FASD also are at high risk for sexually inappropriate behavior. This risk may be complicated by developmental trauma, which can impact understanding of appropriate boundaries and social skills in interpersonal relationships. Youths with FASD need explicit instruction about healthy sexuality and boundaries as well as reminders, redirection, and monitoring.

- Youths with FASD are *vulnerable to victimization*. Provide youths with specific rules around personal boundaries and do not assume problem behaviors are associated with nefarious intent. Youths require clear and concise rules, using simple concrete language.
- Youths with FASD have *reasoning difficulties* and difficulty understanding abstract concepts. They struggle with concepts like ownership (e.g., borrowed, stolen, or found) and time.
- Youths with FASD have *difficulty understanding cause and effect*. Punishment and consequences usually are not helpful and create frustration in youths, caregivers, educators. Use a non-blaming approach and recognize that behaviors do not stem from rational choices. The best approach is supervision and changing the environment to *prevent* problem behavior.
- Youths with FASD often think slowly (*slow cognitive pace*) and may require minutes rather than seconds to respond. Youths with FASD are referred to as "ten-second people in a one-second world." Language is processed more slowly than in neurotypical peers, requiring more time to comprehend. Many affected youths grasp only every third word of normally paced speech. Caregivers and educators are most likely to succeed if they tell these youths what they want them *to do* rather than telling them what *not to do*.

References

American Psychiatric Association. (2013). Diagnostic and statistical manual of mental disorders (5th ed.). Arlington, VA: Author.

Andrews, D. A., & Bonta, J. (2010). *The psychology of criminal conduct* (5th ed.). New Providence: LexisNexis.

Andrews, D. A., Bonta, J., & Hoge, R. D. (1990). Classification for effective rehabilitation: Rediscovering psychology. *Criminal Justice and Behavior, 17*(1), 19–52. https://doi.org/10.1177/0093854890017001004

Baobaid, M., & Ashbourne, L. M. (2016). *Enhancing culturally integrative family safety response in Muslim communities*. New York: Routledge.

Bonta, & Andrews, D. A., Bonta, J., Andrews, D. A. (2016). The Psychology of Criminal Conduct. United Kingdom: Routledge, Taylor & Francis Group..

Bonta, J., & Wormith, J. S. (2013). Applying the risk-need-responsivity principles to offender assessment. In L. A. Craig, L. Dixon, & T. A. Gannon (Eds.), *What works in offender rehabilitation: An evidence-based approach to assessment and treatment* (pp. 71–93). Toronto: Wiley-Blackwell.

Borum, R., & Verhaagen, D. (2006). *Assessing and managing violence risk in juveniles*. New York: Guilford Press.

Brown, J., Carter, M. N., Haun, J., Wartnik, A., & Zapf, P. A. (2019). Fetal alcohol spectrum disorder (FASD) and competency to stand trial (CST): A call on forensic evaluators to become informed. *Journal of Forensic Psychology Research and Practice, 19*(4), 315–340. https://doi.org/10.1080/24732850.2019.1620798

Brown, J., Spiller, V., Carter, M. N., & Asp, E. (2019). Fetal alcohol spectrum disorder (FASD) and confabulation: A call to action and a need for increased awareness, understanding, and training among criminal justice, forensic mental health, and legal professionals. *Dual Diagnosis: Open Access*, 4. Accessed on September 20, 2020, at https://dual-diagnosis.imedpub.com/fetal-alcohol-spectrum-disorder-fasd-and-confabulation-a-call-to-action-and-a-need-for-increased-awareness-understanding-and-train.php?aid=24643

Bower, C., Watkins, R. E., Mutch, R. C., Marriott, R., Freeman, J., Kippin, N. R., et al., (2018). Fetal Alcohol spectrum disorder and youth justice: A prevalence study among young people sentenced to detention in Western Australia. British Medical Journal Open Access, 2018; 8e019605. https://doi.org/10.1136/bmjopen-2017019605.

Campbell, M. A., Schmidt, F., & Wershler, J. (2016). Juvenile risk assessment. In R. Levesque (Ed.), *Encyclopedia of adolescence*. Cham, Switzerland: Springer. https://doi.org/10.1007/978-3-319-32132-5_127-2

Canada, Truth and Reconciliation Commission. (2015). *Honouring the truth, reconciling for the future: Summary of the final report*. http://nctr.ca/assets/reports/Final%20Reports/Executive_Summary_English_Web.pdf

Chasnoff, I., Wells, A. M., & King, L. E. (2015). Misdiagnosis and missed diagnoses in foster and adopted children with prenatal alcohol exposure. *Pediatrics, 135*(2), 264–270. https://doi.org/10.1542/peds.2014-2171

Cook, J. L., Green, C. R., Lilley, C. M., Anderson, S. M., Baldwin, M. E., Chudley, A. E., … Rosales, T. (2016). Fetal alcohol spectrum disorder: A guideline for diagnosis across the lifespan. *Canadian Medical Association Journal, 188*(3), 191–197. https://doi.org/10.1503/cmaj.141593

Conry, J. & Asante, K. O. (2010). Youth Probation Officers' Guide to FASD Screening and Referral. The Asante Centre for Fetal Alcohol Syndrome: Maple Ridge. Downloaded from: https://static1.squarespace.com/static/5afcc5b9e17ba38be3185853/t/5c76fa7a6e9a7f0763056bb1/1551301249598/Youth+Probation+Officers%27+Guide+to+FASD+Screening+and+Referral+%28Booklet+Format%29.pdf.

Crawford, A., Te Hāpuku Te Nahu (Rongomaiwahine rāua ko Kahungunu) L., Peterson, E., McGinn, V., Robertshaw, K., & Tippett, L. (2020). Cognitive and social/emotional influences on adaptive functioning in children with FASD: Clinical and cultural considerations. *Child Neuropsychology, 26*(8), 1112–1144. https://doi.org/10.1080/09297049.2020.1771296

Davis, J. (2019). Developing a model for evidence-based clinical forensic interviewing. *International Journal of Forensic Mental Health, 18*, 3–11.

Ehrenreich-May, J., & Chu, B. C. (2014). Overview of transdiagnostic mechanisms and treatments for youth psychopathology. In J. Ehrenreich-May & B. C. Chu (Eds.), *Transdiagnostic treatments for children and adolescents: Principles and practice* (pp. 3–14). New York: Guildford.

Fast, D. K., Conry, J., & Loock, C. A. (1999). Identifying fetal alcohol syndrome among youth in the criminal justice system. *Journal of Developmental and Behavioral Pediatrics, 20*(5), 370–372. https://doi.org/10.1097/00004703-199910000-00012

Greenspan, S., Brown, N. N., & Edwards, W. (2016). FASD and the concept of "intellectual disability equivalence.". In M. Nelson & M. Trussler (Eds.), *Fetal alcohol spectrum disorders in adults: Ethical and legal perspectives* (pp. 241–266). Cham, Switzerland: Springer.

Greenspan S., Driscoll J.H. (2016) Why People with FASD Fall for Manipulative Ploys: Ethical Limits of Interrogators' Use of Lies. In: Nelson M., Trussler M. (eds) Fetal Alcohol Spectrum Disorders in Adults: Ethical and Legal Perspectives. International Library of Ethics, Law, and the New Medicine, vol 63. Springer, Cham. https://doi.org/10.1007/978-3-319-20866-4_2.

Gudjonsson, G. H. (1997). The Gudjonsson Suggestibility Scales manual. Hove: Psychology Press.

Hand, L., Pickering, M., Kedge, S., & McCann, C. (2016). Oral language and communication factors to consider when supporting people with FASD involved with the legal system. In M. Nelson & M. Trussler (Eds.), *Fetal alcohol spectrum disorders in adults: Ethical and legal perspectives* (pp. 139–147). Cham: Springer.

Hughes, N., Williams, H., Chitsabean, P., Davies, R., & Mounce, L. (2012). *Nobody made the connection: The prevalence of neurodisability in young people who offend*. London: Office of the Children's Commissioner.

Ian Freckelton QC (Barrister, Professorial Fellow in Law and Psychiatry) (2016) Sentencing Offenders with Foetal Alcohol Spectrum Disorder (FASD): The Challenge of Effective Management, Psychiatry, Psychology and Law, 23:6, 815-825, https://doi.org/10.1080/13218719.2016.1258752.

Kruse, A. S., Tippin, G., & Mushquash, C. J. (2014). Transdiagnostic approaches in rural clinical practice. *Psynopsis, 36*, 17–18.

Landgren, V., Svensson, L., Gyllencreutz, E., Aring, E., Gronlund, M. A., & Landgren, M. (2019). Fetal alcohol spectrum disorders from childhood to adulthood: A Swedish population-based naturalistic cohort study of adoptees from Eastern Europe. *British Medical Journal Open, 9*(10), e032407. https://doi.org/10.1136/bmjopen-2019-032407

Lange, S., Shield, K., Rehm, J., & Popova, S. (2013). Prevalence of fetal alcohol spectrum disorders in childcare settings: A meta-analysis. *Pediatrics, 132*(4), e980–e995. https://doi.org/10.1542/peds.2013-0066

McLachlan, K., & Cook, J. (2020). Difficulties in daily living experienced by adolescents, transition-age youth, and adults with fetal alcohol spectrum disorder. *Alcoholism: Clinical and Experimental Research, 44*(8), 1608–1624. https://doi.org/10.1111/acer.14385

McLachlan, K., Gray, A. L., Roesch, R., Douglas, K. S., & Viljoen, J. L. (2018). An evaluation of the predictive validity of the SAVRY and YLS/CMI in justice-involved youth with fetal alcohol spectrum disorder. *Psychological Assessment, 30*(12), 1640–1651. https://doi.org/10.1037/pas0000612

McLachlan, K., Roesch, R., Viljoen, J. L., & Douglas, K. S. (2014). Evaluating the psycholegal abilities of young offenders with fetal alcohol spectrum disorder. *Law and Human Behavior, 38*(1), 10–22. https://doi.org/10.1037/lhb0000037

Novick Brown, N., Connor, P. D., & Adler, R. (2012). Conduct-disordered adolescents with fetal alcohol spectrum disorder: Intervention in secure treatment settings. *Criminal Justice and Behavior, 39*(6), 770–793. https://doi.org/10.1177/0093854812437919

Novick Brown, N., Gudjonsson, G., & Connor, P. (2011). Suggestibility and fetal alcohol spectrum disorders (FASD): I'll tell you anything you want to hear. *Journal of Psychiatry and Law, 39*(1), 39–71. https://doi.org/10.1177/009318531103900103

Novick Brown, N., Wartnik, A. P., Connor, P. D., & Adler, R. S. (2010). A proposed model standard for forensic assessment of FASD. *Journal of Psychiatry and Law, 38*(4), 383–418. https://doi.org/10.1177/009318531003800403

Pei, J., Leung, W. S. W., Jampolsky, F., & Alsbury, B. (2016). Experiences in the Canadian criminal justice system for individuals with fetal alcohol spectrum disorders: Double jeopardy? *Canadian Journal of Criminology and Criminal Justice, 58*(1), 56–86. https://doi.org/10.3138/cjccj.2014.E25

Popova, S., Lange, S., Bekmuradov, D., Mihic, A., & Rehm, J. (2011). Fetal alcohol spectrum disorder prevalence estimates in correctional systems: A systematic literature review. *Canadian Journal of Public Health, 102*(5), 336–340. https://doi.org/10.1007/bf03404172

Popova, S., Lange, S., Burd, L., & Rehm, J. (2014). Canadian children and youth in care: The cost of fetal alcohol spectrum disorder. *Child and Youth Care Forum, 43*, 83–96. https://doi.org/10.1007/s10566-013-9226-x

Popova, S., Lange, S., Poznyak, V., Chudley, A. E., Shield, K. D., Reynolds, J. N., … Rehm, J. (2019). Population-based prevalence of fetal alcohol spectrum disorder in Canada. *BMC Public Health, 19*, 845. https://doi.org/10.1186/s12889-019-7213-3

Price, A., Cook, P. A., Norgate, S., & Mukherjee, R. (2017). Prenatal alcohol exposure and traumatic childhood experiences: A systematic review. *Neuroscience and Biobehavioral Reviews, 80*, 89–98. https://doi.org/10.1016/j.neubiorev.2017.05.018

Streissguth, A. P., Barr, H. M., Kogan, J., & Bookstein, F. L. (1996). *Understanding the occurrence of secondary disabilities in clients with fetal alcohol syndrome (FAS) and fetal alcohol effects (FAE): Final report to the Centers for Disease Control and Prevention (CDC)*. Seattle, WA: University of Washington. Fetal Alcohol & Drug Unit, Tech. Rep. No. 96-06.

Wartnik, A. P., & Carlson, S. S. (2011). A judicial perspective on issues impacting the trial courts related to Fetal Alcohol Spectrum Disorders. Journal of Psychiatry & Law, 39(1), 73–119. https://doi.org/10.1177/009318531103900104.

Chapter 12
Identifying and Providing Alternatives to Detention for Adolescents with Fetal Alcohol Spectrum Disorder in the Juvenile Justice System

Douglas Waite

Abstract Fetal alcohol spectrum disorders (FASDs) are common but rarely diagnosed neurodevelopmental disorders. Although research estimates FASDs occur in up to 2–5% of the general population, the conditions are even more prevalent in the child welfare and juvenile justice systems. Diagnosis helps inform alternatives to detention and appropriate treatment planning to reduce risk of recidivism. This chapter outlines a process for forensic teams to use in identifying young offenders with possible FASD and obtaining appropriate evidence to support diagnosis in court under the most recent diagnostic guidelines. Recommendations for interventions target changing the trajectory of delinquency with treatment plans that recognize neurological impairments and include supportive services that maximize the likelihood of independent pro-social living.

Keywords Juvenile justice · Fetal alcohol spectrum disorders · Alternatives to juvenile detention · Dually involved youths · Foster care

12.1 Introduction

Fetal alcohol spectrum disorders (FASDs) encompass a range of neurodevelopmental disorders that stem from brain damage caused by prenatal alcohol exposure (PAE). PAE interferes with normal fetal brain development and causes static encephalopathy, a permanent neurological disorder that, while not progressive over time, becomes more apparent as age-related developmental expectations increase with chronological age. This chapter highlights neurodevelopmental and

D. Waite (✉)
Mount Sinai Hospital, New York, NY, USA
e-mail: dwaite@bronxleb.org

N. Novick Brown (ed.), *Evaluating Fetal Alcohol Spectrum Disorders in the Forensic Context*, https://doi.org/10.1007/978-3-030-73628-6_12

neurobehavioral challenges common to children with FASD, with a specific focus on identifying both adjudicated and non-adjudicated adolescents within the juvenile justice system. Identification of this neurodevelopmental disability can lead to interventions that maximize independence and reduce risk of re-adjudication by providing alternatives to detention for the large number of juveniles with FASD who enter the criminal justice system each year.

12.2 Prevalence of Fetal Alcohol Spectrum Disorder in the Juvenile Justice System

FASD is extremely common, yet most children and adolescents with this neurodevelopmental disorder are never identified and diagnosed. Prevalence of FASD among children in the general population in the United States is currently estimated to be 2–5% (May et al., 2009). A recent study of first-grade children in four regions of the United States found FASD prevalence rates ranging from 1.1% to 5.0%, with only two of 222 children previously diagnosed with this disorder (May et al., 2018). Prevalence rates among adopted children and children in foster care are at least 16.9% (Lange, Shield, Rehm, & Popova, 2013), with another study finding 70% of children with FASD no longer in the care of either birth parent (Astley, 2010).

Within the juvenile justice system, 23.3% of 287 youths from age 12–18 years who were remanded for forensic psychiatric/psychological evaluation were identified as having an FASD (Fast & Conry, 2009). Only three of these adolescents had been diagnosed previously with FASD. Adolescents with FASD are 19 times more likely to be incarcerated than youths without a neurodevelopmental disorder (Popova, Lange, Bekmuradov, Mihic, & Rehm, 2011). Yet, in a survey of correction systems in the United States that included a total of 3,080,904 inmates, only one inmate had been diagnosed with an FASD (i.e., fetal alcohol syndrome), only one corrections program reported having an FASD screening protocol, and only four programs reported having access to diagnostic services for FASD in the corrections facility (Burd, Selfridge, Klug, & Bakko, 2004).

Though rarely identified, adolescents with FASD typically come to the attention of juvenile justice systems at an early age. Among 415 individuals with FASD, 42% had been involved with the police, charged, or convicted of a crime, with age at first offense most often between 9 and 14 years. Prevalence increased to 60% among adolescents 12 years and older, with the most common offenses including crimes against persons (e.g., theft, burglary, assault, murder, domestic violence, child molestation), followed by running away, property damage, possession/selling, sexual assault, and vehicular crimes (Streissguth, Barr, Kogan, & Bookstein, 1996). Children with FASD tend to have an earlier onset of behavior problems and higher rates of impairment and experience higher rates of victimization (e.g., physical and sexual abuse, domestic violence, and parental substance abuse) compared to children with other neurodevelopmental disorders such as intellectual disability, traumatic brain injury, or pervasive developmental disability (Stinson & Robbins, 2014). The high prevalence of FASD in the juvenile justice system highlights the need to incorporate screening, identification, and intervention as early as possible in the juvenile justice process (Popova et al., 2011). Diagnosis enables proper treatment planning and alternatives to detention by identifying barriers to learning and school completion as well as the need for substance use treatment, anger management, and/or vocational training (Burd, Martsolf, & Juelson, 2004). For example, diagnosis might support special education placement as well as supports for transitioning youths from juvenile hall to the community.

12.3 Effect of Prenatal Alcohol Exposure on the Brain and Development

In 1973, a constellation of facial features, growth impairment, and developmental disabilities stemming from PAE was described as fetal alcohol syndrome (FAS; Jones, Smith, Ulleland, & Streissguth, 1973). Subsequent research over the past 50 years not only confirmed these findings but demonstrated the far-reaching effects of PAE on prenatal and postnatal brain development, including widespread neurodevelopmental consequences in the absence of outward physical manifestations of FAS (i.e., facial abnormalities and growth impairment). PAE's widespread effects on brain functioning, now known collectively as fetal alcohol spectrum disorders (FASD), refer specifically to the neurodevelopmental abnormalities that manifest after birth. Brain damage in FASD is best understood as *static encephalopathy*, a neurological disorder involving permanent injury to the central nervous system that typically is accompanied by functional impairments in sensation, perception, cognition, communication, and adaptive behavior. Symptoms of these impairments often are misdiagnosed as psychiatric or behavioral disorders without awareness of the underlying neurological impairment from PAE. Furthermore, these impairments become more apparent over time as chronologic age surpasses neurodevelopmental abilities.

FASD disorders range from FAS, with a constellation of facial features, growth impairment, and neurodevelopmental disabilities, to the most common diagnosis, alcohol-related neurodevelopmental disorder (ARND), which does not involve outward physical features. At present, only FAS can be diagnosed in the absence of confirmed PAE. Both partial FAS (pFAS), which involves some but not all of the outward physical characteristics seen in FAS, and ARND require confirmation of PAE. Confirming PAE is one of the greatest challenges in establishing an FASD diagnosis. Because of its importance to diagnosis, a separate section of this chapter is devoted to obtaining a history of PAE (see also, Chap. 4 for more detailed information on confirming PAE).

Findings from magnetic resonance imaging (MRI) and autopsy studies support the neurological basis of FASD and define specific areas of the brain that seem preferentially damaged by PAE. Overall volume reductions in the brains of children with FASD have been documented, with effects most prominent in five areas of the brain (Guerri, Bazinet, & Riley, 2009; Moore, Migliorini, Infante, & Riley, 2014; Riley & McGee, 2005; Roebuck, Mattson, & Riley, 1998): the corpus callosum (site of communication across the two hemispheres of the brain, which is associated with verbal learning and executive functioning among other things), the frontal cortex (controls sensory and motor functioning, impulse control, cognition, abstract thought, working memory, speech and language, and visual and hearing perception), the caudate nucleus (participates with the frontal cortex in controlling executive functioning, attention, and response inhibition), the hippocampus (involved in the storage of new memories and participates in spatial learning), and the cerebellum (involved in motor coordination, attention regulation, verbal learning, and memory). In addition to MRI studies, newer functional MRI studies using diffusion tensor imaging (DTI) have found white matter abnormalities associated with functional deficits, including significantly altered neuronal connectivity and decreased function that correlates with decreased integration of various cognitive domains (Wozniak et al., 2017).

Neurodevelopmental impairments stemming from these (and perhaps other) regions of brain malformation lead to childhood developmental delays in speech, learning, social interaction, and gross and fine motor skills (Day, Helsel, Sonon, & Goldschmidt, 2013) as well as impairments in everyday age-expected adaptation to environmental demands, known as adaptive functioning (Mattson, Crocker, & Nguyen, 2011; O'Connor, 2014). Research finds 86% of persons with FASD have IQs above 75 (Streissguth et al., 1996), the widely accepted threshold for intellectual disability (ID). This means when developmental disability services are based on IQ, those with FASD rarely qualify despite deficient adaptive skills that are similar in severity to those seen in ID (Streissguth et al., 1996). While the *Diagnostic Statistic Manual of Mental Disorders, Fifth Edition* (*DSM-5*; American Psychiatric Association (APA), 2013), emphasizes the importance of adaptive functioning over a specific IQ cut-off number in its definition of ID, many states still refuse to recognize an ID diagnosis in the context of borderline to normal IQs. For this reason, highlighting the *brain-based* nature of FASD over a more reductive focus on associated *problematic behaviors* allows a proper perspective regarding the constellation of impairments that form a greater static encephalopathy, a neurological condition that often leads to involvement with the juvenile justice system. This point will become a dominant theme throughout this chapter.

12.4 Crossover and Dually Involved Youth

As previously noted, prevalence of FASD among children in the child welfare system is estimated to be at least 16.9%, with other studies suggesting a much higher rate (Lange et al., 2013). For example, Alaska's comprehensive FASD Project found 65% of children with FASD were in foster care, adoptive homes, or in placements outside their biological parents' care, and a North Dakota FAS Center found 75% of children with FASD were or had been in foster care (Burd, Cohen, Shah, & Norris, 2011). Among 1400 children diagnosed with an FASD, 70% were no longer in the care of either birth parent, 64% had experienced neglect, 34% had experienced physical abuse, and 23.5% had experienced sexual abuse, with an average number of 2.9 home placements. In addition, 19% of children with FASD had four or more home placements (Astley, 2010). Yet, among children in foster care referred for developmental evaluation, 80% of those who met criteria for a medical diagnosis of FASD had never been diagnosed previously with such a condition (Chasnoff, Wells, & King, 2015). Higher FASD prevalence rates for children in foster care suggests a strong correlation among FASD, child welfare involvement, and later involvement with the juvenile justice system.

Parental substance use is one of the primary reasons for child welfare placement. The U.S. Substance Abuse and Mental Health Services Administration (SAMHSA) estimates that nationally, 400,000 births per year are affected by prenatal exposure to alcohol and illicit drugs, representing 10–11% of all live births, with many of these children involved in child welfare systems (Young et al. 2009). The National Survey of Child and Adolescent Well-Being (NSCAW) estimates 61% of infants and 41% of older children in out-of-home care come from families with active alcohol or drug use. This statistic likely underrepresents the impact of parental substance use as 62% of children were placed in foster care due to neglect (Child Welfare Information Gateway, 2014). In many instances, even when parental substance use is not ascertained or recorded at intake, it is a significant contributing factor to child welfare involvement (Waite, Greiner, & Laris, 2018; Young, Boles, & Otero, 2007).

Adolescents with histories of child welfare system placement make up a substantial number of those who become adjudicated as juveniles. Regardless of whether their maltreatment and/or delinquency came to the attention of the child welfare and/or justice systems, 'crossover youths' is a term used to describe adolescents with histories of maltreatment who subsequently engage in delinquent behavior. Dually involved youths simultaneously receive services from child welfare and juvenile justice systems. Both crossover and dully involved youths often have histories of multiple foster care placements and high rates of psychiatric and substance use disorders, and are significantly more likely to remain in the justice system, than peers who have not experienced foster care placements or maltreatment (Herz, Ryan, & Bilchik, 2010). Moreover, compared to youths who live with one or both parents, adolescents in the juvenile system with histories of foster care placement are more likely to be placed in detention while awaiting trial and more likely to be treated harshly within the juvenile justice system (Conger & Ross, 2001). Notably, a study of 300 children found 48% of crossover youths had a neurodevelopmental disability, with causes that ranged from PAE to genetic conditions, perinatal and postnatal birth trauma or injury, socio-emotional deprivation, nutritional deficiency, and toxin exposure such as lead (Baidawi & Piquero, 2020). These children experienced greater cumulative maltreatment and adversity, earlier out-of-home placement and offending onset, more caregiver relinquishment and residential care placement, and a greater volume of charges.

The virulent combination of child maltreatment and neurological damage caused by PAE leads to an especially high risk of juvenile justice involvement. Because many adolescents enter the juvenile justice system after childhood foster care placement(s), and even more experience adverse experiences although never placed in foster care, an understanding of the effects of adverse experiences on brain development in FASD is imperative in defining the complex challenges that often lead to criminal activity. The construct of *developmental trauma disorder* refers to the effects of adverse life experiences on child development that are seen not only in everyday functioning but also in brain anatomy alterations (Van der Kolk, 2017).

Exposure to chronic childhood adversity causes or exacerbates dysfunction in both the autonomic nervous system (responsible for primitive fight-flight and threat detection responses) and hypothalamic-pituitary-adrenal (HPA) system (responsible for regulation of the stress hormone, cortisol). Chronic exposure to cortisol induces changes in the limbic system, the brain region that regulates emotions and urges below the level of consciousness (Teicher, Samson, Anderson, & Ohashi, 2016). Children with FASD, who already have limited adaptive functioning, are especially affected by these subsequent brain changes. Adaptive impairments are intensified, putting these children at high risk of victimization through re-enactment of past traumas, susceptibility to the influence of others because of gullibility, and emotional dysregulation that often manifests as impulsivity and violent behavior.

The high prevalence of neurodevelopmental disorders among crossover and dually involved adolescents clarifies the common pathway from foster care to the juvenile justice system. An FASD diagnosis in childhood can be anticipated to place an adolescent at high risk for involvement with the criminal justice system (Burd, Fast, Conry, & Williams, 2010). Because of brain immaturity, neurotypical adolescents are highly sensitive to peer pressure and immediate gratification and do not have the adult-level capacity to consider the consequences of their actions, make good judgments, and self-regulate in emotionally charged contexts (National Research Council, 2013). When these adolescent traits are further compromised by brain damage due to PAE, each characteristic increases in an almost inevitable trajectory toward involvement with the criminal justice system. Redirecting this trajectory requires more than engaged parents and supportive professionals.

Few support services are in place for youths who cannot function independently or negotiate the challenges of daily life. Developmental disability systems often exclude children and adolescents with FASD diagnoses, seeing their delinquent behavior as manifestations of psychiatric or behavioral problems rather than a neurological disability. The high prevalence of adverse experiences and risk for future juvenile justice involvement in FASD underscores the importance of PAE screening for all children who enter the child welfare system.

12.5 Neurodevelopmental Signs of Fetal Alcohol Spectrum Disorder: Birth and Developmental History

All forensic evaluations should begin with a thorough, structured birth and developmental history. Obtaining a clear timeline should begin with a birth mother's alcohol and/or substance use before, during, and following the discovery of her pregnancy and extend through early developmental milestones, including academic and adaptive function during the elementary school years. For example, complications during delivery, birth defects, or developmental delays can be further investigated in records (e.g., birth and medical records, school records, developmental and mental health evaluations) or medical tests to identify disabilities that might serve as mitigating factors in the forensic setting.

A comprehensive prenatal and birth history is the starting point for a child's developmental trajectory. Generally, such history is best obtained from the birth or adoptive parent when available but also can be obtained from other family members. Birth and medical records add objective details to subjective histories reported by family members. Additional histories provided by caregivers often contain the first signs of early temperament difficulties, sleep and self-regulation disturbances, feeding problems, and delays in motor, speech/language, and social skills that often are absent in medical records.

Initial birth history should include maternal age at birth, neonatal gestational age at birth, birth weight, type of delivery (normal spontaneous vaginal delivery versus Cesarean section), and indications for deliveries other than spontaneous vaginal deliveries (Demirci & Kartal, 2018). It also is important to include questions about the outcomes of previous pregnancies, as miscarriages and stillbirths are more common among women who use alcohol during pregnancy (Sundermann et al., 2019). Important early indicators of impaired emotional regulation and social interaction in the first year of life include overall temperament, amount of crying, response to soothing, sleep pattern, early eye contact with the parent during feeding in the first 3 months, and reactive smiling. Subsequent milestones include age when a child begins to sit alone, walk independently, speak with intelligible words, speak with fully intelligible sentences, and understand and carry out one-step instructions. A constellation of delays across the major developmental domains of gross and fine motor skills, speech and language, social interaction, and adaptive function allows assessment of early developmental challenges that are hallmarks of several neurodevelopmental disorders including FASD, autism, intellectual disability, communication disorder, learning disorder, and attention-deficit/hyperactivity disorder (ADHD).

Children with an FASD often are misdiagnosed in their preschool years with global developmental delay, isolated speech delay, ADHD, or autism until the increasing severity of behavioral challenges during the school years progressively overshadows early developmental delays. For this reason, a diagnosis of another neurodevelopmental disorder in early childhood should never exclude FASD as the primary diagnosis. Also, it never should be assumed that developmental evaluations in early childhood and beyond included FASD as part of the differential diagnosis, as most do not. During the first 3 years of life, many neurodevelopmental disorders appear undifferentiated, overlapping in presentation. Often, young children with FASD do not receive early intervention services because qualifying criteria are too stringent. In such children, developmental challenges become more apparent when chronological age outpaces the trajectory of their developmental abilities.

Early intervention evaluations completed before age 3 provide an objective assessment of specific delays. After age 3, psychoeducational evaluations completed by school systems or other professionals permit detailed assessments of cognitive abilities and specific learning disorders. Children with FASD who have borderline to normal cognitive abilities often have impairments that are not identified in these evaluations, which tend to focus on intellectual ability and academic achievement and neglect standardized measures of adaptive functioning. In the absence of direct adaptive assessment, a significant discrepancy between cognitive ability and academic achievement can reveal adaptive impairment. While many children with learning disabilities have significant gaps between ability to learn (cognitive capacity) and actual achievement (adaptive capacity), those with FASD often are labeled as unmotivated because of associated behavior challenges (e.g., "she could do better if she would just try harder"). Behavioral challenges include difficulties with attention, executive function, and memory, which can lead to frustration for teachers, caregivers, and affected children who seem to learn a task one day "only to forget it the next day." Because of cognitive impairments in multiple domains (e.g., attention, auditory and visual processing, executive function), adaptive difficulties become more apparent over the school years as education increasingly relies on didactic verbal instruction. Common areas of academic challenge for this population include reading comprehension, math calculation, and language, often despite normal IQ (Mattson et al., 2011). Awareness of these challenges is important in evaluating children because poor early school performance not only is a marker of behavioral and cognitive problems but also a predictor of future achievement, truancy, early school dropout, early involvement with the juvenile justice system, and recidivism (Katsiyannis, Ryan, Zhang, & Spann, 2008). Thus, identifying brain-based challenges early on can support academic achievement and reduce rates of both delinquency and recidivism.

As noted above, academic challenges often occur in association with behavioral problems in FASD, which may lead to an ADHD diagnosis as early as the prekindergarten years. Over 60% of children exposed in utero to alcohol exhibit deficits in attention and impulsive behavior (Streissguth et al., 1996). Such children tend to have clinically significant scores on measures of externalizing behavior, which include social difficulties, attention problems, and aggressive behavior that may lead to diagnoses of oppositional defiant disorder (ODD) and/or conduct disorder (CD) as well as ADHD (Mattson et al., 2011). Related histories involve school suspension/expulsion, truancy, and early school dropout. For example, a systematic review of 5984 cases of FASD found 50.2% of the study sample had comorbid ADHD diagnoses (10 times greater prevalence than in the general population), 23.0% had an intellectual disability (23 times greater prevalence), 63% had ODD (five times greater prevalence), 14.1% had depression (four times greater prevalence), 12.3% had psychotic disorders (24 times greater prevalence), and 8.6% had bipolar disorder (five times greater prevalence; Weyrauch, Schwartz, Hart, Klug, & Burd, 2017). By adulthood, externalizing behaviors that manifested in childhood as ADHD, ODD, and CD in this large sample often were eclipsed by depression. In another large study of 473 individuals with FASD, 23% of adults had attempted suicide, and 43% had threatened to commit suicide (Streissguth et al., 1996).

Substance use disorders are common among adolescents in the juvenile justice system with up to 50% of juvenile detention detainees scoring in the elevated range for alcohol and drug use severity (Bukstein, 2000). The additional morbidity of a substance use disorder places adolescents with FASD at further risk of arrest and/or incarceration. Due in part to genetic influences, children of parents with substance use disorders are at especially high risk for substance use disorder themselves (Schuckit, 2009). Interventions at the time of adjudication must address this pervasive, yet often difficult to treat, comorbidity.

12.6 Obtaining Prenatal Alcohol-Exposure History

Alcohol use during pregnancy is extremely common and correlates with the prevalence of FASD. Among pregnant women aged 18–44 years (i.e., child-bearing age), the U.S. Centers for Disease Control and Prevention (CDC) estimates the prevalence of current drinking (at least one alcoholic drink in the previous 30 days) is 11.5% and prevalence of binge drinking (four or more drinks on at least one occasion in the previous 30 days) is 3.9%. Among pregnant women who binge drink, average frequency of binge drinking in the previous 30 days is 4.5 episodes, and average largest number of drinks consumed on any occasion is six drinks (Denny, Acero, Naimi, & Kim, 2019).

Unlike FAS, where sentinel facial features, growth impairment, and neurodevelopmental impairments together are pathognomonic for PAE, other diagnoses under the FASD umbrella require confirmed history of PAE. Thus, for these other disorders, beyond identifying the neurodevelopmental impairments that apply in a particular child's case, the single most important diagnostic task is obtaining PAE history. This task can be challenging (although not insurmountable) due to the stigma associated with alcoholism and specifically with alcohol use during pregnancy. Some research has found that maternal disclosure of alcohol use during pregnancy is considerably less than biological markers of prenatal exposure, such as meconium testing at birth, would suggest. For example, in a study that directly compared the two, PAE prevalence as measured by meconium testing was 4.26 times greater than the rate measured by maternal self-report (Lange, Shield, Koren, Rehm, & Popova, 2014). Unfortunately, meconium testing is not readily available outside of FASD research centers.

While a review of obstetric records may find documentation of alcohol use during pregnancy, obstetricians rarely note such information, and pediatricians seldom record this information (Stoler & Holmes, 1999). Newborn urine toxicology tests obtained in the first 1–2 days after birth usually screen for substances other than alcohol. Moreover, even in cases where substantial alcohol exposure occurred before birth, newborns with significant prenatal alcohol exposure may test negative in blood and urine tests. More recent advances include an ability to test newborns at birth by a method similar to the newborn screening tests currently required in the United States. However, this method remains in the experimental stage and is fraught with legal implications in the case of positive results (McQuire et al., 2016).

Current standards in determining the level of PAE necessary to cause FASD vary. The standard definition is based upon updated diagnostic guidelines for FASD that were developed in collaboration with the National Institute on Alcoholism and Alcohol Abuse (NIAAA), Collaborative Initiative on Fetal Alcohol Spectrum Disorders (CIFASD) and Collaboration on FASD Prevalence. Based upon this standard, one or more of the following conditions must be met to constitute confirmed PAE, and the information must have been obtained from the biological mother or a reliable collateral source, such as a family member, social service agency, or medical record:

- ≥6 drinks/week for ≥2 weeks during pregnancy;
- ≥3 drinks per occasion on ≥2 occasions during pregnancy;
- documentation of alcohol-related social or legal problems in proximity to (before or during) the index pregnancy, such as history of a citation for driving while intoxicated or history of treatment for an alcohol-related condition;
- documentation of intoxication during pregnancy by blood, breath, or urine alcohol content testing;
- positive testing with one or more established alcohol-exposure biomarkers during pregnancy or at birth (e.g., analysis of fatty acid ethyl esters, phosphatidyl ethanol, and/or ethyl glucuronide in maternal hair, fingernails, urine, or blood, or placenta, or meconium); or,
- increased prenatal risk associated with drinking during pregnancy, as assessed by a validated screening tool (e.g., T-ACE, AUDIT; Hoyme et al., 2016).

Notably, pre-pregnancy binge drinking is a strong predictor of both drinking and binge drinking during pregnancy (Ethen et al., 2009). Other characteristics associated with maternal alcohol use during pregnancy include tobacco use during pregnancy, unintended pregnancy, poor prenatal care, and use of substances other than alcohol.

Usually, an interview with the biological mother is the most direct means of establishing an FASD diagnosis. The American Academy of Pediatrics has developed a screening tool for pediatricians that helps guide this interview past defensive responses that may limit disclosure of alcohol use. One important element involves integrating questions about PAE into the prenatal history, which is best accomplished by asking the mother how far into her pregnancy she discovered the pregnancy (American Academy of Pediatrics, 2018). After establishing this time frame, the interview can then proceed:

- Did you have any medical problems during your pregnancy?
- Were you prescribed any medications during pregnancy?
- How many drinks of alcohol per day or week did you typically have before discovering you were pregnant?
- How many drinks of alcohol per day or week did you typically use after you discovered your pregnancy?
- How often did you use any other substances such as cannabis, cocaine, or opioids?

When quantifying amount of alcohol use, it is imperative to determine type of alcohol (e.g., wine, beer, mixed drinks, etc.) as well as how much was consumed over a day or week (Burd et al., 2006) as in the following questions:

- In an average week, how many days per week did you drink?
- On an average drinking day, how many drinks do you have?
- How many days per week did you drink four or more drinks?

Quantifying what constitutes "a drink" can further clarify alcohol consumption, as an 8 oz. glass of wine has far less alcohol than an 8 oz. glass of vodka, but both may be viewed by the birth mother as "one drink." Severity of alcohol exposure depends largely on quantity, frequency, and timing within the gestational period, although other factors also affect the fetus. For example, research has found that maternal stress and adverse experiences, poor maternal health and inadequate nutrition, social isolation, and/or insufficient prenatal care are associated with increased risk of fetal brain damage (Maier & West, 2001; May & Gossage, 2011).

In addition to screening for prenatal alcohol and other substance exposures, developmental history should include any experiences of prenatal or postnatal lead exposure, head injuries that might be associated with traumatic brain injury, seizure disorder, poor growth in height or weight, small head circumference for age at any time in childhood, and other medical problems (including eye abnormalities, hearing loss, congenital heart disease, kidney disease). Family history including developmental delays, serious medical problems, psychiatric illness, substance use disorder, learning challenges, school failure, and incarceration also should be obtained for both birth parents and siblings. Finally, given the high prevalence of physical abuse, sexual abuse, and neglect among adolescents in the juvenile justice system, developmental history should include screening for adverse childhood experiences to rule out additional causes of delinquency.

Past psychological evaluations, psychoeducational evaluations, individualized education plans (IEPs), and any history of past psychiatric diagnoses, medications, or hospitalizations can help clarify specific neurodevelopmental challenges that support diagnosis of an FASD. A history of cognitive impairment with intellectual disability is not required for diagnosis. Rather, a constellation of cognitive and neurobehavioral impairments in domains such as executive function, attention, self-regulation, memory, auditory and visual learning, and adaptive function (e.g., communication, socialization, practical skills) shows the extent to which PAE has affected brain development. Previous psychological evaluations should be supplemented with a current neuropsychological assessment to identify and quantify impairments that may have contributed to the instant offense for juveniles facing adjudication.

12.7 Features of Fetal Alcohol Spectrum Disorder

According to the updated Institute of Medicine's (IOM) diagnostic guidelines (Hoyme et al., 2016), sentinel features for FAS involve two or more of the characteristic facial features. These include the following:

- short palpebral fissures (≤10 percentile for age),
- thin vermilion border of the upper lip (rank 4 or 5 on a racially normed lip/philtrum guide), and,
- smooth philtrum (rank 4 or 5 on a racially normed lip/philtrum guide).

While most children and adolescents with FASD do not have the physical characteristics seen in FAS, thorough physical examination may support another diagnosis under the FASD umbrella. A clinician with experience in dysmorphology should be contacted to complete the physical examination if the evaluating physician lacks such expertise. (A list of clinicians can be found at the resource directory of the National Organization on Fetal Alcohol Syndrome [www.nofas.org]).

Sentinel features of FAS are found in only 10–20% of those with FASD (May et al., 2018). Such features are best appreciated in early childhood and diminish in prominence with age. For this reason, childhood photos that show a relaxed face (not smiling), with the child directly facing the camera, may be helpful. In addition to facial features, growth deficits in height or weight at or below the tenth percentile for age at any time in childhood, using a racial or ethnically appropriate growth curve, can support diagnosis. Review of pictures from early childhood (with the child looking head-on and not smiling) can more clearly show sentinel features of FAS that become less apparent with age. Importantly, absence of facial features or growth deficits does not rule out an FASD as most children with this neurodevelopmental disorder have neither facial features nor growth deficits.

Structural evidence of brain abnormalities may be found either by head circumference that falls below the tenth percentile for age at any time in childhood or brain abnormalities shown in neuroimaging, such as an abnormal MRI. Recurrent nonfebrile seizures are another diagnostic criterion although electroencephalograms (EEGs) may be read as normal even in the face of documented seizure disorder. Forensic evaluators can consider obtaining an MRI with a specific request for measures of the corpus callosum and cerebellar volume and close examination for subtle heterotopias, abnormal gyri, and decreases in cortical volume that otherwise might be easily missed (Wozniak, Riley, & Charness, 2019). These findings are not routinely documented by radiologists and must be specifically requested before evaluation.

In addition to physical findings, neuropsychological testing is required to identify areas of functional impairment. To meet criteria for an FASD, an individual must have impairment in either cognitive ability or behavioral impairment without cognitive impairment. Under the Hoyme et al. (2016) diagnostic guidelines for FASD, impairments are defined as ≥1.5 standard deviations (SDs) below the mean. Cognitive impairments include either global intellectual ability (i.e., full-scale IQ or verbal, performance, or spatial IQ) or impairments in at least two other cognitive domains (e.g., executive functioning, specific learning category, memory, or visual-spatial functioning). Neuropsychological measures such as the NEPSY (a Developmental Neuropsychological Assessment) make evaluation a bit less complicated. Importantly, an IQ score that falls within the borderline or even average range should never exclude an FASD diagnosis (Hoyme et al., 2016).

Because many youths with FASD have borderline or average (and sometimes higher) cognitive abilities, the new Hoyme et al. (2016) guidelines provide for inclusion based upon behavioral impairment without cognitive impairment. The behavioral criterion requires impairments (also ≥1.5 SDs below the mean) in at least two behavioral domains, such as mood or behavioral regulation, attention control, or impulse control. Useful measures to acquire such information include the Vineland Adaptive Behavior Scale, Adaptive Behavior Assessment Scale, Child Behavioral Checklist, or Behavior Assessment Scale for Children, which typically can be readily administered in most psychological evaluations. Children prenatally exposed to alcohol often have deficits in communication, daily living skills, and socialization, evidenced by low standard scores on the Vineland or other measures of adaptive function. In youths with FASD, severe adaptive deficits may be seen in tandem with average cognitive ability (Greenspan, Novick Brown, & Edwards, 2016). *For this reason, IQ threshold scores typically are misleading in FASD as they fail to capture the array of deficits in social and adaptive functioning that persist throughout the lifespan.* Thus, standardized assessment of adaptive functioning is imperative in making an FASD diagnosis.

Other specific malformations are well described in children with FASD. These include cardiac abnormalities (e.g., atrial septal defects, aberrant great vessels, ventricular septal defects, conotruncal heart defects), skeletal problems (e.g., radioulnar synostosis, vertebral segmentation defects, large joint contractures, scoliosis), renal conditions (e.g., aplastic/hypoplastic/dysplastic kidneys, "horseshoe" kidneys/ureteral duplications), eye and vision problems (e.g., strabismus, ptosis, retinal vascular anomalies, optic nerve hypoplasia, abnormal saccadic eye movements), and hearing problems (e.g., conductive hearing loss, sensorineural hearing loss, auditory processing disorder). In forensic cases, examination by a cardiologist, orthopedist, nephrologist, ophthalmologist, and/or an audiologist might be considered to gather supporting evidence. Such malformations may be diagnosed separately as alcohol-related birth defects (ARBD; Stratton, Howe, & Battaglia, 1996).

Finally, to exclude other possible causes of neurodevelopmental disability, a chromosomal analysis with reflex microarray testing and testing for Fragile X should be considered. These can be obtained readily at most major commercial or university laboratories. Neuroimaging also might help rule out additional brain-based disorders, traumatic brain injury, or other abnormalities. Finally, it is important to obtain a thorough substance use history in adolescents, as early-onset alcohol and drug use, if frequent and sustained, may complicate diagnostic formulation.

12.8 Screening

Many families enter the child welfare system through dependency and delinquency courts in the context of familial drug and alcohol abuse and neglect. FASD should be a primary "rule out" condition in such cases, even when neurodevelopmental and neurocognitive impairments are not readily apparent. A child with an undiagnosed FASD is deprived of services and treatments that are known to prevent recidivism and further involvement with the juvenile court system. Consequently, a diagnostic evaluation is critical. Unfortunately, despite the high rate of FASD in foster care, most children in foster care systems in the United States are not screened for FASD by dependency courts or their attorneys.

The Prenatal and Neurodevelopmental Assessment is one of several screening tools that facilitate identification of children and adolescents with a possible FASD (Table 12.1). This measure addresses common developmental and behavioral challenges that can be identified by caregivers during the developmental history and is based upon *DSM-5* (APA, 2013) criteria for neurodevelopmental disorder associated with prenatal alcohol exposure (ND-PAE). ND-PAE criteria show a strong correlation with other diagnostic guidelines for FASD and, like all non-FAS criteria, require confirmed PAE (Kable & Coles, 2018). A copy of this assessment tool is found at the conclusion of this chapter.

Scoring of the neurocognitive, adaptive, and self-regulation domains in the Prenatal and Neurodevelopmental Assessment enables a straightforward risk assessment for neurodevelopmental signs of an FASD while also screening for other possible causes of neurodevelopmental disorders, such as exposure to other substances of abuse, lead exposure, medical conditions and medications taken during pregnancy, and family histories of autism or intellectual disability. Threshold scores may be used as a crude measure of symptom severity, but any adolescent who scores within the range of these thresholds and has a PAE history should be referred for full FASD evaluation. In other words, this screening tool should not be used as a diagnostic assessment but rather as a first step in identifying adolescents who need further evaluation.

The value of using a screening tool in the juvenile justice setting was examined in a study completed in the 17th Judicial District in Colorado (Bisgard, Fisher, Adubato, & Louis, 2010). Out of 718 delinquent youths, PAE was found in 25%. Of those with PAE histories, 43% received an FASD evaluation, and 50% of those youths were diagnosed with an FASD. All subjects diagnosed with an FASD received services, with treatment planning based upon recommendations in the

FASD diagnostic evaluations. These findings suggest all juveniles entering the justice system should be screened for prenatal alcohol exposure and possible FASD.

12.9 Alternatives to Detention

A fundamental philosophical difference between juvenile and adult criminal courts involves advocacy for alternatives to detention in the former. By acknowledging the susceptibility of adolescents to external influences, juvenile courts seek to prevent future criminal behavior by rehabilitating juvenile delinquents rather than inducing law-abiding behavior through punishment for wrongdoing (Osher, Quinn, Kendziora, Woodruff, & Rouse, 2002). While criminal law is based on holding individuals accountable for offense conduct, especially for behavior that harms victims, a developmentally informed juvenile justice system can promote accountability by providing the setting and opportunity for juveniles to accept responsibility for their actions, make amends to individual victims and the community, and participate in community service or other kinds of rehabilitative programs. Restorative justice programs involving victims and adjudication programs that include restitution and peer review of progress are examples of developmentally appropriate instruments of accountability. However, accountability, preventing recidivism, and fairness include ensuring youths are adjudicated only if they are competent to understand the proceedings and assist counsel (National Research Council, 2013). This often is a major challenge for adolescents with FASD, who typically lack the cognitive ability to complete goal-oriented tasks, including the self-regulation required to prevent re-offending as well as competency to stand trial (Brown, Haun, Zapf, & Novick Brown, 2017).

Recognition and remediation for disabilities are governed by the *American Disabilities Act* (United States Department of Justice, Civil Rights Division, 1990) and *Individuals with Disabilities Education Act* (United States Department of Education, 1990). These laws attempt to address discrimination against children with disabilities. For example, Title II of the ADA prohibits “public entities” from discriminating against a “qualified individual with a disability” on account of that disability. From the time a law enforcement officer takes a youths with a disability into custody to the point of final discharge from the system, the youths has a right to accommodation for any disability. Accommodations for disability must both follow the law and help improve outcomes for youths.

Three-quarters of young offenders with FASD have significant cognitive impairments and behavioral and emotional challenges that hinder ability to manage and understand the adjudicative process, which increases likelihood of a judicial finding of legal incompetence (McLachlan, Roesch, Viljoen, & Douglas, 2014). Such a finding speaks to the need for careful assessment of these capacities in juvenile defendants with FASD. For example, this population may be unable to link legal consequences with their criminal behavior. In 2010 and 2013, the Canadian Bar Association (CBA) passed resolutions calling on all levels of government to "allocate additional resources for alternatives to the current practice of criminalizing individuals with FASD" and "improve access to justice" while accommodating FASD (Canadian Bar Association (CBA), 2020). In 2012, the American Bar Association (ABA) passed a resolution to support "passage of laws, and adoption of policies at all levels of government" to better address the needs of those with FASD, advocating for treatment and training to enhance awareness of FASD and its impact on individuals in the child welfare, juvenile justice, and adult criminal justice systems (ABA, 2012). The latter resolution discusses why people with FASD should receive services from developmental disability organizations.

One example of the need for such resolutions is the extreme gullibility of persons with FASD, which can lead to false or exaggerated confessions. Adolescents have the right to pretrial motions that question the voluntariness of their confessions. The U.S. Supreme Court has held that sixth and 14th Amendment rights allow defendants to present evidence "about the physical and psychological environment in which the confession was obtained" (Crane v. Kentucky, 1986; Osher et al., 2002). In addition to significant behavioral problems, adolescents with FASD often are socially inept and inappropriate due to poor understanding of interpersonal boundaries. Impaired language and communication skills are underappreciated in this population, which has serious implications during interrogation, communication with counsel, following and participating in court proceedings, and understanding judicial rulings (Burd et al., 2010).

In 1997, the Center for Effective Collaboration and Practice at the American Institutes for Research concluded that the inability of community institutions (including the juvenile justice system) to respond to cognitive and behavioral impairments contributes to higher arrest rates for youths with disabilities as well as more restrictive and longer placements and higher recidivism rates (Osher et al., 2002). This report acknowledged many issues are interconnected. For example, lack of early intervention (often the case in FASD), early school failure, and school dropout interact with the system's ongoing failure to respond to adolescents with disabilities as their involvement with the criminal justice system progresses. In addition to finding that more restrictive sentences resulted in longer jail terms (often due to behavioral issues during incarceration), the report cited the justice system's failure to address initial criminal involvement as a primary factor in higher recidivism rates. Lack of aftercare was viewed as perhaps the most important determinant in avoiding recidivism.

In three important opinions, the Supreme Court has ruled consistently that imposing the most severe punishments on juveniles violates the ban on cruel and unusual punishment under the Eighth Amendment of the Constitution. The Court based these decisions on developmental research, concluding that because of developmental immaturity, adolescents were less culpable than adults and therefore deserved less punishment (National Research Council, 2013). In *Roper v. Simmons*, the Court held in 2005 that using the death penalty for a crime committed by a juvenile violated the Eighth Amendment's prohibition on cruel and unusual punishment. Five years later in Graham v. Florida (2010), the Court held that a sentence of life without parole for a nonhomicide offense by a juvenile was unconstitutional. In

2012, the Court found in *Miller v. Alabama* that a mandatory sentence of life without parole for a homicide committed by a juvenile was unconstitutional. These decisions not only highlight the Court's insistence on leniency for adolescents but also underscore many issues that allow advocacy for alternatives to detention for adolescents with disabilities.

In contrast to policies that support leniency for adolescents, several methods are used to transfer youths out of the juvenile justice system into the more severe and punitive adult criminal system (National Research Council, 2013). These include judicial waiver (also known as a discretionary waiver), by which juvenile court judges waive jurisdiction over a particular case and transfer it to adult court. A second method involves charging juveniles as adults by legislative exclusion (i.e., automatic transfer), wherein laws are passed that require all youths charged with certain offenses to be prosecuted in criminal court, even if they are below the age of criminal court jurisdiction. A third method is prosecutorial discretion, which involves prosecutors sending certain youthful offenders to juvenile court or criminal court. Prosecutorial discretion, also known as "concurrent jurisdiction," allows serious offenses to be initiated under the simultaneous jurisdiction of adult and juvenile court. Typically, states bear the burden of proving that criteria for transfer of juveniles to criminal court are met. Juveniles can contest waiver motions by challenging or producing evidence.

Notably, Centers for Disease Control and Prevention's (CDC) (2007) Task Force on Community Preventive Services found that transferring juveniles to the adult justice system increased rather than decreased rates of violence. For example, transferred juveniles were 34% more likely to be rearrested for violent or other crimes than juveniles retained in the juvenile justice system (McGowan et al., 2007). In contrast, a community reentry process involving 413 serious adolescent offenders released from juvenile court found those receiving court supervision, community-based support services, and intensive services had lower rates of formal system involvement (Chung, Schubert, & Mulvey, 2007). In addition, court supervision increased the likelihood of positive adjustment during community reentry. Thus, identifying disabilities that might have led to criminal involvement helps ensure adequate support services are in place for aftercare while also adding weight toward leniency in court.

According to model court guidelines developed by the National Council of Juvenile and Family Court Judges (2005), a youth's attorney has responsibility for investigating all circumstances behind allegations, seeking discovery for court records, appointing an investigator, and informing the youths and his/her family about the nature of the proceedings and potential consequences. The guidelines propose that statements made by a juvenile during court intake or the detention hearing should not be admissible at trial. The state is required to prove every element of an allegation beyond a reasonable doubt. If an adjudicatory hearing finds that a juvenile committed a delinquent act, a disposition hearing is scheduled. Once adjudicated, the dispositional hearing allows virtually all information bearing on the youth's life, family, schooling, and disabilities (National Research Council, 2013). Thus, the dispositional hearing offers the best opportunity to present evidence that impairments such as FASD may have contributed to an offense. A review of cases where an FASD diagnosis entered court deliberations found that the diagnosis improved outcomes (Williams, 2006). Conversely, the absence of a diagnosis made it easy for juveniles charged with violent offenses to be tried as adults.

While courts often use an IQ number to determine mitigation, comprehensive medical-legal evaluations can identify the extent to which impairments affect adolescents with FASD and support advocacy for alternatives to detention. Because of severe impairments in adaptive functioning and judgment, sentences for this population should include highly structured living situations that provide close supervision and daily support rather than punishments young offenders might be unable to connect with their crimes. Identification and treatment of co-existing psychiatric and substance use disorders will greatly increase the opportunity to avoid recidivism (Fast, Conry, & Loock, 1999). Although everyday adaptive functioning in this population usually falls within the ID range, many disability organizations do not recognize FASD as a disability when IQ exceeds 70. Consequently, when a 17-year-old adolescent who is age-eligible for placement in the adult criminal justice system has an IQ over 75 but the adaptive skills of a 10-year-old child (Burd et al., 2010), courts and state disability organizations typically dispute the adolescent's disability because of "normal"-appearing cognitive ability. For this reason, the forensic team's task is to educate the court on the nature of FASD as a brain-based disability with substantial adaptive behavior implications.

Attorneys representing clients with FASD should consider arguing that their clients were born with a developmental disability and have permanent brain damage that causes adaptive functioning identical to those with ID despite IQ. In other words, IQ is not the determinant of everyday behavior; adaptive functioning is. Thus, severe impairments in adaptive functioning, even in the presence of an average IQ, are equivalent to ID (Greenspan et al., 2016). Because of substantial adaptive dysfunction, without proper services, many juveniles with FASD are destined to perpetual cycles that include incarceration, unemployment, homelessness, substance abuse, and reincarceration. For this reason, attorneys need to assist and advocate for clients with FASD in applying for Supplemental Security Income (SSI) and developmental disability services. Introducing FASD as a static encephalopathy often is helpful in clarifying the brain-based nature of this disorder, similar to but often more extensive than the postnatal brain damage that occurs in traumatic brain injury.

Alternatives to incarceration include conditional sentences or diversion. Diversion permits treatment planning that can be initiated before adjudication. Conditional sentences permit young offenders to serve time in their homes or other non-criminal settings while obtaining treatment services and working or attending school. When seeking such alternatives, attorneys should be aware that adolescents with FASD will need intense supervision to prevent additional criminal behavior while awaiting adjudication. If courts require incarceration, attorneys should advocate for safeguards to keep inmates with FASD away from the negative influence of peers who will recognize their gullibility and prey upon them (Fast & Conry, 2009). Because people with FASD have great difficulty transitioning back to the community following incarceration, transitional support services must be in place to minimize recidivism. These services include coordinated case management, multidisciplinary court conferencing, permanency planning, stable housing, and support systems (Conger & Ross, 2001).

12.10 Intervention

The primary purpose for establishing an FASD diagnosis is to recommend interventions, reduce recidivism, and maximize opportunities for a productive life. Many adolescents come to the juvenile justice system following previous interventions throughout childhood that targeted behavioral and/or psychiatric challenges, leaving the primary neurological cause of these challenges unrecognized and undiagnosed. Adolescents may have a history of one or more psychiatric diagnoses such as ADHD, oppositional defiant disorder, conduct disorder, depression, anxiety, or posttraumatic stress disorder (PTSD), while a diagnosis of FASD has never been considered. Awareness of the risk factors for prenatal alcohol exposure and its attendant behavioral manifestations allows the forensic team to consider, refer, and obtain an FASD diagnosis. Such a diagnosis not only confers an argument for mitigating factors regarding an offense but guides interventions that are especially important in preventing criminal recidivism and establishing an alternative trajectory toward independence while acknowledging impairments that require ongoing support across the lifespan.

Needs assessment should guide the intervention plan. A study of 726 individuals with PAE in Canada, including 443 adolescents (12–17 years old), 135 transition-aged youths (18–24 years old), and 148 adults (25–60 years old), found high rates of difficulties in daily living, including independent living support needs (63%), alcohol misuse (38%), other substance use (46%), employment problems (37%), legal problems with offending (30%), assisted or sheltered housing (21%), school disruption (18%), legal problems with victimization (4%), and incarceration (3%), with greatest rates for adults and those with low intellectual ability (McLachlan, Flannigan, Temple, Unsworth, & Cook, 2020). This list highlights specific areas for anticipatory guidance in developing treatment and transition plans to address impairments and support individuals with FASD.

The Crossover Youth Practice Model (CYPM) is an example of comprehensive interventions that support adolescents involved with the justice system (Lutz, Stewart, Legters, & Herz, 2015). Developed by Casey Family Programs and the Center for Juvenile Justice Reform at the Georgetown University Public Policy Institute, CYPM addresses the needs of the large number of juvenile offenders in foster care but can be adapted easily to serve adolescents diagnosed with FASD. CYPM uses a strength-based perspective to reduce (a) the number of youths placed in out-of-home care, (b) use of congregate care, (c) the disproportionate representation of youths of color, particularly crossover youths, and (d) the number of youths in foster care who become involved in the juvenile justice system. This model begins with addressing offense charges, case evaluation and planning, coordinated case management and ongoing assessment, and youths permanency, transition planning, and case closure (Lutz et al., 2015). CYPM's focus on transition planning is one example of the extensive services needed for adjudicated adolescents with FASD. Streissguth et al. (1996) identified living in a stable nurturing home with minimal household changes as one of the most important protective factors in FASD. Other protective factors include early diagnosis, eligibility for developmental disability services, and protection from exposure to violence. Juvenile justice system involvement provides an opportunity to establish interventions that promote these protective factors and positive development through diagnosis, application for disability services, and permanency planning to maximize day-to-day stability.

Research suggests two categories of adolescent offenders: those who offend only in their teens and those who continue offending well into their adult years (Moffitt, 1993). In a follow-up study of 728 juvenile offenders, the following risk factors were associated with recidivism: number of past offenses, young age at first offense, stranger victims, criminal behavior in the family, history of physical and emotional abuse, poor treatment adherence, and lack of positive coping strategies (Mulder, Brand, Bullens, & van Marle, 2011). Because adolescents with FASD have many of these risk factors, interventions should be guided by two objectives: ensuring treatment adherence while providing treatments that support development of positive coping strategies. Juveniles affected by FASD need intensive interventions that address social skills, behavioral management, attitudes, and perceptions. Examples include multisystemic therapy and functional family therapy, both of which are especially effective for adolescents with mental health and substance use disorders (Braverman et al., 2011). A structured and closely supervised therapeutic behavioral milieu that uses positive reinforcement rather than punishment is perhaps the most effective alternative to incarceration (Petrenko, 2015).

In addition to identifying and establishing interventions that specifically address the impairments associated with FASD, comorbid mental health disorders must be addressed. In one study of 1024 juveniles in detention, 60% had one or more psychiatric disorders, but only 20% of those with depression and 10% of those with other disorders received treatment (Domalanta, Risser, Roberts, & Risser, 2003). The same study found 36% of detained juveniles were diagnosed with a substance abuse disorder and 27% were diagnosed with alcohol abuse, yet fewer than half who required treatment received appropriate intervention. Similarly, the presence of PTSD and attachment disorders in individuals with FASD, especially those with impairments in emotional dysregulation, present possible targeted interventions that focus on effective coping strategies, psychiatric treatment, and environmental supports to decrease risk during times of increased stress or challenge later in life (Temple, Cook, Unsworth, Rajani, & Mela, 2019). Use of psychotropic medications, when appropriate, can augment comprehensive individualized mental health treatment plans that include individual, group, and family therapy (Penn & Thomas,

2005). Supportive relationships with family, peers, and members of the treatment team significantly increase the likelihood of engaging adolescents in services.

Treatment plans also should address educational and vocational needs. A Survey of Youth in Residential Placement found 21% of juvenile offenders were not enrolled in school at the time they entered custody (Braverman et al., 2011). This rate was more than four times the rate of peers in the general population. In addition, 48% were functioning below grade level, and 25% had been held back a year in school. Up to 61% of these youths reported being expelled or suspended in the year before entering custody. Given the likelihood many of these juveniles had FASD, adjudication was the only opportunity for diagnosis and treatment planning to address their educational needs. Despite the requirement in the IDEA that the educational needs of youths in custody be identified and addressed with special education services if appropriate, only 46% of juveniles reported special education services while in custody (Braverman et al., 2011).

Finally, vocational training and associated support services are crucial for successfully transitioning this population to the community while at the same time minimizing risk of recidivism. Youths with FASD identify this transition period as the most significant challenge in their lives. Because most have been raised in unstable homes with unreliable caregivers, the bridge to adulthood is precarious and fraught with pitfalls. In addition to poor family support, adaptive difficulties in completing age-expected tasks turn simple tasks (e.g., following probation rules and directions, getting to work or appointments on time, interacting appropriately with others) into insurmountable obstacles without appropriate services. Therefore, transition plans should include vocational assessment and employment readiness training (e.g., how to schedule and ensure appointment punctuality, following directions, appropriate workplace social behavior) as well as support in finding employment and job coaching. Adaptive assessments during the diagnostic evaluation process should contain information about specific weaknesses in daily living skills (e.g., hygiene, nutrition, shopping, cooking, paying bills) that also should be addressed during transition. Most adolescents with FASD will need ongoing support and supervision for adaptive tasks that overwhelm capacity as they attempt to meet adult responsibilities.

Although adolescents with FASD may appear confident about managing age-appropriate tasks, this apparent self-confidence often masks impairments in adaptive skills and low self-esteem. Environmental supports are just as important as treatment services. Without ongoing support during transition to adulthood to accommodate deficient executive functioning and associated adaptive impairments, treatment services—no matter how extensive—are unlikely to result in a successful transition to independence and productive integration into society. Independent living programs, subsidized rent programs, and home health-care services in addition to the services addressed earlier in this chapter can facilitate a successful transition to adulthood and maximize independence (Burnside & Fuchs, 2013).

Table 12.1 Prenatal and Neurodevelopmental Assessment Worksheet

Prenatal and neurodevelopmental assessment

Child's name:
Date of birth:
Date of evaluation:
Evaluator:

No.	Symptoms	Never	Sometimes	Often
1.	Forgets to do what he or she was just asked to do	0	1	2
2.	Often loses things	0	1	2
3.	Difficulty following simple directions	0	1	2
4.	Difficulty transitioning from activity to activity	0	1	2
5.	Difficulty remembering recently learned information or skills	0	1	2
6.	Difficulty following multiple-step or verbal instructions	0	1	2
7.	Makes the same mistakes over and over	0	1	2
8.	Clumsy, always bumping into things	0	1	2
9.	Writes letters and words not clearly or backward	0	1	2
10.	Difficulty learning or repeated a grade	0	1	2
11.	Has temper tantrums and outbursts that seem to come out of nowhere	0	1	2
12.	Cannot sit still, always on the go	0	1	2
13.	Difficulty falling asleep or wakes frequently at night	0	1	2
14.	Sensitive to sounds, light, or touch	0	1	2
15.	Difficulty paying attention	0	1	2
16.	Does not think before acting	0	1	2
17.	Difficulty waiting for his or her turn	0	1	2
18.	Hits other children or adults, gets into fights, or yells at adults	0	1	2
19.	Touches other children or adults inappropriately	0	1	2
20.	Takes other's property (toys, food, clothes, money)	0	1	2
21.	Has or previously had a delay in the development of speech	0	1	2
22.	Difficulty following a conversation or reading social cues	0	1	2
23.	Acts younger than his or her age	0	1	2
24.	Overly friendly to strangers	0	1	2

(continued)

Table 12.1 (continued)

25.	Difficulty fitting in with kids in her or his age group, prefers to play with younger children	0	1	2
26.	Gullible and easily talked into doing actions they might not otherwise do	0	1	2
27.	Difficulty understanding consequences of actions	0	1	2
28.	Needs constant reminding to complete daily living skills such as dressing, eating, showering, brushing teeth, using the toilet, or managing a daily schedule	0	1	2
29.	Current or past delay in walking, running, climbing	0	1	2
30.	Difficulty making eye contact when speaking or listening to others	0	1	2
31.	Difficulties with behavior before age 5	0	1	2

Total score: _______________ (scores >30 should be referred for evaluation even in the absence of documented prenatal alcohol exposure)

Screening for prenatal alcohol exposure:

☐ When did you (or the child's birth mother) find out you (she) were (was) pregnant?

☐ How many drinks of alcohol a day/week did you (or the child's birth mother) drink prior to discovering the pregnancy?

☐ How many drinks of alcohol a day/week did you (or the child's birth mother) drink after discovering the pregnancy?

(if birth mother drank 6 or more drinks per week for two or more weeks in pregnancy or greater than 3 or more drinks at one time on two or more occasions during pregnancy, this information constitutes a positive screen.)

Risks for prenatal alcohol exposure:

☐ The birth mother received treatment for alcohol or substance use disorder

☐ The child was previously in foster care or the care of someone other than the child's mother

☐ Child or child's sibling born positive to drugs or alcohol or diagnosed with an FASD

☐ Child/adolescent's report of the birth mother's drinking or drinking-related problems

☐ Other reliable informants report about the mother's drinking or drinking-related problems; specify source: _______________________

☐ Death of mother from complications of alcohol use (e.g., cirrhosis, suicide)

(each of these risk factors is an additive risk for prenatal alcohol exposure, and any positive response should prompt further FASD evaluation.)

References

American Academy of Pediatrics. (2018). *The screening for prenatal exposure to alcohol: An implementation guide for pediatric primary care providers*. https://www.aap.org/en-us/Documents/FASD_PAE_Implementation_Guide_FINAL.pdf

American Bar Association (ABA). (2012). *FASD resolution*. https://www.americanbar.org/groups/public_interest/child_law/resources/attorneys/fasd-resolution/

American Psychiatric Association (APA). (2013). *Diagnostic and statistical manual of mental disorder (DSM-5)* (5th ed.). Arlington, VA: American Psychiatric Association.

Astley, S. J. (2010). Profile of the first 1,400 patients receiving diagnostic evaluations for fetal alcohol spectrum disorder at the Washington State fetal alcohol syndrome diagnostic & prevention network. *Canadian Journal of Clinical Pharmacology = Journal canadien de pharmacologie clinique, 17*(1), e132–e164.

Baidawi, S., & Piquero, A. R. (2020). Neurodisability among children at the nexus of the child welfare and youth justice system. *Journal of Youth and Adolescence*, 1–17. https://doi.org/10.1007/s10964-020-01234-w

Bisgard, E. B., Fisher, S., Adubato, S., & Louis, M. (2010). Screening, diagnosis, and intervention with juvenile offenders. *Journal of Psychiatry and Law, 38*(4), 475–506. https://doi.org/10.1177/009318531003800406

Braverman, P. K., Murray, P. J., Adelman, W. P., Breuner, C. C., Levine, D. A., Marcell, A. V., … Shain, B. (2011). Health care for youth in the juvenile justice system. *Pediatrics, 128*(6), 1219–1235. https://doi.org/10.1542/peds.2011-1757

Brown, J. M., Haun, J., Zapf, P. A., & Novick Brown, N. (2017). Fetal alcohol spectrum disorder (FASD) and competency to stand trial (CST): Suggestions for a "best practices" approach to forensic evaluation. *International Journal of Law and Psychiatry, 52*, 19–27. https://doi.org/10.1016/j.ijlp.2017.04.002

Bukstein, O. G. (2000). Disruptive behavior disorders and substance use disorders in adolescents. *Journal of Psychoactive Drugs, 32*(1), 67–79. https://doi.org/10.1080/02791072.2000.10400213

Burd, L., Cohen, C., Shah, R., & Norris, J. (2011). A court team model for young children in foster care: The role of prenatal alcohol exposure and fetal alcohol spectrum disorders. *Journal of Psychiatry and Law, 39*(1), 179–191. https://doi.org/10.1177/009318531103900107

Burd, L., Fast, D. K., Conry, J., & Williams, A. (2010). Fetal alcohol spectrum disorder as a marker for increased risk of involvement with correction systems. *Journal of Psychiatry and Law, 38*(4), 559–583. https://doi.org/10.1177/009318531003800408

Burd, L., Klug, M. G., Martsolf, J. T., Martsolf, C., Deal, E., & Kerbeshian, J. (2006). A staged screening strategy for prenatal alcohol exposure and maternal risk stratification. *Journal of the Royal Society for the Promotion of Health, 126*(2), 86–94. https://doi.org/10.1177/1466424006063184

Burd, L., Martsolf, J. T., & Juelson, T. (2004). Fetal alcohol spectrum disorder in the corrections system: Potential screening strategies. *Journal of Fetal Alcohol Syndrome International, 2*, e1–e10. http://adaiclearinghouse.net/downloads/Fetal-Alcohol-Spectrum-Disorders-FASD-and-the-Criminal-Justice-System-498.pdf

Burd, L., Selfridge, R., Klug, M., & Bakko, S. (2004). Fetal alcohol syndrome in the United States corrections system. *Addiction Biology, 9*(2), 169–176. https://doi.org/10.1080/13556210410001717060

Burnside, L., & Fuchs, D. (2013). Bound by the clock: The experiences of youth with FASD transitioning to adulthood from child welfare care. *First Peoples Child & Family Review, 8*(1), 40–61. https://fpcfr.journals.publicknowledgeproject.org/index.php/FPCFR/article/view/200

Canadian Bar Association (CBA). (2020). *Fetal alcohol spectrum disorder in the criminal justice system.* https://www.cba.org/getattachment/Our-Work/Resolutions/Resolutions/2010/Fetal-Alcohol-Spectrum-Disorder-in-the-Criminal-Ju/10-02-A.pdf

Centers for Disease Control and Prevention (CDC). (2007). Violence prevention: Policies facilitating the transfer of juveniles to adult justice systems. *Systematic Review.* https://www.thecommunityguide.org/findings/violence-prevention-policies-facilitating-transfer-juveniles-adult-justice-systems

Chasnoff, I. J., Wells, A. M., & King, L. (2015). Misdiagnosis and missed diagnoses in foster and adopted children with prenatal alcohol exposure. *Pediatrics, 135*(2), 264–270. https://doi.org/10.1542/peds.2014-2171

Child Welfare Information Gateway. (2014). *Parental substance use and the child welfare system.* U.S. Department of Health and Human Services (HHS). https://www.childwelfare.gov/pubPDFs/parentalsubabuse.pdf

Chung, H. L., Schubert, C. A., & Mulvey, E. P. (2007). An empirical portrait of community reentry among serious juvenile offenders in two metropolitan cities. *Criminal Justice and Behavior, 34*(11), 1402–1426. https://doi.org/10.1177/0093854807307170

Conger, D., & Ross, T. (2001). *Reducing the foster care bias in juvenile detention decisions: The impact of project confirm.* New York: Vera Institute of Justice. https://www.vera.org/publications/reducing-the-foster-care-bias-in-juvenile-detention-decisions-the-impact-of-project-confirm

Crane v. Kentucky (1986). 476 U.S. 683.

Day, N. L., Helsel, A., Sonon, K., & Goldschmidt, L. (2013). The association between prenatal alcohol exposure and behavior at 22 years of age. *Alcoholism: Clinical and Experimental Research, 37*(7), 1171–1178. https://doi.org/10.1111/acer.12073

Demirci, A., & Kartal, M. (2018). Sociocultural risk factors for developmental delay in children aged 3–60 months: A nested case-control study. *European Journal of Pediatrics, 177*(5), 691–697. https://doi.org/10.1007/s00431-018-3109-y

Denny, C. H., Acero, C. S., Naimi, T. S., & Kim, S. Y. (2019). Consumption of alcohol beverages and binge drinking among pregnant women aged 18-44 years—United States, 2015–2017. *Morbidity and Mortality Weekly Report, 68*(16), 365. https://doi.org/10.15585/mmwr.mm6816a1

Domalanta, D. D., Risser, W. L., Roberts, R. E., & Risser, J. M. H. (2003). Prevalence of depression and other psychiatric disorders among incarcerated youths. *Journal of the American Academy of Child and Adolescent Psychiatry, 42*(4), 477–484. https://doi.org/10.1097/01.CHI.0000046819.95464.0B

Ethen, M. K., Ramadhani, T. A., Scheuerle, A. E., Canfield, M. A., Wyszynski, D. F., Druschel, C. M., & Romitti, P. A. (2009). Alcohol consumption by women before and during pregnancy. *Maternal and Child Health Journal, 13*(2), 274–285. https://doi.org/10.1007/s10995-008-0328-2

Fast, D. K., & Conry, J. (2009). Fetal alcohol spectrum disorders and the criminal justice system. *Developmental Disabilities Research Reviews, 15*(3), 250–257. https://doi.org/10.1002/ddrr.66

Fast, D. K., Conry, J., & Loock, C. A. (1999). Identifying fetal alcohol syndrome among youth in the criminal justice system. *Journal of Developmental and Behavioral Pediatrics, 20*(5), 370–372. https://doi.org/10.1097/00004703-199910000-00012

Graham v. Florida. (2010) 560 US 48.

Greenspan, S., Novick Brown, N., & Edwards, W. (2016). FASD and the concept of "intellectual disability equivalence.". In M. Nelson & M. Trussler (Eds.), *Law and ethics in fetal alcohol spectrum disorder* (pp. 241–266). Amsterdam: Springer.

Guerri, C., Bazinet, A., & Riley, E. P. (2009). Foetal alcohol spectrum disorders and alterations in brain and behaviour. *Alcohol and Alcoholism, 44*(2), 108–114. https://doi.org/10.1093/alcalc/agn105

Herz, D. C., Ryan, J. P., & Bilchik, S. (2010). Challenges facing crossover youth: An examination of juvenile-justice decision making and recidivism. *Family Court Review, 48*(2), 305–321. https://doi.org/10.1111/j.1744-1617.2010.01312.x

Hoyme, H. E., Kalberg, W. O., Elliott, A. J., Blankenship, J., Buckley, D., Marais, A. S., … May, P. A. (2016). Updated clinical guidelines for diagnosing fetal alcohol spectrum disorders. *Pediatrics, 138*(2), e20154256. https://doi.org/10.1542/peds.2015-4256

Jones, K. L., Smith, D. W., Ulleland, C. N., & Streissguth, A. P. (1973). Pattern of malformation in offspring of chronic alcoholic mothers. *Lancet, 301*(7815), 1267–1271. https://doi.org/10.1016/s0140-6736(73)91291-9

Kable, J. A., & Coles, C. D. (2018). Evidence supporting the internal validity of the proposed ND-PAE disorder. *Child Psychiatry and Human Development, 49*(2), 163–175. https://doi.org/10.1007/s10578-017-0738-8

Katsiyannis, A., Ryan, J. B., Zhang, D., & Spann, A. (2008). Juvenile delinquency and recidivism: The impact of academic achievement. *Reading & Writing Quarterly, 24*(2), 177–196. https://doi.org/10.1080/10573560701808460

Lange, S., Shield, K., Koren, G., Rehm, J., & Popova, S. (2014). A comparison of the prevalence of prenatal alcohol exposure obtained via maternal self-reports versus meconium testing: A systematic literature review and meta-analysis. *BMC Pregnancy and Childbirth, 14*(1), 127. https://doi.org/10.1186/1471-2393-14-127

Lange, S., Shield, K., Rehm, J., & Popova, S. (2013). Prevalence of fetal alcohol spectrum disorders in a child care settings: A meta-analysis. *Pediatrics, 132*(4), e980–e995. https://doi.org/10.1542/peds.2013-0066

Lutz, L., Stewart, M., Legters, L., & Herz, D. (2015). *The crossover youth practice model (CYPM): An abbreviated guide*. Washington, DC: Center for Juvenile Justice Reform, McCourt School of Public Policy, Georgetown University. https://cjjr.georgetown.edu/wp-content/uploads/2015/09/CYPM-Abbreviated-Guide.pdf.

Maier, S. E., & West, J. R. (2001). Drinking patterns and alcohol-related birth defects. *Alcohol Research and Health, 25*(3), 168–169.

Mattson, S. N., Crocker, N., & Nguyen, T. T. (2011). Fetal alcohol spectrum disorders: Neuropsychological and behavioral features. *Neuropsychology Review, 21*(2), 81–101. https://doi.org/10.1007/s11065-011-9167-9

May, P. A., Chambers, C. D., Kalberg, W. O., Zellner, J., Feldman, H., Buckley, D., … Hoyme, H. E. (2018). Prevalence of fetal alcohol spectrum disorders in 4 US communities. *JAMA: Journal of the American Medical Association, 319*(5), 474–482. https://doi.org/10.1001/jama.2017.21896

May, P. A., & Gossage, J. P. (2011). Maternal risk factors for fetal alcohol spectrum disorders: Not as simple as it might seem. *Alcohol Research and Health, 34*(1), 15–26. http://pubs.niaaa.nih.gov/publications/arh341/15-26.htm.

May, P. A., Gossage, J. P., Kalberg, W. O., Robinson, L. K., Buckley, D., Manning, M., & Hoyme, H. E. (2009). Prevalence and epidemiologic characteristics of FASD from various research methods with an emphasis on recent in-school studies. *Developmental Disabilities Research Reviews, 15*(3), 176–192. https://doi.org/10.1002/ddrr.68

McGowan, A., Hahn, R., Liberman, A., Crosby, A., Fullilove, M., Johnson, R., … Stone, G. (2007). Effects on violence of laws and policies facilitating the transfer of juveniles from the juvenile justice system to the adult justice system: A systematic review. *American Journal of Preventive Medicine, 32*(Suppl. 4), 7–28. https://doi.org/10.1016/j.amepre.2006.12.003

McLachlan, K., Flannigan, K., Temple, V., Unsworth, K., & Cook, J. L. (2020). Difficulties in daily living experienced by adolescents, transition-aged youth, and adults with fetal alcohol spectrum disorder. *Alcoholism: Clinical and Experimental Research, 44*(8), 1609–1624.

McLachlan, K., Roesch, R., Viljoen, J. L., & Douglas, K. S. (2014). Evaluating the psycholegal abilities of young offenders with fetal alcohol spectrum disorder. *Law and Human Behavior, 38*(1), 10–22. https://doi.org/10.1037/lhb0000037

McQuire, C., Paranjothy, S., Hurt, L., Mann, M., Farewell, D., & Kemp, A. (2016). Objective measures of prenatal alcohol exposure: A systematic review. *Pediatrics, 138*(3), e20160517. https://doi.org/10.1542/peds.2016-0517

Miller v. Alabama. (2012). 567 U.S. 460.

Moffitt, T. E. (1993). Adolescence-limited and life-course-persistent antisocial behavior: A developmental taxonomy. *Psychological Review, 100*(4), 674–701. https://doi.org/10.1037/0033-295X.100.4.674

Moore, E. M., Migliorini, R., Infante, M. A., & Riley, E. P. (2014). Fetal alcohol spectrum disorders: Recent neuroimaging findings. *Current Developmental Disorders Reports, 1*(3), 161–172. https://doi.org/10.1007/s40474-014-0020-8

Mulder, E., Brand, E., Bullens, R., & van Marle, H. (2011). Risk factors for overall recidivism and severity of recidivism in serious juvenile offenders. *International Journal of Offender Therapy and Comparative Criminology, 55*(1), 118–135. https://doi.org/10.1177/0306624X09356683

National Council of Juvenile and Family Court Judges. (2005). *Juvenile delinquency guidelines: Improving court practice in juvenile delinquency cases*. Reno, NV: NCOJFCJ. https://www.ncjfcj.org/wp-content/uploads/2019/10/Juvenile-Delinquency-Guidelines.pdf.

National Research Council. (2013). *Reforming juvenile justice: A developmental approach*. Washington, DC: National Academies Press.

O'Connor, M. J. (2014). Mental health outcomes associated with prenatal alcohol exposure: Genetic and environmental factors. *Current Developmental Disorders Reports, 1*(3), 181–188. https://doi.org/10.1007/s40474-014-0021-7

Osher, D., Quinn, M. M., Kendziora, K., Woodruff, D., & Rouse, G. (2002). *Addressing invisible barriers: Improving outcomes for youth with disabilities in the juvenile justice system*. College Park, MD: Center for Effective Collaboration and Practice, American Institutes for Research. https://files.eric.ed.gov/fulltext/ED471035.pdf.

Penn, J. V., & Thomas, C. (2005). Practice parameter for the assessment and treatment of youth in juvenile detention and correctional facilities. *Journal of the American Academy of Child and Adolescent Psychiatry, 44*(10), 1085–1098. https://doi.org/10.1097/01.chi.0000175325.14481.21

Petrenko, C. L. M. (2015). Positive behavioral interventions and family support for fetal alcohol spectrum disorders. *Current Developmental Disorders Reports, 2*(3), 199–209. https://doi.org/10.1007/s40474-015-0052-8

Popova, S., Lange, S., Bekmuradov, D., Mihic, A., & Rehm, J. (2011). Fetal alcohol spectrum disorder prevalence estimates in correctional systems: A systematic literature review. *Canadian Journal of Public Health, 102*(5), 336–340. https://doi.org/10.1007/bf03404172

Riley, E. P., & McGee, C. L. (2005). Fetal alcohol spectrum disorders: An overview with emphasis on changes in brain and behavior. *Experimental Biology and Medicine, 230*(6), 357–365. https://doi.org/10.1177/15353702-0323006-03

Roebuck, T. M., Mattson, S. N., & Riley, E. P. (1998). A review of the neuroanatomical findings in children with fetal alcohol syndrome or prenatal exposure to alcohol. *Alcoholism: Clinical and Experimental Research, 22*(2), 339–344. https://doi.org/10.1111/j.1530-0277.1998.tb03658.x

Roper v. Simmons. (2005). 541 U.S. 1040.

Schuckit, M. A. (2009). An overview of genetic influences in alcoholism. *Journal of Substance Abuse Treatment, 36*(1), S5–S14.

Stinson, J. D., & Robbins, S. B. (2014). Characteristics of people with intellectual disabilities in a secure U.S. forensic hospital. *Journal of Mental Health Research in Intellectual Disabilities, 7*(4), 337–358. https://doi.org/10.1080/19315864.2014.930549

Stoler, J. M., & Holmes, L. B. (1999). Under-recognition of prenatal alcohol effects in infants of known alcohol abusing women. *Journal of Pediatrics, 135*(4), 430–436. https://doi.org/10.1016/s0022-3476(99)70164-2

Stratton, K., Howe, C., & Battaglia, F. (Eds.). (1996). *Fetal alcohol syndrome: Diagnosis, epidemiology, prevention, and treatment*. Washington, DC: National Academy Press.

Streissguth, A. P., Barr, H. M., Kogan, J., & Bookstein, F. L. (1996). *Final report: Understanding the occurrence of secondary disabilities in clients with fetal alcohol syndrome (FAS) and fetal alcohol effects (FAE)*. Seattle, WA: University of Washington Publication Services.

Sundermann, A. C., Zhao, S., Young, C. L., Lam, L., Jones, S. H., Velez Edwards, D. R., & Hartmann, K. E. (2019). Alcohol use in pregnancy and miscarriage: A systematic review and meta-analysis. *Alcoholism: Clinical and Experimental Research, 43*(8), 1606–1616. https://doi.org/10.1111/acer.14124

Teicher, M. H., Samson, J. A., Anderson, C. M., & Ohashi, K. (2016). The effects of childhood maltreatment on brain structure, function, and connectivity. *Nature Reviews Neuroscience, 17*(10), 652–666. https://doi.org/10.1038/nrn.2016.111

Temple, V. K., Cook, J. L., Unsworth, K., Rajani, H., & Mela, M. (2019). Mental health and affect regulation in fetal alcohol spectrum disorder (FASD): Results from the Canadian National FASD Database. *Alcohol and Alcoholism, 54*(5), 545–550. https://doi.org/10.1093/alcalc/agz049

United States Department of Education (1990) accessed at https://sites.ed.gov/idea/about-idea/

United States Department of Justice, Civil Rights Division (1990), accessed at https://sites.ed.gov/idea/about-idea/

Van der Kolk, B. A. (2017). Developmental trauma disorder: Toward a rational diagnosis for children with complex trauma histories. *Psychiatric Annals, 35*(5), 401–408. https://doi.org/10.3928/00485713-20050501-06

Waite, D., Greiner, M. V., & Laris, Z. (2018). "Putting families first": How the opioid epidemic is affecting children and families, and the child welfare policy options to address it. *Journal of Applied Research on Children, 9*(1), 4. https://digitalcommons.library.tmc.edu/childrenatrisk/vol9/iss1/4.

Weyrauch, D., Schwartz, M., Hart, B., Klug, M. G., & Burd, L. (2017). Comorbid mental disorders in fetal alcohol spectrum disorders: A systematic review. *Journal of Developmental and Behavioral Pediatrics, 38*(4), 283–291. https://doi.org/10.1097/dbp.0000000000000440

Williams, S. J. (2006). *Is there justice in the juvenile justice system?: Examining the role of fetal alcohol spectrum disorders*. U.S. Department of Health and Human Services (HHS), Center on juvenile and criminal justice. *Justice Policy Journal, 3*(1), 1–15. http://www.cjcj.org/uploads/cjcj/documents/is_there.pdf.

Wozniak, J. R., Mueller, B. A., Mattson, S. N., Coles, C. D., Kable, J. A., Jones, K. L., … Sowell, E. R. (2017). Functional connectivity abnormalities and associated cognitive deficits in fetal alcohol spectrum disorders (FASD). *Brain Imaging and Behavior, 11*(5), 1432–1445. https://doi.org/10.1007/s11682-016-9624-4

Wozniak, J. R., Riley, E. P., & Charness, M. E. (2019). Diagnosis, epidemiology, assessment, pathophysiology, and management of fetal alcohol spectrum disorders. *Lancet Neurology, 18*(8), 760–777. https://doi.org/10.1016/S1474-4422(19)30150-4

Young, N. K., Boles, S. M., & Otero, C. (2007). Parental substance use disorders and child maltreatment: Overlap, gaps, and opportunities. *Child Maltreatment, 12*(2), 137–149. https://doi.org/10.1177/1077559507300322

Young, N. K., Gardner, S., Otero, C., Dennis, K., Chang, R., Earle, K., & Amatetti, S. (2009). Substance-exposed infants: State responses to the problem. HHS Pub. No. (SMA) 09-4369. Rockville, MD: Substance Abuse and Mental Health Services Administration.

Chapter 13
Forensic Neuroscience and Violence Risk Assessment in Prenatal Drug Exposure Cases

John Matthew Fabian

Abstract This chapter addresses forensic assessment of persons exposed prenatally to substances of abuse and the relationship of such exposure to violence. In addition to alcohol, this chapter's focus includes other drugs commonly used by high-risk mothers during pregnancy, such as stimulants (methamphetamine, cocaine, 3,4-methylenedioxymethamphetamine [MDMA], commonly referred to as ecstasy), cannabis and nicotine, and opioids such as heroin. The brain-based effects of these substances on postnatal functioning are examined, with particular emphasis on brain-behavior relationships as they affect criminal behavior and violence. This chapter describes how this information may be used in forensic legal proceedings pertaining to mitigation and violence risk assessment and offers an empirically driven and structured violence risk assessment approach that emphasizes distinctive risk factors for offenders with significant prenatal substance use exposure.

Keywords Forensic neuroscience · Prenatal drug exposure · Violence · Risk assessment

13.1 Introduction

There is a myriad of risk factors that place young people at risk for delinquency in adolescence and criminality in adulthood (Fabian, 2009). These risk factors can be considered from a biopsychosocial perspective that includes prenatal exposure to substances of abuse as well as a diverse set of multiple environmental risk factors (Herrenkohl et al., 2000; Herrenkohl, Hawkins, Chung, Hill, & Battin-Pearson, 2001). A risk factor analysis pursuant to the US Department of Justice Office of

J. M. Fabian (✉)
Department of Psychiatry and Behavioral Sciences, University of Texas Health Sciences Center at Houston McGovern Medical School, Houston, TX, USA
e-mail: john@johnmatthewfabian.com

N. Novick Brown (ed.), *Evaluating Fetal Alcohol Spectrum Disorders in the Forensic Context*, https://doi.org/10.1007/978-3-030-73628-6_13

Justice Programs, Office of Juvenile Justice and Delinquency Prevention (OJJDP), risk factor paradigm highlights *individual*, *family*, *school*, *peer group*, and *community* risk factor domains (Shader, 2003). Generally, high-risk youths that engage in juvenile and adult criminality often have high-risk parents who are poorly educated, frequently unemployed, and engage in domestic violence, substance abuse, and criminality. High-risk families often reside in high-risk urban environments with exposure to weapons, guns, and drugs. Offspring in these families are at risk of (a) being exposed to prenatal substance use; (b) experiencing abuse, parental separation, and neglect; (c) having neurodevelopmental conditions such as attention deficit hyperactivity disorder (ADHD) and learning disorder; and (d) developing both conduct disorder and substance use disorders. Thus, prenatal substance abuse by pregnant women places these youths at risk for a number of these negative outcomes.

13.2 Biopsychosocial and Neurodevelopmental Risk Factors in Violence

Fabian (2018) highlighted pre-, peri-, and postnatal violence risk factors in forensic psychological and neuropsychological criminal offender evaluations. Early risk factors leading to neuropsychological impairment are described in Box 13.1.

Box 13.1: Pre-, Peri-, and Post-risk Factors in Violence

1. Young age of mother during pregnancy
2. Low parental education
3. Maternal alcohol, nicotine, and drug use during pregnancy and during labor
4. Infant drug-positive test at birth
5. Mother victimized by domestic violence during pregnancy, causing prenatal vulnerability to central nervous system (CNS) dysfunction
6. Poor maternal diet and medical care during pregnancy
7. Maternal depression and mental illness during pregnancy
8. Fetal maldevelopment, minor physical abnormalities, and fetal alcohol syndrome (FAS).
9. Low birth weight
10. Low heart rate at birth
11. Perinatal birth complications, including oxygen deprivation at birth
12. Parental criminality and substance abuse
13. Parental mental illness
14. Exposure to parental physical abuse and emotional neglect
15. Lack of attachment to primary caregivers
16. Exposure to parental domestic violence between parents

17. Exposure to housing instability and deplorable home conditions
18. Exposure to toxins, lead, parasites, and infection
19. Poor socioeconomic conditions
20. Lack of attachment to community resources
21. Deficient parental and offspring education
22. Lack of parental involvement with the child
23. Substance abuse and dependence history (brain dysfunction is more common among individuals with these problems and more likely to be associated with preexisting neurological conditions)
24. Experience of violent victimization within the community
25. Exposure to polytrauma/polyvictimization and complex trauma
26. Exposure to early head injury and neuropsychological and psychological symptoms of posttraumatic stress disorder (PTSD)
27. History of ADHD
28. History of language-based learning disorders

Thus, it is not unusual to see defendants with mothers who had teen pregnancies characterized by alcohol and drug use, domestic violence, deficient prenatal care, and poor nutrition who then tested positive for substances at birth and delivered infants with potential neonatal abstinence syndrome (NAS), which involves physiological and neurobehavioral symptoms and withdrawal in newborns exposed to psychotropic substances in utero. Their offspring, in turn, suffered from one or more neurodevelopmental disorders in childhood while also witnessing domestic violence and substance use during their childhood years. Certainly, a child's developmental risk for violence is impacted by a diverse set of variables such as these, which ultimately have a dose-dependent interaction.

13.3 Prenatal Nicotine Use

Prenatal exposure to tobacco smoke is associated with numerous adverse health effects in newborns, infants, children, adolescents, and adults. Most empirical studies, including recent epidemiological studies, reveal a higher likelihood of ADHD or ADHD symptoms in prenatally exposed versus nonexposed offspring, yet human and animal studies tend to be ambiguous regarding causality (Tiesler & Heinrich, 2014). Prenatal nicotine exposure is associated with altered brain structure and function in offspring with a proposed biological mechanism related to nicotine's adverse influence on neurotransmitter systems during brain development (Benowitz, Hukkanen, & Jacob III, 2009). Obviously, youths can be affected by prenatal substance use but also by secondhand smoke (Öberg, Jaakkola, Prüss-Üstün, Schweizer, & Woodward, 2010).

Nicotine is an alkaloid chemical compound found in tobacco smoke. Once in the bloodstream, nicotine is dispersed throughout the body to various tissues, including the brain, lungs, and liver, before the liver metabolizes it for excretion from the body through urine. Nicotine can pass through the placental barrier, thereby transferring from maternal circulation to the fetus (Pastrakuljic et al., 1998).

Prenatal exposure to nicotine may be examined via questionnaires administered to birth mothers regarding their prenatal smoking habits, but such inquiry can lead to denial or recall bias, such as fear of admitting such use if aware of the negative health effects. Prenatal exposure also may be measured by exposure-specific biomarkers in the biological matrices of mother and/or child (Cnattingius, 2004). Epidemiological studies in Europe revealed maternal smoking prevalence between 14 and 38% and more recently, researchers (Azagba, Manzione, Shan, & King, 2020) found the prevalence of smoking during pregnancy (SDP) in the United States decreased from 9.2% in 2010 to 6.9% in 2017.

Maternal cigarette smoking is associated with a number of adverse health effects on the newborn in a dose-response relationship. Smoking-related risk factors for newborns include pregnancy complications and preterm delivery, low birth weight, and sudden infant death syndrome (Abbott & Winzer-Serhan, 2012). Secondhand smoke also carries risk. For example, Salmasi, Grady, Jones, and McDonald (2010) conducted a meta-analysis on environmental tobacco smoke exposure and perinatal outcomes, finding significant correlations between environmental tobacco smoke exposure and lower birth weight, congenital anomalies, longer birth length, and smaller neonate head circumference. Prenatal nicotine exposure (PNE) also is associated with lung, respiratory, and cardiovascular developmental problems in children (Bakker & Jaddoe, 2011; Burke et al., 2012).

Regarding cognitive functioning, PNE is associated with decreased head circumference, which may stem from (a) reduction in cortical gray matter and total parenchymal volumes, (b) atypical fractional anisotropy in anterior cortical white matter and in the corticofugal fibers of the internal capsule of the brain, (c) volumetric reduction of the frontal lobes and cerebellum, and/or (d) deficient nicotinic cholinergic receptors in the hippocampus and prefrontal cortex (Zhou et al., 2014). Functionally, PNE is associated with increases in behavioral and cognitive problems (Clifford, Lang, & Chen, 2012). Although association often is found between PNE or prenatal tobacco smoke exposure and ADHD in children (Abbott & Winzer-Serhan, 2012; Rosenthal & Weitzman, 2011), generally, it is difficult to establish causation between PNE/prenatal tobacco smoke exposure and cognitive impairment due to confounding variables such as prenatal exposure to teratogens such as alcohol and biopsychosocial factors (e.g., maternal age, education, intelligence quotient [IQ], socioeconomic status).

In a literature review involving 24 studies published between 1975 and 2002, Linnet et al. (2003) investigated the relationship between PNE and ADHD in children. Most studies reported an increased risk of ADHD in children of smoking mothers, with some studies revealing a dose-response effect in that association. Tiesler et al. (2011) studied 1600 children from a German birth cohort, which supported an association between maternal SDP and hyperactivity or inattention problems in 10-year-olds. In a study involving data from over 8000 children from a birth cohort study, researchers (Langley, Heron, Smith, & Thapar, 2012) compared ADHD symptoms in children age 7.5 years whose mothers smoked during pregnancy with children whose mothers did not smoke but were exposed to paternal smoking. Both maternal and paternal smoking (even in the absence of maternal smoking) was associated with increased ADHD symptoms in offspring, but there was no such association in situations involving passive environmental smoke exposure where neither parent smoked. The authors of this study concluded the association between maternal smoking and ADHD in children may have been confounded by genetic as well as household factors and was, to a lesser extent, attributable to the causal effects of nicotine exposure in utero. In another study, Silva, Colvin, Hagemann, and Bower (2014) found PNE was a risk factor for clinically defined ADHD in offspring who had been prescribed stimulant medication. Comparing the effects of maternal and/or paternal smoking on hyperactivity in 10-year-old children, Keyes, Davey Smith, and Susser (2014) found both maternal and paternal PNE was related to increased hyperactivity. In a study based on a large sample from a national registry, Joelsson et al. (2016) found prenatal smoke exposure was more strongly linked to ADHD comorbid with conduct disorder and oppositional defiant disorder than to ADHD alone.

Of all the factors implicated in causing ADHD, PNE has been found to be the most important risk factor identified to date (Langley, Holmans, van den Bree, & Thapar, 2007). Specifically, research finds that children born to mothers who smoke more than half a pack of cigarettes per day during pregnancy are four times more likely to have conduct disorders and increased rates of oppositional defiant disorder and juvenile delinquency (Button, Thapar, & McGuffin, 2005; Nigg & Breslau, 2007; Wakschlag, Pickett, Kasza, & Loeber, 2006). When considering the effects of prenatal exposure to nicotine on a broad range of externalizing and acting out behaviors, including conduct disorder and antisocial behavior, research generally finds correlations but no causal links, typically due to research methodological limitations (Herrmann, King, & Weitzman, 2008; Wakschlag, Pickett, Cook Jr., Benowitz, & Leventhal, 2002). Notably, research (Gatzke-Kopp & Beauchaine, 2007) has found that nonsmoking women exposed to environmental tobacco smoke during pregnancy as well as pregnant women who actively smoked had children with higher symptom scores for conduct disorder.

Extending the behavioral research, D'Onofrio, Van Hulle, Goodnight, Rathouz, and Lahey (2012) examined whether PNE could predict adolescent antisocial behavior. Based upon a large sample involving 6066 children and mothers from the National Longitudinal Survey of Youth, considered a representative sample of women in the United States, and controlling for statistical covariates, the study found that each additional pack of cigarettes per day predicted greater mean adolescent-reported antisocial behavior symptoms, increased odds of being in the top 10% of those with antisocial behavior, and increased risk of a criminal conviction. Notably, PNE significantly predicted most assessments of offspring antisocial behavior while controlling for measured covariates. However, when siblings exposed to differing levels of PNE were compared, all associations attenuated and fell below the threshold of significance. Results of this study strongly suggested that familial factors rather than the presumed causal influence of PNE accounted for the correlation between PNE and adolescent antisocial behavior in offspring. Finally, in a study that found a direct causal effect between PNE and later conduct problems in offspring, researchers (Gaysina et al., 2013) were able to assess the association in mother-child pairs who differed not only in tobacco smoke exposure during pregnancy but also in genetic relationship. That is, children exposed to maternal smoking in utero were observed to have a higher risk of conduct problems compared to nonexposed children regardless of whether they were genetically related or unrelated to their mothers.

Ultimately, review of the literature here suggests prenatal nicotine exposure detrimentally affects CNS development, predisposing offspring to neurobehavioral deficits measured as irritability or difficult temperament during infancy, poor self-regulation during childhood, and even delinquency during adolescence (Cornelius & Day, 2009). However, since most of the studies examined in this review accounted for the distinct possibility of concomitant prenatal exposure to teratogenic substances, such as alcohol, results are at best tentative. The lone exception was a study (Fried & Watkinson, 1990) that controlled for prenatal exposure to alcohol and cannabis, which found a significant association between PNE and poor language development and lower cognitive scores at both 36 and 48 months after statistically controlling for prenatal alcohol exposure (PAE) and prenatal marijuana exposure (PME).

13.4 Prenatal Marijuana Use

Mothers who smoke cigarettes during pregnancy are at risk of using other substances as well, including cannabis. Between 2002 and 2017, cannabis use by pregnant women in the United States increased from 3.4 to 7.0% (Volkow, Han, Compton, & McCance-Katz, 2019). This increase is not surprising given the legalization of the substance by many states in recent years.

Animal studies involving PME find changes in dopaminergic activity of the corpus striatum, leading to ADHD and changes in locomotion, and changes in the prefrontal cortex, causing cognitive impairment and emotional dysregulation (Roncero et al., 2020; Trezza et al., 2012). Animal studies also find alterations in dopaminergic activity and hypothalamic-pituitary access in the amygdala, commonly involved in emotional regulation (Gray, Day, Leech, & Richardson, 2005). With respect to human studies, it is relevant to know that cannabinoid receptors are present in the placenta and appear in the fetal brain at 14 weeks postconception, increasing in density throughout the third trimester (Roncero et al., 2020). In particular, there are high-density cannabinoid receptors in the frontal lobe and cerebellum, brain structures that are late to mature compared to other brain structures. Studies involving human fetus exposure to cannabis report different effects on the mesocortical limbic system, which regulates emotion (Wang, Dow-Edwards, Anderson, Minkoff, &

Hurd, 2004; Wang, Dow-Edwards, Keller, & Hurd, 2003). Regarding fetal outcomes, use of cannabis in the early and late stages of pregnancy is associated with a high risk of restricted fetal growth, low birth weight, shorter birth length, and smaller head circumference compared to nonexposed samples (El Marroun et al., 2009).

Studies of PME and neurocognitive functioning in offspring tend to find short-term effects in young children. Similar to much of the nicotine and smoke exposure research, cannabis studies rarely account for exposure to other substances. An exception is the previously mentioned study involving neurobehavioral development in 36- and 48-month-old children exposed to nicotine and alcohol as well as cannabis (Fried & Watkinson, 1990). This study found that while relatively low levels of PAE no longer had a significant correlation with outcome variables at 48 months of age, PME was associated with significantly lower scores in verbal and memory domains after adjusting for confounding variables. However, another study (Jaddoe et al., 2012) found no correlation between PME and nonverbal cognitive functioning and language development at 30 months. Day et al. (1994) examined the effects of PME on cognitive development in offspring at age 3, finding significant negative effects on performance during assessment with the Stanford-Binet Intelligence Scale. Extending this research, Day, Leech, and Goldschmidt (2011) found an association between PME and low IQ during the school years as well as decrements in executive functioning (Day et al., 2011). After controlling for current maternal substance use (including alcohol, nicotine, and drugs), household income, home environment, maternal IQ, and child's race, an association between first trimester PME and delinquency at age 14 remained significant.

Using data from the Maternal Health Practices and Child Development (MHPCD) study, researchers (Leech, Day, Richardson, & Goldschmidt, 2003) found three pathways to delinquency: (a) 3-year temperament predicted 10-year temperament, which predicted delinquency; (b) 3-year IQ predicted 10-year IQ, which predicted psychological problems and subsequently delinquency, and (c) behavior problems at age 3 predicted behavior problems at 10 years, which in turn predicted peer substance use, offspring substance use, and then delinquency. This analysis identified correlates of delinquency at age 10, which included race, gender, anxiety, substance use, perceived substance use of peers, IQ, and shyness. PME was correlated with delinquency, although PNE and PAE were not. Day et al. (2011) found a significant association between PME and delinquency in exposed adolescents. The odds ratio for delinquency among those exposed in utero to one or more marijuana joints per day during the first trimester was 1.76, indicating the odds of heavily exposed adolescents being delinquent were nearly double those of adolescents who were not exposed or who were exposed to lesser amounts. The *Generation R Study* (Jaddoe et al., 2012) observed an association between PME and aggressive behavior and attention disorders in girls at age 18 months, which was no longer statistically significant at age 36 months (El Marroun et al., 2011).

As noted above, a major problem in research examining the developmental effects of prenatal substance exposure is the confounding effects of other substances, typically alcohol and cigarettes. While researchers attempt to separate their subjects (mothers) into cohorts and separate groups on the basis of specific substance used, there always is the threat of overlap as many mothers use a combination of these substances during pregnancy (i.e., polysubstance abusers) and may not report such use (Day et al., 2011). Thus, the most that can be said at this point about the research findings regarding PME is such exposure may cause alterations in brain functioning involving the prefrontal cortex and executive functioning; mesolimbic system, striatum, and hypothalamic-pituitary axis; and limbic system (Roncero et al., 2020), with neurocognitive consequences that may last into early adulthood, especially with respect to executive dysfunction (Calvigioni, Hurd, Harkany, & Keimpema, 2014; Wang et al., 2003) and delinquency (Day et al., 2011). However, until and unless research into PME accounts for PAE and other possible teratogens, no definitive conclusions can be reached.

13.5 Prenatal Stimulant Use

Cocaine use by birth mothers places their unborn children at risk for disruptions in brain monoamines, especially dopamine, which leads to permanent changes in specific brain circuits, molecules, and behavior (Martin, Graham, McCarthy, Bhide, & Stanwood, 2016). Among pregnant women ages 15–44, relatively recent research indicates approximately 5.4% report current cocaine drug use (Substance Abuse and Mental Health Services Administration [SAMHSA], 2014). However, the cocaine epidemic emerged in the United States during the 1980s and 1990s, and epidemiological studies around that time revealed that up to 27% of women used cocaine during pregnancy (Frank et al., 1988). This latter prevalence rate has important forensic implications on evaluees born during those decades.

Pregnant women who use cocaine are at an increased risk for premature rupture of membranes, hemorrhage, and spontaneous abortion or fetal death (Handler, Kristin, Davis, & Ferré, 1991). Prenatal cocaine exposure (PCE) places a child at risk for increased prematurity, growth retardation, respiratory distress, seizure, decreased head circumference, low birth weight and decreased length, malformations of the genitourinary tract, cerebral infarction-malformations, and increased risk for sudden infant death syndrome (Bada et al., 2005; Martin et al., 2016). In fact, Mayes reported that infants with PCE had lower birth weights and smaller head sizes when compared with nonexposed infants or infants exposed only to alcohol, tobacco, or marijuana (Mayes, Bornstein, Chawarska, Haynes, & Granger, 1996). PCE also is associated with lower Apgar and neonatal behavioral assessment scores (Martin et al., 2016).

Studies revealing decreases in head circumference typically find behavioral and cognitive deficits in children exposed in utero to cocaine (Martin et al., 2016). Magnetic resonance imaging (MRI) studies have revealed smaller cortical and subcortical structures, including smaller caudate, corpus callosum, and pallidum following PCE (Dow-Edwards et al., 2006; Martin et al., 2016; Rivkin et al., 2008), yet PCE also has been associated with a larger amygdala (Rao et al., 2007). Akyuz et al.

(2014) and Liu et al. (2013) used magnetic resonance imaging (MRI) to examine changes in brain structure following PCE at two separate time points (8- to 10-year-old children and 13- to 15-year-old adolescents). Initial studies of 8- to 10-year-olds revealed a trend toward reduction in overall brain volume in PCE subjects with reduced cortical gray matter in the thalamus and putamen. Size reductions in these brain structures were inversely correlated with amount of cocaine exposure in utero. MRI scans using a smaller cohort of 13- to 15-year-olds determined these volume reductions persisted at least to age 10. Diffuse tensor imaging (DTI) showed PCE was correlated with increased diffusion and frontal brain damage including medial and lateral white matter tracks, suggesting immature development (Warner et al., 2006), and reduction of cortical gray matter in total parenchymal volumes (Rivkin et al., 2008).

PCE is associated with increased risk of seizures in newborns and related changes in brain wave activity (Scher, Richardson, & Day, 2000). In particular, functional MRI studies of school age children ages 8 and 9 show that during a response inhibition task, PCE is associated with greater activation of the right inferior frontal cortex and caudate, but nonexposed children showed greater activation in the temporal and occipital regions (Sheinkopf et al., 2009). While such results suggest PCE may preferentially affect brain regions that control attention and response inhibition, research is mixed on this matter (Hurt et al., 2008), which may stem from failure to account for exposure to teratogens such as alcohol.

Cocaine also has been found to affect brain neurotransmitters. Because the drug binds to monoamine transporters in the fetal brain, research has focused on dopamine, serotonin, and norepinephrine signaling mechanisms (Lidow, Trakht, & Howard, 1999; Martin et al., 2016), with some studies finding alterations in dopamine signaling that have profound lasting effects on the developing brain (Kubrusly & Bhide, 2010; Martin et al., 2016). Animal research, which has the advantage of being able to isolate substance exposure, has found that PCE affects neuronal migration in the developing brain, with long-lasting effects into adulthood (Kosofsky, Wilkins, Gressens, & Evrard, 1994). Another animal study has found that PCE impairs brain-drive neurotrophic factor expression, especially in the mesolimbic dopamine pathway (McCarthy, Brown, & Bhide, 2012). Such impairment appears to persist throughout adolescence and adulthood, potentially producing deficits associated with learning and memory extinction. Martin et al. (2016) point out that brain regions with dopamine-rich connections, such as the prefrontal cortex, anterior cingulate cortex (ACC), or striatum, which are involved in attention or arousal, are often impaired in children exposed in utero to cocaine and do not fully mature until the third decade of life. As a consequence, children with PCE exhibit long-term deficits in arousal, attention, emotional reactivity, and reward processing.

As in PAE, in PCE there appears to be a connection between the timing of gestational cocaine exposure and childhood behavioral problems such that cocaine exposure during the first and second trimesters increases the risk of abnormal responses, and exposure during the second and third trimester reduces motor maturity and muscle tone (Richardson, Hamel, Goldschmidt, & Day, 1996). From a neurocognitive perspective, PCE has been shown to lead to deficits in language development and emotional reactivity and alterations in arousal and attention (Bada et al., 2007; Chasnoff, 1992; Lewis et al., 2007). For example, there is concern that PCE disrupts arousal regulation in orientation, attention, information processing, learning, and memory (Martin et al., 2016; Mayes, Bornstein, Chawarska, Haynes, & Granger, 1996). Notably, children exposed prenatally to cocaine show evidence of inhibition deficits, inability to sustain attention, and executive dysfunction (Espy, Kaufmann, & Glisky, 1995). Neuroimaging studies find longer response latencies and variations in brain activation patterns in exposed versus nonexposed children during executive functioning tasks (Mayes, Molfese, Key, & Hunter, 2005).

Notwithstanding the studies referenced above, predictions that "crack babies" born in the 1980s and 1990s would have reduced intelligence and social skills appear to have been exaggerated. For example, some studies find PCE leads to subtle but significant cognitive deficits in some children (Lambert & Bauer, 2012; Lester & LaGasse, 2010), with more significant inattention and arousal deficits in the context of higher levels of exposure (Carmody, Bennett, & Lewis, 2011), particularly with respect to visual and sustained attention (Heffelfinger, Craft, White, & Shyken, 2002). In particular, cocaine-exposed children show slow responses, make more errors, and exhibit less consolidated learning compared to nonexposed children, which may indicate a broader deficit in procedural learning and spatial working memory (Mayes, Snyder, Langlois, & Hunter, 2007). Impairments in verbal language processing also have been found (Bandstra, Vogel, Morrow, Xue, & Anthony, 2004). With regard to IQ testing in exposed versus nonexposed children, exposed children appear to have decreased perceptual reasoning scores with language deficits, effects that strengthen with higher levels of exposure (Singer et al., 2008).

Behaviorally, PCE places children at risk for self-regulation problems and impaired social and emotional development (Bada et al., 2007; Linares et al., 2006). For example, a study that compared exposed and nonexposed 3-, 5-, and 7-year-old children (Bada et al., 2007) found exposed children exhibited more externalizing behaviors (aggressive or defiant behaviors) and internalizing behaviors (social withdrawal, nervousness, irritability, and fearfulness) at all three ages when controlling for factors such as the environment (but not controlling for exposure to other substances). In this study, exposed children exhibited dulled emotions, less secure attachment, limited social play skills, passive and withdrawn personalities, and rapid mood swings, which increased in direct proportion to level of exposure (Gittler & McPherson, 1990). In a study that used parent and teacher ratings to investigate behavioral differences in exposed versus nonexposed children, Lambert and Bauer (2012) found more internalizing and externalizing behaviors in exposed children. Notably, these results were attenuated by confounding variables (e.g., gender, low socioeconomic status, exposure to domestic violence, caregiver depression, caregiving environment, *and prenatal exposure to other substances such as alcohol and tobacco*). In a meta-analysis that examined the effects of PCE on neurobehavioral outcome, the authors (Held, Riggs, & Dorman, 1999) found small correlations in motor performance and reflexes between cocaine-exposed and nonexposed infants, both at birth and soon after. Unfortunately, the authors failed to note whether potential confounds such as prenatal exposure to other teratogens had been addressed in the underlying studies. Notably, no direct effects of PCE on delinquent behaviors have been found (Gerteis et al., 2011).

Turning to prenatal methamphetamine (crystal methamphetamine, Ice) use, research by Little, Snell, and Gilstrap III (1988) found that exposure to such substances in utero placed pregnancies at risk for increased rates of intrauterine growth retardation and decreased length, weight, and head circumference at birth. Plessinger (1998) found that methamphetamine exposure led to increased frequency of heart defects, cleft lips, congenital atresia, and stillbirths. A number of studies have sought to determine the effects of methamphetamine exposure on brain structure and function. For example, prenatal exposure to this substance appears to be associated with increased volume in subcortical brain structures such as the putamen, globus pallidus, caudate nucleus, and hippocampus (Chang et al., 2004). Chang et al. (2004), who looked at behavior as well as brain structure, found smaller subcortical volumes and noticeable cognitive deficits in exposed children. Although these researchers used small samples of exposed and nonexposed children, the exposed cohort scored lower on measures of visual and motor integration, attention, verbal memory, and long-term spatial memory. In contrast, no differences were found in motor skills, short-delayed spatial memory, and measures of nonverbal intelligence, although methamphetamine-exposed children showed volume reductions in the globus pallidus, hippocampus, and putamen bilaterally, with a trend toward smaller caudate bilaterally.

In a behavioral study, researchers (Smith et al., 2015) using Infant Development, Environment, and Lifestyle (IDEAL) national data found poor inhibitory control in children heavily exposed in utero to methamphetamine, which put them at high risk for impaired executive functioning. Yet, independent of methamphetamine exposure, children with home environments that were responsive to their developmental and emotional needs demonstrated lower risk for internalizing and externalizing behaviors. Roos et al. (2015) used DTI to study white matter integrity and cognitive performance in exposed versus nonexposed children, finding that those in the exposed group had abnormal white matter values correlated with poor motor coordination and general cognitive ability, especially executive functioning. These researchers suggested that disruptions in white matter microstructural integrity in striatal, limbic, and frontal brain regions of exposed children produced significant cognitive implications, especially with respect to executive functioning.

A large research study (Kiblawi et al., 2014) used the IDEAL database to investigate connections between prenatal methamphetamine exposure and neurobehavioral outcomes in newborns and infants. Specifically, the study assessed 34,833 exposed subjects that were identified by self-report and/or more reliable means (i.e., gas chromatography/mass spectroscopy confirmation of amphetamine and metabolites in meconium). Comparison subjects were matched on demographics but denied methamphetamine use. However, both groups included children exposed prenatally to alcohol, tobacco, and marijuana. While no significant differences were found between groups in neurobehavioral ratings at 1 month of age, prenatal exposure to substances other than methamphetamine in both groups rendered results uninterpretable.

Although compared to human subjects, animal studies of drug addiction are a potential source of reliable information about how methamphetamine impacts prenatal brain development but to date, there is a dearth of research on this topic as research using animal models has involved relatively short follow-up periods and small subject samples (Vassoler, Byrnes, & Pierce, 2014). Nonetheless, prenatal methamphetamine exposure is known to affect the nervous system because NAS requiring medical intervention is observed in exposed newborns (van Baar, Fleury, Soepatmi, Ultee, & Wesselman, 1989). Data from developmental studies on infants with such exposure indicate a deceleration in neurobehavioral development pertaining to movement control, decreased excitability, and increased stress levels (Behnke & Smith, 2013; Smith et al., 2008), although recent studies have not found significant differences between exposed and nonexposed children (Shah et al., 2012). In fact, research using electroencephalogram (EEG) data find deficits in newborns tend to disappear during the first month of life (Kiblawi et al., 2014).

Research has not consistently found lower IQs or language delays in children exposed in utero to methamphetamine (Chakraborty et al., 2015). On the other hand, some studies have cited possible issues regarding younger school-aged children having difficulties with social integration and getting along with others as well as lower results on cognitive testing compared to nonexposed children (Billing, Eriksson, Jonsson, Steneroth, & Zetterström, 1994; Jablonski, Williams, & Vorhees, 2016). In addition, exposed children may be at risk for psychiatric symptoms or disorders relevant to depression, anxiety, and emotional instability, which manifest as externalizing behaviors in childhood and adolescence and personality disorders in adulthood (Abar et al., 2013; Kiblawi et al., 2014; Spurlock et al., 1998), as well as ADHD (Holmes et al., 2001; Leech, Richardson, Goldschmidt, & Day, 1999; Raine & Yang, 2006). Notably, prenatal exposure to methamphetamine coupled with hardship during childhood appears to place children at risk for impaired neurodevelopment (Abar et al., 2013; Šlamberová, 2019).

In addition to prenatal exposure to other psychoactive substances that potentially confound the research on methamphetamine exposure in utero (e.g., PAE, PME, PCE, etc.), there also is limited research regarding the effects of genetic mechanisms on behavioral and psychiatric outcomes (Shilling, Kuczenski, Segal, Barrett, & Kelsoe, 2006). As noted above, the benefit here of animal research is that most of these potential confounds can be controlled. For example, when comparing rats to humans, researchers can correlate the time of development of specific brain structures, thereby making it possible to match the growth and maturation process in animal models to corresponding human development (Tomášková, Šlamberová, & Černá, 2020). Research in animal models as well as in humans consistently finds delayed development of motor skills in exposed individuals. Methamphetamine appears to affect human brain development mostly in the second and third trimesters, where it alters serotonergic cells, noradrenergic neurons, and dopaminergic neurons, thereby affecting a number of brain areas relevant to the limbic system as well as the striatum and basal ganglia. (Šlamberová, 2019). Studies in animals and humans reveal prenatal methamphetamine exposure not only affects sensory motor development but learning and memory as well and increases susceptibility to seizures (Tomášková et al., 2020). Importantly, research (Itzhak, Ergui, & Young, 2015) finds that methamphetamine exposure and maternal behavior contribute significantly to offspring at a genetic level, and such epigenetic effects are involved in vulnerability to neuropsychiatric disorders, including addiction (Ary & Komiskey, 1980). Methamphetamine use also causes a wide range of psychiatric and neuropsychiatric effects on mothers, which from an epigenetic perspective place offspring at similar risk (Thompson et al., 2009).

Briefly considering other psychostimulants, such as MDMA/ecstasy, researchers find motor delays in infants in a dose-dependent fashion (Singer et al., 2015). Animal studies reveal prenatal MDMA exposure is related to long-term memory and learning impairments (Skelton, Williams, & Vorhees, 2008). In fact, research involving 136 MDMA-exposed pregnancies supported a four to seven times higher risk of congenital malformations compared to nonexposed pregnancies (McElhatton, Bateman, Evans, Pughe, & Thomas, 1999). Thompson et al. (2009) studied the long-term behavioral consequences of prenatal MDMA exposure in rats, finding such exposure resulted in increased dopaminergic fiber density in the prefrontal cortex, striatum, and nucleus acumens—brain areas that are important to processing novelty, reward, tension, and local motor activity. In particular, adult rats prenatally exposed to MDMA were found to have reduced anxiety, heightened response to novelty, and hyper-attentiveness to environmental cues during spatial learning. Further, Canales and Ferrer-Donato (2014) found prenatal exposure to alcohol and ecstasy altered hippocampal development causing enduring memory deficits in rats.

13.6 Prenatal Opiate Use

The final area of prenatal drug use covered in this chapter includes opiates and heroin. Infants born to narcotic-addicted mothers are at high risk for adverse outcomes including perinatal medical problems, impaired control of interactive and state behavior as well as attachment behavior during early infancy, cognitive and psychomotor deficits during early development, and later disturbances in activity levels, attention span, sleep patterns, and socialization (Householder, Hatcher, Burns, & Chasnoff, 1982). Prenatal heroin exposure has been found to evoke neurochemical and behavioral impairments that reflect disruption of septohippocampal cholinergic function (Slotkin, Seidler, & Yanai, 2003).

With respect to neurobehavioral effects, Hutchings (1982) studied the effects of methadone and heroin exposure in human and animal offspring, finding an acute phase relevant to NAS characterized by increased arousal leading to hyperactivity, disturbed sleep, and increased mood lability in newborns. Although the second phase of the syndrome is less well understood, exposure to heroin—particularly in a pattern of polydrug abuse by the mother—can result in offspring effects that include impaired organization, perceptual abilities, poor self-adjustment, and heightened activity in situations requiring motor inhibition. Studies of preschool children exposed prenatally to methadone showed no effects on intellectual and cognitive functioning despite heightened activity or energy level, impulsivity, brief attention span, and limited persistence (Beckwith & Burke, 2015).

In a recent meta-analysis (Yeoh et al., 2019) that examined cognitive and motor outcomes in children with prenatal opioid exposure, results indicated a negative association between exposure and neurocognitive and physical development from ages 6 to 26 months, a correlation that persisted until adolescence. In another study that compared opioid-exposed to nonexposed newborns, Larson et al. (2019) found lower birth weight and NAS were the most common outcomes. Importantly, NAS is a significant factor to consider on its own (Larson et al., 2019). In fact, researchers who compared children with and without a history of NAS found the NAS group had significantly lower academic scores in every tested cognitive domain and were more likely to be referred for educational disabilities (Fill et al., 2018).

In research regarding prenatal methadone exposure, Davis and Templer (1988) examined cognitive functioning in exposed and nonexposed children between ages 6 to 15, finding lower full-scale IQs in the exposed group. These researchers also found that compared to nonexposed children who lived among drug users, exposed children fared worse in almost every psychosocial area, including anxiety and aggression. Likewise, Soepatmi (1994) reported that compared to nonexposed children, those exposed in utero to methadone and heroin had lower IQ scores and higher total behavior problem scores as well as higher proportions of school problems at age 6.

A meta-analysis by Baldacchino, Arbuckle, Petrie, and McCowan (2014/2015) found impairments in working memory, cognitive impulsivity, and cognitive flexibility in preschool age children with methadone exposure in utero compared to nonexposed children. In particular, these authors found attention and executive functioning were areas of concern. For example, compared to nonexposed children, those exposed to methadone in utero were found to have neuropsychological deficits in executive functioning such as impaired cognitive flexibility, strategic planning, and decision-making. Methadone-exposed children also were found to perform more poorly on neuropsychological tasks of short-term memory and inhibition compared to nonexposed peers (Konijnenberg & Melinder, 2015). Looking at behavior, de Cubas and Field (1993) found methadone-exposed school-aged children had more anxiety and aggression problems than nonexposed children. However, with respect to the effects of prenatal stimulant exposure on delinquency, this author was unable to locate any studies.

In a longitudinal study that examined behavior and attention problems in 8-year-olds exposed to prenatal opioid and other substance use (Nygaard, Slinning, Moe, & Walhovd, 2016), caregivers and teachers reported a broad range of regulatory problems in exposed children, particularly a high level of attention problems. Yet, like most of the studies assessing prenatal substance exposure, these researchers could not isolate the effects of drug exposure in utero. Thus, between-groups differences actually may have been caused by a number of factors in addition to prenatal opioid exposure.

Summarizing the drug exposure studies above, children born to drug-using mothers appear to be at significant risk for detrimental neurobehavioral outcomes. Obviously, many other risk factors come into play in the context of mothers who use and abuse substances during pregnancy. For example, functioning and developmental trajectories in children born to drug-abusing mothers also can be harmed by childhood abuse, severe environmental deprivation, and/or the fact one or both caregivers is addicted (Ornoy, Michailevskaya, Lukashov, Bar-Hamburger, & Harel, 1996). Importantly, not only does the potential impact of prenatal substance exposure involve the pattern and intensity of prenatal exposure to a particular substance, there also is a very high likelihood of polysubstance exposure (Forray, 2016). Ultimately, given the current state of our science and the fact that polysubstance abuse appears to be the rule rather than the exception along with other confounds, such as extent of prenatal care, socioeconomic environment, maternal health and nutrition, exposure to sexually transmitted disease, domestic violence during pregnancy (National Institutes on Drug Abuse (NIDA), 2020), future research will find it quite difficult if not impossible to pinpoint the specific effects of each substance in offspring.

13.7 Prenatal Substance Use, Forensic Neuroscience/ Neurocriminology, and the Law

This section of the chapter addresses how substance use during pregnancy is a risk factor for neurodevelopmental disorders and an important factor in the etiology of violence, both of which should be addressed in violence risk assessments for legal proceedings.

Criminal behavior and violence are multifaceted constructs. There are a number of biopsychosocial risk factors that collectively put individuals at risk for aggression and violence (Beech et al., 2018). Unfortunately, there are many relevant risk factors (e.g., individual, family, academic, peer, and community) that have dose-dependent effects (Shader, 2004), in that the more risk factors one has, the greater the likelihood of negative outcomes, such as violence. For example, Loeber et al. (2005) studied young men who had committed homicide and found predictors of violence in risk factors that involved domains beyond the individual level (i.e., family, school, and demographics). For example, individuals with four or more violence risk factors were six times more likely to later commit violence in comparison with those with under four risk factors. With regard to homicidal violence, individuals with four or more risk factors for homicide were 14 times more likely to later commit homicide than violent offenders with fewer than four risk factors. High-risk mothers who abuse substances also add their own risk factors to the equation, including chemical dependency, early teenage pregnancy, poverty, domestic violence, legal problems, and arrest history (Aizer, 2011; Waters, Roberts, & Morgen, 1997).

As highlighted previously, prenatal and perinatal substance use places offspring at risk for compromised brain development and associated neurodevelopmental disorders, such as ADHD and learning disorders, ultimately placing offspring at further risk for conduct disorder and substance abuse (Wiggs, Elmore, Nigg, & Nikolas, 2016). The literature suggests that prenatal exposure to drugs of abuse puts offspring at risk of neuropsychological impairments in executive functioning, thereby increasing impulsivity, deficient reward processing, and behavioral dysregulation, which in turn contributes to neurodevelopmental disorders such as ADHD and conduct disorder. In fact, the conduct disorder or antisocial behavior often seen in juvenile delinquents can be considered through a neurodevelopmental criminal lens since ADHD and learning disorders place youths at risk for conduct problems (Mohan, Yilanli, & Ray, 2020). Further, ADHD has a causal role in the development of substance use disorders, and both together place a youths at risk for conduct disorder (Eme, 2012) and adult criminality.

Investigating the neurodevelopment of delinquency, Moffitt (1990) found poor neuropsychological test results, especially in the area of executive functioning, were a significant risk factor for juvenile delinquency. Similarly, the Dunedin Research Project, which examined data in a birth cohort of 700 New Zealand males ages 13 to 18, found poor neuropsychological test scores were associated with the early onset of delinquency (Moffitt, 1990). In this study, early-onset offending began before age 13 and persisted at high levels thereafter.

The effects of prenatal substance exposure on adult offspring also have been explored, with some focus on criminality. In a longitudinal study of behavior problems in 21-year-olds who had been exposed in utero to cocaine, researchers (Richardson, De Genna, Goldschmidt, Larkby, & Donovan, 2019) found direct links between exposure and early-onset marijuana use and emotional regulation problems, arrest history, and conduct disorder by age 21. Similarly, in a study (Brennan, Grekin, Mortensen, & Mednick, 2002) that examined the effects of PNE on criminal arrest and substance abuse hospitalization in male and female adult offspring, results indicated significant dose-response correlations between exposure amount and both criminal arrests and psychiatric hospitalizations. These correlations remained significant after demographic prenatal and perinatal risk factors were controlled. As before, such findings should be viewed with caution due to the potential for confounding effects from polysubstance exposure.

When addressing the possible ramifications of prenatal drug exposure(s) in the legal context, practicing forensic neuropsychologists typically receive legal referrals involving the following contexts:

1. Competency to waive Miranda rights;
2. Competency to stand trial (CST);
3. Mental state at the time of the offense, insanity, diminished capacity, and self-defense;
4. Mitigation and disposition at sentencing;
5. Future dangerousness;
6. Violence and sexual violence risk assessment; and

7. Juvenile transfer and waiver.

Some of the above contexts apply to juvenile as well as adult offender criminal proceedings. Regardless of forensic context, it should be emphasized that a multi-source/multimethod database will have a higher level of reliability in court. Therefore, assessment components should include a life history interview as well as testing, review of records (e.g., academic, mental health, and medical), and collateral interviews with family members to obtain gestation, birth, and developmental data.

Neurodevelopmental disorders such as ADHD and learning disorders are prevalent in children with prenatal substance exposure (PSE) and are also prevalent in the criminal justice system (Malmgrem, Abbott, & Hawkins, 1999). PSE compromises brain structure development and associated neurological functioning, leading to cognitive, emotional, behavioral, and social deficits—especially in executive processing of information (American Psychiatric Association (APA), 2013). Typically, PSE and NAS in combination lead to neurodevelopmental disorders, such as ADHD and learning disorder, which place youths at risk for a host of other psychosocial complications that include substance abuse and a variety of psychiatric disorders. In fact, the comorbidity of multiple neurodevelopmental disorders in youths with histories of PSE is profound (DuPaul, Gormley, & Laracy, 2013). While obviously, there are a number of psychosocial risk factors that mediate associations between PSE and negative outcomes, such as neurodevelopmental disorders, forensic neuropsychologists tend to be tasked with conducting examinations that focus on functional brain-behavior relationships involving the following domains: attention, language, visuospatial and perceptual reasoning, auditory/verbal and visual learning and memory, and executive functioning. Often, juvenile evaluees with PSE tend to have impairments involving attention, language, memory, and executive functioning and thus are at higher risk of comorbidities such as learning disorder and ADHD (Goel, 2009) as well as childhood trauma and PTSD. In cases with suspected neurodevelopmental disorders, forensic neuropsychologists should administer a neuropsychological assessment battery that not only involves the aforementioned domains but also includes IQ, academic achievement, both receptive and expressive language, and auditory/listening comprehension pursuant to possible ADHD and learning disorder.

If an evaluee has a neurodevelopmental history, an expanded comprehensive assessment should be mandatory. In assessments involving juveniles and young adults, it also is relevant for neuropsychologists to consider brain immaturity as it relates to frontal lobe development and executive functioning (e.g., impulse control, problem-solving, and decision-making). Forensic neuropsychological assessment, as well as reference to research on issues relevant to a particular evaluee, can educate the trier of fact when making legal decisions.

With respect to mitigation, the forensic neuropsychologist also is investigating etiological factors that may have led to an evaluee's violent acts. Thus, such an assessment also may be germane to plea negotiation and sentencing. In contrast, violence risk assessment not only looks at correlation and causation but at future probability and likelihood violence will reoccur. Violence risk assessment is required in a number of psycholegal referral questions, including juvenile transfer and waiver, sentencing and disposition, probation and parole evaluations, psychiatric conditional release, and future dangerousness proceedings in capital offenses.

13.8 Mitigation

Mitigation in capital cases includes anything a death-qualified jury or judicial panel can consider regarding the moral culpability and death worthiness of a defendant (Fabian, 2009). The US Supreme Court has considered many cases over the last 50 years on this issue to ensure fairness in sentencing. For example, in *Eddings v. Oklahoma* (1982), the Court instructed the sentencer to consider *any* mitigating factors in sentencing deliberation and decision-making, which included the defendant's youths, lack of maturity, difficult family history including severe abuse, and emotional disturbance. Ideally, forensic neuropsychological assessments address neurocognitive and psychological functioning capacity in evaluees, which can be integrated with the social (and criminal) history, psychiatric diagnoses, and neuroimaging, with the ultimate goal of providing the court with mitigation evidence that has a nexus with the criminally violent act.

Along these lines, the neurosciences and neurocriminology are revealing a body of growing evidence involving neural markers and specific elements related to impulsivity and behavioral dyscontrol (Gaudet, Kerkmans, Anderson, & Kiehl, 2016) as well as biomarkers for mental illnesses such as schizophrenia (Du et al., 2012) and psychopathy (Ermer, Cope, Calhoun, Nyalakanti, & Kiehl, 2012). There is a trend in death penalty cases for the appointment of a defense mitigation neuropsychologist, and when there is a history of neurodevelopmental disorder(s), traumatic brain injury, epilepsy, schizophrenia, and/or neurocognitive disorders, neuroimaging also is recommended. The latter may include quantitative MRI, DTI, and positron emission tomography (PET) scan techniques (Blume & Paavola, 2011). Neuroscience practitioners including neurologists, neuroradiologists, and neuroscientists as well as psychologists and neuropsychologists may take part in educating the jury as to the neuroimaging evidence.

13.9 Violence Risk Assessment

There are many definitions of violence. Certainly, mild forms of violence such as hitting and slapping are more prevalent than severe forms such as stabbing, shooting, and other means of killing. Violent threats are considered a form of violence. In addition, there are two recognized types of violence: (a) instrumental, premeditated, and predatory (cold-blooded) versus (b) affective, reactive, or impulsive types (hot-blooded) (Fabian, 2021). Notably, the impulsive and reactive violence type is more prevalent in individuals with mental health issues and neurocognitive impairments, while instrumental and predatory violence tend to be more common in those who are mentally healthier but have antisocial personality disorder and psychopathy (severe criminal personality). It is important for forensic examiners to be aware of these dualities of violence and consider them when assessing past and present violent acts in evaluees.

Forensic mental health experts embarking in the professional practice of violence risk assessment must be well versed in contemporary research in this area. Violence risk methodologies that forensic psychologists typically use include the following (Fabian, 2006):

1. Unguided/unstructured clinical judgment,
2. Structured/guided clinical judgment,
3. Clinical judgment based on anamnestic data,
4. Research-guided clinical judgment,
5. Clinically/research-guided adjusted actuarial assessment,
6. Purely actuarial assessment, and
7. Consideration of base rate data for particular population being assessed.

Unguided and unstructured clinical judgment was popular in the past due to clinician confidence in predicting violence from past acts. Such an approach did not include contemporary evidence-based risk assessment methods and essentially was based solely on professional opinion, intuition, and clinical experience. Because this type of assessment was found to involve a tendency for clinicians to exaggerate an offender's likelihood of recidivism, the result was a large number of false-positive conclusions (falsely saying offenders will recidivate when ultimately they do not) (Bengtson & Långström, 2007). Fortunately, this approach to risk assessment appears to have waned in popularity, replaced in large part by structured/guided clinical judgment, also described as the structured professional judgment (SPJ) approach to violence risk assessment. In fact, the structured/guided clinical judgment approach currently may be the most prevalent risk assessment method as it perhaps has the best predictive validity (Hart, Douglas, & Guy, 2017). This risk assessment method is heavily research-based and relies on evidence-based guidelines that systematically assist forensic examiners in anchoring assessments on empirically sound risk factors related to violent recidivism.

Clinical judgment based on anamnestic data is a risk assessment method wherein forensic examiners identify violence risk factors through a detailed examination of violent and/or threatening behaviors in offender history. This assessment focuses more on the individual and certainly the premise that past behavior predicts future behavior, including violent behavior. However, risk factors unique to a particular evaluee are not necessarily empirically based and therefore have questionable validity in predicting recidivism. Thus, the forensic examiner must pay close attention to the nuances of the offender's past history of violence.

In recent years, actuarial-based risk assessments have grown in popularity. Actuarial-based methods minimize clinical judgment and instead rely on empirically based risk factors for violent recidivism based on group data (Snowden, Gray,

Taylor, & MacCulloch, 2007). Generally considered the most statistically advanced methodology of risk assessment and embraced by some experts because of their perceived statistical strength, others argue that this method reduces or eliminates clinical assessment of psychiatric disorders and symptoms, thereby omitting factors that have a strong influence on the risk of recidivism. Some experts also argue convincingly that actuarial methods tend to ignore or minimize treatment and aging effects.

In future dangerousness risk assessments for death penalty cases, base rate data often are used. Specifically, examiners attempt to determine the probability of violence within a particular population (e.g., death row) and over a particular period of time (Sites, 2007). Base rate data also can be used to predict future dangerousness with other populations as well, such as sex offenders.

This author typically uses a combination of risk assessment methods that include the following: actuarial, SPJ, anamnestic assessment focusing on the offender's prior behavior, psychological and neuropsychological analysis pertaining to psychiatric diagnosis and functional impairments that may be related to violence, and empirically based static and dynamic risk factor assessment. In addition, assessment of psychopathy, a disorder characterized in part by shallow emotional responses, lack of empathy, impulsivity, and increased likelihood for antisocial behavior (Hare, 1996), also is important to consider in evaluating violence risk. The Hare Psychopathy Checklist-Revised (PCL-R; Hare, 2003) is a 20-item instrument used by examiners to score evaluees on several facets of psychopathy (e.g., interpersonal, affective, lifestyle, antisocial). Scoring is based upon a semi-structured interview and record review. The PCL-R has shown solid predictive validity in assessing violence risk (Hare, Clark, Grann, & Thornton, 2000).

It is common in violence and sexual violence risk assessment to consider static risk factors in offenders' histories that are unchangeable and therefore unamenable to interventions and treatment, typically with the greatest weight afforded to prior violent offenses (Coid et al., 2016). In contrast, dynamic risk factors are potentially changeable, such as substance abuse and negative peer associations. Stable dynamic risk factors are elements that gradually change with time, such as personality traits, while acute dynamic risk factors such as drug use may change on a day-to-day basis (Douglas & Skeem, 2005).

Forensic examiners should be aware of contextual measures that also may be applicable in risk assessments. For example, the Spousal Assault Risk Assessment (SARA) pertains to the risk of spousal assault. A structured risk assessment instrument that relies on clinical judgment, the SARA specifically examines risk factors empirically associated with the risk of future domestic violence (Kropp & Gibas, 2010). The instrument has shown modest predictive validity pertaining to domestic violence (Svalin & Levander, 2020).

It also is important to note that violence risk assessment may consider short- and/or long-term estimations and follow-up periods. For example, the Short-Term Assessment of Risk and Treatability (START), is a clinical/forensic SPJ instrument that examines an evaluee's risk level for violence and likelihood of responding positively to treatment (Webster, Nicholls, Martin, Desmarais, & Brink, 2006). The instrument informs examiners regarding multiple risk domains pertaining to everyday psychiatric clinical practice, such as risk to others, suicide, self-harm, self-neglect, substance abuse, unauthorized leave, and victimization. The START is comprised of 20 dynamic items relevant to treatment and risk management, including such things as substance use, mental state, social skills, and coping, with each item rated for evaluees in terms of vulnerability and strength.

13.10 Examples of Violence Risk Assessment Measures

Actuarial risk assessment is in wide use in the United States. Such measures are statistical, empirical, algorithmic, and mechanical in nature, and the variables that comprise risk factors on these instruments are selected because they demonstrate a statistically significant association with violence. Items usually are weighted according to their empirically based strength and association with violence. While mechanical to use, these instruments increase interrater reliability and predictive validity and therefore are less vulnerable to biasing errors associated with clinical judgment.

One of the most widely used actuarial risk assessment instrument with violent offenders is the Violence Risk Appraisal Guide (n.d.), now in its revised version, VRAG-R (vrag-r.org). The original VRAG was a 12-item instrument designed to assess the risk of violent recidivism in men arrested for criminal violence. The measure was developed in a population of 618 violent offenders who were being assessed pretrial in a secure psychiatric hospital in Canada, with half of the sample returning later for treatment and the other half being incarcerated in prison (Harris, Rice, & Quinsey, 1993). During development, approximately 50 variables associated with violent recidivism were considered, which eventually was narrowed down to the 12 most statistically significant items. Items are scored from clinical records rather than structured interviews or questionnaires (Harris, Rice, Quinsey, & Cormier, 2015). The VRAG-R has good predictive validity for violent recidivism and can be used to assess violence risk over a relatively long period of time such as 5 and 15 years (Harris, Rice, & Quinsey, 2016). Each VRAG-R score is associated with a particular risk percentile, such that an individual evaluee's relative risk level can be compared to a large sample of violent offenders (Quinsey, Harris, Rice, & Cormier, 2006). As good as it is, the VRAG-R is a static risk assessment instrument with factors that typically do not change with time or treatment. VRAG-R items include the following:

1. Lived with both biological parents to age 16,
2. Elementary school maladjustment up to eighth grade,
3. History of alcohol or drug problems,
4. Marital status at the time of index offense,
5. Criminal nonviolent history score,
6. Failure on conditional release,

7. Age at index offense,
8. Criminal violent history score,
9. Prior admissions to correctional institutions,
10. Conduct disorder prior to age 1,
11. Sex offending history, and
12. Antisociality based on PCL-R score.

The SPJ approach dates back at least 30 years. This method assists examiners in empirically guiding assessments based on current research on violence risk factors. The most well-known SPJ instrument is the Historical, Clinical, and Risk Management-20 (HCR-20), now in its third version, HCR-20-V3 (Douglas, Hart, Webster, & Belfrage, 2013). The HCR-20 is most often used in forensic applications with correctional, clinical, and forensic psychiatric populations as well as with offenders in institutions or the community (Judges, Egan, & Broad, 2016). The HCR-20-V3 was tested in different countries and in different forensic psychiatric, civil psychiatric, and correctional settings, together involving more than 800 research participants (Douglas et al., 2014). Research shows the HCR-20-V3 has good interrater reliability and predictive validity for community violence at both 6 and 12 months (Douglas, 2014). The following risk domains and factors are included in the HCR-20-V3:

Historical Scale:

H1. Violence
H2. Other Antisocial Behavior
H3. Relationships
H4. Employment
H5. Substance Use
H6. Major Mental Disorder
H7. Personality Disorder
H8. Traumatic Experiences
H9. Violent Attitudes
H10. Treatment or Supervision Response
OC-H. Other Considerations.

Clinical Scale:

C1. Insight
C2. Violent Ideation or Intent
C3. Symptoms of Major Mental Disorder
C4. Instability
C5. Treatment or Supervision Response
OC-C. Other Considerations.

Risk Management Scale:

R1. Professional Services and Plans
R2. Living Situation
R3. Personal Support
R4. Treatment or Supervision Response
R5. Stress or Coping
OC-R. Other Considerations.

(Adapted from Douglas et al., 2013).

As can be seen, HCR-20-V3 items do not specifically mention prenatal substance use, neurodevelopmental disorders, or neurocognitive disorders, although examiners may fill in the gaps with such information under the category for major mental disorder and other considerations. In contrast, actuarial measures such as the VRAG-R do not permit one to "fill in the gaps" with relevant information regarding prenatal exposure(s) or NAS. As noted in other chapters in this book, a large minority of violent offenders have histories involving PDE as well as PAE. Since it is unknown how many (if any) offenders with PAE/PDE (or who have ID, ADHD, and learning disorders as well) comprised actuarial developmental samples, the predictive validity of the VRAG-R and similar measures is less certain. In fact, the only diagnostic risk factors on the VRAG-R are psychopathy and conduct disorder, which overlap as both address antisocial and criminal behaviors. Certainly, an argument can be made that measures such as the VRAG-R are not empirically equipped to assess violence risk in persons with neurodevelopmental disorder associated with prenatal alcohol (or drug) exposure as well as those with ADHD, intellectual disability, and neuropsychological impairments in executive functioning.

13.11 Contextual Violence Risk Assessment

This section introduces a practical risk assessment method for persons with histories of prenatal alcohol and/or drug exposure. As a starting point, forensic experts should be aware of static and dynamic risk factors related to criminality and violence (Andrews & Bonta, 2006) and assess evaluees for such, keeping in mind that a number of empirically sound violence risk factors (e.g., prior violent acts, supervision violations, single marital status, substance abuse) likely apply to any clinical population. Accordingly, powerful research concerning prediction of criminal violent recidivism among mentally disordered offender populations (a meta-analysis involving 35 predictors of general criminal recidivism and 27 predictors of violent criminal recidivism from 64 unique samples) yielded results that showed the major predictors of recidivism were the same for mentally disordered offenders as for non-disordered offenders (Bonta, Law, & Hanson, 1998).

The question then becomes, what is the etiology of violence in a particular offender? Certainly, offenders with PAE/PDE histories will be at jeopardy for many clinical risk factors throughout development. Along those lines and in the spirit of neurocriminology, forensic examiners working with PAE/PDE offenders should be aware of the research highlighted in this and other chapters in this book regarding impulsivity, attention deficits, hyperactivity, and externalizing behaviors in this population, which appear to continue through adolescence and into adulthood in the form of high rates of delinquency, criminal behavior, and substance abuse (Behnke & Smith, 2013). In essence, forensic examiners should have a solid understanding of the short- and long-term effects of prenatal substance use on exposed fetuses as such knowledge lends itself to more reliable individualized risk assessments.

Along these lines, the risk-need-responsivity (RNR) model for offender assessment, rehabilitation, and risk management is frequently implemented with success, especially when offenders are supervised in the community (Andrews, 2012). Essentially, using the RNR model in violence risk assessment matches the level of service to a specific offender's risk to reoffend. The need principle involves determining whether an evaluee has criminogenic needs and if so, targeting those needs in treatment. The responsivity principle involves maximizing the offender's ability to learn from rehabilitative intervention by providing cognitive and behavioral management and adjusting the intervention to match the learning style that best accommodates the offender's motivation, abilities, and strengths. Obviously, the RNR model can be adjusted to address the special needs of offenders with PAE/PDE.

A promising and more recent violence risk assessment instrument called the Classification of Violence Risk (COVR) is a software program designed to estimate violence risk in an acute psychiatric unit or over a short time period (i.e., several months). The instrument is based upon the MacArthur Violence Risk Assessment Study (Monahan et al., 2005, 2007), which involved more than 1000 patients in acute psychiatric facilities who were assessed on 134 potential risk factors for violence and followed up in the community at 20 weeks post-discharge to determine which factors best predicted violence. The outcome of this study yielded a measure capable of assessing the 40 most predictive violence risk factors. The instrument allows for many different combinations of risk factors to ultimately classify a person as either high or low risk and has been shown to have moderate predictive validity (Singh, Serper, Reinharth, & Fazel, 2011). Although promising, the COVR has not been validated to date in offenders with FASD or PDE histories.

Finally, professionals examining violence risk in juveniles should consider using the Structured Assessment of Violence Risk in Youth (SAVRY) (Borum, Lodewijks, Bartel, & Forth, 2010). Similar to the HCR-20, the SAVRY can be used to structure assessments in children and adolescents involved in juvenile court proceedings. The measure contains three risk domains (historical, social/contextual, and individual/clinical risk factors) as well as protective factors and provides operational definitions for risk factors that examiners can apply in a structured fashion. The SAVRY is currently used in a broad range of juvenile settings (Gammelgård, Koivisto, Eronen, & Kaltiala-Heino, 2015) and for young offenders with PAE and/or PDE histories, the SAVRY includes empirically derived developmental and neurodevelopmental risk factors. The SAVRY also can be considered qualitatively when examining adults in order to include a developmental and neurodevelopmental perspective.

13.12 Concluding Remarks

In conclusion, juvenile and adult offenders presenting for forensic neuropsychological evaluation and risk assessment are likely to have neurodevelopmental risk factors if their histories involve PAE or PDE. As noted, forensic experts must be aware of the current research on prenatal substance exposures, including knowing which exposures present the most risk in offspring. Ideally, forensic examiners will receive psychosocial and collateral records that include school, behavior, and academic histories and psychoeducational test performance as well as mental health/medical records and prior criminal history.

For those of you contemplating violence risk assessments with offenders prenatally exposed to substances, this author recommends a SPJ approach using the HCR-20-V3, with consideration of empirically supported dynamic and static risk factors as those outlined by Bonta et al. (1998). Neuropsychological testing as well as clinical assessment are necessary for this population. Moreover, when applicable and accessible, neuroimaging can add structural and functional brain data to fully inform brain-behavior relationships, including violence. For example, when Aharoni et al. (2013) administered a Go/No-Go task to parolees that assessed response inhibition and impulsivity during functional magnetic resonance imaging (fMRI) administration, error-related brain activity during performance of the task prospectively predicated subsequent arrest. In fact, offenders who performed poorly on the task and exhibited low anterior cingulate activity in the prefrontal cortex were rearrested twice as often as offenders with high activity in this brain region. The authors hypothesized that the ACC may be a neurocognitive biomarker for antisocial behavior.

While neurodevelopmental assessment of violence risk is an arduous task with prenatally exposed offenders, just as important is consideration of the risk management process (Coid et al., 2016), especially with a vulnerable population that often needs multiple rehabilitative services due to brain dysfunction and comorbidities. As noted in this chapter, it is not uncommon for forensic mental health professionals who evaluate violent offenders to see evaluees with documented FASD or prenatal drug exposure and complicated histories involving neurodevelopmental and psychiatric disorders in the context of damaged attachments, complex trauma, abuse, head injuries, and polysubstance abuse. Since these complicated individuals do not fit concisely into a traditional risk assessment model, forensic mental health experts must be extremely adept at multitasking: assessing psychiatric diagnoses and neuropsychological functioning pursuant to risk assessment/management and being constant consumers of the research—both the violence risk assessment research *and* the prenatal exposure research.

References

Abar, B., LaGasse, L. L., Derauf, C., Newman, E., Shah, R., Smith, L. M., … Lester, B. M. (2013). Examining the relationships between Prenatal methamphetamine exposure, early adversity, and child neurobehavioral disinhibition. *Psychology of Addictive Behaviors, 27*(3), 662–673. https://doi.org/10.1037/a0030157

Abbott, L. C., & Winzer-Serhan, U. H. (2012). Smoking during pregnancy: Lessons learned from epidemiological studies and experimental studies using animal models. *Critical Reviews in Toxicology, 42*(4), 279–303. https://doi.org/10.3109/10408444.2012.658506

Aharoni, E., Vincent, G. M., Harenski, C. L., Calhoun, V. D., Sinnott-Armstrong, W., Gazzaniga, M. S., & Kiehl, K. A. (2013). Neuroprediction of future rearrest. *Proceedings of the National Academy of Sciences of the United States of America (PNAS), 110*(15), 6223–6228. https://doi.org/10.1073/pnas.1219302110

Aizer, A. (2011). Poverty, violence and health: The impact of domestic violence during pregnancy on newborn health. *Journal of Human Resources, 46*(3–4), 518–538. https://doi.org/10.1353/jhr.2011.0024

Akyuz, N., Kekatpure, M. V., Liu, J., Sheinkopf, S. J., Quinn, B. T., Lala, M. D., … Kosofsky, B. E. (2014). Structural brain imaging in children and adolescents following prenatal cocaine exposure: Preliminary longitudinal findings. *Developmental Neuroscience, 36*(3–4), 316–328. https://doi.org/10.1159/000362685

American Psychiatric Association (APA). (2013). *Diagnostic and statistical manual of mental disorders (DSM-5)* (5th ed.). Arlington, VA: American Psychiatric Association.

Andrews, D. A. (2012). The risk-need-responsivity (RNR) Model of correctional assessment and treatment. In J. A. Dvoskin, J. L. Skeem, R. W. Novaco, & K. S. Douglas (Eds.), *American psychology–law society series: Using social science to reduce violent offending* (pp. 127–156). Oxford: Oxford University Press.

Andrews, D. A., & Bonta, J. (2006). *The psychology of criminal conduct* (4th ed.). Newark, NJ: LexisNexis.

Ary, T. E., & Komiskey, H. L. (1980). Basis of phencyclidine's ability to decrease the synaptosomal accumulation of 3H-catecholamines. *European Journal of Pharmacology, 61*(5), 401–405. https://doi.org/10.1016/0014-2999(80)90082-5

Azagba, S., Manzione, L., Shan, L., & King, J. (2020). Trends in smoking during pregnancy by socioeconomic characteristics in the United States, 2010-2017. *BMC Pregnancy and Childbirth, 20*, 52. https://doi.org/10.1186/s12884-020-2748-y

Bada, H. S., Das, A., Bauer, C. R., Shankaran, S., Lester, B. M., Gard, C. C., … Higgins, R. (2005). Low birth weight and preterm births: Etiologic fraction attributable to prenatal drug exposure. *Journal of Perinatology, 25*(10), 631–637. https://doi.org/10.1038/sj.jp.7211378

Bada, H. S., Das, A., Bauer, C. R., Shankaran, S., Lester, B., LaGasse, L., … Higgins, R. (2007). Impact of prenatal cocaine exposure on child behavior problems through school age. *Pediatrics, 119*(2), e348–e359. https://doi.org/10.1542/peds.2006-1404

Bakker, H., & Jaddoe, V. W. V. (2011). Cardiovascular and metabolic influences of fetal smoke exposure. *European Journal of Epidemiology, 26*(10), 763–770. https://doi.org/10.1007/s10654-011-9621-2

Baldacchino, A., Arbuckle, K., Petrie, D. J., & McCowan, C. (2014/2015). Neurobehavioral consequences of chronic intrauterine opioid exposure in infants and preschool children: A systematic review and meta-analysis [published correction appears in BMC Psychiatry, (2015), 15, 134. https://doi.org/10.1186/s12888-015-0438-5]. *BMC Psychiatry, 14*, 104. https://doi.org/10.1186/1471-244X-14-104

Bandstra, E. S., Vogel, A. L., Morrow, C. E., Xue, L., & Anthony, J. C. (2004). Severity of prenatal cocaine exposure and child language functioning through age seven years: A longitudinal latent growth curve analysis. *Substance Use and Misuse, 39*(1), 25–59. https://doi.org/10.1081/2FJA-120027765

Beckwith, A. M., & Burke, S. A. (2015). Identification of early developmental deficits in infants with prenatal heroin, methadone, and other opioid exposure. *Clinical Pediatrics, 54*(4), 328–335. https://doi.org/10.1177/0009922814549545

Beech, A. R., Carter, A. J., Mann, R. E., & Rotshtein, P. (Eds.). (2018). *The Wiley Blackwell handbook of forensic neuroscience. 2 vols*. Hoboken, NJ: John Wiley.

Behnke, M., & Smith, V. C. (2013). Prenatal substance abuse: Short- and long-term effects on the exposed fetus. *Pediatrics, 131*(3), e1009–e1024. https://doi.org/10.1542/peds.2012-3931

Bengtson, S., & Långström, N. (2007). Unguided clinical and actuarial assessment of re-offending risk: A direct comparison with sex offenders in Denmark. *Sexual Abuse, 19*(2), 135–153. https://doi.org/10.1177/107906320701900205

Benowitz, N. L., Hukkanen, J., & Jacob, P., III. (2009). Nicotine chemistry, metabolism, kinetics and biomarkers. *Handbook of Experimental Pharmacology*, (192), 29–60. https://doi.org/10.1007/978-3-540-69248-5_2

Billing, L., Eriksson, M., Jonsson, B., Steneroth, G., & Zetterström, R. (1994). The influence of environmental factors on behavioural problems in 8-year-old children exposed to amphetamine during fetal life. *Child Abuse and Neglect, 18*(1), 3–9. https://doi.org/10.1016/0145-2134(94)90091-4

Blume, J. H., & Paavola, E. C. (2011). Life, death, and neuroimaging: The advantages and disadvantages of the defense's Use of neuroimages in capital cases—Lessons from the front. *Mercer Law Review, 62*(3), 909–931. https://scholarship.law.cornell.edu/facpub/212

Bonta, J., Law, M., & Hanson, K. (1998). The prediction of criminal and violent recidivism among mentally disordered offenders: A meta-analysis. *Psychological Bulletin, 123*(2), 123–142. 123–142. https://doi.org/10.1037/0033-2909

Borum, R., Lodewijks, H., Bartel, P. A., & Forth, A. E. (2010). Structured assessment of violence risk in youth (SAVRY). In R. K. Otto & K. S. Douglas (Eds.), *International perspectives on forensic mental health. Handbook of violence risk assessment* (pp. 63–79). New York: Routledge/Taylor & Francis Group.

Brennan, P. A., Grekin, E. R., Mortensen, E. L., & Mednick, S. A. (2002). Relationship of maternal smoking during pregnancy with criminal arrest and hospitalization for substance abuse in male and female adult offspring. *American Journal of Psychiatry, 159*(1), 48–54. https://doi.org/10.1176/appi.ajp.159.1.48

Burke, H., Leonardi-Bee, J., Hashim, A., Pine-Abata, H., Chen, Y., Cook, D. G., ... McKeever, T. M. (2012). Prenatal and passive smoke exposure and incidence of asthma and wheeze: Systematic review and meta-analysis. *Pediatrics, 129*(4), 735–744. https://doi.org/10.1542/peds.2011-2196

Button, T. M. M., Thapar, A., & McGuffin, P. (2005). Relationship between antisocial behaviour, attention-deficit hyperactivity disorder and maternal prenatal smoking. *British Journal of Psychiatry, 187*(2), 155–160. https://doi.org/10.1192/bjp.187.2.155

Calvigioni, D., Hurd, Y. L., Harkany, T., & Keimpema, E. (2014). Neuronal substrates and functional consequences of prenatal cannabis exposure. *European Child and Adolescent Psychiatry, 23*(10), 931–941. https://doi.org/10.1007/s00787-014-0550-y

Canales, J. J., & Ferrer-Donato, A. (2014). Prenatal exposure to alcohol and 3, 4-methylenedioxymethamphetamine (Ecstasy) alters adult hippocampal neurogenesis and causes enduring memory deficits. *Developmental Neuroscience, 36*(1), 10–17. https://doi.org/10.1159/000356820

Carmody, D. P., Bennett, D. S., & Lewis, M. (2011). The effects of prenatal cocaine exposure and gender on inhibitory control and attention. *Neurotoxicology and Teratology, 33*(1), 61–68. https://doi.org/10.1016/j.ntt.2010.07.004

Chakraborty, A., Anstice, N. S., Jacobs, R. J., LaGasse, L. L., Lester, B. M., Wouldes, T. A., & Thompson, B. (2015). Prenatal exposure to recreational drugs affects global motion perception in preschool children. *Scientific Reports, 5*, 16921. https://doi.org/10.1038/srep16921

Chang, L., Smith, L. M., LoPresti, C., Yonekura, M. L., Kuo, J., Walot, I., & Ernst, T. (2004). Smaller subcortical volumes and cognitive deficits in children with prenatal methamphetamine exposure. *Psychiatry Research: Neuroimaging, 132*(2), 95–106. https://doi.org/10.1016/j.pscychresns.2004.06.004

Chasnoff, I. J. (1992). Cocaine, pregnancy, and the growing child. *Current Problems in Pediatrics, 22*(7), 302–321. ; discussion 322. https://doi.org/10.1016/0045-9380(92)90027-V

Clifford, A., Lang, L., & Chen, R. (2012). Effects of maternal cigarette smoking during pregnancy on cognitive parameters of children and young adults: A literature review. *Neurotoxicology and Teratology, 34*(6), 560–570. https://doi.org/10.1016/j.ntt.2012.09.004

Cnattingius, S. (2004). The epidemiology of smoking during pregnancy: Smoking prevalence, maternal characteristics, and pregnancy outcomes. *Nicotine and Tobacco Research, 6*(Suppl. 2), S125–S140. https://doi.org/10.1080/14622200410001669187

Coid, J. W., Ullrich, S., Kallis, C., Freestone, M., Gonzalez, R., Bui, L., … Bebbington, P. (2016). *Improving risk management for violence in mental health services: A multi-methods approach*. Southampton (UK): NIHR Journals Library. (Program Grants for Applied Research, No. 4.16.) Section D, Development and validation of new instruments for static and dynamic risk assessment. Retrieved from https://www.ncbi.nlm.nih.gov/books/NBK396455/

Cornelius, M. D., & Day, N. L. (2009). Developmental consequences of prenatal tobacco exposure. *Current Opinion in Neurology, 22*(2), 121–125. https://doi.org/10.1097/WCO.0b013e328326f6dc

Davis, D. D., & Templer, D. I. (1988). Neurobehavioral functioning in children exposed to narcotics in utero. *Addictive Behaviors, 13*(3), 275–283. https://doi.org/10.1016/0306-4603(88)90054-8

Day, N. L., Leech, S. L., & Goldschmidt, L. (2011). The effects of prenatal marijuana exposure on delinquent behaviors are mediated by measures of neurocognitive functioning. *Neurotoxicology and Teratology, 33*(1), 129–136. https://doi.org/10.1016/j.ntt.2010.07.006

Day, N. L., Richardson, G. A., Goldschmidt, L., Robles, N., Taylor, S., & D., S., … Geva, D. (1994). Effect of prenatal marijuana exposure on the cognitive development of offspring at age three. *Neurotoxicology and Teratology, 16*(2), 169–175. https://doi.org/10.1016/0892-0362(94)90114-7

de Cubas, M. M., & Field, T. (1993). Children of methadone-dependent women: Developmental outcomes. *American Journal of Orthopsychiatry, 63*(2), 266–276. https://doi.org/10.1037/h0079429

D'Onofrio, B. M., Van Hulle, C. A., Goodnight, J. A., Rathouz, P. J., & Lahey, B. B. (2012). Is maternal smoking during pregnancy a causal environmental risk factor for adolescent antisocial behavior? Testing etiological theories and assumptions. *Psychological Medicine, 42*(7), 1535–1545. https://doi.org/10.1017/s0033291711002443

Douglas, K. S. (2014). Introduction to the special issue of the HCR-20 version 3. *International Journal of Forensic Mental Health, 13*(2), 91–92. https://doi.org/10.1080/14999013.2014.913746

Douglas, K. S., Hart, S. D., Webster, C. D., & Belfrage, H. (2013). *HCR-20 V3—Assessing risk for violence: User guide*. Burnaby, Canada: Mental Health, Law and Policy Institute, Simon Fraser University.

Douglas, K. S., Hart, S. D., Webster, C. D., Belfrage, H., Guy, L. S., & Wilson, C. M. (2014). Historical-clinical-risk management-20, version 3 (HCR-20V3): Development and overview. *International Journal of Forensic Mental Health, 13*(2), 93–108. https://doi.org/10.1080/14999013.2014.906519

Douglas, K. S., & Skeem, J. L. (2005). Violence risk assessment: Getting specific about being dynamic. *Psychology, Public Policy, and Law, 11*(3), 347–383. https://doi.org/10.1037/1076-8971.11.3.347

Dow-Edwards, D. L., Benveniste, H., Behnke, M., Bandstra, E. S., Singer, L. T., Hurd, Y. L., & Stanford, L. R. (2006). Neuroimaging of prenatal drug exposure. *Neurotoxicology and Teratology, 28*(3), 386–402. https://doi.org/10.1016/j.ntt.2006.03.003

Du, W., Calhoun, V. D., Li, H., Ma, S., Eichele, T., Kiehl, K. A., … Adali, T. (2012). High classification accuracy for schizophrenia with rest and task fMRI data. Frontiers in Human Neuroscience, 6, 145. doi:10.3389%2Ffnhum.2012.00145

DuPaul, G. J., Gormley, M. J., & Laracy, S. D. (2013). Comorbidity of LD and ADHD: Implications of DSM-5 for assessment and treatment. *Journal of Learning Disabilities, 46*(1), 43–51. https://doi.org/10.1177/0022219412464351

Eddings v. Oklahoma, 455 U.S. 104 (1982).

El Marroun, H., Hudziak, J. J., Tiemeier, H., Creemers, H., Steegers, E. A. P., Jaddoe, V. W. V., … Huizink, A. C. (2011). Intrauterine cannabis exposure leads to more aggressive behavior and attention problems in 18-month-old girls. *Drug and Alcohol Dependence, 118*(2–3), 470–474. https://doi.org/10.1016/j.drugalcdep.2011.03.004

El Marroun, H., Tiemeier, H., Steegers, E. A. P., Jaddoe, V. W. V., Hofman, A., Verhulst, F. C., … Huizink, A. C. (2009). Intrauterine cannabis exposure affects fetal growth trajectories: The generation R study. *Journal of the American Academy of Child and Adolescent Psychiatry, 48*(12), 1173–1181. https://doi.org/10.1097/chi.0b013e3181bfa8ee

Eme, R. (2012). Male adolescent substance use disorder and attention-deficit hyperactivity disorder: A review of the literature. *International Scholarly Research Notices: Addiction, 2013*, 15096. https://doi.org/10.1155/2013/815096

Ermer, E., Cope, L. M., Calhoun, V. D., Nyalakanti, P. K., & Kiehl, K. A. (2012). Aberrant paralimbic gray matter in criminal psychopathy. *Journal of Abnormal Psychology, 121*(3), 649–658. https://doi.org/10.1037/a0026371

Espy, K. A., Kaufmann, P. M., & Glisky, M. L. (1995). Neuropsychological function in toddlers exposed to cocaine in utero: A preliminary study. *Developmental Neuropsychology, 15*(3), 447–460. https://doi.org/10.1080/87565649909540761

Fabian, J. M. (2006). A Literature review of the utility of selected violence and sexual violence risk assessment instruments. *Journal of Psychiatry and Law, 34*(3), 307–350. https://doi.org/10.1177/009318530603400304

Fabian, J. M. (2009). Mitigating murder at capital sentencing: An empirical and practical psycho-legal strategy. *Journal of Forensic Psychology Practice, 9*(1), 1–34. https://doi.org/10.1080/15228930802425084

Fabian, J. M. (2018). Forensic neuropsychology and violence: Neuroscientific and legal implications. In A. R. Beech, A. J. Carter, R. E. Mann, & P. Rotshtein (Eds.), *The Wiley Blackwell handbook of forensic neuroscience (2 vols.)* (pp. 837–887). Hoboken, NJ: John Wiley.

Fabian, J. M. (2021). The Neuroscience of predatory and affective violence. In J. M. Fabian (Ed.), *Forensic neuroscience and violence*. Hoboken, NJ: John Wiley. (In Press).

Fill, M.-M. A., Miller, A. M., Wilkinson, R. H., Warren, M. D., Dunn, J. R., Schaffner, W., & Jones, T. F. (2018). Educational disabilities among children born with neonatal abstinence syndrome. *Pediatrics, 142*(3), e20180562. https://doi.org/10.1542/peds.2018-0562

Forray, A. (2016). *Substance use during pregnancy*. F1000Research, 5, F1000 Faculty Rev-887. Retrieved from https://doi.org/10.12688/f1000research.7645.1

Frank, D. A., Zuckerman, B. S., Amaro, H., Aboagye, K., Bauchner, H., Cabral, H., … Levenson, S. M. (1988). Cocaine use during pregnancy: Prevalence and correlates. *Pediatrics, 82*(6), 888–895.

Fried, P. A., & Watkinson, B. (1990). 36- and 48-Month neurobehavioral follow-up of children prenatally exposed to marijuana, cigarettes, and alcohol. *Journal of Developmental and Behavioral Pediatrics, 11*(2), 49–58.

Gammelgård, M., Koivisto, A.-M., Eronen, M., & Kaltiala-Heino, R. (2015). Predictive validity of the structured assessment of violence risk in youth: A 4-year follow-up. *Criminal Behaviour and Mental Health, 25*(3), 192–206. Epub 2014 Jul 5. https://doi.org/10.1002/cbm.1921

Gatzke-Kopp, L. M., & Beauchaine, T. P. (2007). Direct and passive prenatal nicotine exposure and the development of externalizing psychopathology. *Child Psychiatry and Human Development, 38*(4), 255–269. https://doi.org/10.1007/s10578-007-0059-4

Gaudet, L. M., Kerkmans, J. P., Anderson, N. E., & Kiehl, K. A. (2016). Can neuroscience help predict future antisocial behavior? *Fordham Law Review, 85*(2), 503–531. https://ir.lawnet.fordham.edu/flr/vol85/iss2/6

Gaysina, D., Fergusson, D. M., Leve, L. D., Horwood, J., Reiss, D., Shaw, D. S., … Harold, G. T. (2013). Maternal smoking during pregnancy and offspring conduct problems: Evidence from 3 independent genetically sensitive research designs. *JAMA Psychiatry, 70*(9), 956–963. https://doi.org/10.1001/jamapsychiatry.2013.127

Gerteis, J., Chartrand, M., Martin, B., Cabral, H. J., Rose-Jacobs, R., Crooks, D., & Frank, D. A. (2011). Are there effects of intrauterine cocaine exposure on delinquency during early adolescence? A preliminary report. *Journal of Developmental and Behavioral Pediatrics, 32*(5), 393–401. https://doi.org/10.1097/dbp.0b013e318218d9f2

Gittler, J., & McPherson, M. (1990). Prenatal substance abuse. *Child Today, 19*(4), 3–7.

Goel, R. (2009). Delinquent of distracted—Attention deficit disorder and the construction of the juvenile offender. *Law & Inequality, 27*(1), 1–52. http://scholarship.law.umn.edu/lawineq/vol27/iss1/1

Gray, K. A., Day, N. L., Leech, S., & Richardson, G. A. (2005). Prenatal marijuana exposure: Effect on child depressive symptoms at ten years of age. *Neurotoxicology and Teratology, 27*(3), 439–448. https://doi.org/10.1016/j.ntt.2005.03.010

Handler, A., Kristin, N., Davis, F., & Ferré, C. (1991). Cocaine use during pregnancy: Perinatal outcomes. *American Journal of Epidemiology, 133*(8), 818–825. https://doi.org/10.1093/oxfordjournals.aje.a115961

Hare, R. D. (1996). Psychopathy: A clinical construct whose time has come. *Criminal Justice and Behavior, 23*(1), 25–54. https://doi.org/10.1177/0093854896023001004

Hare, R. D. (2003). *Manual for the revised psychopathy checklist* (2nd ed.). Toronto, ON: Multi-Health Systems.

Hare, R. D., Clark, D., Grann, M., & Thornton, D. (2000). Psychopathy and the predictive validity of the PCL-R: An international perspective. *Behavioral Sciences & the Law, 18*(5), 623–645. https://doi.org/10.1002/1099-0798(200010)18:5%3C623::AID-BSL409%3E3.0.CO;2-W

Harris, G. T., Rice, M. E., & Quinsey, V. L. (1993). Violent recidivism of mentally disordered offenders: The development of a statistical prediction instrument. *Criminal Justice and Behavior, 20*(4), 315–335. https://doi.org/10.1177/0093854893020004001

Harris, G. T., Rice, M. E., & Quinsey, V. L. (2016). *Violence risk appraisal guide—Revised, 2013, User guide*. Data Services, Queen's University Library. Retrieved from https://hdl.handle.net/10864/12053

Harris, G. T., Rice, M. E., Quinsey, V. L., & Cormier, C. A. (2015). *The law and public policy: Psychology and the social sciences. Violent offenders: Appraising and managing risk* (3rd ed.). Washington, DC: American Psychological Association. https://doi.org/10.1037/14572-000

Hart, S. D., Douglas, K. S., & Guy, L. S. (2017). The structured professional judgement approach to violence risk assessment: Origins, nature, and advances. In D. P. Boer, A. R. Beech, T. Ward, L. A. Craig, M. Rettenberger, L. E. Marshall, & W. L. Marshall (Eds.), *The Wiley handbook on the theories, assessment, and treatment of sexual offending. (3 vols.)* (Vol. 2, pp. 643–666). Chichester, UK: Wiley Blackwell.

Heffelfinger, A. K., Craft, S., White, D. A., & Shyken, J. (2002). Visual attention in preschool children prenatally exposed to cocaine: Implications for behavioral regulation. *Journal of International Neuropsychological Society, 8*(1), 12–21.

Held, J. R., Riggs, M. L., & Dorman, C. (1999). The effect of prenatal cocaine exposure on neurobehavioral outcome: A meta-analysis. *Neurotoxicology and Teratology, 21*(6), 619–625. https://doi.org/10.1016/s0892-0362(99)00032-x

Herrenkohl, T. L., Hawkins, J. D., Chung, I., Hill, K. G., & Battin-Pearson, S. (2001). School and community risk factors and interventions in child delinquents, development, intervention, and service needs. In R. Loeber & D. P. Farrington (Eds.), *Child delinquents: Development, intervention and service needs* (pp. 211–246). Thousand Oaks, CA: Sage.

Herrenkohl, T. L., Maguin, E., Hill, K. G., Hawkins, J. D., Abbott, R. D., & Catalano, R. F. (2000). Developmental risk factors for youth violence. *Journal of Adolescent Health, 26*(3), 176–186. https://doi.org/10.1016/s1054-139x(99)00065-8

Herrmann, M., King, K., & Weitzman, M. (2008). Prenatal tobacco smoke and postnatal secondhand smoke exposure and child neurodevelopment. *Current Opinion in Pediatrics, 20*(2), 184–190. https://doi.org/10.1097/MOP.0b013e3282f56165

Holmes, L. B., Harvey, E. A., Coull, B. A., Huntington, K. B., Khoshbin, S., Hayes, A. M., & Ryan, L. M. (2001). The teratogenicity of anticonvulsant drugs. *New England Journal of Medicine, 344*(15), 1132–1138. https://doi.org/10.1056/NEJM200104123441504

Householder, J., Hatcher, R. P., Burns, W. J., & Chasnoff, I. (1982). Infants born to narcotic-addicted mothers. *Psychological Bulletin, 92*(2), 453–468. https://doi.org/10.1037/0033-2909.92.2.453

Hurt, H., Giannetta, J. M., Korczykowski, M., Hoang, A., Tang, K. Z., Betancourt, L., … Detre, J. A. (2008). Functional magnetic resonance imaging and working memory in adolescents with gestational cocaine exposure. *Journal of Pediatrics, 152*(3), 371–377. https://doi.org/10.1016/j.jpeds.2007.08.006

Hutchings, D. E. (1982). Methadone and heroin during pregnancy: A review of behavioral effects in human and animal offspring. *Neurobehavioral Toxicology and Teratology, 4*(4), 429–434.

Itzhak, Y., Ergui, I., & Young, J. I. (2015). Long-term parental methamphetamine exposure of mice influences behavior and hippocampal DNA methylation of the offspring. *Molecular Psychiatry, 20*, 232–239. https://doi.org/10.1038/mp.2014.7

Jablonski, S. A., Williams, M. T., & Vorhees, C. V. (2016). Mechanisms involved in the neurotoxic and cognitive effects of developmental methamphetamine exposure. Birth Defects Research. *Part C Embryo Today Reviews, 108*(2), 131–141. https://doi.org/10.1002/bdrc.21130

Jaddoe, V. W., van Duijn, C. M., Franco, O. H., van der Heijden, A. J., van Iizendoorn, M. H., de Jongste, J. C., … Hofman, A. (2012). The generation R study: Design and cohort update 2012. *European Journal of Epidemiology, 27*(9), 739–756. https://doi.org/10.1007/s10654-012-9735-1

Joelsson, P., Chudal, R., Talati, A., Suominen, A., Brown, A. S., & Sourander, A. (2016). Prenatal smoking exposure and neuropsychiatric comorbidity of ADHD: A Finnish nationwide population based cohort study. *BMC Psychiatry, 16*, 306. https://doi.org/10.1186/s12888-016-1007-2

Judges, R., Egan, V., & Broad, G. (2016). A critique of the historical clinical risk-20, version 3, risk assessment instrument. *Journal of Forensic Psychology Practice, 16*(4), 304–320. https://doi.org/10.1080/15228932.2016.1196102

Keyes, K. M., Davey Smith, G., & Susser, E. (2014). Associations of prenatal maternal smoking with offspring hyperactivity: Causal or confounded? *Psychological Medicine, 44*(4), 857–867. https://doi.org/10.1017/S0033291713000986

Kiblawi, Z. N., Smith, L. M., Diaz, S. D., LaGasse, L. L., Derauf, C., Newman, E., … Lester, B. (2014). Prenatal methamphetamine exposure and neonatal and infant neurobehavioral outcome: Results from the IDEAL study. *Substance Abuse, 35*(1), 68–73. https://doi.org/10.1080/08897077.2013.814614

Konijnenberg, C., & Melinder, A. (2015). Executive function in preschool children prenatally exposed to methadone or buprenorphine. *Child Neuropsychology, 21*(5), 570–585. https://doi.org/10.1080/09297049.2014.967201

Kosofsky, B. E., Wilkins, A. S., Gressens, P., & Evrard, P. (1994). Transplacental cocaine exposure: A mouse model demonstrating neuroanatomic and behavioral abnormalities. *Journal of Child Neurology, 9*(3), 234–241. https://doi.org/10.1177/088307389400900303

Kropp, P. R., & Gibas, A. (2010). The Spousal Assault Risk Assessment Guide (SARA). In R. K. Otto & K. S. Douglas (Eds.), *International perspectives on forensic mental health. Handbook of violence risk assessment* (pp. 227–250). Routledge/Taylor & Francis Group.

Kubrusly, R. C. C., & Bhide, P. G. (2010). Cocaine exposure modulates dopamine and adenosine signaling in the fetal brain. *Neuropharmacology, 58*(2), 436–443. https://doi.org/10.1016/j.neuropharm.2009.09.007

Lambert, B. L., & Bauer, C. R. (2012). Developmental and behavioral consequences of prenatal cocaine exposure: A review. *Journal of Perinatology, 32*, 819–828.

Langley, K., Heron, J., Smith, G. D., & Thapar, A. (2012). Maternal and paternal smoking during pregnancy and risk of ADHD symptoms in offspring: Testing for intrauterine effects. *American Journal of Epidemiology, 176*(3), 261–268. https://doi.org/10.1093/aje/kwr510

Langley, K., Holmans, P. A., van den Bree, M. B. M., & Thapar, A. (2007). Effects of low birth weight, maternal smoking in pregnancy and social class on the phenotypic manifestation of attention deficit hyperactivity disorder and associated antisocial behaviour: Investigation in a clinical sample. *BMC Psychiatry, 7*, 26. https://doi.org/10.1186/1471-244x-7-26

Larson, J. J., Graham, D. L., Singer, L. T., Beckwith, A. M., Terplan, M., Davis, J. M., … Bada, H. S. (2019). Cognitive and behavioral impact on children exposed to opioids during pregnancy. *Pediatrics, 144*(2), e20190514. https://doi.org/10.1542/peds.2019-0514

Leech, S. L., Day, N. L., Richardson, G. A., & Goldschmidt, L. (2003). Predictors of self-reported delinquent behavior in a sample of young adolescents. *Journal of Early Adolescence, 23*(1), 78–106. https://doi.org/10.1177/0272431602239131

Leech, S. L., Richardson, G. A., Goldschmidt, L., & Day, N. L. (1999). Prenatal substance exposure: Effects on attention and impulsivity of 6-year-olds. *Neurotoxicology and Teratology, 21*(2), 109–118. https://doi.org/10.1016/s0892-0362(98)00042-7

Lester, B. M., & LaGasse, L. L. (2010). Children of addicted women. *Journal of Addictive Diseases, 29*(2), 259–276. https://doi.org/10.1080/10550881003684921

Lewis, B. A., Kirchner, H. L., Short, E. J., Minnes, S., Weishampel, P., Satayathum, S., & Singer, L. T. (2007). Prenatal cocaine and tobacco effects on children's language trajectories. *Pediatrics, 120*(1), e78–e85. https://doi.org/10.1542/peds.2006-2563

Lidow, M. S., Trakht, T., & Howard, R. L. (1999). Cocaine-induced alterations in the density of monoaminergic receptors in the embryonic guinea pig cerebral wall. *Synapse, 32*(3), 225–237. https://doi.org/10.1002/(sici)1098-2396(19990601)32:3%3C225::aid-syn8%3E3.0.co;2-9

Linares, T. J., Singer, L. T., Kirchner, H. L., Short, E. J., Min, M. O., Hussey, P., & Minnes, S. (2006). Mental health outcomes of cocaine-exposed children at 6 years of age. *Journal of Pediatric Psychology, 31*(1), 85–97. https://doi.org/10.1093/jpepsy/jsj020

Linnet, K. M., Dalsgaard, S., Obel, C., Wisborg, K., Henriksen, T. B., Rodrigues, A., … Jarvelin, R.-R. (2003). Maternal lifestyle factors in pregnancy risk of attention deficit hyperactivity disorder and associated behaviors: Review of the current evidence. *American Journal of Psychiatry, 160*(6), 1028–1040. https://doi.org/10.1176/appi.ajp.160.6.1028

Little, B. B., Snell, L. M., & Gilstrap, L. C., III. (1988). Methamphetamine abuse during pregnancy: Outcome and fetal effects. *Obstetrics and Gynecology, 72*(4), 541–544.

Liu, J., Lester, B. M., Neyzi, N., Sheinkopf, S. J., Gracia, L., Kekatpure, M., & Kosofsky, B. E. (2013). Regional brain morphometry and impulsivity in adolescents following prenatal exposure to cocaine and tobacco. *JAMA Pediatrics, 167*(4), 348–354. https://doi.org/10.1001/jamapediatrics.2013.550

Loeber, R., Pardini, D., Homish, D. L., Wei, E. H., Crawford, A. M., Farrington, D. P., … Rosenfeld, R. (2005). The prediction of violence and homicide in young men. *Journal of Consulting and Clinical Psychology, 73*(6), 1074–1088. https://doi.org/10.1037/0022-006X.73.6.1074

Malmgrem, K., Abbott, R. D., & Hawkins, J. D. (1999). LD and delinquency: Rethinking the "link". *Journal of Learning Disabilities, 32*(3), 194–200. https://doi.org/10.1177/002221949903200301

Martin, M. M., Graham, D. L., McCarthy, D. M., Bhide, P. G., & Stanwood, G. D. (2016). Cocaine-induced neurodevelopmental deficits and underlying mechanisms. Birth Defects Research. Part C. *Embryo Today: Reviews, 108*(2), 147–173. https://doi.org/10.1002/bdrc.21132

Mayes, L. C., Bornstein, M. H., Chawarska, K., Haynes, O. M., & Granger, R. H. (1996). Impaired regulation of arousal in 3-month-old infants exposed prenatally to cocaine and other drugs. *Development and Psychopathology, 8*(1), 29–42. https://doi.org/10.1017/S0954579400006957

Mayes, L. C., Molfese, D. L., Key, A. P. F., & Hunter, N. C. (2005). Event-related potentials in cocaine exposed children during a Stroop task. *Neurotoxicology and Teratology, 27*(6), 797–813. https://doi.org/10.1016/j.ntt.2005.05.011

Mayes, L., Snyder, P. J., Langlois, E., & Hunter, N. (2007). Visuospatial working memory in school-aged children exposed in utero to cocaine. *Child Neuropsychology, 13*(3), 205–218. https://doi.org/10.1080/09297040600888753

McCarthy, D. M., Brown, A. N., & Bhide, P. G. (2012). Regulation of BDNF expression by cocaine. *Yale Journal of Biology and Medicine, 85*(4), 437–446.

McElhatton, P. R., Bateman, D. N., Evans, C., Pughe, K. R., & Thomas, S. H. (1999). Congenital anomalies after prenatal ecstasy exposure. *Lancet, 354*(9188), 1441–1442. https://doi.org/10.1016/S0140-6736(99)02423-X

Moffitt, T. E. (1990). The neuropsychology of juvenile delinquency: A critical review. *Crime and Justice, 12*, 99–169. http://www.jstor.org/stable/1147439

Mohan, L., Yilanli, M., & Ray, S. (2020). Conduct disorder. In *In: StatPearls [Internet]*. Treasure Island (FL): StatPearls Publishing. https://www.ncbi.nlm.nih.gov/books/NBK470238/

Monahan, J., Steadman, H., Appelbaum, P., Grisso, T., Mulvey, E., Roth, L., … Silver, E. (2007). The classification of violence risk. *Behavioral Sciences & the Law, 24*(6), 721–730. https://doi.org/10.1002/bsl.725

Monahan, J., Steadman, H., Robbins, P., Appelbaum, P., Banks, S., Grisso, T., et al. (2005). An Actuarial Model of Violence Risk Assessment for Persons with Mental Disorders. *Psychiatric Services, 56*, 810–815.

National Institutes on Drug Abuse (NIDA). (2020, May 29). *What are the effects of maternal cocaine use?* Retrieved from https://www.drugabuse.gov/publications/research-reports/cocaine/what-are-effects-maternal-cocaine-use

Nigg, J. T., & Breslau, N. (2007). Prenatal smoking exposure, low birth weight, and disruptive behavior disorders. *Journal of the American Academy of Child and Adolescent Psychiatry, 46*(3), 362–369. https://doi.org/10.1097/01.chi.0000246054.76167.44

Nygaard, E., Slinning, K., Moe, V., & Walhovd, K. B. (2016). Behavior and attention problems in eight-year-old children with prenatal opiate and poly-substance exposure: A longitudinal study. *PLoS One, 11*(6), e0158054. https://doi.org/10.1371/journal.pone.0158054

Öberg, M., Jaakkola, M., Prüss-Üstün, A., Schweizer, C., & Woodward, A. (2010). *Second-hand smoke: Assessing the environmental burden of disease at national and local levels. WHO Environmental Burden of Disease Series 18*. Geneva, Switzerland: World Health Organization.

Ornoy, A., Michailevskaya, V., Lukashov, I., Bar-Hamburger, R., & Harel, S. (1996). The developmental outcome of children born to heroin-dependent mothers, raised at home or adopted. *Child Abuse and Neglect, 20*(5), 385–396. https://doi.org/10.1016/0145-2134(96)00014-2

Pastrakuljic, A., Schwartz, R., Simone, C., Derewlany, L. O., Knie, B., & Koren, G. (1998). Transplacental transfer and biotransformation studies of nicotine in the human placental cotyledon perfused in vitro. *Life Sciences, 63*(26), 2333–2342. https://doi.org/10.1016/S0024-3205(98)00522-0

Plessinger, M. A. (1998). Prenatal exposure to amphetamines: Risks and adverse outcomes in Pregnancy. *Obstetrics and Gynecology Clinics of North America, 25*(1), 119–138. https://doi.org/10.1016/s0889-8545(05)70361-2

Quinsey, V. L., Harris, G. T., Rice, M. E., & Cormier, C. A. (2006). *Violent offenders: Appraising and managing risk* (2nd ed.). Washington, DC: American Psychological Association. https://doi.org/10.1037/11367-000

Raine, A., & Yang, Y. (2006). Neural foundations to moral reasoning and antisocial behavior. *Social Cognitive and Affective Neuroscience, 1*(3), 203–213. https://doi.org/10.1093/scan/nsl033

Rao, H., Wang, J., Giannetta, J., Korczykowski, M., Shera, D., Avants, B. B., … Hurt, H. (2007). Altered resting cerebral blood flow in adolescents with in utero cocaine exposure revealed by perfusion functional MRI. *Pediatrics, 120*(5), e1245–e1254. https://doi.org/10.1542/peds.2006-2596

Richardson, G. A., De Genna, N. M., Goldschmidt, L., Larkby, C., & Donovan, J. E. (2019). Prenatal cocaine exposure: Direct and indirect associations with 21-year-old offspring substance use and behavior problems. *Drug and Alcohol Dependence, 195*, 121–131. https://doi.org/10.1016/j.drugalcdep.2018.10.033

Richardson, G. A., Hamel, S. C., Goldschmidt, L., & Day, N. L. (1996). The effects of prenatal cocaine use on neonatal neurobehavioral status. *Neurotoxicology and Teratology, 18*(5), 519–528. https://doi.org/10.1016/0892-0362(96)00062-1

Rivkin, M. J., Davis, P. E., Lemaster, J. L., Cabral, H. J., Warfield, S. K., Mulkern, R. V., … Frank, D. A. (2008). Volumetric MRI study of brain in children with intrauterine exposure to cocaine, alcohol, tobacco, and marijuana. *Pediatrics, 121*(4), 741–750. https://doi.org/10.1542/peds.2007-1399

Roncero, C., Valriberas-Herrero, I., Mezzatesta-Gava, M., Villegas, J. L., Aguilar, L., & Grau-López, L. (2020). Cannabis use during pregnancy and its relationship with fetal developmental

outcomes and psychiatric disorders: A systematic review. *Reproductive Health, 17*, 25. https://doi.org/10.1186/s12978-020-0880-9
Roos, A., Kwiatkowski, M. A., Fouche, J.-P., Narr, K. L., Thomas, K. G. F., Stein, D. J., & Donald, K. A. (2015). White matter integrity and cognitive performance in children with prenatal methamphetamine exposure. *Behavioural Brain Research, 279*, 62–67. https://doi.org/10.1016/j.bbr.2014.11.005
Rosenthal, D. G., & Weitzman, M. (2011). Examining the effects of intrauterine and postnatal exposure to tobacco smoke on childhood cognitive and behavioral development. *International Journal of Mental Health, 40*(1), 39–64. https://doi.org/10.2753/IMH0020-7411400103
Salmasi, G., Grady, R., Jones, J., & McDonald, S. D. (2010). Environmental tobacco smoke exposure and perinatal outcomes: A systematic review and meta-analyses. *Acta Obstetricia Gynecologica Scandinavica, 89*(4), 423–441. https://pubmed.ncbi.nlm.nih.gov/20085532
Scher, M. S., Richardson, G. A., & Day, N. L. (2000). Effects of prenatal cocaine/crack and other drug exposure on electroencephalographic sleep studies at birth and one year. *Pediatrics, 105*(1 Part 1), 39–48. https://doi.org/10.1542/peds.105.1.39
Shader, M. (2003). *Risk factors of delinquency: An overview*. Washington, DC: U.S. Department of Justice, Office of Justice Programs, Office of Juvenile Justice and Delinquency Prevention.
Shader, M. (2004). *Risk factors for delinquency: An overview*. Washington, DC: U.S. Department of Justice, Office of Justice Programs, Office of Juvenile Justice and Delinquency Prevention. https://www.ncjrs.gov/pdffiles1/ojjdp/frd030127.pdf
Shah, R., Diaz, S. D., Arria, A., LaGasse, L. L., Derauf, C., Newman, E., … Lester, B. M. (2012). Prenatal methamphetamine exposure and short-term maternal and infant medical outcomes. *American Journal of Perinatology, 29*(5), 391–400. https://doi.org/10.1055/s-0032-1304818
Sheinkopf, S. J., Lester, B. M., Sanes, J. N., Eliassen, J. C., Hutchison, E. R., Seifer, R., … Casey, B. J. (2009). Functional MRI and response inhibition in children exposed to cocaine in utero. Preliminary findings. *Developmental Neuroscience, 31*(1–2), 159–166. https://doi.org/10.1159/000207503
Shilling, P. D., Kuczenski, R., Segal, D. S., Barrett, T. B., & Kelsoe, J. R. (2006). Differential regulation of immediate-early gene expression in the prefrontal cortex of rat with a high vs. low behavioral response to methamphetamine. *Neuropsychopharmacology, 31*(11), 2359–2367. https://doi.org/10.1038/sj.npp.1301162
Silva, D., Colvin, L., Hagemann, E., & Bower, C. (2014). Environmental risk factors by gender associated with attention-deficit/hyperactivity disorder. *Pediatrics, 133*(1), e14–e22. https://doi.org/10.1542/peds.2013-1434
Singer, L. T., Moore, D. G., Min, M. O., Goodwin, J., Turner, J. J., Fulton, S., & Parrott, A. C. (2015). Developmental outcomes of 3, 4-methylenedioxymethamphetamine (Ecstasy)-exposed infants in the UK. *Human Psychopharmacology, 30*(4), 290–294. https://doi.org/10.1002/hup.2459
Singer, L. T., Nelson, S., Short, E., Min, M. O., Lewis, B., Russ, S., & Minnes, S. (2008). Prenatal cocaine exposure: Drug and environmental effects at 9 years. *Journal of Pediatrics, 153*(1), 105–111. https://doi.org/10.1016/j.jpeds.2008.01.001
Singh, J. P., Serper, M., Reinharth, J., & Fazel, S. (2011). Structured assessment of violence risk in schizophrenia and other psychiatric disorders: A systematic review of the validity, reliability, and item content of 10 available instruments. *Schizophrenia Bulletin, 37*(5), 899–912. https://doi.org/10.1093/schbul/sbr093
Sites, B. (2007). The danger of future dangerousness in death penalty use. *Florida State University Law Review, 34*(3), 959–996. https://ir.law.fsu.edu/lr/vol34/iss3/7
Skelton, M. R., Williams, M. T., & Vorhees, C. V. (2008). Developmental effects of 3,4-methyle nedioxymethamphetamine: A review. *Behavioral Pharmacology, 19*(2), 91–111. https://doi.org/10.1097/FBP.0b013e3282f62c76
Šlamberová, R. (2019). Review of long-term consequences of maternal methamphetamine exposure. *Physiological Research, 68*(Suppl. 3), S219–S231. https://doi.org/10.33549/physiolres.934360

Svalin, K., & Levander, S. (2020). The predictive validity of intimate partner violence risk assessments conducted by practitioners in different settings—A review of the literature. *Journal of Police and Criminal Psychology, 35*, 115–130. https://doi.org/10.1007/s11896-019-09343-4

Slotkin, T. A., Seidler, F. J., & Yanai, J. (2003). Heroin neuroteratogenicity: Delayed-onset deficits in catecholaminergic synaptic activity. *Brain Research, 984*(1–2), 189–197. https://doi.org/10.1016/s0006-8993(03)03152-4

Smith, L. M., Diaz, S., LaGasse, L. L., Wouldes, T., Derauf, C., Newman, E., … Lester, B. M. (2015). Developmental and behavioral consequences of prenatal methamphetamine exposure: A review of the infant development, environment, and lifestyle (IDEAL) study. *Neurotoxicology and Teratology, 51*, 35–44. https://doi.org/10.1016/j.ntt.2015.07.006

Smith, L. M., LaGasse, L. L., Derauf, C., Grant, P., Shah, R., Arria, A., … Lester, B. M. (2008). Prenatal methamphetamine use and neonatal neurobehavioral outcome. *Neurotoxicology and Teratology, 30*(1), 20–28. https://doi.org/10.1016/j.ntt.2007.09.005

Snowden, R. J., Gray, N. S., Taylor, J., & MacCulloch, M. J. (2007). Actuarial prediction of violent recidivism in mentally disordered offenders. *Psychological Medicine, 37*(11), 1539–1549. https://doi.org/10.1017/S0033291707000876

Soepatmi, S. (1994). Developmental outcomes of children of mothers dependent on heroin or heroin/methadone during pregnancy. *Acta Paediatrica (Oslow), 404*(Suppl), 36–39. https://doi.org/10.1111/j.1651-2227.1994.tb13382.x

Spurlock, G., Williams, J., McGuffin, P., Aschauer, H. N., Lenzinger, E., Fuchs, K., … Owen, M. J. (1998). European multicentre association study of schizophrenia: A study of the DRD_2 Ser311Cys and DRD_3 serology polymorphisms. *American Journal of Medical Genetics, 81*(1), 24–28. https://doi.org/10.1002/(SICI)1096-8628(19980207)81:1%3C24::AID-AJMG5%3E3.0.CO;2-N

Substance Abuse and Mental Health Services Administration (SAMHSA). (2014) *Results from the 2013 national survey on drug use and health: Summary of national findings* (NSDUH Series H-48, HHS Publication No (SMA) 14–4863). Rockville, MD: Substance Abuse and Mental Health Services Administration.

Thompson, V. B., Heiman, J., Chambers, J. B., Benoit, S. C., Buesing, W. R., Norman, M. K., … Lipton, J. W. (2009). Long-term behavioral consequences of prenatal MDMA exposure. *Physiology and Behavior, 96*(4–5), 593–601. https://doi.org/10.1016/j.physbeh.2008.12.013

Tiesler, C. M., Chen, C. M., Sausenthaler, S., Heerbarth, O., Lehmann, I., Schaaf, B., … Heinrich, J. (2011). Passive smoking and behavioural problems in children: Results from the LISAplus prospective birth cohort study. *Environmental Research, 111*(8), 1173–1179. https://doi.org/10.1016/j.envres.2011.06.011

Tiesler, C. M. T., & Heinrich, J. (2014). Prenatal nicotine exposure and child behavioural problems. *European Child and Adolescent Psychiatry, 23*(10), 913–929. https://doi.org/10.1007/s00787-014-0615-y

Tomášková, A., Šlamberová, R., & Černá, M. (2020). Influence of prenatal methamphetamine abuse on the brain. *Epigenomes, 4*(3), 14. https://doi.org/10.3390/epigenomes4030014

Trezza, V., Campolongo, P., Manduca, A., Morena, M., Palmery, M., Vanderschuren, L. J. M. J., & Cuomo, V. (2012). Altering endocannabinoid neurotransmission at critical developmental ages: Impact on rodent emotionality and cognitive performance. *Frontiers in Behavioral Neuroscience, 6*, 2. https://doi.org/10.3389/fnbeh.2012.00002

van Baar, A. L., Fleury, P., Soepatmi, S., Ultee, C. A., & Wesselman, P. J. M. (1989). Neonatal behaviour after drug dependent pregnancy. *Archives of Disease in Childhood, 64*, 235–240. https://adc.bmj.com/content/archdischild/64/2/235.full.pdf

Vassoler, F. M., Byrnes, E. M., & Pierce, R. C. (2014). The impact of exposure to addictive drugs on future generations: Physiological and behavioral elects. *Neuropharmacology, 76*(Part B), 269–275. https://doi.org/10.1016/j.neuropharm.2013.06.016

Violence Risk Appraisal Guide. (n.d.). *Violence risk appraisal guide-revised: Official website*. Retrieved from http://www.vrag-r.org/

Volkow, N. D., Han, B., Compton, W. M., & McCance-Katz, E. F. (2019). Self-reported medical and nonmedical cannabis use among pregnant women in the United States. *JAMA, 322*(2), 167–169. https://doi.org/10.1001/jama.2019.7982

Wakschlag, L. S., Pickett, K. E., Cook, E., Jr., Benowitz, N. L., & Leventhal, B. L. (2002). Maternal smoking during pregnancy and severe antisocial behavior in offspring: A review. *American Journal of Public Health, 92*(6), 966–974. https://doi.org/10.2105/AJPH.92.6.966

Wakschlag, L. S., Pickett, K. E., Kasza, K. E., & Loeber, R. (2006). Is prenatal smoking associated with a developmental pattern of conduct problems in young boys? *Journal of the American Academy of Child and Adolescent Psychiatry, 45*(4), 461–467. https://doi.org/10.1097/01.chi.0000198597.53572.3e

Wang, X., Dow-Edwards, D., Anderson, V., Minkoff, H., & Hurd, Y. L. (2004). In utero marijuana exposure associated with abnormal amygdala dopamine D2 gene expression in the human fetus. *Biological Psychiatry, 56*(12), 909–915. https://doi.org/10.1016/j.biopsych.2004.10.015

Wang, X., Dow-Edwards, D., Keller, E., & Hurd, Y. L. (2003). Preferential limbic expression of the cannabinoid receptor mRNA in the human fetal brain. *Neuroscience, 118*(3), 681–694. https://doi.org/10.1016/s0306-4522(03)00020-4

Warner, T. D., Behnke, M., Eyler, F. D., Padgett, K., Leonard, C., Hou, W., … Blackband, S. J. (2006). Diffusion tensor imaging of frontal white matter and executive functioning in cocaine-exposed children. *Pediatrics, 118*(5), 2014–2024. https://doi.org/10.1542/peds.2006-0003

Waters, J., Roberts, A. R., & Morgen, K. (1997). High risk pregnancies: Teenagers, poverty, and drug abuse. *Journal of Drug Issues, 27*(3), 541–562. https://doi.org/10.1177/002204269702700307

Webster, C. D., Nicholls, T. L., Martin, M. L., Desmarais, S. L., & Brink, J. (2006). Short-term assessment of risk and treatability (START): The case for a new structured professional judgment scheme. *Behavioral Sciences & the Law, 24*(6), 747–766. https://doi.org/10.1002/bsl.737

Wiggs, K., Elmore, A. L., Nigg, J. T., & Nikolas, M. A. (2016). Pre- and perinatal risk for attention-deficit hyperactivity disorder: Does neuropsychological weakness explain the link? *Journal of Abnormal Child Psychology, 44*(8), 1473–1485. https://doi.org/10.1007/s10802-016-0142-z

Yeoh, S. L., Eastwood, J., Wright, I. M., Morton, R., Melhuish, E., Ward, M., … Oei, J. L. (2019). Cognitive and motor outcomes of children with prenatal opioid exposure: A systematic review and meta-analysis. *JAMA Network Open, 2*(7), e197025. https://doi.org/10.1001/jamanetworkopen.2019.7025

Zhou, S., Rosenthal, D. G., Sherman, S., Zelikoff, J., Gordon, T., & Weitzman, M. (2014). Physical, behavioral, and cognitive effects of prenatal tobacco and postnatal secondhand smoke exposure. *Current Problems in Pediatric Adolescent Health Care, 44*(8), 219–241. https://doi.org/10.1016/j.cppeds.2014.03.007

Chapter 14
Adults with Fetal Alcohol Spectrum Disorder in the Context of Sexually Violent Predator Involuntary Civil Commitment Psychological Evaluations

Brian R. Abbott

Abstract Prenatal alcohol exposure (PAE) produces a broad range of primary disabilities (i.e., cognitive deficits) that lead to adverse life course outcomes ("secondary disabilities") in children raised in adverse environments. Inappropriate sexual behaviors are a commonly occurring secondary disability, with a large minority of individuals with fetal alcohol spectrum disorder (FASD) displaying sexual aggression. Adults with FASD who commit repeated criminal sexual acts may be subject to legal proceedings for indefinite involuntary civil confinement as sexually violent predators (SVPs) in 21 of the United States and in federal jurisdictions. Studies that have examined the diagnostic practices of psychologists and psychiatrists retained by states to evaluate individuals as SVPs do not recognize FASD as a mental disorder, although extrapolated data reported in this chapter suggest hundreds of individuals petitioned for involuntary commitment as SVPs suffer from undetected FASD. Establishing an FASD diagnosis may provide exculpatory evidence to refute a government petition that an individual suffers from a mental condition affecting emotional or volitional capacity by predisposing the person to committing criminal sexual behavior. This chapter provides a framework for determining whether an FASD diagnosis in persons subject to possible SVP determination meets the legal requirements of a mental condition necessary to indefinitely commit people to civil confinement as SVPs. Recommendations are made for conducting a comprehensive forensic evaluation of this legal issue.

Keywords Sexually violent predator · SVP · Civil commitment · FASD · Alcohol · Sexual aggression

B. R. Abbott (✉)
San Jose, CA, USA
e-mail: brian@dr-abbott.net

N. Novick Brown (ed.), *Evaluating Fetal Alcohol Spectrum Disorders in the Forensic Context*, https://doi.org/10.1007/978-3-030-73628-6_14

14.1 Introduction

Central nervous system (CNS) abnormalities fundamental to FASD produce cognitive deficits (i.e., primary disabilities) that manifest in a range of difficulties, including microcephaly, fine and gross motor deficits, characteristic facial features, growth deficiency, maladaptive behaviors, inattention, and impairments in cognition, including executive functioning and memory (Streissguth, 1997). Primary disabilities place children with FASD at risk for later developing secondary disabilities, which are acquired conditions that cause clinically significant impairment in social, occupational, and/or academic functioning. Secondary disabilities may take the form of dysregulated thinking, feeling, and behavior. Inappropriate sexual behaviors (ISBs) are a commonly observed secondary disability (Anderson, Karding, Reid, & Pei, 2018; Streissguth, Barr, Kogan, & Bookstein, 1996).

ISBs exhibited by persons with FASD may encompass one or more of the following behaviors: improper sexual advances, unwanted sexual touching, exposure, promiscuous or dangerous sexual activity, prostitution, coercive sexual acts, masturbation in unsuitable settings, peeping, and obscene or offensive language (Novick, 1997; Streissguth et al., 1996; Streissguth et al., 2004). Prevalence of ISBs appears to increase over the lifespan, with up to 65% of males with FASD demonstrating some form of ISB (Streissguth et al., 1996; Streissguth et al., 2004). In apparently the only attempt to quantify the extent to which individuals with FASD are reported for sexual crimes, Streissguth et al. (1996) studied 412 children, adolescents, and adults with FASD, discovering that approximately 15% of youths between 12 and 20 years old and an equal proportion of adults between 21 and 51 years old had committed at least one sexual assault. Mela et al. (2020) reported results in a study that compared two groups of criminal offenders with mental disorders, including those referred to forensic psychiatric outpatient clinics with FASD (n = 12) and those without the disorder (n = 33). These researchers discovered virtually equal proportions of the FASD sample (25%) and non-FASD group (27%) had committed sexual crimes. Other than these findings from a small nonrepresentative sample, there are no contemporary prevalence data regarding FASD in persons who commit criminal sexual acts. Nonetheless, it is possible to estimate the rate by applying the lower (0.0091) and upper (0.223) bounds of prevalence rates for FASD in the US corrections system (Burd, Fast, Conry, & Williams, 2010) to current correctional census data. Applying this metric to the most recent correctional census information reported by the US Bureau of Justice Statistics suggests that in 2016 (Carson, 2018), 343,384 individuals were incarcerated (jails and prisons) and under community supervision (parole or probation) for sexual crimes likely had FASD.

In fact, some criminal sexual offending among imprisoned individuals, including those suffering from FASD (Brown & Singh, 2016), is so severe or repetitive it leads prosecutors in nearly half of the United States to file petitions against them for involuntary civil confinement as sexually violent predators (SVPs) upon expiration of their prison sentences. These individuals are alleged to suffer from an SVP-qualifying mental disorder that constitutes an acquired or congenital condition affecting their emotional or volitional capacity in a way that predisposes them to commit criminal sexual acts, and this mental condition makes them sexually dangerous (Abbott, 2017). Data do not exist as to what proportion of individuals involved in the SVP involuntary civil confinement system present with an acquired or congenital condition in the form of FASD, but it is possible to estimate the rate by applying lower and upper prevalence rates for the US correctional system from Burd et al. (2010). As of 2018, there were 6332 individuals committed as SVPs or who were detained awaiting adjudication of their civil confinement petitions in 19 SVP facilities across the United States (Schneider et al., 2018). However, this rate underestimates the total census for two reasons. Two SVP facilities did not respond to the survey. Among the 19 survey respondents, six did not report the number of individuals detained awaiting adjudication of their SVP petitions. Omission of these data from nonreporting facilities likely underestimates the census by approximately 1000 individuals. Given this number, it is estimated between 58 and 1412 individuals housed in SVP civil confinement facilities suffer from FASD. However, FASD appears virtually unrecognized among individuals petitioned or committed as SVP when examining the diagnostic practices of evaluators who support petitions by states' attorneys for SVP civil commitment (Becker, Stinson, Tromp, & Messer, 2003; Levenson, 2004; Lieb, 1996; Perillo, Spada, Calkins, & Jeglic, 2014; Vess, Murphy, & Arkowitz, 2004).

Failure to identify individuals with FASD in the correctional system happens because clinicians are unfamiliar with identifying FASD's primary and secondary disabilities (Brown & Singh, 2016; Burd et al., 2010) as well as other variables in clinical presentation, such as changes in FASD phenotypes over the lifespan, inadequate documentation of prenatal alcohol exposure (PAE), and high rates of postnatal adversity and comorbidities that tend to obscure FASD symptomology (Burd et al., 2010; Mela et al., 2020). It is reasonable to infer that similar reasons contribute to the lack of recognition of FASD as an acquired or congenital condition in SVP diagnostic studies. Consistent with this premise, Brown and Singh (2016) surveyed 100 staff members working in SVP treatment programs around the United States, discovering the 18 individuals who responded lacked adequate knowledge to reliably identify individuals with FASD. While the small number of participants limits generalizability of the outcome, such results are consistent with other studies demonstrating that lack of knowledge regarding the clinical presentation of FASD over the lifespan is a barrier to reliable identification of the condition (Anderson et al., 2018; Burd et al., 2010; Novick Brown, Wartnik, Connor, & Adler, 2010).

Need for accurate diagnosis is paramount in the SVP context because if a requisite mental disorder cannot be substantiated, a person does not qualify for involuntary civil commitment as an SVP. Since 2002, the author has evaluated hundreds of individuals being petitioned for involuntary civil confinement as SVPs across seven states. In this capacity, the author reviewed more than 1500 reports and countless testimony transcripts of psychologists and psychiatrists retained by the government (SVP evaluators) who supported petitions to involuntarily commit persons as SVPs (hereinafter referred to as respondent[s]). This experience revealed many instances where FASD was not recognized in respondents who likely had the disorder.

Consistent with the previously mentioned SVP diagnostic studies (Becker et al., 2003; Levenson, 2004; Lieb, 1996; Perillo et al., 2014; Vess et al., 2004), SVP evaluators who have concluded respondents meet legal criteria for involuntary civil commitment either failed to identify FASD or, when FASD was established by history, failed to appreciate the etiological significance of the disorder in explaining the history of sexual offending that provoked a petition for civil commitment. Instead, these evaluators contorted the primary and secondary disabilities in respondents' FASD to fit the symptom picture of a paraphilic disorder and/or personality disorder because such acquired or congenital conditions appeared logically linked to the emotional or volitional capacity that presumably predisposed people to committing criminal sexual acts. In contrast, when primary and secondary disabilities associated with FASD are recognized and evaluated properly, there is very little basis for forensic evaluators to reasonably conclude FASD affects emotional or volitional control in a way that predisposes an individual to criminal sexual acts. The focus of this chapter is on the intersection of FASD and the SVP mental disorder.

14.2 Overview of Sexually Violent Predator Laws and Forensic Implications as Applied to Fetal Alcohol Spectrum Disorder

Laws in 21 states and at the federal level permit the government to petition individuals for involuntary civil confinement as SVPs after they have served their prison sentences for certain sexual crimes (Knighton, Murrie, Boccaccini, & Turner, 2014). SVP statutes are premised on three underlying legal principles to justify involuntary civil confinement (Scurich & Krauss, 2014), including the existence of proscribed prior qualifying criminal sexual conviction(s), presence of a current SVP mental disorder, and a requirement the SVP mental disorder must cause the person to be likely to commit further criminal sexual acts after release into the community. The only exception to this legal scheme is the federal Adam Walsh Act where chapter 18 of the US Code section 4247(a)(6) presumes an individual is sexually dangerous if he (or she) has a history of at least one of the qualifying sexual crimes and suffers from a current SVP mental disorder. Once civilly committed, a respondent remains in total confinement indefinitely unless he later can prove he no longer suffers from the SVP mental disorder or is no longer sexually dangerous (Scurich & Krauss, 2014).

Except for the legally required history of qualifying sexual crimes, the remaining SVP criteria—an SVP mental disorder that makes the person sexually dangerous—fall under the purview of forensic psychology or psychiatry. Not surprisingly, SVP evaluators typically are the principal witnesses who provide evidence to triers of fact as to whether respondents' clinical presentations fit the SVP mental disorder and likelihood to commit dangerous sexual behavior necessary to justify involuntary civil confinement (Scurich & Krauss, 2014). Psychologists employ a range of psychological methods to assess for the presence of an SVP mental disorder, which may include psychological testing, review of relevant background information, physiological assessment of sexual arousal, diagnostic interview, mental status examination, and differential diagnosis. The general legal definition of an SVP mental disorder is an *acquired or congenital condition that affects emotional or volitional capacity which predisposes the individual to commit dangerous sexual behavior*. It is evident the SVP mental disorder consists of two component parts that can be conceptualized as a sequential contingency. First, the forensic evaluator must determine if the individual suffers from a current acquired or congenital condition. If this element is satisfied, the forensic examiner then must determine whether the acquired or congenital condition affects the individual's emotional or volitional capacity in a manner that predisposes him to engage in dangerous sexual behavior.

SVP laws do not specify or require acquired or congenital conditions to take the form of one or more mental disorder diagnoses contained in the American Psychiatric Association's *Diagnostic and Statistical Manual for Mental Disorders* (*DSM-5*; American Psychiatric Association (APA), 2013; Frances, Sreenivasan, & Weinberger, 2008). However, by convention SVP evaluators rely upon the DSM as foundation to substantiate the presence of an acquired or congenital condition (First & Halon, 2008). Categories of paraphilic disorders and/or personality disorders enumerated in past DSM manuals and the current fifth edition of DSM (*DSM-5*; APA, 2013) typically are specified as the acquired or congenital condition (Becker et al., 2003; Levenson, 2004; Lieb, 1996; Perillo et al., 2014; Vess et al., 2004).

Pedophilia is the most frequently recorded diagnosis among respondents, with prevalence rates ranging between 30 and 63% (Becker et al., 2003; Levenson, 2004; Lieb, 1996; Perillo et al., 2014). *Other specified paraphilic disorder, nonconsent*, is the second most observed paraphilic condition, assigned at rates between 30 and 56% (Becker et al., 2003; Levenson, 2004; Lieb, 1996; Perillo et al., 2014). The diagnosis of *sexual sadism* appears to occur at relatively low prevalence rates that fall between 2.5 and 13.2% (Becker et al., 2003; Levenson, 2004; Lieb, 1996; Perillo et al., 2014). Aside from the already-mentioned three paraphilic disorders reported in the referenced studies, forensic evaluators assign other paraphilic diagnoses (e.g., *voyeurism, exhibitionism, frotteurism, fetishism, masochism, telephone scatalogia*) at much lower rates (range = 1–15%). Among personality disorders reported in SVP diagnostic studies (Becker et al., 2003; Levenson, 2004; Lieb, 1996; Perillo et al., 2014), *antisocial personality disorder* was assigned the most, with an average prevalence rate of 38%, followed by *other specified personality disorder (mixed type)*, which on average was assigned to about one-fifth (21%) of respondents. The remaining specified personality disorders contained in the DSM manuals were diagnosed at much lower rates (≤6.5%). It was not uncommon for respondents to be assigned diagnoses from both the paraphilic and personality classes of mental disorders. Again, no SVP diagnostic studies have reported FASD as an acquired or congenital condition.

As noted, primary and secondary disabilities associated with FASD involve impairments in various areas of cognitive and adaptive functioning that mimic but do not actually represent symptoms of paraphilic conditions and personality disorders. Accurate diagnosis in such situations per *DSM-5* (APA, 2013) is a *neurodevelopmental disorder associated with prenatal alcohol exposure* (*ND-PAE*), which falls under the general category Other Specified Neurodevelopmental Disorder and is coded as 315.8. While ND-PAE satisfies the acquired or congenital condition element of an SVP mental disorder, SVP evaluators would be hard-pressed to reasonably conclude ND-PAE affects emotional or volitional control to predispose persons to commit acts of sexual violence as there is no science to support such a link. Absent substantiation of the sequential contingency, SVP evaluators must conclude a respondent does not present with the required SVP mental disorder.

14.3 Primary and Secondary Disabilities Mimic Paraphilia and Personality Disorders

An often overlooked aspect of the *DSM-5* diagnostic system (APA, 2013) is clinical case formulation; a process by which a clinician takes a thorough history of social, psychological, and biological factors that may have contributed to the development of a specific mental disorder in an evaluee. Accurate clinical case formulation requires evaluators to engage in a process of differential diagnosis, which involves exercising clinical judgment when considering what mental disorder criteria-set(s), if any, best explain clinical presentations. Differential diagnosis is necessary because presenting symptoms may overlap categories of mental disorders or stem from sources other than a mental disorder. First (2014a) presents a useful *DSM-5* differential diagnosis process involving six basic steps: (1) ruling out malingering and factitious disorder, (2) ruling out a substance use etiology, (3) ruling out an etiological medical condition, (4) determining the specific primary disorder(s), (5) differentiating adjustment disorder from the residual other specified and unspecified conditions, and (6) establishing the boundary with no mental disorder. Step three is especially important for individuals suffering from FASD, as the primary disabilities associated with CNS impairments likely are a major contributor of secondary disabilities that mimic mental disorders listed in the *DSM-5*. In such a situation, the diagnosis ND-PAE would be made and designated as "primary," with associated comorbid mental disorders, if applicable, listed as "secondary." As previously noted, differential diagnosis is complicated by the fact individuals with FASD typically suffer from co-occurring mental and personality disorders (Popova et al., 2016).

PAE produces psychological, interpersonal, and social impairments that not only may contribute to the commission of criminal sexual acts (McMurtrie, 2011; Novick Brown et al., 2010; Streissguth et al., 1996) but also mimic paraphilic or personality disorders. PAE has been found to impair executive functioning, adaptive behavior, social skills, and emotional regulation. These deficits coupled with developmental immaturity, social and emotional, may explain how sexual offenders with FASD present clinically in ways that evaluators confuse with paraphilic disorders or personality disorders. The following provides guidance for disentangling the primary and secondary disabilities in FASD that lead to the commission of sexual criminal behavior from paraphilic and personality disorders. These concepts then are illustrated with a case history.

Each specified paraphilic disorder in *DSM-5* (APA, 2013) consists of two primary symptoms, which include a pattern of recurrent, intense sexual arousal involving the paraphilic erotic targets or erotic activity (criterion A) and impairment in functioning caused by the paraphilic arousal pattern (criterion B). A paraphilic disorder cannot be rendered unless both criteria are met, along with any other specified criteria. Language in *DSM-5* stipulates the paraphilic arousal pattern necessary to substantiate criterion A can be assumed rather than affirmed by objective clinical evidence when certain conditions are met. If an individual engages in multiple acts of paraphilic activity and either denies such or refutes any significant or sustained sexual interest in the paraphilia, a clinician can assume criterion A is satisfied if the person has multiple victims. This instruction is referred to as *victim counts*. Thus, for example, when a respondent denies experiencing criterion A arousal to frotteurism, despite having engaged in four separate acts that involved touching or rubbing against four nonconsenting women, an SVP evaluator may diagnose the person with frotteuristic disorder. With the exception of pedophilic disorder, victim count is set at three or more for the other paraphilic conditions that permit this diagnostic practice. The Diagnostic Features section of pedophilic disorder uses the term *multiple victims* without setting a floor as to the exact number of victims. For example, do two victims qualify as multiple victims? Such uncertainty engenders further imprecision in diagnostic accuracy (First, 2010).

Using victim counts instead of objective clinical evidence to diagnose paraphilic conditions effectively gives SVP evaluators license to circumvent the differential diagnosis process in favor of using circular logic to assign a paraphilic diagnosis (First, 2010). When clinical case formulation for a respondent finds primary and secondary disabilities associated with ND-PAE explain his criminal sexual behavior, it would be expected he would not admit during evaluation that he had experienced the criterion A paraphilic arousal pattern. In this situation, a respondent's clinical presentation does not signify refusal to acknowledge paraphilic arousal or interest as the etiology for his criminal sexual behavior. Rather, it portrays an accurate representation of a clinical picture where primary and secondary disabilities associated with FASD motivated criminal sexual conduct. It is intuitively apparent how the victim count method of diagnosis carves out an exception to following the sequential process of differential diagnosis, but it is unjustified because it permits SVP evaluators to bypass step three of the process (First, 2014a), which would recognize ND-PAE as the primary diagnosis over (and perhaps precluding) a paraphilic condition. It is this type of circumvention of the differential diagnosis process that produces unacceptably high rates of false-positive paraphilic diagnoses (First, 2010).

Originally, victim count language for paraphilic disorders was included in proposed *DSM-5* criteria-sets for paraphilias but ultimately omitted because of a lack of broad clinical consensus regarding diagnostic utility (First, 2014b). With the exception of one research study that examined victim counts to identify criterion A of pedophilic disorder (Blanchard, Klassen, Dickey, Kuban, & Blak, 2001), no scientific data or even anecdotal reports support the notion that engaging in certain classes of sexual misconduct involving three or more victims is a valid or reliable method by which to substantiate criterion A of paraphilic conditions. Nonetheless, data in support of using victim counts to substantiate criterion A of pedophilic disorder has been hotly contested, and the following summary of the controversy illuminates the extent to which this procedure produces unacceptably high rates of false-positive diagnoses.

First (2010) criticized inserting victim count language into paraphilic disorder criteria-sets because of lack of established accuracy in identifying true positives and unknown error rates (i.e., false negatives and false positives), as well as concern such language would make it easier for evaluators to ignore differential diagnosis. In a response to First, Blanchard (2010) published Receiver Operating Curve (ROC) analyses from a subset ($N = 998$) of 2715 men seen at an outpatient evaluation and treatment center. The subset sample consisted of individuals at the extreme ends of the entire population, including those who admitted sexual interest in children and those who reported sexual interest in adults. Data for individuals in the mid-range of the sample continuum were omitted from the analysis. Wollert and Cramer (2011) illustrated through mathematical proofs that sampling from the extreme ends of a continuum produced inflated accuracy outcomes. Blanchard then provided the data from the missing subjects to Wollert and Cramer (2011), who recomputed accuracy statistics and found ROC values significantly lower than what Blanchard (2010) had reported. Wollert and Cramer (2011) noted that Blanchard's use of victim counts had resulted in erroneously identifying criterion A pedophilic arousal by 71–91% when considering victim counts between three and six. Blanchard (2011) issued a letter to the editor disputing the findings of Wollert and Cramer (2011) and recomputed what he thought were the proper sensitivity and specificity rates. Favoring Blanchard's (2011) reanalysis over the findings of Wollert and Cramer (2011) results in marginal decreases in false-positive rates to between 64 and 84%. These extremely high false-positive rates when using victim counts to substantiate criterion A pedophilic arousal disproves its clinical utility and does not support circumventing the differential diagnosis process. These findings also raise serious concerns about the validity of victim counts to establish criterion A in other affected paraphilic disorders.

DSM-5 (APA, 2013) presents two procedures for diagnosing personality disorders, the categorical method and dimensional model. Each approach describes a specific personality disorder (e.g., antisocial, narcissistic, borderline) along with categories for recording other types of personality disorders not specified. Despite the divergent theoretical approaches to conceptualizing personality disorders, each model incorporates the differential diagnosis process previously specified by First (2014a), including a consideration that impaired personality functioning may be the product of substance use, a medical condition, or other mental disorder. Establishing a boundary of *no* personality disorder involves determining whether enduring patterns of thinking, feeling, behavior, and relating to others (categorical approach) or impairments in domains of personality functioning (dimensional model) are relatively stable over time, with onset traced to adolescence or early adulthood, and inflexible and pervasive across broad personal and social situations. Personality disorders may share a similar boundary with ND-PAE when primary and secondary disabilities related to FASD are stable and of long duration. Two crucial factors distinguish FASD-related impairments from characteristics due to personality pathology.

First, in FASD the onset of impairments in thinking, feeling, relating to others, and impulse control that mimic pathological personality traits can be traced to childhood as opposed to first becoming evident in adolescence or early adulthood. Second, individuals who suffer from personality pathology do not evidence characteristic FASD CNS neurobiological changes or structural damage that produces cognitive and behavior dysfunction and adaptive impairments, assuming other etiologies have been ruled out (e.g., traumatic brain injury [TBI]). Evaluators should be able to link the primary disabilities associated with FASD to characteristic impairments in psychological and interpersonal functioning manifesting in childhood, with increasing adaptive dysfunction over the course of development into adulthood (Jirikowic, Kartin, & Olson, 2008; Treit et al., 2013). People who exhibit FASD-related impairments in psychological and interpersonal functioning may not manifest the dysfunction in a broad range of personal and social contexts, but standing alone, this clinical manifestation is insufficient to make a differential diagnosis of ND-PAE over a personality disorder.

14.3.1 Case Example

The following case history exemplifies issues related to differential diagnosis in a respondent whose sexual offending behavior was a secondary disability associated with his FASD as opposed to pedophilic disorder and antisocial personality disorder. At the time the author evaluated Mr. Matthews, he was 31 years of age. He had been imprisoned 4 years prior to the evaluation for a parole violation and criminal conviction for possession of child pornography. The state petitioned him for civil confinement as an SVP prior to his scheduled date of parole. His sexual offense history dated to 12 years old when he fondled the penis of a 3-year-old male in a public restroom. Four years later, while in juvenile hall for a nonsexual offense, he fondled the penis of his 14-year-old roommate once. At 23 years old, Mr. Matthews fondled the penis of a 10-year-old male and talked about sexual matters with him. The victim was the brother of Mr. Matthews' peer-age friend. Mr. Matthews had been on parole for about 4 months following conviction for sexually abusing the 10-year-old male when he left his cellular telephone in a public restroom at a truck stop. The store clerk found the telephone, discovered child pornography on it, and called the police. While officers were investigating the matter, Mr. Matthews appeared at the store, asking about the telephone he left behind. Police arrested him. When an officer asked Mr. Matthews to estimate the ages of the persons depicted in the pornographic images on his cellphone, Mr. Matthews responded the images depicted males between 15 and 20 years old, although he believed two images depicted males that were 5 and 8 years old. There was no forensic examination performed on the electronic device, but the officer's report did not question the veracity of Mr. Matthews' age estimates.

Leading up to the time of his arrest, Mr. Matthews had been homeless because he could not find housing compliant with sexual offender residency restrictions. He slept in a car at night, which was when he viewed pornography on his cellular telephone. He frequented the truck stop to use the restroom and purchase food items. He felt emotionally distraught over being homeless.

Records indicated Mr. Matthews had been diagnosed with FASD by a medical doctor at age 3. At that time, the doctor observed dysmorphic facial features and diagnosed him with static encephalopathy (permanent, nonprogressive brain damage) and severe dysarthria (motor speech disorder). An MRI at the time revealed white lesions in the occipital and frontal lobes that likely produced the seizures Mr. Matthews had experienced from childhood on. At the time of his SVP evaluation, he was taking seizure medication and had been seizure-free for a long time. He presented no other medical problems by history or for which he was being treated.

Mr. Matthews' adoptive mother communicated with the birth mother, who confirmed alcohol use during her pregnancy with him. Available history indicated he was easily overwhelmed cognitively by too much auditory and visual stimuli. He suffered from learning disabilities, vision problems, a speech disorder, impaired hearing, and he had sustained five concussions over the course of his life. Tested at a regional center at age 5, he was found to engage in self-abusive behaviors. Intelligence quotient (IQ) scores were within the average to below-average range, although 9 years later, testing with the Wechsler Abbreviated Scale of Intelligence (WASI; Wechsler, 1999) found IQ scores in the borderline range. Additional testing discovered he functioned in the extremely low range in executive functioning, visual and auditory memory, and consolidating information into memory. Testing at age 21 identified other areas of impairment in cognitive functioning not observed at age 5, including impairments in language, attention and concentration, fine motor skills, visual information processing, math, and verbal fluency. Based upon apparent deterioration in cognitive functioning and lack of cognitive testing for 11 years, the author requested a neuropsychological evaluation.

Results of neuropsychological examination revealed Mr. Matthews' full-scale IQ was in the extremely low range according to testing with the Wechsler Adult Scale of Intelligence, Fourth Edition (WAIS-IV; Wechsler, 2008). The author considered these results more accurate than previous findings from the WASI. Neuropsychological assessment also showed Mr. Matthews continued to display clinically significant impairments in attention, learning and memory, and executive functioning. Results from the Gudjonsson Suggestibility Scale found him to be highly suggestible, which his adoptive mother confirmed. The neuropsychological evaluator assessed Mr. Matthews' adaptive behavior with the Vineland Adaptive Behavior Scales, Third Edition (Vineland-3; Sparrow, Saulnier, Cicchetti, & Doll, 2016), wherein data obtained from the adoptive mother indicated substantial impairments in communication, daily living, and socialization. The adoptive mother also completed the Fetal Alcohol Behavior Scale (FABS; Streissguth, Bookstein, Barr, Press, & Sampson, 1998), which assessed domains of communication and speech, personal manner, emotions, motor skills and activities, academic/work performance, social skills/interactions, and bodily/physiologic functions. Results of the FABS were well above the clinical threshold associated with a behavioral profile unique to FASD.

Aside from the sexual crimes he committed, Mr. Matthews also incurred nonsexual criminal violations. He was arrested and convicted for physical assault, brandishing a weapon, parole and probation violations, burglary, theft, forgery, and filing a false report. The theft and burglary offenses involved his repetitively entering a store where he stole homosexual pornography magazines. He stole checks from his adoptive mother and cashed some of them. He violated probation as a juvenile and adult for such circumstances as possessing adult pornography and threatening his adoptive mother with a knife and getting into a physical fight with her. In adolescence, he had displayed verbally abusive and physically aggressive behavior toward staff and peers in residential placement and juvenile hall. He also stole items from other adolescents in placement and repeatedly ran away. In prison, he had one rule violation report for fighting with his cellmate. Aside from the aforementioned behavioral problems, Mr. Matthews presented no signs of mental disorders such as mania, psychosis, or anxiety.

Mr. Matthews' adoptive mother remained supportive of her son throughout his childhood and adult years. She was available to the author and FASD expert for an interview. She consistently advocated for her son to ensure he received appropriate special education services in public school. She consulted experts and educated herself on how to effectively manage her son's behavioral problems during his childhood and adolescence. Generally, she provided a structured, supportive, protective, and nurturing caregiving environment.

During his school years, Mr. Matthews was enrolled in full-day special education due to the emotional, behavioral, and cognitive sequelae associated with his FASD. He displayed mood swings and temper tantrums throughout his school years, but overall, his behavioral adjustment was fair. He dropped out of school in tenth grade after being incarcerated as a juvenile and lost interest in school. He had no peer friendships during adolescence, due to impaired social functioning. Peers teased and taunted him throughout childhood. He reported having several male and female friends as an adult, including two developmentally disabled "girlfriends." He did not date.

Mr. Matthews had been evaluated by numerous examiners over the years by the time the author saw him. He provided inconsistent information regarding the age of onset of certain sexual milestones such as when he started masturbating, his first sexual experience, when he began having sexual feelings, and how he learned about sexual matters. He began to view pornography during adolescence, looking at it regularly, especially over the Internet. He eventually gained access to Internet child pornography, which resulted in his last arrest for a sexual crime. He reported being sexually active with several female peers, according to records. However, when the author questioned him about the extent of his sexual activity, he acknowledged it was limited to kissing. In early childhood, Mr. Matthews had been sexually victimized by his biological mother and her boyfriends and later was sexually victimized by other wards and inmates when he was in custody as a juvenile and adult. He described his sexual orientation as bisexual at the time of the evaluation, with primary sexual interest in women. He denied a history of recurrent, intense, sexually arousing urges or sexual fantasies involving prepubescent children.

Two psychologists for the state evaluated Mr. Matthews and concluded he met legal requirements for involuntary civil commitment as an SVP. Both evaluators diagnosed him with pedophilic disorder, sexually attracted to males, nonexclusive type. One evaluator identified him as suffering from ND-PAE but hedged on its validity because he only had historical information to consider. The other evaluator diagnosed Mr. Matthews with *personality disorder with borderline and antisocial traits*, as well as *speech sound disorder*, *seizure disorder by history*, and *rule out neurocognitive disorder, not otherwise specified*. It is reasonable to conclude the last three diagnoses reflected the evaluator's identification of symptoms associated with ND-PAE, which she misdiagnosed as comorbid mental disorders. The author notes both psychologists for the state had access to the same historical information summarized previously about Mr. Matthews' FASD, with the exception of the neuropsychological testing the author requested. They received the neuropsychological evaluation report well before testifying in Mr. Matthews' trial, and the psychologist who diagnosed ND-PAE changed his opinion to the condition being present rather than *by history*. That evaluator claimed the combination of ND-PAE and pedophilic disorder affected Mr. Matthews' emotional or behavioral capacity, predisposing him to commit sexually violent acts. The other evaluator refused to acknowledge Mr. Matthews suffered from ND-PAE.

Based upon the history summarized above, this author concluded Mr. Matthews suffered from ND-PAE as the *only* mental condition, finding it did not affect his emotional or behavioral capacity, predisposing him to commit sexually violent acts. The author did not find support for a pedophilic disorder diagnosis. For example, the incident involving Mr. Matthews touching the 3-year-old child's penis in the restroom occurred well below the age floor of 16 years for diagnosing the condition. Moreover, there was no evidence Mr. Matthews' actions were sexually motivated. The next incident involved a 14-year-old male in juvenile hall, who was not prepubescent in physical development. The incident with the 10-year-old victim involved multiple episodes of Mr. Matthews fondling the child's penis; however, there was no information this was anything more than impulsive juvenile behavior on his part rather than being motivated by sexual interest in young children. Between the incidents with the 3- and 10-year-old victims, a period of nearly 11 years, Mr. Matthews' records and self-report indicated no apparent pedophilic interests or attempts to sexually abuse prepubescent males, which is inconsistent with someone who allegedly prefers to engage in sexual activity with prepubescent children. Finally, child pornography involved males who primarily were adolescents and two who were prepubescent. Having such a mix of child pornography is inconsistent with someone who exhibits a sexual preference for engaging in sexual activity with prepubescent children.

Rather than a paraphilic condition, personality disorder, combination of ND-PAE and pedophilic disorder or personality disorder, the author determined that possession of child pornography and sexual offending behavior since age 12 years, which was directed toward both prepubescent and pubescent males, were better explained by impairments in Mr. Matthews' cognitive, emotional, and adaptive functioning related to ND-PAE in combination with situational factors at the time of the sexual offenses. Aside from his sexual offending behavior, Mr. Matthews had engaged in other nonsexual criminal behaviors due to developmental delays in cognitive, emotional, and adaptive functioning related to FASD. Moreover, he displayed other impulsive behavior problems during early childhood that became more severe over time after he experienced childhood adversities such as sexual victimization. In the period preceding the child pornography arrest, Mr. Matthews was highly stressed due to being homeless and decompensated psychologically, as evidenced by his poor coping (i.e., viewing pornography of various types, including child pornography). Impaired coping skills were an aspect of his adaptive dysfunction, which further deteriorated in the context of emotional distress. Mr. Matthews' executive function impairments, including boundary confusion, poor judgment, impulse control problems, emotional dysregulation, and difficulty learning from experience and anticipating the consequences of his actions (e.g., harm to others as well as himself) played a central role in his committing repeated criminal sexual acts. This same clinical case formulation fully explains Mr. Matthews' thinking, feeling, and behaving throughout childhood as well as his adult life, which one of the evaluators attributed to pathological personality traits. The author further noted Mr. Matthews' personality functioning was not marked by enduring pathological character traits that were inflexible and pervasive across broad personal and social contexts. In fact, the very behaviors the state evaluator diagnosed as antisocial and narcissistic personality traits actually were evident early in childhood, which precluded their interpretation as personality disorder symptoms (i.e., personality disorders require symptom-onset in the early adult years), and were consistent with the cognitive and adaptive dysfunction seen in FASD.

14.4 Substantiating the Second Element of a Sexually Violent Predator Mental Disorder

Since a diagnosis of ND-FAE qualifies as a congenital condition under the first element of an SVP mental disorder, it is necessary to evaluate whether it affects emotional or volitional capacity predisposing a person to committing criminal sexual acts, hereinafter referred to as serious difficulty in controlling sexually violent behavior (SDIC-SVB). SDIC-SVB is a legal construct that has no analogous conceptualization in psychology, although some attempts have been made to psychologically describe and evaluate SDIC-SVB (Simon, 2015; Winsmann, 2012). Generally, research examining SDIC-SVB has overwhelmingly concluded the construct cannot be accurately and reliably defined, quantified, or measured using psychological principles or theories (First & Halon, 2008; Grinage, 2003; Janus, 2001; Mercado, Schopp, & Bornstein, 2005; Miller, Amenta, & Conroy, 2005; Prentky, Janus, Barbaree, Schwartz, & Kafka, 2006; Rogers & Jackson, 2005). Prentky et al. (2006) succinctly summarized this state of affairs by concluding the assessment of SDIC-SVB could not be further from the realm of competence of psychologists and psychiatrists. Absent valid and precise methods by which to assess SDIC-SVB psychologically, SVP evaluators must turn to the law for guidance.

The US Supreme Court first addressed the legal concepts of volitional and emotional control when addressing the statutory language of SVP law in *Kansas v. Hendricks* (1997), although the Court made no ruling on the subject. However, the Court described how Hendricks demonstrated current indicia of SDIC-SVB as evidenced by his acknowledging he could not control his sexual desires when "stressed out," and the only way for him to stop his sexually offending behavior was to die. Five years later in *Kansas v. Crane* (2002), the Supreme Court issued a ruling regarding SDIC-SVB, holding lack of control did not have to be absolute but,

> [it] is enough to say that there must be proof of serious difficulty in controlling behavior. And this, when viewed considering such features of the case as the nature of the psychiatric diagnosis, and the severity of the mental abnormality itself, must be sufficient to distinguish the dangerous sexual offender whose serious mental illness, abnormality, or disorder subjects him to civil commitment from the dangerous but typical recidivist convicted in an ordinary criminal case.

The *Crane* court went on to characterize volitional impairment as typically involving individuals who found it particularly difficult to control their behavior, providing the example of compulsive, repetitive, and driven behavior. Since *Kansas v. Crane*, some states with SVP statutes have issued rulings regarding SDIC-SVB. Interested readers should be acquainted with SDIC-SVB case law issued by state courts in jurisdictions in which they practice as it is beyond the scope of this chapter to summarize these varying interpretations state by state. The following offers a few examples for illustrative purposes.

The Arizona Supreme Court offers a useful heuristic to identify the dangerous but typical sexual recidivist as an individual who makes a voluntary choice to commit repetitive sexually violent acts (In re the matter of Leon G., 2002). In contrast, an individual who lacks control over his criminal sexual behavior because of a mental disorder that makes him likely to commit sexually violent acts warrants civil confinement as an SVP. The California Supreme Court in *Hubbart v. People* (1999) and California Appeals Court, Third District, in *People v. Buffington* (1999) concluded the condition of SDIC-SVB must be present at the time of commitment, and the respondent should demonstrate recent objective indicia of it. Such rulings, which even predated the *Crane* decision, indicate SDIC-SVB should be present at the time of commitment. In *People v. Williams* (2003), a California court found the respondent exhibited current SDIC-SVB as evidenced by behavior at the time of commitment that involved acts of open masturbation and instances where he cut the crotch of his pants so his penis was exposed. Williams was quoted as saying, "I feel like a fish on a hook and I don't have control" regarding his sexually violent impulses. Two experts subsequently testified he suffered from a largely uncontrollable obsessive drive to rape.

People v. Galindo (2006) also is instructive as it relates to assessing SDIC-SVB in respondents diagnosed with ND-PAE. *Galindo* involved an individual committed for his criminal sexual history because he was found not guilty by reason of insanity (NGRI). This case is relevant to SVP respondents because the California Supreme

Court determined the legal concept of serious difficulty controlling dangerous behavior, whether physical or sexual violence, held the same meaning across the state's various civil confinement laws (In re Howard N., 2005). In *Galindo*, the appeals court reasoned a finding of serious difficulty controlling dangerous behavior was not supported when a respondent simply failed to exercise control over his dangerous behavior because he perceived no reason to do so. That is, failing to control dangerous behavior does not prove deficient ability to do so on its face. Rather, in order to conclude a respondent had serious difficulty controlling dangerous behavior, there must be evidence he *tried but was unable* to control his dangerous behavior and this difficulty was due to an acquired or congenital condition.

Courts in Washington State have held SDIC-SVB reflects a *current* condition. In the case of In re the Detention of Young (1993), the Washington Supreme Court cited a psychological journal article that was instructive in defining SDIC-SVB, which was consistent with the US Supreme Court's conceptualization in *Kansas v. Crane* (2002):

> ... having recurrent, repetitive, and compulsive urges and fantasies to commit rapes. These offenders attempt to control their urges, but the urges become eventually so strong that they act upon them, commit rapes, and then feel guilty afterwards with a temporary reduction in urges, only to have the cycle repeat again. This cycle of ongoing urges, attempts to control them, breakdown of those attempts, and recurrence of the sex crime is similar to the clinical picture presented by exhibitionists, voyeurs, pedophiles, and other traditionally recognized categories of paraphiliacs.

In the matter of In re the Detention of Thorell (2003), the Washington Supreme Court considered five different SVP cases in addressing SDIC-SVB. In analyzing the facts of each case, the Court referenced examples of current SDIC-SVB, such as a respondent who admitted constructing pornographic images and stories about children to promote sexual fantasies, another respondent who continuously tried to solicit sex from other residents who fit his preferred victim profile, a third respondent with a strong compulsion to offend sexually who reported he would continue to do so and conceal his behavior by any means necessary, a respondent who expressed words reflecting current lack of control (e.g., "I'm Mr. Rapo, I have raped 15 people, women, in the past. I'm going to rape again."), and a respondent who estimated he was likely to reoffend in 9 months.

By itself, the presence of a current DSM mental disorder is insufficient to establish SDIC-SVB. A cautionary statement in *DSM-5* (APA, 2013) states that in forensic contexts, clinical diagnoses are an imperfect fit for questions of ultimate concern to the law. That is, a *DSM-5* diagnosis does not necessarily meet the requirements of a legally defined mental disorder, which is the case with an SVP mental disorder. Information needs to be established independent of the DSM diagnosis itself to substantiate the diagnosed condition causes functional impairments that affect the particular legal abilities in question, such as SDIC-SVB. DSM mental disorders do not carry any necessary implications regarding etiology or degree of control over behaviors that may be associated with a particular disorder (APA, 2013). In fact, clinicians are cautioned, "Even when diminished control over one's behavior is a feature of the disorder, having the diagnosis in itself does not demonstrate that a particular individual is (or was) unable to control his or her behavior at a particular time" (APA, 2013, p. 25).

In summary, *DSM-5* mental disorder(s) that constitute an acquired or congenital condition are necessary but insufficient to substantiate an SVP mental disorder. To satisfy the second contingency of an SVP mental disorder, evaluators must establish current evidence of SDIC-SVB independent of the *DSM-5* diagnosis. In order to establish such evidence, focus should be on current functioning at the time of evaluation. If, and only if, current communication and actions reflect SDIC-SVB and such symptoms are logically linked to the acquired or congenital condition, there is meaningful evidence of SDIC-SVB consistent with the legal rulings described above. A helpful key to understanding the condition of SDIC-SVB is whether a respondent attempts to control his sexually violent urges, fails, and reengages in it. This example is not to be construed that SDIC-SVB only can be established if respondents commit sexually violent acts while in custody pending disposition of their SVP petitions, although this can occur, as evidenced by, for example, attempted or completed rapes or repeated acts of frottage involving staff or other respondents. Evaluators also should be alert to how SDIC-SVB commonly manifests in custodial settings, such as viewing pornography or erotica depicting sexual behaviors such as rape, sadism, or drawn images depicting sexually violent acts; deliberately exposing genitalia to staff or masturbating openly with the intent to be seen; acting out sexual delusions; or self-reporting SDIC-SVB.

Importantly, evidence supporting current SDIC-SVB resulting from an acquired or congenital condition must be sufficient to distinguish respondents from dangerous but typical sexual recidivists convicted in ordinary criminal cases (*Kansas v. Crane*, 2002). Presumably, this categorical exclusion would exempt individuals from SVP commitments if their histories of reoffending consisted of multiple types of crimes, not just sexual reoffending. This exclusion begs the question: could not such "versatile" criminals likely meet *DSM-5* criteria for antisocial personality disorder? Indeed, some individuals who commit sexual offenses have been civilly committed as SVPs with only the diagnosis of antisocial personality disorder, despite forensic and legal concerns that such individuals are indistinguishable from up to nearly three-fourths of the prison population in the United States (Zander, 2005). This situation starkly illustrates how most individuals suffering from antisocial personality disorder do not fit the narrow class of individuals who are subject to civil confinement because antisocial personality disorder typically leads to the commission of various types of criminal offenses rather than predisposing individuals to committing sexual crimes alone.

Executive dysfunction and associated social impairment due to PAE produce a wide array of behaviors in people with ND-PAE, including criminal sexual behavior despite repeated sanctions that superficially resemble behavior disorders. DMS-5 cautions against a rush to such judgment in ND-PAE, noting aberrant behavior in the context of deficient executive functioning is not de facto evidence of a behavioral disorder or, by extension, SDIC-SVB. Executive functioning, which involves higher order cognitive skills necessary for adaptive self-regulation, has been found to directly predict adaptive dysfunction in FASD (Schonfeld, Paley, Frankel, &

O'Connor, 2006; Ware et al., 2012). In ND-PAE, it is impairment in adaptive self-regulation that produces repeated sexual misconduct (as well as other repetitive behaviors) rather than an internal cognitive and emotional struggle to control sexually violent urges that end in failure (i.e., committing sexual crimes). Thus, in the context of FASD/ND-PAE, behaviors labeled by state evaluators as SDIC-SVB actually represent adaptive dysfunction due to executive deficiency in weighing and choosing the most appropriate action based upon consideration of potential outcomes and planning courses of action based upon lessons learned from past mistakes. This impaired cognitive-set orients respondents with FASD/ND-PAE to think about intended illegal sexual behavior with a constricted, single-minded focus on immediate rewards, with no thinking about or struggling with previous learning experiences, consequences, and potential impact of the intended action on themselves or others. This core deficit in cause-and-effect thinking is observed in most, if not all, individuals with FASD, largely due to impairment in working memory, a key executive skill that involves holding disparate bits of relevant information in mind and taking this information into account during the process of reflecting before acting (Novick Brown et al., 2010; Streissguth et al., 1991).

In light of the above discussion, two relevant observations regarding the intersection of ND-PAE with SDIC-SVB can be made. First, cognitive deficits typically associated with ND-PAE short-circuit the neurotypical process of reflecting about one's actions before deciding how to act rather than deficient ability to control sexual behavior that the person knows is illegal. Second, the core executive deficits that produce a wide range of maladaptive behaviors in ND-PAE are not limited to illegal sexual behavior. Therefore, executive function impairment does not predispose respondents to committing criminal sexual acts—a factor that is necessary to substantiate the presence of SDIC-SVB.

Returning to the case example, the author ultimately concluded Mr. Matthews' congenital ND-PAE condition did not produce current SDIC-SVB. Rather, he suffered from deficits in executive functioning, which not only contributed to repeated sexual offense behaviors but also to other behavioral problems that did not involve sexual criminal acts. This clinical presentation refuted the notion his executive function deficits predisposed him to committing criminal sexual acts. Moreover, neither documented reports of his adjustment in county jail nor his self-reports during evaluations revealed him expressing words or demonstrating behaviors indicative of current SDIC-SVB. The two psychologists for the state concluded Mr. Matthews demonstrated SDIC-SVB because his sex crimes resembled behavioral symptoms of pedophilic disorder. The evaluators had no evidence of internal indicia (i.e., thoughts, urges, emotions) of pedophilic disorder at any point in Mr. Matthews' life. Moreover, they also lacked any recent external indicia of SDIC-SVB (i.e., comments or acts), which was inconsistent with the forensic cautionary statement in *DSM-5* (APA, 2013). Attempting to support their opinions, the evaluators offered descriptions of Mr. Matthews that never have been reliably associated with sexual recidivism (e.g., lack of remorse and empathy regarding victim harm, impulsive behavior without considering consequences, not being deterred by previous criminal sanctions for sexual offending, and ignoring victim resistance or protests). Such dated observations, even if they hypothetically represented evidence of SDIC-SVB at the time of Mr. Matthews' sexual offending, failed to substantiate current symptoms of an acquired or congenital condition with SDIC-SVB at the time of the evaluations. Moreover, the crime-related behaviors they attributed to SDIC-SVB were characteristic of any violent criminal recidivist and therefore failed to distinguish Mr. Matthews from the dangerous but typical recidivists convicted in ordinary criminal cases who are not subject to civil confinement as SVPs, as required in *Kansas v. Crane* (2002).

14.5 Implications for Forensic Practice

When assessing respondents suspected of having an FASD who are undergoing legal proceedings for civil confinement as SVPs, a team approach to evaluation is recommended. There are two major goals in using such an approach: determining whether a particular respondent does in fact have an FASD and if so, determining whether the FASD condition constitutes an SVP mental disorder. The expert team should involve a psychologist who specializes in FASD who can test and assess the respondent for CNS damage and ND-PAE (i.e., an "FASD expert") and a psychologist qualified to assess the required elements of an SVP mental disorder in the context of ND-PAE (i.e., an "SVP expert").

Attorneys for respondents play an indispensable role in acquiring necessary background information and medical records and can subpoena important records if needed. For example, ND-PAE assessment relies on lifelong behavioral assessment, which requires school and childhood medical records if available as well as interviews with family and others who observed childhood and adolescent behavior. Although many respondents have been imprisoned for decades and consequently have no recent contact with family members, attorneys often are able to use investigators to locate individuals who can provide relevant third-party information regarding two important subjects: PAE and the respondent's developmental history. Obtaining such information is another reason why an FASD expert needs to be involved, as such experts are trained in interviewing families about PAE as well as childhood behaviors typically seen in FASD. Ultimately, each evaluator on the team will send his/her report to the attorney, who is responsible for distributing the reports to all experts and coordinating consultation between experts.

Neuropsychological testing should be comprehensive. In addition to an IQ test, which superficially screens for the possibility of cognitive dysfunction, other domains of testing should include attention, learning and memory, academic achievement/learning, visuospatial construction/reasoning, executive functioning (multiple tests are best, including a test of suggestibility), and adaptive assessment. The latter can involve direct adaptive testing but always should include standardized adaptive assessment with behavior rating measures such as the previously mentioned Vineland. Testing for malingering is essential. It is important that all testing occur prior to an SVP expert examining the respondent. The reason for this sequencing will become apparent later. The reader is referred to Novick Brown et al. (2010) as well as chapters in this book relevant to assessment for comprehensive descriptions of test protocols and results that indicate cognitive impairments associated with FASD. Evaluation by an FASD expert does not address whether a respondent meets legal criteria for civil confinement as an SVP. Invariably during testimony, the state will ask the FASD expert for such an opinion and if the judge overrules objection by the defense attorney, the expert should make it clear that the scope of his/her professional services did not include such assessment.

Prior to examining a respondent, the SVP expert should consult with the FASD expert to understand whether test results and other findings support a diagnosis of ND-PAE. The SVP expert needs to understand a respondent's functional impairments in order to plan a forensic interview that will obtain sufficient information to conduct differential diagnosis. For example, does an acquired or congenital condition involve ND-PAE only or also involve co-occurring mental disorders and/or personality pathology? It is the responsibility of the SVP expert to determine whether the acquired or congenital condition produces SDIC-SVB. As is the case in all high-stakes forensic matters, it is not advisable for psychologists to conduct personality testing as the clinical and normative samples upon which test interpretation is based do not include individuals with FASD. It also should be noted that physiological tests such as polygraphs and penile plethysmographs also have never been empirically validated in people with FASD. Given the high degree of suggestibility often associated with FASD, personality and physiological tests are ill-advised as results may be quite misleading.

After completing the SVP evaluation, FASD and SVP experts should consult regarding clinical case formulation as it relates to respondent sexual offense history and differential diagnosis. Such consultation has become the standard of practice in psychology and psychiatry in the forensic context (e.g., Woods, Freedman, & Greenspan, 2012) as well as the standard of practice in both clinical and forensic contexts involving FASD (Novick Brown et al., 2010). Expert consultation serves at least three important purposes (a) determining whether a respondent suffers from ND-PAE alone or also has comorbid disorders based on data from multiple sources and methodologies; (b) analyzing sexual offense behavior and sexual offense history to ascertain if such data are consistent with the functional impairments in ND-PAE (with or without comorbid mental health disorders) or are better explained by paraphilia and/or personality disorder; and (c) concluding whether the respondent's acquired or congenital condition currently affects emotional or volitional capacity by predisposing him to commit criminal sexual acts.

Regarding testimony in SVP matters, it is necessary for the FASD expert to testify initially about FASD and the ND-PAE diagnosis in the respondent, describing the criteria that support the diagnosis as well as any comorbid disorders. Such testimony will include primary and secondary disabilities associated with the respondent's FASD, with relevant empirical information about the science of FASD. Such testimony lays the groundwork for the SVP expert, who will rely upon the testimony to conclude the respondent suffers from ND-FAE and, if applicable, any comorbid mental condition(s) as well, with particular emphasis on whether the acquired or congenital condition has resulted in current indicia of SDIC-SVB. Presumably by this point, the SVP expert is able to testify how the functional impairments in ND-PAE—in contrast to paraphilic or personality disorders—best explain *all* aspects of the respondent's history over the course of his life, including his sexual offense history, describing how such functional impairments are distinguished from SDIC-SVB.

While the focus of this chapter has been on the SVP mental disorder, the comprehensive assessment process may reveal the respondent suffers from ND-PAE in combination with other mental or personality disorders, and this combination of acquired and/or congenital conditions produces current SDIC-SVB. In this event, SVP experts are responsible for determining whether the diagnosed SVP mental disorder makes the respondent likely to engage in criminal sexual acts if released. It is beyond the scope of this chapter to discuss the complexities and nuances of assessing risk for committing future criminal sexual acts as defined by SVP laws in general and as it relates to respondents who suffer from FASD. Readers who desire such information are referred to peer-reviewed publications on that topic (Abbott, 2011; Janus & Prentky, 2003; Krauss & Scurich, 2013; Mercado & Ogloff, 2007; Rogers & Jackson, 2005).

References

Abbott, B. R. (2011). Throwing the baby out with the bathwater: Is it time for clinical judgment to supplement actuarial risk assessment? *Journal of the American Academy of Psychiatry and the Law, 39*(2), 222–230. http://jaapl.org/content/jaapl/39/2/222.full.pdf

Abbott, B. R. (2017). Sexually violent predator risk assessments with the Violence Risk Appraisal Guide-Revised: A shaky practice. *International Journal of Law and Psychiatry, 52*, 62–73. https://doi.org/10.1016/j.ijlp.2017.03.003

American Psychiatric Association (APA). (2013). *Diagnostic and statistical manual of mental disorders (DSM-5)* (5th ed.). Arlington, VA: American Psychiatric Association.

Anderson, T., Karding, K. D., Reid, D., & Pei, J. (2018). *FASD and inappropriate sexual behavior*. Canada FASD Research Network. Retrieved from https://canfasd.ca/wp-content/uploads/2018/07/CanFASD-Issue-Paper-Inappropriate-Sexual-Behaviour-Final.pdf

Becker, J. V., Stinson, J., Tromp, S., & Messer, G. (2003). Characteristics of individuals petitioned for civil commitment. *International Journal of Offender Therapy and Comparative Criminology, 47*(2), 185–195. https://doi.org/10.1177/0306624X03251114

Blanchard, R. (2010). The specificity of victim count as a diagnostic indicator of Pedohebephilia [Letter to the Editor]. *Archives of Sexual Behavior, 39*(6), 1245–1252. https://doi.org/10.1007/s10508-010-9659-3

Blanchard, R. (2011). Misdiagnoses of pedohebephilia using victim count: A reply to Wollert and Cramer (2011). *Archives of Sexual Behavior, 40*(6), 1081–1088. https://doi.org/10.1007/s10508-011-9835-0

Blanchard, R., Klassen, P., Dickey, R., Kuban, M. E., & Blak, T. (2001). Sensitivity and specificity of the phallometric test for pedophilia in nonadmitting sex offenders. *Psychological Assessment, 13*(1), 118–126. https://doi.org/10.1037/1040-3590.13.1.118

Brown, J., & Singh, J. P. (2016). Perceptions of FASD by civil commitment professionals: A pilot study. *Sexual Offender Treatment, 11*(1), 1–6. http://www.sexual-offender-treatment.org/index.php?id=151&type=123

Burd, L., Fast, D. K., Conry, J., & Williams, A. (2010). Fetal alcohol spectrum disorder as a marker for increased risk of involvement with corrections system. *Journal of Psychiatry and Law, 38*(4), 559–583. https://doi.org/10.1177/009318531003800408

Carson, E. A. (2018). *Prisoners in 2016*. U.S. Department of Justice Bureau of Justice Statistics. Retrieved from https://www.bjs.gov/content/pub/pdf/p16.pdf

First, M. B. (2010). DSM-5 proposal for paraphilias: Suggestions for reducing false positives related to use of behavioral manifestations [Letter to the Editor]. *Archives of Sexual Behavior, 39*(6), 1239–1244. https://doi.org/10.1007/s10508-010-9657-5

First, M. B. (2014a). *DSM-5 handbook of differential diagnosis*. Washington, DC: American Psychiatric. https://doi.org/10.1176/appi.books.9781585629992

First, M. B. (2014b). DSM-5 and paraphilic disorders. *Journal of the American Academy of Psychiatry and the Law Online, 42*(2), 191–201. http://jaapl.org/content/42/2/191; http://jaapl.org/content/jaapl/42/2/191.full.pdf

First, M. B., & Halon, R. L. (2008). Use of DSM paraphilia diagnoses in sexually violent predator commitment cases. *Journal of the American Academy of Psychiatry and the Law, 36*(4), 443–454. http://jaapl.org/content/jaapl/42/2/191.full.pdf

Frances, A., Sreenivasan, S., & Weinberger, L. E. (2008). Defining mental disorder when it really counts: DSM-IV-TR and SVP/SDP statutes. *Journal of the American Academy of Psychiatry and the Law, 36*(3), 375–384. http://jaapl.org/content/jaapl/36/3/375.full.pdf

Grinage, B. D. (2003). Volitional impairment and the sexually violent predator. *Journal of Forensic Science, 48*(4), 861–868. https://doi.org/10.1520/JFS2002087

Hubbart v. People, 19 Cal. 4th 1138 (1999). Retrieved from https://law.justia.com/cases/california/supreme-court/4th/19/1138.html

In re Howard N, 35 Cal. 4th 117 (2005). Retrieved from https://casetext.com/case/in-re-howard-n

In re the Detention of Thorell 149 Wash. 2d 724 (2003). Retrieved from https://casetext.com/case/det-of-thorell

In re the Detention of Young 122 Wash. 2d 1 (1993). Retrieved from https://casetext.com/case/personal-restraint-of-young

In re the matter of Leon G. 59 P.3d 779 (2002). Retrieved from https://www.courtlistener.com/opinion/2621330/in-re-leon-g/

Janus, E. S. (2001). Sex offender commitments and the "inability to control": Developing legal standards and a behavioral vocabulary for an elusive concept. In A. Schlank (Ed.), *The sexual predator: Legal issues, clinical issues, special situations* (pp. 1-2–1-22). Kingston, NJ: Civic Research Institute.

Janus, E. S., & Prentky, R. A. (2003). Forensic use of actuarial risk assessment with sex offenders: Accuracy, admissibility, and accountability. *American Criminal Law Review, 40*(1143), 1–59. http://www.antoniocasella.eu/nume/Janus_2003.pdf

Jirikowic, T., Kartin, D., & Olson, H. C. (2008). Children with fetal alcohol spectrum disorders: A descriptive profile of adaptive function. *Canadian Journal of Occupational Therapy, 75*(4), 238–248. https://depts.washington.edu/fasdpn/htmls/jirikowic-2008.pdf

Kansas v. Crane, 534 U.S. 407 (2002). Retrieved from https://supreme.justia.com/cases/federal/us/534/407/

Kansas v. Hendricks, 521 U.S. 346 (1997). Retrieved from https://supreme.justia.com/cases/federal/us/521/346/

Knighton, J. C., Murrie, D. C., Boccaccini, M. T., & Turner, D. B. (2014). How likely is "likely to reoffend" in sex offender civil commitment trials? *Law and Human Behavior, 38*(3), 293–304. https://doi.org/10.1037/lhb0000079

Krauss, D. A., & Scurich, N. (2013). Risk assessment in the law: Legal admissibility, scientific validity, and some disparities between research and practice. *Behavioral Sciences & the Law, 31*(2), 215–229. https://doi.org/10.1002/bsl.2065

Levenson, J. S. (2004). Sexual predator civil commitment: A comparison of selected and released offenders. *International Journal of Offender Therapy and Comparative Criminology, 48*(6), 638–648. https://doi.org/10.1177/0306624X04265089

Lieb, R. (1996). *Washington State sexually violent predators: Profile of special commitment center residents*. Olympia, WA: Washington State Institute of Public Policy. Retrieved from http://www.wsipp.wa.gov/ReportFile/1235/Wsipp_Washington-State-Sexually-Violent-Predators-Profile-of-Special-Commitment-Center-Residents_Full-Report.pdf

McMurtrie, J. (2011). The criminal justice system's disparate treatment of individuals with fetal alcohol spectrum disorders in cases involving sexual activity. *Journal of Psychiatry and Law, 39*(1), 159–179. https://doi.org/10.1177/009318531103900106

Mela, M., Flannigan, K., Anderson, T., Nelson, M., Krishnan, S., Chizea, C., … Sanjanwala, R. (2020). Neurocognitive function and fetal alcohol spectrum disorder in offenders with mental disorders. *American Academy of Psychiatry and the Law, 48*(2), 1–14. https://doi.org/10.29158/JAAPL.003886-20; http://jaapl.org/content/jaapl/early/2020/02/12/JAAPL.003886-20.full.pdf

Mercado, C. C., & Ogloff, J. R. P. (2007). Risk and the preventive detention of sex offenders in Australia and the United States. *International Journal of Law and Psychiatry, 30*(1), 49–59. https://doi.org/10.1016/j.ijlp.2006.02.001

Mercado, C. C., Schopp, R. F., & Bornstein, B. H. (2005). Evaluating sex offenders under sexually violent predator laws: How might mental health professionals conceptualize the notion of volitional impairment? *Aggression and Violent Behavior, 10*(3), 289–309. https://doi.org/10.1016/j.avb.2003.12.003

Miller, H. A., Amenta, A. E., & Conroy, M. A. (2005). Sexually violent predators: Empirical evidence, strategies for professionals, and research directions. *Law and Human Behavior, 29*(1), 29–54. https://doi.org/10.1007/s10979-005-1398-y

Novick, N. (1997). FAS: Preventing and treating sexual deviancy. In A. P. Streissguth & J. Kanter (Eds.), *The challenge of fetal alcohol syndrome: Overcoming secondary disabilities* (pp. 162–170). Seattle: University of Washington Press.

Novick Brown, N., Wartnik, A. P., Connor, P. D., & Adler, R. S. (2010). A proposed model standard for forensic assessment of FASD. *Journal of Psychiatry and Law, 38*(4), 383–418. https://doi.org/10.1177/009318531003800403

People v. Buffington, 74 Cal. App. 4th 1149 (1999). Retrieved from https://law.justia.com/cases/california/court-of-appeal/4th/74/1149.html

People v. Galindo, 142 Cal. App. 4th 531 (2006). Retrieved from https://casetext.com/case/people-v-galindo

People v. Williams, 31 Cal. 4th 757 (2003). Retrieved from https://www.courtlistener.com/opinion/2625326/people-v-williams/

Perillo, A. D., Spada, A. H., Calkins, C., & Jeglic, E. L. (2014). Examining the scope of questionable diagnostic reliability in sexual violent predator (SVP) evaluations. *International Journal of Law and Psychiatry, 37*(2), 190–197. https://doi.org/10.1016/j.ijlp.2013.11.005

Popova, S., Lange, S., Shield, K., Mihic, A., Chudley, A. E., Mukherjee, R. A. S., … Rehm, J. (2016). Comorbidity of fetal alcohol spectrum disorder: A systematic review and meta-analysis. *Lancet, 387*(10022), 978–987. https://doi.org/10.1016/s0140-6736(15)01345-8

Prentky, R. A., Janus, E., Barbaree, H., Schwartz, B. K., & Kafka, M. P. (2006). Sexually violent predators in the courtroom: Science on trial. *Psychology, Public Policy, and Law, 12*(4), 357–393. https://doi.org/10.1037/1076-8971.12.4.357

Rogers, R., & Jackson, R. L. (2005). Sexually violent predators: The risky enterprise or risk assessment. *Journal of the American Academy of Psychiatry and the Law, 33*(4), 523–528. http://jaapl.org/content/33/4/523

Schneider, J. E., Jackson, R., Ambroziak, G., D'Orazio, D., Freeman, N., & Hebert, J. (2018, October 15). *SOCCPN annual survey of annual sex offender civil confinement programs 2018*. [Paper presentation]. Sex Offender Civil Commitment Programs Network (SOCCPN) 20th Annual Conference, Vancouver, BC, Canada.

Schonfeld, A. M., Paley, B., Frankel, F., & O'Connor, M. J. (2006). Executive functioning predicts social skills following prenatal alcohol exposure. *Child Neuropsychology, 12*(6), 439–452. https://doi.org/10.1080/09297040600611338

Scurich, N., & Krauss, D. A. (2014). The presumption of dangerousness in sexual violent predator commitment proceedings. *Law, Probability, and Risk, 13*(1), 91–104. https://doi.org/10.1093/lpr/mgt015

Simon, E. P. (2015). Psychoanalytic principles as a heuristic framework to bridge the gap between psychology and the law in SVP evaluations: Assessing emotional and volitional impairment. [Special issue]. *International Journal of Law and Psychiatry, 42-43*, 154–167. https://doi.org/10.1016/j.ijlp.2015.08.021

Sparrow, S. S., Saulnier, C. A., Cicchetti, D. V., & Doll, E. A. (2016). *Vineland adaptive behavior scales: Vineland-3 manual* (3rd ed.). San Antonio, TX: Pearson.

Streissguth, A. P. (1997). *Fetal alcohol syndrome: A guide for families and communities*. Baltimore, MD: Paul H. Brookes.

Streissguth, A. P., Aase, J. M., Clarren, S. K., Randels, S. P., LaDue, R. A., & Smith, D. F. (1991). Fetal alcohol syndrome in adolescents and adults. *JAMA: Journal of the American Medical Association, 265*(15), 1961–1967. https://doi.org/10.1001/jama.1991.03460150065025

Streissguth, A. P., Barr, H. M., Kogan, J., & Bookstein, F. L. (1996). *Understanding the occurrence of secondary disabilities in clients with fetal alcohol syndrome (FAS) and fetal alcohol effects (FAE)*. Final Report to the Centers for Disease Control and Prevention (CDC). Seattle, WA: University of Washington. Retrieved from http://lib.adai.uw.edu/pubs/bk2698.pdf

Streissguth, A. P., Bookstein, F. L., Barr, H. M., Press, S., & Sampson, P. D. (1998). A fetal alcohol behavior scale. *Alcoholism: Clinical and Experimental Research, 22*(2), 325–333. https://doi.org/10.1111/j.1530-0277.1998.tb03656.x

Streissguth, A. P., Bookstein, F. L., Barr, H. M., Sampson, P. D., O'Malley, K., & Kogan Young, J. (2004). Risk factors for adverse life outcomes in fetal alcohol syndrome and fetal alcohol effects. *Developmental and Behavioral Pediatrics, 25*(4), 228–238. https://doi.org/10.1097/00004703-200408000-00002

Treit, S., Lebel, C., Baugh, L., Rasmussen, C., Andrew, G., & Beaulieu, C. (2013). Longitudinal MRI reveals altered trajectory of brain development during childhood and adolescence in fetal alcohol spectrum disorders. *Journal of Neuroscience, 33*(24), 10098–10109. https://doi.org/10.1523/JNEUROSCI.5004-12.2013

Vess, J., Murphy, C., & Arkowitz, S. (2004). Clinical and demographic differences between sexually violent predators and other commitment types in a state forensic hospital. *Journal of Forensic Psychiatry & Psychology, 15*(4), 669–681. https://doi.org/10.1080/14789940410001731795

Ware, A. L., Crocker, N., O'Brien, J. W., Deweese, B. N., Roesch, S. C., … Mattson, S. N. (2012). Executive function predicts adaptive behavior in children with histories of heavy prenatal alcohol exposure and attention deficit/hyperactivity disorder. *Alcoholism: Clinical and Experimental Research, 36*(8), 1431–1441. https://doi.org/10.1111/j.1530-0277.2011.01718.x

Wechsler, D. (1999). *WASI: Wechsler Abbreviated Scale of Intelligence*. San Antonio, TX: Psychological Corporation.

Wechsler, D. (2008). *Wechsler Adult Intelligence Scale® (WAIS–IV®)* (4th ed.). San Antonio, TX: Pearson.

Winsmann, F. (2012). Assessing volitional impairment in sexually violent predator evaluations. *Sexual Offender Treatment, 7*(1), 1–14. http://www.sexual-offender-treatment.org/index.php?id=103&type=123

Wollert, R., & Cramer, E. (2011). Sampling extreme groups invalidates research on the paraphilias: Implications for DSM-5 and sex offender risk assessments. *Behavioral Sciences & the Law, 29*, 554–565. https://doi.org/10.1002/bsl.992

Woods, G. W., Freedman, D., & Greenspan, S. (2012). Neurobehavioral assessment in forensic practice. *International Journal of Law and Psychiatry, 35*, 432–439. https://doi.org/10.1016/j.ijlp.2012.09.014

Zander, T. K. (2005). Civil commitment without psychosis: The law's reliance on the weakest link in psychodiagnosis. *Journal of Sexual Offender Commitment: Science and the Law, 1*, 17–82. http://www.sexual-offender-treatment.org/index.php?id=103&type=123

Chapter 15
Evaluating Competency in Defendants with Fetal Alcohol Spectrum Disorder

Kaitlyn McLachlan

Abstract The purpose of this chapter is to provide an overview of the relevance of fetal alcohol spectrum disorder (FASD) in the context of adjudicative competency, from initial interactions with police at arrest through interrogation and adjudication at trial. Individuals with FASD experience contact with the criminal justice system at elevated rates and are overrepresented in forensic, legal, and correctional contexts. The complex range of functional and neurodevelopmental impairments experienced by many individuals with FASD raise concerns about their ability to competently navigate adjudicative proceedings. Growing awareness about FASD among legal professionals and courts, coupled with policy calls to more effectively address their overrepresentation in legal contexts, suggests that forensic clinicians are increasingly likely to be tasked with identifying and evaluating justice-involved individuals with FASD. However, limited FASD training, knowledge, and skill among forensic clinicians, in addition to an array of challenges identifying individuals with FASD in clinical and legal settings, render this a complex task. This chapter begins with a brief overview of adjudicative competency and FASD, followed by practical strategies to support best practices in competency evaluation for forensic clinicians.

Keywords Adjudicative competence · Fetal alcohol spectrum disorder · Rights waiver · Prenatal alcohol exposure · Neurodevelopmental disorder

---

K. McLachlan (✉)
Department of Psychology, University of Guelph, Guelph, ON, Canada
e-mail: kmclac02@uoguelph.ca

N. Novick Brown (ed.), *Evaluating Fetal Alcohol Spectrum Disorders in the Forensic Context*, https://doi.org/10.1007/978-3-030-73628-6_15

15.1 Evaluating Competency

The purpose of this chapter is to provide an overview of the relevance of fetal alcohol spectrum disorder (FASD) in the context of adjudicative competency, from initial interactions with police through interrogation and adjudication. Individuals with FASD experience contact with the criminal justice system at elevated rates and are overrepresented in forensic, legal, and correctional contexts (McLachlan, Flannigan, Temple, Unsworth, & Cook, 2020; Popova, Lange, Shield, Burd, & Rehm, 2019; Streissguth et al., 2004). The complex range of impairments experienced by many individuals with FASD raises concerns about their ability to competently navigate adjudicative proceedings (Brown, Carter, Haun, Wartnik, & Zapf, 2019; Freckelton, 2017; McLachlan, Roesch, Viljoen, & Douglas, 2014). Growing awareness about FASD among legal professionals and courts, coupled with policy calls to more effectively inform justice for this vulnerable population in legal contexts, suggests forensic clinicians are likely to be increasingly tasked with undertaking forensic assessments of justice-involved individuals with FASD (American Bar Association [ABA], 2012; Binnie, Trussler, & Jonsson, 2015; Canadian Bar Association [CBA], 2013; Steering Committee on FASD and Access to Justice, 2016). Currently, limited FASD training, knowledge, and skill among forensic clinicians, coupled with an array of challenges identifying those with the disorder in clinical and legal settings, render this a complex task (Brown et al., 2019; Burd, Selfridge, Klug, & Bakko, 2004; Burd, Selfridge, Klug, & Juelson, 2003; Chudley, Kilgour, Cranston, & Edwards, 2007; McLachlan, Mullally, Ritter, Pei, & Mela, 2020). This chapter begins with a brief overview of adjudicative competency and FASD, followed by practical strategies to support best practices in competency evaluation for forensic clinicians.

15.2 Adjudicative Competency: An Overview

Legal tradition in North America and other common-law jurisdictions recognizes the fundamental importance of ensuring procedural protections through the adjudicative process for defendants accused of crimes (Melton et al., 2018; Reed & Zapf, 2018). The criminal justice system operates on an assumption that defendants must be able to competently navigate the arrest, interrogation, and trial process, and recognizes that proceeding against an incompetent defendant would constitute a fundamental violation of fairness and due process (*Dusky v. United States of America*, 1960; Golding, 2008; Winick, 1983). *Competence*, also referred to as fitness to stand trial in some countries, involves “a defendant’s capacity to understand the criminal justice process and meaningfully participate in the proceedings” (Reed & Zapf, 2018, p. 84). Though modern competency laws vary across jurisdictions, the legal standard for competence in the United States was outlined in *Dusky v. United States of America* (1960), wherein the Supreme Court held a defendant must have present ability to consult with their lawyer with a reasonable degree of rational understanding and have a rational as well as factual understanding of the proceedings against them. Competency definitions in other common-law countries are similarly defined. For instance, in Canada, section 2 of the *Criminal Code* (1985) defines unfit to stand trial as when a defendant is "…unable on account of mental disorder to conduct a defense at any stage of the proceedings before a verdict is rendered or to instruct counsel to do so, and, in particular, unable on account of mental disorder to (a) understand the nature or object of the proceedings, (b) understand the possible consequences of the proceedings, or (c) communicate with counsel." Despite similarities, competency doctrines have evolved somewhat differently across jurisdictions. For instance, whereas US standards require that a defendant possess both factual and rational understanding, Canadian courts have interpreted the standard as requiring only a rational understanding (known at the "limited cognitive capacity" test, *R. v. Taylor*, 1992), resulting in a somewhat narrower standard (Reed & Zapf, 2018). Overall, three broad abilities relevant to adjudicative competence have been identified, including understanding, appreciation, and reasoning (Bonnie, 1992; Poythress et al., 1999; Zapf & Roesch, 2009).

In most jurisdictions, the issue of competency can be raised at any point in the adjudicative process by any party to the proceeding, including the prosecution, defense, or the court, prior to a verdict being reached. Generally, there is a low or conservative threshold for raising the issue of a defendant's competency. Estimates from the United States suggest between 4 and 8% of felony defendants are referred for competency evaluation, although lawyers report competency-related concerns for a higher proportion of their clients (~15%; Beltrani & Zapf, 2020; Hoge, Bonnie, Poythress, & Monahan, 1992). Where concerns about a defendant's competency are raised, one or more mental health professionals may be asked to complete a forensic evaluation. Among those referred, roughly one in four will be found incompetent (Pirelli, Gottdiener, & Zapf, 2011).

Studies evaluating the characteristics of defendants found incompetent underscore high rates of serious psychopathology, including psychosis, in this population (Cooper & Zapf, 2003; James, Duffield, Blizard, & Hamilton, 2001; Pirelli et al., 2011; Viljoen & Zapf, 2002). Defendants with intellectual deficits and/or disability also form a substantial subset of defendants deemed incompetent, with growing recognition of the unique needs and considerations for this population over the last 30 years (Beltrani & Zapf, 2020; Bonnie, 1992; Miller & Germain, 1987). More recently, individuals with FASD also have been identified as a special population warranting additional consideration in the context of adjudicative competence owing to the substantial and complex profile of cognitive deficits, impaired affect and behavior regulation, and comorbid mental health concerns experienced by many with the disorder (Brown, Haun, Zapf, & Novick Brown, 2017; Fast & Conry, 2009; Gagnier, Moore, & Green, 2010; Reid, Kippin, Passmore, & Finlay-Jones, 2020; Roach & Bailey, 2009).

15.3 Fetal Alcohol Spectrum Disorder: A Primer

FASD is a common neurodevelopmental disorder caused by prenatal alcohol exposure (PAE), resulting in a wide range of impairments in neurodevelopmental and affective functioning and, in a small number of cases, sentinel dysmorphic facial features and/or growth restriction (Mattson, Bernes, & Doyle, 2019). FASD is a lifelong condition, requiring a range of individualized supports to promote healthy outcomes for each person in the context of their own strengths and challenges (Harding, Flannigan, & McFarlane, 2019). Estimates of FASD prevalence vary considerably across countries, populations, and settings, and the overall evidence base remains limited with respect to large-scale case-ascertainment studies. Conservative estimates suggest prevalence in North America ranges from 1 to 5% in the general population, with higher rates in subpopulations, including those in special education, child welfare, and criminal justice system settings (Lange et al., 2017; May et al., 2014; May et al., 2018; Popova et al., 2019; Popova, Lange, Shield, et al., 2019). Given high service use and support needs, social and economic costs associated with FASD also are high, ranging from $1 to 2 million USD over the lifetime for an individual with FASD, and in Canada, estimated overall annual costs ranging as high as $9.4 B (Popova et al., 2013; Popova, Lange, Burd, & Rehm, 2015; Thanh & Jonsson, 2015). Of concern, several economic estimates have identified the costs associated with criminal justice system involvement as being among the highest drivers of overall cost (Popova et al., 2015; Thanh & Jonsson, 2015).

Increasing evidence supports considerable concern about elevated rates of FASD in legal contexts. Rates of justice contact among adolescents and adults accessing FASD diagnostic services in the United States and Canada have been estimated to range from 30% to 60% (McLachlan et al., 2020; Streissguth et al., 2004). Further, multiple single-site studies have identified considerable overrepresentation of individuals with FASD in correctional and forensic settings, with estimates ranging from 10 to 36% (Bower et al., 2018; Fast, Conry, & Loock, 1999; Forrester et al., 2015; MacPherson, Chudley, & Grant, 2011; McLachlan et al., 2019). Taken together, current evidence suggests individuals with FASD are 30 times more likely to experience criminal justice system contact, and that youths with FASD are 19 times more likely to be incarcerated compared to those without the disorder (Popova, Lange, Bekmuradov, & Mihic, 2011; Popova, Lange, Shield, et al., 2019). Among studies applying case-ascertainment approaches to identifying youths and adults with FASD in correctional and forensic settings, findings indicate most individuals ultimately diagnosed with FASD had not been identified previously (e.g., Bower et al., 2018; McLachlan et al., 2019). Indeed, rates of missed diagnosis and detection in both the general population and in legal settings are thought to be high owing to numerous factors, including limited knowledge and awareness of FASD among clinicians and legal professionals, insufficient resources to support diagnosis, and substantial stigma associated with FASD and alcohol use in pregnancy (Astley, 2010; McLachlan, Flannigan, Temple, Unsworth, & Cook, et al., 2020; Payne et al., 2005; Wedding et al., 2007). Further, FASD sometimes is described as an *invisible* disability owing to the lack of overt physical signs of disability among most of those with the disorder and complex and variable neurodevelopmental impairments that can be difficult to detect and are successfully masked through adaptive and compensatory strategies (Chudley, 2008; Chudley et al., 2007; Fast & Conry, 2009). Thus, forensic clinicians can anticipate encountering individuals who may have FASD where no previous identification, investigation, or diagnosis has been made (Brown et al., 2017).

15.4 Diagnosis

The term *FASD* is applied as a formal diagnostic label in some jurisdictions (e.g., Canada), while in other areas, FASD is used as an umbrella term (and not a diagnosis) to characterize several PAE-related diagnoses that fall along a spectrum, including fetal alcohol syndrome (FAS), partial FAS (pFAS), and alcohol-related neurodevelopmental disorder (ARND), to list a few (Astley, 2004; Bower et al., 2017; Coles et al., 2016; Cook et al., 2016; Hoyme et al., 2016). Internationally, guidelines also vary with respect to specific diagnostic criteria, although most identify best practices including multidisciplinary team evaluations, assessment of diagnostic features such as the presence of PAE above a risk threshold, neurodevelopmental functioning across multiple domains, and sentinel dysmorphic facial features (Astley, 2004; Bower et al., 2017; Coles et al., 2016; Cook et al., 2016; Hoyme et al., 2016). Several widely used guidelines also consider growth restriction (e.g., Astley, 2004; Hoyme et al., 2016). Differing systems apply varying cut-off scores and criteria around conceptualizing diagnostic indicators such as the level/use patterns of PAE required to surpass an at-risk threshold. There also are differences in the neurodevelopmental domains considered as well as the specific criteria used to indicate when a benchmark for "significant impairment" has been reached. Further, the Fifth Edition of the *Diagnostic and Statistical Manual of Mental Disorders* (*DSM-5*; American Psychiatric Association (APA), 2013) currently includes consideration of FASD and PAE as an exemplar for "Other Specified Neurodevelopmental Disorder—Neurodevelopmental Disorder Associated with Prenatal Alcohol Exposure" (ND-PAE), although the proposed diagnostic criteria for ND-PAE remain in the category of "Conditions for Further Study."

While considerable evidence has accumulated supporting the validity of a range of approaches to diagnosing FASD and identifying the impairments stemming from PAE, clear variations persist across the field. As in all forensic evaluations, clinicians who are either conducting a diagnostic assessment for FASD, or undertaking forensic evaluation with a defendant who may have FASD, must ensure they select and apply an appropriate and evidence-based diagnostic approach, ideally together with a multidisciplinary team and consideration for jurisdictional variations in guidelines and practices. Early and accurate clinical evaluation and diagnosis of FASD form important protective factors that mitigate against risk for a range of adverse outcomes experienced at elevated rates for those with the disorder, including those involved in the criminal justice system (Baldry, Briggs, Goldson, & Russell, 2018; Reid et al., 2020; Streissguth et al., 2004).

FASD is considered a heterogeneous disorder in that wide-ranging variability both between and within individuals frequently is observed (Astley, 2010; Brown, Freeman, Pickett, Watts, & Trnka, 2018; Cook et al., 2016; Mattson et al., 2019; Mela, Coons-Harding, & Anderson, 2019). While there are many commonly observed domains of impairment among those with FASD, individualized consideration is always necessary, particularly with respect to conceptualizing specific areas of deficit that may be of relevance in the forensic context. Regarding neurodevelopment and cognitive impairment, many domains are commonly impacted and have relevance to competence, including overall cognitive or intellectual impairment, academic skills, attention, learning and memory, executive functioning, language, visual-spatial abilities, and adaptive functioning (Brown et al., 2019; Mattson et al., 2019; Mela et al., 2019; Reid et al., 2020; Wozniak, Riley, & Charness, 2019).

Our recent study of 726 adolescents, transition-aged youths, and adults who were evaluated in FASD diagnostic clinics in Canada, including a subset experiencing current legal difficulties with offending (30%), suggests high rates of neurodevelopmental impairment across domains (McLachlan, Flannigan & Temple, 2020). Among those who were ultimately diagnosed with FASD, we found that of 10 domains considered, the average number of impaired domains ranged from five to six. In particular, >75% had significantly impaired global intellectual functioning, executive functioning, and adaptive/social functioning. Similarly, high rates of cognitive deficits across domains of functioning have been demonstrated in justice-involved samples of both youths and adults with FASD (Bower et al., 2018; MacPherson et al., 2011; McLachlan et al., 2019; Mela et al., 2020). Many of these neurodevelopmental impairments have been observed to translate into difficulties understanding complex information, drawing cause and effect connections, learning from consequences, impulsive behavioral presentations, and psychosocial immaturity, including suggestibility—all relevant considerations for competence (Fast & Conry, 2009; Mattson et al., 2019; Novick Brown, Gudjonsson, & Connor, 2011; Streissguth & Kanter, 1997).

Many individuals with FASD also experience additional prenatal exposures and complications, including exposure to other substances, poor prenatal care, and preterm birth (Lebel et al., 2019; Mattson et al., 2019; McLachlan, Andrew, Pei, & Rasmussen, 2015; Streissguth et al., 2004). Comorbidity also tends to be the rule rather than the exception for individuals with FASD. This includes high rates of physical health concerns, along with co-occurrence of mental health problems for as many as 90% of those with FASD, including frequently diagnosed concurrent attention-deficit hyperactivity disorder (ADHD; Pei, Denys, Hughes, & Rasmussen, 2011; Popova et al., 2016). Adverse outcomes and difficulties in daily living are elevated in individuals with FASD, including caregiver disruption, victimization and abuse, involvement in the child welfare system, school disruption, criminal justice system contact, and later, difficulties related to employment and independent living (Lebel et al., 2019; Lynch, Kable, & Coles, 2015; McLachlan, Flannigan & Temple, 2020; Streissguth et al., 2004). Taken together, clinicians should anticipate that individuals with FASD present a complex clinical picture, with a need for fulsome evaluation across multiple domains using an individualized approach, with careful consideration of developmental history irrespective of age at assessment.

15.5 Legal Relevance

Increasingly, overrepresentation of individuals with FASD in criminal justice contexts is being recognized, coupled with growing policy attention focused on better addressing the needs of this population in forensic and correctional contexts (ABA, 2012; Binnie et al., 2015; CBA, 2013; Reid et al., 2020). As such, legal professionals, courts, and forensic clinicians are increasingly likely to be tasked with identifying persons with FASD and ensuring relevant forensic evaluations are conducted to inform key legal questions. Indeed, case law reviews have underscored growing jurisprudence with respect to FASD broadly, including the increasing frequency of PAE and FASD being raised in criminal courts (Chandler, 2015; Douds, Stevens, & Sumner, 2013). Internationally, case law has established the specific relevance of FASD for both youths and adult defendants with respect to arrest rights waiver, admissibility of statements, and adjudicative competency, given the associated complex and intersecting neurocognitive deficits and comorbid mental health difficulties experienced by many with the disorder (Chandler, 2015; Douds et al., 2013; Freckelton, 2016; Reid et al., 2020; Roach & Bailey, 2009). While a comprehensive overview of relevant decisions is beyond the scope of this chapter, readers are directed to recent reviews outlining case law in this area and encouraged to understand relevant FASD case law in their jurisdictions of practice prior to undertaking forensic assessments for this population.

Risk for miscarriage of justice can be great for accused individuals with FASD at many adjudicative stages, including legally invalid arrest/charter waivers, invalid statements and potentially false confessions, and under-recognition of impaired psycholegal abilities relevant to adjudicative competency (Brown et al., 2019; Gagnier et al., 2010; Reid et al., 2020; Roach & Bailey, 2009). Each is reviewed briefly here.

15.6 Police Questioning and Arrest

Legal safeguards are in place from the point police initially approach and question an individual through the process of arrest, interrogation, and detention. Although case law and statutes vary by jurisdiction, common protections include the right against self-incrimination by remaining silent and right to counsel (e.g., *Miranda* warnings in the United States, Charter cautions in Canada). Adolescents in many jurisdictions also are afforded enhanced procedural safeguards owing to their relative developmental vulnerability, such as the right to consult with a parent or other appropriate adult prior to giving a statement (e.g., Youth Criminal Justice Act, 2002). For rights waiver and subsequent statements to be considered valid, they must be provided voluntarily and with full understanding and appreciation for the meaning of each of these rights. True appreciation requires not only that an individual understand the relevance of a given right as it applies in their own situation but also understands the adversarial nature of the interrogative context, the notion that answering questions may lead to self-incrimination, that it may be in one's best interests to not make incriminatory statements, and that a lawyer serves as an advocate working to protect one's interests (Grisso, 2003). Given the knowledge required in this task, it is not surprising that in addition to age, lower or impaired intellectual abilities are a robust predictor of poor rights comprehension (Erickson, Salekin, Johnson, & Doran, 2020; Goldstein, Condie, Kalbeitzer, Osman, & Geier, 2003; McLachlan, Roesch, & Douglas, 2011; Viljoen & Roesch, 2005).

In practice, arrest warnings often are complex and difficult to read, with average required grade-level reading capacity going far beyond the abilities of many individuals in the justice system, calling into question the extent to which even neurotypically functioning adults can understand and thus meaningfully exercise their rights (Eastwood, Snook, & Luther, 2015; Helms & Holloway, 2006; Rogers, Hazelwood, Sewell, Harrison, & Shuman, 2008; Rogers, Hazelwood, Sewell, Shuman, & Blackwood, 2008). Further, it is common for police to simply read the rights warnings to suspects and only briefly query understanding via yes/no prompts. It is easy to see how individuals with FASD, with impaired cognitive and communication skills, may experience substantial difficulty understanding and truly appreciating the significance of these important legal rights. At the most basic level, this population may experience difficulties paying attention to written or oral warnings, and deficits in academic skills such as reading may render the task of understanding a written warning impossible without assistance. Setting aside the issue of whether police have sufficient knowledge to competently evaluate the psycholegal capacities of individuals with FASD, the relative *invisibility* of the disorder may render this task nearly impossible, particularly since many individuals with FASD present an appearance of verbal and social facility coupled with variable neurodevelopmental functioning across domains, which can effectively mask substantial underlying deficits (Abkarian, 1992; Fast & Conry, 2009; Wyper & Rasmussen, 2011). More broadly, experts have identified a critical lack of consideration and referral by defense counsel for evaluation of rights waiver validity in defendants with intellectual disabilities and recommend that all accused persons with intellectual disabilities be referred for such evaluation (Rogers, 2011; Rogers & Drogin, 2014).

15.7 Confessions

In many jurisdictions, police continue to be trained to approach the interrogation process from an adversarial standpoint, with common application of coercive techniques (Cleary & Warner, 2016; Kassin et al., 2010). Confessions reflect one of the most powerful pieces of evidence that ultimately result in convictions, and police officers are explicitly trained in coercive methods designed to extract inculpatory statements (Kassin et al., 2010). Under these conditions, vulnerable suspects such as individuals with FASD likely are at increased risk, not only for making statements against their best interests but also for producing false or inaccurate statements, including false confessions (Freckelton, 2016; McLachlan et al., 2014; Roach & Bailey, 2009). Cognitive and psychosocial impairments commonly experienced by persons with FASD have been identified as risk factors linked with increased vulnerability to coercive interrogation tactics. In addition to multiple cognitive impairments, risk factors include mental health problems and developmental immaturity, such as difficulty thinking strategically and weighing the consequences of decisions, poor future orientation, and impulsivity (Cauffman et al., 2010; Cauffman & Steinberg, 2000; Halpern-Felsher & Cauffman, 2001; Kassin et al., 2010). Indeed, psychosocial and developmental immaturity is a commonly observed characteristic in individuals with FASD, who often are described as functioning at much younger developmental levels relative to same-aged peers (Kully-Martens, Denys, Treit, Tamana, & Rasmussen, 2012). Individuals with FASD also frequently present with challenges related to interpersonal and social skills functioning, such as a tendency to overly trust others, strong desire to please persons in authority, and high levels of suggestibility, all of which may further increase their vulnerability to potentially manipulative or coercive tactics during police interrogation (Allely & Mukherjee, 2019; Fast & Conry, 2004; Novick Brown et al., 2011; Reid et al., 2020).

15.8 Adjudicative Competence

Research has established many risk factors associated with legal capacities relevant to interrogation and adjudication, such as mental health diagnoses and psychopathology, including psychosis, learning disabilities, attention problems and ADHD, and features of externalizing disorders (Goldstein et al., 2003; Pirelli et al., 2011; Ryba & Zapf, 2011; Viljoen & Roesch, 2005). Defendant age, and both functional and intellectual abilities, are particularly robust correlates of the psycholegal abilities relevant to adjudication, such that younger adolescents, particularly those with cognitive deficits, show elevated rates of impairment in psycholegal abilities compared to older adolescents and adults (Cunningham, 2020; Goldstein et al., 2003; Pirelli et al., 2011; Viljoen & Roesch, 2005). Specific impairments, including working memory, processing speed, and poor future orientation, also have been positively associated with overall adjudicative competency, as well as specific facets including appreciation and reasoning (e.g., Cunningham, 2020; Kivisto, Moore, Fite, & Seidner, 2011; Ryba Panza & Fraser, 2015). Notably, as described, rates of these difficulties often are high in individuals with FASD, resulting in a constellation of overlapping risk markers for impaired psycholegal abilities in this population. However, given a traditional focus on major forms of psychopathology in considering adjudicative competence, the pronounced and complex constellation of cognitive deficits in FASD may be underestimated altogether or missed in the context of a focus on signs of serious mental illness.

Legal proceedings and courtrooms can be complex and overwhelming environments with strangers focusing their full attention on defendants facing the considerable stress of life-changing consequences hanging in the balance. The pace of action in courtrooms ranges from a complete standstill to exceptionally rapid events full of incomprehensible legal jargon and procedures, making the process difficult to understand for laypersons. Further, courtrooms can be noisy and busy, with little reprieve from sensory overload. Individuals with FASD often experience problems in processing sensory information and may become overwhelmed in this type of environment (Jirikowic, Olson, & Kartin, 2008). When highly stressed, it is likely that becoming overwhelmed further hinders comprehension, and therefore meaningful participation at trial. Worse, individuals with FASD may engage in contextually inappropriate and impulsive behaviors under such strain, and this may be interpreted as hostile or purposeful by legal professionals and juries (Brown et al., 2019). In addition to deficits in overall intellectual ability, individuals with FASD experience substantial deficits in memory and communication, including both expressive (ability to general verbal output) and receptive (ability to understand what is being communicated auditorially) language skills (Hand, Pickering, Kedge, & McCann, 2015; Mattson et al., 2019; Wyper & Rasmussen, 2011). During a trial, these types of impairments may render a defendant with FASD unable to clearly communicate the facts necessary to mount a successful and fair defense with their lawyer. For example, a lawyer may not be able to "pause" a legal hearing to explain the meaning of lengthy or complex witness testimony. In addition, if the ability to pay attention to or comprehend testimony is impaired, defendants may not be able to signal inconsistencies, false evidence, or other important information to their lawyers, raising concerns about their meaningful participation and ability to communicate with counsel. Difficulties understanding components of a plea agreement, coupled with the earlier described deficits in psychosocial maturity, executive functioning, and decision-making, also may compromise their ability to make reasoned choices during the process of plea decision-making. Beyond the trial context and scope of this chapter, additional competency-related concerns are relevant in jurisdictions that employ the death penalty, including forensic evaluations in that context (Edwards & Greenspan, 2010; Novick Brown et al., 2011; Reed & Zapf, 2018; Wartnik & Carlson, 2011).

While clinical concerns have been raised for some time about psycholegal abilities in persons affected by prenatal exposure to alcohol, empirical evidence regarding these abilities in justice-involved youths and adults with FASD remains sparse. In our 2014 study, we evaluated the psycholegal abilities relevant to police interview and adjudicative competence in 100 justice-involved youths ages 12–23 years, including half with a diagnosis of FASD and half without known PAE or FASD (McLachlan et al., 2014). Using a variety of forensic assessment instruments, findings indicated that among youths with FASD, 90% showed impairment in at least one psycholegal ability, with significantly higher rates of impairment across abilities compared to justice-involved youths without FASD. Considerable within-group variability in psycholegal abilities, overall intellectual ability, and reading comprehension were also evident. Both IQ and reading comprehension emerged as robust predictors of psycholegal abilities, with the FASD diagnosis differentiating participant scores on a forensic assessment instrument evaluating fitness to stand trial, including domains of understanding and communication with counsel. However, given the paucity of empirical study in this area, additional research is warranted to better understand the generalizability of these findings across jurisdictions and in adults.

Various strategies may prove helpful in improving comprehension and communication with legal professionals for defendants with FASD. For instance, where feasible, defense counsel can spend more time with their clients and use strategies including repetition, clarification, and breaking down complex concepts into shorter chunks or ideas. However, lawyers have very limited time to spend with clients, particularly those working in underfunded legal aid programs. Further, the fast-paced nature of typical criminal courtrooms does not lend itself to using these strategies. Among the first of its kind, a special FASD-designated problem-solving court in Manitoba, Canada, recently opened. Personnel ranging from court staff through the lawyers and judge all are FASD-informed, and there are opportunities for a range of accommodations to support meaningful participation during the adjudicative process. Additionally, as a solution-focused court, defendants can be connected with the FASD Justice Program, providing support and navigation with consideration for clinical and community services necessary to support effective sentences and rehabilitation. While evaluation of this program has not been reported yet, the promise of a range of problem-solving courts, including mental health courts and even competency-related subprograms, are being applied with increasing frequency and may provide more optimal adjudicative environments for many individuals with FASD (Heilbrun et al., 2019).

15.9 Forensic Evaluation

Standard models of forensic assessment in the context of adjudicative competence provide an overview of key elements, including identifying and responding to legally relevant referral questions, identifying relevant statutes and common-law in the particular jurisdiction, assessing relevant psychological constructs via clinical assessment, identifying and assessing relevant psycholegal abilities via forensic assessment, synthesizing findings in a report and/or testimony, and ultimately providing relevant information to assist the court (Grisso, 2003; Heilbrun, Grisso, & Goldstein, 2008). Further, specialized ethical guidelines, practice standards, and in some jurisdictions, legislation, provide clear direction regarding the necessary knowledge, skills, and experience required to competently undertake the forensic evaluation process (e.g., American Psychological Association, 2013). Required skills include substantial training in FASD as well as other clinical areas, plus forensic competencies to effectively address legal referral questions (DeMatteo, Marczyk,

Krauss, & Burl, 2009; Grisso, 2003; Heilbrun et al., 2008; Reed & Zapf, 2018). Ultimately, forensic clinicians must be able to effectively navigate both clinical and legal fields while applying ethical and research-informed practices (Reed & Zapf, 2018).

In the context of FASD specifically, increasing evidence suggests a lack of FASD-focused training for mental health professionals may play a contributing role in under-recognition of neurodevelopmental disorders in both clinical and legal settings (Brown et al., 2019; Burd, Fast, Conry, & Williams, 2010). Indeed, surveys focused on FASD knowledge and practice among clinicians find insufficient training and limited knowledge and skill (e.g., Johnson et al., 2010; Wedding et al., 2007). Our recent international survey of 81 forensic mental health clinicians similarly showed that while most had some experience providing forensic assessment and intervention to individuals with FASD, including evaluations of adjudicative competence, the majority identified limited relevant training experiences, gaps in readiness for service provision, and barriers to effectively working in legal contexts with persons who have FASD (McLachlan, Mullally & Ritter, 2020). As such, it is critical for clinicians engaged in competency evaluations to become informed broadly about FASD, which includes seeking out specialized training in order to fully understand and assess the complex array of deficits and needs commonly experienced by this population (Brown et al., 2019; Novick Brown et al., 2011).

15.10 Clinical Evaluation

As described, individuals with FASD present with variable and complex clinical profiles that differ substantially from person to person, marked by considerable within-individual variability in areas of impairment. As such, clinical evaluations of FASD must apply an individualized approach that includes obtaining a comprehensive developmental history with consideration for all relevant pre- and postnatal adversities and evaluating psychopathology and the broad range of intellectual, cognitive, and functional abilities that could impact psycholegal abilities, and ultimately inform judgments of competence. Given the wide-ranging nature of potentially relevant deficits, a multidisciplinary team approach may be required where feasible to ensure complete evaluation (Brown et al., 2019; Novick Brown, Wartnik, Connor, & Adler, 2010).

As indicated, relevant cognitive domains in competency include overall intellectual functioning, attention, academic skills, memory, executive functioning, language, motor and sensory domains, as well as adaptive functioning and social communication (e.g., see Mattson et al., 2019, for a review). The extent to which individuals with FASD exhibit overall cognitive functioning that falls below commonly ascribed cut-off points used to diagnose intellectual disability varies considerably. Our recent study of adolescents, transition-aged youths, and adults diagnosed with FASD found 52% had full-scale IQs below a standard score of 70, although 80% had significantly impaired adaptive functioning (McLachlan, Flannigan & Temple, 2020). Clinicians should carefully assess the full cognitive profile as a pronounced constellation of deficits in multiple domains, particularly attention, executive functioning, memory, language, and adaptive functioning, may surpass the bar of functional impairment commensurate with a finding of intellectual disability, even in the absence of exceptionally low IQ (e.g., McGee, Schonfeld, Roebuck-Spencer, Riley, & Mattson, 2008).

Indeed, the recommendation above for comprehensive neuropsychological assessment mirrors guidance from scholars in the competency field who focus on defendants with intellectual disabilities, noting the risks posed by such defendants with respect to high levels of acquiescence, cooperativeness, and ability to mask deficits, which may render a "cloak of competence" impression in legal contexts (Appelbaum, 1994; Edgerton, 1967). Critically, assessing functional abilities rather than relying solely on IQ scores is required when conducting assessments for individuals presenting with a range of neurodevelopmental disorders such as FASD (Edgerton, 1967). At minimum, comprehensive psychological evaluation should screen for deficits across multiple domains of neurodevelopmental functioning, including adaptive behavior, which may require specialized neuropsychological evaluation if competency evaluators lack such experience (McLachlan, Mullally & Ritter, 2020).

In addition to cognitive functioning, developmental and psychosocial maturity factors must be assessed, particularly given concerns about increased suggestibility and susceptibility to social pressure for defendants with FASD. Similarly, comprehensive evaluation of mental health functioning is indicated given high rates of comorbid psychopathology. In addition, comprehensive assessment of physical health status is important, given high rates of concurrent genetic, chromosomal, and other neurodevelopmental and neurological disorders, such as autism and epilepsy, which may be of relevance to competence (Cook et al., 2016; Popova et al., 2016; Wozniak et al., 2019). Further, rates of psychiatric medication use for individuals with FASD are high and include common polypharmacy concerns (Mela et al., 2018, 2019, 2020). While evidence regarding efficacy of commonly prescribed psychotropic medications for persons with FASD remains limited, elevated rates of adverse events and side-effects in those with intellectual and neurodevelopmental disorders warrant consideration when making determinations about competence remediation and symptom treatment for defendants with FASD (Mela et al., 2018, 2019; Mela, Hanlon-Dearman, et al., 2020). For additional information regarding medication efficacy in FASD, see Chap. 16 in this book.

In practical terms, evaluators should consider implementing appropriate accommodations to ensure defendants with FASD understand the nature and context of the competency evaluation, thereby increasing the likelihood of meaningful and valid assessment. Clinicians with experience providing forensic assessment and intervention services report using a variety of common accommodations when working with justice-involved individuals with FASD, such as using simplified language, open-ended questions with in-depth probing to ensure understanding, and checking comprehension regularly (McLachlan, Wyper, & Pooley, 2013; McLachlan, Mullally & Ritter, 2020). Many evaluators regularly modify evaluation protocols to provide more frequent breaks and/or shorter assessment sessions. Forensic clinicians highlight the importance of interpreting forensic assessment instruments in the context of each defendant's particular cognitive and adaptive profile, referring cases for further specialized assessment as needed, modifying practices based on cultural or other diversity factors, inviting the presence of support persons during assessment, and making environmental modifications, such as lowering lighting and ensuring a quiet and disruption-free assessment area (McLachlan, Mullally & Ritter, 2020).

15.11 Forensic Assessment

As previously mentioned, the focus of competency evaluation involves *current* mental status, which requires assessing specific psycholegal abilities relevant to each defendant's specific legal proceeding (Reed & Zapf, 2018; Zapf & Roesch, 2009). Generally, forensic clinicians must identify the congruence or goodness of fit between a particular defendant's *current* capacities and what is likely to be expected of the person during adjudication. Consequently, these considerations are highly dependent upon dynamic considerations and contextual factors that not only include current functioning but also involve such things as anticipated complexity and duration of the legal proceeding at hand and whether a defendant has access to appropriate clinical and social supports (Birgden & Thomson, 1999; Reed & Zapf, 2018; Zapf & Roesch, 2009). While a prior finding of incompetence may be relevant in informing current evaluation, as in all forensic assessments, it is important clinicians identify the functional deficits thought to underlie impairments in the specific psycholegal abilities relevant to current adjudication (Pirelli et al., 2011; Reed & Zapf, 2018; Zapf & Roesch, 2009). Ultimately, final decisions regarding competency rest with the triers of fact, although courts often accept recommendations made by forensic evaluators (Zapf, Hubbard, Cooper, Wheeles, & Ronan, 2004).

15.12 Forensic Assessment Instruments

In addition to the clinical considerations outlined above, forensic evaluators also obtain extensive information through documented and current collateral interviews with third-party sources, review of legal and other records, and administration of forensic assessment instruments (Archer, Buffington-Vollum, Stredny, & Handel, 2006; McLachlan, Mullally & Ritter, 2020). Several forensic assessment instruments (FAIs) may be used to assess psycholegal abilities relevant to rights comprehension and waiver and adjudicative competency in both youths and adults (Archer et al., 2006; Zapf & Roesch, 2009). While several FAIs have been administered to defendants with intellectual and cognitive disabilities, there is a dearth of research on their psychometric properties in these populations or in FASD (Brown et al., 2019; McLachlan et al., 2014). One FAI, the Competence Assessment for Standing Trial with Mental Retardation (CAST-MR; Everington, 1990), was developed for use with intellectually disabled persons, but this is the only known FAI specifically designed for defendants with neurodevelopmental impairments. Our recent international survey of forensic clinicians found many use a range of FAIs when evaluating adjudicative competence in defendants with FASD (McLachlan, Mullally & Ritter, 2020). Specifically, 43% of clinicians indicated they use competency-related FAIs, and roughly one in five reported using these measures frequently, almost always, or always, when conducting relevant forensic assessments. Given their frequency of use and bearing the aforementioned caveats in mind, several relevant tools are outlined below.

15.12.1 Miranda Rights Comprehension

The *Miranda Rights Comprehension Instruments* (*MRCI*; Goldstein, Zelle, & Grisso, 2011), a revision of Grisso's (1998) *Instruments for Assessing Understanding and Appreciation of Miranda Rights*, comprise a series of measures designed to support forensic clinicians in evaluating capacities to understand and appreciate *Miranda* warnings in the context of waiver validity challenges in youths and adult defendants. The warnings included in the *MRCI* were modeled from a review of sample warnings from police departments across the United States. The measure involves four separate instruments that together address comprehension of Miranda warnings, understanding of relevant vocabulary, and appreciation of the significance of the warnings. The updated instruments follow a standardized administration format, with structured scoring for each instrument. Multiple normative reference samples are available for comparison in the manual. Both Grisso's original instruments and the *MRCI* demonstrate adequate validity and high interrater reliability (Goldstein et al., 2011; Grisso, 1998), and both versions have been studied and applied in a range of youths and adults with cognitive and intellectual disabilities (e.g., Everington & Fulero, 1999; Fulero & Everington, 1995; Lieser, Van der Voort, & Spaulding, 2019; O'Connell, Garmoe, & Goldstein, 2005; Rost & McGregor, 2012). In our study of justice-involved youths with FASD, McLachlan et al. (2014) reported excellent reliability via intraclass correlation coefficients across the four instruments included in Grisso's (1998) original measure, who as noted showed significant impairment across domains.

The Standardized Assessment of Miranda Abilities (SAMA; Rogers, Sewell, Drogin, & Fiduccia, 2013) comprises five measures designed to support forensic psychologists in evaluating a defendant's understanding of Miranda rights. Instruments include a quiz focusing on Miranda knowledge, a measure of vocabulary knowledge, a comprehension assessment relying on paraphrasing, a measure of acquiescence, and a reasoning measure. Examinee scores can be compared to a normative sample of pretrial defendants with pending criminal charges, and psychometric evaluation suggests excellent internal and interrater reliability and good evidence of both content and discriminant validity (Rogers et al., 2013). The SAMA recently was used in a study evaluating *Miranda* abilities in individuals with intellectual disability, with findings generally demonstrating significantly worse performance in all areas compared to the normative sample (Erickson et al., 2020). To our knowledge, no studies have evaluated defendants with FASD using the SAMA.

15.12.2 Competency to Stand Trial

The MacArthur Competence Assessment Tool for Criminal Adjudication (MacCAT-CA; Poythress et al., 1999) evaluates three competence-related abilities (understanding, appreciation, and reasoning) using a standardized administration approach, referencing criterion-based scoring against normative samples that include defendants found both competent and incompetent. Further evaluation of these abilities as they relate to defendants' specific case information must be undertaken given the standardized administration format of the MacCAT-CA. Psychometric characteristics of the MacCAT-CA are well established, including findings from a recent meta-analytic review of four studies with a pooled sample of 1038 participants, which showed the instrument had good internal consistency, excellent interrater reliability, consistently large differences in effect size between competent and incompetent defendants, and both convergent and divergent validity (Blake, Ogloff, & Chen, 2019). However, defendants with intellectual disability, standardized IQ scores falling below 60, and other neurocognitive disorders were excluded from the normative sample. Unfortunately, research applying the MacCAT-CA in defendants with intellectual and other neurodevelopmental disorders is limited. To our knowledge, no studies have used the tool in individuals with FASD, highlighting a need to develop additional psychometric support for using the MacCAT-CA in this population.

The Fitness Interview Test-Revised (FIT-R; Roesch, Zapf, & Eaves, 2006) provides an idiographic approach to evaluating adjudicative competency. Widely used, the FIT-R is a semi-structured interview that provides forensic clinicians a framework for considering competence-related abilities, while allowing flexibility for additional questioning as required. FIT-R items can be scored, although scoring is intended to assist evaluators in conceptualizing and fully assessing domains related to competence rather than for the purpose of comparing individual performance to a normative reference group. In our evaluation of psycholegal abilities relevant to competence, the FIT-R was administered to justice-involved adolescents and young adults with FASD (McLachlan et al., 2014). Although formal evaluation of psychometric considerations was not undertaken, results showed justice-involved youths with FASD had significantly lower average raw scores for Understanding (6.94 vs. 9.48), Appreciation (4.04 vs. 5.08), and Communication (9.66 vs. 11.94) compared to justice-involved youths without FASD, whose scores more closely approximated those reported in prior youths defendants (e.g., Viljoen & Roesch, 2005).

The Evaluation of Competency to Stand Trial-Revised (ECST-R; Rogers, Jackson, Sewell, & Harrison, 2004) is an interview-based FAI designed to support clinicians in evaluating prongs of the US *Dusky* (1960) standard for competency (rational understanding and ability to consult with counsel) for a defendant's own charges and proceedings. The tool applies both semi-structured and structured interview techniques and incorporates a standardized approach for evaluation of feigned incompetency in the context of the defendant's own trial. The tool includes three main scales for evaluating facets of competency, each canvasing areas including consultation with counsel, factual understanding, and rational understanding. The tool also includes a scale comprising items designed to screen for possible feigning. Normative data are drawn from justice-involved adults, though notably, those with IQs <60 were excluded from this sample. Findings from Blake et al.'s (2019) recent meta-analytic review reported results from two studies comprising 511 participants. Psychometric properties were found to be sound, with excellent internal consistency and interrater reliability for each subscale, and good mean inter-item correlations. However, there was insufficient data available to compare scores between competent and incompetent defendants. To our knowledge, research supporting the psychometric properties or use of the tool in defendants with neurodevelopmental disabilities, including those with FASD, remains limited, and caution should be applied when interpreting findings from indicators of feigned incompetency (see additional rational in the subsequent section).

As noted earlier, the Competence Assessment for Standing Trial for defendants with Mental Retardation (CAST-MR; Everington & Luckasson, 1992) is a standardized tool developed to assist evaluators in assessing adjudicative competency in adult defendants with intellectual disability. The instrument includes a range of multiple-choice questions spanning competency domains and is written at a fourth-grade level. The CAST-MR does not appear to have been widely adopted in practice, nor has the tool received a great deal of scrutiny from a research perspective (Blake et al., 2019; Pirelli et al., 2011). Findings from two studies evaluating the CAST-MR with a total sample of 128 participants demonstrated that the instrument showed good internal consistency and excellent interrater reliability. Competency outcome was highly associated with CAST-MR total score. To our knowledge, research using the CAST-MR has not been reported for defendants with FASD.

15.13 Validity, Effort, and Malingering

Performance validity tests (PVTs) and assessment of effort and malingering are important components of neuropsychological and cognitive assessments and necessary to evaluate in forensic contexts where secondary gain potential is high (Miller, Axelrod, Schutte, & Davis, 2017; Reed & Zapf, 2018; Zapf & Roesch, 2009). Studies have specifically assessed validity and feigning of competency-related impairments in the context of FAIs used in competency evaluations, though studies in this area focusing on defendants with neurodevelopmental disabilities, including FASD, remain limited (e.g., Norton & Ryba, 2010; Rogers et al., 2004; Rogers, Henry, Sharf, Robinson, & Williams, 2017). Research on the application of PVT measures that are more broadly designed to be administered in the course of neuropsychological or cognitive assessment in individuals with intellectual disability suggests performance is associated with overall intellectual ability. Further, those with impaired cognitive functioning are more likely to perform worse on such measures compared to those with higher IQs (e.g., Dean, Victor, Boone, & Arnold, 2008). Although some experts caution against using PVTs for individuals with neurocognitive deficits, it nonetheless may be the case that evaluators inadvertently use PVTs or malingering measures with the FASD population given the relative invisibility of the disability (see earlier discussion). To date, and to our knowledge, there is no evidence regarding the validity of FAIs and malingering instruments in individuals with FASD undergoing competency assessment, and a recent brief review yielded no empirical evidence in this area. With respect to general PVT use in FASD, we found that among a sample of 80 justice-involved adults ages 18–40 years with and without FASD, those with diagnosed or possible FASD were more likely to fail *any* single PVT and also failed a greater number of PVTs overall, highlighting a need for caution in practice and additional need for more research examining the applicability of PVT use in forensic assessments of persons with FASD (Mullally, McLachlan, MacKillop, & Pei, 2020). Although empirical evidence remains limited, clinicians identify concerns regarding a tendency for individuals with FASD to confabulate (i.e., providing false or inaccurate information without intent to deceive; Allely & Mukherjee, 2019; Brown et al., 2019; Burd et al., 2010; Freckelton, 2016; Kully-Martens et al., 2012; Novick Brown et al., 2011). Given a likelihood of confabulation in this population, forensic evaluators should carefully differentiate confabulation from intentional deception or malingering (Brown et al., 2014; Mullally et al., 2020; Novick Brown et al., 2010).

15.14 Diversity Considerations

As in all forensic evaluations, clinicians must consider a number of factors related to diversity when conducting competency-related evaluations for individuals with FASD. Forensic clinicians should be knowledgeable about processes related to systematic racism, social determinants of health, and socio-historical factors, which continue to lead to systematic inequities and cause many groups to be overrepresented in the criminal justice system, and consider the impact of these factors in the context of forensic competency evaluations (Riggs Romaine & Kavanaugh, 2019; Shepherd & Lewis-Fernandez, 2016; Weiss & Rosenfeld, 2012). Regarding FASD specifically, historical myths about genetic or cultural susceptibility to the teratogenic impacts of alcohol during pregnancy are not supported by evidence (Mattson et al., 2019). It is critical for forensic clinicians to understand and emphasize to the court that FASD can occur in the context of alcohol use in *any* pregnancy, with higher rates likely impacting communities and individuals marked by inadequate social determinants of health and other system-level inequities that similarly drive the criminalization of minoritized or vulnerable populations (Wolfson et al., 2019). Further, evaluators should select culturally-sensitive and valid instruments and procedures, although many forensic and psychological instruments lack adequate research with diverse populations, rendering this a challenge in practice.

15.15 Competency Restoration

The most common approaches to competency restoration in defendants found incompetent include psychotropic medication, particularly for adults with serious mental illness, which may be accompanied by individual or group therapy targeting competency-related deficits as well as psychoeducational and educational treatment programs (Heilbrun et al., 2019). Cognitive remediation programs also are gaining increasing attention for individuals who have experienced declines in cognitive functioning, often in the context of serious mental illness or neurocognitive disorder (Heilbrun et al., 2019). Recent reviews of the empirical basis supporting best practices and effective competency remediation approaches note a lack of theoretically sound, legally relevant, and methodologically well-designed studies in this area (Gowensmith, 2019; Heilbrun et al., 2019; Pirelli & Zapf, 2020). Further, there remains a dearth of evidence identifying the most effective remediation practices, including methods for predicting remediation outcomes in defendants with intellectual disabilities and cognitive deficits (Heilbrun et al., 2019). This impoverished empirical situation appears to extend to defendants with FASD.

Among the small number of studies that have addressed competence restoration for individuals with intellectual disability, Grabowski (2017) found that while intellectual functioning in a sample of adult defendants was not associated with competency restoration or length of hospitalization for restoration treatment, those with standardized IQ scores falling above a cut-off standard score of 63.5 were more likely to be restored to competency. Anderson and Hewitt (2002) found only one-third of defendants with intellectual disability were restored following competency restoration training, and IQ predicted competency restoration. Specific programs, such as the Slater Method, a specialized program designed specifically for defendants with intellectual disability that features repetition to facilitate learning and retention, also have resulted in variable restoration outcomes (Wall & Christopher, 2012; Wall, Krupp, & Guilmette, 2003).

A particularly critical consideration for defendants with FASD and similar complex neurocognitive deficits involves circumstances where potentially irremediable cognitive deficits increase risk for extended time spent in inappropriate and unnecessary restoration supervision (Heilbrun et al., 2019; Pirelli et al., 2011). While this may not be as critical a consideration for those placed in less restrictive community settings, negative effects associated with more restrictive settings, including custody or mental health placements, coupled with serious deprivation of liberty, warrants important consideration for this vulnerable population (Cunningham, 2020; Pirelli & Zapf, 2020; Reed & Zapf, 2018). For those where a determination of irremediability is found, consideration of whether applicable cases should be stayed or dismissed may be warranted. Further, exploring whether outpatient and community-based competency restoration approaches are appropriate for this population is an important consideration (Heilbrun et al., 2019).

15.16 Conclusion

Increasing recognition of FASD among criminal justice professionals and forensic clinicians, coupled with policy attention aimed at better addressing the needs of defendants with the disorder, suggest that forensic clinicians may be called upon with increasing frequency to undertake a range of forensic evaluations, including adjudicative competency. While research focused on impairments in specific psycholegal abilities relevant to adjudicative competency in this population remains limited to date, courts increasingly are recognizing the relevance of FASD-associated neurodevelopmental and clinical deficits across a range of legal matters, including understanding rights warnings, statement admissibility, and adjudicative competency. Forensic clinicians who conduct evaluations of defendants affected by prenatal alcohol exposure must be FASD-informed, which requires comprehensive evaluation to understand the functional deficits underlying potential impairments in psycholegal abilities. This is particularly important given how often persons with FASD go undetected in legal settings, as well as the relative diagnostic challenge. Future directions for the field include enhanced research to support forensic practice in this area, including better understanding the validity of using FAIs and PVTs with this population in the context of competency evaluation, and additional research to understand competency remediation and restoration efficacy for this population.

References

Abkarian, G. G. (1992). Communication effects of prenatal alcohol exposure. *Journal of Communication Disorders, 25*(4), 221–240. https://doi.org/10.1016/0021-9924(92)90017-Q

Allely, C. S., & Mukherjee, R. (2019). Suggestibility, false confessions and competency to stand trial in individuals with fetal alcohol spectrum disorders: Current concerns and recommendations. *Journal of Criminal Psychology, 9*(4), 166–172. https://doi.org/10.1108/JCP-11-2019-050

American Bar Association (ABA). (2012). *Resolution 112B*. Retrieved from https://www.americanbar.org/news/reporter_resources/annual-meeting-2018/house-of-delegates-resolutions/112b/

American Psychiatric Association (APA). (2013). *Diagnostic and statistical manual of mental disorders (DSM-5)* (5th ed.). Arlington, VA: American Psychiatric Association.

American Psychological Association. (2013). Specialty guidelines for forensic psychology. *American Psychologist, 68*(1), 7–19. https://doi.org/10.1037/a0029889

Anderson, S. D., & Hewitt, J. (2002). The effect of competency restoration training on defendants with mental retardation found not competent to proceed. *Law and Human Behavior, 26*(3), 343–351. https://doi.org/10.1023/A:1015328505884

Appelbaum, K. L. (1994). Assessment of criminal-justice-related competencies in defendants with mental retardation. *Journal of Psychiatry and Law, 22*(3), 311–327. https://doi.org/10.1177/009318539402200301

Archer, R. P., Buffington-Vollum, J. K., Stredny, R. V., & Handel, R. W. (2006). A survey of psychological test use patterns among forensic psychologists. *Journal of Personality Assessment, 87*(1), 84–94. https://doi.org/10.1207/s15327752jpa8701_07

Astley, S. J. (2004). *Diagnostic guide for fetal alcohol spectrum disorders: The 4-digit diagnostic code* (3rd ed.). Seattle: University of Washington.

Astley, S. J. (2010). Profile of the first 1400 patients receiving diagnostic evaluations for fetal alcohol spectrum disorder at the Washington State Fetal Alcohol Syndrome Diagnostic & Prevention Network. *Canadian Journal of Clinical Pharmacology = Journal canadien de pharmacologie clinique, 17*(1), e132–e164.

Baldry, E., Briggs, D. B., Goldson, B., & Russell, S. (2018). "Cruel and unusual punishment": An inter-jurisdictional study of the criminalisation of young people with complex support needs. *Journal of Youth Studies, 21*(5), 636–652. https://doi.org/10.1080/13676261.2017.1406072

Beltrani, A., & Zapf, P. A. (2020). Competence to stand trial and criminalization: An overview of the research. CNS Spectrums. *Cambridge University Press, 25*(2), 161–172. https://doi.org/10.1017/S1092852919001597

Binnie, I., Trussler, M., & Jonsson, E. (Eds.). (2015, February 17). *Legal issues of FASD: Fetal alcohol spectrum disorder*. Proceedings from a consensus development conference. Institute of Health Economics. Edmonton, AB. Retrieved from https://www.ihe.ca/download/legal_issues_fasd_proceedings.pdf

Birgden, A., & Thomson, D. (1999). The assessment of fitness to stand trial for defendants with an intellectual disability: A proposed assessment procedure involving mental health professionals and lawyers. *Psychiatry, Psychology and Law, 6*(2), 2071214. https://doi.org/10.1080/13218719909524963

Blake, G. A., Ogloff, J. R. P., & Chen, W. S. (2019). Meta-analysis of second generation competency to stand trial assessment measures: Preliminary findings. *International Journal of Law and Psychiatry, 64*, 238–249. https://doi.org/10.1016/j.ijlp.2019.04.007

Bonnie, R. J. (1992). The competence of criminal defendants: A theoretical reformulation. *Behavioral Sciences & the Law, 10*(3), 291–316. https://doi.org/10.1002/bsl.2370100303

Bower, C., Elliott, E. J., Zimmet, M., Doorey, J., Wilkins, A., Russell, V., … Watkins, R. (2017). Australian guide to the diagnosis of foetal alcohol spectrum disorder: A summary. *Journal of Paediatrics and Child Health, 53*(10), 1021–1023. https://www.ncbi.nlm.nih.gov/pmc/articles/PMC5658660/

Bower, C., Watkins, R. E., Mutch, R. C., Marriott, R., Freeman, J., Kippin, N. R., … Giglia, R. (2018). Fetal alcohol spectrum disorder and youth justice: A prevalence study among young people sentenced to detention in Western Australia. *BMJ Open, 8*(2). https://doi.org/10.1136/bmjopen-2017-019605

Brown, J., Carter, M. N., Haun, J., Wartnik, A., & Zapf, P. A. (2019). Fetal alcohol spectrum disorder (FASD) and competency to stand trial (CST): A call on forensic evaluators to become informed. *Journal of Forensic Psychology Research and Practice, 19*(4), 315–340. https://doi.org/10.1080/24732850.2019.1620798

Brown, J., Freeman, N., Pickett, H., Watts, E., & Trnka, A. J. (2018). FASD in adult populations: Clinical and forensic considerations. In E. Jonsson, S. Clarren, & I. Binnie (Eds.), *Ethical and legal perspectives in fetal alcohol spectrum disorders (FASD)* (pp. 163–183). Cham, Switzerland: Springer. https://doi.org/10.1007/978-3-319-71755-5_10

Brown, J., Long-McGie, J., Wartnik, A., Oberoi, P., Wresh, J., Weinkauf, E., … Kerr, A. (2014). Fetal alcohol spectrum disorders in the criminal justice system: A review. *Journal of Law Enforcement, 3*(6), 1–10. https://canfasd.ca/wp-content/uploads/2018/01/Brown-2014-FASD-in-the-criminal-justice-system.pdf

Brown, J. M., Haun, J., Zapf, P. A., & Novick Brown, N. (2017). Fetal alcohol spectrum disorders (FASD) and competency to stand trial (CST): Suggestions for a "best practices" approach to forensic evaluation. *International Journal of Law and Psychiatry, 52*, 19–27. https://doi.org/10.1016/j.ijlp.2017.04.002

Burd, L., Fast, D. K., Conry, J., & Williams, A. (2010). Fetal alcohol spectrum disorder as a marker for increased risk of involvement with correction systems. *Journal of Psychiatry and Law, 38*(4), 559–583. https://doi.org/10.1177/009318531003800408

Burd, L., Selfridge, R. H., Klug, M. G., & Bakko, S. A. (2004). Fetal alcohol syndrome in the United States corrections system. *Addiction Biology, 9*(2), 169–176. https://doi.org/10.1080/13556210410001717060

Burd, L., Selfridge, R. H., Klug, M. G., & Juelson, T. (2003). Fetal alcohol syndrome in the Canadian corrections system. *Journal of FAS International, 1*(14), 1–10.

Canadian Bar Association (CBA). (2013). *Resolution 13-12-A: Accommodating the disability of FASD to improve access to justice*. Retrieved from https://www.cba.org/getattachment/Our-Work/Resolutions/Resolutions/2013/Accommodating-the-Disability-of-FASD-to-Improve-Ac/13-12-A-ct.pdf

Cauffman, E., Shulman, E. P., Steinberg, L., Claus, E., Banich, M. T., Graham, S., & Woolard, J. (2010). Age differences in affective decision making as indexed by performance on the Iowa Gambling Task. *Developmental Psychology, 46*(1), 193–207. https://doi.org/10.1037/a0016128

Cauffman, E., & Steinberg, L. (2000). (Im)maturity of judgment in adolescence: Why adolescents may be less culpable than adults. *Behavioral Sciences & the Law, 18*(6), 741–760. https://doi.org/10.1002/bsl.416

Chandler, J. A. (2015). The use of neuroscientific evidence in Canadian criminal proceedings. *Journal of Law and the Biosciences, 2*(3), 550–579. https://doi.org/10.1093/jlb/lsv026

Chudley, A. E. (2008). Fetal alcohol spectrum disorder: Counting the invisible—Mission impossible? *Archives of Disease in Childhood, 93*(9), 721–722. https://doi.org/10.1136/adc.2008.137109

Chudley, A. E., Kilgour, A. R., Cranston, M., & Edwards, M. (2007). Challenges of diagnosis in fetal alcohol syndrome and fetal alcohol spectrum disorder in the adult. *American Journal of Medical Genetics. Part C: Seminars in Medical Genetics, 145C*(3), 261–272. https://doi.org/10.1002/ajmg.c.30140

Cleary, H. M. D., & Warner, T. C. (2016). Police training in interviewing and interrogation methods: A comparison of techniques used with adult and juvenile suspects. *Law and Human Behavior, 40*(3), 270–284. https://doi.org/10.1037/lhb0000175

Coles, C. D., Gailey, A. R., Mulle, J. G., Kable, J. A., Lynch, M. E., & Jones, K. L. (2016). A comparison among 5 methods for the clinical diagnosis of fetal alcohol spectrum disorders. *Alcoholism: Clinical and Experimental Research, 40*(5), 1000–1009. https://doi.org/10.1111/acer.13032

Cook, J. L., Green, C. R., Lilley, C. M., Anderson, S. M., Baldwin, M. E., Chudley, A. E., … Rosales, T. (2016). Fetal alcohol spectrum disorder: A guideline for diagnosis across the lifespan. *CMAJ: Canadian Medical Association Journal, 188*(3), 191–197. https://doi.org/10.1503/cmaj.141593

Cooper, V. G., & Zapf, P. A. (2003). Predictor variables in competency to stand trial decisions. *Law and Human Behavior, 27*(4), 423–436. https://doi.org/10.1023/A:1024089117535

Criminal Code, Pub. L. No. c. C-46 (1985). Retrieved from https://laws-lois.justice.gc.ca/eng/acts/C-46/

Cunningham, K. A. (2020). Advances in juvenile adjudicative competence: A 10-year update. *Behavioral Sciences & the Law, 38*(4), 406–420. https://doi.org/10.1002/bsl.2478

Dean, A. C., Victor, T. L., Boone, K. B., & Arnold, G. (2008). The relationship of IQ to effort test performance. *The Clinical Neuropsychologist, 22*(4), 705–722. https://doi.org/10.1080/13854040701440493

DeMatteo, D., Marczyk, G., Krauss, D. A., & Burl, J. (2009). Educational and training models in forensic psychology. *Training and Education in Professional Psychology, 3*(3), 184–191. https://doi.org/10.1037/a0014582

Douds, A. S., Stevens, H. R., & Sumner, W. E. (2013). Sword or shield? A systematic review of the roles FASD evidence plays in judicial proceedings. *Criminal Justice Policy Review, 24*(4), 492–509. https://doi.org/10.1177/0887403412447809

Dusky v. United States of America, 362 U.S. 402 (1960).
Eastwood, J., Snook, B., & Luther, K. (2015). Measuring the reading complexity and oral comprehension of Canadian youth waiver forms. *Crime & Delinquency, 61*(6), 798–828. https://doi.org/10.1177/0011128712453689
Edgerton, R. B. (1967). *The cloak of competence: Stigma in the lives of the mentally retarded*. Berkeley: University of California Press.
Edwards, W. J., & Greenspan, S. (2010). Adaptive behavior and fetal alcohol spectrum disorders. *Journal of Psychiatry and Law, 38*(4), 419–447. https://doi.org/10.1177/009318531003800404
Erickson, S. L., Salekin, K. L., Johnson, L. N., & Doran, S. C. (2020). The predictive power of intelligence: Miranda abilities of individuals with intellectual disability. *Law and Human Behavior, 44*(1), 60–70. https://doi.org/10.1037/lhb0000356
Everington, C. T. (1990). The competence assessment for standing trial for defendants with mental retardation (CAST-MR): A validation study. *Criminal Justice and Behavior, 17*(2), 147–168. https://doi.org/10.1177/0093854890017002001
Everington, C., & Fulero, S. M. (1999). Competence to confess: Measuring understanding and suggestibility of defendants with mental retardation. *Mental Retardation, 37*(3), 212–220. https://psycnet.apa.org/record/2000-12361-004
Everington, C. T., & Luckasson, R. (1992). *Competence assessment for standing trial for defendants with mental retardation (CAST-MR)*. Columbus, OH: IDS. http://criminal-justice.iresearchnet.com/forensic-psychology/competence-assessment-for-standing-trial-for-defendants-with-mental-retardation-castmr/
Fast, D. K., & Conry, J. (2004). The challenge of fetal alcohol syndrome in the criminal legal system. *Addiction Biology, 9*(2), 161–166. https://doi.org/10.1080/13556210410001717042
Fast, D. K., & Conry, J. (2009). Fetal alcohol spectrum disorders and the criminal justice system. *Developmental Disabilities Research Review, 15*(3), 250–257. https://doi.org/10.1002/ddrr.66
Fast, D. K., Conry, J., & Loock, C. A. (1999). Identifying fetal alcohol syndrome among youth in the criminal justice system. *Journal of Developmental and Behavioral Pediatrics, 20*(5), 370–372. https://doi.org/10.1097/00004703-199910000-00012
Forrester, P., Davis, C. G., Moser, A., MacPherson, P., Gobeil, R., & Chudley, A. E. (2015). *Assessing fetal alcohol spectrum disorder in women offenders*. (Research Report R346). Ottawa, ON: Correctional Service of Canada. Retrieved from https://www.csc-scc.gc.ca/005/008/092/005008-r346-eng.pdf
Freckelton, I. (2016). Fetal alcohol spectrum disorders, expert evidence and the unreliability of admissions during police interviews. *Psychiatry, Psychology and Law, 23*(2), 173–183. https://doi.org/10.1080/13218719.2016.1149898
Freckelton, I. (2017). Assessment and evaluation of fetal alcohol spectrum disorder (FASD) and its potential relevance for sentencing: A clarion call from Western Australia. *Psychiatry, Psychology and Law, 24*(4), 485–495. https://doi.org/10.1080/13218719.2017.1350931
Fulero, S. M., & Everington, C. (1995). Assessing competency to waive Miranda rights in defendants with mental retardation. *Law and Human Behavior, 19*(5), 533–543. https://doi.org/10.1007/BF01499342
Gagnier, K. R., Moore, T. E., & Green, M. (2010). A need for closer examination of FASD by the criminal justice system: Has the call been answered? *Journal of Population Therapeutics and Clinical Pharmacology, 18*(3), e426–e439. https://www.glendon.yorku.ca/timmoore/wp-content/uploads/sites/222/FASDJustice-2011.pdf
Golding, S. L. (2008). Evaluations of adult adjudicative competency. In R. Jackson (Ed.), *Learning forensic assessment* (pp. 75–108). New York, NY: Routledge/Taylor & Francis.
Goldstein, N. E. S., Condie, L. O., Kalbeitzer, R., Osman, D., & Geier, J. L. (2003). Juvenile offenders' Miranda rights comprehension and self-reported likelihood of offering false confessions. *Assessment, 10*(4), 359–369. https://doi.org/10.1177/1073191103259535
Goldstein, N. E. S., Riggs Romaine, C. L., Zelle, H., Kalbeitzer, R., Mesiarik, C., & Wolbransky, M. (2011). Psychometric properties of the Miranda rights comprehension instruments with a juvenile justice sample. *Assessment, 18*(4), 428–441. https://doi.org/10.1177/1073191111400280

Goldstein, N. E. S., Zelle, H., & Grisso, T. (2011). *Miranda Rights Comprehension Instruments (MRCI) Manual*. Sarasota, FL: Professional Resource Press.

Gowensmith, W. N. (2019). Resolution or resignation: The role of forensic mental health professionals amidst the competency services crisis. *Psychology, Public Policy, and Law, 25*(1), 1–14. https://doi.org/10.1037/law0000190

Grabowski, K. E. (2017). *Intellectual disability/intellectual developmental disorder and restoration to competency to stand trial*. Doctoral dissertation, Texas Tech University. Retrieved from http://hdl.handle.net/2346/73132

Grisso, T. (1998). *Instruments for assessing understanding & appreciation of Miranda rights*. Professional Resource Press/Professional Resource Exchange. Retrieved from https://psycnet.apa.org/record/1998-06394-000

Grisso, T. (2003). *Evaluating competencies: Forensic assessments and instruments* (2nd ed.). New York, NY: Kluwer Academic Press/Plenum Press.

Halpern-Felsher, B. L., & Cauffman, E. (2001). Costs and benefits of a decision: Decision-making competence in adolescents and adults. *Journal of Applied Developmental Psychology, 22*(3), 257–273. https://doi.org/10.1016/S0193-3973(01)00083-1

Hand, L., Pickering, M., Kedge, S., & McCann, C. (2015). Oral language and communication factors to consider when supporting people with FASD involved with the legal system. In M. Nelson & M. Trussler (Eds.), *Fetal alcohol spectrum disorders in adults: Ethical and legal perspectives: An overview on FASD for professionals* (pp. 139–147). Cham, Switzerland: Springer International Publishing. https://doi.org/10.1007/978-3-319-20866-4_9

Harding, K., Flannigan, K., & McFarlane, A. (2019). *Policy action paper: Toward a standard definition of fetal alcohol spectrum disorder in Canada*. Canada Fetal Alcohol Spectrum Disorder Research Network, Canada. https://canfasd.ca/wp-content/uploads/2019/08/Toward-a-Standard-Definition-of-FASD-Final.pdf

Heilbrun, K., Giallella, C., Wright, H. J., DeMatteo, D., Griffin, P. A., Locklair, B., & Desai, A. (2019). Treatment for restoration of competence to stand trial: Critical analysis and policy recommendations. *Psychology, Public Policy, and Law, 25*(4), 266–283. https://doi.org/10.1037/law0000210

Heilbrun, K., Grisso, T., & Goldstein, A. (2008). *Foundations of forensic mental health assessment*. Oxford: Oxford University Press. https://doi.org/10.1093/med:psych/9780195323092.001.0001

Helms, J. L., & Holloway, C. L. (2006). Differences in the prongs of the Miranda warnings. *Criminal Justice Studies, 19*(1), 77–84. https://doi.org/10.1080/14786010600616007

Hoge, S. K., Bonnie, R. J., Poythress, N., & Monahan, J. (1992). Attorney-client decision-making in criminal cases: Client competence and participation as perceived by their attorneys. *Behavioral Sciences & the Law, 10*(3), 385–394. https://doi.org/10.1002/bsl.2370100308

Hoyme, H. E., Kalberg, W. O., Elliott, A. J., Blankenship, J., Buckley, D., Marais, A.-S., … May, P. A. (2016). Updated clinical guidelines for diagnosing fetal alcohol spectrum disorders. *Pediatrics, 138*(2), 1–18. https://doi.org/10.1542/peds.2015-4256

James, D. V., Duffield, G., Blizard, R., & Hamilton, L. W. (2001). Fitness to plead: A prospective study of the interrelationships between expert opinion, legal criteria and specific symptomatology. *Psychological Medicine, 31*(1), 139–150. https://doi.org/10.1017/S0033291799002901

Jirikowic, T., Olson, H. C., & Kartin, D. (2008). Sensory processing, school performance, and adaptive behavior of young school-age children with fetal alcohol spectrum disorders. *Physical and Occupational Therapy in Pediatrics, 28*(2), 117–136. https://doi.org/10.1080/01942630802031800

Johnson, M. E., Robinson, R. V., Corey, S., Dewane, S. L., Brems, C., & Casto, L. D. (2010). Knowledge, attitudes, and behaviors of health, education, and service professionals as related to fetal alcohol spectrum disorders. *International Journal of Public Health, 55*(6), 627–635. https://doi.org/10.1007/s00038-010-0186-8

Kassin, S. M., Drizin, S. A., Grisso, T., Gudjonsson, G. H., Leo, R. A., & Redlich, A. D. (2010). Police-induced confessions: Risk factors and recommendations. *Law and Human Behavior, 34*(1), 3–38. https://doi.org/10.1007/s10979-009-9188-6

Kivisto, A. J., Moore, T. M., Fite, P. A., & Seidner, B. G. (2011). Future orientation and competence to stand trial: The fragility of competence. *Journal of the American Academic of Psychiatry and the Law, 39*(3), 316–326.

Kully-Martens, K., Denys, K., Treit, S., Tamana, S., & Rasmussen, C. (2012). A review of social skills deficits in individuals with fetal alcohol spectrum disorders and prenatal alcohol exposure: Profiles, mechanisms, and interventions. *Alcoholism: Clinical and Experimental Research, 36*(4), 568–576. https://doi.org/10.1111/j.1530-0277.2011.01661.x

Lange, S., Probst, C., Gmel, G., Rehm, J., Burd, L., & Popova, S. (2017). Global prevalence of fetal alcohol spectrum disorder among children and youth. *JAMA Pediatrics, 171*(10), 948–956. https://doi.org/10.1001/jamapediatrics.2017.1919

Lebel, C. A., McMorris, C. A., Kar, P., Ritter, C., Andre, Q., Tortorelli, C., & Gibbard, W. B. (2019). Characterizing adverse prenatal and postnatal experiences in children. *Birth Defects Research, 111*(12), 848–858. https://doi.org/10.1002/bdr2.1464

Lieser, A. M., Van der Voort, D., & Spaulding, T. J. (2019). You have the right to remain silent: The ability of adolescents with developmental language disorder to understand their legal rights. *Journal of Communication Disorders, 82*, 105920. https://doi.org/10.1016/j.jcomdis.2019.105920

Lynch, M. E., Kable, J. A., & Coles, C. D. (2015). Prenatal alcohol exposure, adaptive function, and entry into adult roles in a prospective study of young adults. *Neurotoxicology and Teratology, 51*, 52–60. https://doi.org/10.1016/j.ntt.2015.07.008

MacPherson, P. H., Chudley, A. E., & Grant, B. A. (2011). *Fetal alcohol spectrum disorder (FASD) in a correctional population: Prevalence, screening and diagnosis*. Report R-247. Ottawa, ON: Correctional Service of Canada.

Mattson, S. N., Bernes, G. A., & Doyle, L. R. (2019). Fetal alcohol spectrum disorders: A review of the neurobehavioral deficits associated with prenatal alcohol exposure. *Alcoholism: Clinical and Experimental Research, 43*(6), 1046–1062. https://doi.org/10.1111/acer.14040

May, P. A., Baete, A., Russo, J., Elliott, A. J., Blankenship, J., Kalberg, W. O., … Hoyme, H. E. (2014). Prevalence and characteristics of fetal alcohol spectrum disorders. *Pediatrics, 134*(5), 855–866. https://doi.org/10.1542/peds.2013-3319

May, P. A., Chambers, C. D., Kalberg, W. O., Zellner, J., Feldman, H., Buckley, D., … Hoyme, H. E. (2018). Prevalence of fetal alcohol spectrum disorders in 4 US communities. *JAMA, 319*(5), 474. https://doi.org/10.1001/jama.2017.21896

McGee, C. L., Schonfeld, A. M., Roebuck-Spencer, T. M., Riley, E. P., & Mattson, S. N. (2008). Children with heavy prenatal alcohol exposure demonstrate deficits on multiple measures of concept formation. *Alcoholism: Clinical and Experimental Research, 32*(8), 1388–1397. https://doi.org/10.1111/j.1530-0277.2008.00707.x

McLachlan, K., Andrew, G., Pei, J., & Rasmussen, C. (2015). Assessing FASD in young children: Exploring clinical complexities and diagnostic challenges. *Journal of Population Therapeutics and Clinical Pharmacology, 22*(1), e108–e124. https://jptcp.com/index.php/jptcp/article/view/280/232

McLachlan, K., Flannigan, K., Temple, V., Unsworth, K., & Cook, J. L. (2020). Difficulties in daily living experienced by adolescents, transition-aged youth, and adults with fetal alcohol spectrum disorder. *Alcoholism: Clinical and Experimental Research, 44*(8), 1609–1624. https://doi.org/10.1111/acer.14385

McLachlan, K., McNiel, A., Pei, J., Brain, U., Andrew, G., & Oberlander, T. F. (2019). Prevalence and characteristics of adults with fetal alcohol spectrum disorder in corrections: A Canadian case ascertainment study. *BMC Public Health, 19*, 43. https://doi.org/10.1186/s12889-018-6292-x

McLachlan, K., Mullally, K., Ritter, C., Pei, J., & Mela, M. (2020). Fetal alcohol spectrum disorder and neurodevelopmental disorder: An international practice survey of forensic mental health clinicians. *International Journal of Forensic Mental Health*, 1–31. https://doi.org/10.1080/14999013.2020.1852342

McLachlan, K., Roesch, R., & Douglas, K. S. (2011). Examining the role of interrogative suggestibility in Miranda rights comprehension in adolescents. *Law and Human Behavior, 35*(3), 165–177. https://doi.org/10.1007/s10979-009-9198-4

McLachlan, K., Roesch, R., Viljoen, J. L., & Douglas, K. S. (2014). Evaluating the psycholegal abilities of young offenders with fetal alcohol spectrum disorder. *Law and Human Behavior, 38*(1), 10–22. https://doi.org/10.1037/lhb0000037

Mclachlan, K., Wyper, K., & Pooley, A. (2013). *Promising practices in substance abuse treatment for justice involved youth with an FASD*. Maple Ridge, BC: Asante Centre. https://www.asantecentre.org/s/Asante-Substance-Abuse-Study-Executive-Summary-Final.pdf

Mela, M., Coons-Harding, K. D., & Anderson, T. (2019). Recent advances in fetal alcohol spectrum disorder for mental health professionals. *Current Opinion in Psychiatry, 32*(4), 328–335. https://doi.org/10.1097/YCO.0000000000000514

Mela, M., Flannigan, K., Anderson, T., Nelson, M., Krishnan, S., Chizea, C., … Sanjanwala, R. (2020). Neurocognitive function and fetal alcohol spectrum disorder in offenders with mental disorders. *Journal of the American Academy of Psychiatry and the Law, 48*(2), 195–208. https://europepmc.org/article/med/32051201

Mela, M., Hanlon-Dearman, A., Ahmed, A. G., Rich, S. D., Densmore, R., Reid, D., … Loock, C. (2020). Treatment algorithm for the use of psychopharmacological agents in individuals prenatally exposed to alcohol and/or with diagnosis of fetal alcohol spectrum disorder (FASD). *Journal of Population Therapeutics and Clinical Pharmacology, 27*(3), e1–e13. https://doi.org/10.15586/jptcp.v27i3.681

Mela, M., Okpalauwaekwe, U., Anderson, T., Eng, J., Nomani, S., Ahmed, A., & Barr, A. M. (2018). The utility of psychotropic drugs on patients with fetal alcohol spectrum disorder (FASD): A systematic review. *Psychiatry and Clinical Psychopharmacology, 28*(4), 436–445. https://doi.org/10.1080/24750573.2018.1458429

Melton, G. B., Petrila, J., Poythress, N. G., Slobogin, C., Otto, R. K., Mossman, D., & Condie, L. O. (2018). *Psychological evaluations for the courts: A handbook for mental health professionals and lawyers* (4th ed.). New York, NY: Guilford Press.

Miller, J. B., Axelrod, B. N., Schutte, C., & Davis, J. J. (2017). Symptom and performance validity assessment in forensic neuropsychology. In S. S. Bush, G. J. Demakis, & M. L. Rohling (Eds.), *APA handbook of forensic neuropsychology (APA handbooks in psychology)* (pp. 67–109). Washington, DC: American Psychological Association. https://doi.org/10.1037/0000032-005

Miller, R. D., & Germain, E. J. (1987). Evaluation of competency to stand trial in defendants who do not want to be defended against the crimes charged. *The Bulletin of the American Academy of Psychiatry and the Law, 15*(4), 371–379.

Mullally, K., McLachlan, K., Mac Killop, E., & Pei, J. (2020). Performance validity Testing in justice-involved adults with fetal alcohol spectrum disorder. *Journal of the International Neuropsychological Society, 26*(7), 701–713. https://doi.org/10.1017/S1355617720000132

Norton, K. A., & Ryba, N. L. (2010). An investigation of the ECST-R as a measure of competence and feigning. *Journal of Forensic Psychology Practice, 10*(2), 91–106. https://doi.org/10.1080/15228930903446625

Novick Brown, N., Gudjonsson, G., & Connor, P. (2011). Suggestibility and fetal alcohol spectrum disorders: I'll tell you anything you want to hear. *Journal of Psychiatry and Law, 39*(1), 39–71. https://doi.org/10.1177/009318531103900103

Novick Brown, N., Wartnik, A. P., Connor, P. D., & Adler, R. S. (2010). A proposed model standard for forensic assessment of fetal alcohol spectrum disorders. *Journal of Psychiatry and Law, 38*(4), 383–418. https://doi.org/10.1177/009318531003800403

O'Connell, M. J., Garmoe, W., & Goldstein, N. E. (2005). Miranda comprehension in adults with mental retardation and the effects of feedback style on suggestibility. *Law and Human Behavior, 29*(3), 359–369. https://doi.org/10.1007/s10979-005-2965-y

Payne, J., Elliott, E., D'Antoine, H., O'Leary, C., Mahony, A., Haan, E., & Bower, C. (2005). Health professionals' knowledge, practice and opinions about fetal alcohol syndrome and alcohol consumption in pregnancy. *Australian and New Zealand Journal of Public Health, 29*(6), 558–564. https://pubmed.ncbi.nlm.nih.gov/16366068/

Pei, J., Denys, K., Hughes, J., & Rasmussen, C. (2011). Mental health issues in fetal alcohol spectrum disorder. *Journal of Mental Health, 20*(5), 473–483. https://doi.org/10.3109/09638237.2011.577113

Pirelli, G., Gottdiener, W. H., & Zapf, P. A. (2011). A meta-analytic review of competency to stand trial research. *Psychology, Public Policy, and Law, 17*(1), 1–53. https://doi.org/10.1037/a0021713

Pirelli, G., & Zapf, P. A. (2020). An attempted meta-analysis of the competency restoration research: Important findings for future directions. *Journal of Forensic Psychology Research and Practice, 20*(2), 134–162. https://doi.org/10.1080/24732850.2020.1714398

Popova, S., Lange, S., Bekmuradov, D., & Mihic, A. (2011). Fetal alcohol spectrum disorder prevalence estimates in correctional systems: A systemic literature review. *Canadian Journal of Public Health, 102*(5), 336–340. https://doi.org/10.1007/BF03404172

Popova, S., Lange, S., Burd, L., Chudley, A. E., Clarren, S. K., & Rehm, J. (2013). Cost of fetal alcohol spectrum disorder diagnosis in Canada. *PLoS One, 8*(4), e60434. https://doi.org/10.1371/journal.pone.0060434

Popova, S., Lange, S., Burd, L., & Rehm, J. (2015). Cost attributable to fetal alcohol spectrum disorder in the Canadian correctional system. *International Journal of Law and Psychiatry, 41*, 76–81. https://doi.org/10.1016/j.ijlp.2015.03.010

Popova, S., Lange, S., Poznyak, V., Chudley, A. E., Shield, K. D., Reynolds, J. N., … Rehm, J. (2019). Population-based prevalence of fetal alcohol spectrum disorder in Canada. *BMC Public Health, 19*(1), 845. https://doi.org/10.1186/s12889-019-7213-3

Popova, S., Lange, S., Shield, K., Burd, L., & Rehm, J. (2019). Prevalence of fetal alcohol spectrum disorder among special subpopulations: A systematic review and meta-analysis. *Addiction, 114*(7), 14598. https://doi.org/10.1111/add.14598

Popova, S., Lange, S., Shield, K., Mihic, A., Chudley, A. E., Mukherjee, R. A. S., … Rehm, J. (2016). Comorbidity of fetal alcohol spectrum disorder: A systematic review and meta-analysis. *Lancet, 387*(10022), P978–P987. https://doi.org/10.1016/S0140-6736(15)01345-8

Poythress, N., Nicholson, R., Otto, R. K., Edens, J. F., Bonnie, R. J., Monahan, J., & Hoge, S. K. (1999). The MacArthur Competence Assessment Tool—Criminal Adjudication: Professional Manual. Psychological Assessment Resources.

R. v. Taylor, 77 C.C.C. (3d) 551 (Ont.C.A.) (1992).

Reed, A. L., & Zapf, A. (2018). Criminal forensic assessment. In R. Roesch & A. Cook (Eds.), *Handbook of forensic mental health services* (pp. 79–103). New York, NY: Routledge. https://doi.org/10.4324/9781315627823-3

Reid, N., Kippin, N., Passmore, H., & Finlay-Jones, A. (2020). Fetal alcohol spectrum disorder: The importance of assessment, diagnosis and support in the Australian justice context. *Psychiatry, Psychology and Law, 27*(2), 265–274. https://doi.org/10.1080/13218719.2020.1719375

Riggs Romaine, C. L., & Kavanaugh, A. (2019). Risks, benefits, and complexities: Reporting race and ethnicity in forensic mental health reports. *International Journal of Forensic Mental Health, 18*(2), 138–152. https://doi.org/10.1080/14999013.2018.1531094

Roach, K., & Bailey, A. (2009). Relevance of Fetal Alcohol Spectrum Disorder in Canadian criminal law from investigation to sentencing. *University of British Columbia Law Review, 42*(1), 1–68.

Roesch, R., Zapf, P. A., & Eaves, D. (2006). *FIT-R: Fitness Interview Test-Revised: A structured interview for assessing competency to stand trial*. Sarasota, FL: Professional Resource Press/Professional Resource Exchange.

Rogers, R. (2011). Getting it wrong about Miranda rights: False beliefs, impaired reasoning, and professional neglect. *American Psychologist, 66*(8), 728–736. https://doi.org/10.1037/a0024988

Rogers, R., & Drogin, E. Y. (2014). *Mirandized statements: Successfully navigating the legal and psychological issues*. Chicago, IL: ABA Book.

Rogers, R., Hazelwood, L. L., Sewell, K. W., Harrison, K. S., & Shuman, D. W. (2008). The language of Miranda warnings in American jurisdictions: A replication and vocabulary analysis. *Law and Human Behavior, 32*(2), 124–136. https://doi.org/10.1007/s10979-007-9091-y

Rogers, R., Hazelwood, L. L., Sewell, K. W., Shuman, D. W., & Blackwood, H. L. (2008). The comprehensibility and content of juvenile Miranda warnings. *Psychology, Public Policy, and Law, 14*(1), 63–87. https://doi.org/10.1037/a0013102

Rogers, R., Henry, S. A., Sharf, A. J., Robinson, E. V., & Williams, M. M. (2017). Dodging self-incriminations: An examination of feigned Miranda abilities on the SAMA. *Assessment, 24*(8), 975–986. https://doi.org/10.1177/1073191116634206

Rogers, R., Jackson, R. L., Sewell, K. W., & Harrison, K. S. (2004). An examination of the ECST-R as a screen for feigned incompetency to stand trial. *Psychological Assessment, 16*(2), 139–145. https://doi.org/10.1037/1040-3590.16.2.139

Rogers, R., Sewell, K. W., Drogin, E. Y., & Fiduccia, C. E. (2013). *Standardized assessment of Miranda abilities*. Lutz, FL: Psychological Assessment Resources.

Rost, G. C., & McGregor, K. K. (2012). Miranda rights comprehension in young adults with specific language impairment. *American Journal of Speech-Language Pathology, 21*(2), 101–108. https://doi.org/10.1044/1058-0360(2011/10-0094)

Ryba, N. L., & Zapf, P. A. (2011). The influence of psychiatric symptoms and cognitive abilities on competence-related abilities. *International Journal of Forensic Mental Health, 10*(1), 29–40. https://doi.org/10.1080/14999013.2010.550982

Ryba Panza, N., & Fraser, T. (2015). Effects of age, adaptive behavior, and cognitive abilities on competence-related abilities in children and adolescents. *Journal of Forensic Psychology Practice, 15*(2), 138–159. https://doi.org/10.1080/15228932.2015.1009803

Shepherd, S. M., & Lewis-Fernandez, R. (2016). Forensic risk assessment and cultural diversity: Contemporary challenges and future directions. *Psychology, Public Policy, and Law, 22*(4), 427–438. https://doi.org/10.1037/law0000102

Steering Committee on FASD and Access to Justice. (2016). *Final report to Federal/Provincial/Territorial Ministers responsible for justice and public safety*. Retrieved from https://scics.ca/en/product-produit/final-report-to-federalprovincialterritorial-ministers-responsible-for-justice-and-public-safety/

Streissguth, A., Bookstein, F., Barr, H., Sampson, P., O'Malley, K., & Young, J. (2004). Risk factors for adverse life outcomes in fetal alcohol syndrome and fetal alcohol effects. *Journal of Developmental and Behavioral Pediatrics, 25*(4), 228–238. https://doi.org/10.1097/00004703-200408000-00002

Streissguth, A., & Kanter, J. (Eds.). (1997). *The challenge of fetal alcohol syndrome: Overcoming secondary disabilities*. Seattle: University of Washington Press.

Thanh, N. X., & Jonsson, E. (2015). Costs of Fetal Alcohol Spectrum Disorder in the Canadian criminal justice system. *Journal of Population Therapeutics and Clinical Pharmacology, 22*(1), e125–e131.

Viljoen, J. L., & Roesch, R. (2005). Competence to waive interrogation rights and adjudicative competence in adolescent defendants: Cognitive development, attorney contact, and psychological symptoms. *Law and Human Behavior, 29*(6), 723–742. https://doi.org/10.1007/s10979-005-7978-y

Viljoen, J. L., & Zapf, P. A. (2002). Fitness to stand trial evaluations: A comparison of referred and non-referred defendants. *International Journal of Forensic Mental Health, 1*(2), 127–138. https://doi.org/10.1080/14999013.2002.10471168

Wall, B. W., Krupp, B. H., & Guilmette, T. (2003). Restoration of competency to stand trial: A training program for persons with mental retardation. *Journal of the American Academy of Psychiatry and the Law, 31*(2), 189–201. http://jaapl.org/content/31/2/189

Wall, B. W., & Christopher, P. P. (2012). A training program for defendants with intellectual disabilities who are found incompetent to stand trial. *Journal of the American Academy of Psychiatry and the Law, 40*(3), 366–373. http://jaapl.org/content/40/3/366

Wartnik, A. P., & Carlson, S. S. (2011). A judicial perspective on issues impacting the trial courts related to fetal alcohol spectrum disorders. *Journal of Psychiatry and Law, 39*(1), 73–119. https://doi.org/10.1177/009318531103900104

Wedding, D., Kohout, J., Mengel, M. B., Ohlemiller, M., Ulione, M., Cook, K., … Braddock, S. (2007). Psychologists' knowledge and attitudes about fetal alcohol syndrome, fetal alcohol spectrum disorders, and alcohol use during pregnancy. *Professional Psychology: Research and Practice, 38*(2), 208–213. https://doi.org/10.1037/0735-7028.38.2.208

Weiss, R. A., & Rosenfeld, B. (2012). Navigating cross-cultural issues in forensic assessment: Recommendations for practice. *Professional Psychology: Research and Practice, 43*(3), 234–240. https://doi.org/10.1037/a0025850

Winick, B. J. (1983). Incompetency to stand trial: Developments in the law. In J. Monahan & H. J. Steadman (Eds.), *Mentally disordered offenders: Perspectives from law and social science* (Vol. 6, pp. 3–38). Springer Science & Business Media: New York, NY.

Wolfson, L., Poole, N., Ninomiya, M. M., Rutman, D., Letendre, S., Winterhoff, T., … Rowan, T. (2019). Collaborative action on fetal alcohol spectrum disorder prevention: Principles for enacting the truth and reconciliation commission call to action #33. *International Journal of Environmental Research and Public Health, 16*(9), 1589. https://doi.org/10.3390/ijerph16091589

Wozniak, J. R., Riley, E. P., & Charness, M. E. (2019). Clinical presentation, diagnosis, and management of fetal alcohol spectrum disorder. Lancet Neurology, 18(8), P760-P770. doi:https://doi.org/10.1016/S1474-4422(19)30150-4

Wyper, K. R., & Rasmussen, C. R. (2011). Language impairments in children with fetal alcohol spectrum disorders. *Journal of Population Therapeutics and Clinical Pharmacology, 18*(2), e364–e376.

Youth Criminal Justice Act (S.C. 2002, c. 1) (2002). Retrieved from https://www.laws-lois.justice.gc.ca/eng/acts/y-1.5/index.html

Zapf, P. A., & Roesch, R. (2009). *Best practices in forensic mental health assessment. Evaluation of competence to stand trial*. Oxford: Oxford University Press.

Zapf, P. A., Hubbard, K. L., Cooper, V. G., Wheeles, M. C., & Ronan, K. A. (2004). Have the courts abdicated their responsibility for determination of competency to stand trial to clinicians? *Journal of Forensic Psychology Practice, 4*(1), 27–44. https://doi.org/10.1300/J158v04n01_02

Chapter 16
Pharmacotherapy of Fetal Alcohol Spectrum Disorder in the Forensic Context

Mansfield Mela and Richard S. Adler

Abstract Comprehensive assessment and resulting treatment recommendations involving individuals diagnosed with fetal alcohol spectrum disorders (FASD) often include the use of psychotropic medications. Such medications, some with known approved indications, target mental disorders while others, with no approved indications, treat symptoms. Psychostimulants, antidepressants (e.g., selective serotonin reuptake inhibitors—SSRIs), antipsychotics, alpha-adrenergic agonists, and mood stabilizers are reported to have efficacious benefit in FASD. A psychotropic medication algorithm was developed and proposed for use in treating the complex presentation common in those with FASD. The algorithm aligns specific medications to different clusters representing abnormalities in hyperactivity, affect regulation, hyperarousal, and cognitive flexibility. Through a three-step decision tree, choice of medications is simplified, and incidence of polypharmacy is reduced. Another innovation in prescribing psychotropic medications relevant to the forensic setting is the use of dextroamphetamine in treating significant impulsivity in offenders. Potentially relevant to both guilt and sentencing phases, offenders with FASD may benefit from stimulants that mitigate poor impulse control. Consent, compulsory treatment, and formulary coverage are important themes also addressed in this chapter. Medications in the forensic setting raise issues of voluntariness, compulsion, and appropriate use. Therefore, the chapter includes guidance on effectively anticipating medication misuse and diversion. Such efforts should include the role of ancillary professionals, especially pharmacists. Poignant case examples are included. The content in this chapter is applicable to professionals with clinical as well as forensic roles.

Keywords Pharmacotherapy · Stimulants · Algorithm · Consent · Medication · Forensic setting

M. Mela (✉)
Center for Forensic Behavior Science and Justice Studies, Department of Psychiatry, College of Medicine, University of Saskatchewan, Saskatoon, Canada

R. S. Adler
University of Washington School of Medicine, Seattle, WA, USA
e-mail: richadler@fcpsych.com

N. Novick Brown (ed.), *Evaluating Fetal Alcohol Spectrum Disorders in the Forensic Context*, https://doi.org/10.1007/978-3-030-73628-6_16

16.1 Introduction

People with fetal alcohol spectrum disorder (FASD) are overrepresented in the criminal justice system (Flannigan, Pei, Stewart, & Johnson, 2018). Prevalence data from various settings, including correctional facilities (McLachlan et al., 2019), forensic outpatient clinics (Mela et al., 2020), and a youths offender psychiatric inpatient unit (Fast, Conry, & Loock, 1999), reflect rates that are three to nine times those seen in the general population. Clinicians need to be aware of the behavioral indicators of justice-involved persons with FASD. Such knowledge should lead to comprehensive assessment and treatment recommendations, preferably based upon input from a multidisciplinary group of professionals trained in the diagnosis of FASD (Novick Brown, Wartnik, Connor, & Adler, 2010). Ultimately, some treatment recommendations will include the use of psychotropic medications to address various clinical issues.

Clinical features of FASD such as emotional outbursts, agitation, aggression, impaired memory, lack of consequential thinking, and high rates of childhood instability and psychosocial trauma are relevant criminogenic factors. Youths with FASD have significantly higher rates of impairment with regard to competency to stand trial (McLachlan, Roesch, Viljoen, & Douglas, 2014). Due to the *invisibility* of FASD—that is, with only a tenth of those in this population showing any notable physical abnormality and reduced knowledge of the disorder among criminal justice system professionals—many individuals with FASD are not identified. In recent studies, most offenders with FASD entered the criminal justice system without having been diagnosed as children (Flannigan et al., 2018; McLachlan et al., 2019).

Mental health professionals certainly encounter the disruptive behavioral manifestations of FASD in their practices. These behaviors arise from neurocognitive deficits that prenatal alcohol exposure (PAE) produces and are influenced by psychosocial circumstances associated with FASD as well as applicable comorbid medical/emotional diagnoses. In particular, there is a high rate of trauma and posttraumatic stress disorder (PTSD) in those with FASD (Price, Cook, Norgate, & Mukherjee, 2017). Lifelong physical, mental, behavioral, and/or learning disabilities in this disorder have a negative impact on both brain and body. As such, these complex disabilities require proven and effective interventions in order to turn challenges into positive outcomes.

Pharmacotherapy is one of the available interventions in FASD. The rationale for using medications to treat individuals with FASD is informed by target behavioral disturbance(s), stage of legal adjudication, location of the offender (institutional or community), and practitioners' level of expertise with the pharmacotherapy of FASD. With a fifth of persons in the correctional system estimated to experience the consequences of prenatal alcohol exposure (PAE; Flannigan et al., 2018), it is crucial for clinicians to have up-to-date knowledge for optimal management of this population. That said, it is inappropriate to recommend medication for every deficit associated with FASD. Prudent weighing of intervention risks and benefits dictates behavioral and environmental efforts be adequately entertained. However, there are times when judicious use of medications can be pivotally important in reducing aggression, stabilizing and improving mood, correcting tendencies for misperception and distortion, and controlling impulsivity (Mela et al., 2020).

At the current time, there is no regulatory approval for any specific medication in people with FASD. This means prescribers have no option but to consider "off-label" prescription. In the forensic context, given the high level of potential scrutiny from opposing counsel and their retained experts, scientific bases for recommendations and open acknowledgment of limitations need to be stated clearly and explicitly. This chapter aims to assist practitioners in such efforts by presenting current evidence for using psychotropic medications in persons with FASD who are involved in the legal context. The chapter identifies target symptoms for treatment, including symptoms relevant to patient safety as well as safety of the forensic treatment staff and public at large. Although the guidance offered here is informed by findings from non-forensic settings, like most psychotropic medication use, treatments based upon current evidence are reasonably expected to be effective in the forensic context as well.

16.2 Current Evidence for Psychotropic Medications

Over the last two decades, researchers have explored the relationship between utility of psychotropic medications and potential benefits in FASD. Two systematic reviews (Mela et al., 2018; Peadon, Rhys-Jones, Bower, & Elliott, 2009) and other reviews of the literature, especially in forensically involved youths with FASD (Novick Brown, Connor, & Adler, 2012), identified then-current, relative limitations in knowledge about using psychotropic medications in FASD. Regrettably, the practice of pharmacotherapy as it relates to the matter under consideration does not stem from well-designed prospective randomized control trials, which are necessary for regulatory approval. Clinical experience and decision-tree algorithmic guidance are central approaches used to guide pharmacotherapy (Mela, Hanlon-Dearman, et al., 2020; Novick Brown et al., 2012). Reports from the current literature identify several classes of psychotropic medications used frequently in individuals with FASD. In particular, stimulants, antipsychotics, antidepressants, mood stabilizers, and alpha adrenergic agonists are the most commonly prescribed psychotropic medications (Mela et al., 2018).

Rates of attention-deficit/hyperactivity disorder (ADHD) reported in those prenatally exposed to alcohol range from 40 to 75% (Mela et al., 2018) and even higher if the criterion used is "attentional problems." In animal studies, dopamine receptors and transmission are impaired by PAE-induced damage to catecholamine and other neurotransmitter systems (O'Malley, Koplin, & Dohner, 2000; Uban, Comeau, Ellis, Galea, & Weinberg, 2013). Researchers also have found PAE-induced dysfunction in dopamine receptors of the meso-cortical pathway (Cheng et al., 2018; O'Malley & Nanson, 2002). These findings formed the basis for selecting stimulant medications. A review of the literature in youths (Novick Brown et al., 2012) advised clinicians to delineate FASD's contribution to the overall clinical presentation of young offenders in light of the high rate of comorbidity. A number of case series and cross-over randomized control studies demonstrated the value of stimulants, especially amphetamine-based salts, among children and adolescents with FASD. After a trial of methylphenidate (with a response rate of 21%), O'Malley et al. (2000) found a better response rate (67%) using amphetamine in methylphenidate non-responders.

A summary of studies in youths with FASD indicated a positive benefit from stimulants (Mela et al., 2018), albeit in the non-forensic context. Although most published research supports stimulant efficacy in FASD (Mela et al., 2018; Peadon et al., 2009), one pre- and post-study only reported a significant stimulant benefit in youths aged 7–15 years with ADHD when there was no heavy PAE (Infante, Humber, Mattson, & Riley, 2011). Researchers based this finding on three core symptoms in ADHD (motion, attention, and shifts in attention state; Infante et al., 2011). Current evidence clearly recommends using stimulants in FASD in a treatment algorithm and, by extension, consideration of stimulant use in the forensic context generally (Mela, Hanlon-Dearman, et al., 2020).

Disruptive behavior, impulsivity, and disordered self-regulation are important mediators of criminal activity. Psychotropic intervention may be helpful by reducing these intermediary manifestations. In a study of children with FASD, treatment with antipsychotic medications showed a significant reduction in disruptive behavior (Ozsarfati & Koren, 2015). Specifically, when risperidone was added to the treatment regimen to control disruptive behavior, 8 of 10 youths who tried the medication responded positively. Similarly, compared to those treated with stimulants alone, adding antipsychotic medication produced positive outcomes among 77 children who underwent a friendship training program (Frankel, Paley, Marquardt, & O'Connor, 2006). Parents and teachers independently completed an outcome measure (i.e., Social Skills Rating System), which provided subscales for assertion, self-control, and problem behaviors. Although this study involved a group of young children, other studies using second-generation antipsychotics provided additional support for inclusion of such medication in the treatment algorithm (Mela, Hanlon-Dearman, et al., 2020).

16.3 Guidance on Medication Effectiveness

With no empirical studies of psychotropic medication use in the forensic context from which to draw guidance, clinicians should be cautious about interpreting and applying findings from the non-forensic context. However, based upon a literature review regarding medication use in youths with FASD and clinical experience, Novick Brown et al. (2012) summarized advice relevant for the forensic context. In particular, clinicians are advised to note overrepresentation of seizure disorders, comorbid medical conditions, and incidence of increased suicidality with certain medications. Clinicians also should avoid or closely monitor medication(s) associated with lowering seizure threshold (e.g., bupropion), those that impact cardiac conduction (e.g., lithium), and those that can precipitate suicidal ideation, such as SSRIs.

Along similar lines, forensic clinicians should exercise caution in translating findings of effective FASD treatments in non-forensic settings. Recently, a panel of experts arrived at a consensus based upon analysis of existing literature on psychotropic medication use in persons with FASD. Their rigorous 4-year process resulted in a protocol that included four clusters of symptoms (Fig. 16.1). From this, an algorithm (i.e., decision tree) for selecting first- and second-line treatments in FASD was proposed (Mela, Hanlon-Dearman, et al., 2020).

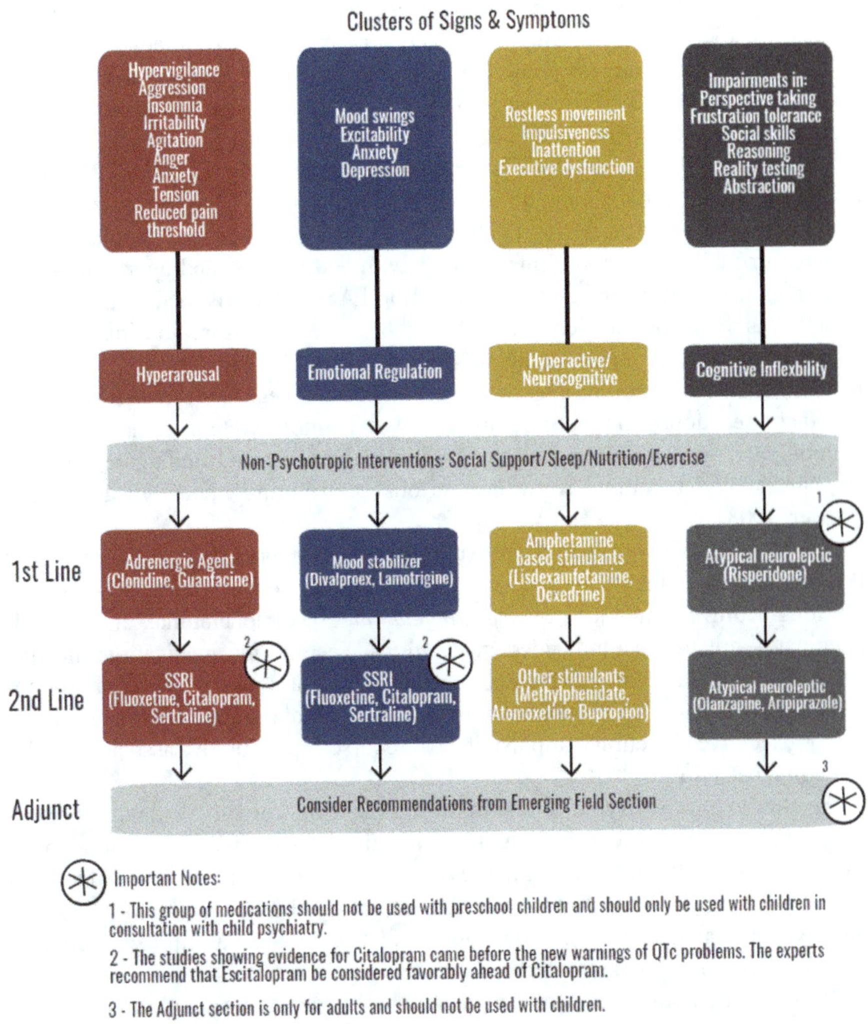

Fig. 16.1 Psychotropic medication algorithm. (Open Access https://jptcp.com/index.php/jptcp/article/view/681)

As an organizing principle (in the clinical setting), focus of treatment was identified as improvement of functioning. The experts recommended that before initiating treatment, it was important to first select the cluster of symptoms constituting the most prominent functional impairment. Naturally, before medications are prescribed, the utility of psychosocial and/or environmental interventions must be considered if at all possible. Additionally, in using the algorithm above, minimizing polypharmacy and, by extension, avoiding the adverse effects of multiple medications must be kept in mind. Of course, these are important considerations irrespective of context—clinical or forensic.

The hyperarousal cluster in the algorithm consists of symptoms that include tension, irritability, fear, hypervigilance, insomnia, and agitation. Related to abnormalities of noradrenergic overstimulation in the subcortical regions of the brain, first-line medications include alpha-adrenergic agonists (i.e., guanfacine and clonidine). If adequate symptom reduction from first-line medications is not achieved, SSRIs are second-line medications. SSRIs also are second-line medications for the second cluster, emotional dysregulation.

The emotional dysregulation cluster is conceptualized as the result of PAE damage in the hippocampus, amygdala, and prefrontal cortex. Mood stabilizers (e.g., carbamazepine, lamotrigine, and valproate) are proposed first-line medications to manage irritability, depressed mood, anxiety, mood swings, and aggression—the most common features of this cluster. In non-FASD contexts, SSRIs are recommended as first-line medications. This is because brain circuitry mapped for aggression identifies neuromodulators associated with ligand-specific receptors (Siever, 2008). Regulating aggression in the cortical regions (reduced serotonin and increased dopamine and noradrenaline) and limbic system (reduced gamma aminobutyric acid [GABA] and increased acetylcholine and glutamate) remains the current understanding regarding various contributing factors in aggression (Siever, 2008).

The hyperactive and neurocognitive cluster is conceptually based upon PAE's downregulation of the dopamine and noradrenaline systems. Stimulants—preferably long-acting formulations of *lisdexamfetamine*, dexamphetamine, and methylphenidate—are the recommended medications. Second-line medications include immediate-release methylphenidate, bupropion, and atomoxetine. Primary symptoms in this cluster include impulsivity, restlessness, and manifestations of disordered executive function. Impulsivity, of course, is strongly associated with offending behavior.

The fourth group of symptoms in the algorithm is the cognitive inflexibility cluster. Symptoms include concrete thinking, impaired abstraction, deficient adaptive function, poor reality testing, and aggression. These symptoms are believed to stem from PAE damage to the dorsolateral and orbitofrontal lobes. Different classes of antipsychotic medications (e.g., risperidone, olanzapine, and aripiprazole) are recommended as first- and second-line choices.

Persons for whom psychotropic medications are being considered should exhibit symptoms that fall into one (or more than one) of the clusters in the algorithm. Capable selection of a specific cluster (by means of consistency with the most prominent and relevant clinical symptoms) is expected to produce benefits that are reasonably similar to outcomes found by the expert panel in its group of clinical patients. Medication-induced improvements should lead to better functioning, the ultimate goal of treatment in FASD.

16.4 Forensic Context Application

Understandably, symptoms targeted for treatment will differ based upon context. For example, impulsivity during the adjudicative process may manifest differently compared to symptom manifestation in custodial settings. In particular, defendants may make statements against their own interest in interviews, impulsively plead guilty, be unable to provide suitable accounts of alleged offenses, or disrupt court proceedings. Any of these symptoms poses a real threat to legal self-interest. In custody, impulsivity may manifest in institutional rule breaking, such as being manipulated into doing the bidding of security threat groups (gangs) or being pressured into settling scores on behalf of others without considering consequences. Such symptoms require careful evaluation in order to develop interventions that effectively target and curb context-dependent behaviors. The decision tree (Fig. 16.1) can help organize treatment planning.

Aggression occurs when environmental conditions align with cognitive and/or psychosocial deficits in a "perfect storm." For example, deficient affect regulation may underlie overly aggressive behavior that is well beyond level of provocation, which has been described in the literature as *catastrophic reaction* (Katz, 2000). In other situations, aggression may stem from deficient executive functioning, hyperactivity, and/or language deficits (e.g., misperceiving or misunderstanding another's actions and jumping to conclusions). Whenever possible, it is helpful to look for patterns in episodes of aggression in order to conceptualize likely etiology. Understanding context-dependent behavior patterns not only assists in masterful pharmacotherapy but also may inform triers of fact regarding relevant factors underlying charged offense conduct. By articulating a working hypothesis that guides approach to pharmacotherapy, positive clinical response may serve as a powerful "proof of concept."

Generally, several psychotropic medications target aggression reduction. In particular, lithium, sodium valproate, and carbamazepine are empirically supported for use in aggression, especially for the impulsive, non-instrumental, reactive type of aggression. Forensically, it is important when addressing aggression to distinguish type, if possible. Other medications such as phenytoin, SSRIs, beta blocking agents like propranolol and pindolol, alpha 2 agents (clonidine and guanfacine), and antipsychotics (e.g., risperidone)—singly or in combination—have different levels of efficacy in reducing aggression. Specific to affect regulation, the negative effects of PAE extend to the hypothalamic-pituitary-adrenal (HPA) axis as well as the prefrontal cortex, causing significant impairments in regulating emotion, social behavior, and empathy that together lead to an unfettered "flight or fight response," which appears to underlie much of the aggression in persons with FASD (Novick Brown et al., 2012).

In a recent review of the literature, an expert-panel recommended mood stabilizers as first-line treatment for affect regulation deficits associated with FASD (Mela, Hanlon-Dearman, et al., 2020). Adopting a similar recommendation in the forensic context for this population has positive implications for improving affect dysregulation and, by extension, reducing aggression. However, because multiple comorbid psychiatric diagnoses are associated with aggression as well as FASD, it is important to evaluate and treat these disorders as well, if warranted. Prominent among disorders likely comorbid with FASD are substance use disorders, bipolar disorder, dementia, psychotic disorders, borderline personality disorder, generalized anxiety disorder, and altered mood and anxiety states (Famy, Streissguth, & Unis, 1998; Weyrauch, Schwartz, Hart, Klug, & Burd, 2017).

Impulsive aggression often is a prominent factor in the offense conduct of persons with FASD. When impulsive aggression is compared to premeditated aggression, fear and anger are two emotions commonly associated with provocation and high levels of autonomic arousal (Scarpa, Haden, & Tanaka, 2010). In addition to fear and anger, persons with FASD may become cognitively "overloaded" by situational complexity, including ambiguity regarding the unpredictability of others' possible actions. While both impulsive and premeditated forms of aggression are observed in the forensic context, the former is associated with common neurobiological deficits in FASD. Given the overrepresentation of trauma in those with FASD, impulsive aggression may occur when environmental cues trigger original trauma.

Should aggression be considered a treatment target for persons with FASD, comorbid conditions should be carefully explored. Such exploration may require referrals to neurologists or psychologists to adequately assess and potentially rule out other conditions associated with aggression apart from FASD. For example, intoxication from various substances and medications, personality disorder (e.g., antisocial or borderline), disruptive disorders (conduct and oppositional defiant disorders), cognitive disorders (dementia with behavioral disturbance), PTSD, intermittent explosive disorder, and personality change due to a general medical condition (Pabis & Stanislav, 1996) are conditions that may predispose one to aggression. Of note, per the fifth edition of the *Diagnostic and Statistical Manual of Mental Disorders* (*DSM-5*; American Psychiatric Association (APA), 2013) and earlier iterations as well, if clinical symptoms are better accounted for by a medical (i.e., organic) condition such as FASD, assigning a personality disorder diagnosis is *not* appropriate.

16.5 Principles for Using Psychotropic Medications in the Forensic Context

16.5.1 Informed Consent

The forensic context presents unique and special considerations with respect to obtaining informed consent. Cognitive dysfunction complicates the informed consent process in FASD. The key organizing principle in this process is obtaining *proper* informed consent, which must be kept front of mind. Evaluees with FASD are known to manifest high levels of suggestibility, poor *true* understanding, disparate comprehension compared to overt verbal fluency, and an excessive desire to please others. These features make this population susceptible to providing consent easily, without necessarily being truly "informed." While informed consent should be obtained at all contact points in the criminal justice system, it is particularly crucial when medications have possible side effects that are significant (e.g., tardive dyskinesia). Therefore, in prescribing medications, information should be presented in simple, concrete, and easy to understand language. Benefits, risks, and side effects should be described without jargon. Information sheets (with bullet points), simplified graphics, and pictorial displays should be considered as helpful visual aids. After establishing a reasonable level of rapport with some passage of time, the nature of evaluee understanding should be assessed and suitably documented. Simple "parroting" of requisite information should not suffice. Thus, it is important to ask evaluees to explain the information in their own words. Finally, if applicable, evaluees should be advised that medication is being prescribed in the form of a "trial," with targeted outcomes to be followed at a pre-determined point in the future.

Once evaluees display appropriate informed consent, that is, they understand the information and have capacity and voluntary agency, written documentation of such is preferred (Appelbaum & Grisso, 1988). Evaluees should be reminded on a regular basis of the right they have to withdraw consent, decline treatment, and review the progress of their treatment. They should be advised explicitly that care will be provided only with their ongoing consent, and their refusal will not be a reason to withdraw care or penalize them except in cases where they are court-ordered or found to lack capacity and to be at risk of harm to self or others. Although the right to refuse medication treatment is not absolutely protected in the forensic context (e.g., compelled medication in competency restoration), rights and avenues for input available to evaluees should be made clear. Careful attention to such foundational issues likely will enhance compliance with prescribed medication. Should adverse effects occur, meticulous attention and documentation of the informed consent process is in everyone's best interest.

In the case of evaluees with comorbid intellectual disability, it is prudent to plan ahead regarding how to effectively convey information and advice about psychotropic medications. Once a decision is made to recommend psychotropic medication, only one medication should be introduced at a time if at all possible. Dosage should start at a low level, and dose titration should be slow, always analyzing risk-to-benefit ratio rather than being overly focused on achieving a specific dose (Ji & Findling, 2016).

16.5.2 Additional Practical Considerations

At times, using medication in the forensic context may be influenced by extreme views in the medical field. Given efficacy in non-forensic contexts, proponents of liberal use of medication point to benefits in restoring competence or improving quality of life. On the other hand, opponents point to purported "atrocities" associated with forced medication, lifelong side effects such as tardive dyskinesia, and dulling of the mind as strong reasons to avoid psychotropic medications altogether (Campinha-Bacote, 2017). Although best interests of the patient is an important consideration, it is not the only concern. Forensic evaluators should be suitably familiar with how larger societal interests (e.g., safety and speedy resolution of criminal charges) impact such matters (Gratzer & Matas, 1994). Not surprisingly, forced medication can be a hotly contested issue. The devil is in the details. Close attention must be paid to which party has the burden of proof and what specific procedures constitute due process. Relevant standards/statutory definitions can differ meaningfully from state to state, in federal versus state venues, and for the specific issues and circumstances at hand.

In addition, practitioners should appreciate the distinction between functioning in a purely clinical role (i.e., attending or treating physician) versus a forensic role. Conventional wisdom is that attending physicians have patient–physician relationships with well-established duties and responsibilities. However, a forensic expert's responsibilities are primarily to the retaining party and to the legal process (including truth and fairness) as codified in various administrative/licensing statutes as well as the cannons/codes of ethics of relevant professional associations. Generally, there is a well-acknowledged *bright line* dictating that a practitioner may not function as both clinician and forensic expert for the same person. Accordingly, a forensic expert should avoid *even the perception of crossing that line* into the domain of providing clinical treatment. This whole arena is rather complicated by what can quickly become a slippery slope. While it seems entirely within bounds for forensic evaluators to make treatment recommendations, it is not unusual for clinical staff who lack expertise to ask for specific guidance. To ensure one is staying "within the lines," it is a good idea to involve counsel for evaluees in medication plans as much as possible. For example, recommendations should be conveyed with a cover letter from counsel, and any direct contact with treatment staff should occur with a properly executed consent for release of information form and prior approval from counsel. Interactions should be fully documented and circulated to clinicians and counsel.

In contrast to the scenario above—in which clinical staff readily adopt treatment recommendations—there also may be truculent refusal to do so. For example, one of the authors (Adler) was involved in a matter that went to the Oregon Supreme Court (Oregon State Hospital v. Butts, 2015). In that matter, Oregon State Hospital refused to comply with a trial judge's directive to prescribe medication to the defendant, who had been adjudicated incompetent to proceed (i.e., not competent to stand trial). After extended litigation and considerable time, even after the decision by the Court, the defendant finally was prescribed medication that restored adjudicative competency. In cases such as this, it can be expected that forensic experts may be called upon to author declarations in support of, testify about, review, and/or oversee use of pharmacotherapy. Of note, medication treatments proposed and possibly administered to evaluees may be excessive, inappropriate, or inadequate for persons with FASD and therefore may require close professional attention. In such cases, an expert's declaration and/or counsel's pleadings may benefit from including relevant journal articles or book chapters to document the proper standard of care.

Physicians prescribing psychotropic medication in forensic settings should appreciate how their positions of power over evaluees with FASD negatively impact the consent process. Untoward pressure may lurk in the background, such as entreaties from ward staff or supervisors. Administrative considerations and/or countertransference reactions from team members play a prominent role in getting physicians to endorse a "need" to treat with medication. Such pressures, which are neither uncommon nor necessarily unfounded, must be balanced with adequate adherence to the concerns articulated above, further ensuring evaluees are engaged as much as possible in decisions to use medication as well as specific choice of medication. Furthermore, medical practitioners need to keep squarely in mind to whom various fiduciary duties are owed.

Recommending medications and writing prescriptions are part of a larger multi-step process by which medications eventually are administered. Managed care entities may consider service utilization, including possible pharmacy carve-outs influencing availability of particular medications, even if they are formally included in formularies. For various reasons, correctional settings may exclude certain medications due to institutional experiences, such as diversion and/or staff abuse of scheduled substances. Delayed release formulations may present budgetary concerns. Some institutions have pharmacists who can be consulted regarding indications, formularies, side effects, and drug interactions.

16.5.3 Compliance

It is worthwhile to educate evaluees in advance about the consequences of noncompliance or other misbehaviors. Psychoeducation, wherein evaluees are provided relevant information of what to expect, is an effective means of managing side effects (Bäuml et al., 2016). Evaluees taking psychotropic medications are more likely to continue with the regimen if they experience side effects they were expecting (Cavezza, Aurora, & Ogloff, 2013). In FASD, all reasonable interventions aimed at medication adherence should be entertained (Marcus, Reilly, Zentgraf, Volpp, & Olfson, 2020). It is important to assess administration details. Expecting persons with neurocognitive deficits to follow a complex regimen is simply a recipe for failure. Therefore, medication regimens should be streamlined as much as possible, especially in contexts requiring reliance on self-medication such as in the community. When self-medication is necessary, available supports should be explored. For example, if evaluees reside in halfway houses or forensic hospitals, 24-h structure and oversight can be very useful. Medication may be prescribed multiple times a day in supervised living environments. However, dispositional "next steps" need to be kept in mind and incorporated into treatment plans.

Forensic and/or correctional settings present a unique set of considerations. Rather than actively seeking medications from physicians for themselves, persons with FASD may be doing the bidding of inmates who are exploiting or manipulating them. History of a substance use disorder is a red flag in anyone requesting medication. Suspicious medication-seeking behaviors include such things as pretending to not recall the names of medication(s) they are seeking or providing the first letter, syllable, or group name of a desired medication. Some individuals may insist no medication provides relief other than the specific medication they are seeking, describing the side effect profiles of approved medications as absolutely intolerable. Some may refuse to try any alternate medication, insisting they do not want to be a "guinea pig" or providing some other illogical reason.

Clinicians contemplating recommending pharmacotherapy also might give some thought in advance to safeguards directed at preventing diversion, including blood level testing or urine screens. If substance use is the main reason for diversion and misuse, persons with FASD can be counseled briefly and encouraged to participate in substance use treatment and psychoeducational groups if available or use 12-step support materials. Of course, such interventions should accommodate the significant cognitive and adaptive limitations in evaluees with FASD. Bluntly put, any attempts to divert medication should be addressed promptly with observation of medication administration and tangible consequences that make it clear diversion will not be tolerated. Selecting medications and formulations with low potential for diversion should be considered. For instance, in the event stimulants are used for hyperactivity and executive function deficiency, non-addictive options often can replace the stimulant. Bupropion, atomoxetine, clonidine, and guanfacine may be adequate replacements in this regard (Mela, Hanlon-Dearman, et al., 2020). Even in the absence of diversion, medication monitoring often is necessary for those with FASD because neurocognitive deficits cause problems with recall, planning, sequencing, and adhering to regimens. Since verbal reports are subject to poor recall and may be unreliable, clear indicia of medication compliance should be implemented.

Soldiering on with a medication that has prominent adverse side effects is rarely necessary, nor is it a successful strategy. Typically, best clinical practice is to directly replace such medication with an alternative agent. Weaning a person off medication should be done with forethought to avoid complications. In fact, clinical experience suggests people with FASD are more apt to experience side effects. Blister packaging or similar pill-packs can support medication crossover (aka cross tapering). The benefits of coordinating with facility staff cannot be overemphasized. For instance, lamotrigine is a medication that requires close monitoring to prevent a fatal dermatological complication. Offenders with FASD in the community could be directed to visit pharmacies in order to receive weekly refills of lamotrigine. Such weekly visits afford opportunities for pharmacists, de facto treatment team members, to check for emerging side effects and support compliance.

16.6 Unique Evaluative Protocol: Impact of Medication on Impulsivity

Impulsivity, a prominent feature in FASD, may be remediated effectively with medication. In a study differentiating impulsive from non-impulsive aggression (Barratt, Stanford, Kent, & Felthous, 1997), event-related potential (ERP) waveform analysis was used to categorize psychophysiological and cognitive variables associated with aggression. Results indicated impulsivity was inversely correlated with P300 ERP amplitudes. In particular, reduced P300 amplitude was found to predict violent versus nonviolent offending patterns in a general population of offenders.

Based upon the study summarized above, one of the authors (Adler) developed an evaluative protocol to address impulsivity in evaluees with FASD. Evaluees who had exhibited impulsivity during previous neuropsychological testing were administered a computer-based test of attention/impulsivity (i.e., one of the commercially available continuous performance tests), along with extrinsic tests of effort/response style. Following testing, 20 mg of dextroamphetamine were administered. This dosage was based upon the usual 0.5–1 mg/kg/day total daily dosing. Since an immediate-release formulation was employed, half of that dosage was administered. The attention test was repeated 90 min after the dexamphetamine was administered, which was the point of maximal effect according to research. Comparing pre- and post-medication performance provided useful individualized information about the impact of pharmacotherapy on attention and impulsivity. Results for each individual who participated in this protocol were relevant not only for planning interventions likely to improve in-custody and out-of-custody adjustment but also for understanding factors leading to subject offenses and informing mitigation regarding prior missed opportunities to ameliorate risk of criminal behavior.

It should be emphasized to legal professionals and juries that medications can be safely administered, monitored carefully, and sufficiently controlled to prevent misuse. Compared to the cost of criminal offending, treatment potentially represents a huge savings to society. One of the authors used the above procedure in what originally was a death penalty matter. Due to the defendant's demonstrated positive response to medication and other compelling neuropsychiatric data, the prosecution withdrew a death penalty charge.

It should be noted that forensic experience with evaluees who have FASD finds a preferential response to amphetamine-based medications versus methylphenidate-based agents. However, this anecdotal finding is not absolute, and there may be dextroamphetamine non-responders for whom a subsequent trial of methylphenidate may be indicated. Data from the pre- and post-medication trial described above constitutes important "baseline" information. If an offender is placed on a non-stimulant, response to the non-stimulant medication can be compared with initial response to a stimulant in order to explore whether effects are equivalent. In the case of non-equivalence, optimizing dosing, use of a stimulant, or combination therapy can be advocated for—credibly and convincingly. If there is contention about such information, this is a protocol the state's expert could be encouraged to undertake.

16.7 Case Example

A young man was facing a possible death penalty in a Western U.S. state. There was a suspicion of PAE, but this was never confirmed. He had a history of sports-related impacts to the head that began early in childhood and continued over a fairly long period of time. During pre-trial incarceration, he was markedly inappropriate with correctional staff, which was extensively documented and expected to work strongly against him at trial. Furthermore, he was noted to have strange, illogical thinking suggestive of a possible pre-psychotic (i.e., prodromal) process. Prior substance use was a complicating factor. In the course of reviewing the case record, it was learned counsel had retained a local private psychiatrist to augment an inadequate level of services available at the jail. Prior to counsel's retaining one of the authors (Adler) as a forensic expert in the case, the private psychiatrist documented her recommendation for an atypical antipsychotic. The forensic expert performed and documented a collateral interview with the private clinician, after which counsel was debriefed.

The antipsychotic medication recommended by the private physician was started after all baseline studies—including quantitative electroencephalography (qEEG)—had been completed. Medication compliance and adequacy were documented by acquiring steady-state trough serum levels. After an extended course on the medication, a follow-up qEEG was obtained. Pre- and post-qEEGs demonstrated improvement consistent with the evaluee's positive clinical (i.e., symptomatic) response. This author (Adler) then testified accordingly, using graphics from the qEEGs in the mitigation phase of trial.

16.8 Conclusion

Justice-involved persons with FASD require a valid, reliable, and readily understood process of diagnosis, assessment, and intervention. Because a significant number of individuals in the criminal, correctional, and forensic settings experience the multifaceted consequences of PAE, evidence-based interventions are much needed. Given the lamentable absence of empirical studies on use of psychotropic medications in the forensic context for those with FASD, interventions must rely upon guidance from use of medications in general practice. Although the FASD psychotropic medication decision tree described in this chapter awaits validation, it represents current available guidance for treatment of this population. Utility of psychotropic medication in forensic settings is enhanced with the approach we have described for detecting and then assessing potential impact of stimulant medication on impulsivity. This evaluative protocol has wide implications and applicability and therefore is worthy of consideration. In our forensic and clinical experience with FASD in Canada and the United States, benefits from proper use of psychotropic medications not only accrue to those with this debilitating disorder but also to their families, correctional staff, and society at large.

References

American Psychiatric Association (APA). (2013). *Diagnostic and statistical manual of mental disorders (DSM-5)* (5th ed.). Arlington, VA: American Psychiatric Association.

Appelbaum, P. S., & Grisso, T. (1988). Assessing patients' capacities to consent to treatment. *New England Journal of Medicine, 319*(25), 1635–1638. https://doi.org/10.1056/nejm198812223192504

Barratt, E. S., Stanford, M. S., Kent, T. A., & Felthous, A. (1997). Neuropsychological and cognitive psychophysiological substrates of impulsive aggression. *Biological Psychiatry, 41*(1), 1045–1061. https://doi.org/10.1016/s0006-3223(96)00175-8

Bäuml, J., Pitschel-Walz, G., Volz, A., Lüscher, S., Rentrop, M., Kissling, W., & Jahn, T. (2016). Psychoeducation improves compliance and outcome in schizophrenia without an increase of adverse side effects: A 7-year follow-up of the Munich PIP study. *Schizophrenia Bulletin, 42*(Suppl. 1), S62–S70. https://doi.org/10.1093/schbul/sbw008

Campinha-Bacote, J. (2017). Cultural considerations in forensic psychiatry: The issue of forced medication. *International Journal of Law and Psychiatry, 50*, 1–8. https://doi.org/10.1016/j.ijlp.2016.09.002

Cavezza, C., Aurora, M., & Ogloff, J. R. P. (2013). The effects of an adherence therapy approach in a secure forensic hospital: A randomised controlled trial. *Journal of Forensic Psychiatry & Psychology, 24*(4), 458–478. https://doi.org/10.1080/14789949.2013.806568

Cheng, Y., Wang, X., Wei, X., Xie, X., Melo, S., Miranda, R. C., & Wang, J. (2018). Prenatal exposure to alcohol induces functional and structural plasticity in dopamine D1 receptor-expressing neurons of the dorsomedial striatum. *Alcoholism: Clinical and Experimental Research, 42*(8), 1493–1502. https://doi.org/10.1111/acer.13806

Famy, C., Streissguth, A. P., & Unis, A. S. (1998). Mental illness in adults with fetal alcohol syndrome or fetal alcohol effects. *American Journal of Psychiatry, 155*(4), 552–554. https://doi.org/10.1176/ajp.155.4.552

Fast, D. K., Conry, J., & Loock, C. A. (1999). Identifying fetal alcohol syndrome among youth in the criminal justice system. *Journal of Developmental and Behavioral Pediatrics, 20*(5), 370–372. https://doi.org/10.1097/00004703-199910000-00012

Flannigan, K., Pei, J., Stewart, M., & Johnson, A. (2018). Fetal alcohol spectrum disorder and the criminal justice system: A systematic literature review. *International Journal of Law and Psychiatry, 57*, 42–52. https://doi.org/10.1016/j.ijlp.2017.12.008

Frankel, F., Paley, B., Marquardt, R., & O'Connor, M. (2006). Stimulants, neuroleptics, and children's friendship training for children with fetal alcohol spectrum disorders. *Journal of Child and Adolescent Psychopharmacology, 16*(6), 777–789. https://doi.org/10.1089/cap.2006.16.777

Gratzer, T. G., & Matas, M. (1994). The right to refuse treatment: Recent Canadian developments. *Journal of the American Academy of Psychiatry and Law, 22*(2), 249–256. https://pubmed.ncbi.nlm.nih.gov/7949413/

Infante, M. A., Humber, C. C., Mattson, S. N., & Riley, E. P. (2011). Effectiveness of stimulant medication in fetal alcohol spectrum disorders. *Alcohol and Alcoholism, 46*(Suppl. 1), i29–i32. https://doi.org/10.1093/alcalc/agr096

Ji, N. Y., & Findling, R. L. (2016). Pharmacotherapy for mental health problems in people with intellectual disability. *Current Opinion in Psychiatry, 29*(2), 103–125. https://doi.org/10.1097/yco.0000000000000233

Katz, I. R. (2000). Agitation, aggressive behavior, and catastrophic reactions. *International Psychogeriatrics, 12*(S1), 119–123. https://doi.org/10.1017/S1041610200006888

Marcus, S. C., Reilly, M. E., Zentgraf, K., Volpp, K. G., & Olfson, M. (2020). Effect of escalating and deescalating financial incentives vs. usual care to improve antidepressant adherence: A pilot randomized clinical trial. *JAMA: Journal of the American Medical Association Psychiatry, 78*(2), 222–224. https://doi.org/10.1001/jamapsychiatry.2020.3000

McLachlan, K., McNeil, A., Pei, J., Brain, U., Andrew, G., & Oberlander, T. F. (2019). Prevalence and characteristics of adults with fetal alcohol spectrum disorder in corrections: A Canadian case ascertainment study. *BMC Public Health, 19*, 43. https://doi.org/10.1186/s12889-018-6292-x

McLachlan, K., Roesch, R., Viljoen, J. L., & Douglas, K. S. (2014). Evaluating the psycholegal abilities of young offenders with fetal alcohol spectrum disorder. *Law and Human Behavior, 38*(1), 10–22. https://doi.org/10.1037/lhb0000037

Mela, M., Flannigan, K., Anderson, T., Nelson, M., Krishnana, S., Chizea, C., … Sanjanwala, R. (2020). Neurocognitive function and fetal alcohol spectrum disorder in offenders with mental disorders. *Journal of the American Academy of Psychiatry and Law, 48*(2), 195–208. http://jaapl.org/content/early/2020/02/12/JAAPL.003886-20

Mela, M., Hanlon-Dearman, A., Ahmed, A. G., Rich, S. D., Densmore, R., Reid, D., … Loock, C. (2020). Treatment algorithm for the use of psychopharmacological agents in individuals prenatally exposed to alcohol and/or with diagnosis of fetal alcohol spectrum disorder (FASD). *Journal of Population Therapeutics and Clinical Pharmacology, 27*(3), e1–e14. https://doi.org/10.3945/ajcn.116.142075

Mela, M., Okpalauwaekwe, U., Anderson, T., Eng, J., Nomani, S., Ahmed, A., & Barr, A. M. (2018). The utility of psychotropic drugs on patients with fetal alcohol spectrum disorder (FASD): A systematic review. *Psychiatry and Clinical Psychopharmacology, 28*(4), 436–445. https://doi.org/10.1080/24750573.2018.1458429

Novick Brown, N., Connor, P. D., & Adler, R. S. (2012). Conduct-disordered adolescents with fetal alcohol spectrum disorder: Intervention in secure treatment settings. *Criminal Justice and Behavior, 39*(6), 770–793. https://doi.org/10.1177/0093854812437919

Novick Brown, N., Wartnik, A. P., Connor, P. D., & Adler, R. S. (2010). A proposed model standard for forensic assessment of fetal alcohol spectrum disorders. *Journal of Psychiatry and Law, 38*(4), 383–418. https://doi.org/10.1177/009318531003800403

O'Malley, K. D., Koplin, B., & Dohner, V. A. (2000). Psychostimulant clinical response in fetal alcohol syndrome. *Canadian Journal of Psychiatry, 45*(1), 90–91.

O'Malley, K. D., & Nanson, J. (2002). Clinical implications of a link between fetal alcohol spectrum disorder and attention deficit hyperactivity disorder. *Canadian Journal of Psychiatry, 47*, 349–354.

Oregon State Hospital v. Butts, 359 P.3d 1187 (Or. 2015).

Ozsarfati, J., & Koren, G. (2015). Medications used in the treatment of disruptive behavior in children with FASD: A guide. *Journal of Population Therapeutics and Clinical Pharmacology, 22*(1), 59–67. https://jptcp.com/index.php/jptcp/article/view/277

Pabis, D. J., & Stanislav, S. W. (1996). Pharmacotherapy of aggressive behavior. *Annals of Pharmacotherapy, 30*(3), 279–287. https://doi.org/10.1177/106002809603000312

Peadon, E., Rhys-Jones, B., Bower, C., & Elliott, E. J. (2009). Systematic review of interventions for children with fetal alcohol spectrum disorders. *BMC Pediatrics, 9*, 35. https://doi.org/10.1186/1471-2431-9-35

Price, A., Cook, P. A., Norgate, S., & Mukherjee, R. (2017). Prenatal alcohol exposure and traumatic childhood experiences: A systematic review. *Neuroscience & Biobehavioral Reviews, 80*, 89–98. https://doi.org/10.1016/j.neubiorev.2017.05.018

Scarpa, A., Haden, S. C., & Tanaka, A. (2010). Being hot-tempered: Autonomic, emotional, and behavioral distinctions between childhood reactive and proactive aggression. *Biological Psychology, 84*(3), 488–496. https://doi.org/10.1016/j.biopsycho.2009.11.006

Siever, L. J. (2008). Neurobiology of aggression and violence. *American Journal of Psychiatry, 165*(4), 429–442. https://doi.org/10.1176/appi.ajp.2008.07111774

Uban, K. A., Comeau, W. L., Ellis, L. A., Galea, L. A., & Weinberg, J. (2013). Basal regulation of HPA and dopamine systems is altered differentially in males and females by prenatal alcohol exposure and chronic variable stress. *Psychoneuroendocrinology, 38*(10), 1953–1966. https://doi.org/10.1016/j.psyneuen.2013.02.017

Weyrauch, D., Schwartz, M., Hart, B., Klug, M. G., & Burd, L. (2017). Comorbid mental disorders in fetal alcohol spectrum disorders: A systematic review. *Journal of Developmental and Behavioral Pediatrics, 38*(4), 283–291. https://doi.org/10.1097/dbp.0000000000000440

Chapter 17
Prosecutorial Decision-Making and Practice: Victims and Witnesses with Fetal Alcohol Spectrum Disorders

Frances Gordon and Erica Madore

Abstract Mental health professionals play an important role in ensuring that victims of crime with fetal alcohol spectrum disorders (FASD) are able to fully participate in the criminal justice system. Because the level of FASD awareness is relatively low among justice professionals, mental health professionals are in a position to educate lawyers, judges, and juries about deficits in FASD that affect a witness' response to crime and their ability to testify at trial. Prosecutors only can effectively guide witnesses and victims through their evidence if they are aware of strategies in use by mental health professionals to overcome communication disabilities associated with FASD. Mental health professionals who are informed about the criminal justice process and role of the prosecutor are better placed to effectively offer their expertise.

Keywords FASD · Fetal alcohol · Witnesses · Victims · Prosecutor · Prosecution · Victimization

17.1 Introduction

This chapter is written for mental health professionals whose expertise in fetal alcohol spectrum disorders (FASD) is sought by criminal justice professionals, specifically prosecutors, in relation to crime victims with FASD.[1] An expert can play a key

[1] The authors, Frances Gordon and Erica Madore, of this chapter wish to acknowledge Doreen Reid, Kathryn Kelly, Eric Schnapper, Diana Goldie, Alicia Wendel, Nancy Fazenda, Kenna Dalrymple, Paul Battin, Emily Yao, Dasein Nearing, Dr. Christine Loock, Ron Friesen, Magistrate Catherine Crawford, and Joanne Boots.

F. Gordon
British Columbia Prosecution Service, Vancouver, Canada

E. Madore (✉)
Mille Lacs County Attorney's Office, Milaca, MN, USA

N. Novick Brown (ed.), *Evaluating Fetal Alcohol Spectrum Disorders in the Forensic Context*, https://doi.org/10.1007/978-3-030-73628-6_17

role in educating criminal justice professionals who are experts at the law but generally have little or no knowledge about FASD. Conversely, many FASD experts have limited understanding of the criminal justice system, particularly the role prosecutors play in the criminal justice system and how to professionally fulfill the role of an expert witness when retained by prosecution. Interactions between mental health and justice professionals can founder if they do not understand each other's roles and knowledge limitations.

Although primarily intended for mental health professionals and prosecutors, the ultimate goal of this chapter's analysis and recommendations is to achieve justice for victims and witnesses with FASD-related disabilities. Both the visible and invisible disabilities associated with FASD create significant challenges for crime victims trying to navigate the criminal justice system. Those best placed to remove these barriers are mental health professionals and prosecutors. Prosecutors are responsible for obtaining justice for all victims of crime by preparing victims for their roles as witnesses in criminal trials and helping witnesses give coherent testimony at trial. Prosecution also means arguing for just sentences by providing judges with comprehensive information about a victim's disabilities and vulnerabilities. At each stage of the criminal justice process, effective intervention with mental health expertise is required to inform prosecutorial practice and judicial decision-making.

The first goal of this chapter is to educate mental health professionals about the prosecutor's role in the criminal justice process as well as the role of the expert witness and unique issues that may affect a victim's capacity to communicate. Such information will help mental health professionals identify strategic intervention points where their expertise can inform decision-making. The second goal is to provide a basic framework for discussion among mental health and justice practitioners. Mental health professionals and prosecutors are invited to collaborate in educating each other about these issues and expanding approaches outlined here in order to enhance access to justice for those with FASD. These are not merely matters of continuing education but of fulfilling legal obligations, both domestic and international.

The scope of this chapter does not permit a comprehensive discussion of all aspects of the criminal justice trial process, which starts with police investigation and ends with sentencing. Rather, it focuses on practical ways in which mental health professionals and prosecutors can effectively work together. Similarly, the chapter describes practical considerations for mental health professionals on how to help courts understand the deficits of victims and witnesses with FASD, especially the effect of impairments on the evidence they provide. We acknowledge that the analysis and recommendations in this chapter are set against the realities of current

---

The term "victim" is used in the literature and in practice in many different contexts. However, in criminal proceedings, until an accused person has been found guilty of an offence by a judge or jury, the person who is alleged to have suffered the wrong is identified as the "complainant." Once the accused's guilt has been proven beyond a reasonable doubt, the term "victim" is used. For the purposes of this chapter, the term "victim" refers to both the complainant and the victim (UK Ministry of Justice. 2011, March).

criminal justice practice in most jurisdictions, such as high case volumes, limited prosecutorial and court resources, and limited knowledge about FASD among justice professionals.

17.2 Need for Greater Fetal Alcohol Spectrum Disorder Awareness Among Mental Health and Justice Professionals

The primary focus in academic and legal research regarding FASD and criminal justice is on offenders, not victims. The same holds true in both American and Canadian caselaw. Thus, in addition to being an invisible disability, FASD largely is invisible in the professional literature as it relates to the law (Cane & Kritzer, 2012). This likely is due to the fact that so few victims of crime with FASD have a formal diagnosis. This problem is compounded by the lack of FASD awareness on the part of justice professionals. However, the number of people in the United States and Canada living with FASD is significant.

The Public Health Agency of Canada estimates 9 of every 1000 births (approximately 350,000 Canadians) are affected by FASD (Canada. Public Health Agency of Canada, 2013, February 21). Unfortunately, it also is well established that persons with disabilities suffer disproportionately high rates of crime victimization. According to the 2014 General Social Survey on Canadians' Safety (victimization), one in 10 people with a mental disability experienced violence in the preceding 12 months, more than double the incidence among the general population (Burczycka, 2014). In the United States, persons with disabilities are three times more likely to be victims of serious violent crimes (such as sexual assault, robbery, and aggravated assault) than persons without disabilities (U.S. Department of Justice, 2017, July). Individuals with cognitive disabilities have the highest victimization rate for total violent crimes (Smith, Harrell, & Judy, 2017).

In many jurisdictions, victims possess similar rights as the accused, including the right to a fair trial. Where mandated by law, prosecutors are required to make best efforts in ensuring these rights are recognized and addressed. For example, in some jurisdictions, legislation codifies a disabled victim's right to use courtroom testimonial aides. In the United States, federal legislation requires equal treatment of disabled persons in the criminal justice system. The Supreme Court of Canada has stated that victims have a constitutional right to a "fair trial."

A review of Canadian and Australian studies on justice professionals' knowledge and awareness of FASD (Flannigan, Pei, Stewart, & Johnson, 2018) concluded that justice professionals generally lacked adequate training about FASD and relevant practice guidelines. In the first Canadian survey of judges and Crown prosecutors in relation to FASD (Cox, Clairmont, & Cox, 2008), 68% of prosecutors reported their main source of information on FASD was mass media. Only 17% of judges and 0% of prosecutors cited any awareness of the 2005 *Canadian Guidelines for FASD*

Diagnosis. The survey further indicated that although the majority of prosecutors and judges believed knowledge of FASD was relevant to their work, a low percentage of judges (40%) and lower percentage of Crown prosecutors (26%) felt prepared to deal with individuals with FASD (Chudley et al., 2005; Cook et al., 2016).

In an Australian study (Mutch, Jones, Bower, & Watkins, 2016), only 8% of judges, lawyers, and law enforcement officials had received formal education on FASD. However, this study also found the judiciary's understanding of the importance of knowledge about FASD in their work was significantly higher than that of legal aid lawyers. Remarkably, 85% of judicial officers agreed that increased knowledge of FASD would assist them in their work, but only 52% of legal aid lawyers perceived that more information about FASD would assist them. Clearly, there is a great need for empirical research that focuses on the current state of the law, practice, and legal strategies related to FASD so as to improve justice outcomes for FASD-affected victims and witnesses.

Judges cannot speculate about whether victims have FASD or how such a disorder might affect them. Without such evidence from mental health experts at trial, unclear testimony or unusual behavior by a victim in court may be misinterpreted by the judge or jury as untrustworthiness. Mental health evidence allows the court to see a victim with FASD as a complete person and make allowances for the person's disabilities.

Since most lawyers and judges know relatively little about FASD, it often falls to mental health professionals to take the initiative. They can do this by identifying the presence of FASD or suspected FASD as a relevant issue for the court. Mental health professionals can educate justice professionals about the symptoms of FASD, particularly about how particular symptoms affect a victim's behavior and ability to communicate effectively. Prosecutors may seek advice from mental health professionals regarding strategies for communicating with affected victims during trial preparation.

In effectively contributing their expertise, the challenge for mental health professionals is to identify mental health information that is relevant to the victim's functioning and also relevant to the trial process. In an ideal world, FASD-informed prosecutors would be able to guide mental health professionals in this regard. However, the reality in high-volume prosecutorial offices is that such guidance rarely will be possible. Accordingly, it is incumbent upon both mental health professionals and lawyers to educate each other about FASD and its relevance to the trial process.

17.3 Prosecutorial Decision-Making: A Summary of Law and Policy

Knowing more about the role of prosecutors in the criminal justice system may assist mental health professionals better understand prosecutorial decision-making. Prosecutors, like all other lawyers, are bound to respect the rule of law and comply with strict ethical standards of conduct. However, they differ from other lawyers in that their function is a matter of public duty that must be discharged in a manner independent of partisan influence. According to the American Bar Association, prosecutors have "the responsibility of a minister of justice and not simply that of an advocate" (American Bar Association (ABA), 2020). Because prosecutors represent the general public rather than individual victims or law enforcement agencies, they assume a quasi-judicial role in not only considering whether cases are supported by the evidence, but also whether it is fair and reasonable under the circumstances in each case to require accused persons to stand trial for alleged crimes. In addition, prosecutors are responsible for ensuring "all available legal proof of the facts is presented" at trial (*R. v. Boucher*, 1954). Therefore, in the case of a victim with neurocognitive disabilities such as FASD, where relevant mental health evidence exists that can explain the disabilities and impact of those disabilities on the victim, such information ought to be presented to the court as part of the prosecution case.

In many jurisdictions, victims of crime and disabled victims are protected by laws aimed at guaranteeing their equal right to a "fair trial." Arguably, a fair trial for a disabled victim is one in which a victim's disabilities are explained and accommodated, so such evidence can be fully heard and understood by the judge or jury. In some jurisdictions, these laws echo the fundamental human rights set out in international instruments such as United Nations conventions, covenants, and declarations.[2]

In the United States, Title II of the *Americans with Disabilities Act* (ADA, 1990) protects persons with disabilities from discrimination in state and local government services, programs, and activities, including law enforcement agencies and justice systems. The ADA requires criminal justice entities, including prosecutors, public defense attorneys, courts, and police, to ensure people with disabilities are treated equally in the criminal justice system and that they have equal opportunity to benefit from safe, inclusive communities. The ADA imposes an obligation to provide reasonable modifications to relevant policies, practices, and procedures and take appropriate steps to communicate effectively with people who have disabilities in order to meet the goals of ensuring public safety and promoting public welfare.

[2] The United Nations, *Universal Declaration of Human Rights* (UDHR) (1948), recognizes the right to equal protection of the law and that "everyone has the right to an effective remedy by the competent national tribunals for acts violating the fundamental rights granted him by the constitution or by law" (article 8). The United Nations, Human Rights, *International Covenant on Civil and Political Rights* (OHCHR) (1966), codifies the right to access to justice providing that "all persons shall be equal before the courts and tribunals" (article 14[1]).

The United Nations, Department of Economics and Social Affairs, *Convention on the Rights of Persons with Disabilities* (CRPD) (2006), Article 5(1), requires recognition of the principle that persons with disabilities are equal before and under the law, and are entitled to equal protection from and equal benefit of the law. Article 13(1) of the Convention specifically directs State parties to ensure the provision of accommodation that facilitate disabled persons' effective participation as witnesses.

The Canadian constitution, the *Charter of Rights and Freedoms* (*Charter*) (Canada. Canadian Charter of Rights and Freedoms, 1982), guarantees equality before and under the law and equal protection and equal benefit of the law for individuals with a mental disability. A victim's constitutional right to "life, liberty and security of the person" in s. 7 of the *Charter* has been interpreted by the Supreme Court of Canada as a victim's right to a fair trial (*R. v. Seaboyer*, 1991). The *Criminal Code* of Canada (Canada, 1970) provides for the right of disabled persons to apply for specific testimonial aids or accommodations to assist them in giving evidence at trial. These aids include use of a previously videotaped police statement as the victim's evidence (s.715.2[1]), use of closed-circuit television (s. 486.2), and assistance from a witness support person (s. 486.1).[3] The *Canada Evidence Act* (1985) provides witnesses with a mental disability the option of providing evidence "by any means that enables the evidence to be intelligible" whenever witnesses have difficulty communicating (Chap. 5, Sect. 10).

While it may be commonplace to speak of a victim "pressing charges" or "dropping charges," it is essential to note that prosecutors do not "represent" the victim in the sense of a solicitor–client or attorney–client relationship. Although victim cooperation is certainly helpful, their consent is not required for initiating or terminating charges. In exercising their discretionary decision-making authority to initiate charges, prosecutors are bound to apply the law and are guided by prosecutorial policies. Laws and policies vary from jurisdiction to jurisdiction. In the United States, the ABA has published general ethical guidelines governing the circumstances in which criminal charges should and should not be brought (ABA, 2020). Prosecution offices at the state or county level in the United States often have internal charging guidelines that respond to local jurisdiction laws and policies. In Canada, many provincial prosecution agencies publish local policies that guide prosecutorial decision-making in a broad range of situations, including initiation and termination of charges.

In common law criminal justice systems, criminal cases begin with a report to a law enforcement agency. In some jurisdictions, the law enforcement agency makes the decision to initiate criminal charges, and in others, the prosecuting authority has this responsibility. Prosecutors do not represent the police and are not required to charge or continue charges in every file presented to them. On the contrary, prosecutors are required to use independent and impartial judgment, bearing in mind the presumption of innocence and standard for conviction in criminal courts (i.e., proof "beyond a reasonable doubt"). "Beyond a reasonable doubt" is the highest burden of proof in any legal context, and it is essential to understand that at trial, a jury does not decide whether the prosecution or the defense version of events is more believable or whether the accused is "probably" guilty. Instead, the jury is asked if they have any reasonable doubt as to the defendant's guilt based upon all of the evidence presented. This high standard requires prosecutors to exercise caution and critical judgment in the pretrial stages of a case in order to protect judicial resources and prevent unfair trials with weak evidence.

[3] Canadian federal and provincial victims' rights legislation specifically provide for the victim's right to request testimonial aides.

In many jurisdictions, prosecution policy provides that the evidence gathered by investigators be evaluated against a two-part test. First, the evidence must be sufficient for a reasonable (or in some jurisdictions, substantial) likelihood of conviction at trial, and second, it must be in the interests of justice to proceed with charges. The test requires that a prosecutor evaluate all evidence with a skeptical view of his or her own case to determine if there are evidentiary weaknesses or viable defenses that may raise reasonable doubt.

In assessing cases, prosecutors only have the information provided by investigators. This information will include written and often recorded versions of witness statements. Prosecutors generally do not engage in independent investigation prior to making decisions to charge because they cannot be direct witnesses to the cases they are charging. As a result, victim capacity to give accurate and reliable evidence is of paramount importance when assessing a case. In particular, a victim's inability to give a clear and cohesive narrative weighs against the likelihood that a judge or jury will convict. This is particularly true in cases that rely solely or heavily upon victim testimony and where physical evidence or third-party witnesses do not exist. This may include very serious offenses, such as sexual assault, domestic assault, and stalking.

In the context of a victim with FASD, the prosecutor needs to assess a number of factors, including severity of the victim's known symptoms and how these disabilities might affect the victim's credibility as a trial witness. For example, it will be of concern to the prosecutor if the victim struggled to answer key questions or provided inconsistent responses to questions in police interviews. Victim statements that demonstrate suggestibility or tendency to confabulate also will raise serious concerns, suggesting the victim's evidence will show similar problems at trial. In assessing whether a case involving a victim with FASD ought to proceed, the prosecutor also must consider the predictable defense argument that FASD-related impairments inherently create reasonable doubt as to the accuracy and reliability of the victim's memory and interpretation of events.

The presence of FASD also may affect when a police report is made. In many cases involving disabled victims, reporting is delayed. Unfortunately, delayed reporting often means that any corroborative physical evidence no longer is available, and corroborating witnesses may have disappeared or forgotten the event. In these cases, the prosecution must be able to present a victim capable of providing a clear, consistent, and comprehensive version of events because such testimony essentially is the only evidence.

When evidentiary weaknesses exist in investigation reports, prosecutors may request that law enforcement follow up on their investigations, or they may decline outright to proceed with charges. In cases involving vulnerable or disabled victims, there is significant public interest in proceeding, so prosecutors should make every effort to ensure investigators have thoroughly explored all potential sources of independent and corroborative evidence. In the case of witnesses with FASD, the presence of mental health reports in the file can help prosecutors understand neurocognitive challenges and ways of supporting victim testimony at trial.

Although victims do not need to consent to charges being brought, charges may be refused or dropped when the loss of victim cooperation results in insufficient evidence to prove the charges. As prosecutions can take months or years, and victims may be pressured by others to "drop the charges," refusal to cooperate is not an uncommon problem, even with neurotypical victims. Because of the substantial public interest in continuing prosecutions involving victims with disabilities, all options for continuing with prosecution should be considered if or when victims do not cooperate. On the other hand, proceeding with criminal charges where there is no reasonable likelihood of conviction is unethical and may taint a prosecutor's credibility with the court or community. When evidence is tenuous and a decision to not initiate charges is made, prosecutors still owe victims the duty of candor and respect, particularly where "the fair and impartial exercise of prosecutorial discretion is at odds with the victim's desires" (Canada. Ministry of the Attorney General, 2020, August, p. 5).

As the prosecutor's role is to seek justice and not merely convictions, there is an ethical obligation to ensure relevant trustworthy evidence is presented to the trier of fact, even if it is damaging to the prosecution's case (*Boucher v The Queen*, 1955; ABA, 2020, 3.8[d]). Before trial, all of the evidence in the prosecutor's possession, including mental health reports, must be disclosed to defense counsel, even if the prosecutor does not intend to present the evidence at trial (Canada, 2014, March 1; Canada, 2019, December 21). If the fact of a victim's FASD diagnosis is material to a case, including to the judge's or jury's assessment of credibility, it can constitute an ethical violation for a prosecutor to fail to disclose such evidence (ABA, 2020, 3.8[g]).

Even when mental health evidence is not favorable to the prosecution case but is potentially relevant to defense, prosecutors have an ethical obligation to disclose the existence of such evidence to defense counsel and call the mental health evidence into evidence at trial.[4] The duty to disclose is an ongoing prosecutorial obligation throughout pretrial and trial. In the course of pretrial preparation, if a mental health professional makes a relevant statement or comment to the prosecutor that is not part of his or her report, this also must be disclosed to defense. Another reason for caution in preparing reports relates to protection of victim privacy. Although the prosecutor's office will review reports and redact personal information, care should be exercised to avoid including personal information not directly related to the legal purpose of the report. This underscores the importance of having a clear understanding of the nature and purpose of an expert's evidence and report. Different rules apply in the case of medical and mental health documents that are not part of investigation files. When these documents remain in the possession of third parties such as doctors or counseling offices, additional protections and specific rules relating to patient privacy will apply to any defense applications for disclosure.

[4] In *R. v. J.A.R.*, 2012 BCPC 241, the prosecution called medical expert evidence on FASD for the purposes of establishing the admissibility of a hearsay statement of a victim. The prosecution advised the court of its ethical duty to call the evidence that would be favourable to the defence.

17.4 Mental Health Experts

Prosecutors may request mental health expertise in a variety of circumstances. For example, when a victim's disability is not severe, a prosecutor may request consultation with a professional familiar with the victim's specific disabilities to advise on strategies for understanding and accommodating the deficits. In such cases, no formal report may be required. Similarly, if a prosecutor intends to apply to the court for testimonial accommodations at trial, an affidavit or solemn declaration supporting the application may be all that is required from an expert. However, in a situation where FASD-related disability is likely to hinder a victim's ability to effectively participate in trial, the prosecutor may request a comprehensive medical-legal report and the expert's participation in trial.

Of course, the nature and purpose of expert reports and testimony will depend upon whether mental health professionals have victim-specific information. Decisions about whether to involve mental health professionals will be contingent on a number of practical constraints, including limited budgets for experts and court schedules which may not accommodate the time required for evaluations and reports. In some cases, such decisions may be contingent on whether prosecutors have sufficient knowledge about FASD to understand the use and value of mental health expertise.

Mental health and medical experts play a special role in court because their specialized technical knowledge allows them to provide opinion evidence to educate judges and juries. Based upon expert opinion, decision-makers are able to make more informed legal decisions. In the United States, witnesses may be qualified as experts if they possess "knowledge, skill, experience, training, or education [that] will help the trier of fact to understand the evidence or determine a fact in issue" (United States, 2021, Rule 702). Experts' opinions must be based upon sufficient facts and data and be the product of reliable principles and methods. Experts also must show they have reliably applied scientific principles and methods to the facts of the case (United States, 2021, Rule 702). In addition, other standard evidentiary rules may apply, such as hearsay (which prohibits using out-of-court statements to prove the truth of the matter asserted) and relevance (whether an expert opinion makes any fact at issue more or less likely to be true). Depending upon the expert–victim relationship, an expert may testify about his or her role in the case, including any assessments conducted and expert reports prepared regarding the victim. The prosecutor may ask the expert questions about the nature of FASD generally and about the victim in particular. However, in most jurisdictions, an expert cannot opine on the question of whether a victim is telling the truth.

Expert evidence offered by the prosecution at trial must comply with that jurisdiction's rules of evidence. The United States' *Federal Rules of Evidence* (2021) sets guidelines regarding experts' written and oral evidence. In the United States, the accused's right to confrontation means the prosecution cannot rely solely on records or affidavits and must call involved experts to testify and be subject to cross-examination (see *Crawford v. Washington*, 2004). For a mental health professional's evidence to be accepted as "expert opinion evidence" in the United States, "the expert's scientific, technical, or other specialized knowledge [must] help the trier of fact to understand the evidence or to determine a fact in issue" (United States, 2021, Rule 702[a]). It is the prosecutor's responsibility to ensure an expert is qualified in a defined area of expertise. Once qualified in that area, the expert cannot give factual or opinion evidence outside that area and may not answer questions that require going beyond his or her defined area of expertise.

The primary duty of an expert is to the court, either the judge or jury. Educating the prosecutor at the pretrial stage is a form of rehearsal for the process of educating the judge or jury at trial. This means the expert is required to translate complex and technical concepts into language understandable by lay people. It requires a fine balance to maintain the high professional standards required of a medico-legal report while also framing and explaining concepts in an understandable manner. As an educator of the judge and jury, the expert is well-placed to draw connections between certain facts in a case and relevant science.

A prosecutor may seek to have evidence about FASD admitted to address a victim's behavior at the time of the incident being tried, such as explaining counterintuitive victim behavior (e.g., why an abused victim did not leave the situation or call police) in domestic assault or sexual assault cases (*People v. Brown*, 2004; *State v. Spigarolo*, 1989). Prosecutors also may offer expert evidence on FASD to help explain why victims are testifying with accommodations or displaying unusual behaviors while testifying that otherwise might suggest untrustworthiness.[5] For example, mental health expert evidence may be helpful in explaining why a victim is easily confused or distracted, avoids eye contact with the judge or jurors, or needs multiple refreshers on his or her police statement.[6] Essentially, mental health evidence can assist to limit uninformed negative judgments about victim credibility whenever victims do not exhibit neurotypical behavior.

When a mental health professional is asked to provide a report and expert evidence at trial regarding a victim with FASD, it is important for the professional to seek clarification from the prosecutor regarding the nature of the expert role and purpose of the expert's evidence. The role of experts who have had no previous provider relationships with victims will differ from the role where experts have participated in previous care, treatment, or assessment of victims. The purpose of expert evidence will depend upon the specific legal issues raised in each case, which are defined by the prosecutor in the context of the facts of the case. It is important for experts to focus their evidence and reports on the legal issues defined by the prosecution. Testifying about aspects of FASD that are not directly relevant to the case may divert the judge or jury from the most essential aspects of the expert's evidence. An expert fully informed about the facts of the case, pertinent legal issues,

[5] *R. v. Pearson* (1994), 95 C.C.C. (3d) 365 (B.C.C.A.) where the court discussed the admission of evidence to explain and supplement a disabled person's evidence.

[6] *R. v. Carroll* [1999] B.C.J. No. 201 where FASD-related memory deficits required accommodations

and possible defenses will be in a better position to assist the prosecutor in identifying the types of expert evidence that may be relevant.

An example of a common legal issue in adult sexual assault cases is whether alleged victims voluntarily consented to sexual activity. In such cases, it is important for experts to understand the law of consent in their jurisdictions in order to frame their evidence around this issue, which will be uppermost in the mind of the tier of fact, either judge or jury. The law of consent in many jurisdictions provides there is no consent if the sexual interaction is the result of abuse of a position of trust, power, or authority. Thus, the law of consent is relevant in the case of victims with FASD who are easily intimidated, have a tendency to acquiesce or cooperate, and are overly eager to please persons they perceive to be authority figures.

In the case of child sexual assault cases, the issue may be the inability of young children with FASD to recount past events. For example, if a prosecutor is seeking to admit a child's disclosure to his or her mother, one legal issue will be whether the child's memory deficit requires admitting the earlier statement, despite evidentiary rules against hearsay and prior statements. In such a case, one purpose of the expert's evidence will be to describe how FASD-related memory deficits affect the child's ability to fully recount past events.

Mental health experts often are needed to inform the court about psycho-legal functioning where competency to testify is an issue. In the United States, there is a general presumption that anyone who can take an oath to tell the truth is competent to testify. However, where victim age or mental disability is an issue, the court may order a separate competency hearing to determine if a witness is capable of testifying (*Kentucky v. Stincer*, 1987). In Canada, expert evidence may be adduced at a competence hearing under s. 16 of the *Canada Evidence Act* (1985) in the case of people with mental disability (*R. v. D.A.I.*, 2012).

Testimonial aids are another matter where mental health expertise may be needed. The law in most jurisdictions provides for use of testimonial aids at trial when a person is under 18 years of age or has a disability that makes it difficult to testify. In such cases, mental health evidence may be required to support prosecution applications to the court for the use of specific testimonial aids. Particularly relevant in the case of victims with FASD-related disabilities, testimonial accommodations might include using a screen or closed-circuit television, a support person, closing the court during testimony,[7] or presenting a previously videotaped statement into evidence at trial.

In some jurisdictions, prosecutors must make pretrial applications to establish the presence of a "mental disability" in order to seek an aid or accommodation at trial. Establishing a mental disability may simply require an affidavit from a mental health professional, or it may require more comprehensive evidence depending upon the nature of the disability and accommodation requested. In American jurisdictions, certain accommodations may conflict with the rules of evidence or

[7] *Ault v. Waid*, 654 F.Supp. 2d 465 (N.D.W. 2009), upholding the use of two-way CCTV and the presence of a guardian ad litem where a child victim was testifying about sexual assault.

standard procedures in a way that could affect the nature of victim testimony. For example, it may be argued by defense counsel that while allowing a victim to testify with his or her prior statement at hand would assist memory and recall, such an accommodation unfairly bolsters victim credibility with inadmissible hearsay. To counter this argument, expert evidence could explain the effects of FASD-related memory deficits on the victim's ability to recall past events.[8]

In addition, victims with FASD may require other accommodations that are more directly related to the specific symptoms in their disabilities (Glowatski & Stewart, 2018). An FASD-informed prosecutor might consider applying for accommodations such as a slow pace for direct and cross-examination, use of concrete sentences and vocabulary that are appropriate to victim cognitive capacity and language skills, frequent short breaks, and reduced sound, light, and movement distractions in the courtroom. Justifying the need for such accommodations requires evidence from mental health experts.[9] In a 2019 survey conducted by the Department of Justice Canada (Hickey & McDonald, 2019), almost half of respondents who participated said prosecutors, judges, and defense counsel resisted using testimonial aids that were provided for in the *Criminal Code*. In addition, 60% of respondents said aids and accommodations needed to be used more often in remote and Indigenous communities. These recent findings highlight the importance of expert evidence as the evidentiary foundation for changes in attitudes of justice professionals and criminal justice systems toward witnesses with disabilities.

Many common law jurisdictions provide for more severe charges and harsher sentences when victims are disabled or particularly vulnerable. For example, in sexual assault cases, defendants may be charged with more severe sexual assault crimes based solely on the fact victims were vulnerable or unable to give consent. In these cases, evidence of victim disability becomes an essential element of the offense, requiring proof beyond a reasonable doubt that often compels expert evidence. Even if disability is not an essential element of a charge, disability-related evidence is highly relevant at the sentencing stage in order to obtain a more severe sentence or counter a defendant's request for leniency. Prosecutors may offer expert evidence of victim disability as one of a number of aggravating factors that judges must take into consideration when deciding appropriate sentences. Expert evidence also may be relevant to prove other aggravating factors such as "the impact of the crime on the victim, considering their age and other personal circumstances, including their health" (Canada. *Criminal Code*, 1970, s. 718.2[a] [iii.1]). Establishing that an adult victim with FASD has the social skills and intellectual ability of a much younger person usually requires expert evidence. The same logic applies where in order to justify harsher sentences, prosecutors must prove that adult victims perceived abusers to be in positions of trust or authority. Because these dynamics also may be relevant to prove the offenses, prosecutors may have obtained

[8] *R. v. A.R.*, [2003] O.J. No. 1320, where the court quotes at length from a medical report on FASD.

[9] The authors are unaware of any examples in the literature or caselaw where the use of these specific FASD-related accommodations have been sought.

relevant testimony from mental health experts during the guilt phase of trial. In such a case, it may not be necessary to obtain similar evidence again at sentencing.

17.5 Adapting a Mental Health Model to the Legal Context: Direct Language/Engage Support System/ Accommodate Needs/Remain Patient

"Advocates must adapt to the witness, not the other way round." Lady Justice Hallett in *R. v. Lubemba; R v. JP* (R. v. Lubemba & R v. JP, 2014).

The conventional model for questioning witnesses is necessarily driven by the nature of legal proceedings: lawyer-controlled, focused, sequential and detail-oriented, and time-sensitive. As this model does not work well in the context of victims with FASD, lawyers need to look elsewhere for an FASD-informed strategy. A communication and interviewing approach that recognizes and accommodates neurocognitive deficits has been developed to guide mental health professionals during assessments of adults with FASD (Brown, Haun, Zapf, & Aiken, 2018). The acronym for this system is Direct Language/Engage Support System/Accommodate Needs/Remain Patient (DEAR). Because this communication approach was designed to accommodate the strengths and weaknesses of adults with FASD, it may provide a useful framework for prosecutors during interviews and at trial.[10]

The following table of symptoms and strategies, although not an exhaustive summary, is a starting point for mental health experts to use in educating prosecutors, judges, or juries about how FASD affects victims. When mental health expertise is not available, this model also is a useful tool for prosecutors to help them guide victims through testimony. It goes without saying that ensuring victims understand lawyers' questions is half the battle. Ensuring lawyers, judges, and juries understand victims' responses is the other half. Although beyond the scope of this chapter, it is hoped this approach will be the subject of future examination.

17.5.1 Direct Language

Many people with FASD are described as "chatty" or superficially talkative. Superficial verbosity often conceals inadequate understanding and confusion when receptive language skills are compromised by FASD (Westrup, 2013). Because expressive language skills affect first impressions, superficial chattiness may lead

[10] In addition to the following guide, prosecutors may find useful and practical interviewing advice in The Advocate's Gateway, an independent UK website, contains Tool Kits for the use of lawyers on all issues related to vulnerable witnesses (Advocate's Gateway, 2020, Welcome, https://www.theadvocatesgateway.org/)

lawyers, judges, or juries to overestimate victim comprehension and ability to respond appropriately to questions. Because social and emotional functioning falls increasingly below chronological age as people with FASD mature (Kully-Martens, Denys, Treit, Tamana, & Rasmussen, 2011), it is advisable to think of adult victims with FASD as younger persons (National Council of Juvenile and Family Court Judges (NCJFCI), 2015). Therefore, consistent use of direct concrete language that avoids abstract concepts is necessary to enhance comprehension.

17.5.2 Engage Support System

Engaging (second element of DEAR) victim service workers and other support persons such as family and friends in criminal trials is particularly important in the case of persons living with FASD. These individuals not only provide support but often can be important collateral sources of information. In the absence of a formal diagnosis about a victim's specific deficits, including communication disabilities, support persons may enlighten the prosecutor about such issues and suggest effective accommodations.

When support persons are used, they should be advised against unintentionally tainting or influencing witnesses by discussing testimony with them. In the context of FASD, this warning is particularly apt due to heightened suggestibility in this population. Weight given to victim testimony at trial will be reduced if there is a suggestion the victim may have been influenced. An equally important rationale for this rule is that any spontaneous statements about the offense made by a victim to anyone before the trial may require another police statement as well as disclosure to defense counsel. Moreover, if the spontaneous statement is inconsistent with the original police statement, it may be used to impeach the victim's evidence at trial and cast doubt on the reliability of his or her evidence.

17.5.3 Accommodate Needs

Accommodation is the third element of DEAR. Of the many neurocognitive deficits associated with FASD that can affect ability to effectively communicate evidence, at least three deficits directly impair testimonial capacity and consequently require accommodation: attention regulation, working memory, and time perception. Attention regulation deficits have been found in 70% of youths with FASD in the juvenile justice context (Fast & Conry, 2009). Therefore, it is quite likely that witnesses and victims with FASD have impaired ability to control and sustain attention during interviews and trial. Appropriate accommodations are necessary in such cases to ensure affected individuals provide relevant and accurate evidence.

Ability to recall and communicate events accurately and reliably at trial is critical if such evidence is to be given proper weight by judges or juries (Gagnier, Moore, & Green, 2011). However, deficient working memory and related impairments in storage, consolidation, and retrieval of information regarding past events are common deficits in FASD that can compromise competent reporting during interviews and testimony. For example, incomplete or variable recall may result in inconsistent or confused narratives of events central to the legal matter. Often, increased susceptibility to suggestion is an unfortunate consequence of such memory deficits (Fast & Conry, 2004; Novick Brown, Gudjonsson, & Connor, 2011). The problem here for interviewers is they may inadvertently speak or act in a way that victims misinterpret as suggesting a particular answer. Related to suggestibility is heightened desire to please by responding in a way that is most likely to achieve this goal. The desire to please is particularly likely when interviewers are authority figures, such as police officers or lawyers (Thiel et al., 2011).

Of significant concern for all justice professionals is a tendency for people with poor working memories to confabulate (Gibbard, Wass, & Clarke, 2003; Novick Brown et al., 2011). Confabulation as it applies to the legal setting involves filling in memory gaps by reconstructing events using both accurate recollections and likely but inaccurate information (Fast & Conry, 2004), which overall can be quite misleading. Confabulation, which typically is unintentional, is distinguished from lying in the cited literature and often is seen in individuals with memory deficits, particularly those with FASD. Confabulation represents memory error and is not deliberate lying because in confabulation, there is no intent to deceive (Metcalf, Langdon, & Coltheart, 2007). Given the importance of witness credibility and reliability, it is of vital importance that mental health experts differentiate between lying and confabulation in witnesses they have evaluated and make this distinction clear to the court.[11] Because judges and juries often conclude that if one part of witness testimony is unreliable, other aspects may be equally unreliable, expert witnesses should be prepared to discuss whether confabulation by a victim at one point during testimony necessarily implies all of the victim's testimony is similarly affected.[12] In response to more general concern about memory deficits, courts have commented on the importance of videotaping statements taken by social workers or police officers in order to avoid any doubt that interviewers may have influenced victim evidence (Moore & Green, 2004).[13] Although the potential for prosecutors to unintentionally influence victims is not mentioned in these decisions, prosecutors should approach any interactions with affected witnesses in a cautious and FASD-informed manner.

Time perception deficits, common in FASD, also are highly relevant in the legal setting as key evidentiary issues in criminal trials require placing events into time-frames with proper sequence. Many persons with FASD will be very confused by questions that include abstract concepts of time (e.g., "this morning," "yesterday," "the day before yesterday," "before," "in a while," "later"). This confusion arises

[11] *R. v. J.A.R.*, 2012 BCPC 241 where the expert distinguished between "an untruth" and confabulation.

[12] *R. v. Inyallie*, [1993] B.C.J. No. 2861 (BCPC) where, notwithstanding inconsistencies in the victim's evidence, the judge found that the essential elements of the evidence about the accused had not varied.

[13] *R. v. Lyons*, 2011 O.J. No. 3596 (S.C), https://www.fasdjustice.ca/cases/witnesses-victims/780-at-trial-r-v-lyons-2011-oj-no-3596-sc.html; and *R. v. R. (A.)[A.R.]*, [2003] O.J. 1320 (Ont. S.C.J.).

because understanding and estimating passage of time is cognitively challenging for this population. Therefore, the difference between "a few seconds" and "a few minutes" may have little or no meaning for a person living with FASD.

17.5.4 *Remain Patient*

The pressure at trial to use court time efficiently means witness examination normally proceeds at a good pace. However, for witnesses with FASD, if pace of questioning does not accommodate their cognitive deficits, direct and cross-examination likely will result in confused witnesses giving incomplete or incorrect answers. Such outcomes are due to the slow processing speed seen in many individuals with FASD. Slow processing speed means witnesses will require minutes rather than seconds to process, understand, and respond to questions (Malbin, 2004). Juxtaposed against this difficulty is the problem that cognitive skills likely deteriorate and confabulation increases when witnesses feel pressured to perform beyond processing capacity (Gagnier et al., 2011).

17.6 Conclusion

In summary, criminal justice systems lacking FASD-informed justice professionals to identify and address the needs of victims and witnesses with such conditions may be responsible for secondary victimization. Mental health professionals play a pivotal role in identifying relevant issues and educating justice professionals on strategies that allow victims with FASD to participate fully in the criminal justice process. On a larger stage, mental health experts play an important role in challenging conventions that ignore or minimize the prevalence and relevance of FASD in the criminal justice system. Several decades ago, mental health professionals played this precise role in another context with tangible success. By bringing scientific and clinical expertise into the courtroom, such experts helped to dispel existing myths and stereotypes surrounding child witness evidence. Today, child-friendly practices that reflect current scientific knowledge are deeply embedded in the law.

Some justice systems have demonstrated a willingness to recognize FASD-related disabilities in their courts. In fact, special FASD courts now exist in some jurisdictions. Several countries have introduced protocols to deal with communication disabilities. For example, legislation in England and Wales has codified the use of "witness intermediaries," who help witnesses with mental disabilities understand what is communicated to them and facilitate their responses to investigators, lawyers, judges, and juries (Cooper & Mattison, 2017). Legislation in New South Wales, Australia, has introduced "narrative evidence power" and "improper questions power" to protect witnesses with mental disabilities from interruptions in their testimony and misleading and oppressive questioning (Nair, 2010; New South Wales, 1995, s. 29[2] and s. 41).

Although FASD awareness in the justice system is increasing slowly over time, clearly much more needs to be done. This chapter has described from a prosecutorial perspective a few developments that have improved understanding of FASD in the legal context. To expand upon ideas discussed in this chapter, Table 17.1 below proposes specific methods for enhancing the way legal professionals interact with victims and witnesses who have, or might have, FASD. The table includes specific empirically based suggestions for addressing deficits that most directly affect capacity to provide relevant and accurate testimony.[14] It is hoped these suggestions provoke thought, discussion, and—hopefully—action among our colleagues in the justice system.

Table 17.1 Guide to enhancing witness trial preparation and trial testimony

Suggestions for prosecutorial witness preparation	
Expressive/receptive communication impairments	
Red flags	Recommendations for prosecutors
Difficulty with abstract thinking (e.g., concrete, repetitive responses to questions) Slow information processing (e.g., hesitation before responding) Behavioral or verbal responses that indicate misunderstanding Expressive language that is stronger than receptive language and comprehension "Chattiness" or use of superficially sophisticated words that mask poor understanding Difficulty providing direct and complete responses to questions Parroting or echoing comments by others without providing contextual information to show adequate understanding Multiple requests for questions or information to be repeated Tangential responses that do not answer questions Inability to provide coherent sequential narrative Forgetfulness	Use concrete language and short sentences. Use active rather than passive voice. Use simple words and phrases. Avoid questions posed in the negative. Include only one query per question. Be alert to any signs a witness is having difficulty understanding. Speak slowly and pause regularly to allow time for processing information. Instead of asking if the witness understands a question, verify comprehension by asking the witness to restate the question in his/her own words. Avoid legal jargon (e.g., "take the stand," "testify," "exhibit," "rights"), double-negatives, and tag questions (e.g., "You were at the party, weren't you?"). Use concrete words that do not require abstract thinking (e.g., "what" questions rather than "how" or "why" questions). Have the witness draw a picture of what happened and then have him/her explain what is happening in the picture.

(continued)

[14] Mental health and justice professionals may also find helpful the discussion in the following article on approaches for working with persons with FASD (Douglas, Hammill, Russell, & Hall, 2012). The Importance of foetal alcohol spectrum disorder for criminal law in practice: Views of Queensland lawyers (p. 153).

Table 17.1 (continued)

Suggestions for prosecutorial witness preparation	
Expressive/receptive communication impairments	
Red flags	Recommendations for prosecutors
Attention regulation impairments	
Impulsive responses before complete questions are asked Disorganized and poorly prioritized responses to questions Losing focus Trouble staying on topic while talking Poor eye contact Excessive restlessness Low frustration tolerance Getting overwhelmed Easily distracted by trivial noises outside the interview room Forgetting to follow through with requests	Pace questioning in interviews and in court. Allow the witness to speak with a minimum of interruptions. Take regular short breaks during interviews and court testimony. Reduce visual and sound distractions in interview room and courtroom (e.g., mute courtroom computers, lower lights, reduce movement of people in and out of the courtroom). Maintain direct eye contact with the witness and frequently call him/her by name to focus attention on the question. Allow the witness to concentrate on a familiar physical activity such as drawing, knitting, or squeezing a stress ball before and during the interview and testimony. Arrange for a distraction-free waiting area for the interview and court appearance.
Memory impairments	
Unable to provide sequential narrative of how he/she was victimized Unable to provide key details about the incident (i.e., who, what, where, when, how) Reporting irrelevant information Voicing uncertainty about important facts Providing inconsistent reports prior to trial Changing information based on questioning Acquiescing easily to whatever is asked Providing *increasing* factual information with each successive interview Reporting unlikely events/scenarios Providing information beyond level of maturity	Build rapport with the witness prior to trial. Explain what will happen at trial and importance of telling the truth. In pretrial interview(s), give the witness permission to indicate when he/she does not understand or know the answer to a question. Explain that asking a question more than once does not mean the witness answered incorrectly. If witness is unable to provide key facts, ask "wh" questions ("who, what, where, when") after exhausting open-ended questions. Ask sensory questions to trigger memories. Advise witness at the start of testimony that ample time will be provided for his/her responses and there is no need to rush. Ask questions that maximize free recall (e.g., "Tell me everything that happened?" "And then what happened?" "Tell me more about…"). Provide sufficient time for processing and responding. Frequently ask witness if he/she needs more time to respond. Consider legal options that will allow the witness to refresh his/her memory during trial. Consider applying for the admission of the witness's video-recorded statement made within a reasonable time of the offense (Canada. *Criminal Code*, 1970, s. 715.2). Do not ask closed-ended or leading questions (e.g., yes/no, either/or, multiple choice) Avoid using language that may unintentionally signal preferred responses to questions. Control tone of voice, facial expressions, and body language to avoid suggesting or reinforcing a particular response. Avoid comments after responses (e.g., "okay," "good," "you're doing really well") that may have a reinforcing effect.

Table 17.1 (continued)

Suggestions for prosecutorial witness preparation	
Expressive/receptive communication impairments	
Red flags	Recommendations for prosecutors
Poor time perception	
Unable to report time frames, duration of instant event, or temporal sequencing Reporting improbable or unlikely time frames	Avoid confusing language relating to time (e.g., "day before yesterday," "several days before that"). Use visual aids in pretrial interviews that enable the witness to demonstrate what happened as he/she explains each event.

References

Advocate's Gateway. (2020). *Welcome*. Retrieved from https://www.theadvocatesgateway.org/

American Bar Association (ABA). (2020). *Model Rules of Professional Conduct. Rule 3.8. Special responsibilities of a Prosecutor. Comment*. Retrieved from https://www.americanbar.org/groups/professional_responsibility/publications/model_rules_of_professional_conduct/rule_3_8_special_responsibilities_of_a_prosecutor/comment_on_rule_3_8/

Americans with Disabilities Act (ADA) of 1990. (42 U.S. § 12101), Pub. L. No. 101-336, 104 Stat. 328 (1990).

Ault v. Waid, 654 F.Supp. 2d 465 (N.D.W. 2009). Retrieved from https://casetext.com/case/ault-v-waid-4

Boucher v The Queen, [1955] S.C.R. 16.

Brown, J., Haun, J., Zapf, P. A., & Aiken, T. (2018). FASD and competency to stand trial (CST): An exploratory review. In E. Jonsson, S. Clarren, & I. Binnie (Eds.), *Ethical and legal perspectives in fetal alcohol spectrum disorders (FASD): Foundational Issues* (pp. 201–227). Cham, Switzerland: Springer International.

Burczycka, M. (2014). Violent victimization of Canadians with mental health-related disabilities. *Juristat, Statistics Canada, 38*(1), 1–21. https://www150.statcan.gc.ca/n1/en/pub/85-002-x/2018001/article/54977-eng.pdf

Canada. (2014, March 1). 2.5. Principles of disclosure. In: *Public Prosecution Service of Canada Deskbook*. Retrieved from https://www.ppsc-sppc.gc.ca/eng/pub/fpsd-sfpg/fps-sfp/tpd/p2/ch05.html

Canada. (2019, December 21). 2.2 Duties and responsibilities of Crown counsel. In: *Public Prosecution Service of Canada Deskbook*. Retrieved from https://www.ppsc-sppc.gc.ca/eng/pub/fpsd-sfpg/fps-sfp/tpd/p2/ch02.html

Canada. *Canadian Charter of Rights and Freedoms*. (1982). s. 15, Part 1 of the *Constitution Act*, 1982, being Schedule B to the *Canada Act 1982* (UK), 1982, c 11.

Canada. *Criminal Code*. (1970). R.S.C. 1970, c. C-34. Retrieved from https://trove.nla.gov.au/work/25084933

Canada. Ministry of the Attorney General. (2020, August). Preamble to the prosecution manual. *Ontario Crown policy manual* (pp. 2–5). Retrieved from https://files.ontario.ca/books/mag-crown-prosecution-manual-en-2020-08-14.pdf

Canada. Public Health Agency of Canada. (2013, February 21). *Canada*. Fact Sheet. Government of Canada Invests to Promote Health, Well-being, and Safety of Canadians. Retrieved from https://www.canada.ca/en/public-health/services/health-promotion/fact-sheet/fasd.html

Canada Evidence Act. (R.S.C. 1985, c. C-5). Retrieved from https://laws-lois.justice.gc.ca/eng/acts/c-5/

Cane, P., & Kritzer, H. M. (Eds.). (2012). *The Oxford handbook of empirical legal research.* Oxford: Oxford University Press.

Chudley, A. E., Conry, J., Cook, J. L., Loock, C., Rosales, T., & LeBlanc, N. (2005). Fetal alcohol spectrum disorder: Canadian guidelines for diagnosis. *CMAJ Network, 172*(Suppl. 5), S1–S21. https://doi.org/10.1503/cmaj.104030

Cook, J. L., Green, C. R., Lilley, C. M., Anderson, S. M., Baldwin, M. E., Chudley, A. E., … Rosales, T. (2016). Fetal alcohol spectrum disorder: A guidelines for diagnosis across the life span. *CMAJ Network, 188*(3), 191–197. https://doi.org/10.1503/cmaj.141593

Cooper, P., & Mattison, M. (2017). Intermediaries, vulnerable people and the quality of evidence: An international comparison of three versions of the English intermediary. *International Journal of Evidence & Proof, 21*(4), 351–370. https://doi.org/10.1177/1365712717725534

Cox, L., Clairmont, D., & Cox, S. (2008). Knowledge and attitudes of criminal justice professionals in relation to fetal alcohol spectrum disorder. *Canadian Journal of Clinical Pharmacology, 15*(2), e306–e313.

Crawford v. Washington, 541 U.S. 36 (2004). Retrieved from https://supreme.justia.com/cases/federal/us/541/36/

Douglas, H., Hammill, J., Russell, E. A., & Hall, W. (2012). The importance of foetal alcohol spectrum disorder for criminal law in practice: Views of Queensland lawyers. *Queensland Lawyer, 32*, 153–164. https://www.researchgate.net/publication/288827361

Fast, D. K., & Conry, J. (2004). The challenge of fetal alcohol syndrome in the criminal legal system. *Addiction Biology, 9*(2), 161–166. https://doi.org/10.1080/13556210410001717042

Fast, D. K., & Conry, J. (2009). Fetal alcohol spectrum disorder and the criminal justice system. *Developmental Disabilities Research Reviews, 15*(3), 250–257. https://doi.org/10.1002/ddrr.66

Flannigan, K., Pei, J., Stewart, M., & Johnson, A. (2018). Fetal alcohol spectrum disorder and the criminal justice system: A systematic literature review. *International Journal of Law and Psychiatry, 57*, 42–52. https://doi.org/10.1016/j.ijlp.2017.12.008

Gagnier, K. R., Moore, T. E., & Green, M. (2011). A need for closer examination of FASD by the criminal justice system: Has the call been answered? *Journal of Population Therapeutics and Clinical Pharmacology, 18*(3), e426–e439. https://jptcp.com/index.php/jptcp/article/view/458

Gibbard, W. B., Wass, P., & Clarke, M. E. (2003). The neuropsychological implications of prental alcohol exposure. *Canadian Child and Adolescent Psychiatric Reviews, 12*(3), 72–76.

Glowatski, K. & Stewart, M. (2018). *Victimization in people with FASD*. Canada FASD Research Network. Retrieved from https://canfasd.ca/wp-content/uploads/2018/07/FASD-and-Victimization-FINAL.pdf

Hickey, S., & McDonald, S. (2019). Testimonial aids knowledge exchange: Successes, challenges and recommendations. *Victims of Crime Research Digest, 12*, 5–13. https://www.justice.gc.ca/eng/rp-pr/cj-jp/victim/rd12-rr12/p5.html

Kentucky v. Stincer, 482 U.S. 730 (1987). Retrieved from https://supreme.justia.com/cases/federal/us/482/730/

Kully-Martens, K., Denys, K., Treit, S., Tamana, S., & Rasmussen, C. (2011). A review of social skills deficits in individuals with fetal alcohol spectrum disorders and prenatal alcohol exposure: Profile, mechanisms, and interventions. *Alcoholism: Clinical and Experimental Research, 36*(4), 568–576. https://doi.org/10.1111/j.1530-0277.2011.01661.x

Malbin, D. V. (2004). Fetal alcohol spectrum disorder (FASD) and the role of family court judges in improving outcomes for children and families. *Juvenile and Family Court Journal, 55*(2), 53–63. https://doi.org/10.1111/j.1755-6988.2004.tb00161.x

Metcalf, K., Langdon, R., & Coltheart, M. (2007). Models of confabulation: A critical review and a new framework. *Cognitive Neuropsychology, 24*(1), 23–47. https://doi.org/10.1080/02643290600694901

Moore, T. E., & Green, M. (2004). Fetal alcohol spectrum disorder (FASD): A need for closer examination by the criminal justice system. *Criminal Reports, 19*(Pt. 1), 99–108. https://www.glendon.yorku.ca/timmoore/wp-content/uploads/sites/222/FASDCrimRep.pdf

Mutch, R. C., Jones, H. M., Bower, C., & Watkins, R. E. (2016). Fetal alcohol spectrum disorder: Using knowledge, attitudes, and practice of justice professionals to support their education needs. *Journal of Population Therapeutics and Clinical Pharmacology, 23*(1), e77–e89.

National Council of Juvenile and Family Court Judges (NCJFCI). (2015). *Fetal alcohol spectrum disorders: Implications for juvenile and family court judges*. Technical Assistance Brief. Reno, NV. Retrieved from https://www.ncjfcj.org/publications/fetal-alcohol-spectrum-disorders-implications-for-juvenile-and-family-court-judges/

Nair, P. (2010). Giving voice in court: Cushioning adversarialism for witnesses with intellectual disabilities. *Current Issues in Criminal Justice, 21*(3), 481–488. https://doi.org/10.1080/10345329.2010.12035862

New South Wales. (1995). *Evidence Act 1995* (NSW), s. 29(2) and s. 41. Retrieved from https://www.legislation.nsw.gov.au/view/html/inforce/current/act-1995-025

Novick Brown, N., Gudjonsson, G., & Connor, P. (2011). Suggestibility and fetal alcohol spectrum disorders: I'll tell you anything you want to hear. *Journal of Psychiatry and Law, 39*(1), 39–71. https://doi.org/10.1177/009318531103900103

People v. Brown, 16 Cal. Rptr. 3rd 447 (2004). Retrieved from https://www.courtlistener.com/opinion/2548176/people-v-brown/

R. v. A.R., [2003] O.J. No. 1320 (SC). Retrieved from https://www.fasdjustice.ca/cases/witnesses-victims/785-at-trial-r-v-ar-2003-oj-no-1320-sc.html

R. v. Boucher (1954), 110 C.C.C. 263 (S.C.C.). Retrieved from https://www.canlii.org/en/ca/scc/doc/1954/1954canlii3/1954canlii3.html

R. v. Carroll [1999] B.C.J. No. 201.

R. v. D.A.I., 2-12 S.C.C. 5, [2012] 1 S.C.R. 149. Retrieved from https://www.canliiconnects.org/en/cases/2012scc5

R. v. Inyallie, [1993] B.C.J. No. 2861 (BCPC). Retrieved from https://www.fasdjustice.ca/cases/witnesses-victims/787-at-trial-r-v-inyallie-1993-bcj-no-2861.html

R. v. J.A.R., 2012 BCPC 241. Retrieved from https://fasdjustice.ca/cases/witnesses-victims/854-at-trial-r-v-j-a-r-2012-bcpc-241-giardini-j.html

R. v. Lubemba [2014] 1 WLR 1579; *R v. JP* [2014] EWCA Crim 2064, para 45. Retrieved from https://www.casemine.com/judgement/uk/5b46f1f72c94e0775e7ef270

R. v. Pearson (1994), 95 C.C.C. (3d) 365 (B.C.C.A.)

R. v. R. (A.)[A.R.], [2003] O.J. 1320 (Ont. S.C.J.)

R. v. Seaboyer, [1991] 2 S.C.R. 577. Retrieved from https://canliiconnects.org/en/summaries/31828

Smith, N., Harrell, S., & Judy, A. (2017). *How safe are Americans with disabilities? The facts about violent crime and their implications*. Brooklyn, NY: Vera Institute of Justice. https://www.vera.org/downloads/publications/How-safe-are-americans-with-disabilities-web.pdf

State v. Spigarolo, 210 Conn. 359 (Conn. 1989). Retrieved from https://casetext.com/case/state-v-spigarolo

Thiel, K. S., Baladerian, N. J., Boyce, K. R., Cantos VII, O. D., Davis, L. A., Kelly, K., … Stream, J. (2011). Fetal alcohol spectrum disorders and victimization: Implications for families, educators, social services, law enforcement, and the judicial system. *Journal of Psychiatry and Law, 39*(1), 121–157. https://doi.org/10.1177/009318531103900105

UK Ministry of Justice. (2011, March). *Achieving best evidence in criminal proceedings: Guidance on interviewing victims and witnesses, and guidance on using special measures*. Retrieved from https://www.cps.gov.uk/sites/default/files/documents/legal_guidance/best_evidence_in_criminal_proceedings.pdf

United Nations. (1948). *Universal Declaration of Human Rights* (UDHR). Retrieved from https://www.ohchr.org/EN/UDHR/Documents/UDHR_Translations/eng.pdf

United Nations, Department of Economics and Social Affairs. (2006).*Convention on the Rights of Persons with Disabilities (CRPD)*. Retrieved from https://www.un.org/development/desa/disabilities/convention-on-the-rights-of-persons-with-disabilities.html

United Nations, Human Rights. (1966).*International Covenant on Civil and Political Rights* (OHCHR). Retrieved from https://www.ohchr.org/Documents/ProfessionalInterest/ccpr.pdf

United States. (2021). *Federal rules of evidence*. Grand Rapids, MI: Michigan Legal.

U.S. Department of Justice. (2017, July). Crime against persons with disabilities, 2009–2015—Statistical Tables. *Bureau of Justice Statistics*. Retrieved from https://www.bjs.gov/content/pub/pdf/capd0915st.pdf

Westrup, S. (2013). Foetal alcohol spectrum disorders: As prevalent as autism? *Educational Psychology in Practice, 29*(3), 309–325. https://doi.org/10.1080/02667363.2013.815114

Chapter 18
Views from the Bench: Fetal Alcohol Spectrum Disorder in the Courtroom

Anthony P. Wartnik, Larry G. Anderson, and Anthony J. FitzGerald

Abstract In this chapter, three judges from the United States, Canada, and New Zealand share their views on a number of challenges fetal alcohol spectrum disorder (FASD) presents in the criminal courtroom. The chapter begins with a look at some of the commonalities between the three common law jurisdictions and then moves to significant differences. The judges address how FASD fits into threshold assessments of criminal responsibility and fitness to stand trial, how courts have developed rules aimed at preventing false confessions and how such rules apply to persons with FASD, rules and issues around how evidence of FASD is presented to the court, and most significantly, how FASD is treated in the sentencing context, including some specific considerations regarding death penalty cases in the United States.

Keywords Fetal alcohol spectrum disorder (FASD) · Neurodevelopmental disorder associated with prenatal alcohol exposure (ND-PAE) · Fitness · Competency to stand trial (CST) · Intellectual disability (ID) · Developmental disorder · Suggestibility · Confabulation · False confession

A. P. Wartnik (✉)
King County Superior Court, Seattle, WA, USA

L. G. Anderson
Provincial Court of Alberta, Edmonton Criminal Division, Alberta, Canada
e-mail: Larry.Anderson@albertacourts.ca

A. J. FitzGerald
District and Youth Court, Auckland District Court, Auckland, New Zealand
e-mail: fitzgea@courts.govt.nz

N. Novick Brown (ed.), *Evaluating Fetal Alcohol Spectrum Disorders in the Forensic Context*, https://doi.org/10.1007/978-3-030-73628-6_18

18.1 Clash with Common Law Fundamentals

Our justice systems are rooted in Anglo Saxon law and based upon a few fundamental beliefs: we are rational beings, we know right from wrong, and we have free will and can foresee consequences. These fundamental underpinnings are reflected in the Supreme Court of Canada decision of *R. v. Ruzic* (2001, p. 715), quoting from *R. v. Chaulk* (1990):

> …this assumption of the rationality and autonomy of human beings forms part of Canadian criminal law: "At the heart of our criminal law system is the cardinal assumption that human beings are rational and autonomous (Ferguson, 1989). This is the fundamental condition upon which criminal responsibility reposes. Individuals have the capacity to reason right from wrong, and thus to choose between right and wrong."
>
> Ferguson (1989) continues: "It is these dual capacities – reason and choice – which give moral justification to imposing criminal responsibility and punishment on offenders. If a person can reason right from wrong and has the ability to choose right or wrong, then attribution or responsibility and punishment is morally justified or deserved when that person consciously chooses wrong" (p. 140).

Our laws are peppered with presumptions reflecting this historical concept, which begins with a general and strong presumption of sanity. Exceptions to this presumption have existed since the 1800s, but historically, the threshold for criminal responsibility has been very low, with few shades of gray. In common law, there is a parallel fundamental presumption that one intends the natural consequences of one's actions, a principle that is applied in criminal courts every day, at virtually every stage of the adjudication process.

Our systems entrench a presumption of innocence, and so we have developed rules around bail, but our bail laws also are grounded in the presumption people act rationally. Bail generally is structured upon the logical premise that if a court threatens adverse consequences for failure to comply with release conditions, accused parties will choose to follow the conditions in order to avoid the consequences. An extension of this logic is an assumption that the harsher the threat of adverse consequences or of more and tighter restrictions, the greater the likelihood of compliance.

The presumption of rational decision-making also is present at the trial stage, infused into rules of evidence. For example, the *confessions rule* is a rule developed in common law to offset risk of a wrongful conviction. This rule states that no confession made to a person in authority can be admitted into evidence unless first it is proven to be voluntary, which historically has meant it must be free of threats or inducements. In its original formulation, this rule assumed no one in his or her right mind would confess to something he/she did not do unless threatened or bribed. In other words, the rule assumes we all think through and recognize the consequences of what we say. At the sentencing stage of a case, the presumption of rationality again figures prominently, especially in concepts such as general and specific deterrence, about which more will be said later. Our sentencing regimes tend to rest upon a principle of "just deserts," which is a logical extension of any system that derives moral and legal authority from the tenets described in *R. v. Ruzic* (2001), above.

The point of these observations is to emphasize how great a challenge our justice systems present to people with FASD accused of crimes and conversely, how great a challenge the condition of FASD presents to our systems' participants. In a consensus conference held in 2013, chaired by Ian Binnie, former justice of the Supreme Court of Canada, the jury found:

> The evidence we have heard is compelling that those with FASD are likely to have a diminished capacity to foresee consequences, make reasoned choices or learn from mistakes. Therefore, their actions are likely to clash with assumptions about human behaviour at almost every stage of the justice system. (Canada, IHE, 2013)

The problem noted above is compounded by the fact FASD often is an invisible condition at first blush, which means the presumption of full competence is routinely applied to affected people with reduced cognitive abilities.

It behooves us to consider that many of the assumptions made about human behavior when our laws were being formed in the nineteenth century have not been borne out by modern developments in science, yet they continue to be the default position absent evidence to displace them. And we tend, or at least it is easy, to revert to default positions, especially when tired and rushed and when the alternative is difficult. If we are to ensure persons with FASD do not get trampled, we must remain ever-vigilant and on occasion have the courage to put old ideas aside in the interests of justice. One judge put it this way:

> The cognitively challenged are before our courts in unknown numbers. We prosecute them again and again and again. We sentence them again and again and again. We imprison them again and again and again. They commit crimes again and again and again. We wonder why they do not change. The wonder of it all is that we do not change. (*R. v. J. H.*, 2002, para. 167)

18.2 A Few Words About Our Adversarial Systems

Before turning to how our respective courts have tried to meet the challenges of FASD, a brief description of criminal courts generally may be of benefit, especially to medical professionals involved in assessments. In fact, the workings of the adversarial process likely are counterintuitive to most health professionals trained in the medical perspective, which includes mental health professionals. For example, criminal courts in a common law system are adversarial in nature. Courts operate on a theory that if two parties (the State and the individual) are equally armed (represented by trained lawyers) and do battle in the sense of putting their strongest case forward before a neutral finder of facts (judge or jury), then the truth will emerge. This system tends to serve us well in determining guilt and innocence. However, once past that stage, either by trial or an admission of guilt, effectiveness of the adversarial model in finding constructive or therapeutic solutions tends to break down. For this reason, many jurisdictions have developed therapeutic courts that incorporate a more individualized and collaborative approach, which is aimed at including a therapeutic component in sentence orders. As long as the rigors of the adversarial process are in place, it can be very difficult to gather and present evidence needed to inform judges in a timely way of the need for a therapeutic approach.

Regardless of whether one is in a therapeutic court or more traditional trial court, it is important for everyone to remember two things: (a) a court's decision is only as good as the information placed before it, and (b) a judge can base his or her decision only on the evidence presented. Unlike most European systems, judges in our systems do not have inquisitorial powers. Although judges may have relevant knowledge from life experience or other sources, a legacy of our adversarial process is the limited extent to which they can rely upon knowledge beyond the evidence presented in the cases before them.

One final point bears mentioning before turning to how FASD has fared in our respective courts. The cases that become published and in turn, sometimes get referenced in later cases or law journals, are a very small fraction of the volumes of cases that go through courts every day. Also, the percentage of cases that actually proceed to trial is very small, usually not more than 5%. Reality is that almost every jurisdiction faces limited resources and crushing volumes, with a large proportion of cases concluded in busy intake dockets. This means that without a great deal of commitment on the part of many people on many levels, starting with decision makers charged with building capacity, frontline workers doing assessments, lawyers, and judges, accused persons with a disability like FASD can easily be left behind and deprived of access to justice. Thus, we all must do our part to pay attention, to act, and to educate.

18.3 Some Common Words of Advice

As the pages that follow will make clear, criminal law has evolved differently in our three jurisdictions, and therefore challenges presented by FASD have been dealt with differently. However, there are a few points the authors of this chapter would like to emphasize for professionals involved in preparing, defending, or prosecuting cases involving accused persons with FASD. First, it is imperative professionals know the relevant law in the jurisdictions where case is being tried. Second, professionals must know the science.

Judges sitting in courtrooms will want to arrive at just results. The role of advocates is to lead judges to such a result within limits permitted by law. Judges likely have a good handle on the law and what is possible within the law but are less likely to know the science. Therefore, the goal for advocates and experts is to translate the relevance and significance of scientific facts to the legal framework within which judges must make rulings. This often requires communicating complex concepts in lay language that judges unfamiliar with the science can understand. Because experts invariably have in-depth knowledge in specialized areas, it is common for them to use acronyms and scientific lingo when communicating with others who have similar training. However, when explaining or eliciting testimony in the courtroom about scientific phenomena such as FASD, it is important to avoid lingo. If specialized terminology must be used, it should be explained in lay terms.[1] It also is important to remain focused on the primary objective sought by calling the evidence. In other words, testimony should be kept relevant and preferably, not repetitive. Judges usually do hear things the first time or will ask for clarity, if not.

18.4 Fetal Alcohol Spectrum Disorder and the Law in New Zealand

Low levels of awareness and uptake, absence of any prevalence studies, lack of diagnostic capacity, and barriers to essential supports and services stand out as major features of the position regarding FASD in the New Zealand justice context. Although the position is better in the Youth Justice system than in the adult criminal courts, we have a long way to go before justice is accomplished for blameless victims of this neurodisability and the community, which should expect that we would be identifying the true underlying cause of offending and properly addressing it so as to reduce risk of reoffending.

18.4.1 Adult Court System

Teina Pora spent 21 years in prison for a rape and murder he confessed to but did not commit. It was not until the Privy Council[2] heard evidence in 2015 from Drs. Valerie McGinn and Craig Immelman regarding Pora's FASD that it became clear why he had made frequently contradictory and often implausible confessions. On the basis of the doctors' evidence about the various ways Pora's FASD impacted his executive functioning, his confessions were found to be unreliable, and the convictions were quashed (*Pora v R*, 2015). This outcome attracted widespread public attention in New Zealand and put the significance of FASD in the criminal justice system in the spotlight in a way that had not happened previously.

Before *Pora*, there had been only a small number of cases in adult criminal courts in New Zealand where evidence of FASD was available. In a 2011 article, Judge Stephen O'Driscoll drew attention to international research showing the close link between FASD and contact with the Youth Justice and Criminal Justice systems (O'Driscoll, 2011, p. 119). Among other things, he expressed concern about how rarely FASD was being recognized by courts in New Zealand at all levels, the very

---

[1] In order to develop skills involved in presenting evidence in the courtroom, it is helpful to understand the historical development of FASD-related law. Two in-depth discussions in this regard are found in Wartnik and Carlson (2011) and Wartnik, Brown, and Herrick (2015).

[2] In 2004, New Zealand severed links to the Privy Council in England and made the Supreme Court in New Zealand the highest court in the country and the final appeal court. However, because *Pora's* convictions predated that change, he was able, with leave, to have his appeal heard there.

limited FASD diagnostic capacity in the country, and lack of any prevalence research. Prior to *Pora*, the very few reported cases in adult courts involving evidence of FASD were for sentencing, and FASD usually was treated as a double-edged sword, justifying some credit in mitigation on the basis of reduced moral responsibility on the one hand but also being viewed as a risk factor requiring protection of the public on the other hand (e.g., *Komene v. NZ Police*, 2009). However, in one case, a man's FASD was the basis for imposing a noncustodial sentence focused on rehabilitation instead of imprisonment for various charges including indecent assault, but FASD was not seen as sufficient justification for a discharge without conviction so as to avoid a second-strike warning under our three-strikes legislation (*NZ Police v. Stipich*, 2012).

Despite the high public profile the *Pora* case has given FASD in the criminal justice context, the disorder continues to have a low profile in New Zealand's adult criminal justice system. Throughout the country there has been only a slight increase in requests for FASD assessments since *Pora* and a correspondingly small increase in the number of cases where evidence of the neurodevelopmental disorder was made available to the court. There also has been very little, if any, increase in diagnostic capacity. A prevalence study still has not been carried out.

Where an FASD diagnosis was available to courts, results have been mixed. In some cases, FASD continued to be viewed as a double-edged sword (*Dodds v. R*, 2016). FASD was the basis for finding reduced moral culpability for murder and together with the man's relative youthfulness, justified a relatively modest discount of 2 years off the minimum period of imprisonment of 15 years and 6 months (*R v. Whiting-Roff*, 2018). In relation to bail, FASD was treated as a factor counting against a defendant in one case because of an anticipated inability to comply (*NZ Police v. Moyle*, 2018), but in another case, FASD was viewed favorably because the bail placement was supported by the neuropsychologist, McGinn, who had diagnosed the defendant's FASD (*R v. Fawcett*, 2018). Evidence regarding the impact of FASD on a defendant's inability to express remorse for offending was reason for the Court of Appeal to find the sentencing judge had erred in not giving this issue proper weight (*Pomare v. R*, 2017).

On a few occasions, an FASD diagnosis was the basis for finding a person to have a mental impairment for the purpose of fitness to stand trial proceedings.[3] In some of those cases, the finding was that the person concerned was unfit to stand trial due to the FASD (*M v. R*, 2019; *NZ Police v. Hansen*, 2020; *NZ Police v. Herbert*, 2019). In *M* v *R*, the judge who decided disposition found it was necessary in the public interest to make the most restrictive order available due to M's high risk of reoffending, which was a consequence of her FASD. An FASD diagnosis was one of the main reasons, together with youths, for a substantial discount of 50% off the starting point of imprisonment for aggravated robbery in *R v Puru* (2018). The defendant's vulnerabilities due to his FASD, which had been described by

[3] A summary of the law regarding fitness in New Zealand is set out below in the section about the Youth Court.

McGinn in her assessment, were described by the judge as being very important to his decision about the discount.

A therapeutic focus was adopted in sentencing a man facing a large number of dishonesty and disorder-type offenses, and intensive supervision was imposed in *NZ Police v Morrison* (2019). In fact, this is one of very few cases where a judge demonstrated, and set out in some detail, awareness of the significance of FASD in the criminal justice context and carefully balanced the competing factors and interests in coming to a result. The judge noted that the type of multidisciplinary management needed in the community for the defendant was beyond the means of the Corrections Department to provide, but he aimed to address that problem by imposing special conditions that were recommended by McGinn, the neuropsychologist who diagnosed the FASD. In *R v Sheers* (2020), an FASD diagnosis was the basis for a finding that it would be manifestly unjust to apply the three-strikes law and impose the maximum sentence of 14 years imprisonment without parole on a charge of aggravated armed robbery, instead allowing eligibility for parole after one-third of that sentence to be retained.

18.4.2 Youth Court

Recognition of the connection between those with FASD and the criminal justice system has been different in the Youth Court in New Zealand in both the pre- and post-*Pora* periods. In fact, diagnoses of FASD in the context of fitness to stand trial proceedings in the Youth Court were appearing from at least 2010 onward (e.g., *NZ Police v. NJ*, 2010; *NZ Police v. UP*, 2011; *R v. BMS*, 2010). That has continued to be the case with FASD being found a mental impairment without necessarily the criteria for intellectual disability (ID) also being established. In some of these cases, young persons were found unfit to stand trial as a result of their mental impairment (i.e., FASD) (e.g., *NZ Police v. KP*, 2017; *NZ Police v. MA*, 2016) but in other cases were found fit to proceed (e.g., *R v. CD*, 2020). FASD also was featuring in sentencing decisions as a reason for adopting a more therapeutic and less punitive approach in the interests of both the young person and the community, given what the FASD research had shown to be most effective in reducing recidivism (*NZ Police v. ED*, 2014). There were two reasons for this situation from this author's (FitzGerald's) point of view.

1. *Fitness to Stand Trial.* The first reason, which also is relevant in the context of adult courts, is that in 2004, the law regarding fitness to stand trial changed significantly. Until then, the only basis for finding a person unfit to stand trial for charges in New Zealand was if he or she had a mental disorder, which meant a mental illness in terms of our Mental Health legislation. Under the *Criminal Procedure (Mentally Impaired Persons) Act* of 2003, which came into force in September 2004, the definition of being unfit to stand trial meant a defendant who was unable, due to mental impairment, to conduct a defense or instruct

counsel to do so. The term "mental impairment" was left undefined in the Act intentionally so as to increase the range of the fitness provision to ensure people with intellectual disabilities were not excluded (see Collins, 2015, p. 816).

At the same time, the *Intellectual Disability (Compulsory Care and Rehabilitation) Act* of 2003 came into force, which provided disposition options for those who were found unfit on account of an ID, the definition of which included a person having a permanent mental impairment that became apparent during the developmental period and which resulted in significantly sub-average general intelligence of 70 or less, with a confidence level of not less than 95%, and significant deficits in adaptive functioning. However, by leaving mental impairment undefined, those with a significant mental health concern that did not satisfy the strict diagnostic criteria for mental disorder ID could be found unfit to stand trial.

Since 2004, the number of fitness cases this author (FitzGerald) has heard in Youth Court where a mental disorder was the mental impairment has been minimal and still in single digits, even after 16 years. The number of cases where the mental impairment was an ID as legally defined is larger but still small and has included young people with FASD. However, the number of young people who had a significant mental impairment that did not satisfy the legal definitions for either mental disorder or ID has been the greatest in number, and those with FASD in particular were represented in this group. Given the "Swiss cheese" nature of the brain damage caused by FASD, it has not been unusual for young people to present with intelligence quotients (IQs) above 70 with the 95% confidence level but whose adaptive functioning scores in several domains were in the extremely low range.

A serious problem for those with FASD who do not have ID is lack of access to adequate supports and services, whether these individuals are found fit or unfit. Although leaving the term mental impairment undefined has allowed people with a wide range of mental health concerns other than mental disorder or ID to be found unfit, adequate options for disposition are largely limited to those with a mental disorder or ID. To make matters worse, if a person found unfit does not have a mental disorder or ID and is not liable to be detained under a sentence of imprisonment (thus ruling out young people in Youth Court), the only order available to a court is to order their immediate release without any ability to impose any terms or conditions on such release. Therefore, for those with high and complex needs and risk factors that require managing, this often is a most unsatisfactory situation. Having been found unfit and in need of significant supports and services but not being mentally disordered or intellectually disabled, these individuals simply are released back to family or caregivers with no support provided. For persons with FASD who are not intellectually disabled, release without support usually means that after going through long, slow, complex fitness proceedings, whether they are found fit or unfit, there is nothing adequate or appropriate as a disposition option to meet their needs or manage risk. An issue that plagued fitness proceedings until the law was amended in 2018, particularly in the Youth Court, was the delay caused by the statutory requirement to hold the hearing to determine involvement in the alleged offending *before* the hearing to determine fitness. In a number of cases, the impact of FASD on a young person's cognitive functioning and serious memory deficits were reasons for charges being dismissed due to the delays that had occurred in such proceedings (see *NZ Police v. NL*, 2017; *NZ Police v. VT*, 2015).

2. *Solution-focused Justice.* The second reason for adopting a more therapeutic and less punitive approach regarding FASD is that from 2007 on, this author (FitzGerald) was presiding over a solution-focused court established in the Auckland Youth Court, known as the Intensive Monitoring Group (IMG), for young people at moderate to high risk of reoffending who had moderate to severe mental health concerns. The mental health criterion was not set with any foresight as to what would be revealed. What we in New Zealand refer to as "solution-focused" courts are the same as the "problem-solving" courts that developed out of Drug Courts started in the United States in the late 1980s. Solution-focused courts in New Zealand involve a non-adversarial, coordinated, inter-agency approach to the cases of young people who meet entry criteria. Many of those who qualified for the IMG were those who had gone through the fitness process and were found to have a mental impairment but however were found fit to stand trial and remain in the Youth Court. Young people with an FASD diagnosis were represented in this group. It also was significant that the Regional Youth Forensic Service (RYFS), which supported the IMG, was able to screen and assess for neurodevelopmental disabilities such as FASD. This was unlike the situation in the adult courts where the forensic service was focused on responding only to persons showing signs of acute mental illness.

   With the benefit of these assessments and input from members of the IMG court team, in particular the health, education, and social work professionals who did not have a direct voice in the conventional adversarial court process, an unmistakable pattern emerged. Alternative explanations were consistently provided for such things as repetitive bad behavior and non-compliance with rules. In addition, alternative options to the sanctions courts normally would impose for such behavior were being suggested, which were shown to be more effective in achieving the desired results. The epiphany these changes caused was a realization that the so-called indicators of criminal recidivism were identical to the indicators of FASD. Experience showed that by following the advice of those who understood the disability and providing structure, support, supervision, keeping things simple, and building on strengths ("the five S's"), remarkably positive change was possible. Other Youth Court judges have had similar experiences. As a result, the profile of FASD in the Youth Court has continued to increase steadily over the past 10 years in a number of respects.

Awareness of the many effects of FASD on young people, including communication disorders and learning disabilities, has prompted a lot of work in the Youth Court to cater to such needs. For example, providing communication assistance to those who need it and making adaptations in court processes has enabled all young people to participate in a meaningful way. Since 2015, work has been ongoing to modify the ways in which information is conveyed to young people so as to make it comprehensible and enable their proper participation in proceedings, with speech-language therapists now essential members of many Youth Court teams. Unlike the situation in adult courts, FASD diagnostic capacity has continued to grow in the Youth Court, with the necessary training provided to some in the Regional Youth Forensic Services. However, adequate capacity has not yet been established nationwide.

18.4.3 Sentencing

An FASD diagnosis has been a significant factor in sentencing decisions in Youth Court in a variety of ways. In all of the following examples, McGinn was the expert who diagnosed the FASD, whose evidence was accepted by the judges involved in reaching their decisions. McGinn was the expert in the vast majority of cases where evidence of FASD was provided to courts at all levels.

First, imposing a community-based therapeutic sentence as opposed to a residential order was preferred in some cases on the grounds that the high stress and over-stimulating conditions of a residence would cause ongoing agitation, worsen emotional volatility, and lead to youths with FASD mimicking antisocial behaviors. This change also was based on literature that showed punishment does not change brain-based behaviors, so young persons would not learn to behave appropriately through ongoing containment in a residence (*NZ Police v. ED*, 2014, supra). In fact, community-based therapeutic interventions that provide a high level of structure and support have been found to be much more effective with the FASD population than residential settings (*NZ Police v. KM*, 2019; *NZ Police v. MQ*, 2019; *NZ Police v. TM*, 2019).

Secondly, in some cases the FASD diagnosis was a reason to justify not transferring young people to adult courts for sentencing to imprisonment because punishment was known to be ineffective in changing behaviors of youths with FASD and likely would increase dangerousness. The provision of a high level of structure and support is much more effective (*NZ Police v. KM*, 2019; *NZ Police v. MQ*, 2019; *NZ Police v. TM*, 2019). A third reason was to explain why little, if any, weight could be assigned to deterrence (*NZ Police v. MQ*, 2019, supra).

Another significant reason for the different response to FASD in the Youth Court is found in the legislation that governs our Youth Justice system (i.e., *Oranga Tamariki Act* of 1989), which not only requires that victims' issues be addressed and young people are held accountable but also requires that young persons' well-being and best interests are a primary consideration and that the underlying causes of their offending are addressed. The scheme of the Act provides for individualized, tailored plans to be made that address all issues and support young people as they move forward on a positive crime-free pathway. The plans are able to be applied in a way that meets the individualized needs of young people with FASD, subject to supports and services being found. There have been numerous cases over the past 10 years or so where this has happened successfully for this population and where plans characterized by the five S's have been adopted.

18.5 Fetal Alcohol Spectrum Disorder and the Law in Canada

In Canada, criminal courts first began to recognize FASD, often by a different name, in the early 1990s. In 1995, a court sentencing an FASD offender accurately observed there were very few reported cases involving FASD (*R. v. Abou*, 1995). Even as recently as 2009, authors of an oft-cited scholarly article on Canadian criminal law noted that judges were only "starting to grapple with the problems presented by FASD throughout the criminal law" (Roach & Bailey, 2010, p. 2). Today, there are many hundreds of reported cases involving FASD, the vast majority of which involve the sentencing context. Besides sentencing, FASD also is relevant in at least four other contexts: threshold criminal responsibility, fitness to stand trial, bail, and admissibility of confessions.

18.5.1 Threshold Criminal Responsibility and Fitness to Stand Trial

In the 1990s, the Canadian *Criminal Code* (*Code*) (1985) was amended significantly with respect to crime and mental health. One change renamed the term "not guilty by reason of insanity" to "not criminally responsible" (NCR). Despite the name change, the idea is still rooted in the same concept as competence to stand trial in the United States, and both are based upon the historic McNaughten test imported from Britain in the 1800s. In Canada, accused persons are presumed to not suffer from a mental disorder. However, section 16 (1) of the *Code* states:

> No person is criminally responsible for an act committed or an omission made while suffering from a mental disorder that rendered the person incapable of appreciating the nature and quality of the act or omission or of knowing that it was wrong.

A similar but different test is applied to determine fitness to stand trial. Section 2 of the *Code* states:

> …*unfit to stand trial* means unable on account of mental disorder to conduct a defence at any stage of the proceedings before a verdict is rendered or to instruct counsel to do so, and, in particular, unable on account of mental disorder to (a) understand the nature or object of the proceedings, (b) understand the possible consequences of the proceedings, or (c) communicate with counsel…

Both tests require that incompetency or inability be based upon a 'mental disorder.'

Courts in Canada never have had difficulty in finding that FASD constitutes a mental disorder. That said, it would be rare for a diagnosis of FASD alone to support a finding of NCR because rarely would FASD alone deprive one of capacity to know right from wrong or appreciate the nature and quality of one's actions.[4] It is more common to find cases in which FASD has been found to support a finding of unfitness to stand trial, although in most of those cases there also is a contributing comorbid condition, and the finding usually is based upon inability to effectively communicate with counsel (e.g., *R. v. Dewhurst*, 2009). The test that generally is accepted when assessing fitness is described as a *limited cognitive capacity test*, which is quite a low standard (see *R. v. Taylor*, 1992). Absent extreme cognitive impairment, a person with FASD rarely will meet this test, which requires only an ability to relate facts, no analytical ability (*R. v. Jobb*, 2008).

Compared to the United States, there are very few cases in Canada where an NCR or unfitness finding is sought by defense, which likely is due primarily to the fact there is no death penalty in Canada. In many cases, even when jail is a likely outcome in the event no finding of NCR is made, defense counsel will choose not to pursue an NCR finding because a successful application runs the risk of an indeterminate restriction of liberty, potentially for a longer period of time than an offender might serve in a jail sentence.

18.5.2 Bail

There is a presumption in Canada that persons accused of crimes should be released from custody pending trial unless charges are in a defined serious category of offenses, they have demonstrated they are not likely appearing in court if released, or there is a substantial likelihood of offending if released. Persons with FASD typically are poor candidates for release pending trial because they often have a history of breaching court orders or failing to appear in court or both. There is little recorded case law that addresses FASD in relation to bail, partly because these matters involve interim applications where decisions must be made quickly, most often in docket courts. However, persons with FASD appear in bail hearings every day across the country.

Two practices are important for helping people with FASD at bail hearings. First, it is important that judges be made aware of the disorder with as much supporting documentation and relevant evidence as possible. This process goes a long way in showing that an accused person's track record is not simply a matter of indifference to court orders but rather adaptive impairment due to a medical condition. The second practice, which is most critical, is to present a plan showing the accused person will have assistance in the community that involves structure, support for staying

[4] *R. v. C.P.F.*, 2006, is an example of where the defence was advanced unsuccessfully; *R. v. Elias*, 2010, is one of the few cases where a lack of fitness was found in part due to the diagnosis of alcohol-related neurodevelopmental disorder (ARND).

focused on release conditions, and help with appointments (e.g., *R. v. T.J.J.*, 2011). It also is not lost on judges that in many cases, persons with FASD often are quite vulnerable in prisons. In other words, safety while on remand is a legitimate consideration (e.g., *R. v. J.H.B.*, 2012).

Going forward, a recent amendment to the *Criminal Code* likely will help persons with FASD in the bail context. Although the amendment does not specifically reference FASD, it does instruct judges and peace officers responsible for deciding whether accused persons should be released to "give particular attention to the circumstances of (a) Aboriginal accused, and (b) accused who belong to a vulnerable population that is over-represented in the criminal justice system and who is disadvantaged in obtaining release under the Part" (Canada, Code, 1985, Section 493.1 *CC*; hereafter *CC*). The latter provision, and possible the first as well, applies to persons with FASD.

18.5.3 Confessions

As already mentioned—and exemplified in the *Pora* decision—people with FASD can be very suggestible or gullible and prone to confabulation, which makes them vulnerable to giving false or exaggerated confessions. In Canada, the "confessions rule" has been expanded over time to include factors such as whether voluntariness was overcome by oppressive circumstances, whether a statement was the product of an operating mind (which simply requires accused persons to understand what they are saying and that they are making statements to police officers who can use such statements to their detriment), and whether, in a few cases, police trickery was involved. The leading authority regarding admissibility of confessions in Canada is *R. v. Oickle* (2000), which emphasizes that when a court is considering whether to admit a statement into evidence, the court must look at the totality of circumstances. Clearly, FASD is a relevant circumstance.

Another area where FASD sometimes underlies applications to exclude self-incriminating evidence is in the context of "Mr. Big scenarios," which often are used by Canadian police to elicit confessions to undercover officers. Under such scenarios, police lead a target into a relationship with an undercover agent posing as an important figure in an organized crime organization. The target person is told that in order to make sure he is worthy of membership in the criminal organization, he will have to confess something serious to "the boss," another undercover agent. Often, persons with FASD are easily manipulated under such a scenario. Courts have not found this police tactic is inherently improper but have excluded confessions in circumstances where there is blatant unfairness or doubt about whether the confession is true versus confabulation or bravado (see *R. v. J.C.*, 2015; *R. v. J.J.G.*, 2015; *R. v. N.R.R.*, 2013).

18.5.4 Sentencing

A few basic observations about sentencing in Canada may help to put the courts' treatment of FASD into context. In Canada, most criminal law is codified in the *Criminal Code*, which applies across the country. This includes a limited number of sentencing provisions that all judges must follow. The *Code* sets out the relevant purpose, principles, and objectives of sentencing that judges must apply and prescribes maximum sentences for all offenses and minimum sentences for a few. Beyond that, guidelines and precedents are established by judges. There are no sentencing grids. Relative to other jurisdictions, sentencing judges in Canada have a great deal of latitude.

The cardinal principle in Canadian sentencing law is proportionality: "A sentence must be proportionate to the gravity of the offence and the degree of responsibility of the offender" (S. 718. 1 *CC*). Aggravating and mitigating factors must be considered (S. 718 *CC*). A second principle is parity, which means "a sentence should be similar to sentences imposed on similar offenders for similar offences committed in similar circumstances" (S. 718. 2(b) *CC*). The *Code* also incorporates the principle of restraint by providing in S. 718.2(d):

> an offender should not be deprived of liberty, if less restrictive sanctions may be appropriate in the circumstances; and (e) all available sanctions, other than imprisonment, that are reasonable in the circumstances and consistent with the harm done to victims or to the community should be considered for all offenders, with particular attention to the circumstances of Aboriginal offenders.

Judges are directed to consider specified objectives, which in part include denouncing unlawful conduct, deterring offenders and other persons from committing offenses, supporting offender rehabilitation, and where necessary, separating offenders from society (S. 718 *CC*).

Three additional factors are important in Canadian sentencing law and potentially important to offenders with FASD. First, if jail sentences are less than 2 years, then a period of probation can be added, but there is no such option for sentences of over 2 years that must be served in a federal penitentiary. Sometimes, courts will adjust sentences one way or the other to allow access to programming that might exist in a particular setting. Second, unique to Canada is the option in some cases to allow sentences to be served in the community rather than jail, subject to strict conditions under a Conditional Sentence Order. Third, a body of law has developed in relation to the sentencing of Indigenous offenders, which flows from the reference to "particular attention to the circumstances of Aboriginal offenders" in s. 718.2(e) above. In a case named *R. v. Gladue* (1999),[5] the Supreme Court noted the over-incarceration of Indigenous people and set factors judges must consider when crafting sentences, factors that recognize the systemic intergenerational effects of colonialism. Thus, references to "Gladue factors" have entered the lexicon of

[5] *R v. Gladue* (1999), later reinforced in *R. v. Ipeelee* (2012).

sentencing law in Canada, and it is not uncommon to see FASD dealt with in conjunction with Gladue factors.

18.5.5 Proportionality: Fetal Alcohol Spectrum Disorder as a Mitigating Factor

It now is well established that FASD will be considered a mitigating factor by sentencing courts, thereby reducing moral blameworthiness. At least six Courts of Appeal in Canada have now expressly confirmed this principle.[6] However, there are at least two strong caveats that run through all these authorities: (a) there must be a basis to support diagnosis, and (b) the court must be able to connect the condition to offense conduct. In *R. v. Ramsay* (2012), the Court emphasized the importance of expert evidence that allows courts to put the relevance of FASD into proper context, stating at paragraph 16:

> Crafting a fit sentence for an offender with the cognitive deficits associated with FASD presents at least two identifiable challenges: accurately assessing the moral blameworthiness of the offender in light of the adverse cognitive effects of FASD; and balancing protection of the public against the feasibility of reintegrating the offender into the community through a structured program under adequate supervision. Medical reports assessing the prospect of the offender's rehabilitation and reintegration into the community are essential to the task and must be carefully analyzed.

The court went on at paragraph 25 to address FASD in the context of proportionality:

> The degree of moral blameworthiness must therefore be commensurate with the magnitude of the cognitive deficits attributable to FASD. The more acute these are shown to be, the greater their importance as mitigating factors and the less weight is to be accorded to deterrence and denunciation, all of which will serve to "push the sentence … down the scale of appropriate sentences for similar offences.[7]

This sliding scale approach has been cited by many later authorities, including several courts of appeal. However, one of the risks in this approach is a potential for courts to look for an easily measurable feature, such as IQ, losing sight of the fact that FASD is a diffuse brain injury wherein multiple domains are affected.

The extent to which an FASD diagnosis is apt to result in sentence reduction based on diminished responsibility will vary from case to case, but it is fair to say that courts have not simply paid lip service to FASD as a mitigating factor. For example, in the recent decision of *R. v. J.P.* (2020), in which the accused person with FASD had conscripted his juvenile nephew's assistance with two robberies, the

[6] See *R. v. R.B.N.* 1190 Canlii 5416, *R. v. Ramsay* (2012) ABCA 257, *R. v. Charlie* (2015) YKCA 3, *R. v. Friesen* (2016) MBCA 50, *R v. Manitowabi*, 2014 ONCA 301 and most recently, *R. v. J.P.* (2020) SKCA 52.

[7] To review the careful application of this sliding scale to an especially severe case of FASD, see *R. v. F.C.* (2012) YKCA 5, at paras. 24-29, 38-43, [2012] 2 CNLR 184.

sentencing judge did not find the offender's FASD to be mitigating, but the Court of Appeal disagreed and reduced the sentence by 2 years. In the *Friesen* decision, the Court of Appeal reduced a manslaughter sentence from 6 to 4 years due to FASD (*R. v. Friesen*, 2016). In *Ramsay*, supra, the sentence was not changed upon appeal, but both courts found the neurological deficits in FASD should reduce the sentence by 3.5–5 years from what the prosecution had sought. In *R. v. Ramalho* (2004), the FASD diagnosis resulted in a Conditional Sentence Order being imposed instead of jail. In *R. v. Soosay* (2012), one of the author's decisions, prosecution sought a global sentence of 33 months in the penitentiary for two robberies and a break-and-enter offense, but the Court imposed an 8-month jail sentence, most of which was served by the time of sentence, followed by a short Conditional Sentence Order and probation.

While cases where FASD has been found to reduce moral culpability are plentiful, there also are cases wherein courts have declined to find reduced culpability, either because the defense was unable to show the behavior at issue was connected to the disorder, or there was no formal diagnosis. Two blunt examples of a court declining to find mitigation absent a report, even where indicia were present, can be found in *R. v. Halversen* (2020) and *R. v. Joamie* (2013). In some cases where circumstances point to FASD, but there is no formal diagnosis, courts still will proceed on the assumption that the disorder applies (e.g., see *R. v. Brown*, 2014; *R. v. C.O.*, 2006; *R. v. Green*, 2013; *R. v. Morgan*, 2013). It is an error to judicially diagnose an FASD (*R. v. Harris*, 2002), but it also would be an error to simply ignore a relevant fact.

18.5.6 Denunciation and Deterrence

Apart from reducing moral blameworthiness, a finding of FASD can operate to reduce, if not displace, the relevance of denunciation and deterrence as objectives. Particularly where evidence finds that an offender is unable to learn from mistakes, control impulses, or connect actions to consequences, denunciation and deterrence are less likely to be given weight. This is particularly so with respect to specific deterrence, which is aimed at reducing recidivism. In most cases where an offender keeps reoffending, a court will apply the *step principle* or *jump principle* by progressively increasing sentences. However, applying this principle to people who cannot connect their offense behavior with sentencing consequences serves no purpose other than locking the person up.

The effect of FASD on the notion of general deterrence, which does not involve the sentence's message to the offender but rather to the public and others of like mind, is less clear-cut. Most courts are loathe to say there is no room for general deterrence, but the emphasis on general deterrence usually will be tempered by an FASD diagnosis. There certainly is no room for an exemplary sentence. As stated in *R. v. Abou* (1995), "it is simply obscene to suggest that a court can properly warn other potential offenders by inflicting a form of punishment upon a handicapped person" (see also *R. v. Ayorech*, 2002; *R. v. Resler*, 2011).

18.5.7 Rehabilitation

There are cases in Canada in which courts have placed little weight on rehabilitation as a factor based on the idea that FASD is not curable or is a life-long disability. Although judges still hear this argument periodically, fortunately these notions have been discredited. The most recent denunciation of such thinking can be found in *J.P.*, supra, discussed above in the context of proportionality. *J.P.* found the sentencing judge was wrong in concluding that rehabilitation only applied when offense behavior was due to curable conditions. Specifically, the higher court found that "the idea of rehabilitation as a sentencing objective has broader meaning than that accorded by the judge" (*R. v. J.P.*, 2020, supra, note 41, at para. 58) and followed another Court of Appeal decision *R. v. Friesen* (2016), supra, to find (para. 36), "Rehabilitation is not limited to the traditional view of correcting the accused's attitude to prevent him from recidivating. It can also deal with finding a way to control and modify the behaviour." Two other decisions that explain how the objective of rehabilitation should apply when sentencing offenders with FASD are *R. v. Charlie* (2015) and *R. v. Kendi* (2011, at para. 11).

18.5.8 Parity in Sentencing

It sometimes is argued that reducing a sentence due to FASD can result in disparate sentences. However, the Canadian Supreme Court has pointed out in the seminal case of *R. v. Ipeelee* (2012, paras. 78–79) that parity does not mean all sentences for similar behavior must be the same but rather there must be a reason for dissimilarity. FASD, if linked to the offending conduct, almost always will be a compelling reason to individualize the sentence.

18.5.9 Dangerous Offenders

There is no question that safety of the community will in many cases trump all other sentencing objectives. In cases where an offender is clearly dangerous, a court may have no choice but to separate the offender from society for a long period of time, even if the reason for dangerousness is beyond the offender's control. In Canada, there is a provision that allows a court to designate a person as a 'dangerous offender,' which may result in an indeterminate jail sentence (Section 753 *CC*). This designation is rare and would not be made without a lengthy hearing and full psychiatric assessment. Unfortunately, the designation has been applied to many offenders with FASD.

When a person is found to be a dangerous offender, an indeterminate sentence is not automatic. For example, a court might impose a determinate sentence combined with a Long Term Offender Order (LTO), which would allow for extremely close and lengthy monitoring following release. In this context, evidence showing an offender can be treated and managed in the community is paramount. See *R. v. M* (2000) for an example of how a court was persuaded that FASD was sufficiently manageable in the community to warrant LTO designation rather than an indeterminate sentence (see also *R. v. Keenatch*, 2019).

18.6 Fetal Alcohol Spectrum Disorder and the Law in the United States

FASD began to present in US courts in the early to mid-1990s as fetal alcohol syndrome (FAS), partial fetal alcohol syndrome (pFAS), and fetal alcohol effects (FAE). In 1994, the Florida Supreme Court recognized the relevance of maternal consumption of alcohol in utero and its dilatory effects upon a developing fetus in *Dillbeck v. State* (1994). In the late 1990s, the Governor of the State of Washington recognized the potential impact of FASD on state resources and created an Advisory Panel on FAS/FAE, chaired by one of this chapter's authors. Consistent with the principles articulated in *Ruzic*, supra, is the discussion in *Dillbeck v. State* (1994):

> Evidence concerning certain alcohol related conditions has long been admissible during the guilt phases of criminal proceedings to show lack of specific intent (and diminished capacity) … (I)f evidence of a self-induced condition such as voluntary intoxication is admissible then so too should be evidence of other commonly understood conditions that are beyond one's control such as epilepsy … Just as the harmful effect of alcohol on the mature brain of an adult imbiber is a matter within the common understanding, so too is the detrimental effect of this intoxicant on the delicate, evolving brain of a fetus held in utero. As with 'epilepsy, infancy or senility,' … we can envision few things more certainly beyond one's control than the drinking habits of a parent prior to one's birth. We perceive no significant legal distinction between the condition of epilepsy … and that with alcohol related brain damage in issue here (as) both are specific commonly recognized conditions that are beyond one's control. (*Dillbeck v. State*, 1994, p. 217)

In 2000, the *Diagnostic and Statistical Manual of Mental Disorders*, fourth edition, text revision (*DSM-IV-TR*; American Psychiatric Association [APA], 2000), recognized FASD was a factor in ID but did not contain a specific mental disorder for the central nervous system (CNS) dysfunction in FASD. The absence of a specific disorder in *DSM-IV-TR* resulted in mental health professionals diagnosing *cognitive disorder not otherwise specified.* This omission was addressed in *Diagnostic and Statistical Manual of Mental Disorders*, fifth edition (*DSM-5*; American Psychiatric Association [APA], 2013), which contained the diagnosis *neurodevelopmental disorder associated with prenatal alcohol disorder* (*ND-PAE*). With ND-PAE, mental health professionals were able to diagnose CNS dysfunction in FASD. *DSM-5* also converted the diagnosis "mental retardation" to "intellectual disability," which is relevant to the subject of FASD.

18.6.1 Effective Advocacy and Presentation of Forensic Evidence

Forensic experts often apply science to answer referral questions and provide facts that are developed and relied upon as evidence. In so doing, forensic experts help judges and juries better understand psycho-legal issues relevant to cases. Although the discussion that follows is based upon experience in US courts, the information applies equally to New Zealand and Canada.

Providing effective advocacy and presentation of effective forensic evidence starts the moment a case first comes to the attention of defense counsel. Capital defense lawyer Cyndy Short (2004) notes:

> What is the formula for success? First, you must form teams that are collaborative in nature and in fact. We must seek a wide array of voices and opinions to challenge our point of view, both lawyers and non-lawyers. We must seek the right resources to help us know the client and all his complexities. We must find a way to infiltrate his world so we can put his experiences into the proper context … We must tell our story from the first witness who takes the witness stand after voir dire to the last witness who testifies before the penalty phase closing. (Short, 2004, p. 8)

This perspective is on point. By its very nature, guilt-innocence and mitigation issues are intertwined, requiring counsel in both processes to engage in close working relationships. There is no reason to represent capital or other criminal defense clients differently under today's bifurcated trial system in the USA (Wartnik, 2011). Yet, many capital defense teams are "teams" in name only. One lawyer prepares guilt/innocence defense, and the other prepares mitigation, as if the two processes involve separate cases … never do the twain meet. This approach does disservice to clients and seriously jeopardizes potential for successful presentation of both guilt-innocence and mitigation phases. One way to bridge the divide is through multidisciplinary teams of diagnostic experts, which happens to be a very effective way to present expert testimony in FASD cases.

18.6.2 Mitigation

The process of developing mitigation evidence in a case must start early to maximize success in educating prosecutors so as to preclude filing or facilitate withdrawal of "death penalty notices." Mitigation also must start early if there is any hope of influencing favorable evidentiary rulings by judges once proceedings begin. This advice is particularly important in cases involving lesser known (and misunderstood) conditions such as FASD, where a number of evidentiary challenges are likely. Challenges may include competency to stand trial (CST), competency to waive Miranda rights, and competency to waive certain trial rights.

Building a team in capital cases begins with bringing mitigation specialists on board at the beginning of a case, so informed decisions can be made expeditiously regarding choices of experts. For example, should individual experts be retained, or does a case require an ensemble team of experts who are accustomed to working together and have established protocols that are compliant with evidentiary rules governing admission of expert testimony (i.e., Daubert or Frye)? Because FASD assessment is somewhat complex and involves both medical and mental health criteria, multiple experts likely are necessary in high-stakes cases. For example, at least one medical expert is needed to assess physiological characteristics such as facial abnormalities and growth deficit as well as order and evaluate neuroimaging evidence (e.g., magnetic resonance imaging, quantitative electroencephalography, diffusion tensor imaging). Psychologists are necessary to administer psychological testing, conduct adaptive assessments, and review all documented information about a defendant's lifelong functioning (including offense conduct) to determine consistency with FASD.

A medical diagnosis only addresses whether a defendant has an FASD, which may be fetal alcohol syndrome (FAS), partial FAS (pFAS), or alcohol-related neurodevelopmental disorder (ARND) under Institute of Medicine guidelines (Institute of Medicine [IOM], 1996; Novick Brown, Wartnik, Connor, & Adler, 2010). In cases using the 4-Digit Code (Astley, 2004), ARND is diagnosed as either static-encephalopathy/alcohol exposed (SE/AE) or neurobehavioral disorder/alcohol exposed (ND/AE). SE/AE is equivalent to severe ARND, and ND/AE is equivalent to moderate ARND (Astley, 2013). In cases involving FASD, psychologists or psychiatrists may address mental state, which as noted is diagnosed as ND-PAE under *DSM-5*, and also may address comorbidities. Psychologists may provide objective test data regarding cognitive limitations and volitional capacity. Psychologists also may assess competency (e.g., CST, Miranda waiver) and address the "nexus" (i.e., poignant connection between FASD diagnosis and subject criminal behavior). The nexus is at the heart of the principle articulated by the court in *Ruzic*, supra, and the judicially recognized reality of FASD articulated by the Supreme Court of Florida in *Dillbeck*, supra.

To date, there has been no challenge to a peer-reviewed model for assessing FASD in the forensic context (Novick Brown et al., 2010), which involves a multidisciplinary team comprised of at least three independent FASD experts (i.e., medical doctor, neuropsychologist, and psychologist), each of whom conducts an assessment in his/her respective field of specialization. Review of capital caselaw involving a collaborative multidisciplinary team (often referred to as the *gold standard*) versus single experts shows the former is the more effective approach. Of course, where offense category and indigent defense funding constraints preclude the expense of multidisciplinary teams, single practitioners also can be effective, particularly with *DSM-5*. In such cases, diagnostic focus on mental state (e.g., neuropsychological testing with adaptive assessment and ND-PAE diagnosis) and either competency assessment or nexus analysis are key.

Referral question(s) provided to forensic experts frame the general direction of the diagnostic assessment process. Therefore, questions must be crafted carefully to address critical factors that support development of effective presentations. Just because a particular defendant has an FASD does not automatically establish a basis for determining he or she lacks capacity to form mens rea. Similarly, an FASD diagnosis alone is insufficient to justify mitigation at sentencing. In order to effectively present a sound basis for verdicts of not guilty due to lack of mens rea or diminished capacity as well as a finding that the disorder constitutes mitigation at sentencing, it is necessary for forensic experts to clearly explain, in terms understandable to the trier of fact, the nexus between the disorder and criminal behavior(s) at issue. Such testimony can properly prioritize the brain damage in FASD over potentially misleading comorbidities that may be present. A case in point is *Williams v. Stirling* (2019), which is discussed later.

Effective expert testimony requires strict adherence to local evidentiary rules governing admission of such testimony (e.g., Daubert, Frye, hybrid of the two). Adherence to evidentiary rules affords protection against prosecutorial allegations that protocols used in the diagnostic process constitute "junk science," which may compel a judicial decision to deny or reject such evidence. Although the junk science objection rarely arises anymore due to the robust nature of FASD science, counsel and experts should be alert to the possibility as a last ditch effort by the prosecution when all else has failed.

18.6.3 Competency to Stand Trial

The first issue likely to be raised once a charge has been filed may be concern on the part of counsel or the court regarding a defendant's CST. In fact, this concern may arise even before counsel becomes aware of facts suggesting a need for FASD investigation. Whenever a CST concern manifests during case proceedings, judges will either order a competency evaluation or authorize funding for such an evaluation. Whoever initiates the process (i.e., defense counsel or judge) usually formulates specific referral question(s) to be answered by an expert. Framing the referral question(s) needs special care in the case of possible FASD (i.e., factors that may make a defendant incompetent must be linked due to the disorder).

When a forensic expert determines a defendant appears incompetent to stand trial, it is defense counsel's responsibility to ensure the judge is educated—not only about the specific factors constituting presumed incompetency but also about the reason for those factors (i.e., FASD). Some judges perceive defendants are competent if they are oriented to time and place and little more. A technique that has proven successful in educating judges about the factors in FASD that compromise CST is for defense counsel to ask questions of experts that are aimed at dispelling myths and misconceptions judges may hold about FASD. Properly presented, experts also can provide illustrative examples of conduct that may at first blush cause judges to think defendants are competent (e.g., driving a car, completing high school with special education services, holding entry-level jobs) but in fact are misleading. Lay witnesses (e.g., teachers, coaches, therapists) can add poignant testimony about firsthand observations of defendants struggling with routine tasks in the community to contextualize and support expert testimony. Counsel will need to proactively explore all areas where a client's relative strengths might be misleading, as one or more of these areas likely will be raised by the prosecution. For example, if a client plays chess, it would be helpful to have the evaluating expert testify that young children are able to play chess, perhaps using a PowerPoint slide depicting an 8-year-old child sitting in front of a chess board.

Standards for competence to stand trial were set by the Supreme Court in *Dusky v. U.S.* (1960), supra. *Dusky* determined the test for competence was whether a defendant had "sufficient present ability to consult with his(/her) lawyer with a reasonable degree of rational understanding, and whether he(/she) has a rational as well as factual understanding of the proceedings against him(/her)." In *Drope v. Missouri* (1975), the Court added an additional prong to the test by requiring defendants also must be able to assist in preparing the defense. Thus, to be competent in the United States, a defendant must be able to (1) consult with a lawyer with a reasonable degree of rational understanding, (2) otherwise assist in the defense, (3) have a rational understanding of the criminal proceedings, and (4) have a factual understanding of the proceedings (White, Meares, & Batchelor, 2014). Incompetence may be due to a change in mental status or additional information that has become known, such as information about functional impairments (Brown, Carter, Haun, Wartnik, & Zapf, 2019).

An important case with respect to CST and FASD is *U.S. v. Duhon* (2000). Authored by a U.S. District Court magistrate in the context of whether a man with mild ID could be restored to competency, the Court found that while restoration therapy might improve capacity to "rote" learn and recite factual legal information, this type of learning was insufficient to establish competence in someone with permanent brain damage. Rather, competence required *rational* understanding of the legal process with ability to apply factual knowledge, not just recite it. This case demonstrates that the permanent brain damage found in persons with FASD as well as ID makes it highly unlikely restoration treatment will produce competency.

18.6.4 Intellectual Disability

Persons with FASD may have comorbid ID, even when IQs are above 70. For defendants in this category, it is important for experts to apply the 5-point standard error of measurement (SEM) to the obtained IQ score and also use the Flynn correction (i.e., downward adjustment of IQ by −0.3 points per year since the year the IQ test was developed). During testimony, experts should explain the lack of precision in test scores, including why it is the standard of practice in mental health to adjust test scores using the SEM as well as the Flynn correction for test obsolescence. See *Hall v. State* (2014) for a cogent analysis of IQ score imprecision and why applying the SEM is essential.

Another effective way to support an ID diagnosis in defendants with FASD and IQs over 70 (+/– 5 points) requires assessment of adaptive functioning, which quantifies performance levels in communication, practical, and social skills that include age equivalencies. For example, based upon such assessment, a defendant with FASD and an IQ of 81 might be equivalent functionally to a 7-year-old child in terms of receptive and expressive communication skills, which is highly relevant to CST. This approach might be used in conjunction with the analysis in *Roper v. Simmons* (2005) and applicable state law involving child capacity to commit crimes. Child capacity is part of our common law, which has been recognized in many states by statute and case law. For example, in Washington State, *State v. Ramer* (2004) discusses RCW 9A.04.050, its child capacity statute, and the seven child capacity criteria as they relate to an adult defendant with FASD: (1) nature of the crime, (2) age and maturity, (3) whether the person evidences a desire for secrecy, (4) whether the person told the victim not to tell (if applicable), (5) whether the person engaged in prior conduct similar to that charged, (6) any consequences attached to such prior conduct, and (7) whether the person made any statements acknowledging his/her behavior was wrong and could lead to detention (note 68). This approach works very well as a way to "connect the dots" following testimony regarding a defendant's adaptive behavior deficits and intellectual performance. [See Chap. 8 in this book for detailed information about adaptive assessment.]

18.6.5 Suggestibility, Confabulation, and False Confession

A study of defendants with ID found 41 individuals who had confessed to crimes they did not commit later were exonerated (Smith, Palloway, Patton, & Beyer, 2008). The study's authors concluded that people with ID were easily manipulated—an issue that is not included in screening tools that measure adaptive behaviors. Susceptibility to suggestibility presents particular problems for defendants with FASD, whether or not they have comorbid ID. Impairments in FASD, particularly executive function deficits and associated social dysfunction, may lead to false confessions or exaggerated confessions where impaired defendants assume more criminal responsibility than is warranted in misguided efforts to protect codefendants. Memory impairments and suggestibility also may result in factual admissions or inconsistencies presumed to be associated with guilt, which create the potential that evidence of innocence will be ineffective with the jury, thereby reducing the possibility of a not guilty verdict. An inherent obstacle in the context of suggestion and confabulation is that US judges and jurors believe strongly in the integrity of law enforcement interrogation as well as the accuracy of overtly voluntary admissions and confessions. Unless interrogations are videotaped, it often is impossible to analyze the nature of questioning that elicited defendant responses.

A good example of the suggestibility problem is found in Cyntoia Brown v. Tennessee (2014). Despite Brown's IQ of 134, her ARND diagnosis was associated with a high level of suggestibility (Novick Brown, Gudjonsson, & Connor, 2011), which led trial counsel to recommend she not testify due to the likelihood she would be led during cross-examination to make statements inconsistent with her police statement. Experts involved in the case indicated that because of the memory and communication deficits in her ARND, Brown was highly inclined to confabulate. Notably, in trial settings, habeas corpus hearings, and hearings on petitions for post-trial relief, presentation of the type of evidence presented by the multidisciplinary team in *Cyntoia Brown* has been demonstratively effective.

Finally, a must-read case is *in re: S.M.S, a Youth*, 2010 MT 18 (S. Ct. of Montana, 2010). S.M.S., a juvenile, was arrested and questioned by police without notice to or the presence of his parent pursuant to a statute permitting such interrogation. During questioning, S.M.S. confessed to a sexual offense involving a younger child. Although the Supreme Court of Montana reviewed the interrogation video, the court issued an opinion that found the police officer's actions appropriate but failed to address whether the officer used leading questions. Testimony regarding the severity of S.M.S.'s FASD-associated cognitive impairments was challenged by the State's expert, and the Court concluded S.M.S.'s confession was voluntary without addressing whether it had been given knowingly and intelligently.

18.6.6 Sentencing

Effectiveness in presenting evidence and recommendations directed at obtaining successful sentencing decisions requires that experts have clear understanding of sentencing laws in case jurisdictions. It is the court's responsibility to make protection of public safety the first priority in sentencing. This priority requires defense counsel to provide courts with assurance that sentences permitting defendants to remain in the community or serve a minimum time in custody are reasonable and appropriate. This "reasonable and appropriate" requirement means sentences must meet the community safety standard as well as serve the best interests of society and defendants. To be effective, defense counsel depend upon testimony from experienced expert witnesses. Experts must be able to explain clearly and in detail that defendants do not present future risk to the community. Experts also must explain why defendants would not present a danger to the community if provided services, providing treatment plans with recommendations of services to reduce risk.

Bail

There are two vehicles in the United States by which defendants may be authorized to remain in the community pending prosecution. First, defendants may be released on personal recognizance, which is based upon certain conditions that include promising to return to court as directed, not being arrested for a new crime, and not having contact with the alleged victim of the charged crime. Second, courts may offer the option of release pending trial under specific conduct conditions, subject to bail paid either in cash or by property bond (e.g., real estate, stocks, bonds). When defendants with FASD are released on either personal recognizance or posting of bail, capacity to abide by court-ordered conditions of conduct largely depends upon their understanding of bail conditions and whether they have support systems for assistance and guidance. To maximize understanding and compliance, conditions should be stated in clear, simple, concrete terms that avoid abstract concepts.

18.6.7 Solution-Focused Justice and Treatment Courts

Treatment courts in the United States use a carrot-or-the-stick approach to divert juvenile offenders and adult defendants out of the criminal justice system. The inducement offered to offenders is that their crimes will be dismissed upon successful completion of specific court-ordered treatments (the carrot). Under this agreement, offenders agree to waive trial and go directly to sentencing if they fail to complete required treatments (the stick). With respect to defendants with FASD who are offered diversion, it is important that the treatment programs use FASD-informed protocols designed to accommodate the learning and adaptive deficits in this population. Otherwise, these defendants likely will get "the stick" because of impairments they have no control over.

18.6.8 Death Penalty

Of the three common law countries we have focused on in this chapter, the United States is the only one that permits defendants who commit capital offenses to be sentenced to death. In 2003, the Supreme Court's decision in *Atkins v. Virginia* (2002), supra, precluded the death penalty for persons with ID, indicating such a penalty would constitute cruel and unusual punishment under the Constitution's Eighth Amendment. However, the Supreme Court left it to the individual states to define ID (referred to as "mental retardation" [MR] at the time of *Atkins*) and establish methodologies for implementing *Atkins*. As a result, states adopted a variety of definitions of MR/ID, which created a situation of unequal justice among the states. For example, a defendant convicted of a capital offense with an IQ of 75 could be found to have MR/ID in one state but not in another state. The defendant would not be subject to the death penalty in the former state but could be executed in the latter state.

The above predicament was caused by some states excluding adaptive behavior deficits from consideration unless the IQ prong was first met. Other states required concurrent consideration of adaptive deficits and IQ but varied with respect to the cutoff point in IQ score (e.g., 70 versus 75). In 2013, *DSM-5* changed the name, definition, and criteria for ID, requiring concurrent consideration of IQ and adaptive behavior deficits and defining "intellectual" functioning as mostly executive function abilities. The Supreme Court in *Hall v. State* (2014), supra, adopted *DSM-5* changes, finding an IQ score was inherently imprecise and subject to adjustment with the SEM and stating at page 7:

> The question this case presents is how intellectual disability must be defined in order to implement these principles and the holding of *Atkins*. To determine if Florida's (IQ score) cutoff rule is valid, it is proper to consider the psychiatric and professional studies that elaborate on the purpose and meaning of IQ scores to determine how the scores relate to the holding of *Atkins*.

Many cases have reinforced the ruling in *Hall*, supra, and refined how courts handle ID (e.g., *Brumfield v. Cain*, 2015; *Webster v. Warden*, 2015; *Moore v. Texas*, 2017, 2019; *Lane v. Alabama*, 2019; *White v. Kentucky*, 2019; and *Williams v. Stirling*, 2019, supra, note 72). *Williams*, in particular, is significant as it involves comorbid ID in the context of underlying FASD. In this case, the Fourth District Court of Appeals found FASD was a brain-based disorder with cause-and-effect implications regarding offense conduct. [See Chap. 2 for more discussion about this case.]

Three years after *Atkins*, the Supreme Court ruled in *Roper v. Simmons* (2005), supra, that juveniles under age 18 could not be executed as this violated the Constitutional prohibition against cruel and unusual punishment in that juveniles lacked maturity and responsibility due to immature brain development. This case has important implications in the context of FASD, where according to research, brain development is delayed significantly (Treit et al., 2013). Thus, the brain of a 25-year-old with FASD likely is years away from mature development.

18.7 Conclusion

Our criminal courts are the vehicles through which people who have offended against society are held to account. There are both substantive and procedural differences from one country to the next and in the case of the United States, from one state to the next. However, to the extent possible, judges in all jurisdictions try to come up with just results. FASD is a spectrum of disorders that challenges the courts in a unique way. FASD often is invisible—masked or overshadowed by other disorders. FASD defies and belies some of the most fundamental tenets of our traditional justice systems. It often is difficult to access resources to both identify and respond effectively to the condition. And, we are learning it is far more prevalent than we ever would have imagined only a decade ago.

It would be unrealistic to think there ever will be a magic bullet to solve the many problems posed by FASD, but we all must do what we can. We need more capacity to diagnose. We need more widespread understanding of relevant issues at all levels. We need courts to follow the science and where old assumptions are shown to be wrong, set them aside. Perhaps most importantly, professionals in legal systems and in the medical community need to work together so that when people are being held to account for their actions, responses are always based upon fact and not assumptions.

References

American Psychiatric Association (APA). (2000). *Diagnostic and statistical manual of mental disorders (DSM-IV-TR)* (4th ed., Text Revision). Washington, DC: American Psychiatric Association.

American Psychiatric Association (APA). (2013). *Diagnostic and statistical manual of mental disorders (DSM-5)* (5th ed.). Arlington, VA: American Psychiatric Association.

Astley, S. J. (2004). *Diagnostic guide for fetal alcohol spectrum disorders: The 4-digit diagnostic code* (3rd ed.). Seattle, WA: University of Washington.

Astley, S. J. (2013). Validation of the fetal alcohol spectrum disorder (FASD) 4-digit diagnostic code. *Journal of Population Therapeutics and Clinical Pharmacology, 20*, e416–e467. https://depts.washington.edu/fasdpn/pdfs/valid2013FAR.pdf

Atkins v. Virginia, 536 U.S. 304. (2002).

Brown, J., Carter, M. N., Haun, J., Wartnik, A., & Zapf, P. A. (2019). Fetal alcohol spectrum disorder (FASD) and competency to stand trial (CST): A call on forensic evaluators to become informed. *Journal of Forensic Psychology Research and Practice, 19*(4), 315–340. https://doi.org/10.1080/24732850.2019.1620798

Brumfield v. Cain, 576 U.S. (2015).

Canada. (1985). *Criminal Code*. (R.S.C., 1985, c. C-46). https://laws-lois.justice.gc.ca/eng/acts/C-46/index.html

Canada. Institute of Health Economics (IHE). (2013). *Consensus Statement of Legal Issues of FASD Conference*. September 20, 2013, Edmonton, Canada. Retrieved from https://www.ihe.ca/publications/consensus-statement-on-legal-issues-of-fetal-alcohol-spectrum-disorder-fasd

Collins, D. (2015). The dilemma caused by delusional defendants. *Victoria University of Wellington Law Review, 46*(3), 811–826. http://www.nzlii.org/nz/journals/VUWLawRw/2015/36.pdf

Cyntoia Brown v. Tennessee, No. M2013-00825-CCA-R3-PC, November 6, 2014.

Dillbeck v. Florida, 643 So.2d 1097 (1994).

Dodds v. R [2016] NZHC 3003.

Drope v. Missouri, 420 U.S. 162 (1975).

Dusky v. U.S., 362 U.S. 402 (1960).

Ferguson, G. (1989). A critique of proposals to reform the insanity defence. *Queen's Law Journal, 14*(1), 135–152.

Hall v. Florida, 572 U.S. 701 (2014).

In re: S.M.S, a Youth, 2010 MT 18 (S. Ct. of Montana, 2010).

Institute of Medicine (IOM). (1996). *Fetal alcohol syndrome: Diagnosis, epidemiology, prevention, and treatment*. Washington, DC: National Academy Press. http://www.come-over.to/FAS/IOMsummary.htm

Komene v. NZ Police, [2009] NZHC 2107.

Lane v. Alabama, No. 1160984 (Alabama S.Ct. 2019).

Moore v. Texas, 137 S.Ct. 1039 (1, 2017) and 581 U.S. (2, 2019).

Moore v. Texas, 139 S.Ct. 666 (2019).

Novick Brown, N., Gudjonsson, G., & Connor, P. (2011). Suggestibility and fetal alcohol spectrum disorders: I'll tell you anything you want to hear. *Journal of Psychiatry and Law, 39*(1), 39–71. https://doi.org/10.1177/009318531103900103

Novick Brown, N., Wartnik, A. P., Connor, P. D., & Adler, R. S. (2010). A proposed model standard for forensic assessment of FASD. *Journal of Psychiatry and Law, 38*(4), 383–418. https://doi.org/10.1177/009318531003800403
M v. R, [2019] NZCA 461.
NZ Police v. ED, [2014] NZYC 122.
NZ Police v. Hansen, [2020] NZDC 26665.
NZ Police v. Herbert, [2019] NZDC 14903.
NZ Police v. KM, [2019] NZYC 436.
NZ Police v. KP, [2017] NZYC 942.
NZ Police v. MA, [2016] NZYC 172.
NZ Police v. Morrison, [2019] NZDC 13977.
NZ Police v. Moyle, [2018] NZDC 1050.
NZ Police v. MQ, [2019] NZYC 456.
NZ Police v. NJ, CRI-092-0400586-587, 5 July 2010.
NZ Police v. NL, [2017] NZYC 662.
NZ Police v. Stipich, CRI-2012-004-003888, 21 December 2012.
NZ Police v. TM, [2019] NZYC 608.
NZ Police v. UP, CRI-2010-204-000314, 5 May 2011.
NZ Police v. VT, [2015] NZYC 819.
O'Driscoll, S. (2011). Fetal alcohol spectrum disorder. *New Zealand Law Journal, 5*, 119–120.
Pomare v. R, [2017] NZCA 155.
Pora v. R, [2015] UKPC 9.
R. v. Abou, 1995 CarswellBC 2923.
R. v. Ayorech, 2002 ABCA 82.
R v. BMS, DC Whangarei; CRI-2010-288-000001, 29 September 2010.
R. v. Brown, 2014 ABPC 236.
R v. CD, [2020] NZYC 34.
R. v. Charlie, 2015 YKCA 3.
R. v. Chaulk, [1990] 3 S.C.R. 1303.
R. v. C.O., 2006 NWTCA.
R. v. C.P.F., 2006 NLCA 70.
R. v. Dewhurst, [2009] YKTC 10.
R. v. Elias, 2010 YKTC 139.
R v. Fawcett, [2018] NZHC 2958.
R. v. F.C., 2012 YKCA 5.
R. v. Friesen, 2016 MBCA 50.
R v. Gladue, [1999] 1 SCR 688.
R. v. Green, 2013 ONCJ 423.
R. v. Halversen, 2020 BCSC 1095.
R. v. Harris, 2002 BCCA 152.
R. v. Ipeelee, 2012 SCC 13.
R. v. J.C., 2015 MBQB 18.
R. v. J. H., [2002] B.C.J. No. 313.
R. v. J.H.B., 2012 ABQB 250.
R. v. J.J.G., 2015 BCSC 77.
R. v. Joamie, 2013 NUCJ 19.
R. v. Jobb, 2008 SKCA 158.
R. v. J.P., 2020 SKCA 52.
R. v. Keenatch, 2019 SKPC 38.
R. v. Kendi, 2011 YKTC 37.
R. v. M, 2000 ONCA 844.
R. v. Morgan 2013 MBPC 99.
R. v. N.R.R., 2013 ABQB 288.

R. v. Oickle, [2000] 2 S.C.R. 3.
R v. Puru, [2018] NZDC 13635.
R. v. Ramalho, 2004 BCCA 617.
R. v. Ramsay, 2012 ABCA 257.
R. v. Resler, 2011 ABCA 167.
R. v. Ruzic, [2001] 1 S.C.R. 687.
R v. Sheers, [2020] NZHC 1596.
R. v. Soosay, 2012 ABPC 220.
R. v. Taylor, [1992] O.J.No. 2394.
R. v. T.J.J., 2011 BCPC 155.
R v. Whiting-Roff (et al.), [2018] NZHC 3239.
Roach, K., & Bailey, A. (2010). The relevance of FASD in Canadian criminal law from investigation to sentencing. *University of British Columbia Law Rev, 42*(1), 1–68. https://www.researchgate.net/profile/Kent_Roach/publication/228263950
Roper v. Simmons, 543 U.S 551 (2005).
Short, C. (2004). Building capital defense teams and uncovering the client's unique stories: The DeLong case. *Warrior. Journal of the Trial Lawyers College*.
Smith, T., Palloway, E. A., Patton, J. R., & Beyer, J. F. (2008). Individuals with intellectual and developmental disabilities in the criminal justice system and implications for transition planning. *Education and Training in Developmental Disabilities, 43*(4), 421–430. https://www.jstor.org/stable/23879673
State v. Ramer, 151 Wash.2d 106 (2004).
Treit, S., Lebel, C., Baugh, L., Rasmussen, C., Andrew, G., & Beaulieu, C. (2013). Longitudinal MRI reveals altered trajectory of brain development during childhood and adolescence in fetal alcohol spectrum disorders. *Journal of Neuroscience, 33*(24), 10098–10109. https://doi.org/10.1523/JNEUROSCI.5004-12.2013
U.S. v. Duhon, 104 F.Supp.2d 663 (W.D. La. 2000).
Wartnik, A. P. (2011, April 21). *Stopping the revolving door of the justice system: Ten principles for sentencing people with FASD*. Williamsburg, VA: National Association of State Judicial Educators.
Wartnik, A. P., Brown, J., & Herrick, S. (2015). Evolution of the diagnosis of fetal alcohol spectrum disorder from DSM-IV-TR to DSM-5: The justice system in the United States—Time for a paradigm shift! In M. Nelson & M. Trussler (Eds.), *Fetal alcohol spectrum disorders in adults: Ethical and legal perspectives, an overview on FASD for professionals* (pp. 151–167). Cham, Switzerland: Springer International.
Wartnik, A. P., & Carlson, S. S. (2011). A judicial perspective on issues impacting the trial courts related to fetal alcohol spectrum disorders. *Journal of Psychiatry and Law, 39*(1), 73–119. https://doi.org/10.1177/009318531103900104
Webster v. Warden, 421 F.3d 308 (2015).
White, A. J., Meares, S., & Batchelor, J. (2014). The role of cognition in fitness to stand trial: A systematic review. *Journal of Forensic Psychiatry and Psychology, 25*(1), 77–99. https://doi.org/10.1080/14789949.2013.868916
White v. Kentucky, 139 S.Ct. 532 (2019).
Williams v. Stirling, 914 F.3d 302 (U.S. CA, 4th Cir., 2019).

Correction to: Evaluating Fetal Alcohol Spectrum Disorders in the Forensic Context

Natalie Novick Brown

Correction to: Chapters 7 & 8 in: Natalie Novick Brown (ed.), *Evaluating Fetal Alcohol Spectrum Disorders in the Forensic Context*, https://doi.org/10.1007/978-3-030-73628-6

This book was inadvertently published with errors; these have been corrected as mentioned below.

On page 168 of Chapter 7, the third paragraph has been replaced with the following one:

In 2013, the American Psychiatric Association (APA) published the fifth edition of the Diagnostic and Statistical Manual of Mental Disorders (DSM-5; APA, 2013). DSM-5 included two elements of particular relevance to FASD. The first was explicit inclusion of the diagnosis neurodevelopmental disorder associated with prenatal alcohol exposure (ND-PAE), which has the DSM-5 diagnostic code 315.8 and ICD-10 code F88 (APA, 2013, p. 86). In fact, ND-PAE is the only specific example provided under the diagnostic entity Other Specified Neurodevelopmental Disorder. No specific diagnostic criteria are provided in this section of DSM-5 and instead, ND-PAE is simply described as "characterized by a range of developmental disabilities following exposure to alcohol in utero" (p. 86).

The updated version of these chapters can be found at
https://doi.org/10.1007/978-3-030-73628-6_7
https://doi.org/10.1007/978-3-030-73628-6_8

N. Novick Brown (ed.), *Evaluating Fetal Alcohol Spectrum Disorders in the Forensic Context*, https://doi.org/10.1007/978-3-030-73628-6_19

On page 209 of Chapter 8, the third paragraph has been replaced with the fol-
lowing one:

Retrospective adaptive assessment is necessary in forensic contexts involving those
who have been incarcerated for long periods of time (Tassé, 2009). In private com-
munication with one of the authors of this chapter, a developer of the Vineland-3
(Celine Saulnier) endorsed retrospective assessment for individuals who have been
out of the community for some time, provided the measure was administered to at
least two individuals to ensure consistency. The accuracy of retrospective adaptive
ratings has been endorsed by AAIDD (Schlock et al., 2010). Another way to verify
accuracy in adaptive ratings is to administer an ancillary measure that includes
validity scales. The Behavior Rating Instrument of Executive Function, Second
Edition (BRIEF-2; Gioia, Isquith, Guy, & Kenworthy, 2015), is a good example of
such a measure and also has the added advantage of including third-party ratings of
executive skills, which often correlate with adaptive scores. The adult version of the
BRIEF-2 (i.e., BRIEF-A; Roth, Isquith, & Gioia, 2005) takes relatively little time to
administer (approximately 15 min) and contains three validity scales that screen for
significant Negativity, Inconsistency, and Infrequency in third-party behavior rat-
ings. Other ways to verify Vineland-3 or ABAS-3 results include consistency with
(a) childhood adaptive ratings documented in school records, (b) neuropsychologi-
cal testing (especially EF), (c) documented anecdotal information, and (d) second-
ary disabilities analysis.

Index

N. Novick Brown (ed.), *Evaluating Fetal Alcohol Spectrum Disorders in the Forensic Context*, https://doi.org/10.1007/978-3-030-73628-6

J

L

M

T

U

V

GPSR Compliance
The European Union's (EU) General Product Safety Regulation (GPSR) is a set of rules that requires consumer products to be safe and our obligations to ensure this.

If you have any concerns about our products, you can contact us on

ProductSafety@springernature.com

In case Publisher is established outside the EU, the EU authorized representative is:

Springer Nature Customer Service Center GmbH
Europaplatz 3
69115 Heidelberg, Germany

www.ingramcontent.com/pod-product-compliance
Lightning Source LLC
Chambersburg PA
CBHW051650290626
47387CB00003B/272
* 9 7 8 3 0 3 0 7 3 6 2 7 9 *